The **Rough Guide** to

Sydney

written and researched by

Margo Daly

with additional contributions by

Paul Whitfield and Ben Connor

D0062872

ROUGH
GUIDES

www.roughguides.com

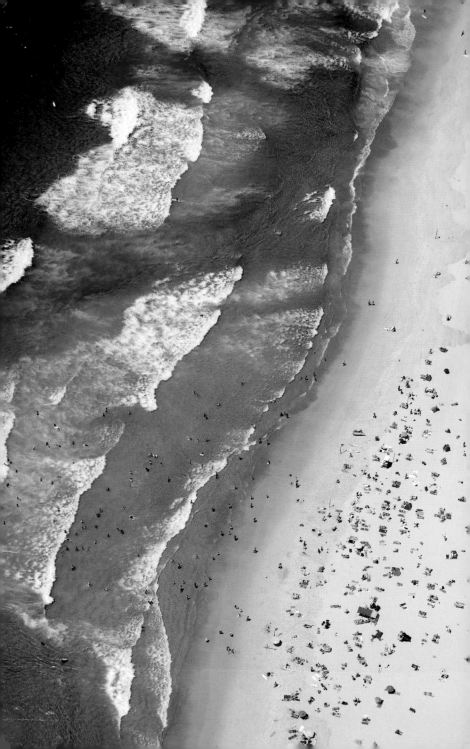

Contents

Sydney style
colour section
following p.112

Sydney festivals
colour section
following p.240

Sydney Opera House **Colour maps**
following p.360

◄◄ Fort Denison ◄ Bondi Beach

Introduction to

Sydney

Draped around the sparkling waters of its glorious harbour, Sydney enjoys a setting that perhaps only Rio de Janeiro can rival, and all the vigour of a world-class city, but still retains a seductive, easy-going charm. Australia's first city, established in 1788, it remains its largest, with a population approaching five million. Despite the creation of Canberra as a purpose-built capital in 1927 – intended to stem the intense rivalry between Sydney and Melbourne – many Sydneysiders still view their city as the true capital of Australia, and in many ways it feels as though it is. There's a tangible sense of history about the old stone walls and well-worn steps in the backstreets around The Rocks, while the sandstone cliffs, rocks and caves among the bush-lined harbour still hold Aboriginal rock carvings, evocative reminders of a more ancient past.

Flying into Sydney provides a thrilling close-up snapshot of the city, as you swoop alongside cliffs and golden beaches, revealing toy-sized images of the Harbour Bridge and the Opera House tilting in a glittering expanse of blue water. Towards the airport the red-tiled roofs of suburban bungalows stretch ever southwards, blue squares of swimming pools shimmering from grassy back yards. The night views are as spectacular, with skyscrapers topped by colourful neon lights and the illuminated white shells of the Opera House reflecting on the dark water as ferries crisscross to Circular Quay.

The city's heritage is balanced by the furious **development** that took place before the 2000 Olympics, heralded as being Sydney's coming-of-age ceremony. This alarmed many locals, who loved their city the way it was,

but the changes brought a greatly improved transport infrastructure, and the $200 million budget improved and beautified the city streets and parks and resulted in a rash of luxury hotels and apartments.

Sydney is in many ways a microcosm of Australia as a whole – if only in its ability to defy your expectations and prejudices as often as it confirms them. A thrusting, high-rise commercial centre in the **Central Business District (CBD)**, a high-profile gay community in **Darlinghurst**, inner-city deprivation of unexpected harshness, with the highest Aboriginal population of any Australian city, and the dreary traffic-fumed and flat suburban sprawl of the **western suburbs**, are as much part of the picture as the beaches, the bodies, the sparkling harbour and the world-class restaurant scene. Similarly, Sydney's sophistication, cosmopolitan population and exuberant nightlife feel a long way from the outback, yet fires are a constant threat to the bush-surrounded city.

Sydney seems to have the best of both worlds – if it's seen at its gleaming best from the deck of a harbour ferry, especially at weekends when the harbour fills with a flotilla of small vessels, racing yachts and cabin cruisers, it's at its most varied in its **neighbourhoods**, with their lively café and restaurant scenes. Getting away from the city centre to explore them is an essential Sydney pleasure. A short ferry trip across to the leafy and affluent North Shore allows access to tracts of largely intact bushland, with bushwalking and native animals and birds right on the doorstep. In summer, the city's sweltering offices are abandoned for the remarkably unspoiled ocean and harbour **beaches** strung around the eastern and northern suburbs, while day-trips outside the city offer a taste of virtually everything to be found in the rest of Australia.

A Saturday in Sydney

The aim is to get to the Saturday Balmain Market at least an hour or two before it closes at 4pm. Start early with a visit to the **Fish Market** (see p.89) at **Pyrmont** – open to the public from 7am, or come for breakfast at the *Fish Market Café* from 5am – then stroll ten minutes to the free-entry **National Maritime Museum** (see p.87) at **Darling Harbour**, which opens at 9.30am. Cross Pyrmont Bridge to spend an hour or two in the brilliant **Sydney Aquarium** (see p.86), before hopping next door to King St Wharf to catch a couple of ferries to Balmain West Wharf (Elliot St). Nearby, Elkington Park on the Parramatta River is the site of one of Sydney's most atmospheric swimming spots, **Dawn Fraser Pool** (see p.113). Wander down Darling Street and head past shops and cafés to the tree-shaded grounds of St Andrew's Church to check out the handmade, home-made and secondhand items for sale at **Balmain Market** (see p.113); don't forget to sample something from the diverse food stalls in the church hall, too. Afterwards, retrace Darling Street west and along Beattie Street for a drink at the classic Balmain boozer the *Exchange Hotel*, or any of the other lively backstreet pubs on a Saturday afternoon. By nightfall, catch the #442 or #445 bus from Darling Street to Balmain East Wharf (Darling St) for the ferry to Circular Quay, which glides underneath the **Harbour Bridge**. Make sure you stand outside to make the most of the views of the lit-up city skyline and the iconic clown's face at **Luna Park** (see p.123), beside Milsons Point Wharf, where you can stop off (the amusement park closes at 11pm, the adjacent heated **North Sydney Olympic Pool** at 7pm). From Circular Quay, catch bus #380 to **Oxford Street, Darlinghurst** (see p.97) and have a drink at a lively gay bar like the *Stonewall* or the *Columbian*, or head for **Victoria Street** to the ever-popular pubs at the *Green Park Hotel* or the *Darlo Bar*. Continue to Darlinghurst Road in **Kings Cross** (see p.94) to follow the traditional weekend crawl past stripclub exteriors and then down the McElhone Stairs (off Victoria St) to **Woolloomooloo** (see p.96), for more good pubs and a late-night pie at *Harry's Cafe de Wheels*.

What to see

Port Jackson, more commonly known as **Sydney Harbour**, carves Sydney in two halves, linked by the **Sydney Harbour Bridge**, the Harbour Tunnel and numerous ferry routes. It's on the south shore, the hub of activity, that you'll find the **city centre** and most of the things to see and do. Many of the classic images of Sydney lie within sight of **Circular Quay**, making this busy waterfront area on Sydney Cove a good point to start discovering the city, with the Opera House and the expanse of the Royal Botanic Gardens to the east of Sydney Cove. It's also near the historic area of **The Rocks** to the west, and prominent museums and art galleries. From Circular Quay south as far as King Street is the **CBD**, with pedestrianized Martin Place at its centre. Just east of Martin Place,

Macquarie Street is Sydney's civic streetscape, lined with fine colonial sandstone buildings including the New South Wales Parliament House. Beyond Macquarie Street, the open space of **The Domain** stretches to the Art Gallery of New South Wales. South of The Domain, **Hyde Park** is very much the formal city park, overlooked by churches and the Australian Museum, and holding a solemn war memorial.

Park Street divides Hyde Park into two; head west along it to reach the ornate town hall, around which Sydney's shopping heart is focused, including the glorious **Queen Victoria Building**. Watching over it all is the Sydney Tower, with 360-degree views from the top. The city's two main thoroughfares, George and Pitt streets, stretch downtown to Central Station and the area known as **Haymarket**, where a vibrant Chinatown sits beside the entertainment area of **Darling Harbour**, with its major museums and attractions.

East of the city centre, following William Street uphill past Hyde Park, is **Kings Cross**, Sydney's red-light district and major travellers' rendezvous, full of accommodation, chic bars, and late-night cafés. The adjacent waterfront area of **Woolloomooloo** is home to a busy naval dockyard and some lively pubs. North and east of "the Cross", you move gradually upmarket, with the **eastern suburbs** stretching along the harbour to Watsons Bay, meeting the open sea at South Head. Running south from the head are the popular and populous **eastern beaches**, from **Bondi** through **Coogee** to Maroubra, ending at La Perouse and the expanse of Botany Bay. Further south brings you to surf territory at Cronulla and the **Royal National Park** across Port Hacking, and a stunning coastal drive down the south coast to Thirroul. Inland from here, the **Southern Highlands** are covered with yet more national parks, punctuated by pleasing little towns such as Bundanoon and Berrima.

◄ Young Sydneysiders

A walking tour of the centre

This five-kilometre walking tour from the city centre to Circular Quay takes in history, architecture, culture, nature and shopping – and there's even time for a swim. Start with a spot of window-shopping at the grand **Queen Victoria Building** (see p.78; Town Hall Station), then head up Market Street past the Art Deco State Theatre – with a possible detour into the David Jones Food Hall for gourmet supplies – and into **Hyde Park** (see p.80). Check out the giant chessboard and Archibald Fountain here, before heading out of the park past St James's Church along Macquarie Street. Soak up convict history for an hour or two at **Hyde Park Barracks** (see p.72), then take a free peek into **NSW Parliament House** (see p.72) and the Mitchell wing of the **State Library** (see p.71). Next, stroll back along Macquarie Street to Sydney Hospital, where you can take a short cut through to The Domain and the free **Art Gallery of NSW** (see p.69). If the weather's fine, you might fancy a dip at **Andrew "Boy" Charlton pool** (Sept–April; see p.69), before continuing on to **Mrs Macquaries Chair** (see p.69) to take in the harbour views. Then take a wander through the nearby **Botanic Gardens** (see p.66) until chucking-out time at dusk, when the possums start frolicking and the fruitbats fly overhead. Afterwards, enjoy a drink and affordable meal at the outside bar at the **Sydney Opera House** (see p.63), or a performance or film at the nearby Dendy Opera Quays **cinema** (see p.224). End the day by strolling along the lively Opera Quays promenade, with its alfresco bars and cafés, to **Circular Quay**, where you can catch a bus, train or ferry back to your hotel.

From the southeast corner of Hyde Park, Oxford Street steams through the gay, restaurant, club and bar strip of **Darlinghurst**, becoming increasingly upmarket through gentrified **Paddington**, which has Centennial Park as its playground. South of Oxford Street, **Surry Hills** is far less gentrified but firmly on the map, with plenty of dining and funky shopping action on Crown Street. Further south, Danks Street in **Waterloo** is another up-and-coming area. The nearby Sydney Cricket Ground and Entertainment Quarter are twin focal points at Moore Park. Southwest of Central Station, Sydney University is surrounded by the café-packed and youthful areas of **Newtown** and **Glebe**. West of Glebe, ugly Parramatta Road heads to Italian-dominated **Leichhardt** and **Haberfield** while the nearby harbour suburb of **Balmain**, once a working-class dock area, has long gone upmarket, but its big old pubs still make for a great pub crawl. Further west, **Sydney Olympic Park** at Homebush Bay, the focus of the 2000 Olympics, is Sydney's geographical heart, and beyond the great sprawl of the western suburbs, the World Heritage-listed **Blue Mountains** offer tearooms, scenic viewpoints and isolated bushwalking.

The bushclad **North Shore** of the harbour is very much where the old money is. From Taronga Zoo to Manly, some wonderful spots can be reached by ferry. North of Manly, the **northern beaches** stretch up to glamorous **Palm Beach**, which looks across to several national parks, including **Ku-Ring-Gai Chase**. Flowing towards Pittwater and Broken Bay is the sandstone-lined **Hawkesbury River**, lined with historic colonial towns. North of here, the **Central Coast** is a weekend beach playground for Sydneysiders, while inland to the northwest the **Hunter Valley**, Australia's oldest and possibly best-known wine-growing region, is set amid idyllic pastoral scenery.

When to go

Since Sydney has such wonderful beaches, the best time to come is between early October and Easter, the official swimming season, when the beaches are patrolled, and outdoor swimming pools open.

During the sunny **spring** months of September and October, the wild flowers are in bloom, and the smell of blossoms such as jasmine fills the warming city streets. November is getting warmer, but the sweltering hot **summer months** are mid-December, January and February. Christmas can often see 40°C in the shade, though it's been known to be cool and overcast; as indicated in the chart below, average summer temperatures are 25°C.

Sydney is subtropical, with high and very oppressive humidity in summer building up to sporadic torrential rainstorms (dubbed "southerly busters" by locals). This is party time, combining high summer with Christmas and New Year festivities, as well as the city's many other festivals and events (see *Sydney festivals* colour section).

▼ The Manly Ferry

April, when the Royal Agricultural Show hits town, is the rainiest month. May, by contrast, is glorious, and you can bet on dry sunny weather and blue skies as Sydney heads for its mild **winter months** of June, July and August. Don't expect bare trees and grey skies – native trees are evergreen and the skies are usually just a less intense blue. Temperatures rarely drop below 10°C, but get colder during the night, and decidedly chilly the further west you go, with frost on the plains heading to the Blue Mountains, where there are rare light snowfalls. Bring a coat, scarf, gloves and woolly hat if you want to go to the mountains in winter; it can get cool at night in summer too. A jumper and jacket should keep you warm enough in the city, where the cafés continue with their outdoor seating, with braziers to radiate heat.

Average daily temperatures and rainfall

	Jan	Feb	Mar	Apr	May	Jun	Jul	Aug	Sep	Oct	Nov	Dec
Max/min (°F)	78/65	78/65	76/63	71/58	66/52	61/48	60/46	63/48	67/51	71/56	74/60	77/63
Max/min (°C)	26/18	26/18	24/17	22/14	19/11	19/9	16/8	17/9	19/11	22/13	23/16	25/17
Rainfall (mm)	89	102	127	135	127	117	117	76	74	71	74	74

17

things not to miss

It's not possible to see everything Sydney has to offer on a short trip – and we don't suggest you try. What follows is a selective taste of the city's highlights: outstanding museums and restaurants, beautiful beaches, exciting festivals and fantastic excursions beyond the city – all arranged in five colour-coded categories to help you find the very best things to see and experience. All entries have a page reference to take you straight into the Guide, where you can find out more.

01 Royal Botanic Gardens Page **66** • Picnic in the beautiful Botanic Gardens, with spectacular views of the harbour, Opera House and Harbour Bridge.

02 **Taronga Zoo** Page **127** • With a superb hilltop position overlooking the city, surrounded by natural bush, this is a fantastic spot to see Australian critters as well as those from further afield.

04 **Powerhouse Museum** Page **90** • With its interactive displays and lavish special exhibitions, Sydney's most stimulating museum is not just for kids.

03 **Drinking** Page **202** • From ultra-chic designer bars to historic watering holes, there's a wealth of places for a great night out in Sydney.

05 **Climbing Sydney Harbour Bridge** Page **54** • Climb the famous coat hanger for great harbour views, or save your money and walk across for free.

07 **Glebe Market Day** Page **107** • This friendly, funky neighbourhood market makes for a great day out; even if you don't buy anything, it's fun just to hang out in the adjacent cafés.

06 **Bondi Beach** Page **133** • One of the best-known beaches in the world, big, brash Bondi is synonymous with Australian beach culture.

08 **Hiking in Sydney Harbour National Park** Page **115** • Follow waterfront trails through the many and varied pockets of astounding natural beauty that comprise this extraordinary national park, for great views of the harbour and city.

09 **Shopping** Page **241** • From stately nineteenth-century Strand Arcade and Queen Victoria Building to cutting-edge Australian designers like Sass & Bide and surfwear shops at Bondi, the shopping opportunities are endless.

10 **Swimming in a seapool** Page **268** • If you'd rather not brave the waves or just want to do a few laps in a beautiful setting, head for one of Sydney's 74 harbour or ocean seapools.

11 **Hunter Valley wineries** Page **290** • Enjoy wine, beauty, gourmet food and a diversity of cultural events in one of Australia's most famous wine-growing regions.

12 **Art Gallery of New South Wales** Page **69** • Visit this vast collection of Australian and European art in an imposing Neoclassical building with stylish modern additions.

13 **The Hawkesbury River** Page **277** • Admire the magnificent sandstone cliffs, and deliver mail to isolated shacks along the Hawkesbury River, on a leisurely cruise.

14 **The Rocks** Page **55** • Classic boozers, enticing markets, stone buildings and narrow cobbled streets in the heart of historic Sydney.

15 **Eating** Page **159** • Sydney's eating scene is ever evolving, but celebrity chefs such as Bill Granger, Luke Mangan, Tetsuya Wakuda, Kylie Kwong and Neil Perry deserve the gongs. From the simplicity of Granger's *bills* (pictured) to the glamour of Perry's *Rockpool*, try them out if you can.

16 **Blue Mountains** Page **294** • The sandstone escarpments, plunging waterfalls and blue gum forests of the World Heritage-listed Blue Mountains make the perfect weekend break from Sydney.

17 **Paddington** Page **98** • With its gorgeous colonial-style houses, Paddington is best explored on Saturday, when the famous market is in full swing.

Basics

Basics

Getting there

Several flights per day arrive in Sydney from Europe, North America and Southeast Asia. Air fares depend on seasonal availability, with the highest rates being for the two or three weeks either side of Christmas. Fares drop during the "shoulder" seasons – mid-January to March and mid-August to November – while the best prices of all are during the low season, April to August.

If Sydney is only one stop on a longer journey, consider buying a **Round-the-World** (RTW) ticket. Some travel agents sell "off-the-shelf" tickets that have you touching down in about half a dozen cities – Sydney is frequently part of the regular eastbound RTW loop from Europe. Figure on £850/US$1500 for a basic RTW ticket including Australia.

Flights from the UK and Ireland

The market for flights between Britain and Australia is among the most competitive in the world, and prices remain low. Qantas, British Airways, Virgin, Emirates, Singapore and Malaysia Airlines all offer **direct flights** to Sydney in 21 to 23 hours. Other airlines may involve a change of plane for connecting flights, and potentially long waits in between, which can make the journey last up to 36 hours. However, it often costs no more to break the journey en route, as detailed below, so it need not be a tedious, seat-bound slog. All direct scheduled flights to Australia depart from London's two main airports, Gatwick and Heathrow, though Singapore Airlines has several weekly flights from Manchester to Singapore that connect with onward flights to Sydney.

Return **fares** to Sydney can start as low as £600 in the low season, with special offers occasionally dropping the price to around £500. In high season Emirates have deals for £700, though you'll need to book well in advance and should otherwise expect to pay £900–1400.

Passengers on Qantas and British Airways can fly from **regional airports** at Aberdeen, Edinburgh, Glasgow, Manchester or Newcastle to connect with international flights at Heathrow for around £50 extra.

An excellent alternative to a long direct flight is a **multi-stopover ticket**, breaking your journey at the airline's stopover points, most commonly in Southeast Asia or in the US, which can cost the same or just a little more than an ordinary return. Unusual routes are inevitably more expensive, but it's possible to fly **via South America** with Aerolineas Argentinas, which offers stops in Buenos

Cruising to Sydney

There's no better way to arrive in Sydney than by **boat**, as can easily be done on a **cruise**. If you're up for a big-spend grand adventure, go with Cunard Line (ⓦwww .cunardline.com), who feature Sydney on multi-week cruises on the luxurious *Queen Mary 2* and *Queen Victoria*. You can embark in Europe or the American east coast, but less costly departure points include Singapore and Hong Kong, which start at around AUS$6000 (including early booking savings). P&O Cruises (ⓦwww.pocruises .com) run similar trips, such as a forty-day trip from Singapore via the Barrier Reef to Sydney, again from around AUS$6000 for an inside cabin.

Princess Cruises (ⓦwww.princess.com) offer more regional cruises, many embarking from Sydney, though that obviously robs you of getting your initial impression of the city from the harbour. Consider a thirteen-day cruise from Auckland, New Zealand, also taking in Wellington, Milford Sound, Hobart and Melbourne (from around AUS$2000).

Aires and Auckland – at least £1000 return – or via Africa with South African Airways, which offers return fares via Johannesburg to Sydney from around £1500, with the added bonus of discounted internal flights to many other African destinations; there are also good deals **via Japan** on All Nippon Airlines (ANA) and Japan Airlines.

Another option is a Round-the-World (RTW) ticket. A good agent such as Trailfinders can piece together sector fares from various airlines: providing you keep your itinerary down to three continents prices range from around £850 for a simple London–Bangkok–Sydney–LA–London deal to well over £1000 for more complicated routings.

There are no direct flights **from Ireland**. Most of the cheaper routings involve a stopover in London and transfer to one of the airlines listed above, though Singapore Airlines has flights ticketed through from Dublin or Cork via London to Singapore and Sydney, while the affiliated companies British Airways and Qantas can ticket from Dublin, Cork and Shannon to Sydney, again via London. In practice it may work out cheaper to make your way to London on a low-cost European airline and fly from there. Fares in low-season are usually around €900, €1200 in high season. For youth and student discount fares, the best first stop is Usit (see p.22).

Flights from the US and Canada

Direct nonstop flights to Sydney from North America are possible from Los Angeles (Air Canada, Qantas, & United), San Francisco (Qantas and United), Honolulu (Qantas), New York (Qantas) and Vancouver (Air Canada). LA to Sydney nonstop takes over fourteen hours. From Los Angeles and San Francisco, expect to pay US$900–1100 for most of the year, rising to more like US$2000–2800 from December to February. United are usually fractionally the cheapest. From Vancouver rates range from CAN$1600–3000.

There's only a slight detour flying via New Zealand with Air New Zealand, whose fares are comparable with the direct carriers. Their routes to Sydney are from Los Angeles, San Francisco and Vancouver through Auckland; and there's a further option of stopovers in

Samoa, Tonga or the Cook Islands on the LA–Auckland route.

Prices are less seasonal if you route through Asia with Cathay Pacific (via Hong Kong from Los Angeles, New York, San Francisco, Vancouver), Malaysian Airlines (via Kuala Lumpur from LA), or Singapore Airlines (via Singapore from LA and New York). All offer low-cost stopovers in their home city. In the off season, Asian rates are higher than the direct Pacific routes, but in the southern summer flying via Asia can save money over flying direct. Cathay generally offer the best rates, charging US$1500–2000 from Los Angeles and San Francisco, US$1600–2300 from New York, and Can$2700–3100 from Vancouver.

Flights from New Zealand

New Zealand–Australia routes are busy and competition is fierce, resulting in an ever-changing range of deals and special offers: check the latest with a specialist travel agent or the relevant airlines' websites. Flying time from Auckland to Sydney is around three and a half hours.

Ultimately, the price you pay for your flight will depend on how much flexibility you want; many of the cheapest deals don't allow date changes. Online, most carriers allow you to book each sector separately, making one-way flights viable.

Qantas and Air New Zealand offer the most flights with price dependent solely on availability and ticket flexibility: book well ahead for the best deals. Qantas fly direct to Sydney from Auckland (from NZ$450), Wellington (from NZ$540), and Christchurch (from NZ$520), while their budget subsidiary Jetstar fly Auckland–Sydney for as little as $160 one-way, though there are additional fees for baggage, paying by credit card etc. Air New Zealand's Sydney flights operate from Auckland (from NZ$520), Hamilton (from NZ$630), Wellington (from NZ$630), Christchurch (from NZ$470), Dunedin (from NZ$700) and Queenstown (from NZ$830).

Pacific Blue, Virgin Blue's New Zealand low-fare carrier, fly direct from Auckland to Sydney with connections from Christchurch and Wellington, from around NZ$450 return. Emirates fly superjumbos on the world's shortest A380 route between Auckland and

Six steps to a better kind of travel

At Rough Guides we are passionately committed to travel. We feel strongly that only through travelling do we truly come to understand the world we live in and the people we share it with – plus tourism has brought a great deal of **benefit** to developing economies around the world over the last few decades. But the extraordinary growth in tourism has also damaged some places irreparably, and of course **climate change** is exacerbated by most forms of transport, especially flying. This means that now more than ever it's important to **travel thoughtfully** and **responsibly**, with respect for the cultures you're visiting – not only to derive the most benefit from your trip but also to preserve the best bits of the planet for everyone to enjoy. At Rough Guides we feel there are six main areas in which you can make a difference:

- Consider what you're contributing to the **local economy**, and how much the services you use do the same, whether it's through employing local workers and guides or sourcing locally grown produce and local services.
- Consider the **environment** on holiday as well as at home. Water is scarce in many developing destinations, and the biodiversity of local flora and fauna can be adversely affected by tourism. Try to patronize businesses that take account of this.
- Travel with a purpose, not just to tick off experiences. Consider **spending longer** in a place, and getting to know it and its people.
- Give thought to how often you **fly**. Try to avoid short hops by air and more harmful night flights.
- Consider **alternatives to flying**, travelling instead by bus, train, boat and even by bike or on foot where possible.
- Make your trips "**climate neutral**" via a reputable carbon offset scheme. All Rough Guide flights are offset, and every year we donate money to a variety of charities devoted to combating the effects of climate change.

Sydney with tickets from NZ$490, and smaller planes from Christchurch direct to Sydney from $430. Less frequent alternatives from Auckland include Aerolineas Argentineas, Malaysian and Thai, who typically charge from around NZ$500.

A huge variety of **packages** to Sydney is available; call or check the websites of any of the agents listed below. The holiday subsidiaries of airlines such as Air New Zealand and Qantas offer short **city-breaks** (flight and accommodation) and **fly-drive** deals for little more than the regular air fare.

Online booking

Ⓦ www.expedia.co.uk (in UK), Ⓦ www.expedia
.com (in USA), Ⓦ www.expedia.ca (in Canada),
Ⓦ www.expedia.co.nz (in NZ)
Ⓦ www.lastminute.com (in UK), Ⓦ www
.lastminute.co.nz (in NZ)
Ⓦ www.opodo.co.uk (in UK)
Ⓦ www.orbitz.com (in US)

Ⓦ www.travelocity.co.uk (in UK), Ⓦ www
.travelocity.com (in US), Ⓦ www.travelocity.ca
(in Canada), Ⓦ www.travelocity.co.nz (in NZ)

Airlines

Aerolineas Argentinas Ⓦ www.aerolineas.com.ar
Air Canada Ⓦ www.aircanada.com
Air China Ⓦ www.airchina.co.uk
Air New Zealand Ⓦ www.airnewzealand.co.nz
All Nippon Airways (ANA) Ⓦ www
.anaskyweb.com
British Airways Ⓦ www.ba.com
Cathay Pacific Ⓦ www.cathaypacific.com
Emirates Ⓦ www.emirates.com
Garuda Indonesia Ⓦ www.garudaindonesia.co.uk
Japan Airlines Ⓦ www.jal.com/en/
Jetstar Ⓦ www.jetstar.com
KLM Ⓦ www.klm.com
Korean Air Ⓦ www.koreanair.com
Malaysia Airlines Ⓦ www.malaysiaairlines.com
Pacific Blue Ⓦ www.flypacificblue.com
Qantas Ⓦ www.qantas.com

Singapore Airlines ⓦwww.singaporeair.com
South African Airways ⓦwww.flysaa.com
Thai Airways ⓦwww.thaiair.com
United Airlines ⓦwww.ual.com
Virgin Atlantic ⓦwww.virgin-atlantic.com

Travel agents

In the UK

Austravel ☎0800/988 4672, ⓦwww.austravel
.com. Specialists for flights and tours to Australia and
New Zealand.

ebookers ☎0871/223 5000, ⓦwww.ebookers
.com. Extensive range of low-fare scheduled flights
to Sydney.

North South Travel ☎01245/608 291, ⓦwww
.northsouthtravel.co.uk. Competitive but ethical travel
agency, offering discounted fares – profits are used to
support projects in the developing world, especially
the promotion of sustainable tourism.

Oz Flights ☎0870/747 11 747, ⓦwww.ozflights
.co.uk. Good deals on southeast Asian airlines.

Quest Travel ☎0845/263 6963, ⓦwww
.questtravel.com. Specialists in RTW and Australian
discount fares.

STA Travel ☎0871/230 0040, ⓦwww
.statravel.co.uk. Worldwide specialists in low-cost
flights and tours for students and under-26s,
though other customers welcome. Also has offices
in Sydney.

Trailfinders ☎0845/058 5858, ⓦwww
.trailfinders.com. Excellent for multi-stop and RTW
tickets, including some unusual routings via South
Africa, the Pacific and the US – their very useful
quarterly magazine is worth scrutinizing for RTW
routes. Well-informed and efficient visa service
available online.

Travel Bag ☎0800/804 8911, ⓦwww
.travelbag.co.uk. Well-established long-haul travel
agent with a good reputation for Australian
coverage. Travel Bag offers some good tour options,
plus some action and eco-oriented trips including
the Great Barrier Reef.

In Ireland

Australia Travel Centre ☎01/804 7100,
ⓦwww.australia.ie. Specialists in long-haul flights.
Trailfinders Dublin ☎01/677 7888,
ⓦwww.trailfinders.ie. Well-informed and efficient
agent for independent travellers; produces a very
useful quarterly magazine worth scrutinizing for
RTW routes.
Usit Dublin ☎01/602 1600, ⓦwww.usit.ie.
Student and youth specialists.

In the US and Canada

Air Brokers International ☎1-800/883-3273,
ⓦwww.airbrokers.com. Consolidator and specialist
in RTW and Circle Pacific tickets.
Airtech ☎212/219-7000, ⓦwww.airtech.com.
Stand-by seat broker; also deals in consolidator fares.
Airtreks.com ☎1-877-AIRTREKS or 415/977-
7100, ⓦwww.airtreks.com. Circle Pacific and
RTW tickets. The website features an interactive
trip planner that lets you build and price your own
RTW itinerary.
Educational Travel Center ☎1-800/747-5551 or
608/256-5551, ⓦwww.edtrav.com. Student/youth
discount agent.
STA Travel ☎1-800/781-4040, ⓦwww.sta-travel
.com. Worldwide specialists in independent travel; also
provide student IDs, travel insurance, car rental, etc.
Student Universe ☎1-800/272-9676 or
1-617/321-3100, ⓦwww.studentuniverse.com.
Competitive student travel specialists, no card or
membership required.
TFI Tours ☎1-800/745-8000 or 212/736-1140,
ⓦtfitours.com. Consolidator with consistently good
deals on flights and accommodation.
Travel Cuts Canada ☎1-800/667-2887, US
☎1-866/246-9762; ⓦwww.travelcuts.com.
Canadian student-travel organization with offices in
many North American cities.
Travelers Advantage ☎1-800/835-8747, ⓦwww
.travelersadvantage.com. Discount travel club; annual
membership fee required (month-long trial $1).
Worldtek Travel ☎1-800/243-1723, ⓦwww
.worldtek.com. Discount travel agency with offices in
several eastern and midwestern states.

In New Zealand

Flight Centres ☎0800/243 5444, ⓦwww
.flightcentre.co.nz. Branches nationwide. Competitive
discounts on air fares plus package holidays and
adventure tours.
STA Travel ☎0800/474 400, ⓦwww.statravel
.co.nz. Branches nationwide. Fare discounts for
students and under-26s, as well as visas, student
cards and travel insurance.

Specialist package and tour agents

In the UK and Ireland

Australia Travel Centre ☎01/804 7100,
ⓦaustralia.ie.
Australian Pacific Touring ☎020/8879 7444,
ⓦwww.aptours.com.

FROM DEEP SEA TO SKY HIGH – THE ONLY PLACE TO SEE AUSTRALIA IN A DAY IS ON THE DISCOVERY TRAIL.

Do the total Aussie experience right in the heart of Sydney on The Discovery Trail! Start at Sydney Aquarium where you'll see the amazing dugongs, walk underwater among sharks and experience Australia's largest Great Barrier Reef exhibit. Head to Sydney Wildlife World, Australia's number one family attraction, where you can have breakfast with the koalas*, feed the kangaroos and walk through nine different Aussie wildlife habitats. And at Sydney Tower you'll enjoy 360 degree views of Sydney, take an amazing virtual reality ride across Australia and venture across breathtaking glass overhangs on Skywalk*.

For tickets, come to Sydney Aquarium, Sydney Wildlife World or Sydney Tower, or visit: myfun.com.au

Sydney Aquarium. Aquarium Pier, Darling Harbour, Sydney. Phone: + 61 2 8251 7800. Open daily 9am-10pm.
Sydney Wildlife World. Aquarium Pier, Darling Harbour, Sydney. Phone: + 61 2 9333 9288. Open daily 9am-Dusk.
Sydney Tower. Centrepoint Podium Level, 100 Market St, Sydney. Phone: + 61 2 9333 9222.
Open Sun-Fri 9am-10:30pm & Sat 9am-11:30pm.

*Breakfast with the koalas and Skywalk are add-ons that come at additional cost.

SAG0129/RG

Explore ☎0845/013 1539, ⓦwww.explore.co.uk.
Lee's Travel ☎0871/855 3388, ⓦwww
.leestravel.com.
World Expeditions ☎020/8545 9030,
ⓦworldexpeditions.co.uk.

In the US and Canada

Abercrombie and Kent ☎1-800/554-7016,
ⓦwww.abercrombiekent.com.
Adventure Center ☎1-800/228-8747, ⓦwww
.adventurecenter.com.
Adventures Abroad ☎1-800/665-3998,
ⓦwww.adventures-abroad.com.
ATS Tours ☎1-888/781-5170, ⓦwww
.atstours.com.
Australian Pacific Tours ☎1-800/290-8687,
ⓦwww.aptours.com.
Destination World ☎1-888/345-4669, ⓦwww
.destinationworld.com.

Goway Travel ☎1-800/387-8850, ⓦwww
.goway.com.
International Gay and Lesbian Travel
Association ☎1-800/448-8550, ⓦwww.iglta.org.
Nature Expeditions International ☎1-800/
869-0639, ⓦwww.naturexp.com.
Qantas Vacations US ☎1-866/914-4359,
ⓦwww.qantasvacations.com.
Swain Australia Tours ☎1-800/227-9246,
ⓦwww.swainaustralia.com.
United Vacations ☎1-888/854-3899, ⓦwww
.unitedvacations.com.

In New Zealand

AAT Kings ☎1-800/500 146, ⓦwww.aatkings
.com.
Contiki ☎0508/266 8454, ⓦcontiki.co.nz

Arrival

The classic way to arrive in Sydney is, of course, by ship (see box, p.19), cruising near the great coathanger of the Harbour Bridge to tie up at the Overseas Passenger Terminal (see p.61) alongside Circular Quay. You're much more likely to be arriving by air, train or bus, however, and the reality of the functional airport, train and bus stations is a good deal less romantic.

By air

Sydney's **Kingsford Smith Airport**, referred to as "Mascot" after the suburb where it's located, is 8km south of the city, near Botany Bay (international flight times ☎13 1223, ⓦwww.sydneyairport.com.au). For transfer between domestic and international terminals, passengers travelling with Qantas or Virgin Blue may be eligible for a free shuttle service (Qantas ☎13 1313; Virgin Blue ☎13 6789). Otherwise you can get a T-Bus (every 30min; $5.50), a taxi ($8–12), or the Airport Link **underground railway** ($5.60), which also connects the airport to the City Circle train line in the heart of Sydney in around fifteen minutes (every 10–15min; one-way $14.40; ⓦwww.airportlink.com.au). A return Airport Link transfer is included in the excellent-value

Sydney Pass tourist transport package (see p.28), which you can buy at the airport train station, Circular Quay and Manly Ferry wharfs, CityRail stations, visitor centres and on Explorer Buses. **Buses** run regularly into the city (see box opposite), while a **taxi** to the city centre or Kings Cross costs $34–38.

Bureau de change offices at both terminals are open daily from 5am until last arrival, with rates comparable to major banks. On the ground floor (Arrivals) of the international terminal, the **Sydney Visitor Centre** (daily 5am until last arrival; ☎02/9667 9386) can arrange car rental and city-bound shuttle bus tickets, and book hotels anywhere in Sydney and New South Wales free of charge at stand-by rates. Most hostels advertise on an adjacent notice board; there's a Freephone

Airport buses

State Transit

State Transit no longer offers dedicated airport buses but a daily commuter route heads east and west from the airport: the **Metroline #400** goes frequently to Bondi Junction via Maroubra and Randwick in one direction, and to Burwood in the other (max cost $5).

Shuttle service – Sydney area

KST Sydney Transporter ℡02/9666 9988, ⓦwww.kst.com.au. Private bus service, dropping off at hotels or hostels in the area bounded by Kings Cross and Darling Harbour. Service leaves when the bus is full ($13 one-way, $22 return). Bookings three hours in advance for accommodation pick-up to the airport.

Coach and shuttle services – central coast and south coast

Aussie Shuttles ℡1300 130 557, ⓦwww.ben-air.com.au. Pre-booked door-to-door service to accommodation anywhere on the central coast ($60–75).

Premier Motor Service ℡13 3410, for bookings outside Australia ℡02/4423 5233, ⓦwww.premierms.com.au. Departs daily at 9.30am & 3.35pm, from the domestic terminal, ten minutes later from the international terminal, to south coast towns as far as Eden ($68). The 3.35pm service continues to Melbourne ($83). Bookings necessary.

line for reservations, and many of them will refund your bus fare; a few also offer free airport pick-ups.

By train and bus

All local and interstate **trains** arrive at **Central Station** on Eddy Avenue, just south of the city centre. From outside Central Station, and neighbouring Railway Square, you can hop onto nearly every major bus route, while from within Central Station you can take a CityRail train to any city or suburban station (see "City transport" on p.26).

All **buses** to Sydney arrive and depart from Eddy Avenue and Pitt Street, bordering Central Station. The area is well set up, with decent cafés, a 24-hour police station and a huge YHA hostel as well as the **Sydney Coach Terminal** (℡02/9281 9366; Mon–Fri 6am–6pm, Sat & Sun 8am–6pm), which has a luggage-storage room ($5–10 per 24hr, depending on size), an internet kiosk and can book accommodation, tours and all coach tickets and passes. You can also store your luggage at Wanderers' Travel, 810 George St, a three-minute walk around the block (daily 8am–8pm; $7 per bag, per day; $30 per week; ℡1800 888 722).

City transport

Sydney's public transport network is reasonably sophisticated and extensive, though train delays are not uncommon and, as the system relies heavily on buses, traffic jams can be a problem. Besides buses and trains, there are ferries, a light rail system and the city monorail to choose from, plus plenty of licensed taxis.

Trains stop running around midnight, as do most regular buses, though several services, such as #380 to Bondi Beach, #373 to Coogee, #151 to Manly, #396 to Maroubra, and #431 to Glebe Point, run through the night (see "Travelling at Night" at ⓦwww.sydneybuses.info/getting-around). Otherwise a pretty good network of **Nightride buses** follow the train routes to the suburbs, departing from Town Hall Station (outside the Energy Australia Building on George St) and stopping at train stations (where taxis wait at designated ranks); return train tickets, Railpasses and Travelpasses can be used, or buy a ticket from the driver. If you're staying more than a few days, it's worth getting a weekly **Travelpass** (see box, pp.28–29). For public transport information, routes, and timetables, contact the **Transport Infoline** ⓣ13 1500 (daily 6am–10pm; ⓦwww.131500 .com.au).

Buses

Within central Sydney, **buses** – hailed from yellow-signed bus stops – are the most convenient, widespread mode of transport, and cover more of the city than the trains. With few exceptions, buses radiate from the centre, with major interchanges at Railway Square near Central Station (especially southwest routes); at Circular Quay (range of routes); at York and Carrington streets outside Wynyard station (North Shore); and at Bondi Junction station (eastern suburbs and beaches).

Single-ride **tickets** can be bought on board from the driver and cost from $1.90 for up to two distance-measured sections, with a maximum fare of $6.10; $3.20 (up to 5 sections) is the most typical fare. Substantial discounts are available with

TravelTen tickets and other travel passes (see box, pp.28–29); these must be validated in the ticket reader next to the front door. Bus **information**, including route maps, **timetables** and **passes**, is available from handy booths at Carrington Street, Wynyard; at Circular Quay on the corner of Loftus and Alfred streets; and at the Queen Victoria Building on York Street. For detailed timetables and route maps, see Sydney Buses' website ⓦwww.sydneybuses.info.

Trains

Trains, operated by **CityRail** (see colour map at back of book), will get you where you're going faster than buses, especially at rush hour and when heading out to the suburbs, but you need to transfer to a bus or ferry to get to most harbourside or beach destinations. There are seven train lines, mostly overground, each of which stops at Central and Town Hall stations. Trains run from around 5am until midnight, with **tickets** starting at $3.20 for a single on the City Loop and for short hops; buying off-peak returns (after 9am and all weekend) saves you up to thirty percent.

Automatic ticket-vending machines (which give change) and barriers (insert magnetic tickets; otherwise, show ticket at the gate) have been introduced just about everywhere. On-the-spot fines for fare evasion start from $200, and transit officers patrol frequently. All platforms are painted with designated "nightsafe" waiting areas, and all but two or three train carriages are closed after about 8pm, enforcing a cattle-like safety in numbers. Security guards also patrol trains at night; at other times, if the train is deserted, sit in the carriage nearest the guard, as marked by a blue light.

Ferries and cruises

Sydney's distinctive green-and-yellow **ferries** are the fastest means of transport from Circular Quay to the North Shore, and indeed to most places around the harbour. Even if you don't want to go anywhere, a ferry ride is a must, a chance to get out on the water and see the city from the harbour. Get the excellent free *Guide to Sydney* by Sydney Ferries (from Sydney Ferry outlets at Circular Quay and Manly wharfs), which gives details of glorious ferry-accessible walks from South Head to Parramatta, or look at the itineraries in "Explore Sydney" at ⓦwww.sydneyferries.info.

Ferries chug off in various directions from the wharves at Circular Quay (see Sydney Ferries map, at back of book); cruises depart from Jetty 6. The popular **Manly Ferry service** leaves Circular Quay for Manly twice an hour between about 5.30am and 11.45pm (11pm on Sun) and takes thirty minutes. Most ferry routes operate until 11.40pm between Monday and Saturday, with the exception of the Darling Harbour service which runs until 10pm, and the Parramatta River, Watsons Bay and Taronga zoo services, which finish in the early evening. Except for the Manly Ferry, services on Sunday are greatly reduced and finish in the early evening around 6pm or 7pm. Timetables for each route are available at Circular Quay or on the Sydney Ferries website (ⓦwww.sydneyferries.nsw.gov.au).

One-way **fares** are $5.20 ($6.40 for the Manly Ferry); return fares are double. The pricier RiverCat to Parramatta costs $7.70. Travelpasses and FerryTen tickets can offer substantial savings – see box on pp.28–29 for details.

Harbour cruises

Almost all of Sydney's wide range of **harbour cruises** leave from Jetty 6, Circular Quay; the rest go from Darling Harbour. While many offer a good insight into the harbour and an intimate experience of its bays and coves, the much cheaper ordinary **ferry** rides are worth experiencing first, and make enjoyable cruises in themselves. The best of these is the thirty-minute ride to **Manly**, but there's a ferry going somewhere worth checking out at almost any time of the day. If you want to splash out, take a **water taxi** ride – Circular Quay to Watsons Bay, for example, costs $110 for up to four passengers (max 20; an extra $11 per person after the first four). Pick-ups are available from any wharf if booked in advance; Water Taxis Combined (☏02/9555 8888, ⓦwww.watertaxis.com.au) also offer half-hour ($250) and hour-long tours ($360) on a sleek, white water taxi (holds up to 20, but 15 is more comfortable) – tour route is negotiable.

The **Australian Travel Specialists** (ATS) at Jetty 6, Circular Quay, and the Harbourside Shopping Centre at Darling Harbour (☏02/9211 3192, ⓦwww.atstravel.com.au), book all cruises. The majority are offered by Captain Cook Cruises (☏02/9206 1122, ⓦwww.captaincook.com.au), and Matilda (☏02/9264 7377, ⓦwww.matilda.com.au), which operate independently but have now combined forces. However, Heritage Cruises, offered by the State Transit Authority (STA; ☏02/9246 8363, ⓦwww.sydneyferries.nsw.gov.au), is a little cheaper. The cruise leaves Wharf 4 at Circular Quay at 1.30pm daily for a

Whale-watching cruises

Whale watching has exploded in Sydney in the last few years. In season – June and July – when you're likely to see migratory humpback or southern right whales, many operators now offer daily whale-watch cruises from Darling Harbour or Circular Quay. Guidelines specify that the cruises must keep a slow speed within 300m of whales, but can approach up to 100m (200m if a calf is present). The average trip takes between three hour thirty minutes and four hours and costs $60–85, but will have as many as 75 passengers on board; most operators guarantee that you'll see whales or receive a refund or second trip. The bigger operators include True Blue Cruises (☏1800 309 672, ⓦwww.sydneywhalewatching.com), and Bass and Flinders Cruises (☏02/9583 1199, ⓦwww.whalewatchingsydney.net), while Sydney Eco Whale Watching (☏02/9878 0300, ⓦwww.austspiritsailingco.com.au), among others, do smaller yacht trips.

ninety-minute tour around the harbour's main attractions, as far as Woolwich in the west and around Shark Island in the east ($30).

Captain Cook Cruises' Middle Harbour Coffee Cruise (daily 10am & 2.15pm; 2hr; $49) is probably the most popular and affordable of the private cruises, offering an intimate experience of the harbour as you venture into quaint little bays and coves (with commentary on history and ecology). If you're willing to splurge, their 2 Night Weekend Escape Cruise ($423 per person) provides an even more pleasurable and intimate introduction to the harbour. Captain Cook also offer cheaper, shorter "highlight" tours on smaller sailing vessels, as well as breakfast, lunch, dinner and cocktail cruises that may take your fancy. Their popular hop-on-hop-off, seven-stop **Sydney Harbour Explorer** loops between Circular Quay, Fort Denison, Taronga Zoo, Shark Island, Watsons Bay, Luna Park and Darling Harbour (daily every 45min; 9.45am–5pm; $35, or discount combination tickets with attractions).

Matilda Cruises, based in Darling Harbour (Aquarium Wharf, Pier 26; ℡02/9264 7377, ⓦwww.matilda.com.au), offer various smaller-scale cruises on sailing catamarans, with large foredecks providing great views. Departures are from Pier 26, Darling Harbour; Wharf 6, Circular Quay; or both. Morning and afternoon "Coffee" cruises include tea, coffee and biscuits (daily 10am & 3pm from Darling Harbour; 2hr; $49); there's a seafood lunch cruise (daily 12.10pm; 2hr; $69); and a sunset cocktail cruise that allows you to watch the city's colours change (Circular Quay daily 5pm; 1hr 30min; $37). They also offer a weekday Lane Cove River ferry ($5.70 one-way; see p.117).

State Transit Authority (STA) travel passes

In addition to single-journey tickets, a vast array of STA **travel passes** are available. The most useful for visitors are outlined below; for more **information** on the full range of tickets and timetables, phone the **Transport Infoline** or check out their website (24hr; ℡13 15 00, ⓦwww.131500.com.au).

Passes are sold at most **newsagents** and at **train stations**. The more tourist-oriented Sydney Passes and Sydney Explorer Passes can be bought at train stations (including airport stations); on board Explorer buses; at State Transit Info booths; and from the Sydney Visitor Centre in The Rocks and Darling Harbour.

Tourist passes
Sydney Explorer Pass (one-day adult $39, ages 4–15 $19, family $97) comes with a map and description of the sights, and includes free travel on any State Transit bus within the same zones as the Explorer routes. The red **Sydney Explorer** (from Circular Quay; daily 8.40am–7.20pm; every 20min) takes in all the important sights in the city and inner suburbs, via 27 hop-on-hop-off stops. The blue **Bondi Explorer** (daily from Circular Quay; 8.30am–6.11pm; every 30min) covers the waterside eastern suburbs (19 stops including Kings Cross, Paddington, Double Bay, Vaucluse, Bondi, Bronte, Clovelly and Coogee). A **two-day ticket** (adult $68, ages 4–15 $34, family $170) allows use of both bus services over two days in a seven-day period.

Sydney Pass (3-, 5- or 7-day passes within a 7-day period; adult $110/145/165, child passes ages 4–15 $55/70/80, family passes $275/360/410) is valid for all buses and ferries including the above Explorer services, the ferry to Manly, the RiverCat to Parramatta, and a return trip to the airport valid for two months with the Airport Link train (buy the pass at the airport train station on arrival). It also covers travel on trains within the central area and discounts at many attractions.

Buses, trains and ferries
Travelpasses allow unlimited use of buses, trains and ferries and can begin on any day of the week. Most useful are the **Red Travelpass** ($38 per week), valid for the city and inner suburbs, and inner harbour ferries (not the Manly Ferry or the RiverCat beyond Meadowbank), and the **Green Travelpass** ($46), which covers all ordinary

More romantic **sailing** options are also available. **Sydney Harbour Tall Ships** (☎1300 664 410, ⓦwww.sydneytallships .com.au), run excursions aboard the *Svanen*, a beautiful three-masted Danish ship, built in 1922, which moors at Campbells Cove. Two-hour "Lunch" and "Twilight" cruises (both $79) sail past iconic harbour sites while guests devour gourmet seafood BBQ offerings. Sydney's oldest sailing ship, the *James Craig*, an 1874 three-masted iron barque, is part of the **Sydney Heritage Fleet** based at Wharf 7, Pirrama Rd, Pyrmont, near Star City Casino, and does six-hour weekend cruises (☎02/9298 3888, ⓦwww.shf.org.au /WhatsOn; Sat & Sun departs 9.30am, returns 4pm; $205; over-12s only; morning and afternoon tea and lunch provided).

With **Sydney by Sail** (☎02/9280 1110, ⓦwww.sydneybysail.com), you can enjoy the harbour from a luxury yacht. Groups are small (from six to twenty), and if you're interested the skipper might even show you some sailing techniques. The popular three hour Port Jackson Explorer cruise sails Sydney Harbour and surrounding inlets (daily 1pm; $150). Departures are from the National Maritime Museum at Darling Harbour, with free entry to the museum thrown in on the day (so buy your ticket in the morning and check out the museum before the afternoon sail). The yachts are also available for charter (see p.267). A number of other businesses also offer private boats to hire for various purposes (visit ⓦwww.sydneyharbourescapes.com.au).

Ocean Extreme offer an alternative to the sedate cruises listed above (☎1300 887 373, ⓦwww.oceanextreme.com.au): hair-raising, small-group (maximum ten) "Extreme Blasts" on an RIB (Rigid Inflatable Boat). Rush Hour ferries. Passes covering a wider area cost between $50 and $60 per week, and monthly passes are also available.

DayTripper tickets ($17) are also available for unlimited travel on all suburban services offered by CityRail, Sydney Buses and Sydney Ferries.

Buses and ferries

The **Blue Travelpass** ($34 per week) gives unlimited travel on buses in the inner-city area and on inner-harbour ferries, but cannot be used for Manly or beyond Meadowbank; the **Orange Travelpass** ($43 a week) gets you further on the buses and is valid on all ferries; and the **Pittwater Travelpass** ($58 a week) gives unlimited travel on all buses and ferries. These travelpasses start with first use rather than on the day of purchase.

Buses

TravelTen tickets represent a twenty percent saving over single fares by buying ten trips at once; they can be used over a space of time and for more than one person. The tickets are colour-coded according to how many sections they cover; the Brown TravelTen ($25.60), for example, is the choice for trips from Leichhardt, Newtown or Glebe to the city. The cheaper Blue TravelTen ($15.20) applies if you get off at, or before, Queen Victoria Building, while the Red TravelTen ($33.60) is the one to buy if you're staying at Bondi.

Ferries

FerryTen tickets, valid for ten single trips, start at $33.50 for Inner Harbour Services, and go up to $48.10 for the Manly Ferry.

Trains

Seven Day RailPass tickets allow unlimited travel between any two nominated stations and those in between, with savings of about twenty percent on the price of five return trips. For example, a pass between Bondi Junction and Town Hall would cost $27.

($80) is an hour-long trip out to the water outside the heads and back; the Bondi Bash ($95) is a ninety-minute trip beyond the heads to Bondi Beach; and Palm Beach Pursuit ($125), a two-hour trip to Palm Beach and back (times based on demand). At speeds of more than 100kph you will regularly, freakily, find yourself airborne. More thrills can be had with **Harbour Jet** (☎1300 887 373, ⓦwww .harbourjet.com), which runs the 35-minute Jet Blast ($65), fifty-minute Sydney Harbour Adventure ($80), and the two-hour Middle Harbour Adventure ($95) (Convention Jetty, Darling Harbour), on a boat that roars along at 75kph, executing 270-degree spins, power breaks and fishtails (times also based on demand). Not for the faint-hearted, it's loathed by the locals.

For cruises that leave from **Manly Wharf**, see p.140.

Monorail and Light Rail

Metro Transport Sydney (☎02/8584 5288, ⓦwww.metromonorail.com.au), a privately owned company, runs the city's monorail and light rail system. STA travelpasses cannot be used on either system.

Metro Monorail is essentially a tourist shuttle designed to loop around Darling Harbour every three to five minutes, connecting it with the city centre. Thundering along tracks set above the older city streets, the "monster rail" – as locals know it – doesn't exactly blend in with its surroundings. Still, the elevated view of the city, particularly from Pyrmont Bridge, makes it worth investing $4.80 (day-pass $9.50) and the ten minutes to do the whole circuit with its eight stops (Mon–Thurs 7am–10pm, Thurs–Sat 7am–midnight, Sun 8am–10pm).

Metro Light Rail runs from Central Station on a fourteen-stop route to Chinatown, Darling Harbour, the fish markets at Pyrmont, Star City Casino, Wentworth Park's greyhound racecourse, Glebe (with stops near Pyrmont Bridge Road, at Jubilee Park, and at Rozelle Bay by Bicentennial Park) and Lilyfield, not far from Darling Street, Rozelle. The air-conditioned light rail vehicles can carry 200 passengers, and are fully accessible to disabled commuters. The service operates 24 hours every ten to fifteen minutes to the casino (every 30min midnight–6am), with

reduced hours for stops to Lilyfield beyond (Mon–Thurs & Sun 6am–11pm, Fri & Sat 6am–midnight). There are two zones: zone 1 stations are Central to Convention Centre in Darling Harbour, and zone 2 is from Pyrmont Bay to Lilyfield. Tickets can be purchased at vending machines by the stops; singles cost $3.20/4.20 for zone 1/zone 2, returns $4.60/5.70, a day-pass costs $9, and a weekly one $22. A TramLink ticket, available from any CityRail station, combines a rail ticket to Central Station with an MLR ticket. If you plan to use the monorail and light rail a lot, it might be worth purchasing a **METROcard** ($30), which gives unlimited rides for seven days on both the monorail and light rail.

Taxis

Taxis are vacant if the rooftop light is on, though they are notoriously difficult to find at 3pm, when the shifts change over. The four major city **cab ranks** are outside the *Four Seasons Hotel* at the start of George Street, The Rocks; on Park Street outside Woolworths, opposite the Town Hall; outside David Jones department store on Market Street; and at the Pitt Street ("CountryLink") entrance to Central Station. Drivers never expect a tip but often need directions – try to have some idea of where you're going. Check that the tariff rate is displayed: tariff 2 (10pm–6am) is twenty percent higher than tariff 1 (6am–10pm). To book a taxi, call ABC (☎13 2522); Legion (☎13 1451); Premier (☎13 1017); RSL (☎13 1581); St George (☎13 2166); or Taxis Combined (☎013 3300). For harbour water taxis, call Water Taxis Combined (☎02/9555 8888).

Driving and vehicle rental

Driving your own vehicle allows you to explore Sydney's more far-flung beaches and national parks and other day-trip areas.

Most foreign **licences** are valid for a year in Australia. An International Driving Permit (available from national motoring organizations) may be useful if you come from a non-English-speaking country. **Fuel prices** fluctuate between 90¢ and over $1 per litre unleaded, from week to week (when the global economy is stable – in times of tumult prices can get as high $1.65), with diesel

Warning: Tags, tolls & passes on Sydney's orbital motorway network

All of Sydney's ten major motorways, which form a convenient orbital network around the city, charge **tolls**. To make matters worse, Sydney has acquired a number of fully electronic motorways over the last few years, causing a great deal of confusion, frustration and unnecessary financial loss to visitors and locals alike. The main culprits are the **Cross City Tunnel**, the **Sydney Harbour Tunnel**, and, most recently, the **Sydney Harbour Bridge**.

Drivers likely to use electronic motorways can choose between purchasing an **E-tag**, which requires a $40 deposit (no refund if marked or not working when returned), or applying for a 1- to 7-day **E-toll** pass (best for short visits) by providing credit card and registration details (number plates are photographed each time a car passes through a toll with a charge subsequently placed on the relevant account). Your car rental company should be able to sort it out for you, but if you're borrowing a car, you can organize it online on the ⓦ sydneymotorways.com website. The E-toll pass incurs a registration fee of $3.30 by phone ($1.50 online) and a supplementary 75¢ video processing fee each time you pay the toll. Should you go through electronic tollbooths without a pass or tag you have 48 hours to acquire a retrospective pass, by phone or online. If you fail to do so, you will incur a fine.

Drivers should be aware that crossing the **Harbour Bridge** or the **Harbour tunnel** in a northerly direction is free, but that briefly joining the Eastern Distributor at the intersection of Moore Park Road and Anzac Parade, Paddington, to connect with the Harbour Bridge or Tunnel (a common occurrence when approaching from the eastern or inner eastern suburbs) incurs the Eastern Distributor toll of $5. For return southbound journeys, the toll on the Harbour Bridge varies: (Mon–Fri 6.30–9.30am $4, 9.30am–4pm $3, 4–7pm $4, 7pm–6.30am $2.50; Sat & Sun $3 by day, $2.50 by night). Southbound on the Sydney Harbour Tunnel costs $4.

With its electronic toll, high (albeit slowly decreasing) rates, and quick travel time, the AUS$680 million **Cross City Tunnel** is both frustrating and pleasing for unsuspecting visitors. Running east–west/west–east beneath the city centre between Darling Harbour and Rushcutters Bay, it links the Anzac Bridge and the Western Distributor at the western end and New South Head Road at the eastern end, and has underground links with the Eastern Distributor (which heads out to the airport). The 2.1km tunnel cuts a thirty-minute traffic-jammed cross-city route to five minutes – but at a cost. The electronic toll is $4.12 each way, or a lot more if you fail to organize an E-pass in time.

slightly cheaper. The **rules of the road** are similar to those in the US and UK. Most importantly, **drive on the left** (as in the UK), remember that seatbelts are compulsory for all, and that the **speed limit** in all built-up areas is 50kph (60kph if signposted; 40kph in school zones during school hours). Outside built-up areas, maximum limits are between 80kph and 110kph. All changes in speed limits are frequently and obviously signed. Whatever else you do in a vehicle, don't drink alcohol to excess; random breath tests are common even in rural areas, especially during the Christmas season and on Friday and Saturday nights. One rule that might catch you out in town is that roadside parking must be in the same direction as the traffic.

Vehicle rental

To **rent** a car you need a full, clean driving licence; usually, a minimum age of 21 is stipulated by the major car-rental companies, rising to 25 for 4WDs. Check any mileage limits or other restrictions, extras and what you're covered for in an accident before you sign. The multinational operators Hertz, Budget, Avis and Thrifty have offices in Sydney. Local firms – of which there are many – are almost always better value, and the bottom-line "rent-a-bomb" agencies go as low as $20 per day; however, these places often have restrictions on how far from Sydney you're allowed to drive. A city-based non-multinational rental agency will supply new cars from around $50 a day with unlimited kilometres.

Four-wheel drives are best used for specific areas rather than long term, as rental (and fuel) costs are steep, starting at around $120 per day. Some 4WD agents don't actually allow their vehicles to be driven off sealed roads, so check the small print first.

You can reserve a vehicle before you arrive with the businesses below, or, once you're in Sydney, from any of the companies listed in "Travel essentials".

Rental companies

Avis ☎+612/8374 2847, 🕸www.avis.com.au
Budget ☎+612/9207 9165, 🕸www.budget .com.au
Hertz ☎+613/9698 2555, 🕸www.hertz.com.au
Thrifty ☎+612/8337 2700, 🕸www.thrifty.com.au

The media

Sydney offers a wide range of print media, a rather American-influenced variety of TV channels, and several radio stations worth tuning in to.

The press

The Fairfax-owned *Sydney Morning Herald* (*SMH*; 🕸www.smh.com.au) is *the* paper to buy to find out what's going on in Sydney. Of its special daily supplements, the most useful are Monday's "The Guide", a programme and review of the week's TV; Tuesday's "Good Living", which focuses on the restaurant, foodie and bar scene; and Friday's entertainment-geared "Metro", with its listings and film, art and music reviews. There are employment and rental sections daily, but the big Saturday edition is the best for these, while Saturday's "Spectrum" includes a two-page spread of events and activities worth checking out that weekend and in the coming week. Sydney also has a tabloid, the Murdoch-owned *Daily Telegraph*. Both Sydney dailies have a lower-brow, ad-packed, multi-section Sunday version, the *Sun Herald* and the *Sunday Telegraph*.

The Murdoch-owned *Australian* is Australia's only national daily (that is, Mon–Sat) newspaper. Aimed mainly at the business community, it has good overseas coverage but local news is often built around statistics; its bumper weekend edition (Sat) is much more lively and interesting.

TV

Australia's first television station opened in 1956 and the country didn't get colour television until 1974 – both much later than other Westernized countries. Australian commercial television, on the whole, isn't particularly exciting unless you're into sport, of which there's plenty, and commercial stations put on frequent ad breaks throughout films. Australian content rulings ensure a high quality of Australian dramas, series and soap operas, some of which go on to make it big overseas, from the Melbourne-set *Neighbours* and *The Secret Life of Us* to *Home and Away*, filmed at Sydney's Palm Beach, and the comic suburban send-up *Kath and Kim*.

There is, however, a predominance of American programmes. Australian TV is also fairly permissive in terms of sexual content compared with the programming of Britain or North America. There are three predictable commercial stations: Channel Seven; Channel Nine, which aims for an older market; and Channel Ten, which tries to grab the younger market with reality-TV programmes like the Australian version of *Big Brother* and some relatively good comedy programmes including the irreverent talk show *Rove Live*. There is also the more intellectually oriented ABC

(Australian Broadcasting Corporation; www .abc.net.au) – a government-funded, national, ad-free station with a British bias. Programming includes the best British comedies, sitcoms and mini-series, some excellent Australian current affairs programmes such as *Foreign Correspondent* and *The 7.30 Report*, the occasional hard-hitting Aussie drama, and shows put together by the politically adept and hilarious *Chaser* team. The lively SBS (Special Broadcasting Service), a mostly government-sponsored, multicultural station, has the best coverage of world news, as well as interesting current affairs programmes, grass-roots talk shows, original Australian dramas (like the impressive *Carla Cametti PD* of early 2009) and plenty of highly entertaining foreign-language films – everything from French dramas, to chilling Japanese thrillers to weird and wonderful Bavarian musicals.

For channel guides, see www .ebroadcast.com.au/tv/, which has links to all the TV stations.

Radio

Sydney's best **radio** is on the various ABC stations, both local and national: Radio National (576 AM) offers a popular mix of arty intellectual topics; 2BL (702 AM), intelligent talk-back radio; News Radio (630 AM), 24-hour local and international news, current affairs, sports, science and finance, also using a diverse range of foreign radio networks including the BBC World Service, the US's National Public Radio (NPR), and Germany's Radio Deutsche Welle; ABC Classic FM (92.9 FM), for classical music; and 2JJJ ("Triple J"; 105.7 FM), which supports local bands and alternative rock – aimed squarely at the nation's youth. You can listen to various ABC radio stations on the web with live or on-demand audio (www.abc.net.au/streaming).

Sydney's "underground" radio station is the university-run – though largely self-supporting – **2SER** (107.3FM; www.2ser.com) which airs a fabulously eclectic mix of shows taking in current affairs and social issues programmes along with a plethora of music shows for different genres, from blues to reggae, Latin, funk, beats, jazz, electronic, hip hop, country, folk, goth and industrial. Koori Radio (93.7FM; www.gadigal.org.au) gives voice to Aboriginal and Torres Strait Island communities in Sydney; the city's only "black" radio station, it plays a great mix of indigenous Australian and world music, and other black musicians.

Travellers with disabilities

Since cheerfully hosting the Paralympics in 2000, Sydney has become adept at welcoming disabled travellers. Disability need not interfere with your sightseeing: the attitude of the management at Sydney's major tourist attractions is excellent, and staff will provide assistance where they can, while most national parks have wheelchair accessible walks.

The Australian federal government provides a national, non-profit, free **information service** on recreation, sport, tourism, the arts, and much more, for people with disabilities, through the National Information Communication Awareness Network (NICAN; ☏02/6241 1220 or 1800 806 769; www.nican.com.au). In addition, the Australian Tourist Commission offices provide a helpline service and publish a factsheet, *Travelling in Australia for People with Disabilities*, available from its offices worldwide (see p.40 for addresses and phone numbers).

Planning a holiday

There are **organized tours and holidays** specifically for people with disabilities (including mobility, hearing, vision and intellectual restrictions). Some arrange travel only, some travel and accommodation, and others provide a complete package – travel, accommodation, meals and carer support (that is, company for the trip). The contacts on p.36 can put you in touch with specialists for trips to Sydney; several are listed in the Australian Tourist Commission factsheet. If you want to be more independent, it's important to become an authority on where you must be self-reliant and where you may expect help, especially regarding transport and accommodation. It is also vital to be honest – with travel agencies, insurance companies and

travel companions. Know your limitations and make sure others know them. If you do not use a wheelchair all the time, but your walking capabilities are limited, remember that you are likely to need to cover greater distances while travelling (often over rougher terrain and in hotter temperatures) than you are used to. If you use a **wheelchair**, have it serviced before you go and carry a repair kit.

Read your **travel insurance** small print carefully to make sure that people with pre-existing medical conditions are not excluded. And use your travel agent to make your journey simpler: airline or bus companies can cope better if they are expecting you, with a wheelchair provided at airports and staff primed to help. A **medical certificate** of your fitness to travel (provided by your

Accessible Sydney – a personal view

Sydney is possibly the most beautiful city in the world, and it's my home town. It's not only a stunning harbourside haven of fabulous dining experiences, designer shopping, divine beaches, spectacular views and truly friendly locals, it's also a very accessible destination. I ride around on an electric blue scooter – no, not a Vespa, unless you squint and fail to notice its three wheels and the place to carry walking sticks. I'm in my thirties and have had rheumatoid arthritis since childhood. Six joint replacements, as well as numerous other surgical procedures, has meant my life has been lived between walking sticks, crutches, wheelchairs and scooters. I've travelled the world with this disability, so I have a pretty good idea of the difficulties visitors to Sydney might face. Take a scooter or wheelchair, a mobile phone, sunscreen, hat, sunglasses and a bottle of water and you're set for an adventure around Sydney.

Stay in **accommodation** close to the Light Rail (see p.36) – it runs 24 hours and links with other accessible modes of transport throughout the city, including the Monorail, trains, buses and ferries. The Light Rail runs from Central Station through Chinatown and the tourist area of Darling Harbour, to the fish markets and then through a couple of inner-city suburbs including Glebe with its cafés, restaurants and pubs. It's a great way to get around – the conductor will spot you, pull out a ramp and direct you to appropriate on-board parking.

If you bring your own wheelchair or scooter to Sydney ensure you take along some spare tubes for your tyres. And if you do get a flat then call the National Roads and Motoring Authority (NRMA; ☏13 11 11) and they'll come and change the tube for you.

You can **hire** everything from raised toilet seats to wheelchairs and crutches. Check out Ⓦwww.accessibility.com.au, an informative site with details on everything from equipment hire and repairs to accommodation and things to do in Sydney.

My perfect Sydney day – an itinerary

You'll need to be up bright and early for the **Growers Markets at Pyrmont Park** in front of Star City Casino, foodie heaven for the Sydneysider. It's held on the first Saturday of the month (7–11am, except Jan). Start off at Central Station on the Light Rail – alight at the Casino and follow the smell of frying bacon and hot coffee until you reach the park by the water. It's always crowded and some of the stalls are on the grass, but it's truly worth the effort and the vendors are always helpful and doctor) is also extremely useful; some airlines or insurance companies may insist on it. Make sure that you have extra supplies of medication – carried with you if you fly – and a prescription including the generic name in case of emergency.

Books that give good overviews of accessible travel in Australia include: *Easy Access Australia*, by Bruce Cameron, a comprehensive guide written by an Australian wheelchair-user for anyone with a mobility difficulty, available over the Internet via ⓦwww.easyaccessaustralia.com.au (AUS$27.45, postage extra, or available from bookshops in Australia); and *A Wheelie's Handbook of Australia* by Australian-based Colin James, which at the time of research was being updated and put into a CD ROM and DVD format (AUS$22.95 includes postage and handling within Australia; ⓦhome.vicnet.net.au/~wheelies).

The disability information resource website has a very useful city guide to Sydney (ⓦwww.accessibility.com.au/sydney/sydney .htm). Most national parks have wheelchair-accessible walks; see ⓦwww.environment .nsw.gov.au/NationalParks/Wheelchair.aspx.

Useful contacts

ⓦ**www.accessibility.com.au** Online city guide with details on the wheelchair accessibility of theatres, cinemas, restaurants, galleries, shopping centres and tourist attractions in the Sydney metropolitan region. ⓦ**www.toiletmap.gov.au** Type a location into the National Public Toilet Map website for immediate info on all accessible toilets nearby.

more than willing to ensure that you get a taste of some of Sydney's finest produce: organic meats, pasta, olives, oils, cheeses and the freshest of bread, fruit, veg as well as strawberries dipped in delectable chocolate.

Get back on the Light Rail and head to the **Sydney Fish Markets**. It can be a bit hair-raising in the car park as locals, tourists and taxis jostle for position but just keep your wits about you and you're in for an experience. Just about everything that swims in the sea is available fresh to take away, or to eat by the waterfront: lobster, sushi, garlic prawn skewers, plain old fish and chips or a fillet of salmon to throw on the barbecue later. There's a bottle shop with a pretty good wine selection, a deli with some fabulous Australian cheeses, and a great fruit shop. All the shops are quite accessible although sometimes you do need to wave a flag to be noticed as the pace can be quite frenetic and sales are quickly made above your head.

Jump back on the Light Rail for a quick trip to **Darling Harbour** which has loads of shops and restaurants. Follow the water around to the other side for a visit to the **Sydney Aquarium** with its Great Barrier Reef exhibition and stunning displays of sea creatures. You can access all areas easily and they have designated toilets, and wheelchairs available for hire.

Take a ferry from adjacent King Street Wharf to **Circular Quay**. Around half of the Sydney ferry wharves are accessible and boarding is simple, although the gradient of the ramp does vary according to the tide. The deckhands are really eager to please which makes getting out on the harbour an easy and fun (not to mention spectacular) thing to do while in Sydney.

Have a sunset drink at the **Opera Bar at the Sydney Opera House** – the sun low in the sky behind the Harbour Bridge and the passing parade of leisure cruisers, tourist boats and government ferries makes for a stunning accompaniment to the drink in your hand. Happy hour indeed. Then catch some culture inside the Opera House itself. All the theatres have accessible seating, the staff are fantastic, plus you get to use the Stage Door entrance so you never know who you might bump into!

After the Opera House, take the train from elevator-accessible Circular Quay Station back to Central. Above all bring some courage and determination with you and never hesitate to ask for help – Australians really are friendly.

Nicole Bradshaw

In the UK and Ireland

Holiday Care ☎0845/124 9971, ⊛www .holidaycare.org.uk. Provides free lists of accessible accommodation abroad, information on financial aid and general assistance in making your holiday happen.
Irish Wheelchair Association Blackheath Drive, Clontarf, Dublin 3 ☎01/833 8241, ⊕833 3873, ⊕iwa@iol.ie. Useful information provided about travelling abroad with a wheelchair.
RADAR (Royal Association for Disability and Rehabilitation) London ☎020/7250 3222, Minicom ☎020/7250 4119, ⊛www.radar.org.uk.
Tripscope The Vassal Centre, Gill Ave, Bristol BS16 2QQ, ☎0845/7585 641. This registered charity provides a national telephone information service offering free advice on UK and international transport for those with a mobility problem.

In the US and Canada

Access-Able ⊛www.access-able.com. Online resource for travellers with disabilities.
Mobility International USA Eugene, voice and TDD ☎541/343-1284, ⊛www.miusa.org. Information and referral services, access guides, tours and exchange programmes.
Society for Accessible Travel & Hospitality (SATH) New York ☎212/447-7284, ⊛www .sath.org. Non-profit educational organization that has actively represented travellers with disabilities since 1976.
Travel Information Service ☎215/456-9600. Telephone-only information and referral service.
Twin Peaks Press Vancouver ☎360/694-2462 or 1-800/637-2256. Publisher of the Directory of Travel Agencies for the Disabled ($19.95), listing more than 370 agencies worldwide; Travel for the Disabled ($19.95); the Directory of Accessible Van Rentals ($12.95); and Wheelchair Vagabond ($19.95), loaded with personal tips.

In Australia

NDS (National Disability Services) Pitt St, Sydney ☎02/9256 3111, ⊛www.nds.org.au. Provides all manner of assistance to people with a disability.
NICAN (National Information Communication Awareness Network) See p.33.
People with Disability Australia Redfern, Sydney ☎02/9370 3100, ⊛www.pwd.org.au. Rights and advocacy organization offers rights-related info, advice and referral services.

Accommodation

Much of Australia's tourist accommodation is well set up for people with disabilities, because buildings tend to be built outwards rather than upwards. New buildings in Australia must comply with a legal minimum **accessibility standard**, requiring that bathrooms contain toilets at the appropriate height, proper circulation and transfer space, wheel-in showers (sometimes with fold-down seat, but if this is lacking, proprietors will provide a plastic chair), grab rails, adequate doorways, and space next to toilets and beds for transfer. There are, of course, many older hotels, which may have no wheelchair access at all or perhaps just one or two rooms with full wheelchair access. Most hotels also have refrigerators for any medication that needs to be kept cool.

Accessible accommodation in Sydney is most likely found in the big chain hotels. Some smaller hotels do provide accessible accommodation, and a large proportion of suburban motels will have one or two suitable rooms. The country around Sydney holds fewer specially equipped hotels, but many motels have accessible units; this is particularly true of those that belong to a chain such as *Choice Hotels* (☎03/9243 2400, ⊛www.choicehotels.com.au). The newest YHA **hostels** are all accessible, and there has been an effort to improve facilities throughout; accessible hostels are detailed in the YHA *Handbook*, or check ⊛www .yha.com.au. **Caravan parks** are also worth considering, since some have accessible cabins. Others may have accessible toilets and washing facilities. Many resorts are also fully designed and equipped for wheelchair travellers, though in all cases it's best to check in advance what facilities are available.

Transport

Post-Olympic improvements in Sydney include many wheelchair-accessible train stations in the Central Business District. Once you get out of the city not all stations have lifts, though many have ramps, and there are plans to make more stations disabled friendly. Check "Station Facilities" on ⊛www.cityrail.info before setting out, or call the Transport Infoline (☎13 15 00). Various accessible bus routes run throughout the city, as well as along major routes into the suburbs. See ⊛www.sydneybuses.info /getting-around/bus-accessibility.htm.

Sydney also has a fleet of **wheelchair taxis**, but be prepared to wait anything from five minutes to hours for one. Call Zero 200 (Wheelchair Accessible Taxis) on ☎02/8332 0200.

Of the major **car-rental** agencies, Hertz and Avis offer vehicles with hand controls at no extra cost, but advance notice is required. Reserved **parking** is available for vehicles displaying the wheelchair symbol (available from local council offices). There is no formal acceptance of overseas parking permits, but states will generally accept most home-country permits as sufficient evidence to obtain a temporary permit (call NICAN for further information). With a permit you can park on meters without paying, stay longer than the norm at some spaces, and use a number of designated parking spots in the CBD.

The "Disabled Access" section on the City of Sydney Council's website includes access maps (Ⓦwww.cityofsydney.nsw .gov.au/AboutSydney/CBDDisabledAccess). Among local councils that will post out mobility maps, showing accessible paths, car parking, toilets and so on, is Randwick Council, which has installed wheelchair accessible ramps at Clovelly and Malabar beaches (30 Francis St, Randwick, NSW 2031; ☎02/9399 0999, Ⓦwww.randwick .nsw.gov.au).

Crime and personal safety

Take the same precautions in Sydney as you would in any other major city in the Western world, though the city's "heavy" areas would seem tame compared to similar areas in Europe or North America.

Drunk males may pose the usual problems on Friday and Saturday nights, though there is no sudden spill out onto the streets as closing times are variable. As in most places, you might find restless teenagers getting themselves into trouble in the city. CCTV cameras have been installed in city areas that often see problems, such as The Rocks, which gets very rowdy on Friday and Saturday nights, and on the George Street cinema strip, which is a popular suburban teenage hangout and a prime area for personal theft. Kings Cross is the red-light district and has a major drug problem. The main strips are crowded but there are assaults and muggings – be careful with your belongings here at any time, and try not to walk down backstreets at night. Nearby Woolloomooloo, though going upmarket, has some troubled public housing, so it's wise to be careful at night.

You're more likely to fall victim to a fellow traveller or an opportunist crime: as **theft** is not unusual in hostels, many provide lockable boxes; if you leave valuables lying around, or on view in cars, you can expect them to be stolen. Be careful with valuables at the beach; either leave them at your accommodation if you are alone, or take turns swimming. There are lockers at Bondi Beach (see p.133) and at Manly (p.141).

Exercise caution, don't forget common-sense streetwise precautions, and you should be fine. At night stay in areas that are well lit and full of people, look like you know where you are going, and don't carry excess cash or anything else that you can't afford to lose.

Rape and serious trouble

If the worst happens, it's best to contact the **Rape Crisis Centre** (24hr; ☎1800 424 017) before going straight to the police. Women police officers form a large part of the force, and in general the police deal sensitively with sexual assault cases.

To avoid physical attack, don't get too relaxed about Australia's friendly, easy-going attitude. The usual defensive tactics apply.

Police stations in central and tourist areas

NSW Police Headquarters are at 1 Charles St, Parramatta. If you have any problems, or need to report a theft for insurance purposes or any other crime, you can drop in here or at a local police station.

For **emergencies** ☏000 (☏112 from mobiles) is a free number, which summons the police, ambulance or fire service. For general enquiries call ☏131 444 or for non-emergencies (to report crime anonymously) call ☏1800 333 000. The following stations near frequently visited areas are open 24 hours:

Balmain 368 Darling St (☏02/9556 0699).

Bondi Beach 91–93 Roscoe St (☏02/9365 9699).

Broadway 3–9 Regent St, Chippendale (☏02/9219 2199).

Darling Harbour 192 Day St (☏02/9265 6499).

Glebe 1–3 Talfourd St, Corner of St Johns Rd (☏02/9552 8099).

Kings Cross 1–15 Elizabeth Bay Rd (☏02/8356 0099).

Manly 3 Belgrave St (☏02/9977 9499).

Mosman 96 Bradleys Head Rd (☏02/9969 1933).

Newtown 222 Australia St (☏02/9550 8199).

North Sydney 273 Pacific Highway (☏02/9956 3199).

Paddington 16 Jersey Rd (☏02/8356 8299).

Randwick 30 Turner St (☏02/9697 1099).

Redfern 30 Turner St (☏02/8303 5199).

The Rocks 132 George St, Corner of Argyle St (☏02/9265 6366).

Surry Hills 151 Goulburn St (☏02/9265 4144).

Town Hall 570 George St (☏02/9265 6595).

Buses are generally safer than trains – on the train, always sit near the guard in the carriage. Pick somewhere to stay that's close to public transport so you don't have to walk far at night – an area with busy nightlife may well be safer than a dead suburban backstreet. If you're going to have to walk for long stretches at night, take a cab unless the streets are busy with traffic and people.

Police and the law

The NSW **Police** Service were identified by a Royal Commission in the 1990s as notoriously corrupt. While matters may have outwardly improved, their reputation has not. Perhaps as a result they tend to keep a low profile; you should have no trouble in your dealings with them. Indeed you'll hardly see them, unless you're out on a Friday or Saturday night when they cruise in search of drink-related brawls.

Watch out, most of all, for **drugs**. A lot of marijuana is grown and its use is widespread, but you'd be foolish to carry it when you travel, and crazy to carry any other illicit narcotic, especially as sniffer dogs now do random searches at Sydney train stations. Driving in general makes you more likely to have a confrontation of some kind, if only for a minor traffic infringement; **drunk driving** is taken extremely seriously, so don't risk it – random breath tests are common around all cities and larger towns.

Lesser potential problems include **alcohol** – there are all sorts of controls on where and when you can drink in public; **smoking**, which is increasingly being banned in public places; and nude or **topless** sunbathing, which is quite acceptable in many places, but absolutely not in others – follow the locals' lead.

If for any reason you are arrested or need help (and you can be arrested merely on suspicion of committing an offence), you are entitled to contact a friend or lawyer before answering any questions. You could call your consulate, but don't expect much sympathy. If necessary, the police will provide a lawyer, and you can usually get legal aid to settle the bill.

Travel essentials

Addresses and floors

The way that addresses are written for apartments (also more commonly known as flats, units or home units) or offices in Australia can cause some confusion. An address given as 4/6 Smith St means Apartment 4, 6 Smith St. Floor levels are usually ground, first, second, third, or ground, level 1, level 2 etc. Basement levels are often called lower ground floor.

Costs

If you've stopped over in southeast Asia you'll find Sydney, with its high standard of living, expensive for daily purchases. Visitors fresh from Europe or US find prices comparable and often cheaper, particularly for accommodation and eating out. Australia is well set up for independent travellers, and a student card (see below) gets discounts on travel and entertainment in Sydney.

If you stay in a hostel, eat in the cheapest cafés and restaurants, and travel by public transport, the absolute minimum daily budget is around $50. Add on sightseeing admissions and a minimal social life and you're looking at at least $100. Staying in decent hotels, eating at moderate restaurants, and paying for tours and nightlife extend your budget to $160–220 per day.

Hostel accommodation will set you back $25–35 per person, while a double room in a moderate hotel costs $130–180. Food is good value: dishes in cheap Asian places cost as little as $10; counter meals in pubs and cafés start from $12; and restaurant mains cost $15–35 depending on the standard. Bottled beer goes for $4–7, while wine starts at around $5 per glass. Renting a car costs around $50 per day; the longer you rent for, the cheaper the daily rate.

A **Goods and Services Tax** (GST) of ten percent, charged on just about everything except fresh foods, is almost always included in quoted prices. Under the Tourist Refund Scheme, visitors can claim GST refunds for goods purchased in Australia as they clear customs, provided individual receipts from any one supplier exceed $300 and the claim is made within thirty days of purchase. Goods must be packed in your hand luggage. Many stores in The Rocks and the airport have a "sealed bag" system that lets you buy goods without paying GST, and the minimum of $300 is waived.

Youth and student discount cards

Once obtained, various official and quasi-official **youth/student ID cards** soon pay for themselves in savings. Full-time students are eligible for the International Student ID Card (ISIC; Ⓦ www.isiccard.com), which entitles the bearer to special air, rail and bus fares and discounts at museums, theatres and other attractions. For Americans there's a

See Sydney & Beyond Smartvisit Card

All the Sydney Visitor Centre tourist offices sell the **See Sydney & Beyond Smartvisit Card** (☎ 1300 661 711, Ⓦ www.seesydneycard.com), which includes admission to forty attractions in Sydney and the Blue Mountains – from Taronga Zoo to a guided tour of the Opera House. If an action-packed, fast-paced itinerary is your thing the card can be good value; it's certainly a convenient way to bypass the queues. The card can be bought for one day (adult $75, child 4–15 years $55), two consecutive days ($135/79), three days ($165/95), and seven days ($225/160). With the last three you can also include a Travelpass giving entry plus almost unlimited use of trains, buses and ferries for two days ($175/99), three days ($225/125), or seven days ($299/199).

To work out whether it's worth buying one, decide what you want to see, check the entry prices in our Guide and compare the total amount to the price of a card.

health benefit, providing up to US$25,000 in emergency medical coverage, plus a 24-hour hotline to call in the event of a medical, legal or financial emergency. The card costs US$22 for Americans; CAN$16 for Canadians; AUS$18 for Australians; NZ$20 for New Zealanders; and £9 in the UK. If you're not a student, but are 26 or younger, you still qualify for the International Youth Travel Card, which costs the same and carries the same benefits. Teachers qualify for the International Teacher Card (same price, some of the benefits). All these cards are available from local student travel agents, or the website. Once you are in Australia, purchasing either an International YHA Card or Backpacker Resorts VIP Card (Ⓦwww.vipbackpackers.com) will give you discounts on relevant hostel accommodation, a host of transport, tours, services, entry fees and even meals; they're worth getting even if you're not planning to stay in hostels.

Electricity

Australia's electrical current is 240v, 50Hz AC. British appliances will work with an adaptor; American and Canadian 110v appliances need a transformer, though most laptops, phone chargers and the like will work fine with just a plug adaptor.

Entry requirements

The Department of Immigration and Citizenship (Ⓦwww.immi.gov.au) handles all applications for entry to Australia, and a great deal can be done through their website. **New Zealanders** visiting Australia do not need any form of visa and can live and work there as long as they like. Everyone else needs some form of **visa**, which will normally allow multiple entries to Australia for a period of twelve months. with a maximum of three months per visit.

Visitors from **European** countries should apply online for an **eVisitor visa** (free). The application takes a few minutes but should be started two weeks before you arrive. You'll be emailed a notification to present with your passport when entering Australia.

Visitors from **Canada**, **USA** and some east Asian countries should apply for an **ETA** (Electronic Travel Authority; Ⓦwww.eta.immi .gov.au), most easily done online or through your travel agent or airline when you book your travel. The ETA application costs AUS$20; if

successful your details will be recorded on the Australian Government system and you'll be waved through on arrival.

Other visitors will need a **tourist visa** (AUS$100), which can last three, six or twelve months, and be applied for online or through your nearest Australian embassy or consulate. Forms can be downloaded from the website.

Longer visas, working visas and extensions

As ETAs and eVisitor visas only allow visits of up to three months, if you want to stay longer it pays to get a tourist visa (see above) in advance. If you're already in Australia on some other visa, you can extend your stay by applying for a new tourist visa, but it will cost AUS$240.

If you need to extend your visa while in Sydney, contact the Department of Immigration and Citizenship, 26 Lee St, near Central Station (☎13 1881). If you're visiting immediate family who live in Australia, apply for a **Sponsored Family Visitor Visa** (AUS$100), which has fewer restrictions. You may be asked to prove you have adequate funds to support yourself – at least AUS$1000 a month.

Twelve-month **Working Holiday Visas** – with the stress on casual employment – are easily available to British, Irish, Canadian, Dutch, German, Italian, Japanese and Korean people aged 18–30. You must arrange the visa before you arrive in Australia, best done online. If there are no complications it should only take a week and the processing fee is AUS$195. Similar conditions apply for US citizens who should apply for the **Work and Holiday Visa** (also AUS$195).

Australian embassies and consulates

For a full list of **Australian embassies and consulates**, consult Ⓦwww.dfat.gov.au /missions/index.html.

Canada Australian High Commission, Suite 710, 50 O'Connor St, Ottawa, Ontario K1P 6L2 ☎613/236-0841, Ⓦwww.canada.embassy.gov.au.

Ireland Australian Embassy, Fitzwilton House, Wilton Terrace, Dublin 2 ☎01/664 5300, Ⓦwww.ireland .embassy.gov.au.

New Zealand Australian High Commission, 72–78 Hobson St, Thorndon, Wellington ☎04/473 6411,

ⓦ www.newzealand.embassy.gov.au; also a consulate in Auckland.

UK Australian High Commission, Australia House, Strand, London WC2B 4LA ℡ 020/7379 4334, ⓦ www.uk.embassy.gov.au; and a consulate in Edinburgh.

US Australian Embassy, 1601 Massachusetts Ave NW, Washington, DC 20036 2273 ℡ 202/797-3000, ⓦ www.usa.embassy.gov.au; and consulates in several other cities.

Foreign consulates in Australia

While all foreign embassies are in Canberra, many countries have consulates in Sydney. For visas for onward travel, consult "Consulates and Legations" in the Yellow Pages. A full list of consulates in Australia can be found at ⓦ www.dfat.gov.au.

Canada Level 5, 111 Harrington St ℡ 02/9364 3000, ⓦ geo.international.gc.ca/asia/Australia.

New Zealand Level 10, 55 Hunter St ℡ 02/8256 2000.

UK Level 16, Gateway Building, 1 Macquarie Place ℡ 02/9247 7521, ⓦ ukinaustralia.fco.gov.uk

US Level 59, MLC Centre, 19–29 Martin Place ℡ 02/9373 9200.

Customs and quarantine

When entering Australia, the duty-free allowance is 2.25 litres of alcohol; 250 cigarettes or 250g of tobacco; and AUS\$900 worth of goods. Strict quarantine laws apply to fruit, vegetables, fresh and packaged food, seed and some animal products, among other things. Most packaged products will be allowed in after inspection but declare anything that may be suspect. For more details consult ⓦ www.daffa.gov.au/aqis.

Insurance

The national healthcare scheme in Australia, **Medicare** ⓦ www.medicareaustralia.gov.au), offers a reciprocal arrangement – free essential healthcare – for citizens of the UK, Ireland, New Zealand, Italy, Malta, Finland, the Netherlands and Sweden. This free treatment is limited to public hospitals and casualty departments; at GPs you pay upfront (about \$55 minimum) with two-thirds of your fee reimbursed by Medicare (does not apply to citizens of New Zealand and Ireland). If you are entitled to free emergency healthcare from Medicare, you may feel that the need for the health element of travel insurance is reduced. In any case, some form of travel insurance can help plug the gaps and will cover you if you lose your luggage or miss a plane.

A typical travel insurance policy usually provides cover for the loss of baggage, tickets and – up to a certain limit – cash or cheques, as well as cancellation or curtailment of your journey. Most of them exclude "high-risk" activities unless an extra premium is paid: depending on the insurer, these can include water sports (especially diving), skiing or even just hiking; check carefully that any policy you are considering will cover you in case of an accident. Many policies can be chopped and changed to exclude coverage you don't need – for example, sickness and accident benefits can often be excluded or included at will. If you do take medical coverage, ascertain whether benefits will be paid as treatment proceeds or only after you return home, and whether there is a 24-hour medical emergency number. When securing baggage cover, make sure that the per-article limit will cover your most valuable possession. If you need to make a claim, keep receipts for medicines and medical treatment; if you have anything stolen, an official statement from the police is a must.

Before spending money on a new policy check whether you are already covered: some all-risks home insurance policies, for example, may cover your possessions against loss or theft when overseas, and many private medical schemes such as BUPA or PPP include cover when abroad, including baggage loss, cancellation or curtailment and cash replacement as well as sickness or accident. Bank and credit cards often have certain levels of medical or other insurance included, and you may automatically get travel insurance if you use a major credit card to pay for your trip (check the small print on this, though, as it may not be of much use).

In Canada, provincial health plans usually provide partial cover for medical mishaps overseas, while holders of official student/teacher/youth cards in Canada and the US are entitled to meagre accident coverage and hospital inpatient benefits. Students will often find that their student health coverage extends during the vacations and for one term beyond the date of last enrolment.

Internet

Public internet access is widespread across Australia and keeping in touch via the web is easy, fast and cheap in Sydney. **Internet cafés** are everywhere, typically charging $3–6 an hour with concessions as well as early-morning happy hours. Many accommodation options – especially **hostels** – also provide terminals for their guests at similar rates (hotels will charge more), although some places still opt for the user-reviled coin-op booths; at some YHAs you buy a card that works like a phonecard. The best machines and setups are what you'd want at home: modern, clean and fast with conventional controls and large screens. Otherwise, **local libraries** almost always provide access, though time is generally limited to one hour and you'll have to sign up in advance on a waiting list. Typically research is free but you pay $2 for thirty minutes if you want to use email, Facebook or other sites. The State Library on Macquarie Street (see p.71), has free-use terminals and wi-fi, though you'll need to obtain a username from the information desk. Darlinghurst Road in Kings Cross is crammed with cut-rate internet places, with rates as low as $2 per hour.

The Global Gossip chain (ⓦwww.globalgossip.com) has three offices in Sydney, plus numerous machines in hostels, 7-Elevens and the like, and more around Australia, New Zealand, Fiji and the UK. Find them near Central Station at 790 George St, near Chinatown; 63 Darlinghurst Rd, Kings Cross; and 37 Hall St, Bondi Beach. Also at Bondi Beach, *Phone.Net Cafe*, 73–75 Hall St (daily 7.30am–9pm; $3 per hr) is a lively café haunt in its own right

The sort of places listed above are increasingly geared up for wi-fi usually either charging the same rate or a flat fee – $10 for 24hr is typical. City libraries have free wi-fi, and even McDonalds now has free wi-fi throughout Australia – you don't even have to buy anything or get an access code.

Laundry

Virtually every accommodation option has a coin-operated laundry and dryer and possibly even a clothesline outside. In any case, busy tourist and residential areas usually have a few laundromats; a load of washing costs $3–4 do-it-yourself at any of these (plus extra for powder and another $3–4 for drying) or a reasonable $8–10 per load to have it washed, dried and folded for you.

Left luggage

Passengers at the Sydney Airport international arrivals hall can leave stuff at SmarteCarte Baggage Storage just near McDonalds (daily 6am–9.30pm; packs $4 for 6hr or $12 for 24hr, surfboards $20 per day, skis $18 per day). The Countrylink luggage room at Central Station accepts articles during the day (daily 6am–8pm; $4.40 per item), but if you need to leave stuff overnight try Wanderers Travel, 810 George St (daily Nov–March 8am–8pm, April–Oct 8am–6pm; ☎02/9280 4933, ⓦwww.wanderers-travel.com) about five minutes' walk west, who charge $7 per day in summer and $5 per day in winter.

You can also leave things at Travellers Contact Point, 7th Floor, Dymocks Building, 428 George Street (Mon–Fri 9am–6pm, Sat 10am–4pm; ☎02/9221 8744, ⓦwww.travellers.com.au) for $5 per item per day, $10–15 per week, or $20–30 per month.

Libraries

City of Sydney Public Library, Customs House, 31 Alfred St, Circular Quay ☎02/9242 8555, ⓦwww.cityofsydney.nsw.gov.au; Monday to Friday 10am to 7pm, Saturday and Sunday 11am to 4pm; State Library of NSW, Macquarie St ☎02/9273 1414, ⓦwww.sl.nsw.gov.au; Monday to Thursday 9am to 8pm, Friday 9am to 5pm, Saturday and Sunday 10am to 5pm.

Living and working in Sydney

If you have a working holiday visa, you shouldn't have too much trouble finding some sort of work, particularly in hospitality or retail. A good starting point is Travellers Contact Point, 7th floor Dymocks Building, 428 George St (Mon–Fri 9am–6pm, Sat 10am–4pm; ☎02/9221 8744, ⓦwww.travellers.com.au), who are well set up to help people to find work, open bank accounts, and find medium to long-term accommodation.

Offices of the government-run Centrelink (☎13 28 50, ⓦwww.centrelink.gov.au) have a database of jobs known as JobSearch;

their most central offices are at 140 Redfern St, corner of George St, Redfern; 137–153 Crown St, Darlinghurst; and 231 Oxford St, Bondi Junction. The private agency Troy's, Level 11, 89 York St (☎02/9290 2955, ⓦwww.troys.com.au), specializes in the hospitality industry. If you have some office or professional skills, plenty of temp agencies take on travellers: look under "Employment Services" in the Yellow Pages.

For a whole range of work, from unskilled to professional, the multinational Manpower (☎13 25 02, ⓦwww.manpower.com.au), is a good bet. Also check out Australia-wide job-seeking networks on the Internet; ⓦwww.seek.com.au is popular. Otherwise, scour hostel notice boards and the *Sydney Morning Herald's* employment pages – Saturday's bumper edition is best.

Mail

Australia's national **postal service** is called Australia Post. Post offices are generally open Monday to Friday 9am to 5pm, but the General Post Office (GPO) in Martin Place has longer hours (Mon–Fri 8.15am–5.30pm, Sat 10am–2pm). There are red post boxes outside post offices and on streets throughout the city. Make sure you put letters in the red box, not the yellow, which is for express post parcels. This guaranteed overnight express delivery service from Sydney to other major cities is handy and relatively inexpensive but ordinary mail is much less reliable: even a letter from Sydney to Katoomba in the Blue Mountains can take two days or more. **International mail** is extremely efficient, taking four to five working days to the UK, four to six to the US, and five to seven to Canada. **Stamps** are sold at post offices and agencies; most newsagents sell them for standard local letters only. A standard letter or postcard within Australia costs 55¢; postcards anywhere in the world cost $1.35; and regular letters start at $2.05 to the US, Canada, or Europe. If you're sending anything bigger in or outside Australia, there are many different services: get some advice from the post office. Large **parcels** are reasonably cheap to send home by surface mail, but take up to three months. Economy Air is a good compromise for packages that you want to see again soon (up to 20kg) – expect a fortnight to Europe. For

more details, go to ⓦwww.austpost.com.au and click on "Calculate postage rates".

You can receive mail at any post office in or around Sydney: address the letter to **Poste Restante** followed by the town or suburb, state of NSW and postcode, but the best address to give friends before you leave is: Poste Restante, GPO Box Centre, Sydney, NSW 2001, Australia. However, the address to pick up this Poste Restante mail is not at the Martin Place GPO but at the post office in the Hunter Connection shopping mall at 310 George St (Mon–Fri 9am–5.30pm), opposite Wynyard Station. You need a passport or other ID to collect mail, which is kept for a month and then returned; it's possible to get mail redirected if you change your plans – ask for a form at any post office. Some smaller post offices will allow you to phone and check if you have any mail waiting.

Most **hostels** and **hotels** will also hold mail for you if it's clearly marked, preferably with a date of arrival, or holders of Amex cards or traveller's cheques can have mail sent to American Express offices.

Maps

For wandering around the centre of Sydney, the maps in this book should be sufficient, but if you crave greater detail, or are staying by the beach or in the inner or outer suburbs, or are driving, you might like to buy something more comprehensive.

The two best maps are UBD's *Sydney Suburban Map* (#262; $10; ⓦwww.ubd-online.com), which gives comprehensive street detail of the CBD and the surrounding suburbs; and HEMA's *Sydney and Region* map ($6.95; ⓦwww.hemamaps.com), which has a slightly wider coverage. The best place to **buy maps** in Sydney is Map World, 280 Pitt St (☎02/9261 3601, ⓦwww.mapworld.net.au; Mon–Fri 9am–5.30pm, Sat 10am–3.45pm).

If you rent a car, make sure the rental company provides a Sydney street directory. The best is UBD's *Sydney Compact* ($19.95; ⓦwww.gregorys-online.com), which has all the detail in a paperback size that can easily fit into a handbag or daypack, at half the price of the larger directories. If you do want a car-sized directory, go for UBD's *Sydney*

& Blue Mountains Street Directory ($39.95), which extends as far as Mt Victoria. For getting out of Sydney, buy Gregory's *200 Kilometres Around Sydney* map ($6.95) for detail of the major tourist drives.

New South Wales's motoring organization, the NRMA, 74–76 King St, City (☎13 11 22, ⓦwww.nrma.com.au), publishes **road maps** of the state, and a useful map of Sydney. All are free to members of associated overseas motoring organizations.

Money

Australia's currency is the Australian dollar, or "buck", divided into 100 cents and shown on currency tables as AU$ or AUD. Colourful plastic notes with anti-forgery clear windows come in $100, $50, $20, $10 and $5 denominations, along with $2, $1 (larger than the $2), 50¢, 20¢, 10¢ and 5¢ coins. Prices are regularly advertised at $1.99 etc, and an irregular bill will be rounded up or down to the closest denomination.

At the time of writing, **exchange rates** were running at AUD2.13 for £1; AUD1.55 for USD1; AUD1.21 for CAN1, AUD0.79 for NZD1 and AUD1.97 for 1 Euro. For the most current exchange rates, consult the useful currency converter website ⓦwww.oanda.com.

Credit and debit cards

For purchases, visitors generally rely on credit cards, particularly Visa and Mastercard/Bankcard, which are widely accepted, though many hostels, campsites and B&Bs will only accept cash. American Express and Diners Club are far less useful. You'll also find credit cards handy for advance booking of accommodation and trips, while with the appropriate PIN you can obtain cash advances through ATMs or over the counter. Remember that all cash advances are treated as loans, with interest accruing daily from the date of withdrawal; there is likely to be a transaction fee on top of this. Debit cards are also widely used, allowing withdrawals from ATMs and payments for goods via EFTPOS (see opposite). Since interest is not charged and the flat transaction fee is usually quite small this may work out a cheaper way to access funds. Make sure you have a PIN that's designed to work overseas.

Traveller's cheques

Traveller's cheques, such as those sold by American Express and Travelex, are no longer the most convenient way to bring your funds into Australia though they do offer more security as they can be replaced if lost or stolen (remember to keep a list of the serial numbers separate from the cheques). Traveller's cheques in US dollars, pounds sterling, Euros and Australian dollars are all widely accepted for exchange at banks and bureaux de change. Take your passport, and check rates and fees as these vary widely.

In the event that cheques are lost or stolen, the issuing company will expect you to report the loss forthwith to their head office in Australia; most companies claim to replace lost or stolen cheques within 24 hours.

Banks and foreign exchange

The major banks with branches countrywide are Westpac (ⓦwww.westpac.com.au), ANZ (ⓦwww.anz.com.au), the Commonwealth (ⓦwww.commbank.com.au) and National Australia (ⓦwww.nab.com.au). Their head branches, all with foreign currency counters, are in the CBD, on and around Martin Place (see p.76). **Banking hours** are Monday to Thursday 9.30am to 4pm, and Friday 9.30am to 5pm, and some branches are now open on Saturday. **ATMs** are usually located outside banks but sometimes in front of ordinary shops in shopping strips. **Bureaux de change** are found in both airport terminals, around Central Station, Darling Harbour and throughout the city centre; only a few in the city are open at the weekend, and the only open ones late at night are at the airport.

If you're spending some time in Sydney, and plan to work, it makes life a great deal easier if you **open a bank account**. This is a fairly straightforward process, though you'll need to take along both your passport and a photo driver's license, as well as any other ID you have, just in case. The Commonwealth Bank and Westpac have the most branches, and their **cards** give you access not only to ATMs but also anywhere that offers **EFTPOS** (essentially debit) facilities. This includes most shops, service stations and supermarkets, where you can use your card to pay directly for goods; some of them will also give you cash (ask for "cash back"). However, bear in mind that **bank fees and charges** can be exorbitant in Australia; most banks allow only a few free withdrawal transactions per month (depending on who you bank with – shop around before you open an account), and you will probably be charged $2 per transaction to use a competing bank's ATM, as well as monthly fees.

Medical assistance

The general ambulance, police and fire emergency number is ☏000 (☏112 from mobiles).

Hospitals

The following hospitals have 24-hour emergency departments: St Vincents Hospital, corner of Victoria and Burton streets, Darlinghurst (☏02/8382 1111); Prince of Wales, Barker St, Randwick (☏02/9382 2222); and Royal Prince Alfred, Missenden Rd, Camperdown (☏02/9515 8141).

Medical centres and clinics

All the following are in areas frequented by travellers; see also "Medical Centres" in the Yellow Pages for the clinic closest to where you're staying.
Broadway Healthcare Level 1 Broadway Shopping Centre, near Glebe (Mon–Fri 9am–7pm, Sat & Sun 11am–5pm; ☏02/9281 5085, ☻www .broadwayhealthcare.com.au). General practitioners plus women's health clinic, pharmacy, dental, eye care and more, no appointment necessary.
Pavilion Plaza Medical Centre Mezzanine Level, 580 George St at Bathurst St (Mon–Fri 7am–9pm, Sat 8am–8pm, Sun 9am–7pm; ☏02/9261 9200) for walk-in consultations (no bookings; $60–80), physio, and X-rays. There's a dentist place next door and a pharmacy (Mon–Fri 8am–7pm, Sat & Sun 10am–4pm).
Sydney Sexual Health Centre Nightingale Wing, Sydney Hospital, Macquarie St (Mon, Tues, Thurs & Fri 10am–6pm, Wed 2–6pm; ☏02/9382 7440). Free, comprehensive and confidential STI, HIV, hepatitis and conselling service.
Travel Doctor Level 7, Dymocks Building, 428 George St, near QVB (Mon, Wed & Fri 9am–5.30pm, Tues & Thurs 9am–8pm, Sat 9am–1pm; ☏02/9221 7133, ☻www.traveldoctor.com.au). Health advice, medical kits, vaccinations and health alerts for overseas travel.

Pharmacy (late-night)

Crest Hotel Pharmacy 91 Darlinghurst Rd, Kings Cross (daily 8am–midnight; ☏02/9358 1822).

Opening hours and public holidays

Business and post office hours are generally Monday to Friday 9am to 5pm. Shops and services, Monday to Saturday 9am to 5pm and until 8 or 9pm on Thursday. Major retailers and many shopping malls in the city and in tourist areas also open on Sunday between 11am and 5pm. Big supermarkets generally open seven days from 8am until 8 or 9pm, though many stay open until midnight. Some close around 4pm on Sundays. In addition, the inner city and suburbs have numerous 24-hour 7/11 convenience type stores/super-markets, often attached to petrol stations.

Specific opening hours for tourist attractions – museums, galleries and historic monuments – are given throughout the Guide. Most open daily, usually between 10am and 5pm. All close on Christmas Day and Good Friday.

Public holidays

When an official holiday falls at the weekend, there may be an extra day off immediately before or after. School holiday dates, when accommodation gets booked up and prices rise, are given on p.235.

Phones

Keeping in touch by phone is easy for travellers to Australia with mobiles rapidly taking over from payphones for local calls, and internet international calls from cybercafés replacing phonecards.

Public holidays

New Year's Day (Jan 1)
Australia Day (Jan 26)
Good Friday
Easter Monday
Anzac Day (April 25)
Queen's Birthday (1st Mon in June)
Bank Holiday (1st Mon in Aug)
Labour Day (1st Mon in Oct)
Christmas Day (Dec 25)
Boxing Day (Dec 26)

Useful phone numbers

Emergency and operator assistance

Fire, police or ambulance ☎000 (☎112 from mobiles)
Local & national directory assistance ☎1223
International directory assistance ☎1225
Operator assistance ☎1234

Special numbers

☎13 xxxx – charged at the local call rate from any landline in Australia.
☎1300 xxx xxx – charged at the local call rate from any landline in Australia.
☎1800 xxx xxx – free from landlines anywhere in Australia.
☎1900 xxx xxx – premium-rated calls usually charged at exorbitant rates.

International calls

To call Australia from overseas, dial the international access code (☎00 from the UK or New Zealand, ☎011 from the US & Canada), followed by ☎61, the area code minus its initial zero, and the number. To dial out of Australia, it's ☎0011, followed by the country code, then the area code (without the zero, if there is one), followed by the number:

Ireland ☎0011 353   US & Canada ☎0011 1
UK ☎0011 44   New Zealand ☎0011 64

Mobile phones

Set up roaming before leaving home, and chances are your mobile will work fine all over Sydney. If you're planning to be here for a while, or expect to make a lot of calls, it will work out cheaper to buy an Australian SIM card (around $10) for your phone and get on a local pre-pay pricing plan. Of course you'll have to tell all your friends your new number, but that may be a small inconvenience for much cheaper calls. If your phone doesn't take SIM cards you could simply buy a basic phone (from $60) which will probably work out cheaper than renting.

Australia has several mobile phone networks. Telstra is the main provider (🌐www.telstra.com.au), with the widest countrywide network coverage, while Vodafone (🌐www.vodafone.com.au) is a long way behind on cross coverage but may work out cheaper solely for urban use in Sydney. Other providers include Optus (🌐www.optus.com.au), 3 (🌐www.three.com.au) and Virgin Mobile (🌐www.virginmobile.com.au). The networks all compete pretty strongly, so check around for the deal that best suits your needs.

Internet calling

For international calls, it is often cheapest to connect over the **internet**, using VOIP technology such as Skype. If you have your own laptop and a wi-fi connection all you'll need is a headset. Alternatively, visit one of the larger internet cafés many of which have several (or all) of their machines set up for VOIP calling. Being shoulder to shoulder with other patrons may limit your privacy, but it beats standing on a draughty and noisy street corner trying to get a phonecard to work.

Landlines

The two major landline operators in Australia are the privatized Telstra and Optus (see above). Their daily rates are pretty similar, but Telstra's coverage is wider. If you have access to someone's domestic landline it always works out considerably cheaper. In practice you're more likely to be using a public phone (mostly operated by Telstra) which, while reducing in number, are still common throughout Sydney. They take coins (local calls are 50¢ flat fee) or slot-in Telstra **phonecards**, sold through newsagents and other stores for $5, $10 or $20. Recently installed Smart payphones also have the capability to send SMS text messages (20¢).

You can also buy Telstra PhoneAway pre-pay calling cards, for use with both private and public phones using a PIN in $10, $20 and $50 denominations. You can make **international calls** from virtually any public Telstra phone as from a private phone (though rates are much higher). Many bars, shops and restaurants have blue **payphones**, but these cost more than a regular call box, and international dialling is not advised because they'll start to gobble money the moment you're connected, even if the call goes unanswered. Whatever their type, payphones do not accept incoming calls. Telstra's unstaffed Telstra Pay Phone Centre, 231 Elizabeth St (Mon–Fri 9am–11pm, Sat & Sun 7am–5pm) has private booths for more privacy and quiet, but bring change or a phonecard with you.

The numerous **account-based phone-cards** available from newsagents and hostels can be a far cheaper way to call cross-country or abroad – from as little as 5¢ a minute. Shop around as deals vary enormously. One card may be super cheap to call Korea but expensive to call the US. Read the fine print: additional charges per call, or per day or for using payphones can soon erode your fantastic deal. One reliable brand is Global Gossip (see "Internet", p.42) who sell their own recharge-able discount phonecard.

Police

For emergencies call ☎000. For non-emergencies call the police assistance line ☎13 1444.

Smoking

Smoking is now banned in most public places including beaches, restaurants and bars, though bars are finding increasingly innovative ways to provide smokers' areas.

Time

Sydney follows Australian Eastern Standard Time (AEST), half an hour ahead of South Australia and the Northern Territory, two hours ahead of Western Australia, ten hours ahead of Greenwich Mean Time (GMT) and fifteen ahead of US Eastern Standard Time. Clocks are put forward one hour on the first Sunday in October and back again on the first Sunday in April for daylight saving.

Don't forget that in the **southern hemisphere the seasons** are reversed. Summer lasts from December until February, winter from June until August.

Tipping

Other than in restaurants, tipping is not customary in Australia, and cab drivers, bar staff (and hairdressers) don't generally expect anything. In fact, cab drivers often round the fare down rather than bother with change. In cafés and cheap-eat restaurants you might leave the change, but most Australians tip in better restaurants when the service has been good, usually around ten percent.

Tourist information

Information on Sydney is easy to get hold of, either from Australian Tourist Commission offices, via the internet or from any tourist offices. For **general research** before you arrive, visit ⓦwww.australia.com, www.visitnsw.com.au or www.cityofsydney.nsw.gov.au.

In Sydney, the **Travellers Contact** Point, 7th floor Dymocks Building, 428 George St ☎02/9221 8744, ⓦwww.travellers.com.au (Mon–Fri 9am–6pm, Sat 10am–4pm), is a one-stop shop for backpackers, with luggage storage, money exchange, internet access, mail forwarding, deals on mobile phones and a travel desk. They're particularly focused on helping people get work, dealing with tax and immigration officials, opening bank accounts, finding accommodation and sorting out medical insurance.

For **parks and wildlife information** visit NPWS, Cadmans Cottage, 110 George St, The Rocks (☎02/9247 5033, ⓦwww.npws.nsw.gov.au).

Tourist information offices

Two **Sydney Visitor Centres** offer comprehensive information, maps, free accommodation- and tour-booking facilities, and sell tourist transport tickets and sightseeing passes. Both are centrally located at The Rocks, on the corner of Argyle and Playfair streets, and at Darling Harbour, beside the IMAX cinema (both daily 9.30am–5.30pm; ☎02/9240 8788 or 1800 067 676, ⓦwww.sydneyvisitorcentre.com).

Tourism New South Wales (☎13 20 77, ⓦwww.visitnsw.com) runs the **City Host information kiosks** (daily 9am–5pm; no phone) at Circular Quay, Martin Place and Town Hall, providing brochures, maps and face-to-face information. Out from the centre, the **Manly Visitor and Information Centre**, by the Manly Ferry Wharf (Mon–Fri 9am–5pm, Sat & Sun 10am–4pm; ☎02/9976 1430, ⓦwww.manlytourism.com.au), is useful for info on Manly and the northern beaches.

Publications

Ask at the tourist offices for *Sydney: The Official Guide*, a free booklet with excellent maps of Sydney and the surrounding areas, plus a CityRail and ferry plan. Several free **listings magazines** are worth picking up at tourist offices: the quarterly *This Week in Sydney* is good for general information, while *TNT Magazine* is the best publication aimed at **backpackers**, giving the lowdown on Sydney on the cheap. **Hostel notice boards** themselves act as an informal network, advertising everything from cars to camping gear.

To get under the skin of Sydney, read Friday's *Sydney Morning Herald* for its "Metro" listings supplement; or buy a copy of the weekly *Time Out Sydney* ($3.95; ⓦwww.timeoutsydney.com.au) whose website is full of good listings and general city info.

Travel agents

Numerous travel agents are dotted all over Sydney, especially in the areas where most visitors hang out.
Backpackers World Travel ☎1800 676 763, ⓦwww.backpackersworld.com.au. Everything from international flights to bus passes. Seven Sydney offices including: 234 Sussex St, City; 10–14 Oxford Square, Darlinghurst; 37 Hall St, Bondi; and 194 Coogee Bay Rd, Coogee.
Flight Centre ☎13 3133, ⓦ www.flightcentre .com.au. Cheap domestic and international air tickets from numerous locations including: 52 Martin Place, City; 88–92 Darlinghurst Road, Kings Cross; and 17 Hall St, Bondi Beach.
STA Travel ☎13 4782 ⓦwww.statravel.com.au. International and domestic flights, tours and accommodation. Branches include 464–480 Kent St, City; 841 George St, Haymarket; 127–139 Macleay St, Kings Cross; 308 King St, Newtown; and Westfield Bondi, corner of Oxford & Grosvenor Sts, Bondi Junction.

YHA Travel ⓦwww.yha.com.au/travel. Budget-oriented travel with outlets at 422 Kent St, City (☎02/9261 1111) and Sydney Central YHA, 11 Rawson Place (☎02/9281 9090).

Weather

We've discussed general weather patterns and given temperature and rainfall statistics on p.10. For four-day forecasts for Sydney and around – as far as the central coast (Gosford), the Blue Mountains, Hawkesbury River – visit ⓦwww.abc.net.au/news/weather/nsw.

Weights and measures

Australia is fully metric, and uses kilometres, kilograms, litres and degrees Celsius. Women's shoe sizes are unique to Australia; for example, Australian women's size 7.5 is roughly equal to a European size 39 and may be up to half a size different from the US/ Canadian 7.5. Men's shoe sizes in Australia are the same as UK sizes – if you're from the US or Canada, ask for one size up from your usual fitting to be safe. Dress sizes are the same as in the UK (but a US 8 is equivalent to an Australian 10).

Women's Sydney

The big events are around International Women's Day in March. Contact the Women's Information and Referral Service (Mon–Fri 9am–5pm; ☎1800 817 227, ⓦwww.women .nsw.gov.au/referral/wirs.htm) for information on this and women's organizations, services and referrals. The Women's Library, 8–10 Brown St, Newtown (Tues, Wed & Fri 11am–5pm, Thurs 11am–8pm, Sat & Sun noon–4pm; ☎02/9557 7060, ⓦwww .thewomenslibrary.org.au), lends feminist and lesbian literature. Jessie Street National Women's Library, housed in the Ultimo Community Centre, 523–525 Harris St (Mon–Fri 10am–3pm; ☎02/9265 9486, ⓦwww.nationalwomenslibrary.org.au), is an archive collecting literature on Australian women's history and writing. The Feminist Bookshop is in Orange Grove Plaza on Balmain Rd, Lilyfield (Mon–Fri 10.30am–6pm, Sat 10.30am–4pm; ☎02/9810 2666, ⓦwww .feministbookshop.com.

The City

The City

Sydney Harbour Bridge and The Rocks

T he rocky outcrop known as **The Rocks**, immediately beneath the **Sydney Harbour Bridge** between Sydney Cove and Walsh Bay, is the heart of historic Sydney. It was here that Captain Arthur Phillip proclaimed the establishment of Sydney Town in 1788, the first permanent European settlement in Australia. Within decades, however, the area had become little more than a **slum** of dingy dwellings, narrow alleys and dubious taverns and brothels. During the 1830s and 1840s, merchants began to build fine stone warehouses in the neighbourhood, but as the focus for Sydney's shipping shifted to Woolloomooloo, it fell into decline once more. In the 1870s and 1880s, the notorious Rocks "pushes", gangs of "larrikins" (louts), would jump – when they weren't beating each other up – from the narrow street named Suez Canal to mug passers-by. Some say its name is a shortening of Sewers' Canal, and indeed this district was so filthy and rat-ridden that whole street fronts had to be torn down in 1900 to contain an outbreak of bubonic plague. In 1924, when construction started on the approaches to the Sydney Harbour Bridge, hundreds of families were again displaced without compensation as great swathes of The Rocks were **demolished**.

Despite its interesting old-world character, The Rocks remained run-down, depressed and depressing until the 1970s, when plans were made to raze the remaining cottages, terraces and warehouses to make way for office blocks. However, thanks largely to opposition from a radical building workers' union, the Builders Labourers Federation (BLF) – and especially its secretary Jack Mundey, now hailed as a hero – the restored and renovated **historic quarter** now ranks among Sydney's major tourist attractions. Despite a passing resemblance to a historic theme park, it's well worth exploring. Apart from the airport, this is the best place for tax-free shopping, and it also holds several world-class restaurants.

It must be admitted, however, that at times the old atmosphere still seems to prevail. Friday and Saturday nights can be so thoroughly drunken that the area has its own, very prominent, police station and officers patrol on horseback. New Year's Eve is riotously celebrated, as fireworks explode over the harbour. The best time to come for a more relaxed drink is Sunday afternoon, when many pubs offer live jazz or folk music.

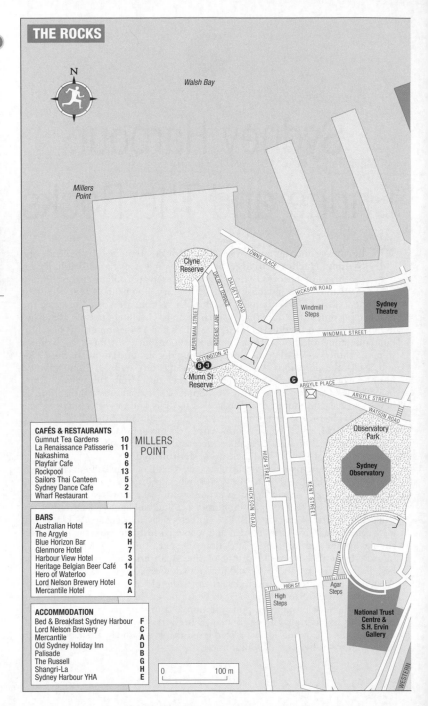

THE ROCKS

N

Walsh Bay

Millers Point

Clyne Reserve

TOWNS PLACE

HICKSON ROAD

Windmill Steps

Sydney Theatre

WINDMILL STREET

MERRIMAN STREET

DALGETY ROAD

ROGERS LANE

PALGETT TERRACE

BETTINGTON ST

B **3**

Munn St Reserve

C ARGYLE PLACE

ARGYLE STREET

WATSON ROAD

Observatory Park

Sydney Observatory

HIGH STREET

KENT STREET

HICKSON ROAD

HIGH ST

HIGH STREET

High Steps

Agar Steps

National Trust Centre & S.H. Ervin Gallery

WESTERN

CAFÉS & RESTAURANTS
Gumnut Tea Gardens	10
La Renaissance Patisserie	11
Nakashima	9
Playfair Cafe	6
Rockpool	13
Sailors Thai Canteen	5
Sydney Dance Cafe	2
Wharf Restaurant	1

MILLERS POINT

BARS
Australian Hotel	12
The Argyle	8
Blue Horizon Bar	H
Glenmore Hotel	7
Harbour View Hotel	3
Heritage Belgian Beer Café	14
Hero of Waterloo	4
Lord Nelson Brewery Hotel	C
Mercantile Hotel	A

ACCOMMODATION
Bed & Breakfast Sydney Harbour	F
Lord Nelson Brewery	C
Mercantile	A
Old Sydney Holiday Inn	D
Palisade	B
The Russell	G
Shangri-La	H
Sydney Harbour YHA	E

0   100 m

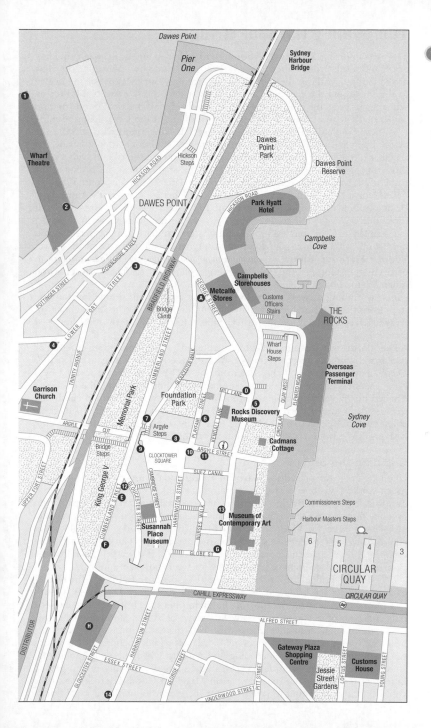

The Sydney Harbour Bridge

The awe-inspiring **Sydney Harbour Bridge** has spanned the water dividing north and south Sydney since the early 1930s. It's hard now to imagine the view of the harbour without the castle-like sandstone pylons that anchor the bridge to the shore, and the crisscross of steel arch against the sky. At 503m, this was, when it was built, the longest single span arch bridge in the world; construction began in 1924 and provided employment throughout the Great Depression.

As New South Wales' Labor-party premier, J.T. Lang, prepared to declare the bridge open in 1932, a dashing horseman, Francis de Groot – royalist fanatic and member of the fascist New Guard – galloped up and cut the ribbon with a sabre. Protesting against Lang's socialist leanings, he declared "I open this bridge in the name of his Majesty the King and all the decent citizens of New South Wales".

Residents of northern England might find the bridge familiar: the tinier Tyne Bridge in Newcastle-upon-Tyne, built in 1929, served as the original model. It took until 1988 for the construction costs of the much larger Sydney project to be finally paid off, but a $3 toll is still charged to drive across, payable as you head south only. It now goes towards maintenance, and the cost of the newer **Sydney Harbour Tunnel**. Running below the bridge, the tunnel, starts south of the Opera House – the ever-increasing volume of traffic had become too much for the bridge to bear.

It costs nothing to **walk** or **cycle** the bridge. Pedestrians should head up the steps from Cumberland Street, reached from The Rocks via the Argyle Steps off Argyle Street, and walk on the eastern side, while the western side is reserved for cyclists.

The "coathanger" requires full-time maintenance, with continuous painting in trademark steel-grey to protect it from rust. Comedian Paul Hogan, of *Crocodile Dundee* fame, worked as a rigger here in the 1970s before being rescued by a New Faces talent quest. If you can't stomach (or afford) to climb the bridge, as detailed below, walk five minutes from Cumberland Street, and then climb 200 steps inside its southeastern pylon, to reach the **lookout point** (daily 10am–5pm; $9.50; Ⓦ www.pylonlookout.com.au). Once there, as well as gazing out across the harbour, you can study a photo exhibition on the bridge's history.

Climbing the bridge

Climbing to the top of **Sydney Harbour Bridge** on the route used by its maintenance workers was once a favoured pastime of drunken students. These days you can do it legally, with **Bridge Climb**, who lead small, specially equipped groups up there from sunrise until night-time daily, roughly every ten to twenty minutes (day climbs Mon–Fri $189, Sat & Sun $199; twilight climbs daily $249; night climbs daily $179; prices rise steeply for two weeks after Christmas; maximum group of 12; no children under 10; Ⓣ 02/8274 7777, Ⓦ www.bridgeclimb.com). Booking ahead is recommended, especially for weekends or in summer.

Two distinct bridge climbs are available. The original **Bridge Climb** leads over the arch of the bridge to its summit, while the newer **Discovery Climb** is a journey through the interior of the arch, offering greater insight into the nuts-and-bolts of its engineering, as well as views of Sydney through the bridge's functional though decorative framework, and the same impressive panoramas from the summit. Both take three-and-a-half hours, but spend only two hours on the bridge itself, slowly ascending and pausing while the guide points out landmarks and engineering details. The initial hour of checking in and getting kitted up in grey *Star Trek*-style suits at the "Base" (5 Cumberland St) can make you feel as if you're about to go into outer space. Anyone with a normal fear of

▲ Sydney Harbour Bridge

heights can take comfort that the climb is not as scary as it looks; you're fully harnessed into a cable system, so there's no way you can fall off. Phobics, however, should definitely refrain.

To prevent anything being accidentally dropped onto cars or passers-by, participants are not allowed to carry anything apart from their glasses, which are attached to the suit, like the handkerchiefs, caps and other provided accoutrements, by special cords. Frustratingly, that also means you can't take your camera up with you. The price of the climb does include one group photo, taken by the guide on top of the bridge – but the cluster of jolly strangers, arms akimbo, invariably crowds out the panoramic background. To get the guide to take a shot that shows you on your own, with the splendours of the harbour behind, you'll need to fork out another $20 (additional shots $10).

The Rocks

The chief delight of **The Rocks** lies in simply exploring the narrow alleys and streets hewn from the original rocky spur. That voyage of discovery involves climbing and descending numerous stairs and cuts between different levels. As you approach from Circular Quay, beyond the impressive Art Deco Museum of Contemporary Art (see p.61), a small sandstone house beside the tiny, grassy Barney & Bligh Reserve makes a good introduction. Built in 1816 for John Cadman, ex-convict and Government coxswain, **Cadman's Cottage**, 110 George St, is the oldest private house still standing in Sydney. It's now the **National Parks and Wildlife Service** bookshop and information centre (Mon–Fri 9.30am–4.30pm, Sat & Sun 10am–4.30pm; ☏02/9247 5033, ⓦwww.environment.nsw.gov.au/nationalparks), providing information about the Sydney Harbour National Park, and taking bookings for guided tours and trips to harbour islands.

Tourist information about The Rocks, Sydney and New South Wales can be picked up at the **Sydney Visitor Centre,** at the corner of Playfair and Argyle streets (daily 9.30am–5.30pm). Further down Playfair Street, at no. 23, **The Rocks**

Walking Tours provides excellent guided tours of the area (Jan Mon–Fri 10.30am & 2.30pm, Sat & Sun 11.30am & 2pm; Feb–Dec Mon–Fri 10.30am, 12.30pm & 2.30pm, Sat & Sun 11.30am & 2pm; $30; bookings ℡02/9247 6678, ⓦwww .rockswalkingtours.com.au).

Campbells Cove to Argyle Street

Wandering north along Circular Quay West, from Cadman's Cottage, past the revamped Overseas Passenger Terminal (see p.61), brings you to **Campbells Cove**. **Campbells Storehouses** here are occupied by small art galleries and fine-dining waterside restaurants that offer great views of the harbour. These beautifully restored sandstone warehouses, built in 1839 to hold everything from tea to liquor, were once part of the private wharf of merchant Robert Campbell. A gorgeous three-masted Danish ship, the *Svanen*, built in 1922, is normally moored here between cruises, adding a Disney-esque atmosphere, while a luxury hotel, the *Park Hyatt*, overlooks the whole area.

A pleasant stroll past the hotel to Dawes Point Park, which extends beneath the Harbour Bridge, brings you to **Dawes Point Reserve,** a favourite spot for photographers, which separates Sydney Cove, on the Circular Quay side, from Walsh Bay. Back at Campbells Cove, climb the Customs Officer's Stairs to Hickson Road to reach **Metcalfe Stores**, a warehouse-turned-shopping complex, dating from around 1912. Exit from the Metcalfe stores onto George Street, where at weekends you can further satisfy your shopping urge at the **Rocks Market** which takes over the Harbour Bridge ends of Playfair and George streets, with more than a hundred stalls – shaded by a long impressive row of sideless, conjoined, geometric marquees on George Street – selling souvenirs, bric-a-brac, and arts and crafts with an Australian slant. Facing George Street (and the market), the *Mercantile Hotel*, one of Sydney's best Irish watering holes (see p.204), along with several welcoming terrace cafés, provides street-side alfresco seating to watch it all unfold. Picturesque leafy back courtyards are tucked away behind the cafés, beneath high sandstone walls and sheer cliffs.

Branching off George Street, narrow **Mill Lane** joins **Kendall Lane**, where the interactive **Rocks Discovery Museum** (daily 10am–5pm; free), makes another great starting point for a random exploration of the area. Its four permanent exhibitions range from Aboriginal and convict history up to the present day, while children's activities are offered seasonally.

Exit the museum on its Quay side, and follow a delightful nineteenth-century stone alleyway, parallel to Kendall Lane, to reach the dungeon-like **Puppetshop At The Rocks**, 77 George St (daily 10am–5pm), which stocks a vast array of marionettes from all over the world, old and new, rudimentary and sophisticated. Alternatively, climb from the museum's Mill Lane entrance to **The Rocks Square** on Playfair Street where on Friday nights in November, during **The Rocks Markets By Moonlight,** Australian artists perform on a temporary stage.

Leafy Argyle Street hosts **The Rocks Farmers Market** on Fridays (10am– 3pm) and Saturdays (9am–3pm), where you can taste-test and/or purchase delectable fresh local produce, including soft and crusty breads, free-range meat and poultry, cheeses, chutneys and other tasty morsels. On the other side of Argyle Street, you can nip down cobbled pedestrian back alleys to such once-sordid streets as Suez Canal and Nurses Walk, or take coffee or lunch in the charming old-world courtyards of *La Renaissance* or *Gumnut Café* (see "Eating"). At 30 Harrington St, Bonza Bike Tours (℡9247 8800, ⓦwww.bonzabiketours .com), provide bike rental (1hr $15, 4hr $35, 24hr $50), and highly recommended cycle tours of the city and Manly ($89–129, 2hr 20min–4hr) – a great way to get to know Sydney.

The Argyle Cut and around

The impressive **Argyle Cut**, which slices through solid stone to the residential and port area of Millers Point, took sixteen years to complete. Convict chain gangs began the task in 1843, carving with chisel and hammer. When convict transportation ended ten years later, the tunnel was still unfinished, and it took explosives and hired hands to complete it in 1859. On the Quay side of the Cut, the **Argyle Steps** climb from Argyle Street to the peaceful pedestrian walkway of **Gloucester Walk**, which passes tiny **Foundation Park**. Descending a steep terraced escarpment, this quaint little park holds the unearthed foundations of cottages that have been given new life by the addition of sculptural installations representing Victorian furniture. Gloucester Walk slowly descends to *The Mercantile* (see "Drinking") on George Street. Its Argyle Street end offers access to the pedestrian entrance of the Harbour Bridge via **Cumberland Street**, home to a couple of classic old boozers, the *Glenmore* and the *Australian Hotel* (see "Drinking"), as well as Bridge Climb.

Down **Gloucester Street** from the *Australian*, a row of four brick terraces at nos. 58–64, built in 1844 and continuously inhabited until 1990, now hold the **Susannah Place Museum** (guided tour only, reserved on ☎9241 1893; Jan daily 10am–5pm; Feb–Dec Sat & Sun 10am–5pm; $8; ⓦwww.hht.net.au). This "house museum" relates the domestic history of Sydney's working class, and includes a re-created 1915 corner store that sells great old-fashioned sweets.

Millers Point

On the western side of the Bradfield Highway (Sydney Harbour Bridge), the mostly residential district of **Millers Point** serves as a reminder of how The Rocks used to be. Many of its homes remain government- or housing-association-owned, and there's a surprisingly real community feel so close to the tourist hype. Of course, the area has its upmarket pockets – like the very swish *Observatory Hotel* on Kent Street, opposite Observatory Hill, and the renovated piers on **Walsh Bay** – but for the moment the traditional street-corner pubs and shabby terraced houses on the hill still evoke the raffish atmosphere that once typified the whole area, and wandering the peaceful leafy streets is a delight.

Lower Fort Street

If you stroll up Lower Fort Street, don't miss the opportunity to have a bevvy in the **Hero of Waterloo** at no. 81 (see "Drinking"), built from sandstone excavated from the Argyle Cut in 1844. It's also worth peeking in at the **Garrison Church** (or Holy Trinity, as it's officially called; daily 9am–5pm; www.thegarrisonchurch .org.au), on the corner of Argyle Street, the place of worship for the military stationed at Dawes Point Fort from the 1840s. The volunteer-run **Garrison Gallery Museum** alongside (Tues, Wed, Fri & Sat 11am–3pm, Sun noon–4pm; free) is housed in the former parish schoolhouse. Century-old photographs, with their ragged barefoot children and muddy dirt roads, gives a good indication of the conditions when Australia's first Prime Minister, Edmund Barton, was educated here. **Argyle Place**, beside the church, holds some pretty terraced houses.

Walsh Bay

The formerly dilapidated old piers that feed off **Hickson Road** at **Walsh Bay** have been transformed in recent years. The first pier, at 11 Hickson Rd, has been taken over by a luxurious hotel, *Sebel Pier One*, while piers 2/3 and 6/7 now hold luxurious apartments with sleek million-dollar yachts and speedboats moored to their sides. Pier 4/5 has long been home to the **Wharf Theatre**, base since 1984 of the prestigious **Sydney Theatre Company** (STC). Former STC luminary

Cate Blanchett is now the company's Artistic Director, along with her husband, playwright Andrew Upton. The complex also holds the internationally acclaimed Sydney Dance Company, and around twenty other smaller arts organizations (see "Performing arts and film").

The dining room and bar of the **Wharf Restaurant** (see "Eating") revel in sublime views across Walsh Bay to Balmain, Goat Island and the North Shore, while you can get closer to the water (and the artists) on the ground floor at the studio-chic *Dance Café* (see "Eating"), which faces across to the luxury apartments on the opposite pier. If you're keen, you can even attend a drop-in **dance class**, ranging in style from hip hop to classical ballet (single classes $18; ☎9258 4818, ⓦwww.sydneydancecompany.com/studios/).

Guided tours of the theatre, including the costume department and a look at set construction, are also available (first and third Thurs of each month 10.30am; 1hr; $8; bookings on ☎02/9250 1795). Sydney's literati converge on the Wharf Theatre complex in May of each year, for the wonderfully sited and mostly free **Sydney Writers Festival** (see "Festivals and events").

Observatory Park

Opposite the Garrison Church, climb the steps from Argyle Street to the well-chosen spot for **Sydney Observatory**, in **Observatory Park**. With its shady Moreton Bay figs, park benches and lawns, the park has a marvellous hilltop view over the harbour and architecture below – on a rainy day enjoy it from the elegant and perfectly sited bandstand. You can also easily reach the park via the Bridge Steps from Cumberland Street, by the Argyle Cut.

Sydney Observatory

When it opened in 1858, the Italianate-style **Sydney Observatory** for which the park is named marked the city's first accurate time standard. Calculating the correct time from the stars, it would signal it to ships in the harbour, and Martin Place's General Post Office, by dropping a ball in its tower at 1pm daily – a custom that still continues. Set among some very pretty gardens, the Observatory holds an excellent modern **museum of astronomy**, and is well worth a visit (museum and gardens daily 10am–5pm; free; ⓦwww.sydneyobservatory .com.au).

A large section of the museum is devoted to the rare astronomical event known as the **Transit of Venus**, when Venus passes over the disk of the sun. That typically occurs around twice per century, most famously spurring Captain Cook's 1769 voyage of exploration, during which he charted Australia's east coast. The most recent transit, on June 8, 2004, was visible from Europe, Africa, Asia and eastern parts of North America, and was the first since 1874. The extensive collection of astronomical equipment, both archaic and high-tech, includes the still-working telescope installed under the copper dome at that time. In the "Stars of the Southern Sky" section, three animated videos recount Aboriginal creation stories, explaining how the stars came to be, from the Milky Way to Orion. The passage of time is also nicely realized, with two parallel interactive monitors showing past (1868) and present panoramic views of the harbour from the perspective of the Observatory dome.

Daytime tours include a 3-D space theatre and telescope (Mon–Fri 2.30pm & 3.30pm; Sat & Sun 11am, noon, 2.30pm & 3.30pm; $7). Daily, two-hour **evening tours** cover the same ground but also feature a lecture and the chance to view the southern sky through telescopes, or see a planetarium show if the weather's bad (tour times vary seasonally; booking essential, usually up to a week in advance, on ☎02/9241 3767; $15).

National Trust Centre and S. H. Ervin Gallery

The **National Trust Centre**, also in Observatory Park south of the observatory, is located in a former military hospital dating from 1815 (Mon–Fri 9am–5pm; ☎9258 0123, ⓦwww.nsw.nationaltrust.org.au). It holds a **café** (daily except Mon 11am–4pm) and a specialist **bookshop** (daily except Mon 10am–5pm) where you can pick up leaflets about other historic buildings and settlements in New South Wales.

The rear of the building, purpose-built as a school in 1850 in neo-Regency style, houses the **S. H. Ervin Gallery** (daily except Mon 11am–5pm; free; entry to special exhibitions $6). Devoted to Australian art, thanks to a 1978 million-dollar bequest, it stages changing exhibitions of scholarly non-mainstream art, focusing on such themes as Aboriginal or women artists.

2

Circular Quay and the Sydney Opera House

At the southern end of Sydney Cove, sandwiched between The Rocks, Sydney's first settlement, and its modern emblem, the Opera House, **Circular Quay** is the launching pad for harbour and river ferries and sightseeing cruises. Less attractively, it's also the terminal for buses from the eastern and southern suburbs, and a major suburban train station to boot, with the ugly 1960s Cahill Expressway also spoiling the views. However, one of the most fantastic of all views of the harbour can be seen from the above-ground platforms of Circular Quay train station, thanks to the partial removal of a wall. A sweeping panorama of the harbour can also be enjoyed from the pedestrian walkway adjacent to the Cahill Expressway, reached by a sleek glass lift from the Quay.

A popular stroll leads from the Quay to the **Opera House** and the Royal Botanic Gardens (see p.66) just beyond, enjoying an ice cream or stopping for some oysters and a beer at a waterfront bar. All the necessities for a picnic in the Gardens, including bubbly and fresh prawns, are on sale at the Quay.

Circular Quay and around

Bustling with commuters all week, "The Quay", as locals call it, is crammed at the weekend with people simply out to enjoy themselves. Restaurants, cafés and fast-food outlets stay open until late and buskers entertain the crowds, while street vendors add to the general hubbub. For intellectual stimulation, just glance beneath your feet as you stroll along: the inscribed bronze pavement plaques of **Writers' Walk** provide an introduction to the Australian literary canon. There are short biographies of writers including Miles Franklin, author of *My Brilliant Career*, Booker Prize-winner Peter Carey, and Nobel Prize-awardee Patrick White, and Germaine Greer, as well as quotations on what it means to be Australian. Notable visitors to Australia, including Joseph Conrad, Charles Darwin and Mark Twain, also feature.

The once-controversial **Opera Quays** development runs the length of **East Circular Quay**, leading up to the Opera House. Locals and tourists promenade along the pleasant colonnaded lower level, with its outdoor cafés, bars and bistros, upmarket shops and Dendy Quays Cinema, all looking out to sublime harbour views.

Besides ferries – the huge range of cruises that start from Circular Quay are detailed on pp.28–29 – the Quay still acts as a passenger terminal for ocean

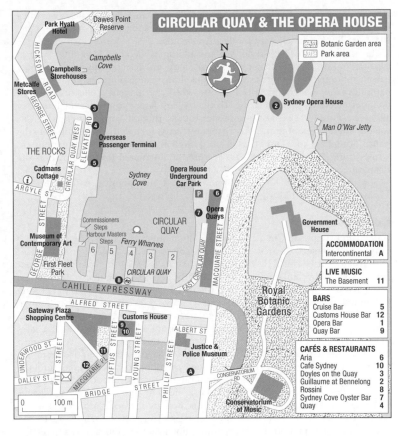

Map labels and legend:

CIRCULAR QUAY & THE OPERA HOUSE

Botanic Garden area
Park area

Park Hyatt Hotel
Dawes Point Reserve
Campbells Cove
Campbells Storehouses
Metcalfe Stores
HICKSON ROAD
GEORGE STREET
CIRCULAR QUAY WEST ELEVATED RD
Overseas Passenger Terminal
THE ROCKS
Cadmans Cottage
ARGYLE ST
STREET
Museum of Contemporary Art
GEORGE STREET
First Fleet Park
Sydney Cove
Commissioners Steps
Harbour Masters Steps
Ferry Wharves
CIRCULAR QUAY
CAHILL EXPRESSWAY
ALFRED STREET
Gateway Plaza Shopping Centre
Customs House
UNDERWOOD ST
PITT STREET
DALLEY ST
MACQUARIE PL
LOFTUS STREET
YOUNG STREET
GEORGE STREET
ALBERT ST
PHILLIP STREET
BRIDGE STREET
Justice & Police Museum
CONSERVATORIUM RD
Conservatorium of Music
Sydney Opera House
Man O'War Jetty
Opera House Underground Car Park
Opera Quays
CIRCULAR QUAY
EAST CIRCULAR QUAY
MACQUARIE STREET
Government House
Royal Botanic Gardens

N

ACCOMMODATION
Intercontinental A

LIVE MUSIC
The Basement 11

BARS
Cruise Bar 5
Customs House Bar 12
Opera Bar 1
Quay Bar 9

CAFÉS & RESTAURANTS
Aria 6
Cafe Sydney 10
Doyles on the Quay 3
Guillaume at Bennelong 2
Rossini 8
Sydney Cove Oyster Bar 7
Quay 4

0   100 m

liners. It's been a long time, though, since the crowds waved their hankies regularly from the **Sydney Cove Overseas Passenger Terminal**, which looks for all the world like the deck of a ship itself. To reach it, head in the opposite direction past the **Museum of Contemporary Art** to **Circular Quay West**; even if there's no ship, take the escalator and the stairs up for excellent harbour views. The rest of the redeveloped terminal is now given over to super-trendy and expensive restaurants and bars such as *Quay* (see "Eating") and *Cruise Bar* (see "Drinking").

Behind the Quay, you can experience a little culture at the renovated **Customs House** on **Alfred Street**, or learn about Sydney's seamy underbelly at the nearby **Justice and Police Museum**.

Museum of Contemporary Art

The **Museum of Contemporary Art** (MCA) on Circular Quay West, with another entrance on 140 George Street (daily 10am–5pm; free; free tours Mon–Fri 11am & 1pm, Sat & Sun noon & 1.30pm; Ⓦ www.mca.com.au), owes its existence to art collector John Power's 1940s bequest to Sydney University to purchase international contemporary art. The burgeoning collection found a permanent home in 1991 in the former Maritime Services Building. As Power left no ongoing funding, the museum has been financially troubled ever since it opened; the free entry is courtesy of corporate sponsorship, and means the MCA is chock-a-block with locals at weekends.

The striking Art Deco-style 1950s building is dedicated to international twentieth- and twenty-first-century art, with an eclectic approach encompassing lithographs, sculpture, installations, film, video, photography, drawings, paintings and Aboriginal art. The museum's permanent collection, which includes pieces by Keith Haring, Bridget Riley, Jasper Johns, David Hockney and Jean Tinguely, is mostly kept in storage, though some emerges for its various themed exhibitions. Recent shows have included solo exhibitions by Yinka Shonibare and Tim Hawkinson, as well as contemporary indigenous art, while young Australian artists have featured in an annual forum known as the Primavera series.

Outdoor tables at the MCA's superbly sited, if expensive, **café** (Mon–Fri 12pm–3pm; Sat–Sun 10am–3pm) overlook the waterfront.

Customs House

Immediately opposite Circular Quay, on Alfred Street, the sandstone and granite **Customs House** is an architectural gem. Constructed in 1845, then redesigned with its current Classical Revival-style facade in 1885 by the colonial architect James Barnet, the building was subsequently neglected for many years. Since being given to the City of Sydney Council in 1994 the structure has undergone two multi-million dollar refurbishments. It now serves as a very stylish "lounge room for the city", and a venue for colourful cultural events and exhibitions. The base of its grand central atrium, visible from all levels, consists of a glass floor covering a continually updated 500:1 scale model of the city. To one side a bright red, waveform, information desk beckons; to the other, multi-directional, red monitor casings and keyboard stands on floor-to-ceiling poles provide internet access, while irregular shaped couches, partial cocoon swivel chairs and an adjustable, lamp-lit, curved reading desk fit out the funky newspaper and magazine salon, which holds daily updated archives of national and international publications. A striking helix staircase and glass elevator lead to the City of Sydney's premier general lending library and exhibition space on the first and second floors, while on the top floor, the sleek interior design of *Café Sydney's* fine dining restaurant (see "Eating") and cocktail bar is complemented by postcard harbour views. Out in front, a newly designed forecourt space incorporates alfresco seating for cafés and bars, buzzing on weekday evenings with post-work euphoria.

Justice and Police Museum

A block east of the Customs House, on the corner of Phillip Street, the **Justice and Police Museum** (late Dec to Jan daily 10am–5pm; Feb–Dec Sat & Sun 10am–5pm; $8; ⓦ www.hht.net.au) is housed in the former Water Police station, an 1856 sandstone building whose veranda is decorated with some particularly fine ironwork.

This social history museum focuses on law, policing and crime in New South Wales. Temporary exhibitions throughout the year explore such themes as the art of tattooing, the effects of drugs on crime, and the relationship between the police and environmental protestors. A mock-up of a nineteenth-century police station and courtroom holds the permanent displays, which include some truly macabre bushrangers' death masks, gruesome confiscated weapons (some used in notorious murders) and other souvenirs of Sydney's murky past.

The Sydney Opera House

The **Sydney Opera House**, such an icon of Australiana that it almost seems kitsch, is just a short stroll from Circular Quay, by the water's edge on **Bennelong Point**. That name comes from Bennelong, a charismatic Iora tribesman, who was initially kidnapped by the early Sydney settlement in a desperate attempt to assist communication with local Iora tribes. Sharp-witted and intelligent, he quickly acquired a great facility with the English language. He later became a much-loved friend of Governor Arthur Phillip, who built a hut for him where the Opera House now stands.

The Opera House is best seen in profile, when its high white roofs, simultaneously evocative of full sails and white shells, give it an almost ethereal quality. Some say the inspiration for its distinctive design came simply from peeling an orange into segments, though perhaps the childhood of Danish architect **Jørn Utzon**, the son of a yacht designer, had something to do with their sail-like shape – he certainly envisaged a building that would appear to "float" on water. He also compared it to a Gothic church and a Mayan temple. Close up, you can see that the shimmering effect is created by thousands of chevron-shaped white tiles.

It took such a feat of structural engineering to bring Utzon's "sculpture" to life that the final price tag of $102 million was fourteen times the original estimate. Now almost universally loved and admired, it's hard to believe quite how controversial the project was, during its long haul from being commissioned after Utzon won an international competition in 1957, to its completion in 1973. Utzon's victory was itself a wonder: Eero Saarinen, the architect of New York's JFK airport terminal, who was on the selection committee, vetoed the shortlist and flicked through the reject pile, pronouncing Utzon's way-out design the work of a genius.

Construction was so plagued by quarrels and scandal – the young son of the winner of the Opera House fund lottery was even kidnapped and murdered, Australia's first such crime – that Utzon was forced to resign in 1966, calling the whole sorry situation "Malice in Blunderland". Many believe that jealous, xenophobic local architects and politicians hounded him out of the country, after a newly elected state government disliked his plans for the interior. It took seven

▲ Sydney Opera House

more years, and three Australian architects, for the interior to be finished, along different lines, and the poor acoustics of the Concert Hall and the inadequate space in the Opera Theatre have troubled the venue ever since.

On the building's twenty-fifth birthday in 1998, a $70 million, ten-year plan was announced to renew and modify the interior. As a gesture of goodwill to make up for past slights, and a real attempt finally to realize his full design, Utzon was invited to be the principal design consultant. Refurbished to his specifications, the Reception Hall was renamed the **Utzon Room** in 2004. The huge sound-absorbing tapestry, Utzon's "homage to Bach", which now hangs on the wall opposite the harbour outlook has allowed the installation of a parquet floor with a pattern echoing the ribbed ceiling. Utzon also re-modelled the western side of the structure, with a colonnade and nine new glass openings, giving previously cement walled theatre foyers a view of the harbour.

Utzon died in November 2008, aged 90. Though he had never seen his master-piece, he was still drawing up plans to renovate the much-maligned Opera Theatre. His business partner and son, Jan, and Sydney-based architect Richard Johnson, with whom he was collaborating, now continue his work.

Around the Opera House

"Opera House" is actually a misnomer: the building is really a performing arts centre, one of the busiest in the world. It holds five performance venues inside its shells, plus two restaurants, several popular cafés and bars, an Aboriginal gallery, and a stash of upmarket souvenir shops.

The focal point is the huge **Concert Hall** (seating 2690), used by the Sydney Symphony Orchestra (SSO). The smaller **Opera Theatre** (1547 seats) serves as the Sydney performance base for Opera Australia (seasons Feb–March & June–Nov), the Australian Ballet (mid-March to May & Nov–Dec) and the Sydney Dance Company (see p.221). Of the three theatrical venues, both the **Drama Theatre** and **The Playhouse** are used primarily by the Sydney Theatre Company (see p.222). The more intimate **Studio** aims to draw in a younger audience, offering cheaper tickets for innovative Australian drama, comedy, cabaret and contemporary dance, performed in an adaptable theatre-in-the-round format.

There's plenty of action outside the Opera House, too. The Mayan- inspired **Forecourt** and Monumental Steps form an amphitheatre for free and ticketed

Goossens and the Genesis of the Opera House

The Sydney Opera House was originally intended as a home for the **Sydney Symphony Orchestra** (SSO). It was the cherished dream of British conductor Sir **Eugene Goossens**, who was invited in 1947 to transform the SSO to world-class status. By 1955, the SSO was considered to be on the world's top ten list, and the whole of Australia was swooning to its radio broadcasts on the Australian Broadcasting Corporation (ABC). However, its only venue was the tiny, draughty and acoustically challenged – albeit splendid – Town Hall.

Like architect Jørn Utzon, Goossens never saw the Opera House. Shortly after being knighted by the Governor General, he left for a holiday to Europe. On his return, he was found to be carrying a huge haul of pornography. Australia's censor-ship laws were notoriously tight, its climate parochial and puritanical, and the £100 fine came with a judgement from the QC that it was "difficult to imagine a worse case...the exhibits speak for themselves...". Hundreds of prominent international and local supporters were appalled at the witchhunt and subsequent career ruination of Goossens, who resigned in disgrace and left for Europe. He died alone on a plane flight in 1962.

concerts – rock, jazz and classical – holding around 5000 people. Sunday is the liveliest day outside, when the **Tarpeian Markets** (10am–4pm), with an emphasis on Australian crafts, are held.

The Opera House holds a number of great **places to eat and drink**. You could choose to dine at one of Sydney's best restaurants, *Guillame at Bennelong*, overlooking the city skyline (see "Eating"), or take a drink at the *Opera Bar* on the lower concourse, with wonderful views from the outside tables and an affordable all-day menu. There's also a sidewalk café, a bistro and several theatre bars.

Opera House tours, performances and packages

The best way to appreciate the Opera House, of course, is to attend an evening **performance** (see p.221). The building is especiallly stunning when floodlit, while once you're inside, the huge windows come into their own, with the dark harbour waters reflecting a shimmering image of the night-time city. Interval drinks certainly aren't like this anywhere else in the world.

If you're not content with gazing at the outside and can't attend a performance, various **guided tours** are available (book on ☎02/9250 7250 or ⓦwww.sydneyoperahouse.com; look out for good-value **Experience Packages**, combining tours, meals, dinner cruises, drinks and performances). One-hour **essential tours** give an overview of the site, looking at the public areas, discussing the unique architecture and visiting one of the venues (daily 9am–5pm; $35). Early-morning, two-hour **backstage tours** include access to the scenery and docks, rehearsal rooms, technical areas, and breakfast in the Greenroom (daily 7am; $150).

3

Royal Botanic Gardens to Macquarie Street

t was Governor Arthur Phillip, at the helm of the new city from 1788 to 1792, who decreed that the picturesquely sited land around the harbour, east of his newly built Government House (now the site of the Museum of Sydney) should always be in the public domain, a great park for the people to enjoy. Over two decades later Governor Lachlan Macquarie formalized his generous idea. The area remains public, but in two distinct parts. To the south and east is the open expanse of **The Domain**, long used for public celebrations and protests. It stretches from the stately strip of civic buildings envisaged by Governor Macquarie on the southern end of **Macquarie Street** to either side of the **Art Gallery of New South Wales** and down to the water alongside Mrs Macquaries Road. West of here lie the much larger and varied expanse of the **Royal Botanic Gardens**, around 30 hectares in all, stretching from the northern end of Macquarie Street to the Opera House and around Farm Cove. Though established in 1816 they were reserved for "the respectable class of inhabitants"; the general public were not allowed in until 1831. Many **paths** run through the gardens and Domain. A popular and speedy route (roughly 15min) starts at the northern gates near the Opera House, then follows the waterfront path to the gates that separate it from The Domain, and climbs the **Fleet Steps** to Mrs Macquaries Chair.

The Royal Botanic Gardens

The **Royal Botanic Gardens** (daily 7am–sunset; free; Ⓦ www.rbgsyd.nsw.gov .au) occupy a huge waterfront area between The Domain and the Opera House, around the headland on Farm Cove where the first white settlers struggled to grow vegetables for the hungry colony. Today's gardeners are much more successful, judging by the well-tended flowerbeds. While duck ponds, a romantic rose garden and a fragrant herb garden strike a very English air, look out for native birds and, at dusk, the fruit bats that fly overhead (see box, p.68) as the nocturnal possums begin to stir. Trees and plants are drawn from all over the world, but it's the huge, gnarled native Moreton Bay figs that stand out. Providing stunning **views** of Sydney Harbour, the gardens are always crowded with workers at lunchtime, picnickers on fine weekends, and lovers entwined beneath the trees.

Within the park's northern boundaries, you can visit the original residence of the governor of New South Wales, and listen to lunchtime recitals at the nearby Conservatorium. Below the music school, the remaining southern area of the gardens holds a herb garden, a cooling palm grove established in the

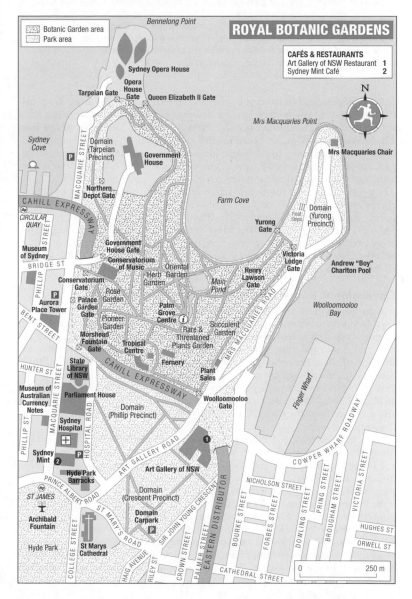

A plague of bats

Cast your eyes around the Royal Botanic Gardens' Palm Grove and you'll soon spot thousands of grey-headed flying foxes hanging from skeletal dying trees. These large bats (which can weigh up to a kilo) come alive in the late afternoon, and head off across the city searching out their favourite foods – fruit and gumtree pollen.

Though abundant here, these bats are listed as vulnerable. The gradual loss of their favoured habitat has forced them to roost in some of Australia's oldest exotic trees, gradually killing the trees in the process.

Following the success of a similar project in Melbourne, the Gardens authorities aim to move the bats with drums and whistles. The plan is to disturb them just enough that the colony gradually moves – metre by metre – to somewhere safe and non-destructive. In a few years the bats may no longer roost here.

1860s, a popular café/restaurant by the duck ponds, and the **Sydney Tropical Centre** (daily 10am–4pm; $5.50) – a striking glass pyramid and adjacent glass arc respectively housing native tropical plants and exotics. Nearby, the **Rare and Threatened Plants** garden boasts the first ever cultivated Wollemi Pine, planted in 1998. The "dinosaur" tree, thought long-extinct, was discovered by a national park ranger in 1994; only 38 naturally propagated such trees exist in the world, growing in the Blue Mountains (see p.308).

Free **guided tours** of the gardens start from the **visitor centre** at the southeast-corner entrance, near the Art Gallery of New South Wales, off Mrs Macquaries Road (daily 9.30am–4.30pm; tours daily 10.30am; 1hr 30min; March–Nov Mon–Fri also 1pm; 1hr). The **Trackless Train**, which runs through the gardens every twenty minutes, picks up from here; the main pick-up point is the entrance near the Opera House and there are also stops along the way (daily 9.30am–5pm; all-day hop-on-hop-off service $10, child $5).

Government House and the Conservatorium of Music

Within the northern boundaries of the Royal Botanic Gardens on Conservatorium Road, the sandstone mansion glimpsed through a garden and enclosure is the Gothic Revival-style **Government House** (grounds daily 10am–4pm; entry by free guided tour only Fri–Sun 10.30am–3pm; tours half-hourly; 45min; ⓦwww .hht.net.au). Built between 1837 and 1845 as the seat of the governor of New South Wales, it's still used for vice-regal receptions and official engagements by the governor, who now lives in a private residence. Designed by Buckingham Palace architect Edward Blore, it's furnished with an impressive array of Australian art and furniture from the past 150 years, including modern works from the major 2007 refurbishment.

South of Government House, just inside the gardens at the end of Bridge Street, the **Conservatorium of Music** is housed in what was intended to be the servants' quarters and stables of Government House. Public opinion in 1821, however, deemed the imposing castellated building far too grand for such a purpose, and a complete conversion, including the addition of a concert hall, gave it the loftier aim of training the colony's future musicians. After a 1990s renovation project uncovered an earlier convict-era site, an archeological dig was incorporated into the final redesign. Duck inside the modern entrance to see the preserved remains of an old drain system and water cistern, or come on Wednesdays during term time, when students give free recitals, which you can combine with a $10 guided tour of the building at 12.30pm. There's also a full program of evening concerts and performances (see ⓦwww.music.uysd.edu.au for details).

The Domain

Wrapped around the eastern and southern sides of the Botanic Gardens, **The Domain** is a large, quite plain, open space divided by the Cahill Expressway. Often filled with people eating lunch under the shady Moreton Bay fig trees, playing volleyball, or swimming in the outdoor Andrew "Boy" Charlton Pool, it's a popular place for a stroll, heading perhaps from the city across to the Art Gallery of New South Wales or down to the harbour for wonderful views from Mrs Macquaries Chair. The Domain has always been a truly public site and Sydney's focus for anti-establishment protests. Since the 1890s, assorted cranks and soapbox revolutionaries have assembled on Sundays for the city's version of **Speakers' Corner**, and huge crowds have registered their disquiet, notably during anti-conscription rallies in 1916 and after the dismissal of the Whitlam Labor government in 1975. Every January thousands of people gather on the lawns to enjoy the wonderful free open-air concerts of the Sydney Festival; in February the Tropfest short film festival takes over the grass, while December sees a night of Christmas carols and the all-Australian line-up of the outdoor rock festival, Homebake (all detailed in "Festivals and events"). The closest **train** stations are Martin Place or St James CityRail.

Mrs Macquaries Chair and "The Boy"

Immediately northeast of the Botanic Gardens on the shores of Farm Cove, the sandstone **Fleet Steps**, built in 1908 to welcome the warships of the American Great White Fleet, climb to Mrs Macquaries Road. Laid out in 1816 at the urging of the governor's wife, Elizabeth, the road curves down from Art Gallery Road to Mrs Macquaries Point, which separates idyllic Farm Cove from grittier Woolloomooloo Bay and its naval base. At the end, the celebrated lookout point known as **Mrs Macquaries Chair** is a two-tier bench fashioned out of the rock, from which Elizabeth could admire her favourite view of the harbour on her daily walk from the original Government House.

On the route down to Mrs Macquaries Point, the **Andrew "Boy" Charlton Pool** (see "Sports and activities") is an open-air, saltwater swimming pool that's safely isolated from the harbour waters on the Woolloomooloo side of the promontory. It enjoys excellent views across to the Garden Island Naval Depot, which is fascinating to watch. "The Boy", as locals fondly call it, was named after the champion swimmer, a Manly local, who turned 17 during the 1924 Paris Olympics, where he won gold in the 1500-metre freestyle. He was beaten at the 400-metre event by Johnny Weissmuller, later the famous Hollywood Tarzan. The pool is a popular hangout for groovy Darlinghurst types (it's quickly reached from Kings Cross via Woolloomooloo by descending the McElhone Stairs from Victoria St) and sun-worshipping gays. The much-glamorized pool has its own café, pilates and yoga classes, and even a weekly biathlon.

Art Gallery of New South Wales

At its southern end, Mrs Macquaries Road crosses the largely covered Cahill Expressway and becomes Art Gallery Road. Running through the southern section of The Domain, it passes the imposing Neoclassical facade, inscribed with the names of Renaissance artists, of the **Art Gallery of New South Wales** (Mon, Tues, & Thurs–Sun 10am–5pm, Wed 10am–9pm; general tours Mon 1pm & 2pm, Tues–Sun 11am, 1pm & 2pm; ⊕ www.artgallery.nsw.gov.au). Started in 1874, the collection was moved into this building in 1897, and has been expanding ever since, most recently in 2003 when a gigantic cube of white glass, dubbed the "lightbox", was grafted onto the eastern Woolloomooloo facade to contain the gallery's Asian collection. Such additions make it light and airy, with good harbour views. As well as a wonderful permanent collection spanning European, colonial, Aboriginal and contemporary art and a very strong programme of temporary exhibits, the gallery hosts the annual **Archibald Prize**, one of Australia's most prestigious art awards. Contestants' works are usually displayed from early March to mid-May each year. The gallery's worthwhile **audio tour** ($5) includes its director talking about his personal favourites.

With its hillside setting, you enter the gallery at Ground Level from where stairs lead down to three lower levels. Ground Level concentrates on a large collection of European art spanning the last thousand years, and includes a vast gilt-framed canvas by Edward John Poynter depicting *The Queen of Sheba before Solomon* in luminous detail, as well as Cezanne's *Bords de la Marne*, bought for over $16 million in 2008, the highest price ever paid by an Australian public gallery.

Revealing a strong northern hemisphere influence, colonial Australian painters often attempted to portray Australia's landscape as some kind of Europeanized Eden. As the nineteenth century progressed, more Australian-ness crept in. Classics to look out for include Frederick McCubbin's *On the Wallaby Track* from 1855, and Rupert Bunny's Impressionist *A Summer Morning* from half a century later. Other highlights include equally classic **Australian paintings**: Tom Roberts' romanticized shearing-shed scene *The Golden Fleece* (1894) and an altogether less idyllic look at rural Australia in Russell Drysdale's *Sofala* (1947), a depressing vision of a drought-stricken town. The precise works on show rotate, but luminaries like Sidney Nolan (typified by *Central Australia*) and Brett Whitely are usually well represented. **Photographs** include Max Dupain's iconic *Sunbaker* (1937), an early study of Australian hedonism that looks as if it could have been taken yesterday.

On Lower Level 3, the **Yiribana** gallery is devoted to the art and cultural artefacts of Aboriginal and Torres Strait Islanders – painting, sculpture, photography and multimedia installations. Join a free one-hour tour (daily 11am plus Wed 7.15pm) to gain an insight into works by artists such as Rusty Peters, Freddie Timms and Lin Onus, who created the lovely *Fruit Bats*, depicting almost a hundred cross-hatched bats hanging from a rotary clothesline.

▲ Art Gallery of New South Wales

Wednesday evening's **"Art After Hours"**, when gallery hours are extended to 9pm, is an especially interesting time to visit. After 5pm, the regular and special exhibitions are accompanied by free talks, films (usually art-house, often rare) and live performances; you'll find up-to-date schedules on ⓦ www.artafterhours .com.au.

The complex also holds an auditorium used for art lectures, an excellent bookshop, a café (Lower Level 1), and a well-regarded restaurant (Ground Level). A pedestrian walkway behind the Art Gallery leads quickly down to Woolloomooloo and its finger wharf on Cowper Wharf Road; as well as restaurants, bars and cafés on the wharf itself, you could eat cheaply at the pie cart, *Harry's Café de Wheels* (for details see "Eating").

Macquarie Street

Lachlan Macquarie, reformist governor of New South Wales between 1809 and 1821, gave the early settlement its first imposing public buildings, clustered on the southern half of his namesake **Macquarie Street**. He had a vision of an elegant, prosperous city, but the Imperial Office in London didn't share his enthusiasm for expensive civic projects. Refused both money and expertise, Macquarie was forced to be resourceful. Many of the city's finest buildings were designed by the ex-convict **Francis Greenway** – the convicted forger who went on to be appointed civil architect, eleven of whose forty edifices survive – and paid for with "rum-money", the proceeds of a monopoly on liquor sales.

Modern Sydney – wealthy and international – shows itself on the corner of Bent and Macquarie streets. The curved glass sails of the ABN AMRO's 41-storey **Aurora Place tower** were completed in 2000 to a design by Italian architect Renzo Piano, co-creator of the extraordinary Georges Pompidou Centre in Paris.

State Library of New South Wales

The **State Library of New South Wales** (Mon–Thurs 9am–8pm, Fri 9am–5pm, Sat & Sun 10am–5pm, Mitchell Library closed Sun; free guided tours Tues 11am & Thurs 2pm; ⓦ www.sl.nsw.gov.au) heads the row of public architecture on the eastern side of Macquarie Street. The complex of old and new buildings includes the 1906 sandstone **Mitchell Library**, its imposing Neoclassical facade gazing across to the Botanic Gardens. Inside the foyer the **Tasman Map** floor mosaic replicates an original drawn by Dutch explorer Abel Tasman in the 1640s and now held in the libraries collection. It depicts the Australian continent, still without an east coast, and its northern extremity joined to Papua New Guinea.

A walkway links the Mitchell Library with the modern building housing the **General Reference Library**. Free exhibitions relating to Australian history, art, photography and literature are held in its vestibules, while a ground-floor **bookshop** offers great Australia-related books. Lectures, films and video shows take place in the **Metcalfe Auditorium** (free and ticketed events; ☎ 02/9273 1414 for details and bookings), which also hosts weekly **free movies** (Thurs 12.10pm) from the extensive film and documentary archive.

Sydney Hospital, NSW Parliament House, and the Royal Mint

Sandstone **Sydney Hospital**, the so-called "Rum Hospital", funded by liquor-trade profits, was Macquarie's first enterprise, commissioned in 1814; the two remaining convict-built original wings therefore form one of Australia's oldest buildings. The central section was pulled down in 1879 when it began collapsing; rebuilt by 1894, the Classical Revival buildings, still functioning as a small general and eye hospital, are also impressive. Peep inside at the entrance hall's flower-themed stained glass and the decorative staircase, or take an interesting short cut through the grounds to The Domain and across to the Art Gallery of New South Wales. Outside on Macquarie Street, the bronze statue of a boar, *Il Porcellino*, is a copy of one from Florence; his nose has long been rubbed shiny for luck by patients and their families.

The northernmost of the hospital's original wings is now the **NSW Parliament House** (Mon–Fri 9.30am–4pm; free guided tours first Thurs of month at 1pm; no bookings but call ☏02/9230 2047 or check Ⓦwww.parliament.nsw.gov.au for parliamentary recesses). Local councils called by the governor started to meet here as early as 1829, so it's by some way the oldest parliament building in Australia. However, not until May 2003 was an Aboriginal Australian elected to the NSW Parliament – Linda Burney, Labor member for multicultural Canterbury as well as minister for Fair Trading, Youth and Volunteering. When Parliament is sitting, you can listen in on the politicians during question time. Foyer exhibitions, on community or public-sector interests and ranging from painting, craft and sculpture to excellent, overtly political photographic displays, change every fortnight or so.

The other hospital wing was converted in response to the first Australian goldrush to become **Sydney Mint** (Mon–Fri 9am–5pm; free). Originally a branch of the Royal Mint, it closed in 1927 and was eventually completely re-developed. It now houses the head office of the Historic Houses Trust, and holds a small display explaining how its re-building combined historic restoration with contemporary architecture.

The on-site *Mint Café* (see "Cafés") extends onto the veranda looking over Macquarie Street.

If you're interested in coins and banknotes, you're better off spending an hour across Macquarie Street at the **Museum of Australian Currency Notes**, 65 Martin Place (Mon–Fri 10am–4pm; free), inside the Reserve Bank of Australia building. That holds everything from chaotic early currency experiments (importing Spanish dollars then punching out the central disc to provide a smaller denomination) to fun cartoons trying to convince the populace of the need to go decimal in 1966, and the polymer banknotes that Australia pioneered in 1988.

The Hyde Park Barracks

Next door to the old Mint, the **Hyde Park Barracks** (daily 9.30am–5pm; $10; Ⓦwww.hht.net.au), designed by convict-architect Francis Greenway to house six hundred male convicts, was built in 1819, again without permission from London. Australia's oldest institutional building, it's among the most complete convict barracks in the former British Empire. Now a museum of Sydney's social and architectural history, it's a great place to visit for a taste of convict life during the early years of the colony. Start on the top floor, where you can swing in re-creations of the prisoners' rough hammocks swinging below exposed beams. Computer terminals allow you to search for information on selected convicts' histories and backgrounds – several of those logged were American sailors nabbed for misdeeds while in Dublin or English ports (look up poor William Pink). Later the barracks took in single immigrant women. Many were Irish; an exhibition on the middle level looks at the lives of over 4000 orphaned Irish girls who passed through between 1848 and 1850, escaping the potato famine.

Ground-floor exhibits explore why the Australian colonies were set up in the first place. The reconstruction of one of the prison hulks that used to line the Thames in London give a clear indication of how bad the situation had become, once Britain could no longer transport its criminals to America after independence.

Look out too for the excellent temporary historical exhibitions, and the room where fittings have been stripped back to reveal the building's original construction.

St James's Church

Opposite the barracks at the very south end of Macquarie Street, **St James's Church** (daily 9am–5pm; ⓦ www.sjks.org.au) marks the northern entry to Hyde Park. The Anglican church, completed in 1824, is Sydney's oldest existing place of worship. It was one of Macquarie's schemes, built to ex-convict Greenway's design. The architect originally planned it as a courthouse, but you can see how his simple plan has been converted into a graceful church. It's worth popping into the crypt (separate entrance on Philip St) to see the richly coloured **Children's Chapel** mural painted in the 1930s.

4

City Centre

Even if you stay in Kings Cross, spend your leisure time at the beach, shop in Paddington and dine all over the inner-city suburbs, you'll inevitably find yourself spending some of your time in the **city centre**, with its major museums and galleries, department stores and grand colonial edifices.

Sydney's **Central Business District**, the high-rise heart of the city often referred to as the CBD, stretches from Circular Quay as far south as King Street. Martin Place is its commercial nerve centre, with its own underground train station, while the **Museum of Sydney** is its most compelling attraction. The region south from here to the Town Hall, where George and Pitt streets are the main thoroughfares, is a shopaholic's oasis, holding all the department stores and several shopping malls, including the celebrated **Queen Victoria Building**; you can walk right through from the underground Town Hall train station into the building's basement levels. The lavish **State Theatre** and the decorative **Town Hall** are also worth a peek, and overlooking it all, with supreme views of the city, is **Sydney Tower**. Several nearby monorail stops can get you here from Darling Harbour.

Hyde Park, the city centre's rest and recreation zone, is three blocks east of the Town Hall across Elizabeth Street. Fenced off by Governor Macquarie in 1810 to mark the outskirts of his township, it's still very much a formal city park with its war memorials and church. Around its perimeter, the natural history-focused Australian Museum, the cathedral, and Sydney's Great Synagogue are book-ended by two well-preserved, very London Underground-like train stations, both opened in 1926 – Museum Station to the south and St James Station to the north.

The short stretch between the Town Hall and Liverpool Street is for the most part teenage territory, a frenetic zone of multi-screen cinemas, pinball halls and fast-food joints. On Friday and Saturday nights, when this area is prone to trouble, there are pleasanter places to choose to catch a film. Things change pace around the junction of Kent Street and Liverpool Street, where Sydney's **Spanish Quarter** (basically a clutch of Spanish restaurants plus a Spanish club) is being crowded out by an emerging **Koreatown**.

Further south, George Street becomes increasingly downmarket as it heads towards Central Station. **Haymarket**, en route, is one of the liveliest areas of the city in the evenings and at weekends, thanks to a bustling **Chinatown**, the presence of students from the University of Technology, and stacks of **backpacker hostels** along with associated travel agents and internet cafés. Here too you'll find the famed **Paddy's Market**, butted up against the southern end of the Darling Harbour development (see Chapter 5).

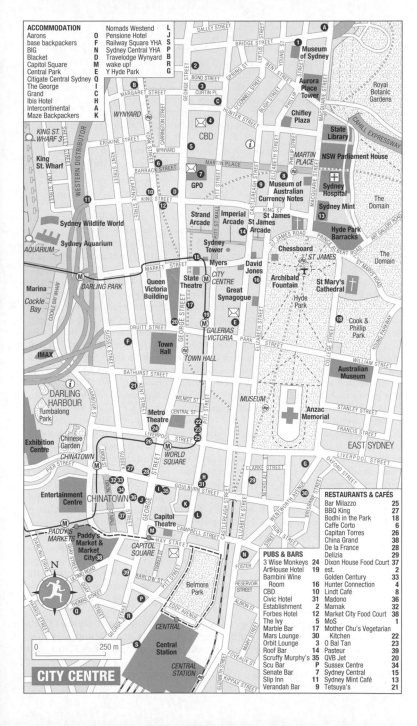

ACCOMMODATION

Aarons	O	Nomads Westend	L
base backpackers	F	Pensione Hotel	J
BIG	N	Railway Square YHA	S
Blacket	D	Sydney Central YHA	P
Capitol Square	M	Travelodge Wynyard	B
Central Park	E	wake up!	R
Citigate Central Sydney	Q	Y Hyde Park	G
The George	I		
Grand	C		
Ibis Hotel	H		
Intercontinental	A		
Maze Backpackers	K		

RESTAURANTS & CAFÉS

Bar Milazzo	25
BBQ King	27
Bodhi in the Park	18
Caffe Corto	6
Capitan Torres	26
China Grand	38
De la France	28
Delizia	29
Dixon House Food Court	37
est.	2
Golden Century	33
Hunter Connection	4
Lindt Café	8
Madono	36
Mamak	32
Market City Food Court	38
MoS	1
Mother Chu's Vegetarian Kitchen	22
O Bal Tan	23
Pasteur	39
QVB Jet	20
Sussex Centre	34
Sydney Central	15
Sydney Mint Café	13
Tetsuya's	21

PUBS & BARS

3 Wise Monkeys	24
ArtHouse Hotel	19
Bambini Wine Room	16
CBD	10
Civic Hotel	31
Establishment	2
Forbes Hotel	12
The Ivy	5
Marble Bar	17
Mars Lounge	30
Orbit Lounge	3
Roof Bar	14
Scruffy Murphy's	35
Scu Bar	P
Senate Bar	7
Slip Inn	11
Verandah Bar	9

CITY CENTRE

0 ___ 250 m

The CBD

As you stroll from Circular Quay to pedestrianized **Martin Place** – the true heart of the city centre – the cramped streets of the CBD, overshadowed by high-rise office buildings, have little to offer. Naturally, office workers keep it lively during weekdays, but once the post-work drinkers have left its smattering of bars it all gets pretty quiet. Smaller, chic-er alternatives have joined the plentiful business hotels in recent years, so this isn't a bad area in which to stay, but unless you can afford the big-spend restaurants you'll have to head down to Haymarket or elsewhere to dine.

If your first stop is the small but nicely formed **Museum of Sydney**, you can wander south from there past the upmarket shopping of **Chifley Plaza** to **Martin Place**.

Museum of Sydney

The **Museum of Sydney,** at the corner of Bridge and Phillip streets (daily 9.30am–5pm; $10; Ⓦ www.hht.net.au), takes an experiential, interactive approach to history, via exhibitions, film, photography and multimedia, which means you may come away feeling less factually informed than you would expect.

Visitors approach the museum across **First Government Place**, a public square on which the foundations of the original Government House, unearthed by an archeological dig in the 1980s, are marked out in different coloured sandstone on the pavement. Built by Governor Phillip in 1788, the house was home to eight subsequent governors of New South Wales before being demolished in 1846. You may fail to notice the foundations altogether, as the eye is naturally drawn instead to the forest of vertical poles at the western end. Entitled *Edge of the Trees*, this emotive sculptural installation was a collaboration between a European and an Aboriginal artist, and attempts to convey the complexity of a shared history that began in 1788. Walk among the "trees" and listen to the commentaries to build up a picture of early colonial Sydney.

The museum itself is built of honey-coloured sandstone blocks, using the different types of tooling available from the earliest days of the colony right up to modern times; you can trace this stylistic development from the bottom to the top of the facade. Inside, you hear a dramatized dialogue between the Eora woman Patyegarang and the First Fleeter Lieutenant Dawes, giving a strong impression of the meeting and misunderstanding between the two cultures. Straight ahead, a video screen projects images of the bush, sea and Sydney sandstone across all three levels, stylistically linking together what is really quite a small museum. Head up to the Level 2 auditorium for short movies of mid-twentieth-century Sydney life and the construction of the Harbour Bridge, then work your way down past wonderful **panoramas** of Sydney Harbour, the **Bond Store Tales** section, in which holographic "ghosts" relate tales of old Sydney as an ocean port, and the **Trade Wall**, full of anecdotes and facts about the goods Sydney imported in its early days – rice from Batavia, cheroots from India, ginger wine from the West Indies and tar from Sweden.

Special exhibits, typically lasting a few months, tend to take up around half the museum space. Recent highlights have included Captain Bligh's Sydney mutiny of 1808, the 1960s' glamour photos of local snapper, David Mist, and Sydney's Lost Gardens.

An excellent **gift shop** stocks a wide range of photos, artworks and books on Sydney. There's no café inside, but *MOS* (see "Cafés") is right next door.

Sydney Architecture Walks (Sept–May; $25; ☎02/8239 2211, ⓦwww
.sydneyarchitecture.org) offer casual two-hour walking tours of the city's modern
architecture, led by young architects and starting from the Museum of Sydney
entrance. The "Sydney" tour (Wed 10.30am) looks at the forces shaping the cityscape
with particular reference to a couple of modern masterpiece skyscrapers, while
"Utzon" (Sat 10.30am) examines the design and construction of the Sydney Opera
House. A third tour, "Harbourings", which only takes place once a month – call for
details – investigates the industrial heritage of The Rocks and the finger wharves of
nearby Walsh Bay. Fee includes admission to the museum.

Chifley Plaza

For a glimpse at how all the wealth generated in CBD might be spent, head
a couple of blocks south along Phillip Street to **Chifley Plaza**, at the corner
with Hunter Street. Stores in Sydney's most upmarket shopping centre include
Leona Edmiston, Max Mara and other exclusive labels. Simeon Nelson's huge
stencil-like **sculpture** of former Australian Labor Prime Minister Ben Chifley
(1945–49), stands on the pleasant palm-filled square outside.

Martin Place

Stretching five blocks between George and Macquarie streets, with its own
underground station, **Martin Place** is a pedestrian mall lined with imposing
banks and investment companies, many with splendid interiors. Street performances take place during summer lunchtimes, while flower and fruit stalls add
colour year-round. The vast Renaissance-style **General Post Office**, designed
by colonial architect James Barnet (also responsible for the Customs House
and Callan Park) and built between 1865 and 1887, with its landmark clock
tower added in 1900, broods over the George Street end of Martin Place in
all its Victorian-era pomp. There's still a small post office on the ground floor,
but the upper floors have been incorporated into a five-star luxury hotel, the
Westin Sydney, the rest of which resides in the 31-storey tower behind. The old
building and the new tower meet in the grand **Atrium Courtyard**, in the
lower ground floor, with its restaurants, bars and classy designer stores.

At the eastern end of Martin Place, Anne Graham's artwork *Passage* is marked
by a fine mist which emerges from ground-level grilles, delineating the outlines
of an early colonial home that once stood there, and creating a ghostly house
on still days.

King Street to Park Street

South of Martin Place, the rectangle between Elizabeth, King, George and Park
streets is Sydney's prime **shopping area**, centred on Pitt Street Mall, with a
couple of beautifully restored **Victorian arcades** – the Imperial Arcade and
the swanky Strand Arcade. It's also home to Sydney's two **department stores**,
the very upscale David Jones, on the corner of Market and Elizabeth streets,
established way back in 1838, and the more populist but still quality-focused
Myers, on Pitt Street Mall. All are overlooked by Sydney skyline's landmark,
Sydney Tower.

Opposite Myers, the **State Theatre** adds a touch of culture, and there's more
shopping in the lovely ornate **Queen Victoria Building** (QVB), which gazes
across Druitt Street at the even more flamboyant **Town Hall**.

Sydney Tower and Oztrek

The 1981 **Sydney Tower**, on the corner of Market and Castlereagh streets (daily 9am–10.30pm, Sat until 11.30pm; adults $25, seniors & students $19.50, child $15; Ⓦ www.sydneytower.com.au), is the tallest poppy in the Sydney skyline. Its observation level is the highest in the entire southern hemisphere, although the management ruefully have to admit that the height of the tower itself, at 305m, is beaten by the spire of the Sky Tower in Auckland, New Zealand, which is 23m taller. The 360-degree view from the observation level is especially fine at sunset; on clear days you can even see the Blue Mountains, 100km away. If, as so often, it's crowded, head instead to the peaceful downstairs **café**, where you can enjoy floor-to-ceiling views along with a cup of tea.

Up on the observation level, the **Skywalk** (daily 9am–8pm every 30–60min; additional $40, kids $30), is a harnessed-up, 45-minute walking tour of the tower's exterior. One of the vertiginous, glass-floored viewing platforms extends right out over the abyss. It obviously imitates the successful Harbour Bridge climb, the original and still the best thrill choice for your money.

The trip up the tower comes packaged with **Oztrek** (included with your ticket) on the ground floor, a tacky "virtual ride" introduction to a clichéd Australia that lasts forty long minutes.

The State Theatre

Near the Sydney Tower the restored **State Theatre**, just across from the Pitt Street Mall at 49 Market St, provides a pointed architectural contrast. Step inside and take a look at the ornate and glorious interior of this 1929 picture palace, where a lavishly painted, gilded and sculpted corridor leads to the lush, red and wood-panelled foyer. To see more – decorations include crystal chandeliers in the dress circle – you'll need to attend a concert or play, or catch June's annual Sydney Film Festival (see "Festivals"). Call ahead to join a **guided tour** (roughly monthly; 1hr 30 min; $15; ℡ 02/9373 6862, Ⓦ www.statetheatre.com.au), or pop into the beautiful little *Retro Café*, attached, for a coffee.

The Queen Victoria Building

The magnificent, domed, Romanesque-style **Queen Victoria Building** (QVB to locals: shops Mon–Wed, Fri & Sat 9am–6pm, Thurs 9am–9pm, Sun 11am–5pm; cafés and restaurants open later; building open 24hr; Ⓦ www.qvb.com.au), takes up the block bounded by Market, Druitt, George and York streets. Built as a market hall in 1898, two years before Queen Victoria's death, the long-neglected building was beautifully restored and reborn in 1986 as an upmarket shopping mall with the focus on fashion, as detailed on p.248. From the bustling food stalls in the basement, its four levels become progressively posher. Coming from Town Hall

Sydney Tower's revolving restaurants

To see the Sydney Tower view without the crowds, put the $25 you've saved towards a meal instead. A couple of **revolving restaurants** are located at the top of the tower; each revolution takes one hour ten minutes, and nearly all the tables are by the windows (bookings on ℡ 02/8223 3800, Ⓦ www.sydney-tower-restaurant.com). For à la carte dining, visit 360 Bar and Dining on Level 1, which serves lunch (Wed–Fri noon–2pm; two courses $68, three courses $75) and dinner (daily from 5.30pm, last entry 8.30pm; two courses $75, three $95, 15 percent surcharge on Sun). On Level 2, the Sydney Tower Restaurant offers buffet lunches (Mon–Sat $49.50, Sun $59.50) and dinners (Mon–Thurs $64.50, Fri–Sun $85).

▲ The Queen Victoria Building

Station, you can walk right through the basement and continue via the Sydney Central Plaza to Myers, emerging on Pitt Street without ever going outside – very cooling on a hot day.

Stern and matronly, a huge **statue of Queen Victoria** herself sits outside the building's Town Hall. She was sourced from the Irish Republic as part of the $75 million restoration, having been wrenched in 1947 from outside the Irish Houses of Parliament in Dublin. A small bronze statue of her favourite dog, Islay, fronts the nearby wishing well.

The **interior** is magnificent, with its beautiful woodwork, mosaic-tiled floors, stained-glass windows, gallery levels, exhibits and antique lifts. A brochure listing all the shops and main features is available from information desks on the ground level and level 2; a one-hour **guided tour** (daily 2.30pm; $10) leaves from the ground-floor information desk.

Two huge and somewhat ugly clocks hang from the ceiling on **level 2**. At the south end, the five-metre-high, one-tonne mechanical **Royal Automata Clock** shows a pageant of British royal history, every hour on the hour, including scenes of Charles I being beheaded. In complete contrast, however, and outdoing it in size and weight, the ten-metre-high, four-tonne **Great Australian Clock** at the northern end comes to life once an hour (on the half hour) with moderately animated displays of scenes from Australian history from the point of view of indigenous people and European settlers. Odd it may be, but it's weirdly compelling.

The Town Hall

In the realm of architectural excess, however, the **Town Hall** (closed for refurbishment until late 2009; Ⓦ www.cityofsydney.nsw.gov.au) is king – you'll find it across from the QVB on the corner of George and Druitt streets. Built during the boom years of the 1870s and 1880s in homage to Victorian England, it has a huge organ inside its Centennial Hall, giving it the air of a secular cathedral. Throughout the interior different styles of ornamentation compete for attention in a riot of colour and detail; the splendidly dignified toilets are a must-see.

This was Sydney's concert hall, home to the Sydney Symphony Orchestra, until the Opera House opened in 1973. The occasional concerts and theatre **performances** still held here set off the splendid interior perfectly, though it's more often used nowadays for public lectures.

Hyde Park and around

From the Town Hall, a short three-block walk leads east to **Hyde Park** along Park Street, which divides the park into two sections. Long and narrow, Hyde Park feels like the continuation of Macquarie Street with its long central axis linking its two principal features. The northernmost of these, the 1932 **Archibald Fountain**, commemorates the association of Australia and France during World War I. Designed by French sculptor François Sicard, it's dripping in Greek and Roman iconography, all gods and minotaurs in a large hexagonal pool. Nearby is a **giant chess set**, where you can challenge the locals to a game.

The southern focus of the main axis is the **Anzac Memorial** (normally open daily 9am–5pm, but closed for renovations as this book went to press; free), Sydney's most potent monument to those fallen in wartime. Fronted by the tree-lined Pool of Remembrance, the thirty-metre-high cenotaph, unveiled in 1934,

The Anzacs

Almost every town in Australia, large or small, has a war memorial dedicated to the memory of the Anzacs, the **Australia and New Zealand Army Corps**. When war erupted in Europe in 1914, Australia was overwhelmed by a wave of pro-British sentiment. On August 5, one day after Great Britain had declared war against the German empire, the Australian prime minister summed up the feelings of his compatriots: "When the Empire is at war so Australia is at war." On November 1, twenty thousand enthusiastic volunteers – the **Anzacs** – left from the port of Albany in Western Australia to assist the mother country in her struggle.

Turkey had entered the war on the German side in October 1914. At the start of 1915, military planners in London (Winston Churchill prominent among them) came up with a plan to capture the strategically important Turkish peninsula of the Dardanelles, with a surprise attack near **Gallipoli**, and thus open the way to the Black Sea. On April 25, 1915, sixteen thousand Australian soldiers landed at dawn in a small bay flanked by steep cliffs; by nightfall, two thousand men had died in a hail of Turkish bullets from above. The plan, whose one chance of success was the element of surprise, had been signalled by troop and ship movements long in advance, thus rendering it useless. Nonetheless, Allied soldiers continued to lose their lives for another eight months without ever gaining more than a feeble foothold.

In December, London finally issued the order to **withdraw**. Eleven thousand Australians and New Zealanders had been killed, along with the same number of French and three times as many British troops. The Turks lost eighty-six thousand men.

Official Australian historiography continues to mythologize the battle for Gallipoli, elevating it to the level of a national legend on which Australian identity is founded. The Anzac soldiers proved themselves heroes of the new nation, their loyalty and bravery evidence of how far Australia had developed. This "birth of a nation" was at the same time a loss of innocence and a national rite of passage: never again would Australians so unquestioningly involve themselves in foreign ventures.

Today, the legend is as fiercely defended as ever. April 25, **Anzac Day**, is commemorated annually, a focal point for Australian national pride. Although it may seem like a one-battle flag-waving ceremony to outsiders, it is akin to Britain's Remembrance Day and the USA's Veterans' Day, a solemn occasion when one is asked to reflect on the sacrifices made by those who fought in all wars.

is classic Art Deco right down to the detail of Rayner Hoff's stylized soldier figures on the exterior. Downstairs, a free, mainly photographic, exhibition looks at Australian wartime experiences. The solemn annual Anzac Day march and wreath-laying takes place here on April 25 (see box opposite).

On the east side of the park, the finely wrought **Great Synagogue**, 187 Elizabeth Street (tours Tues & Thurs noon; $5; Ⓦwww.greatsynagogue.org .au), was consecrated in 1878, and inspired by English synagogues in London and Liverpool. With its strong Gothic and Byzantine influences, domed towers flanking the wrought-iron gates, and big rose window facing Hyde Park, this is Australia's most beautiful synagogue. Tours visit the ornate interior and the A.M Rosenblum Jewish Museum of ritual silverware and vestments.

Along College Street on the east side of the Park, **St Mary's Cathedral** is separated from the **Australian Museum** by the green expanse of **Cook and Phillip Park**.

St Mary's Cathedral and Cook and Phillip Park

Although its foundation stone was laid in 1821, the huge, Gothic, Catholic cathedral of **St Mary's** (Sun–Fri 6.30am–6.30pm, Sat 8am–6.30pm; Ⓦwww .stmaryscathedral.org.au), overlooking the northeast corner of Hyde Park, was completed in 1882. It finally gained the twin stone spires originally planned by architect William Wardell in 1865 for its two southern towers in 1999. The forecourt – a pedestrianized terrace with fountains and pools – provides access to the large **Cook and Phillip Park**, which holds a **recreation centre** with a fifty-metre swimming pool and gym (see "Sports and activities") and an excellent vegetarian restaurant, *Bodhi in the Park* (see "Eating").

The Australian Museum

Facing Hyde Park across College Street, the **Australian Museum** (daily 9.30am–5pm; $12; free 40min highlights tours daily at 11am & 2pm; Ⓦwww .australianmuseum.net.au) is primarily devoted to natural history, with an interest in human evolution and Aboriginal culture. Though the collection was founded in 1827, the building itself, a grand sandstone affair with a facade of Corinthian pillars, wasn't finished until the 1860s, and has been extended several times since. Besides the permanent exhibits described below, it also stages **special exhibitions** throughout the year, for which there's usually an additional charge.

The core of the old museum is the three levels of the **Long Gallery**, Australia's first exhibition gallery, opened in 1855 to a Victorian public keen to gawk at the colony's curiosities. Many classic displays from the ensuing hundred years are still here, Heritage-listed, in contrast with the very modern approach in the rest of the museum.

On the **ground floor**, the impressive **Australia's First Peoples** exhibition looks at the history of Australia's Aboriginal people from the Dreamtime to the more contemporary issues of the Stolen Generation and Freedom Rides. In **Skeletons**, on the ground-floor level of the Long Gallery, a skeletal human goes through the motions of riding a bicycle, for example, and you can admire the elegantly complex bone structure of a python.

Level 1 is given over to **minerals**, while the disparate collections on **level 2** are far more exciting – especially the Long Gallery's **Birds & Insects**, with its chilling contextual displays on dangerous spiders such as redbacks and funnel-webs. On the same floor, adaptation is the key to **Surviving Australia**, which explores how monotremes, marsupials and humans have coped with the extremes of the Australian climate – or not, as in the case of the ancient marsupial lion or the Tasmanian tiger. Ancient beasts also form the bulk of **Dinosaurs** where the fun design-o-saurus programme allows visitors to create their own dinosaurs on screen.

Kids, of course, will love the dinosaurs, and can pass an hour in **Kids' Space**, a fun play-space for under-5s (see p.235 for more on kids at the museum), while adults and older children will appreciate **Search and Discover**, a flora and fauna identification centre with internet access and books to consult.

Haymarket

The section of the city centre south from Liverpool Street down to Central Station is known as **Haymarket**. It is effectively a downmarket southern extension of the CBD, a place that's always alive with students from the University of Technology and backpackers who jam the area's abundant hostels. It is also a heavily East Asian area with its own distinct **Chinatown**, a growing **Koreatown** and plenty of food courts with restaurants offering cuisines from across the continent.

The Light Rail (see p.30) heads through here from Central Station, past Capitol Square and the **Capitol Theatre**. Built as a deluxe picture palace in the 1920s, the theatre now hosts big-budget musicals and ballet under a star-studded ceiling representing the southern skies. To the west, the Light Rail passes the budget shopping area of **Paddy's Market** and the the ugly concrete bunker of the **Sydney Entertainment Centre**, the city's mainstream concert venue (see p.216),

Chinatown

At the northern end of Haymarket, the junction of Liverpool Street and Pitt Street is rapidly becoming the heart of Sydney's **Koreatown** with restaurants popping up all the time. Walk west along Liverpool Street to Kent Street and you're in the fairly lacklustre **Spanish Corner**. Sydney's **Chinatown**, centred on Dixon Street just south of Liverpool Street, is a much more full-blooded affair. No mere tourist attraction, this is a gutsy Chinese quarter, with its share of social problems. Winter 2002 saw unprecedented incidents when several restaurants were wrecked, in front of terrified diners, by rival triad gangs conducting turf wars. Chinese people first began arriving in "New Gold Mountain", as they called Australia, in the 1850s during the time of the gold rushes; most went back after the 1880s, but many stayed on and set up such businesses as wholesaling and running market gardens. Chinatown grew up around what has been the traditional wholesale market area for over 150 years, but Dixon Street was only officially designated as Sydney's Chinatown in 1980.

Through the colourful Chinese gates, **Dixon Street Mall** is the main drag, buzzing day and night as people crowd into numerous restaurants, pubs, cafés, cinemas, food stalls and Asian grocery stores. Chinese New Year (ⓦwww .cityofsydney.nsw.gov.au/cny), at the end of January or early February, is celebrated with gusto: lion dances, Dragon Boat racing, food festivals and musical entertainment compete with the noise and smoke from strings of Chinese crackers.

The southern end of Dixon Street skirts past the undercover **Paddy's Market** (Thurs–Sun 10am–5pm; ⓦwww.paddysmarkets.com.au). Dating from 1869, Sydney's oldest market holds around a thousand stalls, and is a good place to buy cheap vegetables, seafood, plants, clothes and bric-a-brac. Above the old market, the multilevel **Market City Shopping Centre** has a very Asian feel – you could easily imagine yourself in an air-conditioned mall in Bangkok or Kuala Lumpur. There's an excellent Asian food court (see "Eating") next to the multi-screen cinema on the top floor.

Darling Harbour, Pyrmont and Ultimo

mmediately east of the city centre, **Darling Harbour** was named after Ralph Darling, NSW Governor General from 1825 to 1831. Formerly a grimy industrial docks area, it lay moribund until the 1980s, when as part of the Bicentenary Project the state government pumped millions of dollars into regenerating such prime urban real estate. The huge redevelopment scheme around Cockle Bay, which opened in 1988, included the construction of an above-ground monorail as well as a massive shopping and entertainment precinct. In many ways, the old wharves have been very stylishly modernized. The glistening water channels that run along Palm Avenue are beautifully designed, while Darling Harbour and the surrounding areas now hold plenty of attractions. Only since a late-1990s facelift however have Sydney-siders embraced this much-maligned area, after years of sneering at it as tacky and touristy. The addition of King Street Wharf, further north, has further enhanced its array of upmarket cafés, bars and restaurants, and made Darling Harbour more of a fixture on Sydney's nightlife scene.

The eastern side of Darling Harbour, with office and apartment blocks overlooking the yacht-filled waters, blends straight into the CBD. The western side is a different matter. Push beyond the western wharf-side developments and you're onto the Pyrmont–Ultimo Peninsula, an altogether older industrial quarter where the suburbs of **Pyrmont** and **Ultimo** have only recently started to gentrify. There's still a fair way to go, making it an interesting area to wander around, noticing the ongoing changes in between visits to the **Star City Casino**, the **Sydney Fish Market** and the superb **Powerhouse Museum**.

Darling Harbour

Darling Harbour is divided almost in half by **Pyrmont Bridge**, a green-and-cream steel structure built a century ago to connect the city to Pyrmont, and equipped with a swinging section to allow large ships to access Cockle Bay to the south. Effectively the western extension of Market Street, the bridge was turned into a broad pedestrian thoroughfare in the 1980s, and made more graceful with the addition of a sleek **monorail**.

South of the bridge, **Cockle Bay** is flanked on the east by the bars and restaurants of **Cockle Bay Wharf**, with a dress circle of city high-rise apartments behind. On the western shore, the **Harbourside Shopping Centre** huddles below a cluster of rather ugly modern chain hotels, which mainly service attendees

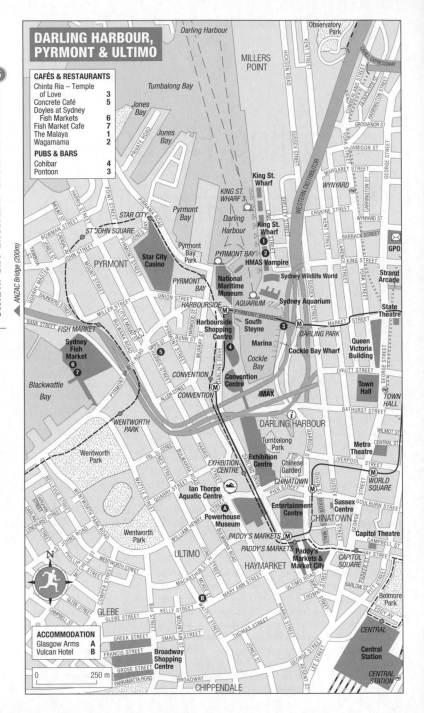

DARLING HARBOUR, PYRMONT & ULTIMO

CAFÉS & RESTAURANTS

Chinta Ria – Temple of Love	3
Concrete Café	5
Doyles at Sydney Fish Markets	6
Fish Market Cafe	7
The Malaya	1
Wagamama	2

PUBS & BARS

Cohibar	4
Pontoon	3

ACCOMMODATION

Glasgow Arms	A
Vulcan Hotel	B

0   250 m

▲ ANZAC Bridge (200m)

Getting to and around Darling Harbour

To walk to Darling Harbour takes only ten minutes from the Town Hall; from the Queen Victoria Building, head down Market Street and along the overhead walkway. Further south there's a pedestrian bridge from Bathurst Street or you can cut through on Liverpool Street to Tumbalong Park; both bring you out near the Chinese Garden.

Alternatively, the monorail (see p.30) runs from the city centre to six stops (Darling Park, Harbourside Shopping Centre, the Convention Centre, Paddy's Markets, Chinatown, World Square and Gallerias Victoria) around Darling Harbour, and has the views to recommend it.

Getting there by ferry from Circular Quay, to the wharf outside the Sydney Aquarium, gives you a chance to see a bit of the harbour. State Transit ferries leave from Wharf 5, and stop at Luna Park, McMahons Point and Balmain en route. The Matilda Ferry runs from the Harbourmaster's Steps, outside the Museum of Contemporary Art, and goes via Luna Park.

To reach Pyrmont by bus from the city, pick up the #443 from Circular or the QVB: it loops through Ultimo, up Harris Street and past the casino to the Maritime Museum. The #449 connects Glebe with Pyrmont, making a road trip past the Broadway shopping centre, the Powerhouse Museum and the casino.

Once you're there, getting around the large harbour area itself takes quite a bit of walking. If you're exhausted, or just for fun, consider hopping on the dinky People Mover train (daily: summer 10am–6pm; winter 10am–5pm; full circuit 20min; $4.50, kids $3.50), which leaves every fifteen minutes from various points around the harbour.

at the many conferences and trade shows held at the Exhibition Centre. If you pop into Harbourside, don't miss the ground-floor **Gavala Aboriginal Art Centre**, near the food court (see p.252), which sells Aboriginal art, clothing, accessories and music.

At the head of the bay, beneath the Western Distributor freeway and all but obscured by an **IMAX cinema**, the **Darling Harbour Visitor Information Centre** dispenses tourist information for the rest of the city and beyond (daily 9.30am–5.30pm; ☎02/9240 8788, ⓦ www.darlingharbour.com.au). It also provides useful details of the many events staged around Darling Harbour, particularly during school holidays, from carols to ethnic community festivals and outdoor Latin dancing bars. Adjoining Tumbalong Park gives access to the peaceful **Chinese Garden**.

Heading north of Pyrmont Bridge, you reach the main body of Darling Harbour, open to the rest of Sydney Harbour at its northern end. Here you'll find its main tourist attractions: **Sydney Aquarium**, the **Sydney Wildlife World** on the city side, and the **National Maritime Museum** over on the Pyrmont shore. Immediately south of the Maritime Museum, moored in the shadow of the bridge, the venerable, twin-funnelled *South Steyne* is a famous harbour ferry that did the "7 Mile" run to Manly from 1938 until 1974, and is now a restaurant.

Tumbalong Park and Cockle Bay

The southern half of Darling Harbour, around **Cockle Bay**, focuses on **Tumbalong Park**, reached from the city via Liverpool Street. Backed by the Exhibition Centre, this is the harbour's "village green", complete with water features, sculptures and public artworks, and serves as a venue for open-air concerts and free public entertainment. The surrounding area can be Darling Harbour's most frenetic – at least on weekends and during school holidays – as most of the attractions, including a free playground and a stage for holiday concerts, are aimed at children.

The Chinese Garden

For a little peace and quiet, head for the adjacent **Chinese Garden** (daily 9.30am–5pm; $6). This "Garden of Friendship", completed for the Bicentenary in 1988 as a gift from Sydney's sister city Guangdong, is designed in the traditional southern Chinese style. Although not large, it feels remarkably calm and spacious, and makes a great retreat from the commercial hubbub. Stroll past the Water Pavilion of Lotus Fragrance to admire the vista across the Lake of Brightness to the pagoda on its hillock, backed by city high-rises, then continue to the traditional tearoom with its views of the polychrome Dragon Wall, where you can enjoy a refreshing green tea as carp swim in the surrounding waters.

IMAX Theatre

The Southern Promenade of Darling Harbour is dominated by the **Imax Theatre** (films hourly from 10am; 2-D & 3-D films, $19.50, kids $14.50; ☎02/9281 3300, ⓦwww.imax.com.au). Its giant eight-storey cinema screen (claimed as the world's biggest) shows a constantly changing programme, with an emphasis on scenic wonders, the animal kingdom and adventure sports.

Sydney Aquarium

If you're not going to get the chance to explore the Barrier Reef, the impressive **Sydney Aquarium** (daily 9am–10pm; $30; ⓦwww.sydneyaquarium.com.au), at the eastern end of Pyrmont Bridge, makes a good substitute.

Displays start with low-key entry-level exhibits on freshwater fish from the Murray–Darling basin. Many of the species on show, such as the oddball platypus, have become increasingly threatened by the impact of drought on Australia's largest river system, while crocodiles typify the northern rivers.

Of the aquarium's three **giant ocean tanks**, the first two cover the Southern Oceans. Plastic-sheathed underwater walkways allow visitors to contemplate sharks, seals and gigantic stingrays swimming overhead. There's a similarly grand approach to the Northern Oceans exhibit, where exotic species from the Great Barrier Reef drift past behind vast sheets of glass. It can be breathtakingly beautiful at quiet times – early or late in the day – when black-and-yellow-spotted butterfly fish drift by, undulating Moon Jellyfish loom into view, iridescent blue starfish glow, and a spotted leopard shark seems uninterested in everything. In front of the final huge floor-to-ceiling tank, you can sit and watch the underwater world while classical music plays.

Yet another section displays dangerous creatures like the moray eel and poisonous sea urchins, and Little Penguins try to keep cool.

Sydney Wildlife World

The large netted room behind the Sydney Aquarium is the free-flying aviary of the **Sydney Wildlife World** (daily 9am–6pm; $30; ⓦwww.sydneywildlifeworld .com.au), a compact urban zoo that makes a perfect topside complement to the aquarium. Animals that you might travel thousands of kilometres to see are

---

Discount tickets

Sydney Aquarium, Sydney Wildlife World and Sydney Tower (see Chapter 3) are managed jointly. All offer a **ten percent discount** for adult, child and family tickets if you book online, a good idea anyway as it saves you queuing at busy times. In addition, assorted combo packages are available, such as seeing all three sights for $68 per adult.

grouped here in replicas of their natural environments: wallabies, kangaroos, cassowaries and wombats roam the compact semi-arid grasslands, while flocks of finches flit about the aviary, their multi-coloured plumage looking too perfect to be real. Elsewhere orange lacewing butterflies go delicately about their business; stick insects contrive to go unseen (and often succeed); Australia's largest lizard, the two-metre-long perentie, struts its stuff; and you can admire the spotted-tailed quoll, the Australian mainland's largest carnivorous marsupial.

This being Australia, wildly venomous nasties abound, notably the Sydney funnel-web **spider**, especially dangerous as it's common in populated areas. Most people don't wish to be reminded that Australia boasts twelve of the world's top thirty most venomous land snakes, including the top three – the inland taipan, the eastern brown and the coastal taipan. They're kept behind glass, thankfully, along with the beautiful red-bellied black snake and the fat pythons typically draped over branches. The latter come out to play during **Reptile Talks** (hourly from 11am; 10–15min; free) – you can even pat one. Other distractions for **kids** include the pinned bug and butterfly collections, and plenty of myth-busting facts.

The place can get very busy, so it pays to come early or late to avoid the crowds and to see the animals at their most active. Even better, book in for the **Koala Breakfast** (Mon–Fri 7.30am; $55), when you get to photograph koalas up really close, have a buffet breakfast as they dine on gum leaves nearby, and are then free to walk around the rest of the exhibits for half an hour before the general public get in.

The National Maritime Museum

On the western side of Pyrmont Bridge, the distinctive modern **National Maritime Museum** (daily 9.30am–5pm, Jan until 6pm; museum free; ⓦwww .anmm.gov.au), topped by a wave-shaped roof, highlights the history of Australia as a seafaring nation, but goes beyond maritime interests to look at how the sea has shaped Australian life. Seven core themed exhibitions cover everything from immigration to beach culture and Aboriginal fishing methods. Highlights include "Merana Eora Nora – First People", delving into indigenous culture, and "Navigators – Defining Australia", which focuses on the seventeenth-century Dutch explorers. Look out for such delights as the replica of the winner of Darwin's Beer Can Regatta, a kind of raft built from hundreds of beer cans (mostly VB, since you ask).

Outside, you can wander along the shore for nothing, relaxing at the pleasant alfresco **café** and strolling north past the Cape Bowling Green Lighthouse to the bronze **Welcome Wall**, which honours Australia's six million immigrants. The real highlights are several **moored vessels**, which charge admission; buy the **Big** ticket ($30, kids $16) if you want to see them all. The **Navy** ticket ($18) gives access to the 1950s destroyer HMAS *Vampire*, which on retirement operated as a naval training ship, and the opportunity to explore deep inside the submarine HMAS *Onslow*, decommissioned in 1999. You can also take a guided tour of the barque *James Craig* ($10), an 1874 square-rigger, and get a sense of Captain Cook's onboard life on the replica HM Bark *Endeavour* ($15). The wharves nearby hold the Sydney Heritage Fleet's collection of smaller restored boats and ships, dating back as far as 1888.

Ultimo and Pyrmont

West of Darling Harbour, the Pyrmont-Ultimo peninsula is in transition: though grimy dereliction has long since been expunged, full gentrification is taking its time.

Harry Seidler

See a white concrete tower block in Sydney, and there's a good chance it was the work of **Harry Seidler**, Australia's best-known Modernist architect, who died in 2006 leaving a distinctive stamp on the city's skyline. Born in Vienna in 1923, he was forced to flee the Nazis as a teenager, winding up first in London and later in Canada and the US. Having studied under Walter Gropius, he is considered a late exponent of the Bauhaus movement, though work with Finnish architect Alvar Aalto and Brazilian Oscar Niemeyer in Rio soon aligned him with **Modernism**. Unornamented design with an emphasis on function underscores his life's work, mostly seen in Australia, where he set up a practice in 1949.

Seidler's first major work, the 50-floor circular **Australia Square** (1961–67) in the CBD, is regarded as the city's first true skyscraper, and remained Sydney's tallest structure until 1976 – visit the top-floor *Orbit Lounge* (see p.206) for a closer look. The use of pre-cast modularized concrete in white became something of a signature, and was seen again a few blocks away at the blockish 67-storey **MLC Centre** (1977), with its distinctive two-storey mushroom, on the corner of Castlereagh Street and Martin Place – Niemeyer's influence to the fore here. Similar themes were explored for the very prominent **Blues Point Tower** (1961) at McMahon's Point, just west of the Harbour Bridge, and for the Australia Embassy in Paris (1973–78). Seidler's final flourish was a beautiful reworking of the old Ultimo Aquatic Centre into the freeform wave shape of the **Ian Thorpe Aquatic Centre** (2001–2007) – in white, of course.

With its shipbuilding yards, a sugar refinery and woolstores, **Pyrmont**, jutting into the water between Darling Harbour and Blackwattle Bay, has long formed an integral part of Sydney's industrial waterfront. This was also Sydney's answer to Ellis Island. During the 1950s, thousands of immigrants disembarked at the city's main overseas passenger terminal here, Pier 13. Today the former industrial suburb, which held a population of only nine hundred in 1988, is being transformed to house twenty thousand, with AUS$2 billion of investment and groovy modern unit blocks and warehouse renovations to show for it. The New South Wales government has sold AUS$97 million worth of property, as part of one of Australia's biggest concentrated sell-offs of land. The area has certainly become glitzier, home to Sydney's **Star City Casino** (see below), and the Channel Ten TV company. Harris Street has filled with new shops and cafés, and the area's old pubs have been given a new lease of life, attracting the young and upwardly mobile alongside the wharfies. The approaches to the spectacularly cabled **Anzac Bridge**, complete with statue of an Australian and New Zealand Army Corps soldier, wing high above the **Sydney Fish Market**.

Heading south along Harris Street you move imperceptibly into **Ultimo**, a residential suburb that increasingly industrialized through the twentieth century. It's now home to the University of Technology campus on either side of Harris Street, and both the television and radio headquarters of the national broadcaster, the ABC. You'll most likely find yourself here to visit the excellent **Powerhouse Museum** or to swim at the **Ian Thorpe Aquatic Centre** (see p.269) with its white tiles and sensual curves.

The best ways to **get around** Pyrmont and Ultimo are the Light Rail and Monorail, though even the Sydney Fish Market is only thirty minutes' walk from the city centre.

Star City Casino

West of the Maritime Museum, on Pyrmont Bay, the palm-fronted **Star City** (Ⓦ www.starcity.com.au) is Sydney's spectacularly tasteless 24-hour casino. As well as the two hundred gaming tables (from Blackjack to Pai Gow – there are heaps of Asian games, and gamblers), a big betting lounge and sports bar, and 1500 noisy poker machines, the building houses over a dozen restaurants, cafés (good for late-night eats) and theme bars, two theatres (see p.222), and a nightclub. The actual casino interior is a riot of giant palm sculptures, prize cars spinning on rotating bases, Aboriginal painting motifs on the ceiling, Australian critters scurrying across a red desert-coloured carpet, and endless flashing poker machines. Dress code is smart casual. You can just wander in and have a look around or a drink, without betting.

Nearby **Pyrmont Bay Park** is a shady spot to rest, and hosts an early morning **Growers Market** (7–11am) on the first Saturday of each month.

To get to the casino, take bus #449 which runs in a loop to and from Broadway in the city via the QVB to the casino and the Exhibition Centre in Darling Harbour, or the #443 which runs from Circular Quay via Phillip and Market streets and the QVB. The Light Rail pulls in right underneath the casino.

Sydney Fish Market

On the corner of Pyrmont Bridge Road and Bank Street, the **Sydney Fish Market** (daily 7am–4pm; Ⓦwww.sydneyfishmarket.com.au) is only ten minutes' walk from Darling Harbour, via Pyrmont Bridge Road. It's the world's second-largest seafood market for variety of fish, after Tokyo's massive Tsukiji market. Come early to see the **auctions** (Mon–Fri only, with the biggest auction floor on Fri): buyers start viewing the fish at 4.30am, auctions begin at 5.30am, and the public viewing platform opens at 7am. Buyers log into computer terminals to register their bids in a Dutch-style auction: the price drops steadily until a bid is made and the first bid gets the fish. You don't get much of a view from the public platform, so seriously consider joining a **tour** (see box, p.90).

You can take away oysters, prawns and cooked seafood, and, if you don't mind being pestered by seagulls, eat picnic-style on waterfront tables watching the boats come in. Everything is set up for throwing together an impromptu meal – there's a bakery, the *Blackwattle Deli*, with an extensive (and tempting) cheese selection, a bottle shop and a grocer. At lunchtime, you can eat in at *Doyles* (see p.185) the casual and slightly more affordable version of the famous *Doyles* fish

▲ Monorail, Darling Harbour

Fish Market tours and the Sydney Seafood School

To get among the action on the auction floor of the **Sydney Fish Market**, and stand amid buyers bidding for sashimi-grade yellow-fin tuna, join one of the informative behind-the-scenes tours (Mon & Thurs 7am; 90min; $20; ☎02/9004 1143). You'll need to wear enclosed shoes and a coffee is included.

The tours also visit the rooms where the Sydney Seafood School (☎02/9004 1111) offers seafood cookery lessons, under the expert tuition of resident home economists as well as guest chefs drawn from the city's top restaurants. These start at $80 for a two-hour course, and range from Thai-style to French provincial. The most popular course, for which you need to book three or more months in advance, is the Seafood Barbecue run at weekends (4hr; $145).

restaurant at Watsons Bay; at the excellent sushi bar; or have dirt-cheap fish and chips or a crack-of-dawn espresso at the *Fish Market Cafe* (see p.184). Retail shops open at 7am.

To get to the fish market, take the Light Rail from Central to Fish Market station on Miller Street. If you arrive on bus #443 from Circular Quay or the QVB, it's a five-minute walk from the corner of Harris Street and Pyrmont Bridge Road.

The Powerhouse Museum

Arguably the best museum in Sydney, the **Powerhouse Museum**, 500 Harris St (daily 10am–5pm; $10, children $5, extra for special exhibitions; Ⓦwww.phm .gov.au; monorail to Paddy's Markets) is located, as its name suggests, in a former power station. A huge and exciting place, spread across four levels – allow several hours for a visit – it combines arts and sciences, design, sociology and technology under the same roof. Each year sees several big temporary exhibitions, with recent themes as varied as "The Lord of the Rings" and "The Untold story of Modernism in Australia", while the much-anticipated "Fashion of the Year" display takes place every November.

Level 3, the museum's entrance level, is dominated by the huge **Boulton and Watt Steam Engine**. The world's oldest rotative steam engine, first put to use in 1785 in a British brewery and used for over a hundred years, it's still operational, and often loudly demonstrated.

Downstairs, the old destination board from Sydney's Central Station is set to look as it would have on a Sunday in 1937, though actually it remained in use until 1982. It overlooks the transport section, including the venerable red-and-cream Rose Bay tram and one of the solar racers that competed in trans-continental races – effectively a streamlined solar panel on wheels.

Elsewhere you'll find ¡*Inspired!*, an excellent design exhibit usually featuring several pieces of furniture by top Australian industrial designer Marc Newsom, including his classic Lockheed Lounge Chair (1986), all aluminium panels riveted into a deliciously organic form.

The **Kings Cinema** on level 2, with its original Art Deco fittings, suitably shows the sorts of newsreels and films a Sydneysider would have watched in the 1930s. Judging by the tears at closing time, the **special children's areas** have proved a great success.

With so much to see, you'll appreciate the inexpensive cafés, one nicely set in the courtyard. The souvenir shop is also worth a browse for some unusual gifts. Free **highlights tours** are available whenever they have spare volunteers.

Inner east

E ast of the city centre, the adjacent neighbourhoods of **Kings Cross** and
Potts Point comprise one of Sydney's major entertainment districts,
and make a popular destination for tourists (particularly backpackers).
With loads of hostels, a few chic hotels, plenty of restaurants and bars of
all kinds, this is a great area to hang out in, as long as you don't mind a fairly
rumbustious atmosphere. While there are few specific sights, you can drop down
to moneyed **Elizabeth Bay** to see inside one of the city's grander houses, and
descend steps to **Woolloomooloo** with its busy naval dockyards and stylish
Finger Wharf.

South of Kings Cross, the **Darlinghurst** and **Paddington** were scruffy
working-class suburbs that were gradually taken over and revamped during the
1970s and 1980s by the young, arty and upwardly mobile – who now have two
teenagers and a Lexus in the garage.

Oxford Street runs southeast from the city through **Taylor Square**, the
heart of gay Sydney, and on through the designer shopping and art gallery
areas of Darlinghurst and Paddington to old-money **Woollahra** and the open
grasslands of **Centennial Park**. It also marks the northern boundary of **Surry
Hills**, which, at least along Crown Street, is beginning to rival Paddington for
gentrification, though it retains a funkier feel. While cutting-edge galleries and
bars are still filling out the Surry Hills backstreets, others are looking south to
go-ahead **Waterloo** and even still-edgy **Redfern**.

Kings Cross and around

Mention **Kings Cross** and most Australians conjure up images of street-corner
hookers, junkies shooting up in back alleys and homeless winos occupying
every second doorway. That may have been true in the 1980s and 1990s, but
times have changed. The brothels have moved out to the 'burbs, an injecting
room has taken the drug abuse off the streets, and most of the homeless are
under the railway viaduct in Woolloomooloo. The rump, so to speak, of the sex
industry is a 700-metre-long strip of Darlinghurst Road where a handful of
strip shows hang on – though even their time is limited, as new places are no
longer allowed to open up.

Kings Cross certainly hasn't become lifeless, however. The place still derives a
slight edginess from the interplay between the disparate groups who stake their
claims – ageing bohemians, strung-out junkies, abstemious backpackers, a few
confused and derelict souls and the upwardly mobile who are increasingly moving
into swank apartments. Somehow "The Cross" manages to cater to them all.

The area is always lively, with places to eat and drink that stay open all hours.
People will still tell you that it's dangerous, but it's no more so than any inner-city

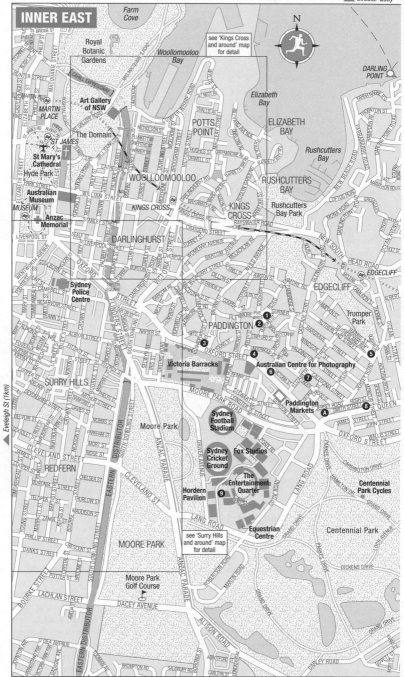

▲ *Circular Quay*

INNER EAST

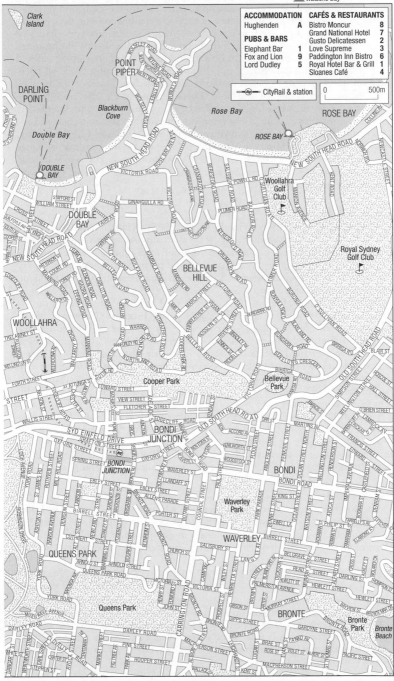

▲ Watsons Bay

ACCOMMODATION	CAFÉS & RESTAURANTS	
Hughenden	**A**	Bistro Moncur	8
		Grand National Hotel	7
PUBS & BARS		Gusto Delicatessen	2
Elephant Bar	**1**	Love Supreme	3
Fox and Lion	**9**	Paddington Inn Bistro	6
Lord Dudley	**5**	Royal Hotel Bar & Grill	1
		Sloanes Café	4

CityRail & station

0   500m

Clark Island

POINT PIPER

DARLING POINT

Blackburn Cove

Rose Bay

ROSE BAY

Double Bay

ROSE BAY

DOUBLE BAY

NEW SOUTH HEAD ROAD

VICTORIA ROAD

Woollahra Golf Club

DOUBLE BAY

BELLEVUE HILL

Royal Sydney Golf Club

WOOLLAHRA

Cooper Park

Bellevue Park

BONDI JUNCTION

BONDI JUNCTION

BONDI

SYD EINFELD DRIVE

OLD SOUTH HEAD ROAD

OXFORD STREET

BONDI ROAD

Waverley Park

QUEENS PARK

WAVERLEY

Queens Park

BRONTE

Bronte Park

Bronte Beach

▶ Bondi Beach (400m)

area with a boozy culture. Come here on a Friday or Saturday night and you may see the odd scuffle and much evidence of excessive alcohol consumption, but the constant flow of people (and police officers) makes it relatively safe. Generally, Kings Cross is much more subdued during the day, with a slightly "hung-over" feel to it; local residents emerge, and it's a good time to hang out in the cafés.

Kings Cross itself is quite small, and hemmed in by a ring of suburbs, all fascinating in their own right. Continue north along Macleay Street or the parallel, leafy Victoria Street and you're into **Potts Point**, where the mid-century apartment blocks are increasingly occupied by chic young things who spend their days (and particularly evenings) hanging out in tasteful cafés and cocktail bars. Drop down the hill to the east, and you're into mostly residential **Elizabeth Bay**, where you might visit Elizabeth Bay House. Over on the western side of Kings Cross, a couple of sets of steps lead down the sandstone escarpment to waterside **Woolloomooloo**, with its naval dockyard and its lovely Finger Wharf, filled with chi-chi bars and restaurants.

Kings Cross

The preserve of Sydney's bohemians in the 1950s, **Kings Cross** became an R&R spot for American soldiers during the Vietnam war, and visiting sailors still troop up from their ships docked at the bottom of the hill in Woolloomooloo. A continuing programme of footpath and shopfront beautification is slowly lending a fresher air, while themed street festivals are becoming more frequent, and bringing in a different crowd.

The "action zone" of Kings Cross centres on **Darlinghurst Road**, from its junction with William Street to the partly paved **Fitzroy Gardens** with its distinctive El Alamein fountain. At weekends, an endless stream of visitors arrive from the suburbs, emerging from the underground Kings Cross station, near the beginning of the Darlinghurst Road "sin" strip, to trawl along the streets licking ice creams as touts try their best to haul them into the remaining tacky strip-joints and sleazy nightclubs. This same strip is increasingly populated with backpacker hostels, budget travel agencies and internet cafés catering to the travellers staying nearby.

A free **walking tour** map, "Passion: Sydney's Wild Side", available from the library at 50 Darlinghurst Road, highlights the area's Art Deco architecture and provides historical background. For a more personal insight into the district's love stories, drug obsessions and murders, join Bounce Walking Tours (daily 5pm; 2hr; $40; ☎1300 665 365, ⓦwww.bouncewalkingtours.com).

Potts Point

From Fitzroy Gardens, **Macleay Street** runs through quieter, upmarket **Potts Point**. With its tree-lined streets, apartment blocks, classy boutique hotels, stylish restaurants, buzzy cafés and occasional harbour glimpses over wealthier Elizabeth Bay, just to the east, this is as close to European-living as Sydney gets. The area

---

Getting to the Kings Cross area

Kings Cross is accessible by train (Eastern Suburbs line) or bus (#311, #324 or #325 from Circular Quay; many others from the city to Darlinghurst Road). It's also not too far to walk, either straight up William Street from Hyde Park, or, for a quieter route, up from the Domain via Cowper Wharf Road in Woolloomooloo, and then up the McElhone Stairs to Victoria Street. To get to Elizabeth Bay House, take bus #311 or walk from Kings Cross Station.

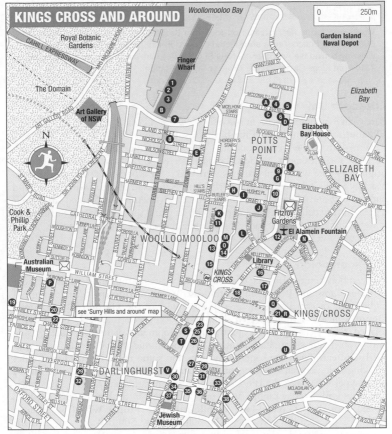

KINGS CROSS AND AROUND

Woolloomooloo Bay

0   250m

ACCOMMODATION		CAFÉS & RESTAURANTS				PUBS & BARS	
Altamont	S	a tavola	31	Harry's Café		Aperitif	16
Backpackers		Almond	34	de Wheels	7	The Bourbon	12
Headquarters	R	Bar Coluzzi	24	La Buvette	6	Darlo Bar	30
Blue Parrot		Bar Reggio	22	Le Petit Crème	26	East Village Hotel	29
Backpackers	G	Bayswater Brasserie	17	Macleay Pizza	10	Green Park Hotel	36
Blue Sydney	B	Beppi's	19	Manta	1	Hugo's	18
Challis Lodge	C	Bill and Toni	20	Minami	9	Lotus	5
The Chelsea	U	bills	38	Onde	33	Peppermint Lounge	15
De Vere	F	Café Hernandez	21	Otto	2	Soho Bar & Lounge	13
Eva's Backpackers	I	Dolcetta	11	Roy's Famous	14	Tilbury Hotel	8
Highfield Private Hotel	O	Fishface	37	Phamish	32	Victoria Room	27
Hotel 59	Q	Fratelli Paradiso	4	Tropicana Caffe	23	Water Bar	3
Jolly Swagman	J	fu manchu	35	Una's	28		
Kanga House	K	Govinda's	25	Victoria Room	27		
Kirketon	T						
Macleay Lodge	D						
Medusa	V						
The Original							
Backpackers Lodge	M						
The Pink House	N						
Quest Potts Point	L						
Simpsons of							
Potts Point	A						
Victoria Court	H						
The Wood Duck Inn	P						
Woolloomooloo Waters							
Apartment Hotel	E						

was Sydney's first suburb, developed land granted to John Wylde in 1822 and Alexander Macleay in 1826. The grand villas of colonial bureaucrats gave way during the 1920s and 1930s to **Art Deco** residential apartments, while the 1950s saw the addition of big, splendid hotels, many of which have been converted into luxury apartments. Beyond Macleay Street, Wylde Street heads downhill to Woolloomooloo; you may spot white-clad sailors and officers here, strolling up through the streets from the naval base.

Elizabeth Bay

Barely five minutes' walk northwest of Kings Cross, well-heeled, residential **Elizabeth Bay** centres on **Elizabeth Bay House**, at 7 Onslow Ave (Fri–Sun 9.30am–4pm; $8; ⓦ www.hht.net.au). This grand Greek Revival villa was built in 1839 for Alexander Macleay, colonial secretary of New South Wales. The original 54-acre waterfront grounds were said to be a botanist's paradise; the large Macleay family, who arrived from Britain in 1826, were obsessed with botany and entomology, and Sydney University's Macleay Museum was formed from their natural history collection. The interior, with its grand spiral staircase, is furnished as it would have been in the early 1840s, while the views from the windows, of the yachts and water of Elizabeth Bay, are stunning.

Woolloomooloo

Wedged between the Botanic Gardens to the west and the sandstone escarpment of Kings Cross and Potts Point to the east, **Woolloomooloo** occupies the old harbourside quarter beside the grey-painted fleet of the **Garden Island Naval Depot**. Once a narrow-streeted slum, Woolloomooloo is quickly being transformed, though its upmarket apartment developments sit uneasily side by side with problematic community housing, and you should still be careful at night in the backstreets. There are some lively pubs and some more old-fashioned quiet drinking holes, as well as the legendary **Harry's Café de Wheels** (see "Eating") on Cowper Wharf Road, a late-closing pie-cart operating since 1945 and popular nowadays with Sydney cabbies and hungry clubbers in the small hours.

Next door, the 400-metre-long **Woolloomooloo Finger Wharf** was built in 1915. For decades, this was where the bulk of New South Wales' wool left for markets overseas, and many new immigrants arrived. As containerization shifted the docks trade elsewhere, the buildings became progressively more picturesquely dilapidated until 1987, when the state government slated them for demolition. They hadn't reckoned on an unprecedented level of public opposition, however, led by the unions who imposed a so-called "green ban" that sought to protect Sydney's natural and built environment from inappropriate development. This effectively stopped the demolition crews entering the site, and eventually the wharf was saved. Some might call it a hollow victory, however, as it has now been fashioned into a posh complex comprising a marina, luxury residential apartments with some A-list tenants, and a bunch of slick restaurants with alfresco dining. All enjoy virtually the same waterside setting but *Otto* and *China Doll* (see "Eating"), are two of the best. There's also the cool *Blue Hotel* (see "Accommodation") and its funky *Water Bar*. The general public are free to wander along the wharf and even go inside: in the centre there's a free exhibition space with a changing theme.

William Street and East Sydney

Eastbound from Hyde Park and the city centre, traffic floods along **William Street**, which flanks the northern side of the Australian Museum and heads straight for the giant neon Coca-Cola sign that heralds Kings Cross. This extremely busy thoroughfare is lined by an uneasy blend of backpacker car and van rental places, and dealerships for Ferrari, Lamborghini and Maserati.

Though the 2005 opening of the Cross City Tunnel was accompanied by grand visions of William Street becoming a European-style boulevard – tree-lined, traffic-calmed, and with wide pavements for café tables and strolling pedestrians – little has happened so far.

The tiny, traditionally Italian suburb of **East Sydney** huddles south of William Street. There are no sights, but the restaurants, cafés and bars clustered along Crown and Stanley streets make this a pleasant area to stop for a drink during the day, or return for a meal later. Less frenetic than nearby Kings Cross and Darlinghurst, it has more of a neighbourhood feel.

Darlinghurst

Hip and bohemian, **Darlinghurst** mingles seediness with hedonistic style. Some art students and clubbers never leave the district, save for a coffee at the Cross or a swim at the "Boy" in The Domain. East of East Sydney, south of Kings Cross and strung out along Oxford Street between Hyde Park and Paddington, it falls into distinct halves. In the north, the restaurants, bars and a couple of chic hotels along the diverging Darlinghurst Road and **Victoria Street** seem like a southern continuation of Kings Cross. It is a classic posing area, boasting the legendary, street-smart *Bar Coluzzi*, the elegantly worn-in lounge-style *Darlo Bar* and up-and-coming dining spots such as *A Tavola* (all listed under "Eating" or "Drinking").

The southern strip along **Oxford Street** and especially around **Taylor Square**, is very much the epicentre of Sydney's very active **gay and lesbian** community (covered in detail in Chapter 16). While some bars and clubs leave you in no doubt whatsoever as to their patrons' sexual orientation, Oxford Street is become increasingly mixed and there are plenty of restaurants and bars where gays and straights mingle comfortably.

Oxford Street's shopping strip, many would argue Sydney's best for labels and funky style, starts at the corner of Victoria Street in Darlinghurst, and doesn't stop until the corner of Jersey Road in **Woollahra**. Two arthouse cinemas – the Academy Twin and the Verona (see "Performing arts and film") – always show the latest local and international alternative flicks, and late-night bookshops Berkelouw (with its fabulous coffee shop upstairs), and Ariel across the street, pack in students and the smart set alike until late.

Sydney Jewish Museum

The impressive **Sydney Jewish Museum**, at 148 Darlinghurst Rd (Mon–Thurs & Sun 10am–4pm, Fri 10am–2pm; $10; Ⓦ www.sydneyjewishmuseum.com.au), is housed in the old Maccabean Hall, which has been a Jewish meeting point since 1923. Sixteen Jews were among the convicts who arrived with the First Fleet, and this high-tech, interactive museum explores over two hundred years of Australian Jewish experience, all briefly covered in an introductory twelve-minute film (screened continuously).

The newly revamped ground-floor exhibits take an interactive approach to Jewish history, traditions and culture, as well as anti-Semitism through the ages. Upstairs, the Holocaust is covered in harrowing detail with Australian

Darlinghurst falls across two of our maps. The northern section is on "Kings Cross and around", while the southern section, around Oxford Street, is on the "Surry Hills" map.

survivors' videotaped testimonies. A map locating just the 180 largest of the estimated five thousand concentration and death camps around Europe in 1944 is displayed above camp uniforms, Star of David identification badges and the pathetic mementoes that people were able to keep hold of. Don't miss the sombre Children's Memorial, dedicated to the 1.5 million children who lost their lives.

Make an effort to join one of the hour-long **guided tours** (daily except Sat at noon; free). These are often led by Holocaust survivors who, at other times, are willing to talk about their experiences.

The museum has a **kosher café** (closed Fri), along with a shop stocking religious objects and books. You can pick up the pamphlet *Guide to Jewish Sydney*, which will help you seek out the **Great Synagogue** in the city centre (see p.81), and the concentration of **kosher** Jewish cafés, butchers and supermarkets on Hall Street in Bondi.

Paddington and Woollahra

From its intersection with South Dowling Street in Darlinghurst, Oxford Street strikes southeast through trendy, upmarket **Paddington** and wealthy, staid **Woollahra** to the verdant expanse of Centennial Park. **Transport** heading in this direction includes **buses** #380 and #389 from Circular Quay, and #378 from Central Station.

Paddington, a slum a century ago, became a popular hangout for hipsters during the late 1960s and 1970s. Yuppies took over in the 1980s, and turned it into the smart and fashionable suburb it remains today: the Victorian-era terraced houses, with their iron-lace verandas reminiscent of New Orleans, have been beautifully restored. Many of the terraces were originally built in the 1840s to house the artisans who worked on the graceful, sandstone **Victoria Barracks** on the southern side of Oxford Street, its walls stretching seven blocks, from Greens Road to just before the Paddington Town Hall on Oatley Road. The barracks are still used by the army, though you can visit a small **museum** (Sun 10am–3pm; $2 donation) of uniforms, medals and firearms. Free **guided tours** (Thurs 10am) also visit the museum, and come complete with army band.

Shadforth Street, opposite the entrance gates, holds many of the original artisans' homes. Follow it north, then turn right on to Glenmore Road to reach **Five Ways**, the focus of an area of pleasant, winding, tree-lined streets that's ideal for a stroll, offering a chance to wander into specialty stores and numerous small art galleries (see "Shopping and galleries"). Refreshments are available around Five Ways, notably at *Gusto* (see "Eating") and the *Royal Hotel* (see "Drinking"), a typically gracious old boozer.

The area's swankiest clothes shopping is around the junction of Glenmore Road and Oxford Street, while Elizabeth Street, which runs off Oxford Street almost a kilometre further southeast, holds yet more classy shops. This latter section of Oxford Street is home to some slightly more mainstream retail action with quality chain clothes stores and arty homeware outlets attracting the see-and-be-seen crowd. Always bustling, the area comes alive on Saturday between 10am and around 4pm, when everyone descends on **Paddington Markets** in the church grounds at no. 395. The markets just keep getting bigger, selling everything from funky handmade jewellery to local artwork, cheap but very fresh flowers and vintage clothes; you can even get a massage or a tarot reading between a cup of coffee and an organic sandwich. Nearby, photo fans shouldn't miss the **Australian Centre for Photography** (see p.253).

▲ Centennial Park

Woollahra, along Oxford Street from Paddington, is even more moneyed and correspondingly staid, with expensive **antique shops** and **art galleries** along **Queen Street** replacing the fashion and funky lifestyle stores of Paddington. Leafy Moncur Street hides the gourmet *jones the grocer* (at no. 68; see p.251), where Woollahra locals gather for coffee at the long central table.

Centennial Parklands

South of Paddington and Woollahra lies the great green expanse known as Centennial Parklands (daily sunrise–sunset; Ⓦ www.cp.nsw.gov.au), stretching from Moore Park in the west to Queens Park in the east. Between them lies, **Centennial Park** which opened its gates to the citizens of Sydney at the Centennial Festival in 1888. With its vast lawns, rose gardens and extensive network of ponds, complete with ducks, it resembles an English country park, but it's reclaimed at dawn and dusk by distinctly antipodean residents, including possums and flying foxes. The park is crisscrossed by walking paths and tracks for cycling, rollerblading, jogging and horseriding: rent a bike or rollerblades nearby, or hire a horse from the adjacent equestrian centre, and then recover from your exertions in the **café** with its popular outside tables (though packed and hideously slow on weekends). In the finer months, you can stay on until dark then catch an outdoor film at the Moonlight Cinema. Pick up a free map from the Park Office (Mon–Fri 8.30am–5.30pm; Ⓣ02/9339 6699) near the café, easily reached from the Paddington gates off Oxford Street (opposite Queen Street).

Adjacent **Moore Park** holds facilities for tennis, golf, bowling, cricket and hockey, along with the **Sydney Cricket Ground** (see below) and Sydney Football Stadium (host to NRL rugby league, A-league soccer, Super 14 rugby and assorted internationals; see p.262). The Parklands also contain the Murdoch-owned **Fox Studios Australia** (no public access; Ⓦ www.foxstudios.com.au), opened in 1998 on the old Showgrounds site, where the Royal Agricultural Society held its annual Royal Easter Show from 1882 until 1997; the show is now held at the Sydney Showground at the Olympic site at Homebush Bay. The eight high-tech film and television sound stages have been put to good use making such movies as *The Matrix*, *Mission Impossible II*, Baz Luhrmann's *Moulin Rouge* and *Episode I* and *II* of the *Star Wars* saga.

Sydney Cricket Ground

The **Sydney Cricket Ground** (☎02/9360 6601, ⓦwww.scgt.nsw.gov.au) is the city's home cricket for pretty much all forms of cricket, at state and international level (see p.263). The venerated institution of the SCG earned its place in cricketing history for Don Bradman's score of 452 not out for NSW against Queensland in 1930, and for the controversy over England's bodyline bowling techniques in 1932–33. Ideally, you would observe today's proceedings from the lovely 1886 Members Stand while sipping an icy gin and tonic – but unless you're invited by a member, you'll end up elsewhere, drinking beer from a plastic cup. Cricket spectators aren't a sedate lot in Sydney, and the noisiest barrackers will probably come from the newly redeveloped Victor Trumper Stand. The Bill O'Reilly Stand offers comfortable viewing until the afternoon, when you'll be blinded by the sun, whereas the Brewongle Stand provides consistently good viewing. Best of all is the Bradman Stand, adjacent to the Members Stand, with a view directly behind the bowler's arm.

Die-hard cricket fans can go on a **tour** of the SCG on non-match days (Mon–Fri 10am, noon & 2pm, Sat 10am; 1hr 30min; $25; ☎1300 724 737, ⓦwww.scgt .nsw.gov.au), which also covers the **Sydney Football Stadium** next door.

The Entertainment Quarter

The southern section of the old Showgrounds is now the **Entertainment Quarter** (ⓦwww.entertainmentquarter.com.au), a modern and rather characterless area of shops, cinemas, a dozen restaurants and a couple of events centres. There's little reason to spend time here unless you are coming for a show, a movie or just need some sustenance when visiting Centennial Park.

The EQ's central focus, the old **Showring** – once the preserve of woodchopping competitions and rodeo events – now stages everything from open-air cinema and circuses, as well as the food- and produce-oriented **Village Market** (Wed, Sat & Sun 10am–3.30pm).

Arcing around the south side of the Showring, **Bent Street** is an anodyne pedestrian promenade. Partly shaded by palms, it's lined with middling restaurants and high-street fashion chains: most stay open daily until 10pm. It also holds the twelve-screen *Hoyts Entertainment Quarter* **cinema complex**, the artier *Cinema Paris* (for both see p.224), and the indoor **Lollipops Playland** (daily 9.30am–6pm; under-1s free; age 1 midweek $10, weekends $14; 2–18 $14; adults $5; ☎02/9331 0811). Two free but less varied playgrounds are just outside.

Visitors on the way to gigs or movies often stop off at the *Fox and Lion* pub (see "Drinking").

Getting to Centennial Parklands

Two buses run along Oxford Street to Paddington Gates, the #378 from Railway Square and Central Station and the #380 from Circular Quay. Alternatively, head straight into the heart of the park from Central Station (#372, #393 or #395). There is plenty of free parking for cars.

To get to the Entertainment Quarter, catch bus #339, #392, #394 or #396 from Central, Wynyard or Town Hall. Once again, there's abundant car parking, this time free for the first two hours.

Getting to Surry Hills

Surry Hills is a short walk uphill from Central Station (Devonshire St or Elizabeth St exit): take Foveaux or Devonshire streets and you'll soon hit Crown Street, or it's an even quicker stroll from Oxford Street, Darlinghurst, heading south along Crown or Bourke streets. Several buses also run to Crown Street from Circular Quay, including the #301 and #303.

6

INNER EAST | Surry Hills

Surry Hills

South of Darlinghurst's Oxford Street and due east of Central Station, **Surry Hills** was traditionally the centre of the rag trade, and what little of it still survives is concentrated along Foveaux Street near Elizabeth Street. The rest of Sydney considered it a slum, with its rows of tiny terraces housing a poor, working-class and predominantly Irish population. These dire and overcrowded conditions were given fictional life in Ruth Park's *The Harp in the South* trilogy (see "Books", p.347), set in the Surry Hills of the 1940s. Postwar immigration from Europe made the area something of a cultural melting pot, while during the 1980s it doubled as a grungy, student heartland, fuelled by cheap bars and cheaper rent.

By the mid-1990s, however, the slickly fashionable scene of neighbouring Darlinghurst and Paddington had finally taken over Surry Hills' twin focal points of parallel **Crown Street**, filled with cafés, swanky restaurants, funky clothes shops and designer galleries, and leafy **Bourke Street**, where a couple of Sydney's best cafés lurk among the trees. As rents have risen, only traffic-snarled **Cleveland Street**, running west to Redfern and east towards Moore Park and the Sydney Cricket Ground (see opposite), and lined with cheap Indian, Lebanese and Turkish restaurants, has retained its ethnically varied population.

Apart from the Brett Whiteley Studio (see below), it holds no particular sights, but it's always good for a coffee, a meal, or a few drinks. On the first Saturday of each month, a lively **flea market** (8.30am–4pm) complete with tempting food stalls, takes over the small Shannon Reserve, on the corner of Crown and Foveaux streets, overlooked by the **Clock Hotel** (see "Drinking"). Expanded beyond all recognition from its 1840s' roots, the hotel typifies the new Surry Hills, with its swish restaurant and bar. So too the *White Horse* (see "Drinking") across the road, which used to have a reputation for shady dealings but is now frequented by the beautiful people, for cocktails and imported beers.

Brett Whiteley Studio

The artistic side of Surry Hills can be experienced at the **Brett Whiteley Studio** at 2 Raper St (Sat & Sun 10am–4pm; free; ℗02/9225 1881, Ⓦwww .brettwhiteley.org); walk about three blocks south from Shannon Reserve, down Crown Street, and it's off Davies Street. By the time he died of a heroin overdose in 1992, aged 53, Whitely was one of Australia's most internationally renowned contemporary painters. Though his subjects included wild self-portraits and expressive female nudes, he's best known for his sensual paintings of Sydney Harbour, as seen from his Lavender Bay home. This former T-shirt factory, which Whitely converted into a studio and living space in 1986, has since his death become a museum and gallery. The only painting permanently on display is 1973's *Alchemy*, a series of multi-media panels, taking up most of two walls, which apparently constitute a snapshot of his state of mind at the time – though it might take you some time to work out just what that was.

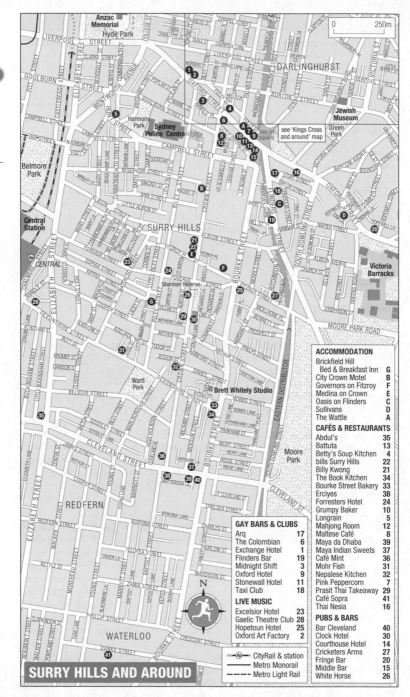

ACCOMMODATION

Brickfield Hill Bed & Breakfast Inn	G
City Crown Motel	B
Governors on Fitzroy	F
Medina on Crown	E
Oasis on Flinders	C
Sullivans	D
The Wattle	A

CAFÉS & RESTAURANTS

Abdul's	35
Battuta	13
Betty's Soup Kitchen	4
bills Surry Hills	22
Billy Kwong	21
The Book Kitchen	34
Bourke Street Bakery	33
Erciyes	38
Forresters Hotel	24
Grumpy Baker	10
Longrain	5
Mahjong Room	12
Maltese Café	8
Maya da Dhaba	39
Maya Indian Sweets	37
Café Mint	36
Mohr Fish	31
Nepalese Kitchen	32
Pink Peppercorn	7
Prasit Thai Takeaway	29
Café Sopra	41
Thai Nesia	16

GAY BARS & CLUBS

Arq	17
The Colombian	6
Exchange Hotel	1
Flinders Bar	19
Midnight Shift	9
Oxford Hotel	3
Stonewall Hotel	11
Taxi Club	18

LIVE MUSIC

Excelsior Hotel	23
Gaelic Theatre Club	28
Hopetoun Hotel	25
Oxford Art Factory	2

PUBS & BARS

Bar Cleveland	40
Clock Hotel	30
Courthouse Hotel	14
Cricketers Arms	27
Fringe Bar	20
Middle Bar	15
White Horse	26

CityRail & station
Metro Monorail
Metro Light Rail

SURRY HILLS AND AROUND

The rest of the displays change three or four times a year, but always with intriguing examples of his work from the state's collection. Upstairs there's a chance to lounge around watching videos of his life and artistic output, and peruse all manner of memorabilia from photos and furniture to his vinyl – the music playing is from his collection. Through the wall is his studio, left chaotically scattered with works in progress.

Waterloo and Redfern

As Surry Hills' gentrification comes ever nearer to completion, galleries in search of cheaper rent, and restaurants out to create a buzz, have gone in search of a new playground. They've found it on **Danks Street**, around its junction with Young Street on the northern fringes of **Waterloo**, 500 metres south of Cleveland Street. A world apart from the uninspiring residential housing that surrounds it, Danks Street is well worth making a little effort to visit, with possible goals including *2 Danks Street Galleries* (see p.252), and such highly regarded cafés as *Café Sopra*.

Long considered Sydney's underbelly, **Redfern**, northwest of Waterloo and less than 2km south of Central Station, has a similarly resurgent feel, with new cafés opening amid the more mundane shops and pubs. Redfern is best known, at least among Sydneysiders, for **Eveleigh Street**, a squalid streetscape of derelict terraced houses and rubbish-strewn streets not far from Redfern train station where Australia's largest urban **Aboriginal community** lives in "the Block". It's the closest Sydney comes to having a no-go zone. The Aboriginal Housing Company, set up as a cooperative in 1973, has been unable to pay for repairs and renovation, and Eveleigh Street stands in shocking contrast to Paddington's cutesy restored terraces and the harbour-view mansions of Sydney's rich and beautiful. Recent demolition of decrepit SP? housing, and the re-location of residents, has upset many of those who want to keep the community together. A full-blown street riot in 2004 is indicative of the tensions, and they may be further fuelled by current plans for indigenous developers to build a 62-house complex on The Block.

Getting to Waterloo and Redfern

Buses #301 & #302 from Circular Quay make a convenient route down Elizabeth Street in the city centre, then right through Surry Hills (down Crown St) and on to Waterloo, where they pass the end of Danks Street.

Redfern has its own CityRail train station, one stop south of Central Station, and is also served by buses #309 & #310 from Circular Quay and Central Station.

Inner west

West of the centre, immediately beyond Darling Harbour, the inner-city areas of **Glebe** and **Newtown** surround Sydney University, their vibrant artistic communities and cultural mix enlivened by large student populations. On a peninsula north of Glebe and west of The Rocks, **Balmain** is a gentrified working-class dock area popular for its village atmosphere and big, old pubs. Up-and-coming **Rozelle** next door has both an art college and a writers' centre in the grounds of waterfront Callan Park, while **Leichhardt** and its neighbour **Haberfield** are the centre of Sydney's Italian community.

Glebe

Right by Australia's oldest university, **Glebe** is simultaneously a café-oriented student quarter; a haven for artists, writers and musicians; a Housing Estate for the poor; and territory for upmarket thirty-somethings with New Age inclinations. Very much the centre of alternative culture in Sydney, it abounds in organic food stores, yoga schools, and healing centres offering every kind of therapy from Chinese massage to homeopathy and flotation tanks. As it runs uphill from **Broadway**, **Glebe Point Road**, the focus of the area, is filled with an eclectic mix of cafés characterized by leafy courtyards, as well as restaurants, bookshops and secondhand and speciality shops, though it turns quietly residential as it slopes down towards the water of Rozelle Bay. The side streets are fringed with renovated two-storey terraced houses with white-iron lacework verandas. Glebe's laid-back, villagey feel makes it a popular **place to**

Getting to Glebe

Buses #431, #432. #433 and #434 run to Glebe from Millers Point, George Street and Central Station: #431 and #434 travel right down the length of Glebe Point Road to Jubilee Park, with #434 back-tracking a little before continuing on to Balmain; #432 and #433 proceed halfway down before turning into Wigram Road, and heading on, via Rozelle, to Birchgrove and Balmain respectively; #370 runs to Glebe from Coogee Beach via the University of NSW and Newtown.

You can also reach Glebe via the Metro Light Rail, which runs between Central Station, Pyrmont, and Lilyfield; the "Glebe" stop is just off Pyrmont Bridge Road (follow Allum Place and Marlborough St to emerge on Glebe Point Rd), while the "Jubilee" stop is at Jubilee Park (follow Victoria Rd and Cotter Lane to emerge at Glebe Point Rd by the YHA). Otherwise a fifteen-minute walk from Central Station leads up Broadway to the start of Glebe Point Road.

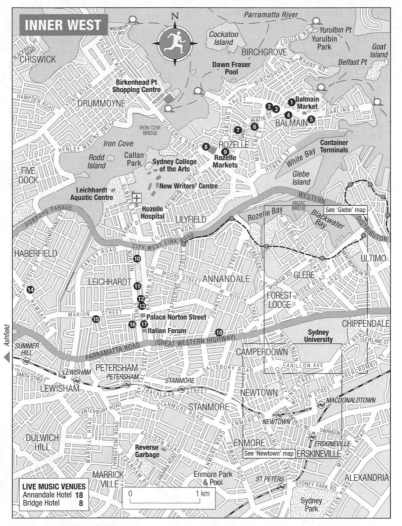

INNER WEST

Parramatta River

Cockatoo Island

Yurulbin Pt
Yurulbin Park

BIRCHGROVE

Goat Island

Belfast Pt

CHISWICK

Dawn Fraser Pool

Birkenhead Pt Shopping Centre

DRUMMOYNE

1 Balmain Market

2 3

4

BALMAIN

5

7

6

Container Terminals

Iron Cove

8 ROZELLE

9 Rozelle Markets

White Bay

Glebe Island

FIVE DOCK

Rodd Island

Callan Park

Sydney College of the Arts

New Writers' Centre

Leichhardt Aquatic Centre

Rozelle Hospital

LILYFIELD

Rozelle Bay

WESTERN DISTRIBUTOR

ANZAC BRIDGE

Blackwater Bay

See 'Glebe' map

HABERFIELD

CITY WEST LINK

LILYFIELD ROAD

10

LEICHHARDT

11

ANNANDALE

GLEBE

FOREST LODGE

ULTIMO

14

12
13

Palace Norton Street

16 17

Italian Forum

15

18

Sydney University

CHIPPENDALE

Ashfield

SUMMER HILL

PARRAMATTA ROAD (GREAT WESTERN HIGHWAY)

CAMPERDOWN

LEWISHAM

PETERSHAM

PETERSHAM

STANMORE

NEWTOWN

MACDONALDTOWN

LEWISHAM

STANMORE

STANMORE ROAD

NEWTOWN

DULWICH HILL

Reverse Garbage

ENMORE

See 'Newtown' map

ERSKINEVILLE

ERSKINEVILLE

MARRICK-VILLE

Enmore Park & Pool

ST PETERS

ALEXANDRIA

Sydney Park

LIVE MUSIC VENUES
Annandale Hotel **18**
Bridge Hotel **8**

0   1 km

CAFÉS & RESTAURANTS						**BARS**			
Adriano Zumbo Patissier	**3**	Elio	**12**	Harvest	**7**	Exchange Hotel	**6**	Monkey Bar	**1**
Berkelouw Café	**16**	Frattini	**15**	La Disfada	**14**	Leichhardt Hotel	**17**	Vanilla Room	**13**
Bar Italia	**11**	Fundamental Food Fresh	**4**	Rosebud	**9**	London Hotel	**5**		
Canteen	**2**	Grappa	**10**						

stay, and it boasts some of Sydney's best hostels, as well as motels and B&Bs (see "Accommodation"); for **longer stays**, check the many café notice boards for flat shares. The handy **Broadway Shopping Centre**, on nearby Broadway, has supermarkets, food shops, a huge food court, record, book and clothes shops, and a twelve-screen cinema. It's linked to Glebe by an overhead walkway from Glebe Point Road, starting opposite one of the street's best cafés, *Badde Manors* (see "Eating").

Sydney University and Victoria Park

Just before the start of Glebe Point Road, on Broadway, **Victoria Park** with its duck pond, huge expanse of lawn and shady trees, has a very pleasant, heated outdoor swimming pool (see "Sports and activities"), with an attached gym and sophisticated café. A path and steps lead up from the park into **Sydney University** (Ⓦwww.usyd.edu.au). Australia's oldest tertiary educational institution, inaugurated in 1850, now caters to more than 46,000 students; famous

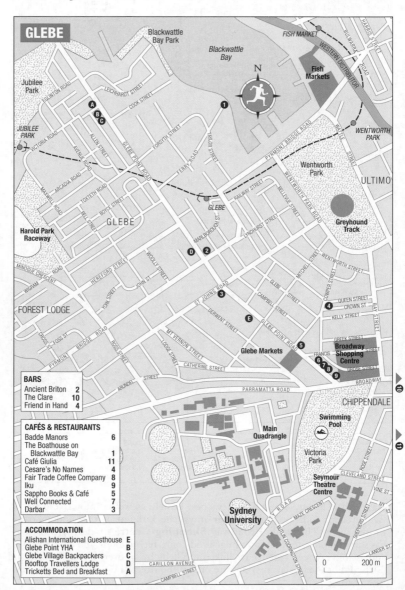

BARS
Ancient Briton	2
The Clare	10
Friend in Hand	4

CAFÉS & RESTAURANTS
Badde Manors	6
The Boathouse on Blackwattle Bay	1
Café Giulia	11
Cesare's No Names	4
Fair Trade Coffee Company	8
Iku	9
Sappho Books & Café	5
Well Connected	7
Darbar	3

ACCOMMODATION
Alishan International Guesthouse	E
Glebe Point YHA	B
Glebe Village Backpackers	C
Rooftop Travellers Lodge	D
Tricketts Bed and Breakfast	A

alumni include Germaine Greer, Clive James, Peter Weir and Jane Campion. Your gaze is drawn from the walkway up to the Main Quadrangle and the stone clock tower, reminiscent of England's Oxford University and complete with gargoyles. The university's cedar-ceilinged, stained-glass-windowed **Great Hall** makes a glorious concert venue. Visitors are free to walk through the gates and wander in the pleasant grounds, which take up a suburb-sized area between Parramatta Road and City Road, running up to King Street, Newtown.

Museum collections

Several **free museums** and **galleries** on campus are worth visiting (all Mon–Fri 10am–4.30pm, Sun 12pm–4pm). The **University Art Gallery** on the Main Quadrangle stages regular temporary exhibitions from its impressive collection of paintings and sculptures by Australian, Asian and European artists. Nearby, the **Nicholson Museum** holds the largest collection of antiquities in Australia, while the **Macleay Museum**, on Science Road, focuses on natural history. It derives from donations from the botany-obsessed Macleay family, who built Elizabeth Bay House, and once owned the largest private insect collection in the world.

Glebe Point Road to Jubilee Park

Glebe itself is at its best on Saturdays, when **Glebe Markets** are in full swing in the shady primary school playground on Glebe Point Road. Local residents love to spend lazy sunny Saturdays wandering Glebe's markets, browsing its bookshops and sipping, supping and socializing in its café courtyards.

As the action stops, a few blocks on, Glebe Point Road trails off into a more residential area, petering out at **Jubilee Park** with its views across the water to Rozelle Bay's container terminal. This pleasantly landscaped waterfront park, complete with huge, shady Moreton Bay fig trees and a children's playground, offers an unusual view of far-off Sydney Harbour Bridge, framed within spectacularly cabled Anzac Bridge.

On the third Sunday of November, the **Glebe Street Fair** takes over Glebe Point Road (from Broadway to Bridge Rd) with bands, eclectic stalls, international food and general frivolity.

Newtown and around

Separated from Glebe by Sydney University and easily reached by train (to Newtown Station), **Newtown** is another up-and-coming inner-city neighbourhood. What was once a working-class district – a hotchpotch of derelict factories, junkyards and cheap accommodation – has been transformed into a trendy but still offbeat area where body piercing, shaved heads and weird fashions rule. Its rich cultural mix includes a vibrant artistic community, large gay and lesbian population, and a healthy dose of students and lecturers from the nearby university. Newtown also has an enviable number of great cafés and pubs, and a wide

Getting to the Newtown area

Buses #422, #423, #426 and #428 run to Newtown from Circular Quay via Castlereagh Street, Railway Square and City Road. They all go down King Street as far as Newtown Station, where the #422 continues to St Peters and the others turn off to Enmore and Marrickville. Bus #370 goes from Coogee Beach to Glebe via Newtown. You can also get to the area by **train** to Newtown, St Peters or Erskineville train stations.

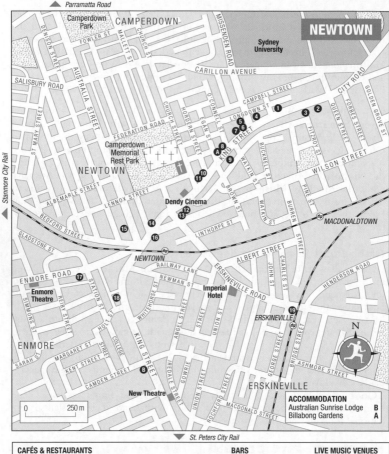

range of restaurants, especially Thai, so it's an agreeable location for an evening meal, late-night drink and midday big-breakfast recovery.

King Street

Gritty, traffic-fumed and invariably pedestrian-laden, **King Street**, Newtown's main drag, is filled with unusual secondhand, funky fashion and speciality and homeware shops, and a slew of bookshops. Littered in between are numerous purveyors of quality caffeine, international restaurants and lively pubs, distinguished by attractive ground-floor and rooftop beer gardens. Newtown used to be a hive of live entertainment, but the number of music venues has severely plummeted in recent decades, making way for ever-insidious slot machines. The stalwart *Sandringham Hotel* (or "Sando"), a Newtown institution, however, continues to host local and touring bands, as do the *Marlborough Hotel*, *@Newtown* and the stylish *Vanguard* (see "Live music and clubs")

During the two-week **Walking the Street** exhibition in September and October, local shop windows are taken over by young, irreverent and in-your-face art. However, the annual highlight comes in November (2nd Sun), when the huge **Newtown Festival** takes over nearby Camperdown Memorial Rest Park, with an eclectic mix of more than 200 stalls and live music on three stages, representing a broad range of styles, including rockabilly punk, blues, funk, hip hop and indie electronica.

South of Newtown train station, King Street becomes less crowded as it heads for a kilometre towards **St Peters** train station. Stroll down to step inside the more unusual speciality shops as well as several small art galleries and yet more book, homeware, furniture, bric-a-brac, retro and young new designer clothes shops. The street is also stacked with culturally diverse restaurants, ranging from Mexican to African, while a couple of theatres and a High School for the Performing Arts, reputed to be one of the top-five performing-arts schools in the world, add a little extra energy.

Enmore Road

Enmore Road, stretching west from King Street, opposite Newtown Station, is a similar mix of speciality shops that testify to a migrant population. Look out for the African International Market at no. 2a, which sells groceries, and skin and hair products; Amera's Palace Bellydancing Boutique at no. 83; Gallery Serpentine at 112–116, with its lustrous gothic threads; and Artwise Amazing Paper at no. 186. **Restaurants** range from Greek to Portuguese, while Alfalfa House, a community grocery cooperative at no. 113, stocks ethically and environmentally sound foods

▲ The Old Fish Shop, Newtown

– largely sourced from local organic and biodynamic farmers. Enmore is generally much quieter than Newtown, except when a big-name band or comedian is playing at the Art Deco **Enmore Theatre**, at no. 130 (see "Performing arts"). When that's closed, you can play board games at the cosy booths of 20s style *Box Office Cafe*. At the end of Enmore Road, Enmore Park hides the **Annette Kellerman Aquatic Centre** and its tiny, heated 33-metre pool (see "Sports and activities"). Combine a swim with a home-made ice cream from *Serendipity Ice Cream*, just across the road at no. 333.

Marrickville

Stretching out beyond Enmore, the vibrant multicultural suburb of **Marrickville** centres on the ugly, bustling commercial strips of Marrickville and Illawarra roads. With locals hailing from a hundred different cultures and speaking more than seventy different languages, it holds some great **places to eat**, particularly Greek and Vietnamese: standouts include the *Corinthian Rotisserie* at 283 Marrickville Rd and *Bay Tinh* at 316–318 Victoria Rd. Among signs of ongoing gentrification are the classy *New Delhi Cafe* (181 Marrickville Rd) and *Post Cafe* (274A Marrickville Rd), both of which offer fine food and coffee.

Marrickville's other notable feature, and of great interest if you're committed to recycling, is **Reverse Garbage**, in the grounds of the Addison Road Community Centre, 8/142 Addison Rd (Mon–Sat 9am–5pm, Sun 10am–4pm; ☎02/9569 3132, ⓦ www.reversegarbage.org.au), which was formed as a cooperative in 1976 by schoolteachers who wanted to save useful industrial discards and off-cuts from landfill to use in arts and crafts projects. The sustainable, not-for-profit business now employs more than twenty people, not just on the shop floor but to run educational workshops, exhibitions and sustainable design shop M.a.d (Make a difference), selling designer reuse products made from recycled material by local eco designers and artists. The warehouses are always being scoured by creative types, from set-builders to artists, and parents with toddlers in tow. To reach Reverse Garbage, catch the #428 **bus** from Circular Quay, Railway Square or Newtown Station.

Leichhardt and Haberfield

In **Leichhardt**, Sydney's "Little Italy", a long strip of Italian businesses, cafés and restaurants stretch out along **Norton Street**, from its starting point at ugly **Parramatta Road**. That said, however, Leichhardt can seem to be more oriented towards serving Italian culture to the broader community than actually living it. An arguably more authentic Italian community resides further west, on Ramsay Street in **Haberfield**, where a sixth of locals were born in Italy and a quarter speak Italian at home (as opposed to Leichhardt's 4.4 percent and 7.2 percent respectively). The quality Italian bakeries, delis, pizza parlours, chocolatiers and coffee shops here provide the sounds, smells and tastes of the real Italy.

Leichhardt

Leichhardt is very much up-and-coming, with shiny, trendy, Italian cafés popping up all along the Norton Street strip. At no. 39, not far from Parramatta Road, the **Italian Forum**, an upmarket shopping and dining centre for all things Italian, showcases the area's economic vitality. Arranged, in typical Italian style, around a central square, or piazza, the Forum is approached by a sheltered commercial alley from Norton Street. Three storeys of residential apartments, with timber shutters and iron-lace balconies, rise above two colon-naded commercial levels. Stylish fashion shops dominate the upper galleria level (and alley), while downstairs on the piazza level, the alfresco tables of a host of mostly Italian eateries venture out into the square; they're hugely popular for lunch on a Sunday when the whole Forum is full of Italian families. The new local library here adds a civic note, while an Italian Cultural Centre, including an auditorium, art gallery and multimedia centre, was due to open as this book went to press.

Further down Norton Street, past the Palace cinema complex (see p.225) and Marion Street, the local council has enhanced the community feel by replacing a parking lane with a raised outdoor dining area used by several cafés and restaurants. This part of Norton Street is taken over on the third Sunday of November by the **Leichhardt Festival**, with numerous stalls, stages and street performances.

To reach Leichhardt, take **buses** #436, #437, #438 or #440 from Circular Quay, George Street in the city, or Railway Square.

Haberfield

The heart of Italian Sydney is in **Haberfield**; catch **bus** #436 from Leichhardt (or from Circular Quay or George St in the city centre). Almost all the houses in this entirely planned suburb are in the classic Australian **Federation Style**, which spread around the country from 1901. As every instance of this elaborate confection is different, you can easily spend an afternoon wandering the leafy streets in admiration.

You won't find a pub in Haberfield, but Italian cafés, restaurants and delis are everywhere, especially on Ramsay Road and Dalhousie Street. One of Sydney's best pizzerias, *La Disfida*, is at no. 109 Ramsay Rd (see "Eating"), while great pasticcerias include *A and P Sulfaro* at no. 119, where you can also sit outside and have a coffee.

Rozelle

From Leichhardt, the #440 bus continues to **Darling Street**, which runs from **Rozelle** right down to Balmain's waterfront. Once very much the down-at-heel, poorer sister of Balmain, Rozelle has now emerged as a highly cultured area with a population of discerning and sophisticated locals. Both the Sydney College of the Arts and the NSW Writers' Centre are based here, in the grounds of the expansive waterfront **Callan Park** on Balmain Road, while Darling Street holds a string of cafés, bookshops, speciality shops, gourmet grocers, restaurants, re-vamped pubs, and designer home-goods stores. A weekend **flea market** takes place in the grounds of the 1877 sandstone Rozelle Primary School, near Victoria Road (Sat & Sun 9am–4pm). A lovely atmosphere pervades as locals mill about

Getting to Rozelle

Buses #432, #433 and #434 to Balmain and Birchgrove also pass along Victoria Road and Darling St on Rozelle's eastern periphery. Buses #440 and #445 run from Norton Street, Leichhardt, to Rozelle; you can also catch #440 from Circular Quay, George Street in the city or Railway Square. The Metro Light Rail runs to Rozelle from Central, Pyrmont or Glebe; the "Lilyfield" stop is about 500m from Balmain Road: follow Catherine Street and Grove Street to emerge opposite the Sydney College of the Arts campus.

the stalls and fragrant international food stands, while jazz bands often play on a raised deck beneath the arching limbs of a camphor laurel down the side. Across the street, glass-walled and alfresco cafés only heighten the appeal (see "Eating").

Callan Park

The site of **Callan Park** was bought by the government for a new lunatic asylum in the 1870s. For the time, it was an enlightened project, under the guiding hand of American doctor Thomas Kirkbride, who believed that the beauty of nature could calm troubled minds. Named for Kirkbride, the Neoclassical buildings that formed the core of the hospital were built from sandstone quarried right here. Designed by colonial architect James Barnet, also responsible for Customs House, they were finished in 1885. Ever since then, the picturesque parklands, sloping down to over a kilometre of waterfront, have been open for public recreation, and attempts by the state government to sell off parcels for development have been stymied by local opposition.

In 1996, the Kirkbride Block was taken over by Sydney College of the Arts, while the still-functioning mental institution, now called Rozelle Hospital, moved to a more ramshackle collection of buildings. The **NSW Writers' Centre** (information and bookings ℡02/9555 9757, 𝕎www.nswwriterscentre.org.au) has for many years occupied the Greek Revival-style Gary Owen House, an information centre and venue for readings and literary events.

Balmain and Birchgrove

Balmain, directly north of Glebe, is less than 2km from the Opera House by ferry, from Circular Quay to Darling Street Wharf. Stuck out on a spur in the harbour, however, and kept apart from the centre by Darling Harbour and Johnston's Bay, its degree of separation has enabled it to retain a slow, villagey atmosphere, making it the favoured home of many writers, film-makers and actors. Like better-known Paddington, Balmain was once a working-class quarter of terraced houses that has gradually been gentrified. Even if the docks at White Bay no longer operate, the pubs that used to fuel the dockworkers still abound: **Darling Street** and the surrounding backstreets are blessed with enough watering holes to warrant a pub crawl – two classics are the *London Hotel* on Darling Street and the *Exchange Hotel* on Beattie Street (see "Drinking" for both). Darling Street also rewards a leisurely stroll, with a bit of browsing in its speciality shops (focused on clothes and gifts), and grazing in its restaurants and cafés.

Getting to and around Balmain and Birchgrove

For a **self-guided tour** of Balmain and Birchgrove, you can buy a *Balmain Walks* leaflet ($2.20) from Balmain Library, 370 Darling St, or the well-stocked *Bray's Bookshop*, at no. 268. The most pleasurable way to **get to Balmain** is to catch a ferry from Circular Quay to Darling Street Wharf in Balmain East, where the #442 bus waits to take you up Darling Street to Balmain proper. Buses #432, #433 and #434 run via George Street, Railway Square (Central) and Glebe Point Road and down Darling Street, with the #432 diverting to **Birchgrove** while the #433 and #434 continue to Balmain; faster from the city is the #442 from the QVB, which crosses Anzac Bridge and heads to Balmain Wharf. **Birchgrove** can also be reached by ferry from Circular Quay or on the speedy #441 from the QVB. You can also catch the #445 from Norton Street in Leichhardt.

Sydney
style

Sydney is a vibrant, cosmopolitan city, where all manner of global influences have been mixed together and reinterpreted with local flair. Thanks to variations in lifestyle, geography, political inclination, wealth, and ethnic origin, different areas of the city have acquired very distinctive flavours, and styles of fashion, art, food, entertainment, design and architecture continue to diverge, cross-pollinate and evolve. From the tanned surfers at Bondi, to experimental artists in Newtown, to old Vietnamese men discussing politics on the crowded streets of suburban Cabramatta, Sydney's many styles are a pleasure to explore.

Glebe Markets ▲

Hanging out in Newtown ▼

Alternative Inner west

In the suburbs of Sydney's **Inner west**, conventions are questioned, sexualities explored, intellects stretched and artistic journeys travelled. **Newtown** and **Glebe** in particular, with their vast array of art and craft galleries, quirky speciality stores, alternative designer and secondhand fashion boutiques, theatres, and live music venues, form the **bohemian heart** of the city. Local students and lecturers gather in cafés, bars and restaurants, largely staffed by struggling poets, actors, musicians and artists. Thai, Vietnamese, Nepalese, Middle Eastern, African, Greek, Spanish and Mexican immigrants have all opened restaurants. Tattoos, body-piercing, grunge, Goth, punk, retro and experimental fashions prevail, as do New Age shops and alternative therapies. Amid all this creativity, curiosity, tolerance and acceptance of diversity, myriad alternative styles flourish.

Trendy Inner east

Sydney's **Inner East**, and especially **Darlinghurst**, is the epicentre of the city's gay culture, hedonistic nightlife and moneyed arts scene. In Oxford Street, Darlinghurst, and Kings Cross – "hip and happening 24 hours a day" – Sydney's trendy and beautiful come out to play, dining in top restaurants, drinking in stylish bars, experimenting with drugs, dressing in the latest fashions and generally having a good time. Straddling mainstream and alternative culture, and home to countless successful commercial artists, designers, photographers and the like, the Inner east abounds in high-street, designer, alternative and secondhand fashion stores, as well as highly regarded art galleries, and stands at the cutting edge of **global cool.**

Ethnic suburbs

Although Sydney as a whole is unequivocally multicultural, most residents of non-western descent live in its inner western and western suburbs, where many hold tightly to their homeland's traditional way of life. Thus the town centre of Cabramatta, in the southwestern suburbs, is a tantalizing mini-Saigon. Vietnamese stores burst onto the streets, with additional produce stacked on makeshift stands or laid out on footpath benches; constant crowds inject chaos and vitality; and the fruits, the fabric, the jewellery, the juices, the delectable restaurant dishes… all are irresistible. The Chinese food halls, restaurants, herbalists and grocery stores of Haymarket's Chinatown are an equally disorienting delight. And it doesn't end there: Haberfield and Leichhardt are the heartland of Sydney's Italian community; Marrickville is Greek; Petersham is Portuguese; and Bankstown and Lakemba, the home of Sydney's Lebanese.

The luxurious harbour

Living in Sydney's harbour suburbs remains the exclusive prerogative of the rich and famous. The cost of living is the highest in Australia, and Nicole Kidman and Russell Crowe are among those who enjoy its many privileges. Mansions with glittering views, private schools, million-dollar yachts, private jetties, golf courses, exclusive shops, foreshore bushwalks and, of course, beaches provide the framework for lives in which style is largely defined by a choice between the best that money can buy. A Federation-style mansion or contemporary glass-and-timber utopia; the latest Maserati or Lexus; a frock from Giorgio Armani or local talent Collette Dinnigan… the list is endless.

▲ Chinatown

▼ The Harbour

Manly Beach ▲
Surfing in style ▼

Beach life

Sydney boasts more than ninety ocean beaches, ranging from Cronulla in the southeastern suburbs to Palm Beach at its northeastern tip.

The two beating hearts of the city's ocean beach experience, however, lie either side of the harbour: Bondi, to the south, where surf-culture meets trendy, ostentatious, eastern suburbia, and the more attractive, harbour-backed Manly, to the north, where designer style and surf-culture mix with longer-established, comfortably affluent, nothing-to-prove locals. At both, stylish beachfront restaurants, funky cafés, and cool waterfront bars buzz with the young and glamorous, while crowds of sun worshippers strip down on the beach, and surfers navigate the water, waiting for the ultimate wave. Real estate prices are high, and the wealthy residents devote their waking hours to the finer things in life – good food, the latest fashion, stylish interior design, as well as, of course, surfing and swimming.

Health and wellbeing are a major focus; vast numbers exercise along the beach, or enjoy coastal cliff walks at twilight, and local café and restaurant menus emphasize healthy ingredients and cooking techniques.

While the communities immediately south of Bondi and north of Manly display much the same characteristics, similarities dwindle the further you go. South from Coogee, the feel is more traditionally working-class, albeit gentrifying fast, while up from Manly, the wealthy northern beaches are dominated by a more sedate atmosphere, and a greater sense of dedication to what's truly important – like surfing.

The best time to come is on Saturday, when the lively **Balmain Markets** occupy the shady grounds of St Andrews Church (7.30am–4pm; see p.253), on the corner opposite the *London Hotel*.

On the Parramatta River side of Balmain, looking across to Cockatoo Island, Elkington Park contains the quaint **Dawn Fraser Swimming Pool** (March–April daily 7.15am–6.30pm, Oct–Nov daily 7.15am–6.15pm, Dec–Feb daily 6.45am–7pm; $3.80), an old-fashioned harbour pool named after the famous Australian Olympic swimmer, a Balmain local. For long, stunning sunsets and breathtaking real estate, meander from here down the backstreets towards water-surrounded **Birchgrove** on its finger of land, where Louisa Road leads to Birchgrove Wharf. Catch a ferry back to Circular Quay from there, or stay and relax in the small park on Yurulbin Point.

8

The harbour

oftily flanking the mouth of **Port Jackson** – Sydney harbour's main
body of water – the rugged sandstone cliffs of North Head and South
Head provide spectacular viewing points across the calm water to the city,
where the Harbour Bridge spans the sunken valley at its deepest point,
11km away. The many coves, bays, points, headlands and islands of the harbour,
and their parks, bushland and swimmable beaches, are enticing destinations.
Harbour beaches are not always as clean as ocean beaches, however, and are
often closed to swimmers after storms. Finding your way by **ferry** is the most
enjoyable way to explore: services run to much of the **North Shore** and to
the harbourfront areas of the **eastern suburbs** and **northwestern suburbs**,
where the conjunction of the Lane Cove and Parramatta rivers creates gorgeous
scenery at well-heeled **Woolwich** and **Hunters Hill**. The somewhat glitzy

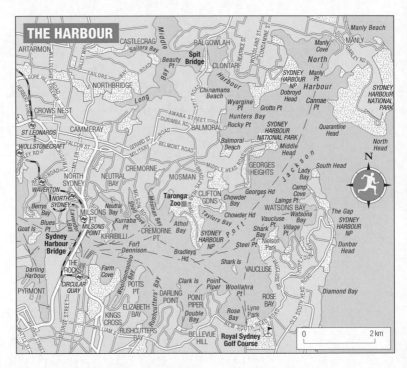

eastern shores are, fundamentally, the haunt of the nouveau riche, while the leafy North Shore is largely the domain of Sydney's old money. Round the corner of Middle Head from the main harbour, the quieter and more secluded coves of Middle Harbour are particularly pleasant.

Sydney Harbour National Park and harbour islands

Pockets of bushland on both sides of the harbour have been incorporated into **Sydney Harbour National Park**, along with five islands: Shark, Clark, Rodd, Fort Denison and Goat. An excellent free National Parks and Wildlife Service (NPWS) **map** detailing the park's various components and its many walking tracks is available at Sydney Visitors Centre or Cadman's Cottage in The Rocks, or the NPWS office in Nielson Park (see p.47 & p.120 respectively). To visit any of the **islands**, it's essential to book in advance; the prices below include the $5 National Parks landing fee.

Shark Island

Though picturesque Shark Island, off Rose Bay, has functioned both as a quarantine area for animals and a storage depot for the Navy, its grassy expanse is now given over to public recreation. Ringed by sandy beaches, with plenty of trees to provide shade, it makes a wonderful family **picnic** spot. Shelter, toilet facilities and drinking water are available, but visitors need to bring their own food. Matilda Cruises (see p.28) run a daily ferry service from Darling Harbour, which calls at Circular Quay fifteen minutes later, then takes another 25 minutes to reach Shark Island (departs Darling Harbour daily 9.30am, 10.15am, 11am, 12.30pm & 2pm, plus 3.30pm Sat & Sun only; departs Shark Island 10.10am, 10.55am, 11.40am, 1.10pm, 2.40pm & 3.25pm, plus 4.10pm Sat & Sun only; $17 return; ☎02/9264 7377, ⓦ www.matilda.com.au).

Clark and Rodd Islands

Clark Island, off Darling Point, which contains some relatively untouched bushland, offers smaller groups a more intimate harbour-island experience. Toilets and drinking water are available, but visitors should bring any food they require, and pack out their own rubbish. The same rules apply to tiny **Rodd Island**, in Iron Cove near Birkenhead Point, which, with its 1920s summerhouses and palm trees, is somewhat reminiscent of a Victorian pleasure ground.

    Access to both islands is via private vessel only. Visitor numbers are restricted by NPWS, so it is essential to book visits and pay the $5 landing fee in advance (☎02/9247 5033, ⓦ www.nationalparks.nsw.gov.au). NPWS produce a list of ferry and water taxi companies approved to land on the islands.

Fort Denison

The most visited of the harbour islands, the visually striking tiny **Fort Denison** originally served as a special prison for the tough nuts that the penal colony couldn't crack. Thanks to the effects of its meagre rations on its unfortunate inmates, it became known as "Pinchgut". When the Crimean War, in the mid-nineteenth century, rekindled former fears of a Russian invasion, the fort was built as part of a defence ring around the harbour.

    The charming stone fort itself, 360 degrees of impressive harbour vistas, a sophisticated self-guided museum, and a surprisingly interesting tide-gauge museum bring history vividly to life on any excursion here. A paid NPWS **guided tour** of the island's Martello tower, however, provides greater insight and depth to the experience (☎02/9247 5033, ⓦwww.nationalparks.nsw.gov.au; Mon & Tues 12.15pm & 2.30pm, Wed–Sun 10.45am, 12.15pm and 2.30pm; 1hr; tour ticket including return ferry $27). Arrive around lunchtime and you'll hear the One O'Clock Gun, originally fired so sailors could accurately set their ship chronometers.

Ferry services leave from Darling Harbour and Circular Quay (daily 9.30am–4pm, every 45min). There's a **café** at the fort, so you don't have to bring a picnic.

Goat Island

Named, somewhat dubiously, for its apparent resemblance to a headless goat, **Goat Island** stands guard over Sydney's shipping channels from its prime position just across the water from Balmain East. The importance of its location was first recognized by the local Cadigal Aboriginal people, who called it Mel-Mel, meaning the eye.

Goat Island is the site of a well-preserved sandstone **gunpowder magazine complex**, built by convicts between 1833 and 1839. Their treatment was harsh: 18-year-old Charles Anderson's refusal to work earned him more than a thousand lashes and a two-year stint chained to a rock ledge, known as Anderson's Couch, which can still be seen today. The island's other architectural relics date from the twentieth century, when it was the headquarters of the Sydney Harbour Trust and later the Maritime Services Board. The original **Harbour Master's Residence** enjoys arguably the best lookout in Sydney, and its rolling lawns are perfect for picnics. You can also make out the footprint of a renowned 1940s **dancehall**; during its heyday, revellers would row across from the mainland to fill the place on Saturday nights. Despite the watchful eye of the dance mistress, who chaperoned the goings-on from the doorway of the hall wielding a broomstick, local folklore credits the adjacent scrubland for the baby boom of the time.

In recent years, the island has only been accessible on NPWS tours. When this book went to press, it was **closed** altogether to allow for maintenance work. For the latest news, contact NPWS (☎02/9247 5033, ⓦwww.nationalparks.nsw .gov.au) or visit Cadman's Cottage.

Cockatoo Island

Sydney Harbour's largest island, at the confluence of the Lane Cove and Parramatta rivers, is **Cockatoo Island**. Having served as a nineteenth-century prison, it became home to some of the Southern Hemisphere's most important naval and commercial dockyards. Many of Australia's best-known warships were launched from the slipways here, and, after the fall of Singapore during World War II, the island became the key ship construction and repair facility in the Pacific Ocean.

After commercial use of the dockyards ceased in 1992, however, the site remained dormant. The Sydney Harbour Federation Trust, an Australian Government agency, has since 2001 been rehabilitating and restoring historic sites, improving public accessibility, promoting the island's aboriginal, convict and maritime history, and more recently opening up facilities for such cultural events as the 2008 Biennale of Sydney, and All Tomorrow's Parties, curated by and featuring Nick Cave & the Bad Seeds, in 2009. The island also now hosts what must surely be one of the world's most unique **campgrounds** (see p.171).

The *Muster Station Café* (Mon–Fri 7.30am–5pm, Sat–Sun 9.00am–4pm), at the ferry dock, provides meals, snacks and drinks and a free brochure for an engaging self-guided tour of the shipbuilding site and convict prison. Guided tours are also available on Sundays (11.15am & 1.15pm; 1hr 30min; $18; ☎02/8969 2100).

Two **ferry** routes serve the island from Circular Quay. The Parramatta route (8–18min; departs Circular Quay Mon–Fri 8.20am–1.50pm, Sat & Sun 8.50am–1.45pm; returns Mon–Fri 2.55pm–8pm, Sat & Sun 2.15–7.25pm) stops at Cockatoo Island before continuing on to Sydney Olympic Park and Parramatta (☎02/13 1500, ⓦwww.sydneyferries.info). Cockatoo Island has recently been added to the Woolwich & Balmain ferry route, thus making an enjoyable combined Hunters Hill/Woolwich (see below) and Cockatoo Island day-trip possible. Woolwich ferries from Circular Quay that stop at Cockatoo Island don't leave until the afternoon, and are much slower as they make more stops (18–28min; hourly, 1.25–9.30pm). Continuing on from Cockatoo Island to Woolwich on this service, a five-minute journey, is worth considering, however. Ferries from Woolwich bound for Circular Quay (every 30–60min, 6.12am–12.48pm), also arrive at Cockatoo Island after a quick five-minute journey

Lane Cove River

Some of Sydney's prettiest suburbs lie on the **Lane Cove River**, which connects with Parramatta River at the western tip of the harbour, near Cockatoo Island. Exclusive **Hunters Hill** and **Woolwich** are located on a peninsula, where the Parramatta River on its southern side and the Lane Cove River to the north side merge with the harbour. As Lane Cove River meanders north from Hunters Hill, a valley of bushland between North Ryde and Chatswood forms **Lane Cove National Park**.

Hunters Hill and Woolwich

While not technically on the harbour, **Hunters Hill** and **Woolwich**, with their tree-lined streets, enchanting historic houses and views over wide, languorous rivers, provide a salubrious harbour-like setting for an afternoon stroll. And in truth both rivers do look very much like the harbour itself, with eastward harbour views to the bridge and the city. Writers Jan Morris, Bill Bryson and Australia's revered Ruth Park have gushed over their respective perambulatory experiences here, and in 2004 actress Cate Blanchett was sufficiently impressed to purchase a $10 million Hunters Hill mansion.

The best way to explore the area is to catch a **ferry** from Circular Quay to Woolwich's **Valentia Street Wharf**, take bus #538 up the hill to Hunters Hill Town Hall on Alexandra Street, then slowly wander back to the wharf. Jumping on this ferry from Cockatoo Island to Woolwich (5min) is worth considering, however.

Step inside the town hall, which dates from 1866, to pick up a **Hunters Hill Village Walk** map (Mon–Fri 8.30am–4.30pm; map also available on ⓦwww.huntershill.nsw.au). The trail takes in numerous heritage-listed buildings and houses including the tiny, adorable, National Trust-owned **Vienna Cottage**, built in 1871, with its picturesque adjoining park and orchard (38 Alexandra St; entry Sun 11am–4pm; gold coin donation; ⓦwww.nationaltrust.org.au).

On the corner of Alexandra and Ferry streets, the two-storey former **Garibaldi Inn**, was constructed by an Italian stonemason in 1861. This gorgeous historic structure and its equally attractive adjacent buildings – separated by paved courtyards and a striking jacaranda tree – form an appealing commercial precinct that holds a gourmet deli, its affiliated alfresco café (serving top-notch coffee and pastries), and fashion, homeware, antique and gift shops. Additional refreshment is available further towards the wharf, at the end of Woolwich Road, in the form of a drink and simple pub food at

Woolwich Pier Hotel, fine-dining Japanese restaurant *Koi* (with a superb oriental escapist interior) and the much-lauded, but far from cheap, pan-Italian restaurant *Cucinetta Ristorante*.

Truly to appreciate Hunters Hill and Woolwich, walk wherever whim dictates, but be sure to venture down regularly to the northern – Lane Cove River – shoreline. Besides enjoying its views, you could perhaps sneak a peak or two at its jaw-dropping waterfront mansions.

Lane Cove National Park

Lane Cove National Park (☎02/8448 0400; CityRail to Chatswood, then bus #545) offers riverside walking tracks, a wildlife shelter and boat rental. You can camp or stay in en-suite cabins at an adjoining caravan park (see box, p.171). The park can also be accessed by Delhi Road, Lane Cove Road or Lady Game Drive.

Rushcutters Bay to South Head

Rich and exclusive suburbs line the harbour's hilly southeast shores. The area around **Darling Point**, the enviable postcode 2027, is the wealthiest in Australia, its waterfront mansions and yacht clubs enjoyed by residents such as Nicole Kidman and Lachlan Murdoch. A couple of early nineteenth-century mansions, **Elizabeth Bay House** and **Vaucluse House**, allow visitors an insight into the lifestyle of the pioneering upper crust. The ferry to Rose Bay offers a good view of the pricey modern real estate, as well as access, after a steep hill climb, through the pretty Hermitage Foreshore to beautiful **Nielson Park**. Surrounded by cute coves and bushy bays, **Watsons Bay**, also accessible by ferry, has an attractive park, great seafood, and spectacular views of the harbour. Equally impressive views of the Pacific (and harbour) are available from **South Head**, and The Gap, near by.

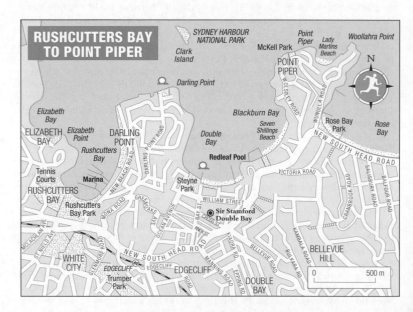

Buses #324 and #325 from Circular Quay, via Pitt Street, Kings Cross and Edgecliff, cover the places listed below, heading to Watsons Bay via New South Head Road; #325 detours at Vaucluse for Nielson Park.

Rushcutters Bay

Just ten minutes' walk northwest from Kings Cross train station, **Rushcutters Bay Park** is set against a wonderful backdrop of the yacht- and cruiser-packed marina in the bay. You can take it all in from the tables outside the very popular *Rushcutters Bay Kiosk* (good coffee and café food). Gangs of friends book out the **tennis courts** at the Rushcutters Bay Tennis Centre (see "Sports and activities"), but if you don't have anyone to play, the friendly managers will try to provide a hitting partner for you. It also has a nice little coffee bar, with outdoor tables beneath vines and a resident squawking galah.

Woollahra Council has developed the 5.5km (3hr) Rushcutters Bay to Rose Bay harbour **walk** (see box, p.121), which takes in exclusive streets, pretty parks and harbour views.

Darling Point and Double Bay

Northeast from Rushcutters Bay, **Darling Point** is according to the tax office Australia's wealthiest postcode zone. McKell Park at the point enjoys wonderful views across to Clark Island and Bradleys Head, both part of Sydney Harbour National Park; to get there, follow Darling Point Road, catch a ferry from Circular Quay (Mon–Fri only), or take bus #327 from Edgecliff Station.

The next port of call for both bus and ferry adventurers is **Double Bay**, dubbed "Double Pay" for obvious reasons. The noise and traffic of New South Head Road is offset by the quiet picturesque "village", where some of Sydney's most exclusive shops are bursting with imported designer labels and expensive jewellery. The eastern suburbs' socialites meet on **Cross Street, Knox Street** and the small pedestrian lanes that feed them, where well-groomed women in Armani outfits sip coffee at swanky pavement cafés.

If all this sounds like a turn-off, Double Bay's real delight is **Redleaf Pool** (daily Sept–May dawn–dusk; free), a peaceful, shady harbour beach – one of the cleanest – enclosed by a wooden pier that you can wander around, dive off or just laze on. You can swim out to pontoons and do the same. The excellent *Redleaf Pool Café*, on the escarpment overlooking the beach, is famed for its fruit salad and coffee.

A **ferry** from Circular Quay (Wharf 4) stops at both Darling Point and Double Bay; otherwise, catch bus #323, #324 or #325, also from Circular Quay, or, for a better service to Darling Point, the #327 from Martin Place, Edgecliff or Bondi Junction stations.

Rose Bay

The ferry to **Rose Bay** from Circular Quay gives you a chance to check out the waterfront mansions of **Point Piper** (birthplace of opera singer Joan Sutherland) as you skim past. Buses #324 or #325 also run here.

Rose Bay itself is quite a haven of exclusivity, home to the verdant expanse of the members-only Royal Sydney Golf Course. Directly across New South Head Road from the course, waterfront **Lyne Park** has since the 1930s provided welcome distraction in the form of a **seaplane** service. Planes can be chartered to go to Palm Beach, Berowra Waters, Ku-Ring-Gai Chase National Park and the Hunter Valley with the option of fine dining, wine-tasting and golf upon arrival, or you can just take a scenic flight over Sydney (Ⓦwww.seaplanes.com.au; ☏020/9388 1978). Rose Bay is also a popular **windsurfing** spot, with equipment rental from Rose Bay Aquatic Hire (see p.267).

▲ Seaplane at Rose Bay

Woollahra Council has developed an eight-kilometre (4hr 30min) **harbour walk** from Rose Bay to Watsons Bay via the cliffs, coves and bushland of the Sydney Harbour National Park (see "Coastal walks" box opposite).

Nielson Park

Extensive, tree-filled **Nielson Park**, on Shark Bay, is one of Sydney's true delights. Don't worry about Shark Bay's ominous name, it's netted, and makes a great spot for a daytime swim, a night-time skinny-dip, a picnic, or refreshment at the pretty waterfront, Federation-style kiosk café. A decorative Victorian mansion within the park, **Greycliffe House**, built for William Wentworth's daughter in 1852, is now the headquarters of Sydney Harbour National Park; if the ranger is around (usually 10am–4pm) pop in for information on waterfront walks. With views across to the city skyline, the park is a popular venue to watch the New Year's Eve fireworks display, while its position is also ideal to view the yachts racing out for the heads on Boxing Day (see "Festivals and events").

To get to Nielson Park, catch bus #325 from Circular Quay or trek through the waterfront national park on the **Hermitage walking track,** a 1.5km path from Bay View Road, up the hill from Rose Bay – jump off the #324 or #325 at Rose Bay Convent on New South Head Road. The walk takes about an hour, with great views of the Opera House and Harbour Bridge, some lovely little coves to swim in, and a picnic ground and sandy beach at yacht-filled **Hermit Point**.

Vaucluse House and Parsley Bay

Beyond Shark Bay, Vaucluse Bay shelters the magnificent Gothic **Vaucluse House** and its lush garden estate on Wentworth Road (Fri–Sun 9.30am–4pm; $8; grounds daily 10am–5pm), with the handsome *Vaucluse House Tearooms* open during museum hours for light meals and refreshment. The house dates from 1803, but its most famous owner was the influential Australian-born explorer, barrister and reformer **William Wentworth** who lived here between 1829 and 1853. William's mother was a former convict, his father a doctor with a dubious past, while he himself was a member of the first party to cross the Blue Mountains (see p.294). The house is restored to the middle period of the Wentworths' occupation, and holds some of the original furniture and family possessions.

To reach Vaucluse House, walk from Nielson Park along Coolong Road, or take bus #325 right to the door. From Christison Park off Old South Head in Vaucluse, a one-hour coastal walk heads to Watsons Bay (see box below).

Narrow, cliff-sided **Parsley Bay** lies beyond Vaucluse Bay. The shady park here is a popular picnic and (shark-netted) swimming spot, with the bay's cliffs crossed by a picturesque pedestrian suspension bridge. A delightful waterside path, cut into the base of the eastern cliff, leads to the bay's entrance, offering numerous opportunities to venture into the water along the way. Behind the park a bush reserve provides rewarding little bush track strolls.

Watsons Bay

Watsons Bay, on the finger of land that culminates in South Head, with an expansive sheltered harbour bay on its west side, and the treacherous cliffs of The Gap on its ocean side, was one of the earliest settlements outside Sydney Cove. Robert Watson was among the first signalmen to man the clifftop flagstaffs nearby, in 1790, and within two years the bay was the focus of a successful fishing village. The suburb has retained a villagey feel, with quaint old wooden fishermen's cottages still adorning the tight streets around Camp Cove. It makes an appropriate location for the long-established fish restaurant, *Doyles* (see "Eating"), right out on the bay by the old Fishermans Wharf (see p.197), which is now a ferry wharf accessible from Circular Quay by both the Rocket Harbour Explorer (Ⓦ www.matilda.com.au) and Sydney Ferries.

In fact *Doyles* has virtually taken over the waterfront here, with two restaurants, a takeaway fish-and-chip shop, and a seafood bistro in the bayfront beer garden of the adjacent *Doyles Watsons Bay Hotel* (which offers luxurious accommodation – see p.166). Should you opt for takeaway, the relaxing grassy expanse of the adjoining waterfront Robertson Park is great for a picnic, affording superb views across the harbour and assorted bush-clad peninsulas to the concrete vertical climb

---

Coastal walks

Woollahra Council (☎ 02/9391 7000, Ⓦ www.woollahra.nsw.gov.au) publishes brochures, also downloadable, that detail three waterside walks: the 5.5km (3hr) Rushcutters Bay to Rose Bay harbour walk (see p.119); the 8km (4hr 30min) harbour walk from Rose Bay to Watsons Bay (see opposite); and the 5km (3hr) cliffside walk from Vaucluse to Watsons Bay and South Head (see above).

On the southern, ocean side of the South Head peninsula, **Christison Park**, off Old South Head Road in Vaucluse, is the start of a magnificent coastal cliff walk that heads north to the sheer drop of The Gap near Watsons Bay (2.3km) and on to South Head and the beach at Camp Cove. Serene, white-painted **Macquarie Lighthouse** stands at the north end of Christison Park, was built in 1883, to the same plan as Australia's first lighthouse, erected here in 1818. The original designer, convict-architect Francis Greenway, was pardoned for his efforts.

The walk continues through **Lighthouse Reserve**; the **signal station** at its north end, facing out over Dunbar Head, was built in 1848. A watchpost was set up here from the colony's very earliest days, to alert the Sydney Town community, by use of flags, of ships arriving in the harbour. Continuing north, the rocks below the cliffs of **Signal Hill Reserve** wrecked the *Dunbar*, in 1857; the sole survivor, of 122 on board, was dragged up **Jacob's Ladder**, the jagged cleft in the cliffs here. The path heads up to **Gap Park**, where the *Dunbar*'s anchor is on display. Continue north through Sydney Harbour National Park to South Head (5km from Vaucluse), or cross Military Road to reach the settlement of Watsons Bay.

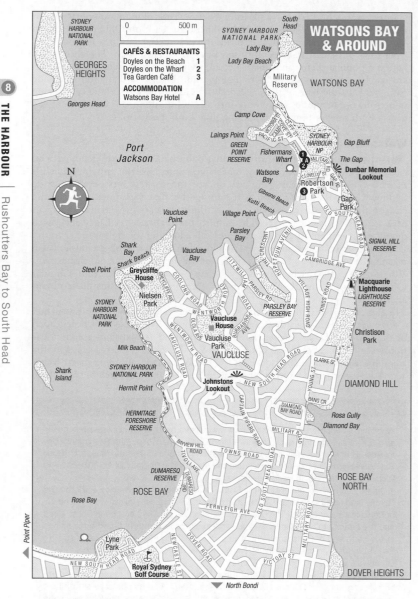

Cafés & Restaurants
Doyles on the Beach   1
Doyles on the Wharf   2
Tea Garden Café   3

ACCOMMODATION
Watsons Bay Hotel   A

of Sydney's city skyline. Equally salubrious is the pavement and grassy lawn of *The Tea Gardens Café* (see "Eating").

The Gap and Camp Cove

Spectacular ocean (and harbour) views can be enjoyed just a two-minute walk from *Doyles* through Robertson Park, across Gap Road to **The Gap**, where the high cliffs here are notorious as a venue for suicides (buses terminate just opposite – #324, #325 and faster #L24 from Circular Quay, and #380 from Circular Quay via Bondi Beach).

A walking **track** leads north from here to South Head via another chunk of **Sydney Harbour National Park**. En route, you can detour up the road at the HMAS *Watson* Military Reserve to look at the Memorial Chapel (daily 9am–4pm), where a picture window frames beautiful water views. The track heads back to the bay side, and onto Cliff Street, which leads to pretty **Camp Cove**, a tiny, palm-fronted, un-netted harbour beach from which vantage point all harbour shores visible are leafy national park; a small kiosk serves refreshments. Camp Cove can also be reached by walking along the beach at Watsons Bay, then along Pacific Street and through Green Point Reserve.

South Head

Steps climb from the northern end of Camp Cove to a boardwalk that leads to **South Head** (a 470m circuit), the lower jaw of the harbour mouth, again affording fantastic views of Port Jackson and the city. Along the way, Sydney's best-known **nude beach**, Lady Jane (officially "Lady Bay" on maps), is a favourite gay hangout. At the base of a steep bushy escarpment, this is one of the harbour's prettiest beaches, but it's hardly private: a lookout point on the track provides full views, and ogling tour boats cruise past all weekend. From Lady Bay, a further fifteen minutes' walk brings you to South Head itself, along a boardwalk that passes nineteenth-century fortifications, historic lighthouse cottages, and the picturesquely red-and-white-striped **Hornby Lighthouse**.

The North Shore

Home to much of Sydney's "old money", the **North Shore** of the harbour is noticeably more affluent than the rest of the city. **Cremorne Point, Clifton Gardens** and **Balmoral** in particular hold some stunning waterfront real estate, priced to match. The North Shore's main stem, the unattractive Military Road, which weaves its way west to east along the North Shore peninsula (wedged between Port Jackson and Middle Harbour), is lined with numerous pricey restaurants and tempting patisseries plus a few good cafés. A surprising amount of harbourside bushland remains intact, providing superb accessible examples of Australian native flora and fauna set against a backdrop of glittering harbour and city views – with **Taronga Zoo** superbly sited amid it all. A ride on any ferry can be a real joy, allowing you to gaze at beaches, bush, yachts and swish harbourfront houses.

North Sydney

Though it's easy enough for white-collar workers to get into the city, **North Sydney** has a busy high-rise office district of its own, on the north side of the Harbour Bridge. You'll also find a famous amusement park, a gloriously sited swimming pool, and a museum devoted to Mary MacKillop, Australia's saint-in-waiting. Get here in a couple of minutes by **train** from Circular Quay to Milsons Point or North Sydney stations; take the **ferry** to Milsons Point Wharf; or even **walk** straight across the Harbour Bridge from The Rocks. Just north of North Sydney (by bus #200 up the Pacific Highway or train to St Leonards), **Crows Nest** has recently become a hot spot for fine eateries, and is worth visiting for that reason alone (see p.197)

Luna Park

North Sydney has been associated with pure fun since the 1930s – you can't miss the huge laughing clown face, beside the Bridge on Lavender Bay at

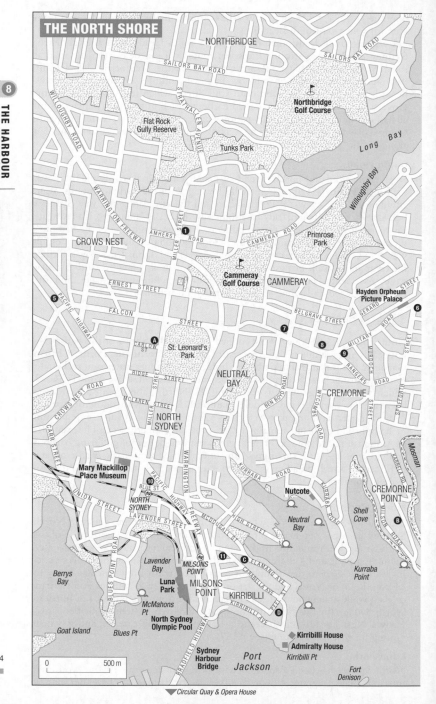

THE NORTH SHORE

NORTHBRIDGE

SAILORS BAY ROAD

SAILORS BAY ROAD

STRATHALLEN AVENUE

WILLOUGHBY ROAD

WARRINGTON FREEWAY

Flat Rock Gully Reserve

Tunks Park

Northbridge Golf Course

Long Bay

Willoughby Bay

CROWS NEST

AMHERST ST

MILLER STREET

❶

ROAD

CAMMERAY ROAD

Primrose Park

Cammeray Golf Course

CAMMERAY

ERNEST STREET

FALCON

❺

PACIFIC HIGHWAY

STREET

BELGRAVE STREET

GERARD

STREET

Hayden Orpheum Picture Palace

❻

CARLOW ST

Ⓐ

St. Leonard's Park

❼

❽

❾

MILITARY

MURDOCH ROAD

STREET

RIDGE STREET

STREET

NEUTRAL BAY

BANGOR

STREET

CREMORNE

MCLAREN STREET

MILLER STREET

NORTH SYDNEY

BEN BOYD ROAD

WYCOMBE ROAD

STREET

SPOFFORTH STREET

Mosman

CARR STREET

CROWS NEST ROAD

KURRABA ROAD

Mary Mackillop Place Museum

❿

BLUE ST

NORTH SYDNEY

PACIFIC HIGHWAY

WARRINGTON FREEWAY

Nutcote

KURRABA ROAD

KAHIBAH RD

MILSON ROAD

CREMORNE POINT

LAVENDER STREET

MCDOUGALL ST

HIGH STREET

Neutral Bay

Ⓐ

Shell Cove

Ⓑ

Berrys Bay

Lavender Bay

Luna Park

MILSONS POINT

⓫

Ⓒ

FLAMANG AVE

CARABELLA AVE

Kurraba Point

BLUES POINT ROAD

McMahons Pt

North Sydney Olympic Pool

MILSONS POINT

KIRRIBILLI

KIRRIBILLI AVE

Ⓓ

Goat Island

Blues Pt

BRADFIELD HIGHWAY

Sydney Harbour Bridge

Port Jackson

◆ **Kirribilli House**
■ **Admiralty House**

Kirribilli Pt

Fort Denison

0   500 m

▼ *Circular Quay & Opera House*

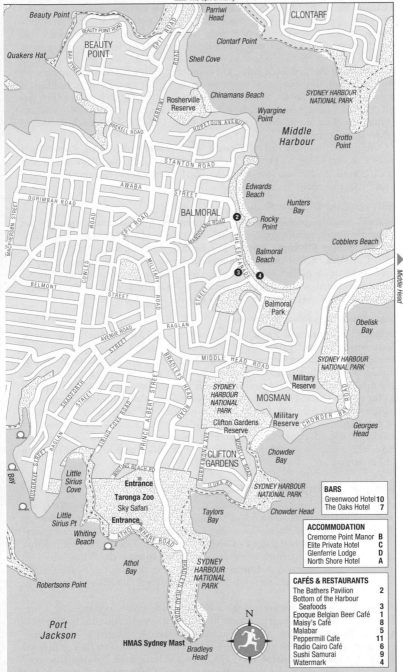

BARS
| Greenwood Hotel | 10 |
| The Oaks Hotel | 7 |

ACCOMMODATION
Cremorne Point Manor	B
Elite Private Hotel	C
Glenferrie Lodge	D
North Shore Hotel	A

CAFÉS & RESTAURANTS
The Bathers Pavilion	2
Bottom of the Harbour Seafoods	3
Epoque Belgian Beer Café	1
Maisy's Café	8
Malabar	5
Peppermill Cafe	11
Radio Cairo Café	6
Sushi Samurai	9
Watermark	4

Milsons Point, that belongs to **Luna Park** (hours vary, see website for details: Fri–Mon opens at 10am or 11am, closes at 4pm, 6pm, 9pm, 10pm or 11pm; usually closed Tues–Thurs; entry free, individual rides $10, unlimited ride day-pass $48, child $25–38, depending on height; Ⓦ www.lunaparksydney.com).

Generations of Sydneysiders have walked through the clown's grinning mouth, while the park's old rides and conserved 1930s fun hall, complete with period murals, slot machines, silly mirrors and giant slippery dips, hold great nostalgia value for locals. Several rides, especially the Ferris wheel, which has the Harbour Bridge as a backdrop, offer sensational water views – it's worth coming for these alone – while newer rides, like The Big Slash, are thrill-packed adventures for teenagers.

Getting to Luna Park can be pleasant too: the **ferry** to Milsons Point Wharf from Circular Quay or Darling Harbour pulls up right outside. You can also catch a **train** to Milsons Point, on the North Shore Line. Beyond the park, a boardwalk runs right around Lavender Bay.

North Sydney Olympic Pool

Sydney's most picturesque public swimming pool stands next door to the amusement park, again enjoying terrific views of the Harbour Bridge. The heated **North Sydney Olympic Pool** (Mon–Fri 5.30am–9pm, Sat & Sun 7am–7pm; $5.80), on Alfred South Street, remains open year round, with an indoor 25-metre pool as well as the older 50-metre outdoor one, plus a gym, sauna, spa, and café. An expensive, contemporary Australian restaurant, *Aqua* (Ⓣ02/9964 9998), overlooks the pool – be prepared to be gazed at by diners as you swim your laps.

Mary MacKillop Place Museum

Beyond Luna Park and the pool, the Catholic-run **Mary MacKillop Place Museum** is housed in a former convent at 7 Mount St (daily 10am–4pm; $8; Ⓦ www.marymackillopplace.org.au). It provides an unexpectedly broad-minded look at the life and times of Australia's first would-be saint – who was beatified in 1995 and is buried here – and at sainthood itself. MacKillop was a nun whose charitable educational work began in Penola in the Coonawarra region of South Australia during the 1860s. Mary, the co-founder of the order of the Sisters of St Joseph, ran more than seventeen free Catholic schools to encourage the education of children from poor backgrounds. To come straight here, take a train to North Sydney station and walk five minutes' north along Miller Street.

Kirribilli, Neutral Bay and Cremorne Point

Just east of the Harbour Bridge, immediately opposite the Opera House, **Kirribilli** on Kirribilli Bay is a mainly residential area. It does at least host a great **market** on the fourth Saturday of the month, in Bradfield Park and the Burton Street tunnel (7am–3pm), the best and biggest of several rotating markets on the North Shore (see "Markets"). On Kirribilli Point, the **Kirribilli House** is the Prime Minister's official Sydney residence. **Admiralty House**, next door, is the Sydney home of the Governor General, and is where the British Royal family stay when they're in town.

Following the harbour around from Kirribilli you come to Careening Cove, where the Ensemble Theatre, which has featured – and continues to feature – many of Australia's most esteemed actors, is pleasantly situated in a converted boatshed on a pier over the water (see "Performing arts and film"). Around the next point lies **Neutral Bay**. Five minutes' walk from Neutral Bay ferry wharf via Hayes Street and Lower Wycombe Road, **Nutcote**, 5 Wallaringa Ave

(Wed–Sun 11am–3pm; $8), was the home for 45 years of May Gibbs (1877–1969). An author and illustrator, Gibbs wrote a famous Australian children's book about two little gum nuts who come to life, *Snugglepot and Cuddlepie*, published in 1918 and an enduring classic. The house appears much as it would have in the 1930s, filled with cute and colourful examples of her numerous projects, all of which young children will adore.

A short walk from Nutcote on Kurraba Point, the **Kurraba Point Reserve** is a pretty place for a picnic, where a perforated stone rail along a steep cliff-edge, and trees, rising from beneath, nicely frame a fine view across the harbour. Gently falling lawns offer numerous benches and rock formations to sit and enjoy it all. Higher up the hill of the reserve, near a gnarled and ancient Morton Bay fig, there's an attractive stone-rimmed play area for the kiddies.

Bush-covered **Cremorne Point**, jutting into the harbour and offering arguably better views than Kurraba Point, is also worth a jaunt. Catch the ferry from Circular Quay and, walking westward, on the Cremorne Point Foreshore Walk, you'll find MacCallum pool, a gorgeous little open-access sea pool surrounded by timber decking with a fine view across the harbour to the Opera House and the city. From here, you can walk right around the point to Mosman Bay (just under 2km), or continue westward to **Shell Cove** (1km). Along this trail, foreshore mansions and recently regenerated bush – with pink-limbed redgums, curved sandstone cliffs and boulders covered in lichen – beautifully complement pretty Shell Cove and, of course, the glittering harbour.

Taronga Zoo

Mosman is most famous for **Taronga Zoological Park**, in a fabulous hilltop position overlooking the city on Bradleys Head Road, (daily 9am–5pm; $39, ages 4–15 $19, family $98.50, under-4s free; ⓦwww.taronga.org.au). The wonderful views and the natural bush surrounds are as much the point of coming as the chance to see such animals as bounding Australian marsupials, native birds (including kookaburras, galahs and cockatoos), reptiles, and sea lions and seals from the sub-Antarctic. Exotic beasts from around the world include the much-photographed giraffes, who stick their necks out across a sublime harbour view, and the formidable Komodo dragon and aptly titled other-worldly green basilisk lizard at **Reptile World**.

Established in 1916, the zoo has come a long way from its old-time roots and the animals now live in more natural habitats. You can get close to kangaroos and wallabies in the **Australian Walkabout** area, while the **koala house** offers eye-level views. Although you can get even closer by paying to have your photo taken patting a koala, for a guaranteed **hands-on experience** with a native animal, take a VIP Aussie Gold Tour, which gives small groups a session with a zookeeper, who guides you through the Australian animals (daily 9.15am & 1.15pm; 1hr 30min–2hr; $80, child $41; includes zoo entry; book 24hr in advance on ⓣ02/9978 4782).

Keeper talks and feeding sessions take place throughout the day; show times are available online or when you arrive. The zoo also hosts concerts on summer evenings, also detailed on its website.

Ongoing **redevelopment** is due to continue until 2012. Most of the creatures are still on show, however, though some are in temporary displays. The newest exhibits are **Great Southern Oceans**, featuring a seal-show theatre and dramatic underwater seal and penguin viewing areas; the **Wollemi Pine** area, where six small and ultra-rare pines (see p.308) are growing among warm-temperate rainforest species; and **Wild Asia**, the stylish new Mod-Asian home for Taronga's elephants and, among others, some very groovy small-clawed otters.

The best way to come to the zoo is by **ferry** from Circular Quay to the Taronga Zoo Wharf (every 30min). "Zoo Pass", a return ferry/zoo entrance combination sold at Circular Quay, can save you money ($44; ages 4–15 $21.50; ⓦ www.sydneyferries.info/). The zoo has a lower entrance near the wharf on Athol Road. It's better to start your visit from the upper entrance, however, so you can spend several leisurely hours winding your way back downhill to the ferry. The **Sky Safari** cable car, a short walk from inside the lower entrance gate, is a particularly scenic way of achieving that aim – whisking you over eucalypts and zoo animals, with magical views across the harbour, before depositing you near the upper entrance gate (unlimited cable-car rides are included in the entry fee). You can also get here by **bus** #247 from Wynyard or the QVB.

Bradleys Head to Chowder Bay

Beyond the zoo, at the end of Bradleys Head Road, **Bradleys Head** itself is marked by an enormous mast that towers over the rocky point. The mast once belonged to HMAS *Sydney* (1912), an Australian battleship, which successfully defeated the German cruiser, SMS *Emden*, off the Cocos Islands during World War I – not to be confused with the World War II battleship HMAS *Sydney* (1934), the remains of which were recently recovered from the Indian Ocean. It's a peaceful spot with a dinky lighthouse and, of course, a fabulous view back over the south shore. A colony of ring-tailed possums nests here, and boisterous flocks of rainbow lorikeets also visit.

The headland comprises another large chunk of **Sydney Harbour National Park**; in fact you can walk here along the six-kilometre Ashton Park **walking track**, which starts near the ferry wharf, opposite the zoo entrance, and continues past Athol Hall, beyond the headland to Taylors Bay and Chowder Head, to finish at **Clifton Gardens**, where there's a jetty and sea baths on **Chowder Bay**.

Wandering the streets of Clifton Gardens is fun too. The high hillside mansions are arguably the most beautiful and superbly sited on the harbour, surrounded as they are by the national park – and especially ravishing **Taylors Bay**, with its lush, unadulterated, wilderness shoreline.

Middle Harbour

The two sides of **Middle Harbour**, Port Jackson's largest inlet, are joined across the narrowest point at **The Spit**. The Spit Bridge opens regularly to let tall-masted yachts through, and that's much the best way to explore its pretty, quiet coves and bays; several cruises pass by (see p.28). Crossing the Spit Bridge, you can walk all the way to Manly Beach along the ten-kilometre Manly Scenic Walkway (see p.265), while buses #143 and #144 connect Spit Road with Manly Wharf, taking a scenic uphill route overlooking the Spit marina.

Middle Head

Between Clifton Gardens and Balmoral Beach, a military reserve and naval depot at **Chowder Bay** blocked coastal access to **Georges Head** and the more spectacular **Middle Head** on foot for over a century, although they could always be reached by road. However, since the military's recent withdrawal from the site, walkers can now trek all the way between Bradleys Head and Middle Head. You can also reach it by walking from Balmoral Beach, below. The old military settlement of Middle Head, dating back to the Napoleonic wars, but of fundamental strategic importance between 1870 and the mid-twentieth century, is now open to visitors. Numerous large circular cement depressions for rotating artillery, perfectly situated to fend off enemy ships entering the harbour, are joined by interlinking passageways and tunnels leading to bunkers. With impressive views of the heads, it's a stimulating and dramatic location at which to imagine a nineteenth-century naval invasion. Monthly NPWS **tours** explore the underground fortifications (fourth Sun of each month; 10.30am; 2hr; $13.20).

Pretty little "gay friendly" and "clothing free" **Obelisk Beach** is tucked between Georges Head and Middle Head, and backed by bush, while tiny **Cobblers Beach** on the Hunters Bay side is also nudist. Both make peaceful, secluded alternatives to the more famous Lady Jane at South Head.

Balmoral Beach and around

The bush setting of Middle Head and Grotto Point Reserve across the water to the north helps lend **Balmoral**, on Hunters Bay, the wealthy country village feel that makes it so popular with families. There's something very Edwardian and genteel about palm-filled, grassy **Hunters Park**, its castellated esplanade and rotunda (bandstand), still used for Sunday jazz concerts or summer Shakespeare recitals. The civilized air is enhanced by the pretty white-painted **Bathers Pavilion** at the northern end, now a restaurant and café (see "Eating").

There are really two beaches at Balmoral, separated by the island-like **Rocky Point**, an attractive picnic spot, joined by a charming arched stone bridge across the sand from the esplanade. Takeaways along the Esplanade (the road parallel to the beach here) include an excellent fish'n'chip shop (see "Eating"), a quiet café, and a fine bottle shop – all you need for a day at the beach. South of Rocky Point, the "baths" – actually a netted bit of beach with a boardwalk and lanes for swimming laps – have been here in one form or another since 1899; you can rent sailboards and catamarans and take lessons from the nearby sailing club (see p.267). This end of the beach is great for kids; the big trees actually shade the sand, and there's a popular playground and a kiosk selling ice creams.

To get to Balmoral, catch a **ferry** from Circular Quay to Taronga Zoo Wharf and then bus #238 via Bradleys Head Road, or, after 7pm from Monday to Saturday, the ferry to South Mosman (Musgrave St) Wharf, at nearby Mosman, then bus #233.

Chinamans beach

The hillside houses overlooking Balmoral command some of the highest price tags in Sydney. To stroll through more prime real estate, head for **Chinamans Beach**, via Hopetoun Avenue and Rosherville Road.

9

Ocean beaches

Sydney's beaches are among its great natural joys, key elements in the equation that makes the city special. Both water and sand are remarkably clean – people actually fish in the harbour, and don't just catch old condoms – while at Long Reef, just north of Manly, you can find rock pools teeming with starfish, anemones, sea snails and crabs, and even a few shy moray eels. Various spots offer good **snorkelling and diving** (see "Sports and activities"), especially the underwater nature trail at Gordons Bay. In recent years, humpback whales have been regularly sighted from the Sydney headlands in June and July on their migratory path from the Antarctic to the tropical waters of Queensland, and Southern Right whales even occasionally make an exciting appearance in the harbour itself – three whales cavorting in 2002 caused a sensation (for more information, consult the Australian Museum website – ⓦ www.livingharbour.net).

This chapter covers both the **northern beaches** – north of the harbour entrance from **Manly** thirty kilometres up to Barrenjoey Heads and Palm Beach – and the **eastern beaches**, which stretch south from **Bondi** to Maroubra.

Bondi Beach

Bondi Beach is synonymous with Australian beach culture – indeed the mile-long curve of golden sand must be one of the best-known beaches in the world. It's the closest ocean beach to the city centre; you can take a train to Bondi Junction and then a ten-minute bus ride, or drive there in twenty minutes (parking is another story). Big, brash and action-packed, it's probably not the best place for a quiet sunbathe and swim, but the sprawling sandy crescent is truly spectacular. Red-tiled houses and apartment buildings crowd in to catch the view, many of them erected in the 1920s when Bondi was a working-class suburb.

Although still residential, Bondi is now among Sydney's trendiest suburbs, with escalating real estate and rental prices, and a thriving café and restaurant scene packed out with the young and fashionable. It also hosts the Saturday night "hoon" culture when suburban youngsters drive their souped-up cars up and down Campbell Parade, and makes an alternative to the city centre for weekend drinking and dining. Backpackers create another large part of the culture, drinking and otherwise, especially in summer when they turn Christmas Day into a big beach event (see "Festivals and events").

You can reach Bondi on **bus** #333, #380 or #389 from Circular Quay via Oxford Street and Bondi Junction, or take the train directly to Bondi Junction, then transfer to these buses or to the #333, #380 or #382.

Campbell Parade and Hall Street

Beachfront **Campbell Parade** is both cosmopolitan and highly commercialized, lined with alfresco cafés, bars, restaurants, music, fashion and surfwear shops. On Sunday the **Bondi Markets** (10am–5pm; Ⓦwww .bondimarkets.com.au) – in the grounds of the primary school on the corner of Campbell Parade and Warners Avenue, facing the northern end of the beach – place great emphasis on fashion and jewellery.

You'll find the locals' favourite cafés and more day-to-day shops and facilities on the calmer side streets. **Hall Street**, heading gently uphill from Campbell Parade, is Bondi Beach's real nerve centre, with a post office (and public phones), banks, bakeries, supermarkets, assorted kosher delis and butchers and other shops that serve the area's Jewish community, cyber-cafés, laundries, bookshops (try *Zabriskie Booksellers* at no. 3 for new books and *Gertrude & Alice Cafe Bookstore* at no. 46 for secondhand) and some great cafés.

Bondi Park and the Bondi Pavilion

Between Campbell Parade and the beach, grassy (though mostly shadeless except for the few picnic group shelters) **Bondi Park** slopes down to the promenade, and is always full of sprawling bodies feasting on fish'n'chips and being mobbed by seagulls. Along the promenade, a popular concrete **skate and BMX** park hosts competitions throughout the year. For places to rent roller-blades, see "Sports and activities".

The focus of the promenade, the arcaded, Spanish-style

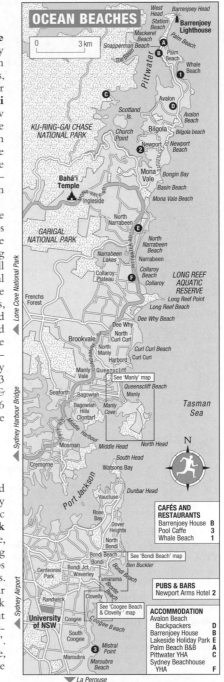

OCEAN BEACHES

0   3 km

West Head
Barrenjoey Head
Station Beach
Barrenjoey Lighthouse
Mackerel Beach
Snapperman Beach
Palm Beach
Pittwater
The Basin
Whale Beach **1**
Scotland Is.
Avalon
Avalon Beach **D**
Church Point
Bilgola
Bilgola beach
Newport **2**
Newport Beach
KU-RING-GAI CHASE NATIONAL PARK
Bahá'i Temple
Ingleside
Mona Vale
Bongin Bay
Basin Beach
Mona Vale Beach
North Narrabeen **E**
North Narrabeen Beach
GARIGAL NATIONAL PARK
Narrabeen Lakes
Narrabeen
Collaroy Plateau
Collaroy Beach
Collaroy **F**
Frenchs Forest
LONG REEF AQUATIC RESERVE
Long Reef Point
Long Reef Beach
Dee Why
Dee Why Beach
North Curl Curl
Brookvale
Curl Curl Beach
North Manly
Harbord
Curl Curl
Manly Vale
Queenscliff
See 'Manly' map
Queenscliff Beach
Seaforth
Bagowlah
Manly
Bagowlah Hills
Manly Cove
Clontarf
Tasman Sea
Middle Harbour
Mosman
Middle Head
North Head
Cremorne
South Head
Watsons Bay
N
Vaucluse
Dunbar Head
Port Jackson
Rose Bay
Dover Heights
North Bondi
Bondi Beach
See 'Bondi Beach' map
Ben Buckler
Bondi Jct.
Bondi
Centennial Park
Waverley
Tamarama
Bronte
Randwick
Clovelly
See 'Coogee Beach & Clovelly' map
University of NSW
Coogee
South Coogee
Coogee Beach
Mistral Point **3**
Maroubra
Maroubra Beach
La Perouse

Lane Cove National Park
Sydney Harbour Bridge
Sydney Airport

CAFÉS AND RESTAURANTS
Barrenjoey House   **B**
Pool Caffe   **3**
Whale Beach   **1**

PUBS & BARS
Newport Arms Hotel **2**

ACCOMMODATION
Avalon Beach Backpackers   **D**
Barrenjoey House   **B**
Lakeside Holiday Park   **E**
Palm Beach B&B   **A**
Pittwater YHA   **C**
Sydney Beachhouse YHA   **F**

131

Rose Bay (2km) ▲   Vaucluse (4km) & Watsons Bay (5km) ▲

BONDI BEACH & TAMARAMA

Bondi Junction (1.5km) ▲

Bondi Junction (2km) ▲

◄ C (200m) & B (250m)

OAKLEY ROAD

WARNERS AVE

SEVEN WAYS

BLAIR STREET

OLD SOUTH HEAD RD

SIMPSON STREET

CURLEWIS STREET

ROSCOE STREET

WELLINGTON STREET

HALL STREET

O'BRIEN STREET

LAMROCK COX AVE

BEACH ROAD AVENUE

GLASGOW AVE

WARNERS AVENUE

HASTINGS

BRIGHTON

RAMSGATE AVENUE

BLAIR STREET

NORTH BONDI

WALLACE PARADE

MILITARY ROAD

BOULEVARD

Bondi Golf Course

Bondi Markets

BONDI BEACH

Bondi Pavilion

Bondi Park

PARK DRIVE

QUEEN ELIZABETH DRIVE

Children's Pool

RAMSGATE AVENUE

BRIGHTON BLVD

HASTINGS PARADE

Skate Park

Bondi Beach

Ben Buckler

GOULD STREET

CAMPBELL PARADE

NOTTS AVE

SANDRIDGE ST

BONDI

FRANCIS STREET

SIR THOMAS MITCHELL ROAD

EDWARD

CASTLEFIELD

BONNARA AVE

DENHAM

GLEN ST

IMPERIAL

BONDI ROAD

DUDLEY ST

WILGA ST

FLETCHER ST

CARLISLE ST

DELLVIEW ST

Bondi Baths & Bondi Icebergs

TAMARAMA

SLSC

PACIFIC AVE

THOMPSON ST

TAMARAMA MARINE DR

HEWLETT ST

BRONTE MARINA DR

Marks Park

Mackenzies Pt

Mackenzies Bay

Bronte Park

Bronte Beach

BRONTE RD

PACIFIC ST

BRONTE

MACPHERSON ST

Bronte Baths

N

0   250 m

PUBS & BARS

Beach Road Hotel	1
Bondi Icebergs Club	19
Bondi Social	15
Hotel Bondi	5
Ravesi's	B

CAFÉS & RESTAURANTS

The Bogeyhole Café	21
Bondi Social	15
Bondi Trattoria	16
Brown Sugar	2
The Earth Food Store	7
Gelato Bar	9
Gelbison Pizzeria	14
Gertrude & Alice Cafe Bookstore	6
Gusto	12
Icebergs Dining Room and Bar	19
Lamrock Café	13
Lauries Vegetarian	17
North Bondi RSL	10
North Bondi Italian Food	10
No Names	1
The One That Got Away	18
Sejuiced	8
Sabbaba	4
Sean's Panarama	3
Swell	20
Speedo's	11

ACCOMMODATION

Bondi Beachouse YHA	E
Bondi Serviced Apartments	C
Noah's Backpackers	D
Ravesi's	B
Swiss-Grand	A

▼ Waverley Cemetery (100m) & Clovelly (600m walk)

Bondi Pavilion, was built in 1928 as a deluxe changing-room complex. It's now a community centre where workshops, classes and events take place, from drama and comedy in the theatre and the Seagull Room (the former ballroom) to daytime dance parties, open-air cinema and the outdoor Bondi Short Film Festival in the courtyard (Ⓦ www.waverley.nsw.gov.au). Downstairs in the foyer, photos of Bondi's past include some classic beach images of men in 1930s bathing suits. There's even a community-access **art gallery** (daily 10am–5pm; free) featuring changing exhibitions by local artists, and some alfresco cafés and restaurants. In September, the Festival of the Winds, Australia's largest **kite festival**, takes over the beach (see "Festivals and events").

The beach

Surfing is part of the Bondi legend, the big waves ensuring that there's always a pack of damp young things hanging around, bristling with surfboards. However, the beach is carefully delineated, with surfers using its southern end, so if you're not surfing yourself you shouldn't have to fear catapulting surfboards. There are two sets of flags for swimmers and boogie-boarders. Families congregate at the northern end near the shallow sheltered saltwater pool (free), popular with kids, which has a park with barbecues and a playground above; everybody else uses the middle flags. The beach is netted and there hadn't been a **shark attack** for eighty years until the upsurge in attack reports around Sydney during the summer of 2008–2009. Despite the sudden worldwide notoriety, only one, non-fatal, incident occurred at Bondi, and most people are content to continue swimming.

If the sea is too rough, or if you want to swim laps, head for the sea-water swimming pool at the southern end of the beach under the **Bondi Icebergs Club** on Notts Avenue, with a fifty-metre lap pool, kids' pool, gym, sauna, massage service and poolside café (pool Mon–Wed & Fri 6am–6.30pm, Sat & Sun 6.30am–6.30pm; $4.50). The Icebergs Club has been part of the Bondi legend since 1929 – members must swim throughout the winter, and media coverage of their plunge, made truly wintry by the addition of huge chunks of ice, heralds the first day of winter. The very dilapidated club building was knocked down and rebuilt in 2002; the top floor houses the posh *Icebergs Dining Room and Bar*, while the floor below holds the club's less salubrious *Icebergs Bistro* (for both see "Restaurants"), which shares the fabulous view over pool and beach.

Topless bathing is condoned at Bondi though a group of conservative councillors recently tried to get it banned on the grounds of obscenity. Either way, it's a far cry from conditions up to the late 1960s when stern beach inspectors were

▲ Bondi Beach

Bondi's surf lifesavers

Surf lifesavers are what made Bondi famous, so naturally there's a bronze sculpture of one outside the Bondi Pavilion. The surf lifesaving movement began in 1906 with the founding of the Bondi Surf Life Bathers' Lifesaving Club in response to the drownings that accompanied the increasing popularity of swimming. From the beginning of the colony, swimming was harshly discouraged as an unsuitable bare-fleshed activity. However, by the 1890s swimming in the ocean had become the latest fad, and a Pacific Islander introduced the concept of catching waves or bodysurfing that was to become an enduring national craze. Although "wowsers" (teetotal puritanical types) attempted to put a stop to it, by 1903 all-day swimming was every Sydneysider's right.

The bronzed and muscled surf lifesavers in their distinctive red and yellow caps are a highly photographed, world-famous Australian image. Surf lifesavers (members of what are now called Surf Life Saving Clubs, abbreviated to SLSC) are volunteers who work the beach at weekends, so come then to watch their exploits – or look out for a surf carnival; lifeguards, on the other hand, are employed by the council and work all week during swimming season (year-round at Bondi).

constantly on the lookout for indecent exposure. If you want to join in the sun and splash but don't have the gear, Beached at Bondi, below the lifeguard lookout tower, rents out everything from umbrellas, wetsuits, cozzies and towels to surfboards and body-boards. It also sells hats and sun block and has lockers for valuables.

The eastern beaches

Sydney's eastern beaches stretch from **Bondi** down to **Maroubra**. Many people find the smaller, quieter beaches to the south of Bondi more enticing, and a popular walk or jog leads right around the oceanfront and clifftop **walking track** to Bondi's smaller, less brazen but very lively cousin **Coogee** (about 2hr 30min). The track also includes a fitness circuit, so you'll see plenty of joggers and other fitness enthusiats. En route you'll pass through gay favourite **Tamarama**; family-focused, café-cultured **Bronte**; narrow **Clovelly**; and a popular diving and snorkelling spot, **Gordons Bay** (see "Sports and activities"). Randwick Council has designed the "Coastal Walkway" from Clovelly to Coogee and beyond to more downmarket Maroubra, with stretches of boardwalk and interpretive boards detailing environmental features. A free guide-map can be picked up at tourist offices or downloaded at ⓦwww.randwickcitytourism.com.au.

It is now also possible to walk all the way **north** from Bondi to **South Head** along the cliffs, as missing links in the pathway have been connected with bridges and boardwalks.

Tamarama

From Bondi Beach, walk past the Bondi Icebergs Club on Notts Avenue round Mackenzies Point, through Marks Park, until you reach the modest and secluded **Mackenzies Bay**. Next is **Tamarama**, a deep, narrow beach favoured by the smart set and a hedonistic gay crowd ("Glamarama" to the locals), as well as surfers. As the surf here is very rough, the flags are often taken down and swimmers advised not to enter the water – hence the sun-worshipping rather than swimming crowd. Topless sunbathing is also common. Apart from the small Surf Life Saving Club, which offers drop-in Pilates classes, the intimate beach has a popular café, and a small grassy park (not very shady) with picnic shelters, barbecues and a basic children's playground.

The **Sculpture by the Sea festival** turns the walk between Bondi and Tamarama into a temporary art gallery for ten days every October (see "Festivals and events"). The walk takes about fifteen minutes, or if you want to come here directly, hop on bus #360 or #361 from Bondi Junction.

Bronte

Walk through Tamarama's small park and follow the oceanfront road for five minutes to reach the next beach along, **Bronte Beach** on Nelson Bay, also easily accessible on bus #378 from Central Station via Oxford Street and Bondi Junction. More of a family affair, with a large green park, a popular café strip and sea baths, the **northern end** as you arrive from Tamarama holds inviting flat-rock platforms, popular as fishing and relaxation spots, while the beach is cliff-backed at this point, providing some shade. The **park** beyond is extensive, shaded by Norfolk Island pines; a **mini-train ride** for small children (Sat & Sun 11am–4pm) has been operating since 1947, while further back there's an imaginative children's playground. In the secluded and peaceful Bronte Gully to the rear, kookaburras are a common sight and lorikeets often bathe in the waterfall.

At the **southern end** of the beach, palm trees lend a holiday feel as you relax at one of the outside tables of Bronte Road's cafés – there's a clutch of eight to choose from, plus a fish'n'chip shop. Back on the water at this end, a natural rock

Beach and sun safety

Don't be lulled into a false sense of security: Sydney's beaches have perils as well as pleasures. Some beaches are protected by special shark nets, but they don't keep out jellyfish such as bluebottles, which can suddenly swamp an entire beach; listen for loudspeaker announcements that will summon you from the water in the event of shark sightings or other dangers.

Pacific currents can be very strong indeed – inexperienced swimmers and those with small children would do better sticking to the sheltered harbour beaches (see "The Harbour" and "Kids' Sydney") or sea pools at the ocean beaches. Ocean beaches are generally patrolled by surf lifesavers during the day between October and April (all year at Bondi): red and yellow flags (generally up from 6am until 6pm or 7pm) indicate the safe areas to swim, avoiding dangerous rips and undertows. It can't be stressed strongly enough that you must try to swim between the flags – people have drowned in strong surf. If you do get into difficulty, try to stay calm and raise one arm above your head as a signal to be rescued. It's hard not to be impressed as surfers paddle out on a seething ocean that you wouldn't dip your big toe in, but don't follow them unless you're confident you know what you're doing. Surf schools can teach you the basic skills and enlighten you on surfing etiquette and lingo: see "Sports and activities" for recommended schools. You can check daily surf reports on ⓦwww.realsurf.com.

The strength of the southern sun shouldn't be underestimated: follow the local slogan and Slip (on a shirt), Slop (on the sun block), Slap (on a hat). The final hazard, despite the apparent cleanliness, is pollution. Monitoring shows that it is nearly always safe to swim at all of Sydney's beaches – except after storms, when storm water, currents and onshore breezes wash up sewage and other rubbish onto certain beaches (usually harbour beaches) making them – as signs will indicate – unsuitable for swimming and surfing. To check pollution levels, call the Beachwatch Bulletin on ☏1800 036 677 or check out ⓦwww.environment.nsw.gov.au).

A final note: topless bathing for women is accepted on many beaches but disapproved of on others, so if in doubt, do as the locals do. There are two official nude beaches around the harbour (see p.123 & p.129).

enclosure, the "Bogey Hole", makes a calm area for snorkelling and kids to swim in, and there are rock ledges to lie on around the enclosed sea swimming pool known as **Bronte Baths** (open access; free), often a better option than the surf here, which can be very rough.

A pleasant five-minute walk continues past the Bronte Baths to **Waverley Cemetery**, a fantastic spot to spend eternity. Established in 1877, it contains the graves of many famous Australians, with the bush poet contingent well represented. **Henry Lawson**, described on his headstone as poet, journalist and patriot, languishes in section 3G 516, while **Dorothea Mackeller**, who penned the famous poem "I love a sunburnt country", is in section 6 832–833.

Clovelly and Gordon's Bay

Beyond Waverley Cemetery – another five-minute walk – on the other side of the ominously named Shark Point, is sheltered, channel-like **Clovelly Bay**, with concrete platforms on either side and several sets of steps leading into the very deep water. Rocks at the far end keep out the waves, so the bay is popular with lap-swimmers – there's a free swimming pool, too – and snorkellers; you're almost certain to see one of the bay's famous blue gropers under the surface. A grassy park – Burrows Park – with several terraces extends far back and makes a good spot for a picnic. The divinely sited *Seasalt Café* (see "Cafés") next to the surf club gets packed at weekends, while on Sunday afternoons and evenings the nearby *Clovelly Hotel* (see "Drinking") is a popular hangout for locals and travellers, with free live music and a great bistro. Otherwise, go for the rock-bottom-priced drinks and fab views at the beachside *Clovelly Bowling Club*, just near *Seasalt Café*, also on the walk route. To get to Clovelly directly, take bus #339 from Millers Point via Central Station and Albion Street, Surry Hills; #360 from Bondi Junction; or the weekday peak-hour X39 from Wynyard.

Gordon's Bay

Rock-hopping from Clovelly around to equally narrow **Gordon's Bay** can be a little tricky – the shoreline is backed by high sandstone cliffs with some rocky tunnels to pass through – so you're probably better off sticking to the road route along Cliffbrook Parade. The secluded rocks are popular with locals for peaceful fishing or sunbathing, and rescuing stranded tourists tends to shatter the equilibrium. Unsupervised, undeveloped Gordons Bay itself is not a pretty beach, but another world exists beneath the sheltered water: the protected **underwater nature trail** makes it diving and snorkelling heaven (see "Sports and activities" for diving operators). From here, a walkway leads around the waterfront to Major Street and then on to **Dunningham Reserve**, overlooking the northern end of Coogee Beach; the walk to Coogee proper takes about fifteen minutes in all.

Coogee

Coogee is another long-popular seaside resort, almost on a par with Manly and Bondi, and has had a reputation for entertaining Sydneysiders since Victorian times. These days, it's popular with young travellers, who flock to its stack of backpackers' hostels.

With its hilly streets of California-style houses looking onto a compact, pretty beach enclosed by headlands, Coogee has a snugness and friendly local feel that its cousin Bondi just can't match – there's something more laid-back and community-oriented about it, and you can happily wear your old shorts to the beach. Everything is close to hand: beachside **Arden Street** is dominated by the extensive *Coogee Bay Hotel*, one of Sydney's best-known

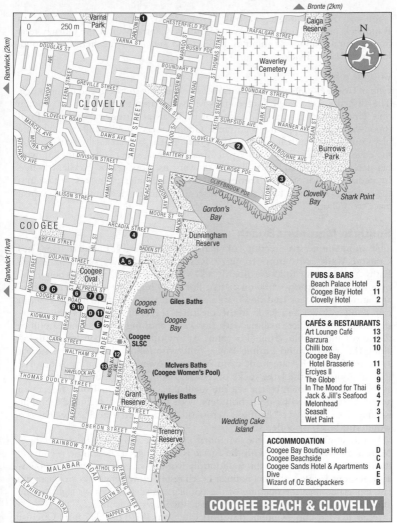

PUBS & BARS

Beach Palace Hotel	5
Coogee Bay Hotel	11
Clovelly Hotel	2

CAFÉS & RESTAURANTS

Art Lounge Café	13
Barzura	12
Chilli box	10
Coogee Bay Hotel Brasserie	11
Erciyes II	8
The Globe	9
In The Mood for Thai	6
Jack & Jill's Seafood	4
Melonhead	7
Seasalt	3
Wet Paint	1

ACCOMMODATION

Coogee Bay Boutique Hotel	D
Coogee Beachside	C
Coogee Sands Hotel & Apartments	A
Dive	E
Wizard of Oz Backpackers	B

COOGEE BEACH & CLOVELLY

music venues, while the main shopping street, **Coogee Bay Road**, runs uphill from the beach and has a choice selection of coffee spots and places to eat plus a big supermarket.

Between the imaginatively modernized promenade – a great place to stroll and hang out – and the beach, a grassy park holds free electric barbecues, picnic tables and shelters. The beach is popular with families (there's an excellent children's playground above the southern end; see "Kids' Sydney") while at the northern end the *Beach Palace Hotel* is a 1980s' restoration of the 1887 Coogee Palace Aquarium. In its heyday, its gigantic dance floor could accommodate three thousand pleasure-seekers; today the hotel is a popular drinking spot for backpackers, who crowd its oceanfront balcony.

You can reach Coogee on **bus** #373 or #374 from Circular Quay via Randwick, or #372 from Eddy Avenue, outside Central Station; the journey time from Central is about 25 minutes. Buses #313 and #314 run here from Bondi Junction via Randwick.

Coogee's baths

One of Coogee's chief pleasures is its baths, beyond the southern end of the beach. The first, the secluded, volunteer-run McIvers Baths, traditionally for women only (and boys up to age 3), is known by locals as **Coogee Women's Pool** (noon–5pm; 20¢). Opposite its entrance, Grant Reserve holds a full-on adventure playground. Just south lies the 1917 **Wylies Baths**, a unisex saltwater pool on the edge of the sea (daily: Oct–April 7am–7pm, May–Sept 7am–5pm; $3), with big decks to lie on and solar-heated showers; its kiosk serves excellent coffee. Immediately south of there, **Trenerry Reserve** is a huge green park jutting into the ocean; its spread of big, flat rocks offers tremendous views and makes a great place to chill out.

South to Maroubra Beach

The most impressive section of Randwick Council's **Eastern Beaches Coastal Walk** starts from Trenerry Reserve, immediately south of Wylie's Baths. You initially follow a boardwalk where interpretive panels detail the ongoing regeneration work on native flora and highlight the returning bird and animal life. Steps lead down to a rock platform full of small pools – you can wander down and look at the creatures there, or swim in a large tear-shaped pool. It's quite thrilling with the waves crashing over, but be careful of the waves and the blue-ringed octopus. At low tide you can continue walking along the rocks around Lurline Bay – otherwise follow the streets inland for a bit, rejoining the waterfront from Mermaid Avenue. Jack Vanny Memorial Park is fronted by the large rocks of Mistral Point, a great spot to sit and look at the water, and down by the sea the small, pleasant **Mahon Pool** (free; open access) is surrounded by great boulders, with an unspoiled, secluded feel. The isolated *Pool Caffe* (see "Eating") across the road on Marine Parade makes a wonderful lunch or coffee spot.

At the southern end of the Memorial Park, the kilometre-long stretch of **Maroubra Beach** begins. With the Anzac Rifle Range at the southern end and the far-off sound of gunfire, this traditionally working-class suburb, with its down-at-heel shops, has never been a popular beach resort. However, things are changing fast, especially since the opening of the popular, casual *Pavilion Cafe* right on the sand on Marine Parade in the former kiosk; the views are fantastic.

To get to Maroubra by public transport, catch **bus** #376 or #377 from Circular Quay, Eddy Avenue at Central Station, Randwick or Coogee, the #396 from Circular Quay, or the #317 from Bondi Junction station.

Manly

Manly, perched on an isthmus behind North Head at the northern mouth of the harbour, is doubly blessed with both ocean and harbour beaches. This combination, and its easy accessibility from central Sydney, give it the feeling of a holiday village still within the city limits. A day-trip to Manly, rounded off with a dinner of fish'n'chips, offers a classic taste of Sydney life.

When Captain Arthur Phillip, the commander of the First Fleet, was exploring Sydney Harbour in 1788, he saw a group of well-built Aboriginal men onshore, proclaimed them to be "manly", and named the cove in the process. During the Edwardian era it became fashionable as a recreational retreat from the city, with the promotional slogan "Manly – seven miles from Sydney, but a thousand miles from care".

The best way to arrive, the ferry from Circular Quay, deposits you at Manly Wharf with its adjacent sheltered, harbour beach. From there, **The Corso**, Manly's pedestrian main drag, runs 400 metres to the ocean beach, **South Steyne**, with its iconic stand of Norfolk Pines lining the shore.

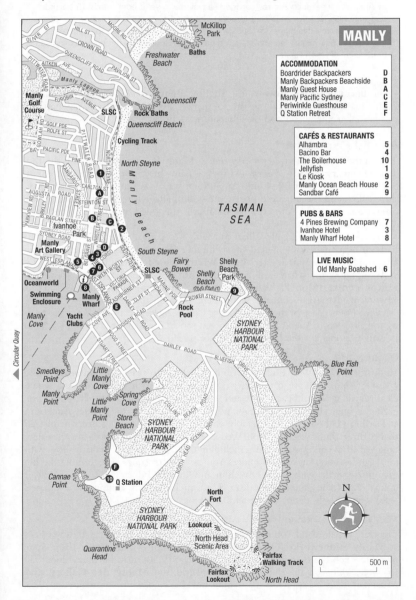

MANLY

ACCOMMODATION
Boardrider Backpackers — D
Manly Backpackers Beachside — B
Manly Guest House — A
Manly Pacific Sydney — C
Periwinkle Guesthouse — E
Q Station Retreat — F

CAFÉS & RESTAURANTS
Alhambra — 5
Bacino Bar — 4
The Boilerhouse — 10
Jellyfish — 1
Le Kiosk — 9
Manly Ocean Beach House — 2
Sandbar Café — 9

PUBS & BARS
4 Pines Brewing Company — 7
Ivanhoe Hotel — 3
Manly Wharf Hotel — 8

LIVE MUSIC
Old Manly Boatshed — 6

0   500 m

Water activities and cruises

Manly Wharf is a hub for adventure activity, with three watersports companies. Manly Parasailing (℡02/9977 6781, ⓦwww.parasail.net; Oct–April only) offers Sydney's only parasailing experience: a ten-minute "lift" costs $79 if you're on your own, but the $129 tandem is more fun; expect to be on the boat for an hour. Manly Boat & Kayak Centre (℡0412/622 662, ⓦwww.manlykayakcentre.com.au) is here daily October to April and weekends the rest of the year; single kayaks cost from $15 per hour, and they also rent five-seater motorboats ($65 for 1hr, $220 all day). All year round, Sydney Ocean Adventures (℡1300 374 278, ⓦwww.sydneyoceanadventures.com .au) operate fifty-minute, adrenalin-fuelled powerboat tours ($75) through crashing surf to the cliffs of North Head.

The beautiful **Fairy Bower** and **Shelley Beach** make a refreshing change from the main beach, while to the south rises **North Head** with its national parkland, harbour views and old quarantine station.

Around Manly Wharf

Taking the thirty-minute ferry trip out to Manly has always been half the fun. The legendary **Manly Ferry** (Mon–Fri 6am–11.45pm, Sat 8am–11.45pm, Sun 8am–11pm; every 30–40min; $6.40 each way) has run from Circular Quay since 1854, and the huge old boats come complete with snack bars selling the ubiquitous meat pie. After the ferries finish, the #151 **night bus** runs from Wynyard station.

Ferries terminate at Manly Wharf in Manly Cove, near a small section of calm harbour beach where the netted-off swimming area is popular with families. Like a typical English seaside resort, **Manly Wharf** housed a tacky funfair until a few years ago; now the wharf is all grown-up, with a swathe of cafés and shops and **visitor centre** (Mon–Fri 9am–5pm, Sat & Sun 10am–4pm; ℡02/9976 1430, ⓦwww.manlytourism.com.au). While here, pick up the excellent, free *Sydney's Northern Beaches Map* or the three *Walking Coastal Sydney* maps that cover the coast up to Palm Beach. An excellent time to visit is over the Labour Day long weekend in early October, for the **Jazz Festival** (see p.259).

Oceanworld

Walk north along West Esplanade from the wharf to reach **Oceanworld** (daily 10am–5.30pm; $18.50; ℡02/8251 7877, ⓦwww.oceanworld.com.au), where clear acrylic walls hold back the water so you can saunter along the harbour floor, gazing at huge sharks and stingrays. While not a patch on the Sydney Aquarium at Darling Harbour, it's considerably cheaper and kids love it. Divers hand-feed sharks three times weekly (Mon, Wed & Fri at 11am) and there's always a new range of shows and guided tours, including the Dangerous Australians show with local (and deadly) snakes and spiders. You can also organize dives among the big grey nurse sharks with Shark Dive Extreme (qualified diver $185, refresher diver course $220 and unqualified diver $250, including all equipment, awareness lecture and 30min diving in the tank; bookings ℡02/8251 7878).

Manly Waterworks and Manly Art Gallery and Museum

Opposite Oceanworld, you may well hear screams from the three giant waterslides at **Manly Waterworks** (Oct–Easter Sat, Sun, school & public hols 10am–5pm, plus Dec–Feb Sat 6–9pm; 1hr $14.50, all day $19.50; must be over 120cm tall to enter). Between the slides and Oceanworld, the **Manly Art Gallery and Museum** (daily except Mon 10am–5pm; free) has a collection started in the 1920s of Australian paintings, drawings, prints and etchings, and a stash of fun beach memorabilia including huge old wooden surfboards and old-fashioned swimming costumes. Much of the space is given over to changing exhibits, often well worth half an hour of your time.

Manly Scenic Walkway

One of the finest harbourside walks anywhere in Sydney is the **Manly Scenic Walkway** (10km one-way; 3–4hr; mostly flat) which follows the harbour shore inland from Manly Cove all the way west to Spit Bridge on Middle Harbour, where you can catch a bus (#180 and many others) back to Wynyard station in the city centre (20min). This wonderful walk takes you through some of the area's more expensive neighbourhoods before heading into a section of **Sydney Harbour National Park** (free entry), passing successive small beaches and coves – perfect for stopping off for a dip – Aboriginal middens and some subtropical rainforest. The walk can easily be broken up into six sections with obvious exit/entry points; pick up a map from the Manly Visitor Information Centre or NPWS offices.

The town and beaches

Northeast of Manly Wharf, **The Corso** cuts directly across the isthmus 500 metres to South Steyne beach. It is lined with surf shops, cafés, bakeries, restaurants and pubs, and even has Coles supermarket not far from the Wharf. The streets hereabouts are lively and interesting, particularly **Belgrave Street**, Manly's alternative strip, with good cafés, interesting shops, yoga schools and the Manly Environment Centre at no. 41, whose aim is to educate the community about local biodiversity and issues affecting it.

On **South Steyne** beach, Manly Beach Hire rents out just about anything to make the beach more fun, from surfboards to snorkel sets, and they also have lockers for your valuables. A six-kilometre shared pedestrian and **cycle path** begins at South Steyne and runs north to Seaforth, past North Steyne Beach

▲ Manly Beach

and Queenscliff. You can rent mountain bikes from Manly Cycles (see p.270) or Manly Bike Tours, 2 West Promenade, who also offer a two-hour **guided bike tour** around interesting corners of Manly (daily 10.30am; $55; T02/8005 7368, Wwww.manlybiketours.com.au).

For a more idyllic beach, follow the footpath from the southern end of South Steyne around the headland to Cabbage Tree Bay, with two very pretty – and protected – green-backed beaches at either end: **Fairy Bower** to the west (where you'll find *The Bower* Café) and **Shelley Beach** to the east (home to *Le Kiosk*), both cafés are listed under "Eating".

North Head

You can take in more of the Sydney Harbour National Park at **North Head**, the harbour mouth's upper jaw, where the short but circuitous Fairfax Walking Track leads to three splendid viewpoints, including the **Fairfax Lookout**. A regular #135 **bus** leaves from Manly Wharf for North Head or you can simply drive up there. Right in the middle of this national park is a military reserve centred on the historic **North Fort**, a curious network of tunnels built into the headland during the Crimean War in the nineteenth century, as a reaction to fears of a Russian invasion. It takes around an hour and a half to wander through the tunnels of the **National Artillery Museum**, with the obligatory guide (Wed–Sun 10am–4pm; $11; Wwww.northfort.org.au).

Q Station

There's a modern twist to historic Sydney at **Q Station** (T02/ 9977 5145, Wwww.qstation.com.au), a recent reincarnation of the old Quarantine Station, on the harbour side of North Head. Between 1832 and 1984, arriving passengers and crew who had a contagious disease were set down at Spring Cove to serve forty days of isolation at the station, all at the shipping companies' expense. Sydney residents, too, were forced here, most memorably during the plague that broke out in The Rocks in 1900, when 1828 people were quarantined (104 plague victims are buried in the grounds). The site, its buildings still intact, has recently become a kind of historic luxury resort, with the old quarantine accommodation turned into hotel rooms (see p.167).

You can't just wander around the site: instead the emphasis is on interpretation, and you're encouraged to join a tour or attend a performance (see below), most of which take place at weekends. Otherwise you're limited to spending a few minutes in the **Luggage Store Visitor Centre** (daily 9.30am–4pm; free), looking at the sandstone where detainees carved inscriptions in English and Chinese, and visiting the *Boilerhouse Restaurant* – no bad thing in itself (see "Eating").

The **Day Tour** (Sun 2.30pm; 2hr; $35) offers a general sense of the station, while **40 Days** (Sat 3pm, Sun 11am; 2hr; $35), takes a more interactive approach, with clues to guide you around as you get a sense of what went on here during the 1918 flu epidemic. Entertaining, if not entirely convincing, **ghost tours** come in three guises: the child-friendly *Family Ghosty* (Fri & Sat 6.30pm; 2hr; $34, kids $22); the more nerve-wracking *Adult Ghost Tour* (Wed & Thurs 8pm, Sat 9pm; 2hr 30min; $44), which tours the site's more haunted locales; and the *Spirit Investigator* (Fri 8.30pm; 2hr 30min; $44) on which a medium takes you ghost-hunting.

There's a more traditional appeal to *Defiance* (Fri 8pm, Sat 3pm & 8pm; early bookings $35, otherwise $50–65), a genuinely entertaining "immersion" play in which you're sucked into the experience of life at the quarantine station during the 1881 smallpox epidemic, the 1900 bubonic plague, the 1918 Spanish Influenza pandemic and a projected Avian Flu epidemic in 2020. The two-act show is performed in buildings where some of the events it depicts took place – the former laundry (with old clothes as seat covers) and the re-created former hospital. Ned Cratchley, the professional rat-catcher, is particularly convincing.

You can get a water shuttle direct to Q Station ($26 return) from King Street Wharf, but tour **packages** are often better value. Try: the shuttle with bubbly, *Defiance* and dinner at the *Boilerhouse* (Sat 5–11pm; $99); or the shuttle, *40 Days* and lunch at the *Boilerhouse* (Sat 10am–4pm, Sun 12.45–6.15pm; $99).

The northern beaches

From Manly northwards, one gorgeous stretch of sand follows the next for thirty kilometres along Pittwater Road, all the way up to **Palm Beach** – some long and open, others sheltered and secluded, and therefore more favoured by the locals. Most suburbs on the way north hold a strip of shops with simple takeaways and some trendier cafés and bars, as well as the odd golf course and larger picnic areas. Pick up the excellent, free *Sydney's Northern Beaches Map* from the Manly visitor centre (see p.140) or check out the associated website, Ⓦ www.sydneybeaches.com.au.

The northern beaches can be reached by regular **bus** from various city bus terminals or from Manly ferry wharf; routes are detailed throughout the text below.

Freshwater to Narrabeen

Freshwater, sitting snugly between two rocky headlands on Queenscliff Bay, just beyond Manly, is one of the most picturesque northern beaches. There's plenty of surf culture around the headland at **Curl Curl**, and a walking track leads from Huston Parade at its northern end, above the rocky coastline to the curve of **Dee Why Beach**. Dee Why provides consistently good **surf**, while its sheltered lagoon makes it popular with families. Beyond the lagoon, windsurfers and kiteboarders gather around Long Reef, where the point is surrounded by a wide rock shelf creviced with rock pools and protected as an aquatic reserve – it's well worth a wander to peek at the creatures within. Bus #136 and #156 from Manly Wharf, or #151, #169 and #178 from outside the QVB in the city, will bring you to here.

The long, beautiful sweep of **Collaroy Beach**, with its popular YHA (see "Accommodation"), shades into idyllic **Narrabeen Beach**, backed by the extensive, swimmable and fishable **Narrabeen Lakes**, popular with anglers, kayakers and families; there's also a good campsite (see box, p.171). No train lines lead to the northern beaches, but both Collaroy and Narrabeen can be reached by bus #183 from Wynyard station or bus #190 from Railway Square and Wynyard station. Several other buses also go to Collaroy, including the #151 from outside the QVB and the #156 and #159 from Manly Wharf, and buses continue all the way up the coast with stop-off points at the more popular sites.

Mona Vale to Avalon

Beyond Narrabeen, **Mona Vale** is a long, straight stretch of beach with a large park behind and a sea pool dividing it from sheltered **Bongin Bay**, whose headland reserve, and rocks to clamber on, make it ideal for children. At Ingleside, 5km inland from Mona Vale, in the middle of the Ku-Ring-Gai Chase National Park, the domed nine-sided **Bahá'í Temple**, 173 Mona Vale Rd (daily: Jan 9am–7pm; Feb–Dec 9am–5pm; Ⓦ www.bahai.org.au), sits amid extensive gardens. It is one of only seven in the world (with an eighth currently being built in Chile).

The Bahá'í faith teaches the unity of religion, and Sunday services (11am) read from texts of the world's main religions; a small visitor centre explains more. The temple is easy to reach by car, but there's no useful public transport.

After Bongin Bay, the **Barrenjoey Peninsula** begins, with calm **Pittwater** (see p.276) on its western side and ocean beaches running up its eastern side until it spears into Broken Bay. **Newport** boasts a fine stretch of ocean beach between two rocky headlands but is better known for the *Newport Arms* (see p.211), with its beer garden and huge deck overlooking Heron Cove at Pittwater. Unassuming **Bilgola Beach**, nestled at the base of a steep cliff next to Newport, is one of the prettiest northern beaches, with its distinctive orange sand. From Bilgola Beach, a trio of Sydney's best beaches, for both surf and scenery, run up the eastern fringe of the hammerhead peninsula: **Avalon** and **Whale** beaches are popular surfie territory, while more fashionable **Palm Beach** caters to visiting celebs and Sydneysiders escaping the city.

Avalon and Whale Beach

Avalon Beach, 5km north of Mona Vale, is another lovely strand, this time backed by pleasant shops and eateries that run perpendicular from the beach on Avalon Parade; *Allo Allo* at no. 24 is a licensed café with good, moderately priced food, free wi-fi and Sunday jazz. If you want to stick around, wander up the road to the *Avalon Beach Hostel* (see "Accommodation").

Backed by bush-covered hills and reached by three kilometres of winding road, **Whale Beach**, 8km further north via Barrenjoey Road and Whale Beach Road, has a secluded feel. It's much less of a settlement, with a rock swimming pool at the southern end, and can be a slice of paradise on a summer's day. It holds the inevitable Surf Life Saving Club, but, sadly, the only beachside café is currently closed.

Palm Beach

If you continue to follow Whale Beach Road north you'll reach **Palm Beach** which, living up to its name, is a hangout for the rich and famous, including plenty of international celebs seeking some Australian sunshine. To blend right in, you too can arrive Hollywood-style on a seaplane from Rose Bay (see p.119). The ocean beach, on the western side of the peninsula, leads a double life as "Summer Bay" in the famous, long-running Aussie soap *Home and Away*, which regularly features the picturesque **Barrenjoey Lighthouse** and bush-covered headland (part of Ku-Ring-Gai Chase National Park).

Most of the dozen or so shops and cafés cluster around Palm Beach Wharf on the Pittwater side. A kilometre north, **Barrenjoey Head**, a sandstone peninsula that marks the southern entrance to Broken Bay, is topped by the 1881 **Barrenjoey Lighthouse** (Sun 11am–3pm with half-hour tours every 30min; $3; ☎02/9472 9300), which can be reached by a steep walking path (2km return; 40–60min; 110m ascent) from the car park at the base. You're rewarded by a stunning panorama of Palm Beach, Pittwater and the Hawkesbury River.

The bulk of Ku-Ring-Gai Chase National Park lies west across Pittwater, and can be visited with Palm Beach and Hawkesbury River Cruises (☎041 446 6635, ⓦwww.sydneysceniccruises.com). **Cruises** leave from the wharf on the eastern, Pittwater side of the peninsula (11am–3.30pm, 1hr lunch break at Bobbin Head; $40); they also offer general transport to Patonga (see p.282). Alternatively, the Palm Beach Ferry Service (☎02/9974 2411, ⓦwww.palmbeachferry.com .au) runs from Palm Beach Wharf via The Basin to Mackerel Beach, reaching picnicking and camping spots on Pittwater (departures roughly hourly 9am–5pm, until 8pm on Fri; $12.60 return).

Beside the wharf, calm Snapperman Beach is fronted by yachts and a shady park, usually full of people on rugs lapping up the atmosphere. Barrenjoey Road nearby holds a few interesting **shops** to browse, selling Indian clothes and accessories, funky secondhand furniture and women's clothing. You can **eat** and drink well at *Barrenjoey House* (see "Eating"), or pick from the café-style dishes at popular *Swelter Café*, or, for less cash, get takeaways from *Palm Beach Fish & Chips* and throw down your own rug on the grass. Both *Barrenjoey House* and *Palm Beach Bed and Breakfast* offer excellent **accommodation** (see "Accommodation").

Buses #190 and #L90 run up the peninsula from Railway Square at Central via Wynyard to Avalon, continuing to Palm Beach via the Pittwater side; change at Avalon for bus #193 to Whale Beach. Bus #L88 goes from Central and Wynyard to Avalon, and the #187 from Milsons Point in The Rocks to Newport.

The southern and western outskirts

S
ydney's mostly unattractive **western suburbs** cover the flat plains that lead towards the Blue Mountains, the ultimate destination of most travellers heading west. The city's first successful farming area, **Parramatta**, on the Parramatta River (a pleasant ferry ride from Circular Quay), holds a cluster of historic colonial buildings not swallowed up by development and there are several **wildlife parks** out this way. Sydney Olympic Park in Homebush (accessed on the same Parramatta River ferry), at which the highly successful 2000 Olympics were held, has been transformed into an attractive sport, entertainment, recreation and nature precinct. To the southwest, surrounded by red-brick suburbia, the town centre of **Cabramatta** is Sydney's Saigon in miniature, its three or four blocks of bustling commerce and community so authentically Vietnamese as to be geographically disconcerting. The **southern suburbs** of Sydney offer pockets of beauty and interest at **La Perouse** and **Botany Bay National Park**, while **Cronulla** boasts a superb surf beach.

South

Arranged around huge **Botany Bay**, the southern suburbs of Sydney are seen as the heartland of red-roofed suburbia. Popular perceptions of Botany Bay are coloured by its proximity to an airport, a high-security prison (Long Bay), an oil refinery, a container terminal and a sewage outlet. Yet the surprisingly clean-looking water is fringed by quiet, sandy beaches and the marshlands shelter profuse birdlife. Whole areas of the waterfront, from **La Perouse** to the **Kurnell Peninsula** where Captain Cook first dropped anchor, belong to **Botany Bay National Park**, while large stretches on either side of the Georges River form a State Recreation Area. Beyond Botany Bay lies the beach surburb of **Cronulla**, and the Royal National Park (see p.315) is just across the water.

La Perouse

Tucked into the northern shore of Botany Bay where it meets the Pacific Ocean, **La Perouse** contains Sydney's oldest Aboriginal settlement, the legacy of a mission. The suburb took its name from the eighteenth-century French explorer, **Laperouse**, who set up camp here for six weeks, briefly and cordially meeting Captain Arthur Phillip, who was making his historic decision to forgo swampy Botany Bay and move on to Port Jackson. After leaving Botany Bay, the Laperouse expedition was never seen again. A grassy headland, between the pretty swimming beaches of Congwong Bay and Frenchmans Bay, features the fort-like sandstone **Macquarie Watchtower** and the excellent **Laperouse Museum**, and provides access to walks in Botany Bay National Park and the nineteenth-century fortifications of bridge-accessed Bare Island. Views from the headland juxtapose shimmering white-sand beaches and impressive wilderness with Botany Bay's somewhat apocalyptic-looking industrial shoreline.

La Perouse is at its most lively on **Sunday** (and public hols) when, following a century-old tradition, Aboriginal people come down from the surrounding

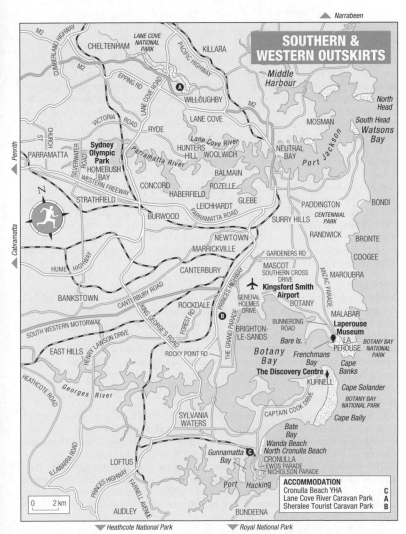

areas to sell boomerangs and other crafts, and demonstrate snake-handling skills and boomerang throwing on the headland.

There are a few places to eat, including the popular, casual and affordable *Paris Seafood Cafe* at 51 Endeavour Avenue, where you can eat in or get take-away fish'n'chips to enjoy in the park. Quality coffee and tasty Mediterranean cuisine at stylishly appointed, *Tony's at La Perouse*, 1599 Anzac Parade, comes with cushioned alfresco seating overlooking the park and museum, while the idyllic veranda of the federation-style *Boatshed Cafe* sits right over the water with a white-sand beach arcing from below and cranes punctuating the distant shoreline.

To get to La Perouse, catch bus #394 from Circular Quay via Darlinghurst and Moore Park, or #393 from Railway Square via Surry Hills and Moore Park, or the #L94 limited stops from Circular Quay.

The Laperouse Museum

At least, is there any news of Monsieur de Laperouse?

Louis XVI, about to be guillotined, 1793

Perched on the grassy headland like a dignified manor house, the striking, crimson Victorian-era building that holds the NPWS-run **Laperouse Museum** (Wed–Sun 10am–4pm; $5.50) is a beauty. Tracing Laperouse's voyage in great detail, the displays within are enlivened by relics from the wrecks, exhibits of antique French maps, and copies of etchings by the naturalists on board. The voyage was commissioned by Louis XVI in 1785 as a purely scientific exploration of the Pacific to rival Cook's voyages, and strict instructions were given for Laperouse to "act with great gentleness and humanity towards the different people whom he will visit". After an astonishing three-and-a-half-year journey through South America, the Easter Islands, Hawaii, the northwest coast of America, and past China and Japan to Russia, the *Astrolabe* and the *Boussole* struck disaster – first encountering hostility in the Solomon Islands, and then in their fate after they sailed from Botany Bay on March 10, 1788. Their disappearance remained a mystery until 1828, when relics were discovered on Vanikoro in the Solomon Islands; the wrecks themselves were found in the Solomons only in 1958 and 1964. An additional exhibition looks at local Aboriginal history and culture.

Bare Island

You can take a tour of the nineteenth-century fortifications on **Bare Island** (Sun 1.30pm, 2.30pm & 3.30pm; 45min; $5; no booking required, wait at the gate to the island), joined to La Perouse by a thin walkway. The tours provide a good historical grounding on Australian military history while informatively introducing the site's nineteenth-century gun emplacements and artillery relics, erected amid fears of a Russian invasion. Bare Island's most recent claim to fame was a brief appearance in *Mission Impossible II*.

Botany Bay National Park

The headlands and foreshore surrounding La Perouse have been incorporated into the northern half of **Botany Bay National Park** (no entry fee) – the other half is across Botany Bay on the Kurnell Peninsula (see below). A **visitor centre**, in the same building as the museum (Wed–Sun 10am–4pm; ☎02/9311 3379), provides details of walks, including a fine one past **Congwong Bay Beach** to Henry Head and its lighthouse (5km round trip). It's also worth having a close-up look at the small fort-like Macquarie Watchtower. Built in 1820, Australia's first customs house is now the oldest building on the Bay's shores, but it's not possible to go inside.

Whale watching

Humpback whales and southern right whales are now regularly sighted from Sydney headlands and surf beaches during June and July, on their migratory path north from the Antarctic to breeding grounds in the tropical waters of Queensland. Whales even occasionally appear in Sydney Harbour itself – three southern right whales frolicking under the Harbour Bridge in 2002 caused a sensation as city offices emptied out and sightseers flocked to the shores. The whales swim close to shore on their trip north and can be spotted without binoculars; while they do head the same way back south in summer, they are much further from shore.

The best and most popular whale-watching spot is **Cape Solander** in the southern Kurnell half of Botany Bay National Park, but any headland or beach with a good ocean view is fine (there are several superb lookout points on North Head and South Head). Cape Solander is where the official whale count is taken – only 298 whales were counted in 1998, but in 2006, thanks presumably to the ban on whaling, the count had soared to 1608. Essentially this is the most southern point of Sydney before the Royal National Park extends southwards, and the first obvious place to sight the whales as they head north. From here, it could take two and a half hours for the same whale to reach Bondi Beach, and another three hours or so for it to be spotted along the northern beaches at the popular site of Long Reef.

Whale spotting from land takes patience. You might have to sit for at least three hours before your first "blow " (humpbacks spout a rounded vapour, while that of the southern right whale is v-shaped), though the more commonly seen, lunge-feeding humpback is very energetic, and spouting might be followed by dives, the waving of fins and arcing through the water. Since it can be windy and cold, make sure you bring a beanie hat and a warm jacket, food supplies, and something to sit on. To get the most out of the experience, get hold of a pair of decent binoculars.

For more information, check out the IFAW (International Fund for Animal Welfare) website at ⓦwww.ifaw.org. For details of whale-watching cruises, see "Basics ", p.27.

From La Perouse, you can see across Botany Bay to Kurnell and the red buoy marking the spot where Captain James Cook and the crew of the *Endeavour* anchored on April 29, 1770, for an eight-day exploration. Back in England, many refused to believe that the unique Australian plants and animals they had recorded actually existed – the kangaroo and platypus in particular were thought to be hoaxes.

Captain Cook's Landing Place is now the south head of **Botany Bay National Park**. To get here, take the train to Cronulla and then Kurnell Bus Services route #987. The informative **Education Centre** (Mon–Fri 10am–4pm, Sat & Sun 9.30am–4.30pm; car entry fee $7; ⓣ02/9668 8431) looks at the wetlands ecology of the park and tells the story of Cook's visit and its implications for Aboriginal people.

Indeed the political sensitivity of the spot, which effectively marks the start of the decline of an ancient culture, has led to the planned renaming of the park to Kamay-Botany Bay National Park, "Kamay " being the original Dharawal people's name for the bay. Set aside as a public recreation area in 1899, the heath and woodland is unspoiled, and holds some secluded swimming beaches; you may even spot parrots and honeyeaters. One of the main attractions in this half of Botany Bay National Park is whale watching from **Cape Solander** in June and July (see box above).

Cronulla

On the other side of the Kurnell Peninsula sits **Cronulla**, Sydney's most southern beach suburb and the only beach accessible by train. The locals call it "God's country", and it definitely has the atmosphere of a holiday village rather than a community just half an hour's drive from the CBD. Steeped in surfer culture, everything about the suburb centres on water sports and a laid-back beach lifestyle, from the multitude of surf-gear shops and outdoor cafés on the beachfront to the surfrider clubs and boating facilities on the bay. Despite this, or perhaps because of it, racist attitudes and consequently racial tension between locals and visiting non-Anglo Sydney residents has been very much a problem in Cronulla in recent years. In December 2005, a spontaneous anti-Muslim protest led to days of violent **riots** between Middle Eastern youths and locals, which were subsequently publicized around the world (see "History"). However, while formerly a haven for panel vans and all-night campfire parties, Cronulla has in the last decade or so been growing increasingly trendy and upmarket – restaurants are serving more than fish'n'chips and pizza, the run-down red-brick beach houses are disappearing, and the prime beachfront real estate is fast being bought up and built on. Town houses and multi-storey mansions with million-dollar price tags have done nothing to change the relaxed beach vibe, however, with walkers and joggers out every morning on the sand and the standard cluster of surfers still gathering on the point to check out the swell.

Cronulla is set on a peninsula with the ocean on one side and the calmer **Gunnamatta Bay** on the other; the outcrop forms one side of the heads at the entrance to the Port Hacking River. The long arch of Bate Bay is Sydney's longest beach at 4.8km. There are four **patrolled beaches** at the south of this strip – **North Cronulla**, **Elouera** and **Wanda** on the main arc of sand, and the smaller and more protected **South Cronulla** beach in its own inlet to the south. Each has a **surf club** with facilities and canteens, and **car parking** extends right along this stretch of coast. As the only Sydney beach directly accessible by train (40min from Central Station on the Sutherland line), **South Cronulla** can become quite crowded. It's also protected from the wind and most tidal rips so many families bring their children here to swim. The beach is 300 metres from Cronulla **train station**, at the southern end of the main shopping strip, Cronulla Street. A pedestrianized mall further down, Cronulla Street houses, along with its side streets, a handful of hip young **café-bars**, including *Nulla Nulla*, at no. 75 and *Grind Expresso* at no. 6 on Surf Street, which continues on to a park fronting the beach. Facing the sea, on the right, the Cronulla Sports Complex has a heated indoor pool and gym (℡02 9523 5842). *Melon Blue Health Bar*, next to the complex and practically in the ocean, is good for a tasty wrap or revitalizing fresh juice, while around the cliff walkway, past the ocean pool, on the southern tip of South Cronulla beach, stylish, glass-walled *Sealevel Restaurant and Bar* serves delicious seafood and modern Australian dishes with a view (and price tag) to match. Check out *Alley Break Cafe* next door for appetising, but simpler and more affordable food.

Around Cronulla

Heading south, a well-trodden footpath, **The Esplanade**, follows the coastline around to Bass and Flinders Point, and beyond to Salmon Haul Bay and Hungry Point. Across the mouth of the Hacking River, the small artist community of **Bundeena** nestles on the edge of the **Royal National Park**. Cronulla National Park Ferry Services runs ferries to Bundeena from Cronulla Marina on Tonkin Street, behind the train station.

Past **Bass and Flinders Point**, at low tide the path can be followed right around the headland, down the back of the promontory and across the sand to **Gunnamatta Park**. The large park is a popular and sheltered BBQ spot with a sizeable amphitheatre, which in summer hosts Shakespeare in the Park performances. The calmer inlet is filled with yachts and run-about dinghies, and is a good place to paddle a surfski, kayak, or swim in the netted-off ocean pool.

West

For over fifty years, Sydney has been sliding ever westwards in a monotonous sprawl of shopping centres, brick-veneer homes and fast-food chains, along the way swallowing up towns and villages, some of which date back to colonial times. The first settlers to explore inland found well-watered, fertile river flats, and quickly established agricultural outposts to support the fledgling colony. **Parramatta**, **Liverpool**, **Penrith** and **Campbelltown**, once separate communities, have now become satellite towns inside Sydney's commuter belt. Yet, despite Sydney's advance, bushwalkers will still find plenty of wild west to explore. Three wildlife parks keep suburbia at bay, and the beauty of the **Blue Mountains** is a far cry from the modernity of Sydney. Heading west, however, now starts for many travellers with a visit to the Olympic site at **Homebush Bay**.

Sydney Olympic Park at Homebush Bay

The main focus of the 2000 Olympics was **Sydney Olympic Park** at **Homebush Bay**, a down-at-heel working-class area in the city's west, far removed from the glamour of Sydney's harbour. Virtually the geographical heart of a city that sprawls westwards, Homebush Bay already held some heavy-duty sporting facilities, including the State Sports Centre and the Aquatic Centre. The **Sydney Olympic Park Authority (SOPA)** has turned Sydney Olympic Park into a recreation and sporting complex that hosts major sporting events, popular music concerts, free outdoor movies, multicultural festivals, school holiday and weekend children's activities, and Sydney Festival-related events. For details call ☎02/9714 7888 or check ⓦwww.sydneyolympicpark .com.au.

The most pleasant way to get out to Olympic Park is to take a ferry up the Parramatta River, jumping on a connecting #401 bus from Sydney Olympic Park Ferry Wharf to Olympic Park Station (on Dawn Fraser Avenue, a few minutes' walk to the ANZ Stadium on Olympic Boulevard). The second-best option is the direct **train** from Central to Olympic Park station, which runs four times daily on weekdays (at weekends change at Lidcombe station, from where trains depart every 10min). Parking stations at Sydney Olympic Park charge $4 per hr with a maximum daily charge of $20. To get around the extensive site, there are 35km of **cycleways**, including those in Bicentennial Park. **Bike hire** is available (contact the Visitor Centre – see below; from $12 per hour, $22 half-day), and bikes are permitted on trains and ferries (charges apply during peak hours). Get information from the **Sydney Olympic Park Visitor Centre**, near Olympic Park station on Showground Rd (daily 9am–5pm; ☎02/9714 7888), which also offers a self-guided audio tour (daily 9am–4pm; $20; headsets must be returned by 4.45pm). Guided **Segway tours** are also available on weekends (Sat & Sun 11am & 2pm; 1hr $55, 2hr $99). Cafés, restaurants and convenient stores, on Dawn Fraser Avenue, by the station, offer refreshments.

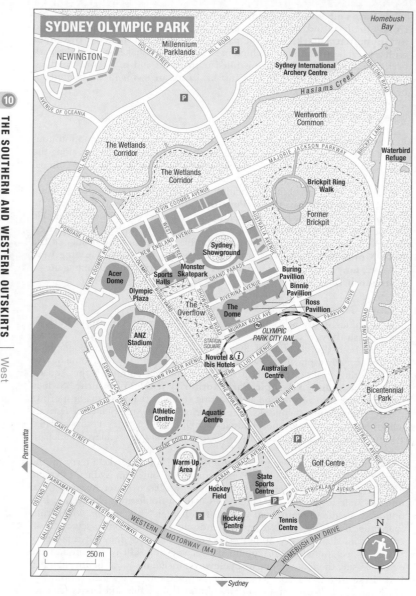

SYDNEY OLYMPIC PARK

Homebush Bay

NEWINGTON

Millennium Parklands

Sydney International Archery Centre

Haslams Creek

Wentworth Common

Waterbird Refuge

The Wetlands Corridor

The Wetlands Corridor

MARJORIE JACKSON PARKWAY

Brickpit Ring Walk

Former Brickpit

Sydney Showground

Acer Dome

Sports Halls

Monster Skatepark

Buring Pavillion

Binnie Pavillion

Olympic Plaza

The Overflow

The Dome

Ross Pavillion

ANZ Stadium

STATION SQUARE

OLYMPIC PARK CITY RAIL

Novotel & Ibis Hotels (i)

Australia Centre

Bicentennial Park

Athletic Centre

Aquatic Centre

FIGTREE DRIVE

Warm Up Area

Golf Centre

Hockey Field

State Sports Centre

Hockey Centre

Tennis Centre

WESTERN MOTORWAY (M4)

PARRAMATTA (GREAT WESTERN HIGHWAY) ROAD

▲ Parramatta

0   250 m

N

▼ Sydney

An **observation centre** on the seventeenth floor of the *Novotel Hotel*, on Olympic Boulevard between ANZ Stadium and the Aquatic Centre, provides an overview of the site (daily 10am–4pm, but sometimes closed for events; $5; ☎8762 1111).

Visiting the sporting venues

The AUS$470-million Olympic site centred on the 110,000-seat **Telstra Stadium** (recently renamed **ANZ Stadium**), is the venue for the opening and closing ceremonies, track and field events, and marathon and soccer finals. It's still Sydney's largest stadium, though an AUS$68-million overhaul has reduced the number of seats to 83,500, which is more realistic for its use as an Australian Rules football, cricket, rugby league, rugby union, soccer and concert venue. Tours of the stadium, with commentary, run daily when other events are not taking place (hourly 10.30am–3.30pm; $28.50, child $18.50; turn up at Gate C; ℡02/8765 2300, ⓦwww.anzstadium.com.au).

Cuddly Koalas: wildlife parks around Sydney

Though it's no longer legal to pick up and hold a **koala** in New South Wales' wildlife parks, photo-op "patting" sessions are still on offer. Several hands-on wildlife experiences on the outskirts of Sydney are listed on pp.236–237. Also see Taronga Zoo (p.127) and the Australian Reptile Park (p.281).

At **Featherdale Wildlife Park,** 30km west of the city centre off the M4 motorway between Parramatta and Penrith (217 Kildare Rd, Doonside; daily 9am–5pm; $20, child $10; ⓦwww.featherdale.com.au), patting koalas is the special all-day attraction. To get there by public transport, take the train from Central to Blacktown station then bus #725.

The **Koala Park Sanctuary**, 25km north of Sydney, not far from the Pacific Highway on Castle Hill Road, West Pennant Hills (daily 9am–5pm; $19, child $9; ⓦwww .koalapark.com.au), was established as a safe haven for koalas in 1935 and has since opened its gates to wombats, possums, kangaroos and native birds of all kinds. Koala-feeding sessions (daily 10.20am, 11.45am, 2pm & 3pm) are the patting and photo-opportunity times. You can get there by train from Central to Pennant Hills station, then bus #651 or #655 towards Glenorie (Mon–Sat).

▲ Koala Park

Across Olympic Boulevard from the stadium, children may be interested in the indoor and outdoor ramps at **Monster Skate Park**, where participants in "Ride With A Pro" clinics get a one-hour group training session with a professional skate or BMX rider (Sat & Sun 9am & 10am; $20; equipment provided; booking required; ⓦwww.monsterpark.com.au).

Just south of the stadium, if no event is taking place at the **Sydney Olympic Park Sports Centre** (daily 9am–5pm; ☎02/9763 0111, ⓦwww.sports-centre .com.au/), you can visit the **NSW Hall of Champions**, devoted to the state's sporting heroes (same hours; free). Nearby stands the **Sydney Olympic Park Aquatic Centre** (April–Oct Mon–Fri 5am–8.45pm, Sat & Sun 6am–6.45pm; Nov–March Mon–Fri 5am–8.45pm, Sat & Sun 6am–7.45pm; swim & spa $6.60; ☎02/9752 3666, ⓦwww.sydneyaquaticcentre.com.au; also see p.269 for more detail).

On the south side of the site, you can watch tennis tournaments (the big one is the Medibank International, second week of Jan) or hire a court at the **Sydney Olympic Park Tennis Centre** (Mon–Fri 8am–10pm, Sat & Sun 8am–5pm; racquets $5 each; ☎02/9764 1999, ⓦwww.sydneytenniscentre.com .au). Alternatively, head to the **Archery Centre** (in the northeast of the site) for some target practice (daily except Mon 10am–4pm; $20 per hr; ⓦwww .archerycentre.com.au).

Bicentennial Park and the Brickpit Ring Walk

The huge **Bicentennial Park**, opposite the Olympic site, opened in 1988. More than half of the expanse is conservation wetlands – a delightful, zigzagging boardwalk explores thick subtropical mangroves and you can observe a profusion of native birds from a hide. Around 8km of cycling and walking tracks facilitate appreciation, and the odd dramatic steel sculpture is a nice touch.

Just northwest of Bicentennial Park, across Bennelong Parkway, the **Brickpit Ring Walk** is a surprise; its space-age elevated walkway juxtaposes dramatically with an old brickpit, and manages, through its many artistic panel displays and sensor-triggered audio, to impart an unexpected depth and complexity. Sparkling illumination on the pit's relevance to social history, geology, palaeontology, ecology, zoology and the use of its water reservoir for the Olympic Park's impressive water reclamation scheme make it well worth a visit, with a lot to take in.

Parramatta

Situated on the Parramatta River, a little over 20km upstream from the harbour mouth, **Parramatta** was the first of Sydney's rural satellites – the first farm settlement in Australia, in fact. The fertile soil of "Rosehill", as it was originally called, saved the fledgling colony from starvation with its first wheat crop of 1789. It's hard to believe today, but dotted here and there among the malls and busy roads a few early nineteenth-century public buildings and original settlers' dwellings still survive, and warrant a visit if you're interested in Australian history. Parramatta is now the headquarters of many government agencies and has a multicultural community and a lively **restaurant scene** on its main drag, Church Street.

You can **stop off** in Parramatta on your way west out of Sydney – a rather depressing drive along the ugly and congested Parramatta Road – or endure the dreary thirty-minute suburban train ride from Central Station. Much the most enjoyable way to get here, however, is on the sleek RiverCat **ferry** from Circular Quay up the Parramatta River (1hr; $7.70 one-way).

Parramatta's wharf on Phillip Street is just a couple of blocks from the helpful visitor centre, by the convict-built Lennox Bridge within the **Parramatta Heritage Centre**, on the corner of Church and Market streets (daily 9am–5pm; ☎02/8839 3300). This details local Aboriginal and colonial history, and hands out free **walking route maps** to help you find the historical attractions detailed below. The colourful paved Riverside Walk, which leads from the ferry wharf to the centre in around ten minutes, is decorated with Aboriginal motifs and interpretative plaques that tell the story of the Burramatagal people.

A block south of the visitor centre, the area around the corner of Church and Phillip streets has become something of an **"eat street"**. Its twenty cafés and restaurants, ranging from Filipino through Chinese and Malaysian to Japanese, reflect Parramatta's multicultural mix.

Getting around Parramatta is easy, thanks to a **free bus** service, the Loop, which continuously circles in and around the city centre (stops at Parramatta Wharf; every 10min; for details visit ⓦwww.parracity.nsw.gov.au).

Historic buildings

Parramatta's most important historic feature is the National Trust-owned **Old Government House** (Tues–Fri 10am–4.30pm, Sat & Sun 10.30am–4pm; $8), the oldest remaining public edifice in Australia, in **Parramatta Park** by the river. To get there from the visitor centre, turn left on to Marsden Street, cross the river, then go right on to George Street. Entered through the 1885 gatehouse on O'Connell Street, the park – filled with native trees – rises up to the gracious old Georgian-style building. Built between 1799 and 1816, it served as the viceregal residence until 1855; one wing has been converted into a pleasant teahouse.

Three other historic attractions are close together: from Parramatta Park, follow Macquarie Street and turn right at its end on to Harris Street. Running off here is Ruse Street, where the aptly named **Experiment Farm Cottage** at 9 Ruse St (Tues–Fri 10.30am–3.30pm, Sat & Sun 11am–3.30pm; $5.50), another National Trust property, was built on the site of the first land grant, given in 1790 to reformed convict James Ruse. On parallel Alice Street, at no. 70, **Elizabeth Farm** (Fri–Sun 9.30am–4pm; $8) dates from 1793 and claims to be the oldest surviving home in the country. The farm was built and run by the Macarthurs, who bred the first of the merino sheep that made Australian wealth "ride on a sheep's back"; a small **café** serves refreshments. Nearby **Hambledon Cottage**, 63 Hassel St (Wed, Thurs, Sat & Sun 11am–4pm; $4), built in 1824, was part of the Macarthur estate.

Cabramatta

In Sydney's southwest, central **Cabramatta** emerges from a bland suburban sprawl as an unexpected replica of an ugly, yet vibrant and exciting, city centre in **Vietnam**. Cluttered around John Street and Park Road, a profusion of retailers are complemented by an inexorable flow of Vietnamese and Chinese locals old and young, buying and selling, or simply sitting around smoking cigarettes.

The highly communal nature of Vietnamese culture, where life is lived on chaotic streets, means that entering Cabramatta can seem like your first day in an Asian country. Vietnamese jewellery, fabric and clothing shops squeeze against each other and spill out onto the street, while the glass walls of DVD/CD shops are plastered with garish pop-culture ads. Street stands and benches sell cane juice, sweets and vegetables, and the **food** is exceptional, with restaurants, like *Thanh Binh* (52 John St) and *Tan Viet Noodle House* (2–3 100 John St), to rival the best in Vietnam. On a hot day, consider *Cabra Café*, up a small lane from 66–68 John Street, where a refreshing *Café Suadae* (espresso, crushed ice and condensed milk) will authentically top off your experience. Cabramatta is accessible from Central Station on CityRail.

Listings

Listings

Accommodation

S
ydney has a tremendous number of places to stay, and fierce competition helps to keep prices down. Finding a bed for the night is only a problem during peak holiday periods – from Christmas to the end of January, during Mardi Gras in late February/early March, and over Easter. At those times you'll definitely need to **book ahead**.

Many places offer a discount for **weekly bookings**, and may also reduce prices considerably in **low season** (roughly May–Oct, school holidays excepted). Rates are inflated during the peak holiday season from Christmas and through January and other school holiday periods (see box, p.235 for school vacation times). Many of the larger city-centre hotels, and increasingly smaller places, operate **dynamic pricing** whereby rates vary daily according to demand. Booking well in advance can often get you a good deal, but prices also drop at the last minute at quiet times.

Our prices are given in Australian dollars and indicate the price for a **double room in high season**, excluding these peak times. We've divided our accommodation listings into the following categories: hotels, motels and pubs; B&Bs and guesthouses; and hostels. All accommodation is marked on the relevant chapter maps throughout the Guide.

Where to stay

The listings below are arranged by area. For short visits, you'll want to stay in the **city centre** or the immediate vicinity: The Rocks, the CBD and Darling Harbour have the greatest concentration of expensive hotels but also several backpackers' hostels, while the area around Central Station and Chinatown, known as Haymarket, has some cheaper, more downmarket places and an ever greater concentration of mega-hostels including two huge YHAs.

One excellent place to stay is **Kings Cross**, which is only a ten-minute walk from the city, has its own train station and is always alive with people eating, drinking and clubbing. In recent years, it has shaken off the worst of its renowned red-light and drug-abuse sleaze, and has become popular once again with backpackers, who frequent the dense cluster of hostels and cheap hotels in The Cross and along leafy Victoria Street. Fashionable restaurants and bars are forever opening up in adjacent **Potts Point**, **Woolloomooloo** and **Darlinghurst**, while the buzz has attracted a cluster of chic boutique hotels and refined B&Bs to the area.

To the west, leafy, more peaceful **Glebe** is another slice of prime backpackers' territory, featuring a large YHA hostel, as well as several other backpackers' places and a number of small guesthouses.

▲ Intercontinental Hotel

If you're staying longer, consider somewhere further out, on the **North Shore**, for example, where you'll get more of a wealthy resident's feel for Sydney as a city. **Kirribilli**, **Neutral Bay** or **Cremorne Point** offer serenity and maybe an affordable water view as well: they're only a short ferry ride from Circular Quay. Large old private hotels (as opposed to pubs, which are also called hotels and often offer rooms) in this area are increasingly being converted into guesthouses. **Manly**, tucked away in the northeast corner of the harbour, is a seaside suburb with ocean and harbour beaches and a concentration of hostels, as well as more upmarket accommodation, just thirty minutes from Circular Quay by ferry. The **eastern suburbs** also have a couple of great beachside locations close to the city, **Bondi** and **Coogee**. Both offer hostels and budget accommodation.

Hotels, motels and pubs

The term "**hotel**" does not necessarily mean the same in Australia as it does elsewhere in the world – traditionally, an Australian hotel was a pub, a place to drink which also had rooms above. Some budget options now use the term **private hotel**, to distinguish themselves from licensed establishments. The city's larger **international hotels**, concentrated in The Rocks and the CBD, charge around $150 to $250 for a double room, or from $400 up for the best five-star establishments. Rates in Kings Cross and nearby Potts Point and Woolloomooloo are much lower, with budget hotels charging around $60 to $110 (cheaper rooms share bathrooms), three- or four-star hotels from $140 to $180, and some very chic boutique hotels from $170 to $310.

Motels, such as those we've listed in Glebe and Surry Hills, charge around $105 a night. Plenty of **pubs** have cleaned up their act and offer pleasant old-fashioned rooms, usually sharing bathrooms. The main drawback can be noise from the bar; ask for a room well away from the action. Rates average $120.

Holiday apartments can be very good value for a group, and are perfect for families, but are generally heavily booked. We have listed serviced apartment hotels that offer overnight rates in the general listings below, while holiday apartments that give weekly rates only, and are mostly unserviced, feature in the box on p.166.

The Rocks

See map on p.52 for locations.

Lord Nelson Brewery Corner of Argyle and Kent sts ℡02/9251 4044, ⓦwww.lordnelson .com. Circular Quay CityRail/ferry. B&B in a historic pub (see p.203). The ten very smart Colonial-style rooms are mostly en suite, and come with all mod cons. Prices vary according to size, position and shared or en-suite bathroom arrangements: best is the corner room with views of Argyle St. Meals served in the upmarket brasserie. Continental breakfast included. $130–190.

Mercantile 25 George St ℡02/9247 3570, ⓔmerc@tpg.com.au. Circular Quay CityRail/ferry. A stash of fab rooms upstairs in Sydney's best-known Irish pub, right on the edge of The Rocks near the Harbour Bridge, are always booked out – get in early. Original features include huge fireplaces in several rooms, all furnished in Colonial style. Several have bathrooms complete with spa baths. Cooked breakfast included. Rooms $110, en suite $140.

Old Sydney Holiday Inn 55 George St ℡02/9252 0524, ⓦwww.holidayinn.com. Circular Quay CityRail/ferry. In a great location right in the heart of The Rocks, this 4.5-star hotel has eight impressively designed levels of rooms around a central atrium, which creates a remarkable feeling of space. The best rooms have harbour views but the rooftop swimming pool (plus spa and sauna) also gives fantastic vistas. There's 24hr room service. From $342.

Palisade 35 Bettington St, Millers Point ℡02/9247 2272, ⓦwww.palisadehotel.com. Circular Quay CityRail/ferry. This magnificent tiled pub, standing like an observatory over Millers Point, was due to re-open shortly, following major refurbishments, as this book went to press. The owners promise that the downstairs bar will maintain its casual, old-fashioned allure, while ten new five-star suites, occupying three floors, with fantastic views of the inner harbour and the Bridge, will be available. A new restaurant on the rooftop with 360° views of Darling and the Bridge was also under construction. Suites expected to cost between $350 and $400.

Shangri-la 176 Cumberland St ℡02/9250 6000, ⓦwww.shangri-la.com. Circular Quay CityRail/ferry. Luxurious five-star hotel on 36 floors with more than five hundred rooms – all with fantastic harbour views from huge windows. The best panorama, however, is from the top floor Horizons Bar (see "Drinking"). Facilities include a gym, indoor pool, spa, sauna and several restaurants and bars. Hefty prices start at $400.

Circular Quay

See map on p.61 for location.

Intercontinental 117 Macquarie St ℡02/9253 9000, ⓦwww.intercontinental.com. Circular Quay CityRail/ferry. The old sandstone Treasury building forms the lower floors of this 31-storey five-star property, with stunning views of the Botanic Gardens, Opera House and harbour. The café/bar is the perfect place for everything from champagne to afternoon tea, and there are three other eateries, plus a pool and gym on the top floor. Parking is $25 per night. Rooms cost from $300 for city view and $375 harbour view.

City centre

See map on p.75 for locations.

Blacket 70 King St ℡02/9279 3030, ⓦwww.blackethotel.com.au. Town Hall or Wynyard CityRail. Stylish four-star small hotel (42 rooms) in a converted nineteenth-century bank, where original features such as the 1850s staircase contrast with the minimalist modern interiors in muted charcoals, blues and off-whites. Suites come with designer kitchenettes and there are also loft suites, two-bedroom apartments and a suite with its own terrace. The basement bar, *Privilege*, is very trendy, and the smart on-site restaurant serves a buffet breakfast ($9). Rates start at $200, rising to $410 for the terrace suite.

Central Park 185 Castlereagh St ℡02/9283 5000, ⓦwww.centralpark.com.au. Town Hall CityRail. A small, chic, 3.5 star hotel in a great location amid the city bustle (near the Town Hall and Hyde Park), though rooms remain quiet. Larger rooms have king-size beds and smart and spacious bathrooms with big bathtub and shower. The smaller standard rooms are still spacious but minus the tub; all come with sofa, desk, a/c, kitchenette with sink, kettle, crockery, fridge and iron. The small lobby café runs daytime only, but there's a 24hr reception. Dynamic pricing $150–210.

Grand 30 Hunter St ☏02/9232 3755, ⓦwww .merivale.com.au. Wynyard CityRail. Very well-sited budget accommodation occupying several floors above one of Sydney's oldest, but not necessarily nicest, pubs (open until 1am Thurs–Sat). Pub and hotel have separate entrances, while rooms (all sharing bathrooms) are brightly painted, with colourful bed covers, fridge, kettle, TV, heating and ceiling fans. From $100.

Travelodge Wynyard 7–9 York St ☏02/9274 1222 or 1300 886 886, ⓦwww.travelodge.com .au. Wynyard CityRail. Central position for both the CBD and The Rocks. This 22-storey, 3.5-star hotel has the usual motel-style rooms but excels with its spacious studios, which come with kitchen area, CD player, voicemail and safe. Small gym; 24hr room service; pleasant café-brasserie. Cheaper weekend packages available. Dynamic pricing, typically rooms $120–190, studios $200–235.

Y Hyde Park 5–11 Wentworth Ave ☏9264 2451 or 1800 994 994, ⓦwww .yhotel.com.au. Museum CityRail. Surprisingly stylish and very comfortable YWCA (both sexes welcome) in a great location just off Oxford Street and near Hyde Park. The huge range of rooms cater to all levels of traveller, from four-bed dorms (made-up beds with towel, no bunks), standard hotel rooms either with shared bathroom or en-suite, and deluxe rooms that come with a pamper pack and plunger coffee. There's no common kitchen, but facilities include a café (7am–1.30pm), a laundry, pay wi-fi throughout, and a light breakfast included. Dorms $35, singles $76, rooms $100, standard en suite $142, deluxe $152.

Haymarket

See map on p.75 for locations.

Aarons 37 Ultimo Rd ☏02/9281 5555 or 1800 101 100, ⓦwww.aaronshotel.com.au. Central

CityRail. A modern makeover doesn't quite hide the ageing fabric of this large, 3-star hotel right in the heart of Chinatown, with its own modern café downstairs. Colourful feature walls add a splash to comfortable en-suite rooms, all with TV, a/c and fridge. The least expensive are internal, small and box-like, with skylight only, while the courtyard rooms are considerably larger and have their own balconies. Parking (around the corner) costs $21. Rooms $135–165, courtyard rooms $190–200.

Capitol Square Capitol Square, corner of Campbell and George sts ☏02/9211 8633, ⓦwww .rydges.com/capitol-square. Central CityRail. Affordable 3.5-star hotel in a National Heritage-listed building right next to the Capitol Theatre and cafés, and across from Chinatown. Small enough not to feel impersonal and run by international chain *Rydges*, so room decor is modern if a little chintzy. In-house restaurant serves Asian and European food. Buffet breakfast. Parking $25. Dynamic pricing, rooms $130–200.

Citigate Central Sydney 169–179 Thomas St ☏02/9281 6888 or 1800 252 588, ⓦwww .mirvachotels.com. Central CityRail. The city's most affordable 4.5-star hotel, in a modern, architecturally interesting 18-storey tower that's fronted by the charming nineteenth-century facade of the site's former hospital. In a quiet street near Central Station, Chinatown and the fringes of Darling Harbour. Modern decor is plain enough to suit all tastes. Heated outdoor swimming pool and spa; terrace garden with BBQ area; 24hr room service. $165–200.

The George 700A George St ☏02/9211 1800 or 1800 679 606, ⓦwww.thegeorge.com.au. Central CityRail. Budget private hotel on three floors opposite Chinatown, with four girls' dorms and one boys' four-share available too. Bargain rooms – some en suite – have a/c, and are clean and acceptable, but staff are unhelpful. Facilities include a small share kitchen/TV room, free broadband and a laundry. Dorms $26–29, single $61, double $78, en suite with TV $105.

Ibis Hotel 384 Pitt St ☏02/8267 3111, ⓦwww.ibishotels.com.au. Central CityRail. Modern, clean-lined, 17-floor budget hotel with tiny, comfortable rooms equipped with shower and flatscreen TVs. Buffet continental breakfast ($18) and off-street parking ($25 per 24hr) plus in-room wi-fi ($18 per 24hr). Dynamic pricing, but expect $110–140.

Pensione Hotel 631–635 George St ☎02/9265 8888 or 1800 885 886, Ⓦwww.pensione.com.au. **Central CityRail.** Stylish 68-room budget hotel opposite Chinatown that couldn't be more centrally located. The building has some well-preserved nineteenth-century features but the style overall is minimalist. Cheaper rooms are smaller, but come with cable TV and a mosaic-tiled bathroom. Facilities include a small guest kitchen and laundry, and internet access throughout. Rooms for around $115, at weekends more like $150.

Darling Harbour, Ultimo and Pyrmont

See map on p.84 for locations.

Glasgow Arms 527 Harris St, Ultimo ☎9211 2354, Ⓦwww.glasgowarmshotel.com.au. **Central CityRail.** Handy for Darling Harbour, and opposite the Powerhouse Museum, this pleasant pub with courtyard dining has good-value accommodation upstairs. Double-glazed windows are handy now the bar closes as late as 3am. The high-ceilinged, en-suite rooms – nicely decorated down to the polished floorboards – are a/c with TV and radio. Light in-room breakfast included. $135.

▲ Intercontinental Hotel

Vulcan Hotel 500 Wattle St, Ultimo ☎02/9211 3283, Ⓦwww.vulcanhotel.com.au. **Haymarket Lightrail or bus #443 or #449 from QVB.** Classy reworking of a heritage-listed 1894 former pub in a quiet part of Ultimo, close to Darling Harbour and Haymarket. The smallish rooms in the old wing (some with bathtubs), and the larger modern rooms, are all decorated in muted tones and come with a/c and fridge; some have kitchenettes. The *Hummingbird* restaurant downstairs serves breakfast (not included); free overnight parking on the street, or off-street at $20. Weekend rates are $10 higher. Old wing $139, new wing $169.

Kings Cross, Potts Point and north Darlinghurst

See map on p.95 for locations.

Altamont 207 Darlinghurst Rd ☎1800 991 110, Ⓦwww.altamont.com.au. Excellent, well-sited small hotel that combines effortless style with modest prices. The casual ambience is aided by the relaxed lobby area with bar and pool table. Rooms come with polished concrete floors, nicely chosen furniture and tiled bathrooms; some have small courtyards. Spacious loft rooms get a king bed and DVD player, plus there's a guest lounge, tiny communal kitchen and spacious rooftop garden overlooking Kings Cross. Late checkouts are okay, there's limited off-street parking ($15 per 24hr) and wi-fi throughout ($20 for your whole stay). Last-minute rates down to $99, but typically $140–150.

Challis Lodge 21–23 Challis Ave, Potts Point ☎02/9358 5422, Ⓦwww.budgethotelssydney.com. **Kings Cross CityRail.** Budget hotel in a wonderful old mansion with polished timber floors throughout. The location is great, on a quiet, tree-filled street a short walk from Woolloomooloo and Kings Cross that's a step away from cool cafés and a couple of trendy restaurants. All rooms have TV, fridge and sink, while the hotel has a laundry but no kitchen. Rooms $70, en suite $80, $110 with balcony.

De Vere 44–46 Macleay St, Potts Point ☎02/9358 1211, Ⓦwww.devere.com.au. **Kings Cross CityRail.** Rooms in this 3.5-star hotel are comfortable if a little drab, though all come with a/c and some have balconies. You can't fault the location, close to cafés, restaurants and transport. Third- and fourth-floor rooms enjoy stunning views of Elizabeth Bay; rooms with kitchenette are also available, and there's a suite with a spa. Breakfast room (buffet-style), guest laundry and 24hr reception. Dynamic pricing but expect standard room $180, with kitchenette $265, spa suite $320.

Highfield Private Hotel 166 Victoria St, Kings Cross ☎1800 285 534, ⓦwww .highfieldhotel.com. Kings Cross CityRail. Very clean and secure 32-room budget hotel, well located amid the hostels on leafy Victoria Street. Rooms are well equipped with fans, heating and sinks, but are smallish and a little dark. Three-bed dorms also available. Tiny kitchen/common room with TV, microwave, kettle and toaster; no laundry but there's one a few doors down. Dorms $25, rooms $65.

Hotel 59 59 Bayswater Rd, Kings Cross ☎02/9360 5900, ⓦwww.hotel59.com.au. Kings Cross CityRail. Little hotel, reminiscent of a pleasant European pension, with a friendly owner and just nine small and very clean if slightly dated a/c rooms. Quiet leafy location, but close to the action; delicious cooked breakfasts (included) are served in a downstairs café. Very popular, so book in advance. One family room (sleeps four) has a small kitchenette and bathtub. $99–121, family room $132.

Kirketon 229 Darlinghurst Rd ☎1800 332 920, ⓦwww.kirketon.com.au. Kings Cross CityRail. Not just location, location, but high in the fashion stakes too, thanks to swish, meticul-ously designed yet understated interiors. Corridor flatscreens showing Keaton and Chaplin movies beckon you to the luxury beyond the chic bar. Beautiful staff, slick service and a stack of great restaurants and cafés on the doorstep. Standard room $169–189, premium $185–235.

Macleay Lodge 71 Macleay St, Potts Point ☎02/9368 0660, ⓦwww.budgethotelssydney .com. Kings Cross CityRail. Don't expect anything fancy from this budget option, but it's perfectly fine and in a fab spot in the midst of Potts Point's café and restaurant scene. Rooms share bathrooms and come with sink, plates, cutlery, kettle, fridge, cheap furniture and TV. The best ones have access to the balcony. Seventh-night-free weekly rates. Single room $60, double $65.

Medusa 267 Darlinghurst Rd, Darlinghurst ☎02/9331 1000, ⓦwww.medusa.com.au. Kings Cross CityRail. This grand Victorian-era terrace houses one of Sydney's swankiest

boutique hotels, close to Oxford St and very popular with gay guests. Interiors by architect Scott Western, known for his innovative use of colour, with cutting-edge furnishings and fixtures. All eighteen guest rooms have luxurious marble bathrooms, sleek kitchenettes, CD and DVD players (plus discs). Deluxe rooms come with chaise longues and access to the stunning interior courtyard. Rooms $310 to $420; specials available.

Quest Potts Point 15 Springfield Ave, Kings Cross ☎02/8988 6999, ⓦwww.questpottspoint .com.au. Recently converted from a chic hotel, just steps from everything Kings Cross has to offer, these 68 serviced apart-ments come in three levels of space and luxury, all with flatscreen TV and broadband, and most with kitchenette. Good on-site restaurant and rooftop terrace. Standard room $165, superior $205.

Woolloomooloo

See map on p.93 for locations.

Blue Sydney 6 Cowper Wharf Rd ☎02/9331 9000, ⓦwww.tajhotels.com/sydney. Bus #311 from Circular Quay CityRail. One of Sydney's hippest luxury boutique hotels, with bags of colourful contemporary style and fantastic service and facilities. On the redeveloped finger wharf, it couldn't be any closer to the water and is a dream choice for a splurge. One end of the wharf is an apartment complex and a marina, and it's lined by great restaurants and cafés. *Blue*'s spacious, striking lobby often hosts art exhibitions, and its lush *Water Bar* is among Sydney's trendiest (see "Drinking"). The rooms have everything including a CD player, big-screen TV with internet, writing desk and coffee-maker; loft rooms have a lounge or work area downstairs and bedroom and bathroom upstairs. There's 24hr room service plus day spa, indoor heated pool and gym. Online packages can save up to 25 percent. Rack rates range from $340 for a rafter room (minimal view), to $500 for a loft suite.

Woolloomooloo Waters Apartment Hotel 88 Dowling St ☎1300 364 200, ⓦwoolloomooloo -waldorf-apartments.com.au. Kings Cross CityRail. Serviced studio, one- and two-bedroom apartments, many with balcony views over Woolloomooloo Bay or the city. Pool, spa and sauna. Light breakfast in the ground-floor *Waldorf Lounge* included. Cheaper weekly rates available. Studio from $170; one-bedroom apartment from $200, two-bedroom from $270.

South Darlinghurst, Paddington and Surry Hills

See map on p.102 for locations.

City Crown Motel 289 Crown St, Surry Hills ☎02/9331 2433 or 1800 358 666, ⊛www .citycrownmotel.com.au. Bus #301–303 from Circular Quay CityRail or Castlereagh St. Fairly typical motel, in a great location. The smart units are a/c with free in-house movies and the bonus of a large balcony looking onto Crown St. One self-catering unit sleeps six. Parking $15, must be pre-booked: enter on Reservoir St. $105–135.

Medina on Crown 359 Crown St, Surry Hills ☎1300 633 462, ⊛www.medina.com.au. Bus #301–303 from Circular Quay CityRail or Castlereagh St, City. The 85 tastefully decorated one- or two-bedroom serviced apartments come with well-equipped kitchen, laundry and balcony, a/c, lounge suite, and dining area. There's also an on-site café (*bills*), gym, sauna, swimming pool. 24hr reception and free covered parking. *Medina* offer various other Sydney apartments; see p.166. Rooms $260, private apartments $340.

Sullivans 21 Oxford St, Paddington ☎02/9361 0211, ⊛www.sullivans.com.au. Bus #378 from Central CityRail; #380 from Circular Quay CityRail. Medium-sized contemporary private hotel in a trendy location, run by staff tuned into the local scene (free guided walking tour of Paddington included). Comfortable, modern en-suite rooms with TV and phones. Free (limited) parking, garden courtyard and swimming pool, in-house movies, free internet, free bicycles, fitness room, laundry, 24hr reception, tour-booking service, and a café open for a huge and delicious breakfast. Rooms $165, family rooms $180.

The Wattle 108 Oxford St, corner of Palmer St, Darlinghurst ☎02/9332 4118, ⊛www .sydneywattle.com. Bus #378 from Central CityRail; #380 from Circular Quay CityRail. Long-running gay-friendly hotel, in the thick of the Oxford St action – with all this so close, there's no need for a bar or breakfast facilities. The a/c, en-suite rooms have seen

better days, but it's clean and spacious, and the rooftop area has spectacular city and harbour views. Weekdays $110, weekends $130; spa suites $165/$200.

Glebe

See map on p.106 for location.

Rooftop Travellers Lodge 146 Glebe Point Rd ☎02/9660 7711, ⊛users.tpg.com.au/glebe146. Bus #431, #433 or #434 from Central CityRail. Reasonably priced motel in the heart of Glebe. On three floors (no lift), the very light, spacious and clean a/c rooms have plain but updated decor. Most have a double and a single bed, a PC and free broadband. The rooftop courtyard has city views and BBQ. Parking included. Dorms $27; rooms $109.

Newtown

See map on p.108 for location.

Australian Sunrise Lodge 485 King St ☎02/9550 4999, ⊛www.australiansunriselodge .com. Newtown City-Rail. Inexpensive and well-managed small, private hotel with guest kitchen, well positioned for King St action but with good security. Single and double rooms, shared bathroom or en suite, come with TV, fridge and toaster. Ground-floor rooms are darker, smaller and cheaper, while the sunny rooms on the top two floors have cute balconies. En-suite family rooms also available. Rooms $99, en suite 119.

The Harbour

Elite Private Hotel 133 Carabella St, Kirribilli ☎02/9929 6365, ⊛www.elitehotel.com.au. Milsons Point CityRail or ferry to Kirribilli Wharf. Bright place surrounded by plants offering good rooms with sink, TV, fridge and kettle. Most share bathrooms, some more expensive ones have a harbour view. Small communal cooking facility but no laundry; quaint garden courtyard. Cheaper weekly rates. $66–88.

North Shore Hotel 310 Miller St, North Sydney ☎02/9955 1012, ⊛www.smallanduniquehotels .com. Bus #207 or #208 from Clarence St, City and North Sydney City Rail. Two-storey mansion with balconies in a quiet location opposite St Leonards Park, 10min walk or a short bus ride from cafés and restaurants.

The following places rent out **apartments**, generally for a minimum of a week with rates decreasing rapidly as your stay lengthens. All are completely furnished and equipped, though only where we explicitly say so are they serviced, and a few require guests to provide linen and towels: check first. Expect to pay $400–800 per week, depending on the size and the season. In addition, we've listed several **hotels** that offer serviced apartments or self-catering studios by the night in our "Hotels" section – see *Bondi Serviced Apartments* (p.166), *Coogee Sands Hotel & Apartments* (p.167), *City Crown Motel* (p.162), *De Vere* (p.163), *Hotel 59* (p.164) and *Quest Potts Point* (p.164). All **hostels** also have communal self-catering facilities – see p.162 for details – while on-site vans and cabins at caravan parks are another affordable option (see box, p.171).

Enochs Holiday Flats 25 Wallis Parade, Bondi ☎02/9388 1477. Bus #380 or #389 from Bondi Junction CityRail. One-, two- or three-bedroom apartments, all close to Bondi Beach, sleeping four to six people: $400–800 weekly, depending on the size, season and length of stay.

Medina Apartment Hotels ☎02/9356 1000 or 1300 633 462, ⓦwww.medina.com.au. Upmarket studio or one-, two- and three-bedroom serviced apartments with resident managers and reception in ten salubrious locales around Sydney – Lee Street near Central Station, Kent Street and Martin Place in the CBD, King Street Wharf at Darling Harbour, Surry Hills, Double Bay and others. All include undercover parking. From $150 per night.

Park Beachside Apartments 190 Arden St, Coogee ☎02/9315 7777, ⓦwww .parkbeachside.com.au. Bus #372 from Central CityRail or #373 or #374 from Circular

En-suite rooms or family studios sleeping four, all with a/c, TV, fridge, hot drinks and telephone. Shared kitchen and laundry; breakfast available. $85–115.

Stamford Plaza Double Bay 33 Cross St, Double Bay ☎02/9362 4455, ⓦwww.stamford.com.au. Ferry to Double Bay Wharf. See map, p.118. Deluxe hotel in a great spot amid the wealthy village atmosphere of Double Bay, surrounded by posh fashion shops, sidewalk cafés and restaurants. Georgian antiques and artworks fill the halls and stairways, while fantastic harbour views dazzle from deluxe rooms and a gorgeous rooftop pool deck – the height of luxury. $180–665.

Watsons Bay Hotel 1 Military Rd, Watsons Bay ☎02/9337 5444, ⓦwww.watsonsbayhotel.com .au. Ferry to Watsons Bay Wharf. If money is not an issue, this is for you. Tasteful luxury suites provide floor-to-ceiling views across a shimmering harbour, punctured by bush-clad shoreline peninsulas and crowned, in the distance, by the city's CBD. Easy access to *Doyles* restaurant, Watsons Bay Wharf, Camp Cove, South Head and the Gap. Harbour views start from $370. $210–605.

Bondi

See map on p.132 for locations.

Bondi Serviced Apartments 212 Bondi Rd, Bondi ☎02/8837 8000 or 1300 364 200, ⓦwww.bondi-serviced-apartments.com.au. Bus #380 from Bondi Junction CityRail. Good-value serviced motel studio apartments, 10min walk to either Bondi Junction or Bondi Beach, but in the thick of the local shops and on bus routes. All units are a/c, have clean modern furniture, TV, phone, kitchen and come with sea-view balconies; some have been stylishly decorated, while some of the cheaper older-style apartments lack views. The rooftop pool has far-off ocean views. Parking included; cheaper weekly rates. From $105.

Swiss-Grand Corner of Campbell Parade and Beach Rd, Bondi Beach ☎02/9365 5666, ⓦwww.swissgrand.com.au. Bus #380 from Bondi Junction CityRail. Five-storey, 4.5-star hotel opposite the beach, which looks tacky from the outside – like a giant wedding cake – but is luxurious within. Some rooms have great ocean views. Health club, gym, rooftop and indoor pools, two bars and restaurants, free parking.

Quay CityRail. Several spacious, well-set-up studio and one-, two- and three-bedroom apartments near the beach, all fully furnished with laundry and linen. From $700 per week for the smaller units, $1000 per week for the larger properties; cheaper quarterly leases available.

Raine and Horne 160 Pacific Highway, North Sydney ℡02/9925 1200, ⓦwww .accommodationinsydney.com. Fully furnished modern executive apartments fitted out by interior designers, on the leafy North Shore: North Sydney, Kirribilli, Milsons Point and McMahons Point. All have TV, DVD, CD player, telephone; several have spas, pools or gyms. Rates are much cheaper if you stay for at least a month but the one-off cleaning fee is pricey: $150 for studios and one-bedders, $225–295 for larger apartments. Studios from $550 per week, one-bed from $675, two-bed from $800, three-bed from $1500.

Sydney City Centre Furnished Apartments 7 Elizabeth St, near Martin Place ℡02/9233 6677, ⓦwww.accommodationsydneycity.com.au. Martin Place CityRail. Fully equipped open-plan studio apartments sleeping up to three; kitchenette, laundry, TV, DVD and fans; basic, but in an excellent location. A good choice for long-stayers, as the minimum rental is sixteen weeks; $300 weekly, streetview $350.

Ultimate Apartments 59 O'Brien Street, Bondi ℡02/9365 7969, ⓦwww.apartments bondibeach.com. Bus #380 or #389 from Bondi Junction CityRail stops right outside. Fully furnished studio apartments (with fairly small kitchens) 700m from the beach, with weekly cleaning, swimming pool and Foxtel TV. No groups. $100–110 per night for stays over two weeks; $110–155 in Dec, Jan & Feb.

Sea-view rooms start around $310, though cheaper packages are available from $200.

Coogee

See map on p.137 for locations.

Coogee Bay Boutique Hotel 9 Vicar St ℡02/9665 0000, ⓦwww.coogeebayhotel.com.au. Bus #372 from Central CityRail, #373 or #374 from Circular Quay CityRail. New hotel attached to the rear of the older, sprawling *Coogee Bay Hotel*. Rooms – all with balconies, half with ocean views – look like something from *Vogue Interior*; luxurious touches include marble-floored bathroom and minibars. Cheaper "heritage wing" rooms in the old hotel are noisy at weekends but just as stylish; several offer splendid water views. Parking included and there's a 24hr reception. The pub has an excellent brasserie, several bars and a nightclub. Heritage rooms $140, boutique rooms $250–290.

Coogee Sands Hotel & Apartments 161 Dolphin St ℡02/9665 8588, ⓦwww.coogeesands.com.au. Bus #372 from Central CityRail, #373 or #374 from Circular Quay CityRail. Very pleasant, spacious self-catering studios and one-bedroom apartments, some with beach

views. Studios $180, ocean-view studios $240, apartments $220–280.

Manly

See map on p.139 for locations.

Manly Pacific Sydney 55 North Steyne, Manly ℡02/9977 7666, ⓦwww.accorhotels.com. Ferry to Manly Wharf. Beachfront, multi-storey, 4-star hotel with 24hr reception, room service, spa, sauna, gym and heated rooftop pool. You pay for it all, and more for an ocean view, which is spectacular. Rooms $200, with sea view $300, suites $300–660.

Q Station Retreat North Head, Manly ℡02/9976 6220, ⓦwww.qstation.com.au. Ferry to Manly Wharf. Stylishly modernized rooms in a wonderfully peaceful former quarantine station where first- and second-class passengers might once have been obliged to spend a month or more. Most rooms have harbour views, best seen from wicker chairs on the broad verandas. Those in the old First Class precinct enjoy the best views of all, though you'll need to don a robe and wander along the veranda to reach your separate personal bathroom. Private bathroom $290, en suite $350.

B&Bs and guesthouses

Guesthouses (and **B&Bs**, which are usually cheaper) are often pleasant, renovated old houses. Prices vary around $115–190 per room for those that share bathrooms (and possibly kitchen facilities), or $145–330 for en-suite rooms. B&Bs in the South Darlinghurst and Surry Hills area tend to be particularly gay-oriented or gay-friendly.

The Rocks

See map on p.52 for locations.

Bed & Breakfast Sydney Harbour 140–142 Cumberland St ☏02/9247 1130, ⓦwww.bedandbreakfastsydney.com. Circular Quay CityRail. Charming brick building, close to the start of the Harbour Bridge, which began life as a boarding house in 1901, and is now a friendly, local-family-run, nine-bedroom B&B. The whole place is furnished in period style from Australian hardwood timber recycled from a Colonial courthouse, with original features including the cedar doors and staircase. Every room is different; one has a kitchenette and all have top-of-the-range mattresses. The cooked breakfast can be eaten in the sitting room, but most guests prefer to hang out in the gorgeous, peaceful garden courtyard, kept warm by braziers in winter. Thick walls and double insulated windows keep out bridge-traffic noise. $155–249

The Russell 143A George St ☏02/9241 3543, ⓦwww.therussell.com.au. Circular Quay CityRail/ferry. Charming, small National Trust-listed hotel with Colonial-style decor. The small rooms that share bathrooms are very popular, and great value for the area, while the best of the en-suite rooms enjoy views of the Quay or access a private interior courtyard. Rooftop garden, sitting room (with a library of local books), and a downstairs restaurant serving complementary continental breakfast. Shared bathroom $150–190, en suite $245–290.

Kings Cross, Potts Point and north Darlinghurst

See map on p.95 for locations.

The Chelsea 49 Womerah Ave, Darlinghurst ☏02/9380 5994, ⓦwww.chelsea.citysearch .com.au. Kings Cross CityRail. In a tastefully decorated terraced house in the leafy residential backstreets of Darlinghurst, this guesthouse is in a quiet location but not far from the action. Rooms are either in contemporary or French Provincial style; most come with queen-sized beds, but some deluxe ones, including a couple of suites have king-sized beds; singles share bathrooms but have sinks. All rooms have fridge, kettle and TV, and rates include a light courtyard breakfast. Single $94, standard double $143, deluxe $155, suites $165–195.

Simpsons of Potts Point 8 Challis Ave, Potts Point ☏02/9356 2199, ⓦwww .simpsonshotel.com.au. Kings Cross CityRail. Small, beautifully restored personal hotel, designed in 1892 for a parliamentarian. Carpeted and quiet, the twelve comfortable rooms, all en suite, are elegantly furnished with antiques and have a/c, fridges and irons. A couple have bathtubs, there's free wi-fi throughout, and breakfast (included) is served in a sunny conservatory. $235, spa suite $330.

Victoria Court 122 Victoria St, Potts Point ☏02/9357 3200, ⓦwww.victoriacourt .com.au. Kings Cross CityRail. Boutique hotel in two interlinked Victorian terraced houses; very tasteful and quiet, if overly floral. En-suite rooms with all mod cons, some with balconies; buffet breakfast included, served in the conservatory. Secure parking a bonus. Dynamic pricing but generally rooms from $150, deluxe $250.

Woollahra

See map on p.95 for location.

Hughenden 14 Queen St ☏02/9363 4863, ⓦwww.hughendenhotel.com.au. Bus #378 from Central CityRail; #380 from Circular Quay CityRail. Old-fashioned Victorian-era guesthouse, built in 1876, decorated to retain its nineteenth-century charm, including such features as servants' bells and black marble fireplaces. Situated opposite Centennial Park and close to the *Paddington*. Pet-friendly. Weekday $160, weekend 190, suites $280–330, full breakfast included.

South Darlinghurst and Surry Hills

See map on p.102 for locations.

Brickfield Hill B&B Inn 403 Riley St, Surry Hills ☏02/9211 4886, ⓦwww.brickfieldhill.com.au. Central CityRail or bus #301 from Circular Quay CityRail. In a terraced house, 5min walk from Oxford St and convenient for Surry Hills' diverse cafés, restaurants and bars, this ornate four-storey terrace recalls a bygone Victorian era, with antique-style furnished rooms, window drapes, chandelier lights and either four-poster or half-tester beds. Three rooms share a bathroom, and one is en suite. Free wi-fi, optional breakfast for $15. Rooms $115, en suite $145.

Governors on Fitzroy 64 Fitzroy St, Surry Hills ☏02/9331 4652, ⓦwww.governors.com.au. Bus #378 from Central CityRail; #380 from Circular Quay CityRail. Long-established gay B&B in a restored Victorian terrace a few blocks from Oxford St. The three rooms, each with its own distinct style, share two bathrooms but have their own sinks. A full cooked breakfast is served in the dining room or the garden courtyard. Guests – mostly men – can also meet and mingle in the spa. $135.

Oasis on Flinders 48 Flinders St, Darlinghurst ☏02/9331 8791, ⓦwww.oasisonflinders.com.au. Bus #397–399 from Circular Quay CityRail. Small men-only nudist B&B retreat in a three-storey terraced house. Two rooms share a bathroom, the other is en suite; all have ceiling fans, TV and video. Spa and sun deck in the courtyard. Continental help-yourself-breakfast included. Very civilized noon checkout time. Room $120, en suite $150.

Glebe

See map on p.106 for locations.

Alishan International Guesthouse 100 Glebe Point Rd ☏02/9566 4048, ⓦwww.alishan.com.au. Bus #431, #433 or #434 from Central CityRail. Restored Victorian mansion in a handy spot at the bottom of Glebe Point Rd. Rather bland but very clean en suite, motel-style rooms plus one furnished in Japanese fashion (minus an actual futon), plus four- and six-bed dorms (though this is a peaceful, not a party, option). Facilities include a kitchen, airy common room, garden patio and BBQ area. Wi-fi available. A very spacious family room sleeps six, cots are available and children are most welcome. Dorms $26–33, rooms $99–115.

Tricketts Bed and Breakfast 270 Glebe Point Rd ☏02/9552 1141, ⓦwww.tricketts.com.au. Bus #431, #433 or #434 from Central CityRail. Luxury B&B in an 1880s mansion. Rooms – en suite – are furnished with antiques and Persian rugs, and the lounge, complete with a billiard table and leather armchairs, was originally a small ballroom. A self-contained one-bedroom garden apartment has its own veranda. Delicious, generous and sociable breakfast. $198–245.

The Harbour

Cremorne Point Manor 6 Cremorne Rd, Cremorne Point ☏02/9953 7899, ⓦwww.cremornepointmanor.com.au. Ferry to Cremorne Point Wharf. Huge restored Federation-style villa, with slightly incongruous bright-blue facade. Nearly all the rooms are beautifully appointed en-suite doubles, with TV, fridge, kettle and a fan, though a few small singles simply have their own toilet and sink. Pricier rooms have harbour views as does the guest balcony. Communal kitchen and a laundry. Rates include continental breakfast. Reception sells bus and ferry passes and books tours. Singles from $87, doubles $185–295.

Glenferrie Lodge 12A Carabella St, Kirribilli ☏02/9955 1685, ⓦwww.glenferrielodge.com. Milsons Point CityRail or ferry to Kirribilli Wharf. Made-over Kirribilli mansion (built 1892), clean, light and secure with 24hr reception. Rates include a continental breakfast whether you're in a three-share dorm, cramped single, double or family room; all share bathrooms. Some pricier rooms have their own balconies, offering glimpses of the harbour; guests can also hang out in the garden and on the guest verandas. Facilities include a TV lounge, laundry and dining room with free tea and coffee. Dorms $45, rooms $129–149.

Bondi

See map on p.132 for location.

Ravesi's Corner of Campbell Parade and Hall St ☏02/9365 4422, ⓦwww.ravesis.com.au. Bus #380 or #389 from Bondi Junction CityRail. The first-floor restaurant and most rooms at this boutique hotel have glorious ocean views. The facade is pure 1914, but interiors are totally modern; well thought-out rooms (twelve in all) have minimalist decor and most of those on the second floor have French windows opening onto small balconies; split-level and penthouse suites have spacious ones. Large, popular bar at ground level. Standard $240, beachfront $325.

Coogee

See map on p.137 for location.

Dive 234 Arden St, Coogee Beach ☎02/9665 5538, 🅦www.thedivehotel.com. Bus #372 from Central CityRail, #373 or #374 from Circular Quay CityRail. Far from living down to its name, this is a wonderful 16-room hotel in a renovated former boarding house opposite the beach. In the lovely interior, clean modern lines complement original Art Nouveau tiling and high, decorative-plaster ceilings, and a pleasant, bamboo-fringed courtyard (with discreet guest laundry) opens out from a spacious breakfast room for buffet breakfasts (included). Two larger rooms at the front have splendid ocean views; one at the back has its own balcony. All have funky little bathrooms, CD players, cable TV, queen-size

▲ Dive

beds and a handy kitchenette with microwave and crockery. Free internet and wi-fi. Standard $170, ocean view $250.

Manly

See map on p.139 for location.

Periwinkle Guesthouse 18–19 East Esplanade ☎02/9977 4668, 🅦www .periwinkle.citysearch.com.au. Ferry to Manly Wharf. Pleasant 18-room B&B in a charming, restored 1895 villa on Manly Cove. Close to the ferry, shops and harbour, and a perfect base for swimming, sailing or just watching the lorikeets. All rooms, furnished in Colonial style, have fridge, fans, and electric blankets, some have big bathtubs; larger family rooms are available. Guest kitchen, laundry, courtyard with BBQ and car park. Shared-bath single $112, double $137; en suites from $167.

Northern beaches

See map on p.131 for locations.

Barrenjoey House 1108 Barrenjoey Rd, opposite Palm Beach Wharf ☎ 02/9974 4001, 🅦www.barrenjoeyhouse.com.au. Simple but elegant rooms in a lovely old building above the restaurant of the same name. Most rooms get Pittwater views, and a buffet continental breakfast is served in the lounge. Two-night minimum on summer weekends. Shared bathroom $180, en suite $220.
Palm Beach B&B 122 Pacific Palm Rd, Palm Beach ☎02/9974 1608, 🅦www.palmbeachbandb .com.au. Bus #L90 from Central CityRail or Wynyard CityRail. Incredibly friendly, slightly quirky B&B (antique cars are scattered about the front lawn), perched on a hilltop in a sought-after street. All rooms have balconies and water views of either Pittwater or the ocean, and the emphasis is on relaxing and unwinding. Not all the four simply furnished rooms are en suite. $185–205.

Hostels

All **hostels** have a laundry, kitchen, and common room with TV unless stated otherwise. Most provide sheets and blankets, so sleeping bags are increasingly unnecessary. Office hours are generally restricted, typically 8am–noon and 4.30–6pm, so call to arrange an arrival time. The contiguous areas of **Kings Cross** and **Potts Point** hold a heavy concentration of hostels. Avoid the dodgy places that spring up overnight on Darlinghurst Road; nearby leafy Victoria

Campsites around Sydney

Several well-equipped **caravan parks** are scattered around Sydney, where you can either **camp** or stay in a self-catering **van** or **cabin** (both of which usually require guests to supply their own bed linen). The four closest to the centre are listed below. Typical peak-season camping rates are $30–34 for two people in an unpowered site, $36–45 for a powered site.

Lakeside Holiday Park Lake Park Rd, Narrabeen ☎1800 008 845, ⊛www .sydneylakeside.com.au. Bus #L90 from Wynyard CityRail then 10min walk. See map, p.131. Spacious campground in a great spot by Narrabeen Lakes, 26km north of the city on Sydney's northern beaches. Camp kitchens and coin-operated gas barbecues, and a supermarket 10min walk away. Powered sites ($45), campervan sites with private bathroom ($55), and modern two-bedroom villas ($210–240); all are en suite, with linen included. Prices increase 20 percent on peak holiday weekends.

Cockatoo Island Camping Cockatoo Island, Sydney Harbour ☎02/8898 9774, ⊛camp@cockatooisland.gov.au. Accessed by ferry on the Parramatta River Service or Woolwich service. See map, p.114. One of the world's most uniquely sited campgrounds, right in the middle of Sydney Harbour, affording magnificent views of the city across the water. Kitchen, BBQs, fridges, solar-powered showers and access to the island's café. An all-in package including tent, mattresses, chairs and a lantern costs $75; unpowered sites $45.

Lane Cove River Tourist Park Plassey Rd, North Ryde ☎02/9888 9133, ⊛www .lanecoverivertouristpark.com.au. Train to Chatswood then bus #545. See map, p.147. Wonderful bush location beside Lane Cove National Park, right on the river, 14km northwest of the city in Sydney's northern suburbs. Great facilities include a bush kitchen (with fridge), TV room, wi-fi and swimming pool. Campsites, $34 without power, $36 with; en-suite cabins $121.

Sheralee Tourist Caravan Park 88 Bryant St, Rockdale, 13km south of the city ☎02/9567 7161. Train to Rockdale station then 10min walk. See map, p.147. Small basic park, close to Sydney Airport and the city, and six blocks from Botany Bay, with good, clean facilities and friendly staff. Campsites $30–35, Caravans $45, Cabins $60.

Street and the backstreets of Potts Point offer a more pleasant atmosphere. **Glebe** is a laid-back, inner-city locale, while the beachside hostels at **Bondi**, **Coogee** and **Manly** provide immediate access to a great Aussie beach lifestyle. If you're planning to stay a few weeks, test out a few of these areas before settling in one place – you might be surprised at what you find. Most prices remain fairly stable throughout the year, though hostels often raise their prices by around 25 percent through December and January, and frequently offer winter discounts such as four nights for the price of three. Private rooms cost between $65 and $100 for a shared bath, or $90–115 for an en suite, while dorm beds usually cost $28, though rates can range from $22 to $40. *Alishan Guesthouse* (p.169), *Glenferrie Lodge* (p.169) and *Highfield Private Hotel* (p.164) also offer dorm beds.

The Rocks

See map on p.52 for location.

Sydney Harbour YHA 106–128 Cumberland St, The Rocks ☎02/9261 1111, ⊛www .sydneyharbouryha.com.au. The only budget accommodation in The Rocks, this 106-bedroom YHA should be open by the time you read this – check the website – and will double as an innovative Archaeology Education Centre known as the Big Dig. The structure is suspended over early nineteenth-century structural remains (where 750,000 artefacts have been found) uncovered during the 1990s.

City centre

See map on p.75 for location.

base backpackers 477 Kent St ☎02/9267 7718 or 1800 24 BASE, ⓦwww .basebackpackers.com. Town Hall CityRail. Huge, modern 360-bed hostel, in a good location near the Town Hall, and well set up with two TV rooms, laundry and internet, plus a renovated kitchen. Globetrotting women can enjoy their "Sanctuary", a women-only section featuring all the comforts of home, including hairdryers in the bathrooms, Aveda haircare products and feather pillows. Well-furnished a/c rooms and dorms, (four-, six-, eight- and ten-bed), all sharing bathrooms. Dorms $26–34, rooms $89.

Haymarket

See map on p.75 for locations.

BIG 212 Elizabeth St ☎1800 212 244, ⓦwww.bighostel.com. Central CityRail. Stylish 155-bed boutique hostel that's just a 5–10min walk from Central Station, Chinatown or Oxford Street. Sunny rooms have extra-thick glass, good curtains and contemporary decor in natural colours; all are a/c with TV and video, but lack lamps and phones. The ground-floor lobby doubles as the common area, with designer lounges and a high-tech guest kitchen where the free buffet continental breakfast is served. There's a great roof-terrace BBQ area, guest laundry, a couple of free bikes, no charge for luggage storage, free wi-fi throughout plus a couple of free terminals. Six- and eight-bed dorms $28–29, en suite 4-shares $32, en-suite rooms with DVD $89–96.

Maze Backpackers 417 Pitt St ☎02/9211 5115, ⓦwww.mazebackpackers.com. Central CityRail. With charming original 1908 features, this huge hostel is a good choice if you're after one of their many tiny single rooms. The atmosphere is sociable and all rooms and dorms (four- to eight-bed) have ceiling fans, but stark fluorescent lighting and shared bathrooms. The kitchens are small and lack facilities, but there are all sorts of drink discounts and offers (sometimes including airport transfers if you stay 3 or more nights). 24hr reception. Dorms $26–28, single rooms $55, doubles $72.

Nomads Westend 412 Pitt St ☎02/9211 4588 or 1800 013 186, ⓦwww.westendbackpackers.com. Central CityRail. Bright, contemporary hostel in a large renovated hotel close to Central Station and Chinatown. Common areas are spick-and-span, with funky furniture and there's a big modern kitchen and dining area, and a pool table. The young, local, clued-up staff organize tours and nights out. All dorms (4- and 6-beds) have bathrooms, except for the one enormous 28-bed affair affectionately known as "the Church" for its stained-glass window. Many rooms have a/c: request these in summer, as there are no fans. Travel centre and internet café downstairs. 24hr reception. Big dorm $24, 4- and 6-shares $29–31, rooms $82, en suite $87.

Railway Square YHA 8–10 Lee St, corner of Upper Carriage Lane ☎02/9281 9666, ⓔrailway@yhansw.org.au. Central CityRail. It's all about location, and this modern stylishly designed hostel in a historic 1904 industrial building is literally next to the tracks of Central Station – some dorm rooms are in actual train carriages and you can look out over the early-morning commuters. A swimming pool/spa, internet café and kiosk serving light meals, travel centre, excellent noticeboards and planned activities, funky indoor and outdoor common areas and heated floors in the bathrooms make it all very comfortable. Dorms $34–40, rooms $98, en suite $108.

Sydney Central YHA 11–23 Rawson Place at Pitt St, opposite Central Station ☎02/9281 9111, ⓔsydcentral@yhansw.org.au. Central CityRail. Very successful YHA, in a central listed building that's been transformed into a huge and snazzy hostel, where all the beds (more than 550) are almost always full. Hotel-like facilities but very sociable. Spacious four- and six-bed dorms and twins sharing bathrooms or en-suite twins and doubles. Wide range of amenities, including employment desk, travel agency, rooftop pool, sauna, BBQ area and nightly movies. 24hr reception. Licensed bistro plus the cute, popular *Scu Bar* (see p.206) in the basement. Some parking ($20). Maximum stay 28 days. For longer stays use the YHA at Glebe. Dorms $35–40, standard twins $100, en-suite twins and doubles $114.

wake up! 509 Pitt St, opposite Railway Square ☎02/9288 7888, ⓦwww.wakeup .com.au. Central CityRail. The catchy name goes perfectly with the oh-so-trendy atmosphere of this mega-backpackers' complex (more than 500 beds). The vibrant interior sits inside a characterful, century-old corner building. Highly styled, right down to the black-clad staff in the huge foyer with its banks of internet terminals and travel/jobs desk. Fairly plain rooms are light-filled and well furnished; only nine doubles are en suite. Dorms (4-, 6-, 8- and 10-bed) have lockers, there's a laundry on every floor and security is very good. Facilities include a streetside café and an underground late-closing bar and eatery serving $7 steak dinners. The best feature is the huge modern kitchen, on a corner with gigantic windows overlooking busy Railway Square. Pay wi-fi throughout. Dorms $28–36, rooms $98, en suite $108.

Kings Cross, Potts Point and East Sydney

See map on p.95 for locations.

Backpackers Headquarters 79 Bayswater Rd, Kings Cross ☎02/9331 6180, ⓦwww .headquartershostel.com.au. Kings Cross CityRail. In a quieter position close to Rushcutters Bay, this hostel is well run but showing some cracks around the edges. No doubles, but plenty of large, bright, partitioned dorms for six or ten people, with firm mattresses, fans, heaters and mirrors. Usual amenities plus big-screen TV in the lounge, sun deck and BBQ area on the rooftop. Excellent security, with good prospects for organizing short-term work. Dorms $22.

Blue Parrot Backpackers 87 Macleay St, Potts Point ☎02/9356 4888, ⓦwww .blueparrot.com.au. Kings Cross CityRail. This family-run hostel, in a great position in the trendy (and quieter) part of Potts Point, occupies a sunny, airy and brightly painted mansion. One appealing feature is the huge courtyard garden out back with wooden furniture and big shady trees, looking onto a heritage building, though evening curfews have been introduced to give the neighbours a break. Mostly six- and eight-bed dorms, plus a few shared-bath doubles. Common room has cable TV, gas fire and free internet and wi-fi. Dorms $28–32, rooms $90.

Eva's Backpackers 6–8 Orwell St, Potts Point ☎02/9358 2185, or 1800 802 517, ⓦwww.evasbackpackers.com.au. Kings Cross CityRail. It's worth paying the extra couple of dollars to stay at this excellent family-run hostel away from Darlinghurst Road's clamour. Colourful and clean rooms and common areas. Four-, six- and ten-bed dorms; four-shares have bathrooms. Peaceful rooftop garden with table umbrellas, greenery,

BBQ area and fantastic views over the Domain. The street-level guest kitchen/dining room, feels like a café and is conducive to socializing, though this isn't a "party" hostel. Free internet and wi-fi throughout. Dorms $30–36, shared-bath rooms $80–90.

Jolly Swagman 27 Orwell St, Kings Cross ☎02/9358 6400, ⓦwww.jollyswagman.com.au. Kings Cross CityRail. Vibrant, long-established hostel geared towards the louder, livelier backpacker. Organized social events range from sports to pub crawls; in-house travel centre, good notice boards and work connections. Along with the usual communal facilities, every room has its own fridge and lockers; there are also four- to six-bed dorms. Cheap licensed café with internet access out front. 24hr reception. Dorms $30, rooms $80.

Kanga House 141 Victoria St, Kings Cross ☎02/9357 7897, ⓦwww.kangahouse.com. au. Kings Cross CityRail. On leafy Victoria St, this terraced-house hostel may have fairly ordinary facilities – though it's regularly repainted – but the city views from the back rooms are tremendous, taking in the bridge and Opera House. Besides free wi-fi and internet, there's a free continental breakfast, free airport pickups if you stay three nights and free Sunday BBQ in the sunny courtyard. Staff are friendly, the atmosphere is laid-back and it's still among the cheapest hostels in the Cross. Dorms are four-, six- and eight-bed and doubles have sink, TV, microwave and fridge. Dorms $22–25, rooms $63–70.

The Original Backpackers Lodge 160–162 Victoria St, Kings Cross ☎02/9356 3232 or 1800 807 130, ⓦwww.originalbackpackers.com. au. Kings Cross CityRail. In a spacious Victorian mansion with ornate ceilings, chandeliers and artwork throughout, this upscale hostel tends to have a quieter clientele. A large kitchen and café-style courtyard back onto clean lounge and common areas with comfy chairs, internet and cable TV. All rooms have TV and fridge, and security lockers and a laundry are available at the 24hr reception. A new wing holds small but stylish en-suite doubles with TV/DVD. Dorms (6-, 8- or 10-bed) $28, rooms $75, en suite $90.

The Pink House 6–8 Barncleuth Square, Kings Cross ☎02/9358 1689 or 1800 806 385, ⓦwww.pinkhouse.com.au. Kings Cross CityRail. Attractive pair of converted mansions with big dorms – up to ten-bed – and a few doubles, some with en-suite sink and shower but none with toilet. All the expected amenities plus cable TV in the common room, cheap wi-fi and garden courtyards with BBQ. Friendly and very peaceful but also close to the action across the strip. Dorms $24–28, rooms $75, en suite $95.

The Wood Duck Inn 49 William St, East Sydney ☎1800 110 025, ⦿www .woodduckinn.com.au. Homely 57-bed hostel run by two switched-on brothers in a great spot right near the Australian Museum and Hyde Park. The dingy and seemingly endless flights of concrete steps are off-putting, but you emerge onto a sunny rooftop, the nerve centre of the hostel, with fantastic park and city views. Here you'll find the all-day reception-cum-bar, BBQ, a small but functional kitchen (plenty of fridge space), laundry and a TV/dining room with quirky surfboard tabletops. Accommodation is on the floors below; expect polished wood floors, citrus-coloured walls and high ceilings. Spacious, clean dorms (mostly 4- and 6-bed) have fans, good mattresses and cage lockers under the bunks. Lots of activities, including free lifts to the beach. Dorms $24.

Glebe

See map on p.106 for locations.

Glebe Point YHA 262 Glebe Point Rd ☎02/9692 8418, ⓔglebe@yhansw.org.au. Bus #431, #433 or #434 from Central CityRail. Reliable YHA standard hostel where helpful staff organize lots of activities. Sleeps just over 150, in a mix of private rooms – no en suites – as well as four- and five-bed dorms. All the usual facilities plus a pool table, luggage storage and roof terrace with city views. Dorms $26–33.50, rooms $68.

Glebe Village Backpackers 256 Glebe Point Rd ☎02/9660 8133 or 1800 801 983, ⦿www.glebevillage.com Bus #431, #433 or #434 from Central CityRail. Three large old houses with a mellow, sociable atmosphere, more akin to that of a guesthouse than a hostel – the generally laid-back guests socialize in the leafy street-side fairy-lit garden. Free Sunday BBQ's, weekend pancake breakfasts, and wine and cheese Friday evenings sweeten the deal. Staffed by young locals who know what's going on around town. Doubles and twins plus four-, six-, ten- or twelve-bed dorms. Dorms $28–30, rooms $90.

Newtown

See map on p.108 for location.

Billabong Gardens 5–11 Egan St, off King St ☎02/9550 3236, ⦿www.billabonggardens .au. Newtown CityRail. In a quiet street but close to the action, this long-running purpose-built hostel is arranged around a peaceful inner courtyard with swimming pool; though there's competition these days, it's still the best hostel in Newtown, with excellent communal facilities. It offers clean dorms (4- to 6-bed; most with bathrooms), single ($50), twin, double and motel-style en suites with free wireless and free internet in the lounge. Parking is limited and metered in Newtown, so there's a daily charge for the popular undercover car park. Dorms $25–27, rooms $70, en suite $90.

Bondi

See map on p.132 for locations.

Bondi Beachouse YHA 63 Fletcher St ☎02/9365 2088, ⓔbondi@bondibeachouse.com.au. Bus #380 from Bondi Junction CityRail. Converted from a former student boarding house, this beach YHA is closer to Tamarama Beach than Bondi, but benefits from being slightly removed from the latter's often overly frenetic atmosphere. The cafés, restaurants and shops of Bondi Rd are close by. Well run and fully equipped. Sunny internal courtyard with BBQ, and a rooftop deck with fabulous ocean views. Spacious high-ceilinged dorms (4-, 6- and 8-bed, with lockers); all rooms have ceiling fans, some are en suite, with fridges and kettles. Small, but well-equipped kitchen, free use of surfboards and bodyboards. Regular free surfing talks. Book ahead to get a beach-view room, for same price. Dorms $32, rooms $80, en suite $90.

Noah's Backpackers 2 Campbell Parade, Bondi Beach ☎02/9365 7100 or 1800 226 662, ⦿www .noahsbondibeach.com. Bus #380 from Bondi Junction CityRail. Huge hostel opposite the beach. Fantastic ocean views from the rooftop deck with a BBQ area and kitchen conveniently on hand. Beach-view rooms with sink, TV, fridge, fan and chair. Four-, six- and eight-bed dorms have sinks and lockers (bring own lock). Clean and well run but with cramped bathrooms. On-site bar serving bargain meals, TV room and pool table. Excellent security. Dorms $24–27, rooms $60, beach-view $70.

Coogee

See map on p.137 for locations.

Coogee Beachside 178 Coogee Bay Rd, Coogee ☎02/9315 8511 or 1800/013 460, ⓦwww .sydneybeachside.com.au. Bus #372 from Central CityRail, #373 or #374 from Circular Quay CityRail. Airy old two-storey house, pleasantly renovated, with wooden floors and managed in conjunction with *Wizard of Oz*, next door. All rooms and four- and six-bed dorms come with TV, in-house videos and fans but share bathrooms. Doubles and family rooms also have fridge. There's a small well-equipped kitchen but you have to go next door to use the common room, so everyone hangs out in the big, sunny back garden. Up the hill from the beach but handy for shops and the supermarket. Dorms $30, rooms $90.

Wizard of Oz Backpackers 172 Coogee Bay Rd, Coogee ☎02/9315 7876, ⓦwww .wizardofoz.com.au. Bus #372 from Central City-Rail, #373 or #374 from Circular Quay CityRail. Top-class hostel run (along with *Coogee Beachside*) by a friendly local couple in a big and beautiful Californian-style house with a huge veranda and polished wooden floors. Spacious, vibrantly painted dorms with ceiling fans, and some well-set-up doubles. TV/video room, dining area, modern kitchen, good showers and big pleasant backyard with BBQ. Dorms $30, doubles $60.

Manly

See map on p.139 for locations.

Boardrider Backpackers 63 The Corso, Manly ☎02/9977 6077, ⓦwww.boardrider.com.au. Ferry to Manly Wharf. Clean hostel in a great spot on the Corso (entry round the back), only metres from the surf beach and even closer to the just-renovated *New Brighton Hotel*. Several rooms and dorms have balconies, some with ocean views, but the constant pub and club action at street level can make it noisy at night. Modern facilities include a large, well-equipped kitchen and dining area, large common room, rooftop terrace with BBQ, lockers in the bedrooms and good security; some nice en suites. Dorms $30, rooms $110, en suite $130.

Manly Backpackers Beachside 28 Raglan St, Manly ☎02/9977 3411, ⓦwww .manlybackpackers.com.au. Ferry to Manly Wharf. Lively modern hostel in a purpose-built two-storey building one block from the surf. One of the few hostels that manages to be both clean and fun, this place has free internet access, a spacious well-equipped kitchen and outside terrace with BBQ, beach toy rental and offers nightly events. Attracts long-staying surfers. Four- and six-bed dorms, and doubles all share bathrooms; the best dorm is at the front with a balcony. Cheaper rates outside the summer season. Dorms $35, rooms $100.

Manly Guest House 6 Steinton St, Manly ☎02/ 9977 0884, ⓦwww.manlyguesthouse.com.au. Ferry to Manly Wharf. A little further from the action on the Corso, but still only a few steps to the beach, this backpacker hangout holds singles, doubles and family rooms (all shared bathroom) but no dorms. Everyone shares a kitchen and TV lounge and there's free internet and wi-fi. Single $60, double $120.

Northern beaches

See map on p.131 for locations.

Avalon Beach Backpackers 59 Avalon Parade, Avalon ☎02/9918 9709, ⓦwww.avalonbeach .com.au. Bus #L88 or #L90 from Central CityRail or Wynyard CityRail. This hostel has seen better days, but its atmosphere, and location at one of Sydney's best and most beautiful surf beaches, still make it worth considering, especially if you're here to surf, like many of the longer-stay guests. Built mainly of timber, it has an airy beachhouse feel with breezy balconies, warming open fires in winter, and plenty of greenery and rainbow lorikeets to gaze at. Dorms (4- and 6-bed) and rooms have storage area and fans. Boat trips and surfboard rental can be organized. Excellent local work contacts and weekly rates available. Dorms $25, rooms $66.

Sydney Beachhouse YHA 4 Collaroy St, Collaroy Beach ☎02/9981 1177, ⓦwww.sydneybeachouse .com.au. Bus from Manly Ferry Wharf: #151, #155 or #156; bus from Central CityRail and Wynyard CityRail: #L88 or #L90. Purpose-built YHA hostel with a casual, relaxed attitude, just across the Pittwater Rd from the beach. Heated outdoor swimming pool, sun deck, BBQs, open fireplaces, video lounge and games and pool rooms. Four- to six-bed dorms plus several doubles (some of them en-suite family rooms). Though too far out for your entire Sydney stay (45min bus ride from the city), it's a good base for kicking back on the sand or exploring the northern beaches

Staying longer

If you're staying longer than a month, consider a **flat-share** as an alternative to hotels or hostels. You'll feel more at home and it will probably cost less.

The average shared-house room price is around $160 per week (usually two weeks in advance, plus a bond/deposit of four weeks' rent; you'll usually need your own bed linen and towels). Furnished Property Group (☎02 8669 3678, ⓦwww.furnishedproperty .com.au) have a wide range of places, both leased rooms in guesthouses in all the best areas, and furnished apartments (stays of 3–12 months). Sleeping With The Enemy, 617 Harris St, Ultimo (☎1300 309 468, ⓦwww.sleepingwiththeenemy.com), organizes travellers' house-shares (aimed at under-28s) in fully equipped inner-city houses with up to eight others. Rooms are mostly singles and twins and go for $180 a week for a minimum one-month stay. There's a $300 bond and the rate includes all bills including free internet and wi-fi. Other good bets include Wednesday and Saturday's real-estate section of the *Sydney Morning Herald*, and café notice boards, especially in King Street in Newtown, Glebe Point Road in Glebe, or Hall Street, Bondi Beach.

You may feel quite vulnerable when renting in a strange city. For information on lease agreements and **tenants' rights**, contact the NSW Tenants Union (☎02/9251 6590, ⓦwww.tenants.org.au).

– bikes are free for guests – and kayaking and sailing can be organized. Free use of boogie- and surfboards with surfing lessons for weekly guests and didgeridoo lessons on offer. Internet available. Free parking. Dorms $30, rooms $80, en suite $120.

Cronulla

See map on p.147 for location.

Cronulla Beach YHA **40 Kingsway, Cronulla** ☎9527 7772, ⓦwww.cronullabeachyha.com.au.

Cronulla CityRail. No fuss, friendly hostel in unpretentious surf-side suburb, 2min from the sand and even less to the shops and restaurants in Cronulla Mall. Well situated for day-trips to the Royal National Park. Internet, pool table and TV/video available, and you can grab a free boogie board for a horizontal surf. Four- and six-bed dorms, all with fans and lockers, and private en-suite rooms. Dorms $30–32, rooms $95.

ACCOMMODATION | Hostels

12

Eating

Sydney has blossomed into one of the great food capitals of the world, and its fantastic range of cosmopolitan cafés and restaurants cover every imaginable cuisine. Quality is uniformly high, with the freshest produce, meat and seafood always on hand, and a culinary culture of discerning, well-informed diners. The places we've listed below barely scratch the surface of what's available and, as the restaurant scene is highly fashionable, businesses rise in favour, fall in popularity and close down or change names and style at an astonishing rate. Popular online user-contributor sites with generally fresh customer reviews, and often helpful menu recommendations, include Ⓦwww .eatability.com.au and grabyourfork.blogspot.com.

This chapter is divided regionally, with each suburb's offerings further divided into **cafés** and **restaurants**. Sydney can thank its sizeable Italian population for having elevated **coffee-drinking** to the status of a serious pastime, and the thriving **café** scene covers everything from traditional espresso joints to classy brunch haunts that border on restaurant standards. In the local coffee lingo, a flat white is a cappuccino without the froth; a café latte is a milkier version usually served in a glass; a long black is a regular black coffee; and a short black is an espresso (transformed with skill by a splash of milk into a layered *macchiato*). Any of these will cost $2.80–3.50, and, except for in the most traditional Italian joints, are also available with soya milk. Most cafés are open for breakfast, particularly those in the beach areas, and some stay open until the small hours. All those listed are inexpensive, many serving delectable main courses for as low as $10.

Establishments listed under **restaurants** are places you're more likely to go for an evening meal. You'll come across the terms "**contemporary Australian**", "modern Australian" or "Pacific Rim" in various restaurant descriptions. These refer to an adventurous blend of influences from around the world – mostly Asian and Mediterranean – combined with fresh local produce (occasionally even including kangaroo, emu and crocodile); the result is a dynamic, eclectic and very healthy cuisine. An average Sydney restaurant main **costs** about $20; top dollar at the city's finest is around $50. Be aware that most establishments apply a ten percent **surcharge on Sundays**.

Almost all restaurants and an increasing number of cafés are **licensed**. Many places allow you to **BYO** (Bring Your Own) wine or beer, but will probably add a corkage charge ($1–2 per person). Several **pubs** have well-regarded restaurants, where meals rarely cost more than $16, with huge steaks likely to be at the top of the menu. All New South Wales's restaurants are **nonsmoking**, except for at reception areas and outside tables.

The style of dining differs greatly by area, so we introduce the culinary character of each suburb throughout this chapter. Broadly, the **city centre** caters to business-lunching execs and on-the-go office workers. As you head north, the

Sydney features many diverse enclaves, often in far-flung suburbs, where you can sample authentic cuisines from around the world and buy imported goods from local shops and delis. Where the areas are detailed in the text, we give page references; where they are not, we have provided transport details to point you in the right direction.

African On King Street, Newtown (see p.108).

Chinese In the Chinatown section of Haymarket (see p.82), and in Ashfield (Ashfield CityRail).

Greek In Marrickville (see p.110), Earlwood (bus #409 from Ashfield CityRail), and Brighton Le Sands (bus #302 or #303 from Circular Quay CityRail).

Indian On Elizabeth Street and Cleveland Street in Surry Hills (p.101), and on King Street, St Peters (p.109).

Indonesian On Anzac Parade, Kingsford and Kensington (bus #393 or #395 from Central CityRail).

Italian On Stanley Street in East Sydney (p.97), Norton Street in Leichhardt (p.110), Ramsay Street in Haberfield (p.111), and Great North Road, Five Dock (bus #438 from Central CityRail).

Japanese There's a concentration at Bondi Junction (Bondi Junction CityRail), Neutral Bay, and Crows Nest (bus #273 from WynyardCityRail).

Jewish On and around Hall Street, Bondi (p.131).

Korean In Campsie (Campsie CityRail) and Haymarket, near the intersection of Liverpool Street and Pitt Street.

Lebanese On Elizabeth Street and Cleveland Street in Surry Hills, in Punchbowl (Punchbowl CityRail), and Lakemba (Lakemba CityRail).

Portuguese At New Canterbury Road, Petersham (Petersham CityRail);

Spanish On Liverpool Street in the city.

Turkish On Elizabeth Street and Cleveland Street in Surry Hills (p.101).

Vietnamese Concentrated in Cabramatta, far west of the CBD (14 stops from Central CityRail); superb restaurants are clustered along Park Road and John Street, just west of Cabramatta Station.

area around **Circular Quay**, **The Rocks** and the **Opera House** is well set up for tourists, with a selection of mid-range places on which floats the cream of Sydney's fine dining, often with stupendous harbour views.

South of the CBD, **Haymarket** is home to lots of cheap joints (many Chinese, Korean, Malaysian and Vietnamese), along with East Asian food courts and some quality Chinese restaurants. In marked contrast, modern and airy restaurant/bars line the rejuvenated waterfront of swish **Darling Harbour**, immediately west.

The **inner east** holds perhaps the broadest selection of cafés and restaurants, with notable concentrations along **Challis Avenue** in Potts Point, **Victoria Street** and **Oxford Street** in Darlinghurst and **Crown Street** in Surry Hills. The **inner west** offers more of the same diversity and quality, with a less fashion-conscious and more relaxed quality to your dining experience in areas such as **King Street** in Newtown, **Glebe Point Road** in Glebe, and the **Darling Street strip** running from Rozelle to Balmain. The inner western suburbs of **Leichhardt** and **Haberfield**, a little further out, host fine examples of Italian cuisine.

On the **North Shore**, **Military Road**, running from Neutral Bay to Mosman; **Miller Street**, from North Sydney to Cammeray; and the intersection of the Pacific Highway and Willoughby Rd at Crows Nest are also popular grazing grounds. By the sea, **Bondi Beach**, **Coogee** and **Manly** all have countless café and dining options.

The Rocks

The quality of café offerings in The Rocks has improved greatly over the last few years, with some finely brewed coffees and a broad selection of meals to be had in charming alfresco locations. But **pubs** still rule supreme, with many serving great light meals and bar snacks at lunchtime. Restaurants, on the other hand, are of the very expensive, award-winning variety. See map, p.52.

Cafés, snacks and light meals

Gumnut Tea Gardens 28 Harrington St
⑦02/9247 9591. Circular Quay CityRail/ferry.
Popular lunchtime venue in historic Reynolds Cottage. Munch on delicious gourmet meat-pies and ploughman's lunch in the serene leafy courtyard, or sip tea in the antiquated lounge. Live jazz on Fri night and Sun lunch. BYO. Daily 8am–5pm, plus dinner Wed–Fri.

Playfair Cafe Shop 21 Playfair St ⑦02/9233 8899. Circular Quay CityRail/ferry. In a quaint old-meets-new pedestrian street, this stylish hole-in-the-wall place, with its alfresco mod-plastic tables and chairs and box-cushion seating beneath a perspex awning, serves the best coffee in The Rocks, as well as tasty frittatas, sandwiches, wraps and burgers. Daily 8am–5pm.

La Renaissance Patisserie 47 Argyle St
⑦02/9241 4878, ⑩www.larenaissance.com.au.
Circular Quay CityRail/ferry. Relax beneath pretty parasols between hedges and stone walls covered in creeper vines in the adjoining courtyard to *Gumnut Tea Gardens*, or enjoy alfresco seating on leafy Argyle St. The house-made French pastries, pies and baguettes are expensive but delectable and the coffee isn't bad either. Daily 8.30am–6pm.

Sydney Dance Cafe Pier 4, Hickson Rd, Millers Point. Circular Quay CityRail/ferry. A relaxing spot for a coffee or a light meal on the ground level of the Wharf Theatre complex, home to the Sydney Dance Company, with water views and an interesting, arty crew of fellow customers. Mains $11.50–23.50. Mon–Sat 7.30am–8pm.

Restaurants

🏃 **Nakashima 7 Cambridge St, The Rocks. Circular Quay CityRail/ferry.** A great-value Japanese restaurant tucked away on a quaint pedestrian street near the Argyle Cut. Things are a bit cramped inside, but the outside tables are ideal. Enjoy complimentary sake and authentic Japanese food, good enough to satisfy a *yakuza* – try the pork *maki*, eel roll sushi, or soft-shell crab salad…and, above all, the tempura. Tues–Fri 12–2.30pm & 6–9.30pm.

🏃 **Rockpool 107 George St, The Rocks** ⑦02/9252 1888. Circular Quay CityRail/ferry. Owned by top chef Neil Perry, raved-about seafood and other contemporary creations make this one of Sydney's best dining spots. With mains ranging $52–65, however, it's definitely splurge material. Licensed. Tues–Sat 6–10pm.

Sydney's star chefs

Sydney's top restaurants have long had a high international reputation, mastering the east-meets-west fusion for which contemporary Australian cuisine is so well known. The ingredients are the freshest available, the interiors come straight out of the latest style magazines, and the city's top **chefs** are regularly poached to work overseas. Many have become TV stars or publishing legends, endorsing products or producing their own commercial food range. For the moment, the stars of Sydney's restaurant scene are: Neil Perry at *Rockpool* (see above); Tetsuya Wakuda at *Tetsuya's* (p.182); Bill Granger at *bills* (p.185); Guillaume Brahimi at *Guillaume at Bennelong* (p.180); Matthew Moran at *Aria* (p.180); Kylie Kwong at *Billy Kwong* (p.191); Martin Boetz at *Longrain* (see p.191); Peter Doyle at *est.* (p.182); Luke Mangan (consultant chef for Sir Richard Branson) at *glass* at the Hilton; Peter Gilmore at *Quay* (p.181); Damien Pignolet at *Bistro Moncur* (p.189); Sean Moran at *Sean's Panaroma* (p.199); and Serge Dansereau at *The Bathers Pavilion* (p.197).

Sailors Thai Canteen 106 George St, The Rocks. Circular Quay CityRail/ferry. The long stainless-steel communal table in this George St-level canteen looks onto an open kitchen, where the chefs chop away to produce simple delectable meals. Housed in a restored home for sailors, this is the cheaper version of the much-praised, pricey downstairs restaurant (℗02/9251 2466 for bookings). Come early for dinner in the canteen. Mains $21–28.50. Licensed. Mon–Sat noon–10pm.

Wharf Restaurant Pier 4, Hickson Rd, Millers Point ℗02/9250 1761, next to the Wharf Theatre. Circular Quay CityRail/ferry. Enterprising modern cuisine (lots of seafood), served in an old dock building with heaps of raw charm and a harbour vista; bag the outside tables for the best views. Cocktail bar open from noon until end of evening performance. Mains $26.50–32. Mon–Sat 12–3pm & 6–10pm.

Circular Quay and the Opera House

Food options around the Quay and Opera House are generally of the fine dining variety. The best restaurants couple exceptional cuisine with fantastic views of the Harbour Bridge, Opera House and harbour. There are a number of Quay-side cafés at which to appreciate the view with an overpriced coffee and pastry, but for cheaper eats try a pub or the Gateway Gourmet Food Court, which offers a wide choice of snacks and light meals (see box, p.184). See map, p.61.

Cafés, snacks and light meals

Rossini Wharf 5, Circular Quay ℗02/9247 8026. Circular Quay CityRail/ferry. Quality alfresco Italian fast food while you're waiting for a ferry or just watching the quay. *Panzerotto* – big, cinnamon-flavoured and ricotta-filled doughnuts ($7) – are a speciality. Pricey but excellent coffee. Licensed. Daily 7am–11pm.

Sydney Cove Oyster Bar Circular Quay East ℗9247 2937. Circular Quay CityRail/ferry. En route to the Opera House, the quaint little building housing the bar and kitchen was once a public toilet, but don't let that put you off. The outdoor tables right on the water's edge provide a magical location to sample Sydney Rock Pacific oysters ($22 per half-dozen), or come for the coffee, a cake and the view. Licensed. Daily 8am until late.

Restaurants

Aria 1 Macquarie St, East Circular Quay ℗02/9252 2555. Circular Quay CityRail/ferry. On the first floor of the Opera Quays building (aka the much-maligned "Toaster" – see p.60), the 200-seater *Aria* has knock-out harbour views, one of Sydney's best chefs, Matthew Moran (dishing up modern Australian fare), and wonderful service to recommend it. The interiors are also pretty slick. All this comes at a price, with mains at $42–49, but there are more affordable set lunch menus and pre-theatre dinners (5.30–7.30pm; one/two/three courses $36/58/72). Mon–Fri noon–2.30pm & 5.30–11.30pm, Sat 5–11.30pm, Sun 6–10.30pm.

Cafe Sydney Level 5, Customs House, 31 Alfred St, Circular Quay ℗02/9251 8683. Circular Quay CityRail/ferry. Though the overpriced food here has never been that highly rated (wide-ranging, from a tandoor oven to French- and Greek-inspired dishes), *Cafe Sydney* is firmly on the tourist agenda thanks to the jaw-dropping views of the Harbour Bridge and Opera House from its balcony. Service is great and the atmosphere is fun, especially with the live jazz on Fri nights. Mains $24–38. A drink at the bar is an affordable option. Mon–Fri noon–late, Sat 5pm–late, Sun noon–3pm.

Guillaume at Bennelong Sydney Opera House, Bennelong Point ℗02/9241 1999. Circular Quay CityRail/ferry. French chef Guillaume Brahimi has fused his name with the enduring *Bennelong*, the Opera House's top-notch restaurant. If you want to have one splash-out romantic meal in Sydney, come here. The restaurant fills one of the iconic building's smaller shells, with dramatic rib-vaulted ceilings, huge windows providing stunning harbour views, and sensuous lighting. With mains at around $35, this is not the priciest in town, but if you can't afford it, just opt for a drink at the bar. Pre-theatre meals at $55 (two courses) and $65 (three courses). Mon–Wed & Sat noon–3pm, Thurs & Fri noon–3pm & 5.30pm–late.

Peter Doyle @ the Quay Overseas Passenger Terminal, Circular Quay West ☎02/9252 3400. **Circular Quay CityRail/ferry.** Downtown branch of the Watsons Bay seafood institution (see p.197; branch at Sydney Fish Market p.185); pricey but excellent, with great harbour views from the outdoor waterfront tables. You'll

probably need to book. Licensed. Mains $28–60. Daily 11.30am–3pm & 5.30–10pm.

Quay Upper Level, Overseas Passenger Terminal, Circular Quay West ☎02/9251 5600. **Circular Quay CityRail/ferry.** Breathtaking views of Sydney's icons, the bridge and the Opera House, accompany exquisite modern Australian food from one of the city's most talented chefs, Peter Gilmore. Vying for the crown of Sydney's best restaurant, and understandably very expensive, with mains from $38. Licensed. Mon, Sat & Sun 6–10pm, Tues–Fri noon–2.30pm & 6–10pm.

Royal Botanic Gardens to Macquarie Street

There are not many dining options in and around the Botanic Gardens, though you'll find a few other places along Macquarie Street. See map, p.67.

Cafés, snacks and light meals

 Sydney Mint Café 10 Macquarie St ☎02/9233 3337. **Martin Place CityRail.** Excellent little café, very central but restfully set in the 1814 former Sydney Mint building with plenty of seating on the broad first-floor veranda overlooking Macquarie Street. While lovely for a slightly pricey coffee and cake, it excels at contemporary lunches (11am–2.30pm; mains $25–30) and a High Tea (2.30–4pm) of savoury tarts, scones with strawberry jam and double cream and, of course, tea (bubbly is optional). Mon–Fri 9am–4pm.

Restaurants

Art Gallery of NSW Restaurant The Domain ☎02/9225 1819. **St James CityRail.** With a great harbour view from a modern interior, this classy modern Australian restaurant makes an excellent place for a break when you're exploring the Domain, the Botanic Gardens or the art gallery itself, particularly for High Tea. Mains mostly $25–30; for something more casual, the Gallery Café fits the bill nicely. Restaurant Mon–Fri noon–4pm, Sat & Sun 10am–4pm; café Mon, Tues & Thurs–Sun 10am–4.30pm, Wed 10am–8.30pm.

City centre

Sydney's city centre offers a wide range of eating options, from cosmopolitan food courts with an array of cheap, tasty snacks and light meals (see p.184), through the last few Italian espresso bars, to a couple of the city finest restaurants. Nearly all city centre pubs also serve great light meals and bar snacks at lunchtime, or head for the scrummy snacks and light meals in the wonderful David Jones Food Hall (see "Shopping", p.248). See map, p.75.

Vegetarian Sydney

Just about every café menu caters well for veggies, as do most contemporary restaurants menus. The following are specifically or virtually entirely **vegetarian**: *Badde Manors* (p.193), *Bodhi in the Park* (p.182), *Harvest* (p.195), *Iku* (p.193), *Maya Indian Sweets* (p.190), *Mother Chu's Vegetarian Kitchen* (p.183) and *Sloanes* (p.189).

Cafés, snacks and light meals

Bar Milazzo 379 Pitt St ☎02/9264 8644.
Museum or Town Hall CityRail. One of
Sydney's last classic Italian hole-in-the-wall
cafés. Great for panini and espresso.
Mon–Fri 7am–6pm.

🏃 **Bodhi in the Park** Cook and Phillip Park,
College St ☎02/9360 2523. **Museum**
CityRail. Top-notch Chinese vegetarian and
vegan food, with the focus on delicious *yum
cha* (dishes $9–18), predominantly using
organic and biodynamic produce. A good
option if you've just been for a swim in the
adjacent park pool, or for a visit to the
nearby Australian Museum; the outside
seating is a treat on a sunny day. Licensed.
Daily 10am–10pm.

Caffe Corto 10 Barrack St ☎02/9279 0070.
Martin Place CityRail. Breakfasts, baguettes,
antipasti and salads, but mostly just
excellent coffee in this diminutive Italian-style
café with a few tables out front. Mon–Fri
7am–4.30pm.

Lindt Café 53 Martin Place ☎02/8257 1600.
Martin Place CityRail. In something of a
coup for Sydney, the world's first *Lindt
Café* opened its doors in the CBD in 2004,
bringing the renowned Swiss chocolati-
er's temptations to a sit-down audience.
A surprisingly creative and tasty range
of gourmet sandwiches are on offer at
lunchtime ($12) but the stars of the show are
the to-die-for desserts ($11 for the coffee,
chocolate and almond Opera Cake) and the
dark iced chocolate drinks ($7). You can
even come here early for breakfast ($5–12).
Chocaholics beware, this experience is
definitely not for the calorie-shy. Mon–Fri
7.30am–6pm, Sat & Sun 10am–5pm.

MoS 37 Phillip St ☎02/9241 3636. **Circular**
Quay CityRail. Local lawyers and business
lunchers flock to this contemporary café/
restaurant, wedged under the Museum
of Sydney and opening out on to First
Government Place. Salads, pasta dishes,
bruschetta and beer-battered fish (mains

mostly $25–30) are typical, but *MoS*
also makes an agreeably peaceful spot
for a (reasonably priced) coffee at other
times or a tasty weekend breakfast.
Licensed. Mon–Fri 7am–9pm, Sat & Sun
8.30am–5pm.

QVB Jet Corner of York and Druitt sts ☎02/9283
5004. **Town Hall CityRail.** Very lively Italian
café/bar on the corner of the QVB building
looking across to the Town Hall, with big
windows and outdoor seating providing
people-watching opportunities. The coffee
is predictably excellent, and the menu is big
on breakfast. For the rest of the day, choose
from pasta, pizza and risotto (mains around
$18) plus soups, salads and sandwiches.
Licensed. Mon–Fri 7.30am–11pm, Sat 9am–
midnight, Sun 10am–7pm.

Restaurants

est. Level 1, Establishment Hotel, 252 George St
☎02/9240 3000. **Wynyard CityRail.** Above one
of Sydney's most deluxe bars (*Establishment*; see p.205), this restaurant is firmly
in Sydney's top tier, its decor giving a
modern twist to the Neoclassical columns
and ceiling. The food, by renowned chef
Peter Doyle, is contemporary Australian,
but has a French slant. Very expensive,
with mains around $45 at lunch, $53 at
dinner. Licensed. Mon–Fri noon–2.30pm &
6–10pm, Sat 6–10pm.

🏃 **Tetsuya's** 529 Kent St ☎02/9267 2900,
ⓕ9799 7099, ⓦwww.tetsuyas.com. **Town
Hall CityRail.** Stylish premises – a Japanese
timber interior and a beautiful Japanese
garden outside – and the internationally
renowned chef Tetsuya Wakuda creating
exquisite Japanese/French-style fare. As
Sydneysiders will attest, an evening here is a
once-in-a-lifetime culinary experience and the
month-long waiting list is worth it to sample
the ten-course dégustation menu ($195);
wine teamed with each course starts from
$70. Licensed and BYO. Tues–Fri 6–11pm,
Sat noon–3pm & 6–11pm.

Haymarket

With heaps of backpacker hostels and a captive student population, budget
dining is dominant in Haymarket, particularly East Asian places. There are a
few pricier Chinese places around Chinatown and even a small Spanish quarter
where tapas and paella reign. See map, p.75.

Cafés, snacks and light meals

De la France 605–609 George St ⓣ02/9267 6744. Museum CityRail. When Haymarket's Chinese, Korean and Vietnamese restaurants just don't hit the spot, head for this corner French-ish café good for a daytime baguette or a leisurely evening coffee at the outside tables. Daily 24hr.

Delizia 148 Elizabeth St ⓣ02/9283 0599. Museum CityRail. A high-ceilinged deli-café bustling with black-clad staff: the gleaming glass counters groan with pasta dishes, and the shelves are stacked with gourmet goods. It looks pricey, but there's nothing much over $12 on the menu. With a secondhand literary bookshop tucked out the back, there's nothing else like it in the city. The tables and lounge chairs among the bookshelves create a private haven. Mon–Fri 6am–5pm, Sat & Sun 8am–4pm.

Madono 404 Sussex St ⓣ02/9211 3534. Central CityRail. Basement Japanese place. Nip in for an excellent-value dinner set menu (from $17), a *wagyu* beef *shabu shabu* or groaning sashimi boat. Even cheaper for lunch. Licensed. Daily 11am–10.30pm.

Mamak 15 Goulburn St ⓣ02/9211 1668. Garden Plaza Monorail. Queues often form at this budget Malaysian place, but there's entertainment while you wait watching them whip up super flaky *roti canai*. Buy a few dishes to share, such as tangy fish curry, stir-fried beans in shrimp paste or *nasi goreng* (all $10–16) and leave space for the impressive, conical sweet *roti* with ice cream. Delicious. BYO ($2 a bottle). Tues–Sun noon–3pm & 6–10.30pm.

Mother Chu's Vegetarian Kitchen 367 Pitt St ⓣ02/9283 2828. Central CityRail. Gaining a reputation fast, this Taiwanese Buddhist restaurant is set in suitably plain surroundings and, true to its name, is family-run. Though traditionally onion and garlic aren't used, the inexpensive eats aren't bland and it's perfect for vegetarians. Don't try to BYO – there's a no-alcohol policy. Mon–Sat noon–3pm & 5–10pm.

Pasteur 709 George St ⓣ02/9212 5622. Central CityRail. They mysteriously dropped "pho" from the name, but *phô* (Vietnamese rice noodle soup, served with fresh herbs, lemon, bean sprouts and meat) is exactly what you get at this popular though simple eatery. Most noodles (mainly pork, chicken and beef) cost $10, and there's nothing over $12. Refreshing pot of jasmine tea included. BYO. Daily 10.30am–9.30pm.

Restaurants

BBQ King 18 Goulburn St ⓣ02/9267 2433. Central CityRail. Late-night hangout of rock stars and students alike, this unprepossessing but always packed Chinese restaurant does a mean meat dish, as suggested by the name and the BBQ ducks hanging in the window. A large vegetarian list on the menu caters to the crowds scattered across various rooms and communal tables. Inexpensive to moderate. Licensed. Daily 11.30am–2am (last orders 1.30am).

Capitan Torres 73 Liverpool St ⓣ02/9264 5574. Town Hall CityRail. Atmospheric and enduring Spanish place with old-country charm – white walls and wrought iron – specializing in seafood. A fresh display of the catch of the day helps you choose, but it's hard to pass up old favourites from the tapas menu such as chorizo and garlic prawns (dishes mostly $12–16), or the authentic paella. Sit downstairs at the bar or upstairs in the restaurant. Licensed. Daily noon–3pm & 6–11pm.

China Grand Level 3, Market City complex, corner of Quay and Haymarket sts ⓣ02/9211 8988. Central CityRail. Locals flock to this massive, 800-seater Cantonese establishment, serving some of Sydney's best *yum cha* (tapas-style dishes). Despite its size, you may well have to queue if you haven't booked. Licensed. Daily 10am–11pm.

Golden Century 393 Sussex St, City ⓣ02/9281 1598, ⓦwww.goldencentury.com.au. Central CityRail. Seafood is the thing here, and it's very fresh – you can watch your potential dinner swimming around in the tanks. Be adventurous – try the oysters sitting on black moss ($15), or the raved-about *pipis* (shellfish) in *xo* sauce ($18). And you can eat as dawn approaches – this one's open very late. Keep an eye out for visiting rock stars – it's also a favourite after-show haunt. Licensed and BYO. Daily noon–4am.

O Bal Tan 363A Pitt St ⓣ02/9269 0299. Central CityRail. This bustling Korean barbecue restaurant is tucked down a back alley in the burgeoning Koreatown, but it is easy

Food courts

Some of Sydney's best cheap eats, with hot dishes at $6–10, are to be found in the multitude of cosmopolitan food courts in city shopping malls, mainly along the Pitt Street Mall. Those around Chinatown are also good, serving everything from Japanese to Vietnamese, and of course Chinese food. .

Dixon House Food Court basement level, corner of Little Hay and Dixon streets. Central CityRail. Chinese noodles, Cambodian, Indian, Thai, Indonesian, Malaysian, Japanese and Korean plus a cane juice bar. Daily 10.30am–8.30pm. See map, p.84.

Gateway Gourmet Quayside Shopping Centre, ground floor, bounded by Alfred St, Reiby Place and Loftus St, Circular Quay. Circular Quay CityRail/ferry. Pizza, pasta, seafood, patisserie, healthy sandwiches and Asian food. Business hours. See map, p.61.

Hunter Connection 310 George St, City. Wynyard CityRail. Fantastic and frenetically busy first-floor food court, with a sushi bar, sandwiches, noodles, pasta, Vietnamese, Korean, Tandoori and Chinese food. Business hours. See map, p.75.

Market City Food Court Level 3, Market City Shopping Centre, corner Quay and Thomas sts, Haymarket. Central CityRail. Almost entirely Asian – Japanese, Chinese, Malaysian, Indian, Cambodian, Thai and Singaporean. The best stall is McLuksa – the spicy coconut noodle soups that give it its name are delicious. Daily 10am–10pm. See map, p.84.

Sussex Centre 401 Sussex St, Haymarket. Central CityRail. First-floor food court: Vietnamese, Korean BBQ, Thai, Japanese, several Chinese and a juice bar. Daily 10am–9.30pm. See map, p.84.

Sydney Central 450 George St, City. Town Hall CityRail. Buzzing basement food court beneath Myer department store. Enter from Pitt St Mall or via the QVB. Mon–Wed 7am–7pm, Thurs 7am–10pm, Sat 8am–7pm, Sun 10am–6pm. See map, p.75.

to find by following the crowds. Steel "elephants' trunks" suck away the vapours of grilled meat, eel, and plenty of offal.

Be adventurous, share several dishes and expect to pay $25–30 a head. Daily 11am–midnight.

Darling Harbour, Pyrmont and Ultimo

Sitting on the broad pavements overlooking the yacht-bobbing waters is the essence of dining around Darling Harbour. Most places are mid-range and expensive restaurant/bars. If you need something cheaper, head over to the "Food courts" (see box above) and budget Asian places around Haymarket and Chinatown. See map, p.84.

Cafés, snacks and light meals

🏃 **Concrete Café** 224 Harris St, Pyrmont ☎02/9518 9523. Fish Market Light Rail. If you can't face being monstered by seagulls dining outside the Fish Market – and fancy better coffee – retreat a couple of hundred metres to this minimalist café, where outside tables catch the morning sun. Tuck into the likes of baked eggs with chorizo and red capsicum and chutney on sourdough ($11), or roast pumpkin and

haloumi salad ($14). Mon–Fri 7am–4pm, Sat & Sun 8am–4pm.

Fish Market Cafe Sydney Fish Markets, Pyrmont ☎02/9660 4280. Fish Market Light Rail. Come to watch the early morning fish-market action (or just head here after a very late night out), and grab breakfast and coffee. Excellent-value seafood platter with Kilpatrick oysters, lobster tails and inexpensive fresh fish'n'chips later in the day. Mon–Fri 4am–4pm, Sat & Sun 5am–5pm.

Restaurants

Chinta Ria – Temple of Love Roof Terrace, 201 Sussex St, Cockle Bay Wharf, Darling Harbour ⊤02/9264 3211. **Town Hall CityRail.** People still queue to get in here (bookings lunch only) years after opening, as much for the fun atmosphere – a blues and jazz soundtrack and decor that mixes a giant Buddha, a lotus pond and Fifties-style furniture – as for the moderately priced Malaysian food. Any of the curries (mostly $22–25) will satisfy, but ask for extra chilli if you want a real kick. Quick, helpful service, including a mobile phone call-back system for busy nights, when patrons are sent to the bars elsewhere in the Darling Harbour restaurant complex. Licensed and BYO ($10 per bottle). Daily noon–2.30pm & 6–11pm.
Doyles at Sydney Fish Markets Sydney Fish Markets, Pyrmont ⊤02/9552 4339. **Metro Light Rail to Fish Market.** A very casual and more affordable lunch-only version of Watsons Bay's famous fish restaurant; you sit at metal tables and order at the counter. Daily specials from the best fish-market offers served all day. BYO. Mon–Fri 11.30am–2.30pm, Sat & Sun 11.30am–3pm.
The Malaya 39 Lime St, King St Wharf, Darling Harbour ⊤02/9279 1170. **Town Hall CityRail.** Popular, veteran Chinese–Malaysian place in swish water surrounds, serving some of the best and spiciest *laksa* in town (chicken or vegetable *laksa* $20, king prawn version $24). Seafood dishes are definitely worth a try. Licensed. Mon noon–3pm & 6–9pm, Tues–Sat noon–3pm & 6–10pm, Sun 6–9pm.
wagamama 10/45 Lime St, King St Wharf. Town Hall CityRail. Huge high-tech Japanese noodle bar based on the London model: young trendy staff equipped with a computerized ordering system, communal tables and no bookings – which can mean long queues, though service and turnover is fast. No desserts. Average main $17. Licensed but only a basic drinks list, which includes sake. Mon–Thurs noon–10pm, Fri & Sat noon–11pm, Sun noon–11pm.

Inner east

The **inner east** holds probably Sydney's greatest concentration of cafés (including several late-night options; see box, p.192) and restaurants, supplemented by an equally vast range of pubs and bars that serve great light meals (see "Drinking"). The area around Kings Cross is perhaps the most diverse, with everything from budget cafés and backpacker haunts to some of the most chic new establishments around. There's a more staid, moneyed feel to places listed under Paddington and Woollahra, while South Darlinghurst offers great Asian restaurants frequented by the Oxford Street gay set, and rapidly gentrifying Surry Hills is always turning up something new and interesting.

Kings Cross, Potts Point, Woolloomooloo, East Sydney and north Darlinghurst

See maps, p.92 and p.95.

Cafés, snacks and light meals

Bar Coluzzi 322 Victoria St, Darlinghurst ⊤02/9380 5420. **Kings Cross CityRail.** "50 years young and still going strong" announces the sign over this famous Italian café; it is tiny but always packed with a diverse crew of regulars spilling out onto wooden stools on the pavement and partaking of the standard menu of focaccias, muffins, open bagels and, of course, coffee. You can watch from a safe distance at the trendier, though equally tiny and very popular *Latteria* next door. Daily 5am–7pm.
bills 433 Liverpool St, Darlinghurst ⊤02/9360 9631. **Kings Cross CityRail.** Owned by celebrity chef Bill Granger, this sunny corner café–restaurant in the quieter, terraced backstreets of Darlinghurst is among Sydney's favourite breakfast spots. A mix of people gather around the large central table to spend hours lingering over ricotta hotcakes with honeycomb butter and banana, muffins and newspapers. Though not cheap (hotcakes $16.50), breakfast is definitely worth it. Modern Australian lunches start at about $17.

Licensed & BYO. Mon–Sat 7.30am–3pm, Sun 8.30am–3pm.

Cafe Hernandez 60 Kings Cross Rd, Kings Cross ☎02/9331 2343. Kings Cross CityRail. Veteran Argentinian-run 24hr coffee shop. Relaxed and friendly with a dark, old-fashioned ambience, you can dawdle here for ages and no one will make you feel unwelcome. Popular with taxi drivers and a mixed clientele of locals who don't mind looking out onto the busy road. Spanish food is served – *churros*, tortilla, *empanadas* and good pastries – but coffee is the focus. Daily 24hr.

Harry's Café de Wheels Corner of Cowper Wharf Rd and Brougham St, Woolloomooloo ☎02/9357 3074. Kings Cross CityRail. Sometimes there's nothing like a good old-fashioned pie; this little cart has been serving them up to the famous and ordinary alike for over sixty years now. Some gourmet and vegetarian options have made it onto the menu, but the pie floater – a standard meat pie with potato, mashed peas and gravy for $5.30 – remains the favourite, at any time of day or night. Mon & Tues 8.30am–2am, Wed & Thurs 8.30am–3am, Fri 8am–4am, Sat 9am–4am, Sun 9am–1am.

La Buvette 35 Challis Ave, Potts Point ☎02/9358 5113. Kings Cross CityRail. Hole-in-the-wall coffee stop next door to the *Spring Espresso Bar*. Sidewalk seating is almost interchangeable and both are packed with mid-morning caffeine seekers. *La Buvette* features well prepared Sydney breakfast favourites plus

▲ Paddington cafés

a blackboard menu of unusual dishes such as baked egg with spinach, sun-dried tomatoes, goat cheese and caramelized onion ($15), or vanilla French toast brioche ($12.50). Daily 6am–5.30pm.

Le Petit Crème 118 Darlinghurst Rd, Darlinghurst ☎02/9361 4738. Kings Cross CityRail. Aim for a veranda table for breakfast at this friendly and thriving French café; it's always crammed inside. Renowned for huge, good-value filled baguettes, as well as steak frites, omelettes, home-made paté, *pain au chocolat* and big bowls of *café au lait*. Bread and pastries are baked on the premises and can be smelled down the road. Mon–Sat 7am–3pm, Sun 8am–3pm.

Macleay Pizza 101 Macleay St, Potts Point ☎02/9356 4262. Kings Cross CityRail. Unassuming pizza bar: great prices and great pizzas. Mon–Sat noon–1.30am, Sun 3pm–1am.

Minami 87C Macleay St, Potts Point ☎02/9357 2481. Kings Cross CityRail. Blink and you'll miss this tiny, authentic Japanese noodle bar, where you'll find Japanese residents and visitors alike squeezed around one large counter; popular choices include *ramen*, *yakisoba* and *kushikatsu*, with most items $9–12. BYO. Mon–Fri noon–3pm & 6–10.30pm, Sat & Sun noon–10.30pm.

Tropicana Caffe 227 Victoria St, Darlinghurst ☎02/9360 9809. Kings Cross CityRail. The birthplace of the Tropfest film festival (see box, p.225) this hugely popular café packs in trendies, junkies and everyone in between. Don't come for the decor, which is clinical, but for the choose-your-own sandwich fillings and pasta toppings, plus great breakfasts (mostly $10; served until 4pm) and hearty daily specials. Licensed. Daily 5am–11pm.

Una's 340 Victoria St, Darlinghurst ☎02/9360 6885. Kings Cross CityRail. Cosy two-roomed open café and restaurant that's been here for years, dishing up schnitzel, dumplings, sauerkraut and other almost authentic Austrian dishes that are cheap (mostly around $18), plentiful and tasty. The very popular big breakfasts are served until 2.30pm. Licensed & BYO. Mon–Sat 7.30am–10.30pm, Sun 8am–10pm.

Restaurants

a tavola 348 Victoria St, Darlinghurst ☎02/9331 7871. Kings Cross CityRail. Polished copper globe lamps over a long communal table define the main room at

▲ a tavola

this stylish Italian pasta restaurant. The blackboard menu is handwritten almost daily depending on what's fresh, but expect a modern approach to traditional dishes such as rabbit-stuffed hand-made ravioli. Everything is superbly done, salads and desserts are delicious and if you don't fancy shoulder-to-shoulder dining, go for the separate tables in the rear courtyard. Mains mostly $25–38. Licensed. Mon–Thurs & Sat 6–11pm, Fri noon–3pm & 6–11pm.

Almond Bar 379 Liverpool St, Darlinghurst ☎02/9380 5318. Kings Cross CityRail. If you want a belly-filling felafel, go elsewhere, but for delicate Middle Eastern food (the owners are of Syrian descent), served in intimate modern surrounds, then this is the place. Kick off with dips (*baba ghanouj*, *labne* and *za'atar*; $19), then move on to small plates of *sumbusic* (pastry filled with lamb, pine nuts and onion; $14) or *kofta* ($15). Always bustling – and tiny, so booking is recommended. Licensed. Tues–Thurs, Sat & Sun 5–11pm, Fri noon–11pm.

Bar Reggio 135 Crown St, East Sydney ☎02/9332 1129. Kings Cross CityRail. Hugely popular neighbourhood Italian joint serving good food (including crisp-based pizzas from $13) in sizeable portions to an eager and rowdy clientele. Not a place for a romantic dinner. BYO ($1 a head). Daily noon–11pm.

Bayswater Brasserie 32 Bayswater Rd, Kings Cross ☎02/9357 2177. Kings Cross CityRail. Busy, upmarket French-style brasserie consistently rated for its interesting modern food (changing seasonal menu) – a long-time hangout for Sydney's media types. Mains $30–40. Licensed. Mon–Thurs, Sat & Sun 5–11pm, Fri noon–3pm & 11pm.

Beppi's 21 Yurong St, East Sydney ☎02/9360 4558. Kings Cross CityRail. Old-fashioned service and cosy surrounds – especially the wine cellar, where you can dine amid the floor-to-ceiling bottles of often very expensive wine – have kept this restaurant thriving since 1956. Solid Italian food, including veal scaloppini and various pastas, make it a first-class night out, though service can be a little curt. Mains around $40. Mon–Fri noon–3pm & 6–11pm, Sat 6–11pm.

Bill and Toni 74 Stanley St, East Sydney ☎02/9360 4702. Kings Cross CityRail. This atmospheric, cheap-and-cheerful Italian restaurant (mains $9–15) with balcony tables is an institution, and there's generally a queue snaking up the stairs to get in. Once you're finally seated beneath the Italian landscape murals, huge servings of simple home-made pasta and sauces hit the spot. The separate café downstairs, a popular Stanley St local (daily 7am–midnight), serves tasty Italian sandwiches. BYO. Daily noon–2.30pm & 6–10.30pm.

Dolcetta 165 Victoria St, Potts Point ☎02/9331 5899. Kings Cross CityRail. Tiny, down-to-earth Italian restaurant with a couple of tables on the street overlooking the fashionable Dov restaurant. All dishes under $15. BYO. Mon–Sat 6am–10pm, Sun 7am–4pm.

Fishface 132 Darlinghurst Rd, Darlinghurst ☎02/9332 4803, takeaway ☎9332 4809. Kings Cross CityRail. This tiny place is one spot where size doesn't matter, and where the excellent range of pricey seafood (mains $30–36) speaks for itself. All the fish is supremely fresh, and fish'n'chips served in a paper cone, pea soup with yabby tails, or any of the sushi prepared before your eyes, will make you forget you're in the city and nowhere near the sea. Licensed and BYO. Mon–Sat 6–10pm, Sun 6–9pm.

Fratelli Paradiso 12–16 Challis Ave ☎02/9357 1744. Kings Cross CityRail. This place has got everything, from gorgeous wallpaper and a dark furniture fit-out, to flirty waiters and a diverse wine list. There's even an adjoining bakery, which runs out of stock by lunchtime most days. And the food's amazing, if a little pricey – calamari, veal, pizza and pastries – with a blackboard menu that changes daily to complement the great standard menu. Licensed. Mon–Fri 7am–11pm, Sat & Sun 7am–6pm.

fu manchu 249 Victoria St, Darlinghurst. Kings Cross CityRail ℡02/9360 9424. Perch yourself on red stools at stainless-steel counters to enjoy stylish but inexpensive Chinese and Malaysian noodles and noodle soups in this small, popular diner. Seasonal specials add variety to a standard but tasty menu, featuring organic chicken and many vegetarian options. BYO only. Mon–Fri noon–3pm & 5.30–10.30pm, Sat & Sun 5.30–10.30pm.

Govinda's 112 Darlinghurst Rd, Darlinghurst ℡02/9380 5155. **Kings Cross CityRail.** Legendary among in-the-know locals, this Hari-Krishna run restaurant-cum-cinema offers excellent, mostly Indian all-you-can-eat vegetarian buffet for a bargain $19.80. Soup, lentils, pasta and curry, plus for an extra $8.80 a new-release or classic movie at the attached cinema, with its huge comfy couches (see p.226). Dinner nightly from 5.45pm, and two screenings at 7pm and 9 or 9.30pm.

Manta The Wharf, 6 Cowper Wharf Rd, Woolloomooloo ℡02/9332 3822. **Kings Cross CityRail.** Some of the city's finest seafood, in a great waterside setting with city views. With entrées approaching $30 and mains into the forties, prices are high and service isn't always what it might be, but the food is delicious and the location stellar. Daily noon–3pm & 6–10pm.

🏃 **Onde 346 Liverpool St, Darlinghurst** ℡02/9331 8749. **Kings Cross CityRail.** Thankfully there's a bar and cushions for waiting on the ledge outside this French-owned restaurant down a Darlinghurst side street, as regulars keep returning and bookings are not accepted. Everyone wants to try the outstanding and very authentic bistro-style food, starting with soups and patés and moving through to mains such as steak frites or confit of duck, and always a special fish dish. Portions are generous and moderately priced (mains $25–28), service is excellent and desserts decadent. Licensed, with many wines by the glass. Daily 5–11pm or midnight.

🏃 **Otto The Wharf, 6 Cowper Wharf Rd, Woolloomooloo** ℡02/9368 7488. **Kings Cross CityRail.** Otto is the sort of restaurant where agents take actors and models out to lunch, and a well-known politician could be dining at the next table. Trendy and glamorous, with yachts bobbing almost within arms' reach, but it's the exquisite and expensive Italian cuisine – very fresh seafood and top-of-the-range everything else – coupled with friendly service and a lively atmosphere, that keeps them coming back. Mains around $35–45. Licensed. Daily noon–3pm & 6–11pm.

Phamish 50 Burton St, Darlinghurst ℡02/9357 2688. **Bus #378 from Central CityRail, bus #380 from Circular Quay CityRail.** Diners spill out on to a large concrete suburban courtyard at this popular Vietnamese place. The usual wait to order at the counter is worth it for great-value rice paper rolls ($10), salt and pepper squid ($17) and chicken, chili and lemongrass ($17). BYO at $2 per head. Daily except Mon 6–10pm.

Roy's Famous 176 Victoria St, Potts Point. Kings Cross CityRail. It's all about the meal deal at this backstreet backpacker hangout, with Sunday Roast for two people with a bottle of wine at $39 (from 6pm) and the Wednesday Pasta night, with garlic bread and glass of wine for $19.50 (from 6pm). Hearty regular menu, two-for-one drinks daily 5.30–6.30pm, and a friendly atmosphere. Daily 7am–10pm.

🏃 **The Victoria Room Level 1, 235 Victoria St, Darlinghurst** ℡02/9357 4488, ⓦwww.thevictoriaroom.com. **Kings Cross CityRail.** Dark, moody and fashioned in the style of the British Raj, this bar-restaurant, with its patterned wallpaper and mismatched but comfortable antique sofas and Chesterfields, is rapidly becoming an institution. The space is separated into a slick bar area where a couple of long tables keep the beautiful crowd back from diners enjoying imaginative *tapas*-style morsels in the homely restaurant. Inspired mains include warm salad of chorizo, squid, chickpeas, capsicum, coriander and preserved lemon ($18), pork and fennel sausages on puy lentils ($21), or a huge antipasto plate ($24). High Tea (Sat 2–4pm, Sun 1–5pm) is also served ($35, $40 with bubbles, $45 with champagne). Licensed. Tues–Thurs & Sun 6pm–midnight, Fri & Sat 5pm–2am.

See p.251 of "Shopping" for details of Woollahra's foodie focus, *jones the grocer*, which has a small eat-in café section. For locations, see map, p.93.

Cafés, snacks and light meals

Gusto Delicatessen 2A Heeley St, Five Ways, Paddington ☎02/9361 5640. Bus #378 from Central CityRail, bus #380 from Circular Quay CityRail. Sit at the breakfast bar at this relaxed local café tucking into mushrooms on sourdough, a croissant and coffee, or one of the salads, quiches and cold meats from the counter. Mon–Sat 7am–5pm.

Love Supreme 180 Oxford St, Paddington ☎02/9331 1779. Bus #378 from Central CityRail; bus #380 from Circular Quay CityRail. Delicious, thin-based pizzas (three sizes: $14, $19 & $25) served in a sometimes frenetic atmosphere. Try Ya Basta! (ham, pumpkin, chilli and pecorino) with a rocket salad and a delicious dessert. Always popular; on hot days, when it gets pretty stifling, you may prefer to take away. No bookings. Mon–Fri 5.30–10pm, Sat & Sun 10am–4pm & 5.30–11pm.

Sloanes Café 312 Oxford St, Paddington ☎02/9331 6717. Bus #378 from Central CityRail; bus #380 from Circular Quay CityRail. Though the emphasis in this veteran café is on good, unusual vegetarian food, moderately priced, some meatier dishes have slipped onto the menu, including a BLT with guacamole to die for; the fresh juice bar has always been phenomenal. The stone-floored dining room opens onto the street for views of Saturday's market action; for more peace, eat out back under vines in the delightful courtyard. Breakfast and lunch served all day. BYO. Daily 6am–5pm.

Restaurants

Bistro Moncur Woollahra Hotel, 116 Queen St, Woollahra ☎02/9363 2519, ⓦwww.woollahrahotel.com.au. Bus #378 from Central CityRail, #380 from Circular Quay CityRail. Stalwart of the Sydney fine-dining scene, this classic, though pricey, French bistro is fighting back the competition with the superb cooking of chef Damien Pignolet. Most mains around $40. No bookings. Licensed. Mon 6–10.30pm, Tues–Sun noon–3pm & 6–10.30pm.

Grand National Hotel 161 Underwood St, corner of Elizabeth St, Paddington ☎02/9963 4557. Bus #378 from Central CityRail, bus #380 from Circular Quay CityRail. A grand pub-restaurant that has moved with the times and is now dishing up fine contemporary fare, with old-fashioned attentive service. Bookings are essential on weekends, Sunday lunch being a peak time for locals recovering from the night before. Mains $26–35. Tues–Thurs 6–10.30pm, Fri & Sat noon–3pm & 6–10.30pm, Sun noon–3pm & 6–9pm.

Paddington Inn Bistro 338 Oxford St, Paddington ☎02/9380 5913, ⓦwww.paddingtoninn.com.au. Bus #378 from Central CityRail, bus #380 from Circular Quay CityRail. Busy upmarket pub-bistro with a tasty menu, from salt and pepper squid ($16) to lamb shoulder ragout ($23). The decor of textured glass, cushioned booths, polished concrete floors and fabric-lined walls is dark but comfortable, and perfect for a few long hours spent over drinks, dinner and dessert. Packed on Saturdays, as it's opposite the market, but there's a good crowd most nights. Mon–Thurs noon–3pm & 6–10pm, Fri noon–3pm & 6–9pm, Sat noon–4pm & 6–9pm, Sun 1–9pm.

Royal Hotel Bar & Grill Royal Hotel, 237 Glenmore Rd, Five Ways, Paddington ☎02/9331 5055, ⓦwww.royalhotel.com.au. Bus #389 from Circular Quay CityRail. Grand old triple-storey pub-restaurant, with antiques and classic cornicing, which serves mouthwatering steaks. Eating on the veranda is a real treat, with views over the art gallery and Five Ways action below. They don't take bookings and tables fill fast, but the slick upstairs cocktail lounge, *Elephant Bar* (see p.209), means even the wait for a seat can be enjoyable. Mon–Fri noon–3pm & 6–10pm, Sat noon–10pm, Sun noon–9pm.

South Darlinghurst, Surry Hills and Waterloo

See map, p.102.

Cafés, snacks and light meals

Abdul's 563 Elizabeth St, corner of Cleveland St ☎02/9698 1275. Bus #393, #395 from Central CityRail. Here since 1968, this cheap Lebanese option is a late-night, post-pub institution. Eat in or take away with dishes from $8 and mixed plates from $18; belly-dancing Fri & Sat nights. BYO.

Mon–Wed & Sun 10am–midnight, Thurs–Sat 10am–2am.

Battuta 179 Oxford St, Darlinghurst ☏02/9331 3229. Bus #378 from Central CityRail, bus #380 from Circular Quay CityRail. With a broad-ranging, largely gay clientele, this Oxford St favourite serves dependably good Italian food (chicken parmigiana for $17 or salmon risotto for $20) and coffee in a location that ensures you'll miss none of the street life. Licensed & BYO. Mon–Thurs & Sun 7am–11.30pm, Fri 7am–3am, Sat 24hr.

Betty's Soup Kitchen 84 Oxford St, Darlinghurst. Bus #378 from Central CityRail, bus #380 from Circular Quay CityRail. As the name suggests, soup is the speciality; continually changing specials make for a cheap but filling meal, served with damper bread (an Australian campfire staple). They also serve very simple but cheerful mains like thicker stews, sausages or fish fingers with mash, pasta and salads, plus delicious home-made ginger beer or lemonade and desserts. Nothing over $15. Licensed and BYO. Mon–Thurs & Sun noon–10.30pm, Fri & Sat noon–11.30pm.

bills Surry Hills 359 Crown St, Surry Hills ☏02/9360 4762. Bus #301–303 from Circular Quay CityRail or Castlereagh St. Sister of *bills* Darlinghurst branch (see p.185), this relaxed place serves equally good breakfasts and stays open for bistro dinner (perhaps steak frites, or fish cakes; mains mostly $23–28), or just a glass of wine. Licensed. No bookings. Daily 7am–10pm.

The Book Kitchen 255 Devonshire St, Surry Hills ☏02/9310 1003. Bus #301–303 from Circular Quay CityRail or Castlereagh St. Great all-day dining (and a little cook-book browsing) in this casual café converted from a garage. Organic and free-range products are used where possible in out-of-the-ordinary dishes such as soft-boiled eggs with Vegemite soldiers ($10), kipper omelette with pickled carrot ($16), and dry aged beef on rye, with fig and beetroot relish and onion rings ($17). Licensed. Mon–Thurs & Sun 8am–4pm, Fri & Sat 8am–4pm & 6.30–10pm.

🏃 **Bourke Street Bakery** 633 Bourke St, Surry Hills ☏02/9699 1011. Bus #301–303 from Circular Quay CityRail or Castlereagh St, City. Superb cakes, breads and pastries are the reason to detour to this exemplary street-corner bakery-café. Just three mini-tables inside, but the seats outside catch the afternoon sun and are great for tucking into a flaky *pain au*

chocolat or a pear and rhubarb tart. Mon–Fri 7am–6pm, Sat & Sun 8am–5pm.

Grumpy Baker 151 Oxford St, Darlinghurst ☏02/9380 4177. Bus #378 from Central CityRail, bus #380 from Circular Quay CityRail. For coffees, breads, pies and pastries, there's no ignoring this popular street café in the heart of the gay strip. Mon–Fri 6am until late, Sat & Sun 24hr.

Maltese Cafe 310 Crown St, Surry Hills. Bus #301–303 from Circular Quay CityRail or Castlereagh St, City. Established in the early 1940s, this café is known for its delicious (and ridiculously cheap at $1.50) Maltese *pastizzi* – flaky pastry pockets of ricotta cheese, plain or with meat, spinach or peas – to eat in or take away. Also enormous servings of fresh lasagne and other pastas ($9). No alcohol. Tues–Sat 9am–8pm, Sun & Mon 9am–6pm.

Maya Indian Sweets 470 Cleveland St, Surry Hills. Bus #393 or #395 from Central CityRail. This very cheap, authentic South Indian cafeteria-style restaurant (you pay at the counter) is always popular with local Indian families, especially at weekends for the exquisite vegetarian food, including *dosas*, *chaat* salads, *paneer kulcha*, *thalis* and more. Great-value weekday specials ($8, Fri $10) and a vast display of very sickly Indian sweets. BYO. Daily 10.30am–10.30pm.

🏃 **Café Mint** 579 Crown St, Surry Hills ☏02/9319 0848. Bus #301–303 from Circular Quay CityRail or Castlereagh St, City. Wonderful smart-casual café that gives a Mediterranean–Middle Eastern twist to the usual urban breakfasting scene. Try the beautifully presented Turkish breakfast of roast tomato, spinach, boiled egg, olives, grilled haloumi & *za'atar* toast ($14.50). Also open for lunch and dinner, when you might tuck into beef cheek with merguez sausage, white beans, preserved lime and figs ($23). Licensed. No bookings or credit cards. Mon 7am–5pm, Tues–Sat 7am–9.30pm.

Mohr Fish 202 Devonshire St, Surry Hills ☏02/9318 1326. Bus #301–303 from Circular Quay CityRail or Castlereagh St, City. This tiny but stylish and convivial fish'n'chip bar, with stools and tiled walls, packs in the customers, and provides fresh, well-priced, well-prepared and sometimes distinctive seafood options. Pop into the pub next door and they'll come and fetch you when a table is free – you can even bring your drink in with you. BYO. Daily 10am–10pm.

Café Sopra 7 Danks St, Waterloo ☎02/9699 3174. Bus #301–303 from Circular Quay CityRail or Castlereagh St. Gain entry through the spacious Fratelli Fresh produce market and *provedore*, then order off the blackboard at this wonderful modern Italian café. Dishes such as butternut pumpkin, roast garlic and mozzarella risotto, and braised squid with peas and potatoes keep punters coming back for more. They don't take bookings so aim for a less busy time. Most mains $15–22. Licensed. Tues–Fri 10am–3pm, Sat 8am–3pm.

Restaurants

Balkan Continental Restaurant 209 Oxford St, Darlinghurst ☎02/9360 4970. Bus #378 from Central CityRail, bus #380 from Circular Quay CityRail. For almost forty years this bustling Croatian place has been chargrilling inside the front window, luring Sydneysiders in with good-value traditional continental favourites like schnitzels and mixed grills with potato, onion and cabbage salad, plus an extensive range of excellent fish and seafood. Be sure to try Balkan specialities such as *cevapci* (spicy skinless sausages), but save room for dessert. Licensed and BYO. Lunch and dinner Mon & Wed–Sun.

Billy Kwong 355 Crown St, Surry Hills ☎02/9332 3300. Bus #301–303 from Circular Quay CityRail or Castlereagh St, City. It's a fight for a table but worth the wait when traditional Chinese cooking gets a stylish modern slant at this restaurant run by celebrity chef Kylie Kwong. The space itself – lots of dark polished wood and Chinese antiques but brightly lit and with contemporary fittings – complements the often adventurous combination of dishes and flavours. Scallops, jellyfish, prawn wontons, plus *wagyu* beef, all with unusual sauces, are highlights. Mains from $26, but mostly $37–49. No bookings. Licensed and BYO ($10 corkage). Daily 6–11pm.

Erciyes 409 Cleveland St, Surry Hills ☎02/9319 1309. Bus #393 or #395 from Central CityRail. This busy, inexpensive, family-run Turkish restaurant, serves delicious *pide* – a bit like pizza – with thirty different toppings, many vegetarian, for around $10: try the *pynirli*, with feta, egg and parsley. They also serve cabbage rolls, stuffed eggplant and other cheap and tasty options, including delicious dips. A takeout section caters to those who didn't book. Belly dancing Fri & Sat nights. Licensed & BYO. Daily 11am–midnight.

Forresters Hotel 336 Riley St, Surry Hills ☎02/9211 2095. Central CityRail. While the menu includes roasted barramundi ($22) and chicken burrito ($15), the *Forresters* is best known for great steaks, with legendary specials Mon & Tues, when $7 buys a 200g sirloin steak with chips and salad. Wed sees a $10 pizza, and on Thurs they serve $8 cocktails. The three-level pub itself is very pleasant, with an unpretentious crowd. Licensed. Daily 11am–11pm or later,

Longrain 85 Commonwealth St, Surry Hills ☎02/9280 2888. Central CityRail. As much a cool cocktail bar as a restaurant, this popular spot is all warm, sensuous woods – big communal tables made of jarrah, black Japanese-style floorboards and pine walls. Superb Thai food, among the best in Sydney, and a hip clientele. Most mains $23–38. Bookings for lunch only. Licensed. Mon–Fri noon–2.30pm & 6–11pm, Sat & Sun 6–11pm.

🏃 **Mahjong Room 312 Crown St, Surry Hills ☎02/9361 3985. Bus #301–303 from Circular Quay CityRail or Castlereagh St, City.** Eat at real Chinese mahjong tables in this excellent Hong Kong Chinese restaurant. A cheaper alternative to nearby *Billy Kwong*, it serves a few more staples, like fresh tiger prawns and sugar peas in XO sauce ($23), and Peking duck with pancakes ($24). The three rooms are usually teeming and the atmosphere is casual. Licensed. BYO Mon–Wed only. Mon–Sat 6–10.30pm.

Maya da Dhaba 431 Cleveland St, Surry Hills ☎02/8399 3785. Bus #393 or #395 from Central CityRail. The more upmarket, non-vegetarian version of the phenomenally

▲ Billy Kwong

Loads of places in Sydney cater to hungry night owls, or those in need of a late-night caffeine fix, and some are open **24 hours**. At Circular Quay, *City Extra* – fronting the wharfs (between wharfs 2 and 3) – is a 24-hour licensed coffee shop. There's a **late-night food court** at the Star City Casino in Pyrmont (see p.88); nearby at the **Sydney Fish Market** you can start the day at 4am at the Italian-run *Fish Market Café* (see p.184). **Chinatown** holds several late-night options, such as *BBQ King* (p.183) and *Golden Century* (p.183). **Kings Cross** has the 24-hour *Café Hernandez* (see p.186) and late-closing *Macleay Pizza* (see p.186). At nearby **Woolloomooloo**, *Harry's Café de Wheels* (see p.186) has dished up pies until the small hours for nearly sixty years. On the **North Shore** you'll find *Maisys Cafe* (p.196), open 24hr.

popular veggie *Maya Indian Sweets* (see p.190) across the street. This one is also noisy and crowded, but it's much comfier, and decor extends to craft-covered walls. The tender goat curry and the Goan fish curry in particular are superb, and prices are low, with nothing over $17. Daily noon–11pm.

Nepalese Kitchen 481 Crown St, Surry Hills ☎02/9319 4264. **Bus #301–303 from Circular Quay CityRail or Castlereagh St, City.** Just walking into this staple of the Surry Hills scene is peaceful – all cosy wooden furniture, religious wall hangings and traditional music. Inexpensive specialities include goat curry, served with the freshly cooked relishes that traditionally accompany such mild Nepalese dishes (mains $12–16), and the simple but delicious *momos* (handmade dumplings stuffed with spicy chicken and vegetables or cheese and spinach). Lots of vegetarian options, and a lovely courtyard for warmer nights. BYO ($1.10 per person). Daily 6–10.30pm.

🏃 **Pink Peppercorn 122 Oxford St, Darlinghurst** ☎02/9360 9922. **Town Hall or Museum CityRail.** This place keeps springing up on critics' lists of favourite eating holes. It might have something to do with the unusual Laotian-inspired cooking

– which ranges from spicy chicken with yoghurt dressing to the signature stir-fried king prawns with veggies and pink peppercorns, and speciality lamb dishes – or the hip layout, complete with pictures of traditional monks on the back wall. Mains $21–25. Daily 6pm–midnight.

Prasit Thai 413 Crown St, Surry Hills ☎02/9698 5522. **Bus #301–303 from Circular Quay CityRail or Castlereagh St, City.** Be prepared for some inexpensive spicy Thai taste sensations amid the sage colour scheme. Since entrées are available cheaply by the portion, you can attempt to work your way through the delicious repertoire; plenty of vegetarian options too. Mains (mostly $12–15) cover the usual soups, curries and stir fries. Licensed. Daily noon–3pm & 5.30–10pm.

🏃 **Thai Nesia 243 Oxford St, Darlinghurst** ☎02/9361 4817. **Bus #378 from Central CityRail, bus #380 from Circular Quay CityRail.** Ever-popular low-key place serving delectable Thai dishes. Get the juices flowing with the betel leaf with prawn ($3.50 each), then choose from the likes of pumpkin chicken curry ($16) or roast duck salad ($18). It's all great value, and attracts a strong gay following. BYO ($2 per head). Daily 5.30–10.30pm.

Inner west

Stretching from Newtown and Glebe west to the very Italian Leichhardt and Haberfield, and harbourside Balmain, the inner west has a well-established café culture, with plenty of casual eateries and some great, often multicultural, restaurants and pub bistros. The area's pubs also usually serve up bar snacks and light meals; for more options, see p.210 of "Drinking".

Glebe

See map, p.106.

Cafés, snacks and light meals

Badde Manors 37 Glebe Point Rd ℡ 02/9660 3797. Bus #431, #433 or #434 from Central CityRail. Veteran vegetarian corner café with timber booths and the ambience of an early twentieth-century American diner. Always packed, especially for weekend brunch. One of the best cafés on this strip, with delicious cakes, cheering chai, and inexpensive and generous portions of tasty vegetarian chow. Mon–Fri 8am–midnight, Sat 8am–1am, Sun 9am–midnight. Kitchen closes at 10pm Sun–Fri, 11pm Fri–Sat.

Café Giulia 92 Abercrombie St, Chippendale ℡ 02/9698 4424 Central CityRail. Funky, easy-going café, hidden away in the backstreets of Chippendale, serving sensational coffee and a varied menu of beautifully cooked food that plays pretty arpeggios on your palate – breakfast is always good, and the Greek lamb salad is a winner. The interior is cool and artistic, while the sunny courtyard makes a perfect spot to laze with friends or a paper. Tues–Fri 6.30am–4pm, Sat & Sun 8am–3pm.

Fair Trade Coffee Company 33 Glebe Point Rd, Glebe ℡ 9660 0621. Bus #431, #433 or #434 from Central CityRail. Warm earth tones, indigenous artifacts, delightful ambience, funky music and dishes from around the world – Columbia, Morocco, Indonesia and the Middle East are all featured. Nothing over $17, plenty of vegetarian options, and the all-day cooked breakfast is a winner. Promotion of the Fair Trade standards is also a plus. Daily 7am–10pm.

Iku 25A Glebe Point Rd ℡ 02/9953 1964. Bus #431, #433 or #434 from Central CityRail. (Also at 612A Darling St, Rozelle; 168 Military Rd, Neutral Bay; 279 Bronte Rd, Waverly; & 62 Oxford St, Darlinghurst). Glebe's original *Iku* proved so popular it keeps branching out. Healthy but delicious macrobiotic meals and snacks, all vegetarian or vegan (the $3.50 rice balls and $8.50 macro burgers are popular), plus health-giving teas like the tasty anti-oxidant "Bancha". While the interior's a little bright, the leafy outdoor timber-tiered courtyard is very relaxing. Mon–Fri 11am–10pm, Sat 11am–8pm, Sun noon–7.30pm.

Sappho Books & Café Glebe Point Rd ℡ 02/9552 4498 Bus #431, #433 or #434 from Central CityRail. Colourful graffiti and murals (remnants of a gritty past) combine beautifully with luminous rainforest plants, timber lattice sidewalks, parasols and a sail shelter in this quintessential Glebe courtyard café, joined to a secondhand bookstore. Great coffee is the focus, but the paninis are cheap'n'tasty ($7–10), the grilled haloumi salad comes with pine nuts and tzatziki (salads $11–13) and who could say no to hot toasted banana bread with ricotta ($5). You can even down it all in arm's reach of the galaxy in the sci-fi and fantasy book room adjoining the courtyard Mon–Fri 8am–7pm, Sun 9am–7pm.

Well Connected 35 Glebe Point Rd ℡ 02/9566 2655. Bus #431, #433 or #434 from Central CityRail. At this funky and popular café, you can choose from pavement tables, sofas or balcony seats upstairs. With breakfast served until 5pm, when dinner starts, people blow in and out all day. Simple good-value menu – Turkish-bread sandwiches, burgers, pastas and salads – and generous servings. Try the chocolate lasagne for dessert. Mon–Fri 7.30am–10pm. Sat & Sun 7.30am–11pm.

Restaurants

The Boathouse on Blackwattle Bay End of Ferry Rd, Glebe ℡ 02/9518 9011. Bus #431, #433 or #434 from Central CityRail. Atmospheric restaurant located in a former boatshed, with fantastic views across the bay to Anzac Bridge and the fish markets opposite. Fittingly, seafood is the thing here, from ten different kinds of oysters to the raved-about snapper pie ($48). One of Sydney's finest fish restaurants; very expensive but worth it. Licensed. Tues–Sun noon–3pm & 6.30–10pm.

Cesare's No Names Friend in Hand Hotel, 58 Cowper St, Glebe ℡ 02/9660 2326. Bus #431, #433 or #434 from Central CityRail. Excellent, cheap Italian restaurant in the gazebo and beer garden of the characterful backstreet pub (see p.210). Generous pasta meals from $10 and pricier meaty main courses like schnitzels. Mon–Sat noon–3pm & 6–10pm, and Sun 6–8.30pm.

Darbar 134 Glebe Point Rd ℡ 02/9660 5666. Bus #431, #433 or #434 from Central CityRail. A cavernous old sandstone building with stone pillars and arched stone doors and windows provides a gorgeous setting for a surprisingly inexpensive – but superb – Indian meal. Mains average $18–20. Licensed and BYO. Mon noon–2.30pm, Tues–Sun noon–2.30pm & 5–10.30pm.

Newtown

See map, p.108.

Cafés, snacks and light meals

Campos Coffee 193 Missenden Rd, just off King St ☏02/9690 0294. Newtown CityRail. Superb coffee (possibly the best in Sydney) is the thing in this pocket-sized timber café – roasted, blended and ground in-house, and served up to perfection by trained baristas. The only nibbles on offer are a few delicious biscuits and morsel-sized pastries. Mon–Fri 7am–4pm, Sat 8am–5pm.

Citrus 227 King St ☏02/9557 3582. Newtown CityRail. An arched ceiling gives an appealing tunnel effect, while big white circular prism lightshades and sleek earth-tone design features generate a cosy atmosphere. Friendly service and huge servings of delicious food – the Mediterranean-inspired chicken-breast burger and steak sandwich are stand-outs. BYO. Mon–Thurs & Sun 8am–10pm, Fri & Sat 8am–midnight.

El Bahsa 233 King St ☏02/9557 3886. Newtown CityRail. Renovated Lebanese coffee lounge, with comfy cushioned booths and a funky retro-Seventies aesthetic. Good-value meals, both international and Lebanese, plus house-made traditional sweets. Mon–Thurs 5–11pm, Fri & Sat 9am–12pm, Sun 9am–11pm.

Tamana's North Indian Diner 196 King St ☏02/9519 2035. Newtown CityRail. Cheap, tasty fast meals to eat in or take away. Licensed and BYO. Mon–Wed 11.30am–10.30pm, Thurs–Sat 11.30am-11pm, Sun 11.30am–10.30pm.

Urban Bites 70–72 King St ☏02/9565 5888. Newtown CityRail. A diverse menu with great coffee, tongue-tingling pastas ($13–23), hearty burgers ($14.50) and serious sugar-for-your-bowl desserts; locals and the University crowd flock to the charming paved side courtyard with shiny timber tables and parasols to watch the world go by. The lively atmosphere inside is highlighted by a colourful photomontage of staff and customers. Daily 7am–late.

Vargabar 10 Wilson St ☏02/9517 1932. Newtown CityRail This tiny café – all

lime greens, purples and polished timber furniture – is a true treasure. A big fold-back window with cushioned seats and outside stools gives it a community feel; if the 1940s' pin-ups and the lounge and jazz music oozing from the stereo can't relax you, a shrink might be necessary. Staff are authentically nice, the food is great, but most of all, the coffee is exceptional (try the coffee frappe on a hot day). Mon–Fri 7am–6pm, Sat & Sun 8am–6pm.

Restaurants

Green Gourmet 115–117 King St ☏02/9519 5330. Newtown CityRail. Loud, busy and cheap Chinese vegan restaurant, which always has plenty of Asian customers, including the odd Buddhist monk. The Buddhist owner's creativity is particularly reflected in the divine tofu variations. To get a taste of everything, there's a nightly buffet or *yum cha* at weekend lunches, or you can order off the menu at lunch and dinner (mains around $15). The same people run the excellent Vegan's Choice grocery next door. Sun–Thurs noon–3pm & 6–10pm, Fri–Sat noon–3pm & 6–11pm.

Kilimanjaro 280 King St ☏02/9557 4565. Newtown CityRail. Newtown is the focus of a small African community, with the African International Market providing supplies at 2A Enmore Rd, just around the corner. This long-running Senegalese-owned place serves authentic and simple dishes that span Africa – from West African marinated chicken to North African couscous. Inexpensive, casual and friendly atmosphere, with African art and craft adorning the walls. BYO. Sun–Thurs noon–3pm & 6–10pm, Fri–Sat noon–3pm & 6–11pm.

Oscillate Wildly 275 Australia St, Newtown ☏02/9517 4700. Newtown CityRail. Newtown has plenty of fine eateries, but if you're looking to treat yourself with some tasty contemporary cuisine, the eight-course degustation menu here ($95) is exceptional. Vegetarian version available. Tues–Sat 6–10pm.

Steki Taverna 2 O'Connell St, off King St ☏02/9516 2191. Newtown CityRail. Atmospheric and moderately priced Greek taverna, with exquisite food, and live music and dancing at weekends – when you'll need to book. Courtyard dining is also an option. Licensed. Wed–Thurs 6.30–11pm, Fri–Sun 6.30pm–3am.

Sumalee Thai **Bank Hotel, 324 King St** 🕾 **02/9565 1730. Newtown CityRail.** Great Thai restaurant, which takes over the sleek mod-Asian designed lower beer garden of the Bank Hotel. Large servings (easily satisfying two) and spot-on flavours. Licensed. Sun–Thurs noon–10.30pm, Fri & Sat noon–11pm.

Thanh Binh 111 King St 🕾 **02/9557 1175. Newtown CityRail.** The Vietnamese food at this Newtown offshoot of the celebrated Cabramatta original is just as fresh, delicious and inexpensive. The roll-your-own rice paper rolls are sensational (and fun). Licensed and BYO. Tues–Thurs 5.30–10.15pm, Fri 5.30–11pm, Sat noon–11pm, Sun noon–10pm.

Leichhardt

See map, p.105.

Cafés, snacks and light meals

Bar Italia 169 Norton St, Leichhardt 🕾 **02/9560 9981. #440 from Central CityRail.** This is like a community centre, with the day-long comings and goings of Leichhardt locals, and positively packed at night. The focaccia, served during the day, comes big and tasty, and coffee is spot-on. Some of Sydney's best *gelato*; pasta from $13, plus more substantial meat dishes ($16.50–20). Shady courtyard out the back and a very cosmopolitan raised street deck out front. BYO. Daily 9am–midnight, kitchen closes 11pm.

Berkelouw Café 70 Norton St 🕾 **02/9560 5144. Bus #438 or #440 from Central CityRail.** Another bookshop/café combo where erudition is acquired and applied as much to the practical tasks of coffee creation as it is to colourful conversation. Explore the extensive book selection then grab a table and chair on the footpath outside or in a comfy interior lounge, and get those neurons sparking with a creamy nutty latte as you settle down to tackle *War and Peace*. Daily 7.30am–5pm.

Restaurants

Elio 159 Norton St, Leicchardt. #440 from Central CityRail 🕾 **9560 9129.** This very stylish Italian restaurant is perfect for a romantic evening or special celebration. Shiny timber floors and chairs, bright white tablecloths, a gorgeous lattice-tinged courtyard out back

and joy-inducing sophisticated food (mains $24.50–35.90) Mon–Thurs, Sat & Sun, Fri noon–2.30pm & 6–10pm.

Frattini 122 Marion St, Leichhardt 🕾 **02/9569 2997. Bus #438 or #440 from Central CityRail.** Popular and very busy Italian restaurant run by a genial family. Modern, airy space, old-fashioned service and moderately priced food. The fish is recommended, especially the whitebait fritters. BYO. Mon–Thurs noon–3pm & 6–9.30pm, Fri noon–3pm & 6–10pm, Sat 6–10pm.

Grappa 267 Norton St, Leichhardt 🕾 **02/9560 6090. Bus #438 or #440 from Central CityRail.** Among Little Italy's liveliest restaurants, with a busy open kitchen, a huge dining area and gregarious staff. The wood-fired oven takes pride of place and turns out tasty Italian sausage, pizza and pasta, plus more sophisticated and expensive mains ($31.50–39), including the signature slow-roasted duck. Licensed and BYO. Mon & Sat 6–10pm, Tues–Fri & Sun noon–3pm & 6–10pm.

Harvest 71 Evans St, Rozelle 🕾 **02/9818 4201. Bus #440 from Central CityRail.** Established in the 1970s, this vegan and vegetarian restaurant has kept up with the times, dipping into Vietnamese, Japanese, Italian and a whole range of cuisines. The moderately priced food is delicious, desserts decadent and the coffee gets the thumbs-up. Licensed and BYO. Tues–Sat 6–10pm.

🏃 **La Disfada 109 Ramsay St, Haberfield** 🕾 **02/9798 8299. Bus #438 from Central CityRail.** A little off the beaten track in Sydney's true Italian heartland, but reckoned to serve the best wood-fired pizza in town, as well as delicious pasta; no bookings so you might have to queue. Alfresco dining too. BYO. Wed–Sun 6–10pm.

Balmain and Rozelle

See map, p.105.

Cafés, snacks and light meals

Adriano Zumbo Patissier 296 Darling St 🕾 **02/9810 7318. Bus #432, #433 or #434 from Central CityRail.** Narrow slither of a place, with a wide selection of seriously divine cakes and pastries direct from the magical hands of a Paris-trained pastry master. Takeaway only. Mon–Sat 8am–6pm, Sun 8am–4pm.

Canteen 332 Darling St, Balmain 🕾 **02/9818 1521. Bus #432, #433 or #434 from Central CityRail.** Airy, high-ceilinged café with whitewashed walls, inside the old Working Men's Institute. Simple food: the generous baguettes, burgers and salads, and big cooked breakfasts are especially popular at weekends, when customers spill out onto the sunny outside tables. Order and pay at the counter. Mon–Fri & Sun 7am–5pm, Sat 6am–5pm.

Fundamental Food Fresh 266 Darling St, Balmain. Bus #432, #433 or #434 from Central CityRail. Funky modern space with a sliding glass front and two long rows of tables to each side – both with comfy cushioned wall seating. Always packed on weekends. Great breakfasts until 4pm, and the massive seafood Sizzling Platter ($26 – but large enough to share) comes highly recommended. Mon 7.30am–5pm, Tues–Sun 7.30am until late.

Rosebud 654 Darling St, Rozelle ☎02/9555 8999. Bus #432, #433 or #434 from Central CityRail. In a glorious modernized Federation corner building (1908), this very chic and expansive café is the perfect respite after a jaunt through Rozelle's weekend market, opposite. The inside/outside appeal of its massive fold-back windows and periphery-bound alfresco tables and chairs, its spacious interior's timber floors, sleek finishings and inspired murals, and the constant buzz of happy patrons, make this a perfect venue for great coffee and exceptional food – but quality is never cheap. Mon & Tues 7am–5pm, Wed–Fri 7am–5pm & 6pm until late, Sat 8am–5pm & 6pm until late, Sun 8am–4pm.

The harbour

For fine dining on the harbour, be sure to visit Watsons Bay and Balmoral where the appeal of delectable food is heightened by some of Sydney's most impressive water geography. While outwardly unassuming, Crows Nest plays host to a number of fine restaurants and cafés and is worth visiting for this reason alone. Several **pubs** around the harbour, in Neutral Bay, Watsons Bay, and North Sydney, serve good snacks and light meals. All have great **beer gardens**; see the box on p.211 and also the *Greenwood Hotel* on p.212.

Cafés, snacks and light meals

Bottom of the Harbour Seafoods 21 The Esplanade, Balmoral Beach ☎02/9969 7911. Bus #229 from North Sydney. An exceptionally good take-away, a little on the expensive side, but worth it. Regress into a child-like state with lightly battered fish'n'chips, yummy prawn cutlets, creative salads or something from the grill. A licensed sit-down breakfast/lunch bistro attached caters to more adventurous taste buds: try the truffle toast or zucchini fritters. Eat in on comfortable cushioned chairs, or take away and dine in Edwardian comfort on the grass overlooking one of Sydney's most picturesque harbour beaches. Mon–Thurs 9am–8.30pm, Fri–Sun 9am–9pm.

Maisy's Cafe 164 Military Rd, Neutral Bay ☎02/9908 4030. Bus #227–230 from North Sydney CityRail or bus #151, #184, #188, or #190 from City. Cool hangout on a hot day or night, with funky interior and music and great coffee. Good for breakfast – from mixed berry yoghurt ($8) to eggs Benedict ($13). The quesadillas are also a treat, as are the vegetarian frittata. BYO, ten percent surcharge for early hours at weekends. Open 24hr.

Peppermill Cafe 30 Glen St, Milsons Point ☎02/9954 1444. Milsons Point CityRail. A good place to recharge after walking over the Harbour Bridge or wandering through Kirribilli Markets, offering tasty pies, pastas and pancakes; BYO & licensed. Mon–Fri 7am–6pm, Sat & Sun 8am–4pm.

Tea Garden Cafe 8 Marine Pde, Watsons Bay ☎02/9337 6733. Ferry or water taxi from Circular Quay to Watsons Bay. A picturesque, parasol-protected, paved alfresco courtyard, backed by a bright green lawn and vibrant garden, with a cute shaded play area (with toys) for the children and a killer view across the harbour. Affordable too: big breakfast ($16), asparagus bruschetta ($13.50), nutella crepes ($12), focaccias ($10). Daily 9.30am–4.30pm.

Restaurants

The Bathers Pavilion 4 The Esplanade, Balmoral Beach ☎02/9969 5050. Bus #229 from North Sydney CityRail. Indulgent beach-house-style dining in the former (1930s) changing rooms on Balmoral Beach. The very pricey restaurant-and-café double-act is presided over by one of Sydney's top chefs, Serge Dansereau. Three-course, fixed-price dinner menu in the restaurant for $125 (from $110 lunchtime). Weekend breakfast in the café is a North Shore ritual – expect to queue – while the wood-fired pizzas are popular later in the day. Licensed. Café daily 7am–midnight, restaurant daily noon–2.30pm & 6.30–10pm.

Doyles on the Beach 11 Marine Parade, Watsons Bay ☎02/9337 2007; also Doyles Wharf Restaurant ☎02/9337 1572. Ferry or water taxi from Circular Quay to Watsons Bay. The former is the original of the long-running Sydney fish-restaurant institution, but both serve great if overpriced seafood and have delicious views of the city across the water. The adjacent boozer serves pub versions in its beer garden, and offers slightly more affordable takeaway options. Mon–Sat noon–3pm & 6–9.30pm, Sun noon–3pm & 6–9pm.

Epoque Belgian Beer Café 429 Miller St, Cammeray ☎02/9954 3811. Bus #202, #207 or #208 from Wynyard CityRail. A slice of Belgium in Sydney, with a Belgian owner and original wood panelling and fittings. Hoegaarden, Leffe Blonde and Brune, and Stella Artois on draught, plus almost forty other beers by the bottle. With room for just eighteen people at the bar, book a table and come to eat. Mussels, of course, are the thing, served with frites and mayo, or try the satisfying *andouillettes* (sausage) and mashed potato, all moderately priced. Mains $23.50–29.50. Licensed. Sun–Thurs noon–10pm, Fri & Sat noon–10.30pm.

Malabar 334 Pacific Highway, Crows Nest, ☎02/9906 7343. Bus #200 from North Sydney CityRail. Fantastic cafés, restaurants and bars are popping up regularly in this zone at the junction of the Pacific Highway and Willoughby Rd, north of North Sydney, which can also be reached by walking down the Pacific Highway from St Leonards CityRail. Drop by this Southern Indian place for saliva-inducing samosas and curries, then explore the surrounds for desserts or drinking. Good vegetarian options. Mon & Tues 5.30–11pm, Wed–Sun noon–3pm & 5.30–11pm.

Radio Cairo Cafe 83 Spofforth St, Cremorne ☎02/9908 2649. Bus #227–230 from North Sydney CityRail or bus #151, #184, #188, or #190 from City. Oozing African exotica – with African arts, crafts and artefacts, and ornate brass-framed flat-screen monitors playing Tarzan, Tin Tin and Casablanca movies – this funky café, directly opposite the fabulous Orpheum cinema, features a creative and varied menu with a strong emphasis on African tastes, complemented by a suburb selection of wines and cocktails (like the Cosmic Cairo). Mains $16.75–23.75. Licensed and BYO. Daily 6–10pm.

Sushi Samurai Shop 5, 197 Military Rd, Neutral Bay ☎02/953 4059. Bus #227–230 from North Sydney CityRail or bus #151, #184, #188, or #190 from City. With decor like a moody science-fiction movie scene this stylish Japanese restaurant is great value for money, serving excellent sushi and mains, like the popular "pork belly Peking duck style" winning the praise and loyalty of locals. Daily noon–3pm & 5.30–10pm.

Watermark 2A The Esplanade, Balmoral Beach ☎02/9968 3433. Bus #247 or #230 from North Sydney CityRail to Mosman Junction, then #257 or #238 from Taronga Zoo Wharf, or after 7pm bus #233 from Mosman South (Musgrave St) Wharf. For a memorable Sydney meal, both for location and food (modern Australian), you can't go wrong here. It offers views right across the water, a terrace to dine on under the sun or stars, a stylish interior and fabulous service (mains $33–39). Licensed. Mon–Thurs noon–3pm & 6.30–10pm, Fri noon–3pm & 6–10pm, Sat 8–10.45am, 12.30–3.30pm & 6–10pm, Sun 8–10.45am & 12.30–3.30pm.

Ocean beaches

From Bondi south to Maroubra, and from Manly north to Palm Beach, the **ocean beaches** hold a stash of great cafés and relaxed eating places: early breakfasts are a beachside speciality. Most local **pubs** also serve bar snacks and light meals, see p.213 of "Drinking" for more options.

Bondi and Bronte

See map, p.132.

Cafés, snacks and light meals

The Bogeyhole Café 473 Bronte Rd, Bronte ⓣ02/9389 8829. Bus #378 from Central/ Bondi Junction CityRail. Long-established café offering breakfast until 3pm and assorted lunch specials from $9. Top-notch iced coffee beneath a gorgeously ornate pressed-metal ceiling – don't forget to look up. Packed at weekends. Daily 7am–4pm.

The Earth Food Store 81A Gould St, Bondi Beach ⓣ02/9365 5098. Bus #380 from Bondi Junction CityRail. More a shop than a café but a good spot for veggie and organic snacks, takeaway espresso, grocery supplies and to peruse the excellent notice board. Mon–Fri 7am–6.30pm, Sat & Sun 7am–6pm.

Gelato Bar 140 Campbell Parade, Bondi Beach ⓣ02/9130 4033. Bus #380 from Bondi Junction CityRail. A gleaming window display of creamy continental cakes and strudels lures beach-goers to this Hungarian-run place, which has been serving up Eastern European dishes since 1958, as well huge portions of cake and *gelato*. Old-fashioned coffee-lounge decor. Mon–Fri & Sun 8am–11pm, Sat 8am–midnight.

🏃 **Gertrude & Alice Cafe Bookstore** 46 Hall St at Consett Ave, Bondi Beach ⓣ02/9130 5155. Bus #380 or #389 from Bondi Junction CityRail. It's hard to decide if *Gertrude & Alice's* is a café or a secondhand bookshop. With small tables crammed into every available space, a big communal table and a comfy couch for lounging, browsers can struggle to get to the books at busy café times. A homely hangout with generous, affordable servings of Greek and Mediterranean food, great cakes, coffee and a hubbub of genial conversation. Daily 7.30am–9.30pm.

Gusto 16 Hall St, Bondi Beach ⓣ02/9130 4565. Bus #380 or #389 from Bondi Junction CityRail. This deli-café creates quite a Bondi scene, with its cosmopolitan crew of regulars and travellers blocking the pavement outside. Excellent coffee, delicious edibles piled high, and a separate deli counter, too. There's just enough room for a few more people to perch on stools inside and along the front. Good notice board. Daily 6am–7pm.

Lamrock Cafe 72 Campbell Parade, corner of Lamrock Ave, Bondi Beach ⓣ02/9130 6313. Bus #380 from Bondi Junction CityRail. Stalwart

lively Bondi café. The unpretentious local crowd comes for magnificent ocean views, uncomplicated food – *panini*, salads, pasta, burgers and fish'n'chips – and breakfasts. Umbrella-covered tables outside, cushions inside. Licensed. Daily 7am–9pm.

Lauries Vegetarian 286 Bondi Rd, Bondi ⓣ02/9365 0134. Bus #380 from Bondi Junction CityRail. Excellent veggie takeaway with a couple of eat-in tables. Daily noon–10pm.

The One That Got Away 163 Bondi Rd, Bondi ⓣ02/9389 4227. Bus #380 from Bondi Junction CityRail. Award-winning takeaway fish shop that even sells kosher fish and sushi; also BBQ grills and fish'n'chips. A small eat-in section serves salads and unusual yam chips. Daily 8am–9pm.

Sejuiced Bondi Pavilion, Bondi ⓣ02/9300 0253. Bus #380 from Bondi Junction CityRail. Sunbathers stroll up from the beach for delicious fresh juices, smoothies and frappes to slake their thirst. Plenty of snacky food too, with Turkish-bread focaccia and salads. Daily 6.30am–7pm.

🏃 **Sabbaba** 82 Hall St, Bondi ⓣ02/9365 7500. Bus #380 or #389 from Bondi Junction CityRail. Excellent value non-kosher Israeli-run café (*sabbaba* is Hebrew for "great" or "cool") in the heart of Bondi's small Jewish quarter. Great felafel (around $9), grilled chicken, salads, tabouleh and a selection of gooey baklava made from all sorts of different nuts. Daily from 11am until 8pm or later.

Speedo's 126 Ramsgate Ave, North Bondi ⓣ02/9365 3622. Bus #380 or #389 from Bondi Junction CityRail. Totally casual café bang opposite the north end of the beach, where locals and their kids and dogs hang out, with no busy road to spoil the view. The inexpensive breakfast specials are very popular; expect long waits for your order. Daily 5.30am–6pm.

Restaurants

Bondi Social 1st Floor, 38 Campbell Parade, Bondi Beach ⓣ02/9365 1788. Bus #380 from Bondi Junction CityRail. You could easily miss the sandwich-board sign that leads you to this hidden gem, but a million-dollar balcony view of the beach awaits the diner who wants to escape the melee of the Campbell Parade pavement. The interior is wood-rich and dimly lit at night; the mood promises romance, and the interesting, world-ranging menu (mains $11–15) includes such dishes as spiced kangaroo with sweet potato,

spinach and native berry jus. Licensed.
Mon–Fri noon–late, Sat & Sun 8am–late.

Bondi Trattoria 34B Campbell Parade, Bondi
Beach ☎02/9365 4303. Bus #380 from Bondi
Junction CityRail. Considering the setting,
with outdoor seating overlooking the beach,
Bondi Tratt is not at all expensive. Come to
take in the view and the invariably buzzing
atmosphere over breakfast, lunch and dinner,
or even a coffee. Serves contemporary
Australian and Italian food. Licensed & BYO.
Mon–Fri 7am–10pm, Sat & Sun 8am–10pm.

Brown Sugar 106 Curlewis St, Bondi ☎02/9130
1566, ⓦwww.brownsugarbondi.com.au. Bus
#389 from Bondi Junction CityRail. A stroll from
the northern end of the beach, this little café
is tucked in a quiet residential street around
the corner from the North Bondi shops.
The decor is funky distressed, the staff
– cooking at the open kitchen – suitably
sweet, and the atmosphere comfortable
and relaxed. Locals straggle in for the very
good breakfast menu (mostly $9–14); the
chefs have an interesting way with eggs,
from green eggs (with pesto) to Moroccan
(with spiced capsicum), and the pancakes
come with a week's supply of fruit. Lunch
on toasted Turkish sandwiches, salad and
pasta, and the dinner menu features a
delicious array of Mod Oz mains ($29–32)
such as Scotch fillet with braised shallots
and shitake mushrooms. Tues–Thurs
6.30pm until late, Fri–Sun 8.30am–2.30pm
& 6.30pm until late.

Gelbison Pizzeria 10 Lamrock Ave, Bondi Beach
☎02/9130 4022. Bus #380 from Bondi Junction
CityRail. Popular "breezy" pizzeria with sea
views from a couple of pavement tables. The
pizzas get the critical thumbs-up and range
from traditional to inspired – the potato and
garlic one is surprisingly good. Big range of
pasta, too ($13–17). Book later in the week,
as the place fills up fast. BYO. Mon–Thurs &
Sun 5–10pm, Fri & Sat 5–11pm.

🏃 **Icebergs Dining Room and Bar** 1 Notts
Ave, Bondi Beach ☎02/9365 9000.
Bus #380 from Bondi Junction CityRail. In the
renovated Bondi Icebergs Club building, this
restaurant has got it all – the views, the sharp
surrounds, the celebs and cuisine to put it
in Sydney's top ten. Don't expect all that to
come cheap, though; the Mediterranean-
style mains are $40–50, but, hey, you only
live once. Valet parking $30. Tues–Sat
noon–3pm & 6.30–9.30pm, Sun noon–3pm
& 6.30–8.30pm.

North Bondi RSL 120 Ramsgate Ave, North Bondi.
Bus #380 or #389 from Bondi Junction CityRail.
Cheap drinks, low-cost bistro meals ($11–20)
and uninterrupted beach views make an
unbeatable combination at this formerly
near-deserted but now prettied-up RSL
club. Licensed. Mon–Thurs noon–midnight,
Fri–Sun 10am–midnight.

🏃 **North Bondi Italian Food** 118 Ramsgate
Ave, North Bondi ☎02/9300 4400. Bus
#380 or #389 from Bondi Junction CityRail.
In a suburb with fierce competition, this
trattoria has perhaps the best combination
of gorgeous beach views and wonderful
food at reasonable prices. Try the warm
beef, salsa and chilli panini ($17), or the
rigatoni with pork sausage, sage and garlic
sauce ($27). For quiet dining eat early, or
come late when the vibe amps up and the
fashionable set arrive. Licensed. Mon–Thurs
6–11pm, Fri–Sun noon–4pm & 6–11pm.

No Name Beach Road Hotel, 71 Beach Rd at
Glenayr Ave, Bondi ☎02/9130 7247. Bus #389
from Bondi Junction CityRail. *The* choice for a
big, filling, cheap and tasty Italian feast after
a day at the beach. Eat in the sunny beer
garden. Pasta $10, mains like veal in tomato
sauce $14. Licensed. Daily noon–10pm.

Sean's Panaroma 270 Campbell Parade,
Bondi Beach ☎02/9365 4924. Bus #380 or
#389 from Bondi Junction CityRail. A funky,
relaxed little restaurant across from the
north end of the beach. Sean Moran's food
is some of the best and most inventive in
Sydney – the blackboard menu reflects the
latest inspirations, though Mediterranean
is the touchstone. Mains around $40.
Licensed & BYO (corkage $20 per bottle).
Wed–Fri 6.30–9.30pm, Sat noon–3pm &
6.30–9.30pm, Sun noon–3pm.

Eastern beaches: Clovelly, Coogee and Maroubra

See map, p.137.

Cafés, snacks and light meals

Art Lounge Café 275 Arden St, Coogee
☎02/9665 2500. Bus #372 from Central Cityrail,
#373 or #374 from Circular Quay CityRail. Well
worth the short walk up the hill, just south of
the beach. Sink into a soft chair, lose yourself
in the paintings, bring yourself round with a
coffee, and restore your energy with an all-
day breakfast or gourmet burger that won't
break the bank. Wed–Sun 8am–4pm.

Barzura 62 Carr St, Coogee ☎02/9665 5546. Bus #372 from Central CityRail; #373 or #374 from Circular Quay CityRail. Fantastic spot with ocean views, this popular café–restaurant serves a wholesome breakfast until 1pm, snacks until 7pm, with pasta deals 5–7pm, and restaurant meals – from seafood spaghetti to grilled kangaroo rump – at lunch and dinner. Unpretentious though stylish service encourages a local crowd and it's always packed. Lunch dishes cost $12–18, dinner mains $25–30. Licensed and BYO. Daily 7am–11pm.

Erciyes II 262 Coogee Bay Rd, Coogee ☎02/9664 1913. Bus #372 from Central CityRail; #373 or #374 from Circular Quay CityRail. This casual eat-in or takeaway place has delicious $5 *pide* – Turkish-style pizzas – halal kebabs and just-baked bread and tasty dips that are perfect for a beach picnic. BYO. Daily 10am–midnight.

The Globe 203 Coogee Bay Rd, Coogee ☎02/9665 9495. Bus #372 from Central CityRail; #373 or #374 from Circular Quay CityRail. Relaxed local daytime hangout serving good organic coffee and interesting, healthy food, from gourmet sandwiches to Mediterranean-slanted mains. Daily 8am–4pm.

In The Mood For Thai 224 Coogee Bay Rd, Coogee ☎02/9664 4788. Bus #372 from Central CityRail; #373 or #374 from Circular Quay CityRail. Crap name but delicious soups, curries and noodle dishes served in chic modern surrounding with dim lighting. Try the lemongrass and kaffir-lime-leaf steamed mussels with basil ($15). Daily noon–11pm.

Melonhead 256 Coogee Bay Rd, Coogee ☎02/9664 3319. Bus #372 from Central CityRail; #373 or #374 from Circular Quay CityRail. The smell of fresh fruit wafts down the street from this fantastic juice bar. Custom-made smoothies, crushes and milkshakes, plus enticing salads and Turkish rolls, and good coffee. Daily 6am–8pm.

The Pool Caffe 94 Marine Parade, Maroubra ☎02/9314 0364. Bus #376 or #377 from Circular Quay CityRail. In a quiet residential spot opposite the Mahon sea pool on the Coogee–Maroubra coastal walk, this café has a relaxed holiday feel. Breakfast on organic porridge and fresh-fruit plates, have a coffee with fresh muffins, biscuits and cakes, or tuck into more expensive restaurant-style meaty modern food, often with an Indian or Italian flavour (bookings recommended weekends). Mains from $17. Mon & Tues 8am–3pm, Wed–Sat 8am–10pm, Sun 8am–6pm.

Restaurants

Chilli Box 205 Coogee Bay Rd, Coogee ☎02/9665 2044. Bus #372 from Central CityRail, #373 or #374 from Circular Quay CityRail. Follows the current trend for Thai food – choose your noodles, choose your flavours. Good fresh ingredients, the clatter of woks, and plenty of other diners make this a great place for a cheap feed. Mostly $15–17 with lunch specials until 4pm. BYO. Daily 11.30am–10pm.

Coogee Bay Hotel Brasserie 212 Arden St, Coogee ☎02/9665 0000. Bus #372 from Central CityRail, #373 or #374 from Circular Quay CityRail. Very reasonably priced pub food, with an interesting menu, but traditionalists can cook their own steaks on the barbie, and breakfast is available. Licensed. Daily 6.30am–10.30pm.

Jack & Jill's Seafood 98 Beach St, Coogee ☎02/9665 8429. Bus #372 from Central CityRail, #373 or #374 from Circular Quay CityRail. This down-to-earth fish restaurant is a local legend. Come here to enjoy beautifully cooked fish from the basic battered variety to tasty tandoori perch. Mains cost $14–23. BYO (corkage $2.50 per head). Daily from 5pm, Sun from noon.

Swell Restaurant 465 Bronte Rd, Bronte ☎02/9386 5001. Bus #372 from Central CityRail, #373 or #374 from Circular Quay CityRail. One of the few Bronte café-restaurants to open in the evening down at the beach. Sit inside for the latest in sharp interiors, or out on the pavement for the million-dollar Bronte Beach view. With plenty of competition around, prices are very reasonable for what you get. Dinner mains $28–32. Licensed. Daily 7am–10pm.

Wet Paint 50 Macpherson St, Waverley ☎02/9369 4634. Bus #372 from Central CityRail, #373 or #374 from Circular Quay CityRail. Everything about this off-the-beaten-track place says it's an old faithful. The menu never changes much, the decor has a frayed homeliness and the delicious Cajun-slanted cooking is all done within a few metres of your seat. Very reasonable at $18–27 for mains. Licensed & BYO. Tues–Sat 6–10pm.

Manly and the northern beaches

See map, p.139.

Cafés, snacks and light meals

Bacino Bar 1A The Corso, Manly ☎02/9977 8889. Ferry to Manly Wharf. All-day café with a wide range of mainly Italian food, including standard lasagne, pasta and risotto (all $9), and some Australian favourites too. The lounge area and communal tables upstairs add to the beachside vibe. Licensed and BYO. Mon–Sat 6am–5pm, Sun 7am–5pm.

Jellyfish 93 North Steyne, Manly ☎02/9977 4555. Ferry to Manly Wharf. Away from the bustle around the Corso but still right across the road from the beach, this casual café serves breakfast until 4pm, great coffee and has a heap of outside seating. Licensed & BYO. Daily 7am–11pm.

Sandbar Café 1 Marine Parade, Shelly Beach ☎02/9977 4122. Ferry to Manly Wharf. If you can't afford to dine at the adjacent parent restaurant, *Le Kiosk* (see opposite), fish'n'chips from the attached takeaway makes an excellent alternative. Licensed. Mon–Fri 9am–4pm, Sat & Sun 9am–5pm.

Restaurants

Alhambra 54 West Esplanade, Manly ☎02/9976 2975. Ferry to Manly Wharf. You can't miss this place, opposite the wharf, when you get off the ferry. The owner is from Spanish Morocco, and the food is both authentic North African and Spanish – tapas, paella, *merguez* sausage, lamb and fish *tagines*, seven-vegetable couscous, and a chicken version of *b'stilla* all feature and are well priced. They even have flamenco dancers on Fri and Sat nights, and a classical Spanish guitarist on Thurs evenings. Licensed & BYO. Mon & Tues 6pm until late, Wed–Sun noon–3pm & 6pm until late.

Barrenjoey House 1108 Barrenjoey Rd, opposite Palm Beach Wharf ☎ 02/9974 4001, ⓦwww .barrenjoeyhouse.com.au. Upmarket guesthouse and restaurant, where sitting and gazing across the bay with a glass of wine in hand is almost mandatory. This might accompany a refined lunch or dinner of Hawkesbury rock oysters ($18 a half-dozen) followed by lobster, scallop and saffron risotto ($35). Licensed. Mon–Fri noon–3pm & 6–10pm, Sat & Sun noon–11pm.

The Boilerhouse Q Station Retreat, North Head ☎02/9976 6220. See p.143 for transport details. The mix of harbour views and the semi-industrial feel of this former boiler house for the old quarantine station makes a great setting for quality contemporary dining that's particularly satisfying when combined with a pre-prandial drink in the old engine house and a Q Station tour or play. Fine for lunching on goats' cheese salad or an elegant pasta dish (around $20), a full meal (mains $26–38) or just a coffee and a muffin. Tues–Fri 11.30am–11pm, Sat 8am–11pm, Sun 8am–4pm.

Le Kiosk 1 Marine Parade, Shelly Beach ☎02/9977 4122, ⓦwww.lekiosk.com.au. Ferry to Manly Wharf. The coastal walk from Manly Wharf to secluded Shelly Beach is a delight in itself, and *Le Kiosk* has just the right laid-back beach-house feel and a contemporary menu strong on seafood (mains $30–35) which doesn't quite match the quality of the view. Licensed. Mon noon–3pm, Tues–Sun noon–3pm & 6pm until late.

Manly Ocean Beach House Ocean Promenade, South Steyne, Manly ☎02/9977 0566. Ferry to Manly Wharf. The only restaurant on the water side of North Steyne enjoys uninterrupted beach views through its floor-to-ceiling windows. This stylish place packs them in, from breakfast (around $15), through to ever-so-elegant dinners. The ocean breeze makes the perfect accompaniment for mains such as blue-eyed cod on gnocchi with wild mushrooms ($35), or Sydney rock oysters ($20 a half dozen), and they serve delectable champagne cocktails ($12). Licensed. Daily 7am–10pm.

Out of Africa 43–45 East Esplanade, Manly, opposite Manly Wharf ☎02/9977 0055. Ferry to Manly Wharf. The zebra-skin seat-covers and tribal spears, masks and colourful photos put you in the mood for this modern-Moroccan-cum-African place serving the likes of "Couscous Royale" (for two people; $45), and fish *tagine* ($26), all prepared traditionally. Licensed. Mon–Wed 6–10pm, Thurs–Sun noon–4pm & 6–11pm.

Pacific Thai Cuisine 2nd Floor, 14 South Steyne, corner of Victoria Parade. Manly ☎02/9977 7220. Ferry to Manly Wharf. Offering crisp decor and fantastic views of the beach from its upstairs location, this inexpensive Thai restaurant serves fresh favourites, spicy seafood dishes, salads and vegetarian options. Licensed & BYO. Daily 11.30am–3pm & 5.30–10pm.

13

Drinking

A ustralians have a reputation for enjoying a drink or two, and most such activity takes place in hotels, more commonly known as **pubs**. After languishing for many years in a wilderness of serviceable though mainly bland pubs, Sydneysiders woke up one day to find a fashionable, renovated pub (the more hip of which are referred to as bars) on almost every corner, serving interesting food and offering everything from poetry readings and art classes to groovy Sunday-afternoon jazz or DJ sessions. This means that the choice of a drinking hole is wide, and you can be assured of finding one to suit any mood and taste. Determined not to be outdone by fashionable bars and cocktail lounges, traditional old **hotels** have upped the ante themselves, by employing renowned chefs and putting on food that's a cut above the old pub-grub fare.

In Sydney's funkier pubs (or bars) the *mixologist* – bartenders with a knack for a good cocktail – are seemingly ubiquitous, and imported beers common than not. For the other end of the spectrum, keep an eye out for RSL and Tradesmen's clubs, where the drinks remain ridiculously cheap, the food is honest, and conversation with the regulars always a treat. If you like to drink in historic surrounds, you can also choose from numerous Art Deco pubs.

Typically, pubs have at least one public bar (traditionally rowdier) and a lounge bar (more sedate), a pool table, and in some cases a beer garden. Many offer meals, either in a restaurant or bistro setting, or served up informally at the bar. Ten percent of the world's **poker machines** are found in New South Wales, however, and the noisy, money-eating things have taken over many Sydney pubs. We have chosen places where these monsters are absent, or at least few and unobtrusive. Some pubs and bars have 24-hour licences, though few actually stay open continuously (we have indicated those that have them, and their normal hours of operation). Standard **opening hours** are Monday to Saturday 11am until 11pm or midnight, and Sunday 11am until 10pm, but many places stay open until at least 2am or later, particularly on Friday and Saturday nights. **Smoking** at bar or service counters has been banned in New South Wales and a designated non-smoking area must be provided within at least one bar area.

Draught **beer** is served in a ten-ounce (half-pint) glass known as a **middy** (around $3) or a fifteen-ounce **schooner** (around $4.20). Imports such as Guinness and Stella cost a bit more. Three local beers readily available on tap are Toohey's New, a pretty standard lager; Toohey's Old, a darker, more bitter brew; and Reschs, a tastier, Pilsner-style beer. Upmarket places may only serve beer in bottles, costing from $6. Wine by the glass is available at many places, usually from $6, but expect to pay at least $8.50 for something choicer. Cocktail bars are very popular, and many offer **happy hours** (times given in reviews) that make a great chance to catch the sunset over cheap drinks; outside these times a cocktail will set you back $10–16.

A few **CBD** bars are closed on Saturday and most also close Sunday (the big nights out downtown are Thurs and Fri). **The Rocks**, with its huge range of popular old hotels and bars, is a fair option on any night, though it does attract a boisterous, beery crowd. Better choices for a cool, gay or arty scene include **Darlinghurst**, **Kings Cross and Potts Point** or nearby **Surry Hills**. You can get a drink any time, day or night, in **Kings Cross** and the old neighbourhood pubs of **Balmain** make for a great pub crawl. The best seaside drinking spots are **Bondi**, **Coogee**, **Watsons Bay**, **Manly** and **Newport**. Some pubs serve such good food that we have listed them separately in the "Eating" chapter. Likewise, some pubs listed in the "Live music and clubs" chapter also rank among the city's best watering holes.

The Rocks

Australian Hotel 100 Cumberland St, The Rocks. Circular Quay CityRail/ferry. Convivial corner hotel that seems always to be full of Brits. Inside, original fittings give a lovely old-pub feel, while outside tables on the footpath provide a genial atmosphere to take in the neighbourhood's historic charm. Known and loved for its Bavarian-style draught beer brewed in Picton, plus delicious gourmet pizzas with extravagant toppings that extend to native animals – emu, kangaroo and crocodile.

The Argyle 18 Argyle St, The Rocks. Circular Quay CityRail/ferry. A seamless and cinematic blend of the best of the past and the best of the future in a vast multi-zoned glass, stone and timber playground. Early nineteenth-century wool stores have been transformed with chic cubic furniture, sleek bars, impressive use of recycled timber and a suspended glass DJ booth. The numerous Bavarian beers are definitely worth a sample and the diverse food and cocktail menus deliver. Daily 11am–late.

Blue Horizon Bar 36th Floor, Shangri-La Hotel, 176 Cumberland St, The Rocks. Circular Quay CityRail/ferry. The mega-expensive top-floor lounge in this five-star hotel boasts a stunning 270-degree view – the Opera House, Darling Harbour, Middle Harbour and Homebush Bay to the Blue Mountains. Dress smart to get in. Mon–Thurs & Sun 5pm–late, Fri 3pm–late, Sat noon–late.

Glenmore Hotel 96 Cumberland St, The Rocks. Circular Quay CityRail/ferry. Unpretentious, inexpensive breezy pub perched over The Rocks, with great views from large windows in the public bar and spectacular ones from the rooftop beer garden, where large groups gather every night. A handy refresher

before or after the Harbour Bridge walk – it's opposite the pedestrian walkway entrance – serving unfussy, reasonably priced pub grub.

Harbour View Hotel 18 Lower Fort St, The Rocks. Circular Quay CityRail/ferry. Sibling to Balmain's stately *Exchange Hotel*, this three-storey renovated gem puts you right under the bridge – and close enough from the top balcony cocktail bar to raise a glass to the grey-overall-clad bridge climbers making their way back from the summit. The crowd is mixed, and better for it although drinks are a little pricey. Fine-dining restaurant upstairs.

Heritage Belgian Beer Café 135 Harrington St, The Rocks. Circular Quay CityRail/ferry. So authentic and Continental you'll forget you're in Sydney, with more than forty draught and bottled beers, plus oysters and other hearty European food. The whole atmosphere is conducive to a long session with good mates. Daily noon until late.

Hero of Waterloo 81 Lower Fort St, Millers Point, The Rocks. Circular Quay CityRail/ferry. One of Sydney's oldest pubs, built in 1843 from sandstone dug from the Argyle Cut (see p.57), this place reeks of history. The atmosphere is aided by a complete absence of TVs, blazing fireplaces in winter, simple meals and folk, dirty blues, trad Irish and jazz almost every night. Check out the classic ageing jazz quartet, the Heroes of Waterloo, on weekend afternoons.

Lord Nelson Brewery Hotel 19 Kent St (corner of Argyle St), Millers Point, Circular Quay Cityrail/ferry. Brewing six of its own beers since 1987, this pub is a beer-lover's paradise and attracts a unique and interesting crowd. Recommended tipples include the Three Sheets and the Old Admiral. Mon–Sat 11am–11pm, Sun noon–10pm.

Bars with views

Several Sydney pubs and bars offers wonderful harbour and beach **views**. The best are at the *Blu Horizon Bar* at the *Shangri-La* (see p.205) and at the *Glenmore Hotel* (p.203), both in The Rocks; *Cruise Bar* (below) around Circular Quay; the *Opera Bar* (see opposite) at the Opera House; *Orbit Lounge* in the Australia Square tower in the city centre (p.206); and by the beach at *Bondi Icebergs Club* (p.213) and *Coogee Bay Hotel* (p.211).

Mercantile Hotel 25 George St, The Rocks. Circular Quay CityRail/ferry. High-spirited Irish pub where Sydney's

best-poured Guinness accompanies filling bistro meals. Outdoor tables are great for watching the weekend market crowds.

Circular Quay and Sydney Opera House

While Sydney Opera House has several bars, including the very swish one at its top-notch restaurant, *Guillaume at Bennelong*, plenty of other bars may distract you as you walk around the concourse.

Cruise Bar Level 2, Overseas Passenger Terminal, Circular Quay West. Circular Quay CityRail/ferry. With glass walls providing an uninterrupted (unless by a passing cruise liner) view of the harbour and Opera House, the location of this fun and bright bar ensures it's popular with the young and urbane. You'll need to dress well, but drink prices aren't exorbitant, and cocktail classes are offered for the keen mixer. Daily 11am–late.

Customs House Bar 19 Macquarie Place, off Bridge St. Circular Quay CityRail/ferry. Ground-floor bar in an attractive building (circa 1826) fronting onto a city square near Circular Quay (but not at Customs House itself). A suited crowd spills out of the doors and schmoozes among the palm trees and statues. Cheap bar lunches. Mon–Thurs 11am–10pm, Fri 11am–11pm; closed Sat & Sun.

Opera Bar Lower Concourse Level, Sydney Opera House. Circular Quay CityRail/ferry. Stunningly located, like a tiered deck beneath the Opera House sails, with alfresco bar, tables and stylish parasols overlooking the Quay, the Bridge and the harbour, and a sleek glass-walled interior – the *Opera Bar* is almost perfect. All the more so for the entertainment, with some of Sydney's best DJ and live music nightly from 8.30pm and 2pm weekends, and a delectable bar-snack menu.

Quay Bar Ground floor, Customs House. Circular Quay CityRail/ferry. The stylish dark timber and cream-walled interior, with its

suspended industrial shelving over a central marble-top bar, is a looker. Outside, the expansive forecourt bar area is the winner however, with white parasols, timber high tables and a sleek industrial-chic bar oozing Continental alfresco sophistication. Come at twilight to take in the surrounding buzz of the city, while relaxing with a tasty affordable appetizer, exotic cocktail or simple, lip-smackingly good cold beer.

▲ Opera Bar

City centre and Haymarket

See map, p.75.

ArtHouse Hotel 275 Pitt St. Town Hall CityRail. Ⓦ www.thearthousehotel.com.au. Set in the grand nineteenth-century School of Arts Building in the middle of the CBD, this high-ceilinged space does more than just sell drinks. The main bar, *The Verge*, is a dramatic converted chapel. The polished wooden floorboards and beautiful Victorian-era design extend through four ever-changing rooms, which feature new and sometimes famous artworks. *ArtHouse* lives up to its name with life-drawing classes in the library (Mon at 6pm; $3), art exhibitions, short-film screenings and guest DJs. Both bar and restaurant food are moderately priced and taste great. Mon–Wed 11am–midnight, Thurs 11am–1am, Fri 11am–3am, Sat 5pm–6am, closed Sun.

Bambini Wine Room 185 Elizabeth St Ⓣ 02/9283 7098, Ⓦ www.bambinitrust .com.au. There's a refined yet far from stuffy feel to this chic modern bar with its pared-back Rococo styling. It features a fabulous wine list, and a great range of cocktails (around $16) such as the exquisite kumquat and green tea spiced mojito, or the Pash On, with vodka, poire William, passionfruit and fresh mint. Mon–Fri 3pm–late, Sat 5.30pm–late.

CBD 75 York St, corner of King St. Wynyard CityRail. Glamorous and swanky ground-floor bar in a renovated Victorian building, popular with an after-work crowd. The hotel covers four floors, which include an award-winning modern Australian restaurant and two other bars. Mon–Fri 11.30am–11pm or later, Sat 5pm–1am or later.

Civic Hotel 388 Pitt St, corner of Goulburn St Ⓣ 02/8267 3186, Ⓦ www.civichotel.com.au. **Town Hall CityRail.** Beautiful 1940s Deco-style pub, its original features perfectly preserved. Kick off your evening in the stylish main saloon which has DJs at weekends, then either head upstairs to the glamorous restaurant or down to the clubby *Civic Underground* with its white booths and fine sound system, mainly used for techno and house gigs: check website for upcoming events. A handy meeting point for Chinatown and George St cinema forays. Mon–Sat noon–11pm or later.

Establishment 252 George St. Circular Quay CityRail. The huge main room boasts an extraordinarily long marble bar, white pillars, high decorative ceilings, and an atrium and fountain at the back. Despite the size, it gets jam-packed, particularly on Thurs nights (when it's free champagne for ladies before 7pm) and Fri, when the door policy is very strict – glam for girls, smart (even suits) for guys. On level 4, *Hemmesphere*, is a sophisticated Ottoman Empire-themed bar room with cushions and lavish couches, and a drinks list to match. On-site ballroom, a world-class restaurant *est.* (with top chef Peter Doyle), *Tank* nightclub (p.219) and thirty-odd luxurious hotel rooms complete the deluxe options. Mon–Fri 11am–late, Sat 6pm–late.

Forbes Hotel 30 York St at King St. Wynyard CityRail. Atmospheric, century-old corner hotel with a lively, resolutely untrendy downstairs bar. Upstairs is more sedate, with a pool table and plenty of window seating – the best spot is the tiny cast-iron balcony, with just enough room for two. Happy hour Mon–Fri 5–6pm. Very popular Thurs & Fri nights. Mon–Thurs 11am–11pm or later, Fri & Sat 11am–5am.

The Ivy 320–330 George St Ⓣ 02/9240 3000. **Wynyard CityRail.** The beautiful people (and plenty of wannabes) flock to The Ivy, a massive complex of over a dozen bars and restaurants including everything from the glitzy IvyBar to the intimate Den cocktail bar and even the Pool Club with private cabanas around an open-air swimming pool. Dress sharp and join the queue (which snakes around the block at weekends) to get past the goons at the door.

Marble Bar 259 Pitt St Ⓦ www .marblebarsydney.com.au. **Town Hall CityRail.** A sightseeing stop as well as a great place for a drink: this was the original 1893 basement bar of the *Tattersalls Hotel*, and the stunningly ornate *fin de siècle* interior features Italian marble. It was preserved when the *Hilton Hotel* was built in 1973 and the *Marble Bar* was encased in concrete during major renovations in 2005, emerging more splendid than ever. Drinks are modestly priced, Tuesday is comedy night (from 6.30pm; $15 entry, including a drink), Wed & Thurs (7–10pm) have live jazz, and Fri & Sat feature funk and R&B (10pm–1am). (Also check out the glamorous *Zeta Bar* on Level 4, above.) Free entry. Mon–Thurs 5–11pm, Fri & Sat 3pm–2am.

Mars Lounge 16 Wentworth Ave, Surry Hills. Museum CityRail. With high ceilings, red-and-black decor, moody lighting, and heaps of seating – from booths to stools – *Mars* is both comfortable and stylish. DJ choices are eclectic and there's a different emphasis each night, from funky, retro-flavoured jazz, world grooves, Latin, Seventies funk and uplifting house through to electronica. Wed is comedy night. Mediterranean menu, including lots of shareable platters. Wed 5pm–midnight, Thurs 5pm–1am, Fri 5pm–3am, Sat 7pm–3am, Sun 6pm–1am.

Orbit Lounge Level 47, Australia Square, 264 George St. Wynyard CityRail. Australia's first Manhattan-style skyscraper, designed by perhaps Sydney's best-known architect Harry Seidler, was built in 1968, and the fifty-storey building remained Sydney's tallest for many years. The views from the revolving bar are best when darkness falls and the city is dramatically lit up. It's much easier to get in here than into the crowded *Blue Horizon Bar* (see p.203); dress code is smart casual. The drinks list is very James Bond (try the delicious Maserati cocktail, $18), and there's bar food if you're peckish. Open all night when custom justifies it.

Roof Bar Roof Level Skygarden, 77 Castlereagh St, Sydney. Town Hall CityRail. After a hard day shopping in the Pitt St Mall and surrounding centres, this Balinese-inspired rooftop bar is a breath of fresh air, literally, as you sit among the high-rises and look down at the bustling streets below. Very zen-like water features and a wooden sundeck make things relaxing, and the drinks are reasonable too. Mon–Fri noon–10pm or later.

Scruffy Murphy's 43 Goulburn St. Central CityRail. Rowdy, late-closing Irish pub with Guinness on tap, naturally; phenomenally popular, particularly with travellers and expats, who come for the nightly free covers bands and hearty home-cooking, including

$6 meal deals. Just around the corner from Central Station. Open until around 4am most nights.

Scu Bar 4 Rawson Place, off Pitt St. Central CityRail. This is the basement bar of the adjacent YHA, but it's open to all-comers. Not surprisingly, it's most popular with the area's many backpackers. Crab racing on Mon nights, and a party theme Thurs. Affordable pub prices and a casual atmosphere.

Senate Bar Lower ground floor, 1 Martin Place. Martin Place CityRail. Elegant, stylish bar below the old GPO, where lawyers and bankers come to sip on imported beers. Sandstone walls and funky ottomans provide a sophisticated feel. The good-value $12 curry-of-the-day lunch, which includes a drink, draws the punters in during the day. Mon–Wed noon–10pm, Thurs & Fri noon–11pm, closed Sat & Sun.

Slip Inn 111 Sussex St, corner of King St. Town Hall CityRail. Famous as the place where Tasmanian Mary Donaldson met her Prince Frederick of Denmark back in 2000, this huge three-level complex holds several bars, a bistro and a nightclub, the *Chinese Laundry*, overlooking Darling Harbour. A young style-conscious crowd still comes here, but it's dropped some of its past pretension. The front bar has a poolroom, while downstairs a boisterous beer garden fills up on sultry nights, with the quieter, more sophisticated *Sand Bar* alongside. Excellent wine list, with lots by the glass, and bar food including Thai. Mon–Thurs noon–midnight, Fri noon–3am, Sat 5pm–3am. Closed Sun.

3 Wise Monkeys 555 George St, corner of Liverpool St. Town Hall CityRail. A good mix of Sydneysiders and travellers come for the relaxed pub atmosphere, beers on tap, pool tables, live music and DJs. Daily 10am or 11am to 3am or 4am.

Verandah Bar 60 Castlereagh St. Town Hall CityRail. A lively after-work crowd packs out the *Verandah* on Fridays, when it's impossible to appreciate the wonderful spacious, white and shiny glass interior. You'll need to get in early for a prime position on the namesake veranda overlooking Pitt St, or in one of the great booths. If you're after a quiet chat, this isn't for you. Mon–Fri noon–11pm.

Darling Harbour

The eastern shore of Darling Harbour – Cockle Bay Wharf and King Street Wharf – is pretty much a continuous line of largely similar, modern, lively restaurant-bars. Go where feels good on the night, or follow our suggestions below. As well as these places you can also drink 24 hours in **Darling Harbour** at the *Star City Casino* (see p.88) and at *Home* nightclub (p.219), which has its own waterfront bar. The *Glasgow Arms Hotel*, opposite the Powerhouse Museum, is a pleasant spot for a drink, too. See map, p.84.

Cohibar Harbourside Shopping Centre, Darling Harbour ☎02/9281 4440. Harbourside Monorail. Classy cocktail bar across the water from the main Darling Harbour strip topped by a "cigar loft" that's perfect for a leisurely Cohiba (they're available in six grades) with great city views. Limited bar food, and DJs at weekends. Daily 10am–midnight.
Pontoon Cockle Bay Wharf, Darling Harbour. Town Hall CityRail. This open-fronted bar

with outdoor tables feels like one big, lively beer garden, right on the water opposite the marina and with big umbrellas to shade you from the sun. Attracts a young casual crowd, despite the upmarket restaurants surrounding it, and is a great place to wait for a table at *Chinta Ria* (on the level above; see p.185). Daily until late.

Inner east

Sydney's **inner east**, and Darlinghurst especially, holds the biggest concentration of places to drink, from fun pubs where you can play pool to some of the city's hippest bars. Many gay bars are also worth checking out: the legendary *Taxi Club* (p.231) makes a weird and wonderful place to end a big night out.

Kings Cross, Potts Point and Woolloomooloo

Kings Cross is very much a weekend party place with numerous bars from backpacker hangouts to chic cocktail bars and clubs, which we've listed in the "Live music and clubs" chapter. Down the hill, **Woolloomooloo** holds a couple of boisterous pubs plus the *Water Bar* and the *Tilbury Hotel*. See map, p.95.

Aperitif 7 Kellett St, Kings Cross ☎02/9357 4729. Kings Cross CityRail. Push through the restaurant to reach this sophisticated wine and cocktail bar, decorated in warm tones with Spanish tiles. European wines (many by the glass) are a strong point, but there's no lack of Aussies either and the bar staff know their way around them. The Moroccan/Mediterranean cuisine is excellent, too, and good value with exquisite mains under $30. Daily except Tues, 6pm–midnight or much later.

The Bourbon 24 Darlinghurst Rd, Kings Cross. Kings Cross CityRail. This infamous 24hr Kings Cross drinking hole was recently given a swish new upgrade, which unfortunately has done little to deter some of the colourful regulars. The place first opened in 1968 to attract US soldiers on R&R, and has become notorious for late-night "incidents", often including well-known sporting and media personalities. The addition of a terrace section upstairs (*The Cross*) and a lounge bar at the back, means more people are stopping off for a meal and to take in the still slightly low-rent ambience. Nightly happy hours (6–9pm) and $10 steaks all day are a big hit. Bands every night (usually cover bands) and DJs play retro at weekends. Mon–Fri 10am–6am, Sat & Sun 9am–6pm.
Hugo's 33 Bayswater Rd, Kings Cross. Kings Cross CityRail. Two venues in one. *Hugo's Lounge*, a very cool restaurant and beautiful bar, complete with ottomans to loll on, has a very decadent Oriental feel. It attracts a beautiful crowd and can be hard to get into. Good reason then to head downstairs

to stylish *Hugo's Bar Pizza* for superb cocktails, great pizzas and more. Prices aren't cheap, but on Sunday afternoons (3–6pm) they do half-price cocktails and pizza. Tues–Sat 5pm–late, Sun 3pm–late.

Lotus 22 Challis Ave, Potts Point. Kings Cross CityRail ☎02/9326 9000. Style and substance combine in the back room of the *Lotus Bistro*, and the padded snake-skin walls and retro wallpaper will put you in the mood for love, or at least a famous Lotus martini. Cocktails are a speciality, and there's an extensive list – enough to keep you happy all night, if you can afford it. Tues–Sat 6pm–late.

Peppermint Lounge 281 Victoria St, Kings Cross. Kings Cross CityRail. Decor is sexy and plush in this European-style bar, with plenty of couches and private booths to relax in. A young funky crowd enjoy deep house and hip hop. Wed & Thurs 6pm–4am, Fri & Sat 6pm–5am, Sun 6pm–3am.

Soho Bar & Lounge Piccadilly Hotel, 171 Victoria St, ⓦ www.sohobar.com.au Kings Cross. Kings Cross CityRail. Trendy Art Deco pub on leafy Victoria St, looking better than ever after yet another refurbishment. The ground-floor *Gold Room Bar* is the most fancy, but locals head to the upstairs *Leopard Room* (Fri & Sat only) to hang out on the back balcony and sample the seasonally updated cocktail menu. The attached nightclub, *Yu*, runs Thurs–Mon 10pm–6am.

Tilbury Hotel Corner of Forbes St and Nicholson St. Kings Cross CityRail. The beer garden isn't huge, but it's good-looking, opening up from the polished wood and leather furniture café-restaurant area behind the bar. Customers come not only for the hip atmosphere, but for the food – fruity breakfasts and lunches Mon–Sat 7am–4pm & Sun 10am–noon, plus nightly BBQs for $9–14. Sunday Sessions in summer include live jazz and soul and some surprise big-name artists. Mon–Thurs 7am–11pm, Fri 7am–midnight, Sat 9am–midnight, Sun 9am–10pm.

Water Bar W Hotel, Cowper Wharf Rd, Woolloomooloo. Kings Cross CityRail. The bar of Sydney's hippest hotel, this place is fabulously located in a dramatically renovated old iron-and-timber finger wharf. The sense of space is sensational, the lighting lush, and the sofas gorgeously designed and comfortable. A favourite with local celebrities, the pricey drinks (cocktails from $17) and the extortionate cost of the snacks are just about worth it for the architecture and ambience.

Darlinghurst and East Sydney

Several restaurants in **Darlinghurst** also have their own separate bars, including the dark and moody *Victoria Room* (see p.188). See maps, p.92 and p.102.

Courthouse Hotel 189 Oxford St, Darlinghurst. Bus #378 from Central CityRail, #380 from Circular Quay CityRail. Overlooking Taylor Square, the street-level bar of this pub often stays open 24hr. Totally undiscriminating – you may find yourself here in the wee hours amid an assortment of young clubbers and old drunks – and with cheap drinks. Wakes up around 1am. Mon–Thurs until 3am, Fri & Sat 24hr.

Darlo Bar Royal Sovereign Hotel, corner of Darlinghurst Rd and Liverpool St, Darlinghurst. Kings Cross CityRail. Popular Darlinghurst meeting place, with a lounge-room atmosphere. Comfy colourful chairs and sofas have a 1950s feel, though there aren't enough to accommodate the mixed and unaffected crowd who come to play pool or just curl up under the lamps and chat. Drinks, including the house wines, aren't expensive. At night you can order from the menus of local eateries (Thai, pizza, etc), and they'll fetch the food for you. Daily 10am–midnight.

East Village Hotel 234 Palmer St, corner of Liverpool St, Darlinghurst. Kings Cross CityRail. Downhill from the main Darlinghurst bar and café action, this beautifully tiled corner pub, built in 1917, sits alone in a grittier sleazy backstreet area – tables on the street provide a glimpse of the street life. The bar is self-consciously stylish, with wooden floors and red ottomans but the crowd is appealingly eclectic and nipping in for a beer is just fine. Mon–Sat noon–midnight, Sun noon–10pm.

Green Park Hotel 360 Victoria St, Darlinghurst. Kings Cross CityRail. A Darlinghurst stalwart, thanks partly to the pool tables in the back room and TVs over the doors, but mainly to the unpretentious vibe. There's nothing decorating the walls, the bar couldn't be more unassuming and humble bar tables with stools and a few lounge chairs accommodate the regular arty crowd. Very popular with gay men on Sunday evening.

Middle Bar 1st floor, Kinsela's, 383 Bourke St, Darlinghurst. Bus #378 from Central CityRail, #380 from Circular Quay CityRail. Formerly a deluxe Art Deco funeral parlour, *Kinsela's* has long been a lively drinking and dancing spot. The *Middle Bar* is seriously sexy, from its lush decor and sunken seating area to the young good-looking crowd who drink here. It's generally only open Fri (9pm–3am; $20) for R&B night, and Sat ($10) when it is more casual. You can gaze at the action in Taylor Square from the open-air balcony. The less glamorous ground-floor bar is open nightly.

Victoria Room Level 1, 235 Victoria St, Darlinghurst. Kings Cross CityRail. Classy cocktail bar that's all potted palms, Victorian wallpaper and dim lighting. Delicious drinks, and supper is served on Fri & Sat from 11pm (see p.188).

Paddington and Woollahra

In addition to the listings below, two lively drinking spots reviewed in the "Eating" chapter, the *Paddington Inn* and the *Grand National Hotel*, shouldn't be overlooked. See map, p.92.

Elephant Bar Royal Hotel, 237 Glenmore Rd, Paddington. Bus #389 from Circular Quay CityRail. The top-floor bar of this beautifully renovated Victorian-era hotel has knockout views of the city, best appreciated at sunset (happy hour 5.30–6.30pm). The small interior is great, too, with fireplaces, paintings and elephant prints. As it gets crowded later on, people cram onto the stairwell and it feels like a party. Mon–Thurs & Sun 5pm–11pm, Fri & Sat 3pm–midnight.

Fox and Lion The Entertainment Quarter, Centennial Park. Bus #339, #392, #394 or #396 from Central, Wynyard or Town Hall. On the way to a gig or movie in this area, people often stop off in this large modern bar with decent meals and plenty of TV screens showing sports or music videos.

Fringe Bar Unicorn Hotel, 106 Oxford St, Paddington ⓦ www.thefringe.com.au. Bus #389 from Circular Quay CityRail. The brown leather ottomans and multitude of chandeliers give a modern, almost exclusive, air to what is really quite a straightforward boozer. Reasonably priced drinks, good pub meals and pizzas (mostly $10–13) are a major draw but there's something on every night, such as comedy

on Mon, trivia or all-you-can-eat pizza for $10 on Tues. See website for details. Wed–Sat noon–3am, Sun–Tues noon–midnight.

Lord Dudley 236 Jersey Rd, Woollahra. Bus #389 from Circular Quay CityRail. Sydney's most British-style pub, complete with fireplaces, fox-hunting pictures, dark wood furniture – and a dartboard. The eighteen beers on tap include Newcastle Brown Ale and Guinness as well as lots of Aussie brews, while the bistro serves up hearty British grub. You can while away winter afternoons playing scrabble or backgammon in the comfy overstuffed chairs. Mon–Wed 11am–11pm, Thurs–Sat 11am–midnight, Sun noon–10pm.

Surry Hills

Surry Hills is packed with great pubs. A couple listed in the "Live music and clubs" and "Eating" chapters – the lively *Hopetoun Hotel* (p.217) and the sprawling cheap-eats venue *Forresters Hotel* (p.191) – are also fun drinking spots. The nearest station to the suburb is "City".

Bar Cleveland Corner of Cleveland and Bourke sts. Bus #372, #393 or #395 from Central CityRail. Huge plate-glass windows open onto the busy, gritty street, and punters come in for an authentic urban brew. Trivia competition on Mon, Wed $9 cocktails (6–9pm) and $10 meals (Mon–Wed only) bring in assorted colourful locals. Mon–Thurs & Sun 10am–2am, Fri & Sat 10am–4am).

Clock Hotel 470 Crown St, Surry Hills. Central CityRail or bus #301–303 from Circular Quay CityRail or Castlereagh St. Classy former pub where fashionable clientele are draped around the chocolate-coloured lounge bar and fill the booths and tables downstairs. It's a popular venue for after-work drinks, while the restaurant really excels, with prime seating on the veranda and a satisfying menu of burgers, tapas, pasta and risotto dishes (mains $15–25) and plenty of swish touches. Mon–Fri noon–3pm & 5–10pm, Sat & Sun noon–10pm.

Cricketers Arms 106 Fitzroy St, Surry Hills. Central CityRail or bus #301–303 from Circular Quay CityRail or Castlereagh St, City. Just down the road from the live music scene at the *Hopetoun* (see p.217), the *Cricketers* has an equally dedicated clientele. A young,

DRINKING | Inner east

offbeat crowd – plenty of piercings and shaved heads – cram in and fall about the bar, poolroom and tiny beer garden, yelling at each other over a funky soundtrack. Hearty bar snacks and a bistro. Mon–Sat noon–midnight, Sun noon–10pm.

White Horse 381–385 Crown St, Surry Hills. Central CityRail or bus #301–303 from

Circular Quay CityRail or Castlereagh St, City. Well-appointed two-storey bar, with open fires and ottomans, enough space to take the crowds, and an open, light balcony that sets it apart from other local bars. The staff really know their stuff and can whip up a delicious cocktail to go with either the swanky menu, or the cheaper bar food.

Inner west

The areas around the Sydney University – **Glebe**, **Chippendale** and **Newtown** – have always held plenty of lively pubs. Further west, **Leichhardt** and **Balmain** also have some great boozers, and the latter makes a good place for a bar crawl.

Glebe

Ancient Briton 225 Glebe Point Rd. Bus #431–434 from Central CityRail. Lively pub, popular with the area's travellers, now refurbished into a stylish boozer. The sleek upstairs "Pacific Penthouse" sports the world's largest fishtank bar, professional poker tournaments (daily 2pm & 7.30pm), DJs on weekend nights, live jazz, soul, and blues Thurs night and world music Sun afternoon. The food is Asian and modern Australian (check out the $10 deals) and goes down well in the Spanish-style courtyard.

The Clare 20 Broadway, Ultimo. Bus #431–434 from Central CityRail. Like a spacious retro lounge-room filled with comfy vintage couches and lightshades from antique furniture auctions; visiting this old amber-tiled pub, a short walk from Glebe, is the equivalent of a Newtown warehouse party experience. Local gig posters line the bar, the toilets are strewn with gritty graffiti, and the outside smoker's quarter, with its beer-keg tables and trippy mural, is as cinematic as a New York alley. Effortlessly cool.

Friend in Hand 58 Cowper St, corner of Queen St, Glebe ☎02/9660 2326. Bus #431–434 from Central CityRail. Character-filled pub in the leafy backstreets of Glebe, where all manner of curious objects dangle from the walls and ceilings of the public bar; a popular haunt for backpackers. Diverse entertainment in the upstairs bar (where you can also play pool) includes poetry, stand-up comedy and crab-racing nights – call to check what's on. A good Italian restaurant serves pasta from $10 (closed Sun lunch).

Chippendale and Newtown

In addition to the watering holes included here, the *Lansdowne Hotel* in **Chippendale** opposite Victoria Park has a great little cocktail bar upstairs and popular pool tables downstairs, while the *Sandringham Hotel* ("Sando") has long been one of **Newtown**'s favourite places to drink.

Bank Hotel 324 King St, Newtown. Newtown CityRail. Smart-looking pub, next to Newtown station, that's open late and always packed with arty local residents and visiting musos. The cocktail bar out back leads onto fantastic timber decking (lovely in summer) – with a great Thai restaurant, *Sumalee Thai*, in the leafy beer garden below.

Kuleto's 157 King St, Newtown. Newtown CityRail. Lively three-level but cosy cocktail bar, packed with inner-city types for the great two-for-one cocktails during happy hour (Mon–Fri 6pm–7.30pm, Sat 6pm–7pm). Dimly lit, earth-toned and comfy, and now equipped with a funky rooftop deck bar overlooking the city.

Marlborough Hotel 145 King St, Newtown. Newtown CityRail. A local favourite for a pre-dinner drink and a hangout for students from nearby Sydney University, the "Marly" is benefiting from almost a decade of major structural work. It's a spacious pub with a great beer garden and several bars, including a very stylish upstairs bar with a big breezy balcony (great for watching Newtown street life). Also a popular, good-value restaurant, serving diverse meals with an Italian slant. Cover bands Fri & Sat, trivia nights Wed. 24hr licence.

The Rose 54 Cleveland St, Chippendale. Bus #423, #424, #426 or #428 from Central CityRail. This funkily decorated pub near

Victoria Park is a real treasure, despite its unpromising location at the traffic-laden end of Cleveland St. A mock-Renaissance ceiling mural overlooks the busy interior bar, while the spacious, partly covered beer

Legendary beer gardens

Many Sydney pubs feature outdoor drinking areas, perfect for enjoying the sunny weather. These five, however, are outright legends:

The Coogee Bay Hotel Arden St, Coogee ⓦ www.coogeebayhotel.com.au. Bus #372 from Central CityRail or #373 or #374 from Circular Quay CityRail. Loud, rowdy and packed with backpackers from the nearby hostels, this enormous pub is legendary in the eastern suburbs. There's a huge beer garden (also open in winter when they crank up the heaters) where revellers can buy jugs of beer and cook their own meat in the garden from 9.30am until late. Among the five other bars is a big-screen sports bar for all international sporting events. Events include foam parties and a big Australia Day bash.

Watsons Bay Hotel 10 Marine Parade, Watsons Bay ⓦ www.watsonsbayhotel.com .au. Ferry to Watsons Bay Wharf or bus #324 or #325 from Edgecliff CityRail. Watsons Bay is Sydney's not-so-well-kept secret, and the *Watsons Bay Hotel* is the best place to experience it – a seat in the sun with a cool beer, fresh fish'n'chips from the renowned *Doyles* kitchen or a steak from the BBQ, and uninterrupted views across the harbour to the city. The hours will just disappear.

The Mean Fiddler corner of Commercial and Windsor rds, Rouse Hill ⓦ www.meanfiddler .com.au. No public transport. About an hour's drive from Sydney's CBD, the *Fiddler* is off the beaten track; you'll need your own transport but a day out here is not misspent. You might consider dropping in on a return drive along the Bells Line of Road from the Blue Mountains. Join the huge crowds at the 170-year-old Irish pub and sample the range of attractions – small, intimate rooms, open fires, live sport in the sports bar, and one of Sydney's best beer gardens – a large courtyard with cook-your-own-steaks and help-yourself salad bar by day and live entertainment at night.

▲ Newport Arms

Newport Arms Hotel Beaconsfield St, Newport ⓦ www.newportarms.com.au. Buses #L87, #L88, or #L90 from Wynyard CityRail. A famous beer garden pub, established in 1880 (and now claimed as Australia's largest) where crowds gather every afternoon to relax on the huge deck looking out over Heron Cove at Pittwater. Grab a gourmet pizza or bowl of pasta (under $20), something from the grill ($20–33), or a salad ($18). Good for families, with a children's play area. Always heaving at weekends, on major holidays and when everyone's watching a big game on the large outdoor screen.

The Oaks Hotel 118 Military Rd, Neutral Bay ⓦ www.oakshotel.com.au. Bus #247 or #263 from Wynyard CityRail. Generations of locals have spent Friday and Saturday nights in the North Shore's most popular pub, crowded out back beneath the giant oak tree that shades the large beer garden. Cook your own (expensive) steak, or order a gourmet pizza from the restaurant inside.

garden out back is a stylish, bustling hive of hip locals and students (doubling as a modern Australian eatery, with exceptionally good pizzas). Good wine list, available by the glass.

ZanziBar 323 King St, Newtown. Newtown CityRail. Three levels make for a three-in-one experience at this central Newtown watering hole. The spacious ground level oozes indie cool with a floor-to-ceiling poster-montage sidewall, circular high tables and stools and staff with attitude. The first floor's illicit red, mod-Eastern design, is all high-class Asian brothel, while the rooftop, with its iron-lace furniture, spot lighting and succulents, is an open-air temple to Middle Eastern cool – and a fantastic sunset spot. There's a great Spanish tapas menu, good-value mains (nothing over $15) and simple pizzas ($10) till late. Mon–Thurs 10am–4am, Fri 10am–6am, Sat 10am–5am, Sun 10am–midnight.

Balmain and Leichhardt

Exchange Hotel Corner of Beattie & Mullens sts, Balmain. #432–434 from Central CityRail. Classic, very popular Balmain backstreet corner pub, built in 1885, with a vast, stylish and comfortably furnished wrought-iron balcony upstairs, and gourmet pizzas. Relax with a beer or combine a hearty breakfast with a Bloody Mary on the balcony at the *Bloody Mary Breakfast Club* on weekend mornings (Sat & Sun 10am–3pm).

Leichhardt Hotel 95 Norton St, Leichhardt. Bus #438 or #440 from Central CityRail. With a courtyard opening onto the busy Italian restaurant strip and a first-floor balcony also providing a vantage point, the newly incarnated *Leichhardt Hotel* is a very slick designer pub. Its dramatic contemporary interior includes a huge Caravaggio-style mural, a modern Italian restaurant (bar snacks also available) and a good selection of Italian bottled beers. Mon–Wed until midnight, Thurs–Sat until 3am, closed Sun.

London Hotel 234 Darling St, Balmain. Bus #442 from Darling St ferry or the QVB. Convivial old British-style pub, with a high veranda overlooking the Saturday market. Attracts a typically mixed Balmain crowd.

Monkey Bar 255 Darling St, Balmain. Bus #442 from Darling St ferry or the QVB. Stylish, crowded bar with an atrium restaurant, the *Cicheti*, serving top-notch Italian tapas. There's a small stage for the loud, free live music – blues, soul, jazz or acoustic rock (Wed & Sun). Inexpensive bar menu and a big selection of wines by the glass.

Vanilla Room 153 Norton St, Leichhardt. Bus #438 or #440 from Central CityRail. Norton St is known for its Italian restaurants and pizza joints, not its swish bars, but this newly decked-out space fits right in with the surrounding trattorias. Red ceilings, dark floorboards and dim lanterns lend an air of mystery to the extensive rows of exciting wine bottles glinting behind the bar. Cheap pizzettas too. Closed Mon.

The harbour

Three of the best places to drink around the harbour, **Watsons Bay**, **Newport** and **Neutral Bay**, are listed in the "Legendary beer gardens" box on p.211.

Greenwood Hotel 36 Blue St, North Sydney. North Sydney CityRail. A former school, this gorgeous old sandstone building has been turned into a very pleasant, extensive pub, where sunny courtyards serve as havens from the corporate bustle of the North Shore's high-rise business district. Four bars, one of which includes a restaurant serving lunch (modern Australian); you can also eat outside, and pizza and bar snacks are available in the evenings. From Thurs to Sun there's much more of a party atmosphere; the best time to come is on Sun, when around 1500 trendy young people flock to the day club, which takes over the whole pub (noon–10pm); between twelve and fifteen DJs in three different areas, including the courtyard, play everything from funky house to hip hop ($15). Thurs night is free with hip hop, R'n'B and house DJs (8pm–late; happy hour 8–10pm), as is "Retro" Friday (5pm until late).

Ocean beaches

Whether for a casual afternoon of drinking and watching the surf roll in, or an evening of dancing and partying beside the sea, Sydney's beachside pubs have the location and the facilities to ensure a good time will be had by all.

Bondi and the eastern beaches

In addition to the places listed below, the *North Bondi RSL* is also a lively drinking hole (see p.199). See map, p.132.

Beach Palace Hotel 169 Dolphin St, Coogee Ⓦ www.beachpalacehotel.com.au. Bus #372 from Central CityRail & #373 or #374 from Circular Quay CityRail. Home to a young and drunken crowd, made up of locals, beach babes and backpackers. Five bars, two restaurants and a great view of the beach from the balcony under the distinctive dome. DJs on the middle level (Wed & Thurs 8pm–1am, Fri & Sat 10pm–3am) and on the top floor (Thurs & Fri 8pm–midnight), entrance for which is free except on Sat after 10.30pm, when it's $6.

Beach Road Hotel 71 Beach Rd, Bondi Beach Ⓦ www.beachrdhotel.com.au. Bus #389 from Bondi Junction CityRail. Huge, stylishly decorated pub with a bewildering range of bars on two levels and a beer garden. Popular with both travellers and locals for its good vibe. Entertainment, mostly free, comes from rock bands, DJs, soul nights and roots/dub/reggae Thurs: see website for details. The hotel also holds a cheap Italian bistro, *No Name* (see p.199), and an upmarket contemporary Australian restaurant. Daily until midnight or later.

Bondi Icebergs Club 1 Notts Ave, Bondi Beach ☏ 02/9130 3120. Bus #380 from Bondi Junction CityRail. Effectively the clubrooms of the Icebergs swimming club, this straightforward bar and bistro shares the same fabulous view as the much flasher *Icebergs Dining Room* on the floor above. Out-of-towners just need to show a photo ID, sign themselves in and settle down for a beer and everything from a fry-up breakfast to half a dozen oysters ($15) or a rump steak and chips ($22). Cover bands often play at weekends. Mon–Fri 11am–late, Sat & Sun 9am–late.

Bondi Social Level 1, 38 Campbell Parade, Bondi Beach. Bus #380 from Bondi Junction CityRail. One floor up from the busy Bondi strip, but a world away from the bikini shops and bikini-clad locals. Recycled timber interiors add a warm, cutting-edge flavour – not a bad place to kick back with a cocktail or beer and take in the unrivalled view out to sea.

Clovelly Hotel 381 Clovelly Rd, Clovelly Ⓦ www.clovellyhotel.com.au. Bus #360 from Bondi Junction CityRail. Known to the locals as the "Cloey", this huge hotel, perched slightly away from the beach, has four bars and a fantastic, very popular bistro complete with a great terrace eating area with views over the water. Free live bands play Fri–Sun, a DJ spins platters on Sat night, or you can relax at the pool tables and upstairs deck. Mon–Sat 10am–midnight, Sun 11am–10pm.

Hotel Bondi 178 Campbell Parade, Bondi Beach. Bus #380 from Bondi Junction CityRail. Huge pub dating from the 1920s, with many intact original features, seating outside and an open bar area where locals hang out with sand still on their feet. Sedate during the day but at night an over-the-top, late-night backpackers' hangout. Always the last to close. Mon–Sat 10am–4am, Sun 10am–midnight.

▲ Bondi Icebergs Club

Ravesi's **Campbell Parade, corner of Hall St, Bondi Beach. Bus #380 from Bondi Junction CityRail.** This corner spot, looking across to the beach, houses a very popular and stylish bar attached to the boutique hotel above (see p.169). Huge windows ensure full people- and ocean-watching opportunities. There's a dress policy in the evening but you can get away with beach gear by day. Beer on tap, albeit pricier than elsewhere. Wine by the glass starts from $7. A basement bar opens Thurs–Sun, and there's a bistro-style restaurant and cocktail bar upstairs.

Manly

See map, p.139.

4 Pines Brewing Company **43 The Esplanade, Manly ☎02/9976 2300, ⓦwww.4pinesbeer .com.au. Ferry to Manly Wharf.** Slick yet casual modern bar that's all polished concrete floors, recycled timber tables and a harbour-view deck that catches the afternoon sun. Its own microbrewery produces toothsome handcrafted beers, typically including a pale ale, a bitter, a *hefeweizen* (wheat beer),

and a *kolsch* (light ale from Cologne), plus seasonal brews. Good modern bar meals for around $20. Daily 11am–11pm or later.

Ivanhoe Hotel **27 The Corso, Manly. Ferry to Manly Wharf.** This huge Corso pub combines several bars with a nightclub and brasserie over four floors, and includes a terrace and balcony where you can take in some sun. Locals and backpackers crowd the place out, from the old-timers in the public bar, to the smartly dressed twenty-somethings in the lounge bar. Pool tables, $11 cocktails and a pizza kitchen ensure a merry atmosphere, and there's various live music and also free DJs Fri & Sat nights. Generally Mon–Wed until midnight, Thurs until 1am, Fri & Sat until 3am, Sun until midnight.

Manly Wharf Hotel **Manly Wharf, Manly ☎02/9977 1266, ⓦwww.manlywharfhotel .com.au. Ferry to Manly Wharf.** Modern, light and airy pub that makes a great spot to catch the afternoon sun and sunset over the city. With four bars there's something to suit everyone, including the *Harbour Bar* restaurant serving great seafood (the $130 platter is huge and fabulous), grills ($18–30) and pizza ($20). Daily 11am–midnight.

Live music and clubs

t's easy enough to find out exactly what's going on in Sydney's music and club scene. The *Sydney Morning Herald* lists music events in Friday's "Metro" supplement, and Saturdays "Spectrum" lift, while the *Daily Telegraph's* Friday. "T-Music" lift is aimed primarily at 18–24s. Free magazines with information on more alternative goings-on – clubbing, fashion and the like – plus band interviews and reviews, can be found in the cafés, record shops and boutiques of Surry Hills, Darlinghurst, Glebe and Newtown. The well-written *Drum Media* (with an online gig guide at ⓦ www.drummedia.com.au) and *The Brag* have weekly listings and informed reviews, and *TNT* magazine has a listings section, too; *3D World* (ⓦ www.threedworld.com.au) covers the clubbing scene. *City Hub*, a politically aware, free, weekly newspaper, also has an excellent events listing section, while *Time Out Sydney* is a weekly magazine with detailed listings and things to do for fun and entertainment. There's also a handy web-based gig guide prepared by ABC Radio's youth station Triple J (ⓦ www.abc.net.au/triplej/gigs). Also check the useful website ⓦ www.sydney.citysearch.com.au, a kind of listings mag on the net, with plenty on the music and club scene.

Live music

Australia in general, and Sydney in particular, has a well-deserved reputation for producing quality **live bands**: the thriving pub scene of the late 1970s and early 1980s produced a spectrum of great acts, from indie stars Nick Cave, the Church and the Triffids, to globe-straddling stadium-shakers like INXS, ACDC and Midnight Oil. Sadly, however, Sydney's live music scene has passed its boom era, and pub venues keep closing down to make way for the dreaded poker machines.

However, there are still enough venues to nourish a steady stream of local, interstate and overseas acts passing through each month, peaking in summer with several huge open-air **festivals**. Besides the big concert halls, Sydney's live music action still centres around **pub** venues. Pub bands are often free, especially if you arrive early (bands generally go on stage around 9.30–10.30pm, earlier on Sun); otherwise, $5–8 is a standard entry fee for local bands, $12–15 for the latest interstate sensation and upwards of $20 for smaller international acts. Late Sunday afternoon and early evenings are notably laid-back – an excellent time to catch some funk or mellow jazz bands, which are usually free.

Concert venues

Acer Arena **Olympic Blvd, Sydney Olympic Park**
ⓣ 02/8765 4321, ⓦ www.acerarena.com.au.

Homebush CityRail. Sydney's biggest venue, holding up to 21,000 people, the Acer Arena, at the Olympic site at Homebush, has hosted everything from Kiss and the Rolling

Always check gig guides, as venues often sell tickets independently, depending on the size and scope of the show. In addition, Sydney has several **booking agencies**:

Ticketek (☏13 2849, ⓦwww.ticketek.com.au) have outlets in the CBD at Hum, 55 Oxford St; Ticketek@Park, 50 Park St; and the Theatre Royal.

Ticketmaster7 (☏13 6100, ⓦwww.ticketmaster7.com) can be found at the State Theatre, Market St, CBD, and Sydney Entertainment Centre at Darling Harbour.

Moshtix (☏1300 438 849, ⓦwww.moshtix.com.au) have central outlets including Utopia Records, 233 Broadway, and The Music Shop, Shop 5050, Level 5, Westfield, 500 Oxford St, Bondi Junction.

Fish Records (ⓦwww.fishrecords.com.au) also sells tickets to selected gigs in-store; see "Shopping" for locations.

Stones to Supercross Masters motorcycle extravaganzas. Due to its location, there's not much to do after a show, but for the big performances there's nowhere better.

Capitol Theatre 13 Campbell St, Haymarket ☏02/9320 5000. Central CityRail. Refurbished, older theatre with balcony seating and room for around 2000 people. The *Capitol* hosts musicals and even ballet, but crooners and mellow pop groups occasionally appear here.

Enmore Theatre 118–132 Enmore Rd, Enmore ☏02/9550 3666, ⓦwww.enmoretheatre.com. au. Newtown CityRail. A pleasingly intimate, old-world Art Deco theatre venue for 1500 people – dingier than the *Capitol*, a fact which sits comfortably with its location, near to inner-city Newtown. Acts like Elvis Costello, the Pogues, Kraftwerk and the Cranberries are among notables to have played here while comedians (like Chris Rock and Eddie Izzard) have also appeared here.

Hordern Pavilion Driver Ave, Entertainment Quarter ⓦwww.playbillvenues.com. Big enough without lacking atmosphere (capacity 5500), the Hordern has hosted everyone from Moby to Destiny's Child and Justin Timberlake. The dance party after Mardi Gras is held here every year.

Metro Theatre 624 George St ☏02/9550 3666, ⓦwww.metrotheatre.com.au. Town Hall CityRail. Purpose-designed to handle everything from musicals to bands and dance parties, the Metro is exceptionally well laid out and has an excellent sound system; holds up to 1200 people.

State Theatre 49 Market St ☏02/9373 6655, ⓦwww.statetheatre.com.au. Town Hall CityRail. This 2000-seat theatre is decked out perhaps a bit too opulently in marble and

statuary, but performers who insist on a bit of grandeur play here. No dancing on the top balcony.

Sydney Entertainment Centre Haymarket, beside Darling Harbour ☏02/9320 4200, ⓦwww .sydentcent.com.au. Central CityRail. Soulless, 12,000-seat arena with video screens and a good sound system – Sydney's most popular indoor venue, for big international acts.

Pub venues

As well as the places listed below, which are well known as live music venues, many of the **pubs and bars** reviewed in the "Drinking" chapter also have regular music or dance nights: see the *Opera Bar* at the Opera House, the *Civic Hotel* in the city, the *Marlborough Hotel* in Newtown, the *Monkey Bar* in Balmain, in Bondi, the *Beach Road Hotel* and the *Bondi Icebergs Club*, in Manly the *Ivanhoe Hotel* and the *Old Manly Boatshed*, and the *Newport Arms Hotel* in Newport.

Annandale Hotel Corner of Nelson St and Parramatta Rd, Annandale ☏02/9550 1078, ⓦwww.annandalehotel.com. Bus #438 & #440 from Central CityRail. A showcase for indie bands, from up-and-comers to headline international acts, through rock, funk, metal and groove, with a capacity of 450. Music most nights (door $5–15).

The Basement 29 Reiby Place, Circular Quay ☏02/9251 2797, ⓦwww .thebasement.com.au. Circular Quay CityRail/ ferry. This dark and moody venue is an institution that attracts the great and rising names in jazz, funk, acoustic and world music as well as a roster of the world's most renowned blues performers. To take in a show, book a table and dine in front of the low stage; otherwise, you'll have to stand all night at the bar at the back. Recorded broadcasts on the internet.

Brass Monkey 115A Cronulla St, Cronulla ☏02/9544 3844, ⓦwww.brassmonkey.com.au. Cronulla CityRail. This small jazz and music club attracts some big names, who often play *The Basement* and then head south for a more intimate show here. Cover charge depending on act, but food, beer and good wine is reasonable.

Bridge Hotel 135 Victoria Rd, Rozelle ☏02/9810 1260. Bus #440 from Central CityRail. Legendary inner-west venue specializing in blues, jazz and pub rock, with the occasional big-name international act (B.B. King and Jon Cleary have played here) but mostly local performers. Laid-back, no-frills atmosphere.

Excelsior Hotel 64 Foveaux St, Surry Hills ☏02/9211 4945, ⓦwww.excelsiorhotel .com.au. Central CityRail. Something of a musos' pub with live music playing to around 150 people nightly, free on Mon but otherwise around $10 in. Musical styles range from jazz (three nights per week) to hard rock, with the odd open mic night. Sun evening from 6pm is usually a jam session, and decent bistro food is always available.

Gaelic Theatre Club 64 Devonshire St, Surry Hills ☏02/9211 1687, ⓦwww.thegaelic.com. Central CityRail. Anything and everything plays at the *Gaelic Club* – one night there's DJs and dance music, the next heavy metal or hard-core punk – which makes it one of Sydney's more interesting live venues, and fully licensed too. Only open when there's a show, but can go on until 5am.

🎤 **Hopetoun Hotel** 416 Bourke St, corner of Fitzroy St, Surry Hills ☏02/9361 5257, ⓦwww.myspace.com/hopetounhotel. Central CityRail. One of Sydney's best venues for the indie band scene; everyone wants to play at "The Hoey", and the new, young bands get to mix it up with local, interstate and international acts all playing in the small and inevitably packed front bar (Mon–Sat from 7.30pm; cover charge depends on the act, normally $6–10, though sometimes free). DJs on Sun (5–10pm; $6). Popular pool room, a drinking pit in the basement, and an inexpensive little restaurant upstairs (meals $9–16). Closes midnight.

@ Newtown Petersham RSL Club, 52 Enmore Rd, Newtown ☏02/9557 5044. Newtown CityRail. Another multilevel venue with diverse line-ups, from DJs, to rock, funk and indie bands – there's usually something going on somewhere. Open daily, gigs various times.

Old Manly Boatshed 40 The Corso, Manly ☏02/9977 4443. Ferry to Manly Wharf. Characterful and grungy late-night basement bar overflowing with Manly Surf Club paraphernalia, popular with both backpackers and local regulars. Live music nightly (Tues–Thurs & Sun 8.30pm, free; Fri & Sat 9.30pm, $10) – Wed is the night for emerging songwriters – except for Mon, when there's stand-up comedy (8.30pm; $8–12). Food is served until midnight – the bistro-style menu includes good-value steaks ($17) and fajitas $22 for 2). Mon–Sat 6pm–3am, Sun to midnight.

Oxford Art Factory 38–46 Oxford St, Darlinghurst ☏02/9332 3711, ⓦwww.oxfordartfactory.com. Kings Cross CityRail. Andy Warhol-inspired cultural focal point and arts space with an industrial feel. As well as running a bar and cutting-edge art gallery they put on an enormously wide range of shows from album launches and avant-garde plays to gigs that might be anything from relatively well established rock, funk and punk to DJ nights. Cost varies. Check website for listings.

Rose of Australia Hotel 1 Swanson St, Erskineville ☏02/9565 1441. Erskineville CityRail Trendy inner-city types mix with Goths, locals and gays to sample favourites of the pub circuit. Line-up changes regularly, and there are no set days for performances. Check *Drum Media* for details and catch anything from an original rock act through to a country cover band. Music is from 9pm and is usually free.

Sandringham Hotel 387 King St, Newtown ☏02/9557 1254. Newtown CityRail. "The Sando" features local and interstate indie bands, who play on the stage upstairs (daily 8–11pm, $5–15 – big shows $20) or on the small corner stage downstairs (free; Wed, Thurs & Sat 7.30pm–9pm).

The Vanguard 42 King St, Newtown ☏02/9557 7992. Newtown CityRail. Billed as bringing jazz, blues and roots to Newtown, this 1920s-style venue – resplendent in ubiquitous, seemingly illicit, crimson – with restaurant and cocktail bar, attracts big-name international acts, plus excellent raw local talent. It's incredibly relaxed, and…groovy baby. Most acts play 7–11.45pm.

Sydney hosts big outdoor rock concerts throughout spring and summer, but the **Big Day Out**, in late January, is the original and most commercial (around $140 plus booking fee; ⓦwww.bigdayout.com). Held at the showground at the Sydney Olympic Park at Homebush Bay (see p.151), it features big international names such as Neil Young, the Arctic Monkeys and the Prodigy as well as local talent like Something for Kate and the Drones, and attracts crowds of more than fifty thousand.

Homebake (around $95; ⓦwww.homebake.com.au) is a huge annual open-air festival in The Domain (see p.69) in early December, with food and market stalls, rides and a line-up of more than fifty famous and underground Australian bands from Powderfinger to Grinspoon.

Peats Ridge Festival, a three-day camping and fun-filled fiesta climaxing on New Year's Eve, takes place in the beautiful Glenworth Valley, off the F3, about an hour's drive northwest from Sydney Harbour Bridge ($300; ⓦwww.peatsridgefestival.com.au). Featuring two hundred Australian and international musical artists across eight stages, plus two venues dedicated to theatre, cabaret and comedy, this is a big one. There are workshops in everything from martial arts to juggling; a massive international food fair; workshops and entertainment for the kids; horseriding, kayaking and swimming opportunities; and a disco tent for nocturnal grooving.

Good Vibrations, in the spacious leafy surrounds of Centennial Park in mid-February gets bigger and better each year. In 2009, a day of fun, beer and jaw-dropping beauty was elevated by the likes of Fat Boy Slim, Roni Size, The Roots and local sensation, The Presets (despite the rain and mud) into a veritable festival utopia, which will no doubt be sustained (if not somehow bettered) in the years to come.

The inauguration of the Australian incarnation of **All Tomorrows Parties** (ⓦwww .atpfestival.com) on Cockatoo Island (featuring Nick Cave and the Bad Seeds) took place in 2009, and **Days Like This Music Festival** (ⓦwww.dayslikethis.com.au) at the Entertainment Quarter (featuring Morcheeba, Public Enemy and DJ Vadim). Both festivals were hugely successful, with many fingers now crossed in the hope that they return.

The **Manly International Jazz Festival** runs over the Labour Day long weekend in early October. Free outdoor stages include one on the scenic harbourfront and one on the oceanfront, while a number of indoor concert venues charge admission. The wide-ranging guests of previous years have included a Slovenian band playing Gypsy swing, a Japanese jazz orchestra and an Italian trio, plus well-known local, US and UK acts. You can get advance details from Manly Council (ⓦwww.manly.nsw.gov.au).

For other musical events through the year, see the "Festivals and events" chapter.

Clubs

From dark den to opulent fantasy, Sydney's thriving **club scene**, frequented by international DJ celebrities and impressive local DJ talent, is likely to satisfy. A long strip of clubs stretches from Kings Cross to Oxford Street and down towards Hyde Park. Along with the places listed below, most of the clubs in our Gay and Lesbian listings have fairly mixed clientele; although we've listed these separately – see p.231 – the divisions are not always clear. There are also clubs attached to several of the pubs we've listed – see *Soho Bar* for *Yu* – and some pubs actually transform into clubs, such as the hugely popular Sunday day club that takes over the entire *Greenwood Hotel* in North Sydney (see p.212), even the beer garden. Most other pubs and bars don't push things quite so far, but DJs are fast taking over from the live music scene, and you'll find people dancing at least one night a week in the city at the *Art House Hotel* (p.205); in Newtown at the *Marlborough Hotel* (p.210); and by the beaches at the *Clovelly Hotel* (p.213), the *Beach Palace Hotel* in Coogee (p.213) *and Beach Road Hotel* in Bondi.

Many of the clubs listed below are open to different promoters, so have different styles on different nights. Check gig guides and listings, and look out for posters on the streets. The club scene can be pretty snobby, with door gorillas frequently vetting your style, so pull out your finest holiday threads and be sure to do some sprucing. Admission ranges from $10 to $30, depending on the club and DJ; many stay open until 5am Saturday morning and until 6am Sunday morning.

Candy's Apartment 22 Bayswater Rd, Kings Cross ☏02/9380 5600, Ⓦwww.candys.com.au. Kings Cross CityRail. The most happening place in town, this music-portal transforms itself every night with the coolest DJs playing gigs early and then churning out fresh dance mixes as the night progresses. A good option after checking out the Kings Cross strip. Entry $10–20. Wed–Sun 8pm until late.

Civic Underground 388 Pitt St, Haymarket ☏02/8080 7000, Ⓦwww.civichotel.com.au. Town Hall CityRail. There's a great, friendly vibe at this stylish basement venue (see "Drinking"), where house and techno rule. Seventies-inspired decor with plush white seating and great cocktails. Mainly Fri & Sat nights. $15–20 in.

Club 77 77 William St, East Sydney ☏02/9361 4981, Ⓦwww.myspace.com /club_77. Kings Cross CityRail. The big DJ nights are Fri and Sat (Thurs nights gets some great live acts) at this intimate and relaxed club. Drinks are cheap and a swag of regulars come here for the progressive and rare funk, experimental and house music. It's scene-free clubbing, and they pack 'em in. $10.

Havana 169 Oxford St, Darlinghurst ☏02/9331 7729, Ⓦwww.havanaclub.com.au. Bus #378 from Central CityRail or #380 from Circular Quay CityRail. Pitched somewhere between a sumptuous loungey bar and a club, this intimate venue is all pale wood and suede booths clustered near several bars dotted around the dance floor. Tunes are an eclectic mix of electronica, disco and old-school funk and the latest house, generally attracting a more mature crowd. Fri & Sat 9pm until late.

Home 101 Cockle Bay Wharf, Darling Harbour ☏02/9266 0600, Ⓦwww .homesydney.com. Town Hall CityRail. Sydney's first really big club venture, the lavish *Home* can cram 2000 punters into its cool, cavernous interior, which

also features a mezzanine, a chill-out room, and outdoor balconies. Decks are often manned by famous DJs, drinks are expensive, and staff beautiful. The place gets packed with a younger crowd on Fri for its flagship night "Sublime", with four musical styles across four levels. On Sat, "Together at Home" plays progressive and funky house. Fri & Sat 11pm until gone daybreak. $20–25.

Le Panic 20 Bayswater Rd, Kings Cross ☏02/9368 0763. Kings Cross CityRail. The former site of nightclub *Sugareef*, an extreme makeover has *Le Panic* aiming to be a one-stop-shop for late-night partying, with the sizeable dance floor still open for boogying but now surrounded by a bar and comfy booths with food on offer. A private and exclusive lounge off to the side acts as a chill-out room. Thurs & Sun 9pm–1am, Fri & Sat 9pm–6pm. $15.

Tank 3 Bridge Lane, off George St, City ☏02/9240 3000, Ⓦwww.tankclub.com.au. Wynyard CityRail. This is for the glamorous industry crowd – fashion, music and film aficionados. If you don't belong, the style police will spot you a mile away. All very "funky" – from the house music played by regular or guest DJs to the mirrors and wash basins in the toilets. Three amazing bars and a VIP section. Attire is smart casual to street wear, but attitude and good looks override the dress code. Fri & Sat 10pm–6am. $15–20.

The World 24 Bayswater Rd, Kings Cross ☏02/8324 0100, Ⓦwww.theworldbar.com. Kings Cross CityRail. With a relatively relaxed door policy, *The World* is popular with a fun, party-loving crowd of travellers, who jive to a pleasing mix of funk and house grooves in a pleasant Victorian-era building with a big front balcony. The atmosphere throughout is lively, if a little beery in the front bar. Mon–Thurs & Sun noon–4am, Fri & Sat noon–6am. $15, free before midnight (10pm Fri & Sat).

Performing arts and film

From Shakespeare to gay film festivals, Sydney's arts scene takes itself seriously while managing never to lose its sense of fun. Free summertime outdoor performances, such as the Sydney Festival's **Symphony in The Domain** (see p.257), are among the year's highlights, as Sydneysiders turn out in their thousands to picnic and share in the atmosphere.

For **listings** of **what's on** at the venues below, check the *Sydney Morning Herald's* Friday supplement "Metro", or the "Planner" in Saturday's *Spectrum*. Also check any of the diary-style magazines available at the tourist offices, or the website ⊛ www.sydney.citysearch.com.au. To buy tickets for performing arts events, either contact the venues direct or book through Ticketek, the main **booking agency**, or Ticketmaster7; details of both can be found on p.216.

Classical music, opera and ballet

The **Sydney Opera House** is the centre of high culture in Sydney. While it's not necessary to don tie-and-tails or an evening dress when attending a performance, it's still about the only place you're likely to see locals in formal attire.

All Sydney's most prestigious performing arts companies have Opera House seasons. The **Australian Ballet**, which features contemporary as well as classical dance (tickets from $70; ⊛ www.australianballet.com.au), shifts between Sydney and Melbourne – it's based in the latter, but performs regularly at the Opera House. **Opera Australia** (full-view tickets from $103; ⊛ www.opera-australia.org.au) also alternates between the two cities, with Opera House seasons in either the Concert Hall or the Opera Theatre from January to March and June to September. The **Sydney Symphony Orchestra** (tickets from $35; ⊛ www.sso.com.au) performs at the Sydney Opera House Concert Hall and the City Recital Hall.

City Recital Hall Angel Place, between George and Pitt sts. Martin Place CityRail. On-site box office ☏ 02/8256 2222, ⊛ www.cityrecitalhall .com. Opened in 1999, this classical music venue, right next to Martin Place, was specifically designed for chamber music, and is the major concert venue for the renowned Australian Brandenburg Orchestra (⊛ www .brandenburg.com.au; tickets from $55), who use seventeenth-century instruments and original scores in their baroque and classical concerts. The hall seats 1200, but on three levels, giving it an intimate atmosphere.
Conservatorium of Music Off Macquarie St, in the Botanic Gardens ☏ 02/9351 1438, ⊛ www.usyd.edu.au/su/conmusic. Circular Quay CityRail/ferry. Students at the "Con", a prestigious branch of Sydney University,

▲ Inside the Opera House

give lunchtime recitals every Wed at 1.10pm during term time in Verbrugghen Hall (donation). Other concerts, both free and ticketed (anywhere from $10 up to around $45) involve students and staff here and at venues around town; check website for details.

St James's Church King St, beside Hyde Park ☎02/9232 3022, ⓦwww.sjks.org.au. St James or Town Hall CityRail. This beautiful little Anglican church has long been associated with fine music. It has its own director of music and a highly acclaimed semi-professional chamber choir, whose repertoire extends from Gregorian chants to more contemporary pieces. The choir can be heard every Sun morning at 11am and on the last Sun of the month at 4pm. St James's music programme also includes lunchtime concerts (Wed 1.15pm; 30min; $5 donation requested).

Sydney Opera House Bennelong Point ☎02/9250 7777, ⓦwww.sydneyoperahouse.com. Circular Quay CityRail/ferry. Sydney's prestige venue for opera, classical music and ballet. Forget quibbles about acoustics or ticket prices – it's worth going just to say you've been. The huge Concert Hall, seating 2690, is home to the Sydney Symphony Orchestra and also hosts opera; the smaller Opera Theatre (1547 seats) hosts opera, ballet and contemporary dance. See p.222 for details of performances at the Opera House's three theatrical venues.

Town Hall Corner of Druitt and George sts ☎02/9265 9007, ⓦwww.cityofsydney.nsw.gov.au. Town Hall CityRail. Centrally located concert hall (seats 2000) with a splendid high-Victorian interior; hosts everything from chamber orchestras to bush dances and public lectures. Closed for major refurbishment as this book went to press, but should reopen by the time you read this.

Theatre

Sydney's thriving theatre scene produced many of the stars that presently grace the Hollywood firmament. Cate Blanchett, Geoffrey Rush and Hugo Weaving all started here, and regularly return to participate in local productions alongside

Contemporary dance companies

Bangarra Dance Theatre Pier 4, Hickson Rd, Millers Point ☎02/9251 5333, ⓦwww.bangarra.com.au. Formed in 1989, Bangarra's innovative style fuses contemporary movement with the traditional dances and culture of the Yirrkala Community in Arnhemland. They are based at the same pier as the Wharf Theatre, but perform at other venues in Sydney and tour nationally and internationally – call or check their website for the latest details.

Sydney Dance Company Pier 4, Hickson Rd, Millers Point ☎02/9221 4811, ⓦwww.sydneydance.com.au. Graeme Murphy, Australia's doyen of dance, was at the helm here from 1976 to 2007, and his successors continue to set the standard with ambitious sets and beautifully designed costumes. The company is based at the Wharf Theatre but tours nationally and internationally.

equally impressive developing talents. Prices for mainstream theatre performances are fairly high, from $25 to $70 for the best seat at a Sydney Theatre Company performance; tickets in smaller, fringe venues cost from around $25.

Major venues

Capitol Theatre 13 Campbell St, Haymarket ☎ 02/9320 5000, ⓦ www.capitoltheatre.com .au. Central CityRail. Built as a deluxe picture theatre in the 1920s, the Capitol was saved from demolition and beautifully restored in the mid-1990s. The 2000-seater now hosts big-budget musicals, ballet and opera, which you watch from beneath its best feature, the deep blue ceiling spangled with the stars of the southern skies.

Seymour Theatre Centre Corner of City Rd and Cleveland St, Chippendale ☎ 02/9351 7940, ⓦ www.seymour.usyd.edu.au. Bus #422, #423, #426 or #428 from Central CityRail. Opened in 1975 and refurbished in 2000, this three-theatre multi-purpose performing arts venue was a businessman's bequest to Sydney University for a venue for musical and dramatic arts. From lectures by eminent writers to plays from the university's Dramatic Society and offbeat comical musicals, the Seymour's range is varied and often interesting. The main stage, the 788-seat York Theatre, hosts everything from serious imported theatre such as Steven Berkoff's *Shakespeare's Villains* to international piano competitions and the Sydney Peace Prize lecture. The smaller Everest Theatre's acoustics are designed for musical events, from classical pianists to contemporary dance (seats 419–605), while the Downstairs Theatre is the informal studio space (seats 150–200). The new 120-seater cabaret room, Sound Lounge, hosts improvised jazz from SIMA (Sydney Improvised Music Association) on Fri and Sat nights (9pm–midnight; $20); light meals and drinks are offered during performances.

Star City Casino 20–80 Pyrmont St, Pyrmont ☎ 02/9657 9657, ⓦ www.starcity.com.au. Star City Light Rail. Sydney's Vegas-style casino has two theatres catering to popular tastes. The technically advanced Lyric Theatre, seating 2000, stages big musical extravaganzas imported from the West End and Broadway such as *Saturday Night Fever*, while the smaller Star City Showroom puts on more offbeat musicals – like the *Rocky Horror Picture Show* – and comedy.

▲ National Theatre

Theatre Royal MLC Centre, King St, City ☎ 02/9224 8444, ⓦ www.theatreroyal.net.au. Martin Place CityRail. Imported musicals and blockbuster plays in a Harry Seidler-designed building opened in 1976; seats 1180.

Drama and performance

Belvoir St Theatre 25 Belvoir St, Surry Hills ☎ 02/9699 3444, ⓦ www.belvoir.com.au. Central CityRail. Highly regarded two-stage venue for a wide range of contemporary Australian and international theatre. Company B, the resident theatre company, is one of Australia's most innovative and productive, and tours nationally and abroad.

Ensemble Theatre 78 McDougall St, Milsons Point ☎ 02/9929 0644, ⓦ www.ensemble.com.au. Milsons Point CityRail. Australian contemporary and classical plays.

Sydney Opera House Bennelong Point ☎ 02/9250 7777, ⓦ www.sydneyoperahouse.com. Circular Quay CityRail/ferry. The Opera House holds three theatrical venues: the Playhouse and the Drama Theatre show modern and traditional Australian and international plays mostly put on by the Sydney Theatre Company, while the smaller, theatre-in-the-round Studio (which has the most affordable ticket prices), is flexible in design and offers an innovative and wide-ranging programme of contemporary performance – theatre, cabaret, dance, comedy and hybrid works.

Wharf Theatre Pier 4, Hickson Rd, Millers Point ☎ 02/9250 1777, ⓦ www.sydneytheatre.com.au. Circular Quay CityRail/ferry. Home to the highly regarded Sydney Theatre Company (STC) –

which produces Shakespeare and modern pieces and has two theatres here – and to the Sydney Dance Company (SDC; see box, p.221). Atmospheric waterfront location, and a well-regarded restaurant, bar and café – see p.180. The 850-seater Sydney Theatre, diagonally opposite, also puts on STC and SDC performances.

Fringe and repertory

New Theatre 542 King St, Newtown ☎02/9519 3403, ⓦwww.newtheatre.org.au. Newtown or St Peters CityRail. Formed in 1932. Professional and amateur actors perform contemporary dramas with socially relevant themes.

NIDA 215 Anzac Parade, Kensington ☎02/9697 7613, ⓦwww.nida.edu.au. Bus #390–394 from Central CityRail. Australia's premier dramatic training ground – the National Institute of Dramatic Art – where the likes of Mel Gibson and Judy Davis started out. Student productions are open to the public as well as talent-spotters.
Performance Space 245 Wilson St, Eveleigh. ☎02/8571 9111, ⓦwww.performancespace .com.au. Central CityRail. Stages experimental performances.
Stables Theatre 10 Nimrod St, Darlinghurst ☎02/9361 3817, ⓦwww.griffintheatre.com.au. Kings Cross CityRail. Home to the Griffin Theatre Company, whose mission is to develop and foster new Australian playwrights.

Comedy and cabaret

Sydney's comedy scene is pretty quiet these days, but there are a couple of good venues, and drag shows can always be found along Darlinghurst's Oxford Street, particularly on Thursday nights. See p.217 for details of the *Old Manly Boatshed*, which puts on comedy on Monday nights.

Friend in Hand 58 Cowper St, Glebe ☎02/9660 2326. All westbound buses from Railway Square, Central CityRail. Every Thurs at 7.30pm this iconic Sydney pub plays host to "Mic In Hand", a friendly night of comedy, featuring a mix of amateur and professional comedians – past luminaries include Will Anderson and Sarah Kendall. "Word In Hand", a poetry night on the first Tues of every month, has also been known to get quite comical.
Sydney Comedy Store Entertainment Quarter Driver Ave, Moore Park ☎02/9357 1419,

ⓦwww.comedystore.com.au. Bus #373. #374, #376, #377, #392, #394, #396, #397, #399 from Circular Quay CityRail/ferry, or #339, #372, #374, #376, #397, #399 from Central CityRail (Eddie Ave). International (often American) and Australian stand-up comics Tues–Sat; open from 8.15pm; shows start 8.30pm. Meals aren't available inside, but nearby restaurants offer discounts for ticket-holders. Booking recommended. Tues & Wed $15, Thurs $20, Fri $27.50, Sat $29.50.

Cinema

Sydneysiders love going to the pictures, and in recent years Hollywood itself has come to town in the shape of the Fox Studios site, which offers superb facilities and filming locations in the heart of the city, plus sixteen cinema screens. During the summer you can watch films **outdoors**, either at one of Sydney's open-air cinemas (see box, p.226), or at its lively film festivals. The commercial movie centre of Sydney is two blocks south of the Town Hall at 505–525 George Street, where you'll find the two big **chains** – Hoyts (☎02/9273 7431, ⓦwww.hoyts.com.au) and Greater Union (☎02/9267 8666, ⓦwww.greaterunion.com.au) – under one roof. This is mainstream, fast-food, teenager territory and there are much nicer places to watch a film. Other more pleasantly located Hoyts can be found at the Broadway Shopping Centre, on Broadway near Glebe (☎02/9211 1911), and at Fox Studios, and there's a Greater Union in the Westfield Shopping Centre in Bondi Junction

Film festivals

Sydney's great **film festivals** provide opportunities to catch a movie in a number of attractive settings, some of them outdoors.

Sydney Film Festival

Held annually over two weeks in **early June**, the **Sydney Film Festival** is an exciting programme of features, shorts, documentaries and retrospective screenings from Australia and around the world. Founded at Sydney University in 1954, the festival struggled with prudish censors until freedom from censorship for festival films was introduced in 1971. From the early, relaxed atmosphere of picnics on the lawns between screenings, it has gradually moved off-campus, to find a home from 1974 in the magnificent State Theatre (see p.78). Films are now also shown at various other venues, including the wonderfully sited three-screen Dendy Quays in Circular Quay, Greater Union on George Street, the Metro Theatre (across the street), and The Studio at the Opera House among others.

The more provocative line-up of films at the Greater Union and Metro Theatre aims to attract an under-35 audience to the festival on a single or packaged ticket basis. Single **tickets** cost $17 in 2008, but are expected to decrease in future. Selected packages of five to ten films are available with significant savings, or there are twenty- and fifty-film Flexi Passes. **Subscriptions** for the State Theatre programme range from one week's daytime unreserved stalls seating, to two weeks' reserved dress circle night-time screenings. For up-to-date information on pricing and a programme, call or drop in to the festival office at suite 102, 59 Marlborough St, Surry Hills (Mon–Fri 9am–5pm; ☎02/9318 0999, ⊛www.sydneyfilmfestival.org).

Flickerfest and Tropfest

Sydney also hosts two short-film festivals, both of which echo the young and irreverent attitude that once fuelled the Sydney Film Festival. Stars above and the sound of waves accompany the week-long **Flickerfest International Short Film Festival** (☎02/9365 6888, ⊛www.flickerfest.com.au; session ticket $15, season pass $120),

(Level 6, 500 Oxford St ☎02/9300 1555). Standard tickets cost around $16, but Tuesdays are reduced–price (around $10) at all Hoyts and Greater Union/ Village cinemas and their suburban outlets, and Monday or Tuesday at the arthouse and local cinemas listed below.

Main venues

Cinema Paris Entertainment Quarter Moore Park ☎02/9332 1633, ⊛www.hoyts.com.au. **Bus #339 from Central CityRail.** Hoyts' "arthouse" option; a pleasant four-screen cinema that also puts on mini film festivals (Spanish, Mexican) and events throughout the year. $16, Tues $10.

The Dendy 261 King St, Newtown ☎02/9550 5699, ⊛www.dendy.com.au. **Newtown CityRail.** Trendy four-screen cinema complex with attached café, bar and bookshop, showing prestige new-release films. Discount day is Tues, but if you're staying in Sydney longer, and will be living or working nearby, it's worth investing in a Club Dendy card ($15 for twelve months)

which discounts tickets to $10 and gives a ten percent discount on numerous theatre tickets, shops, restaurants and bars. The newer three-screen Dendy Quays is superbly sited at 2 East Circular Quay (☎02/9247 3800).

Hoyts Entertainment Quarter Moore Park ☎02/9332 1300, ⊛www.hoyts.com.au. **Bus #339 from Central CityRail.** Twelve-screen multiplex digital surround-sound showing mainstream new releases, and occasional international premieres. Six of the screens have a special deluxe section, La Premiere, aimed at couples, where custom-made sofa seats for two have wine holders and tables for food – you can buy bottles of wine and cheese plates, while soft drinks and popcorn are included held in early January in the amphitheatre of the Bondi Pavilion; foreign and Australian productions are screened, including documentaries.

The **Tropfest** (☎9368 0434, ⓦ www.tropfest.com.au) is a competition festival for short films held annually on the last Sunday of February. Its name comes from the *Tropicana Café* on Victoria Street, Darlinghurst, where the festival began almost by chance in 1993 when young actor John Polsen persuaded his local coffee spot to show the short film he had made. He pushed other film-makers to follow suit, and the next year a huge crowd packed themselves into the café. Nowadays the entire street is closed to traffic to enable an outdoor screening, while cafés along the strip screen films on TVs inside, but the festival has grown enormously over the years and the focus of the event has now moved to the Domain, with live entertainment from 3pm and huge crowds turning up to picnic on the grass and watch the free 8pm screening of sixteen finalist films from around seven hundred entries. Each state capital also screens the event simultaneously in venues ranging from cafés to parks. The films (maximum seven minutes) must be specifically produced for the festival, and to this end an item that must feature in the shorts is announced a few months in advance of the entry date; in 2009 it was "spring" – however you wanted to interpret it. The judges, who turn up for the screenings, are often famous international actors, which adds some excitement, while Polsen himself, still the festival's director, has made it as a Hollywood director with his films *Swimfan* (2002) and *Hide and Seek* (2005). You can see him acting in *Mission Impossible II* alongside Tom Cruise.

Other film festivals

Other Sydney film festivals include the **World of Women (WOW) Film Festival** (ⓦ www.wift.org/wow/), held over five days in early October at the Chauvel Cinema, Paddington – and surrounding venues. A **Gay and Lesbian Film Festival** takes place in late February as part of the Sydney Gay & Lesbian Mardi Gras (see p.228), while French, Italian, Spanish and Greek film festivals run at the Palace Cinemas – look out for ads and see below.

in the ticket price ($33, Tues $23). Normal tickets $16 (Tues $10).

IMAX Theatre Southern Promenade, Darling Harbour ☎02/9281 3300, ⓦ www.imax.com.au. **Town Hall CityRail.** State-of-the-art giant eight-storey-high cinema screen showing a choice of six films (many of them 3D) designed to thrill your senses. Films under 1hr cost $19.50, over 1hr $25. Films hourly 10am–10pm.

Palace Academy Twin 3A Oxford St, corner of South Dowling St, Paddington ☎02/9361 4453, ⓦ www.palacecinemas.com.au. **Bus #378 from Central CityRail or #380 from Circular Quay CityRail.** One of a chain of inner-city cinemas (see "Norton" and "Verona" below) showing foreign-language, arthouse and new releases, with discounts on Mon. If you're going to be in Sydney for a while, consider joining their Movie Club ($18 for twelve months), which gives discount-price ($11) tickets anytime for yourself and a friend; it doesn't take long to recoup the cost.

Palace Norton Street 99 Norton St, Leichhardt ☎02/9550 0122, ⓦ www.palacecinemas.com.au. **Bus #438 & #440 from Central CityRail.** This cinema has a bookshop and café, and hosts an Italian film festival during late Sept and early Oct, as well as French, Spanish, Greek and German film festivals. Discount Mon ($9.50).

Reading Cinema Level 3, Market City Shopping Centre, Haymarket ☎02/9280 1202, ⓦ www.readingcinemas.com.au. **Central CityRail.** Mainstream five-screen multiplex in a great spot in the heart of Chinatown close to Central Station. Adjacent Asian food court and bar handy for quick pre- or post-movie meals. Cheap day Tues, discounts daily before 6pm.

Verona 17 Oxford St, corner of Verona St, Paddington ☎02/9360 6099, ⓦ www.palacecinemas.com.au. **Bus #378 from Central CityRail or #380 from Circular Quay CityRail.** Arthouse and foreign-language films, plus new releases. Also has a trendy first-floor bar.

In the summer, two open-air cinemas set up shop. From November to the end of March, the **Moonlight Cinema**, in the Centennial Park Amphitheatre on Oxford Street (Woollahra entrance; Tues–Sun, films start 8.30pm, tickets from 7pm for $17 or bookings online for $15; Ⓦ www.moonlight.com.au; bus #378 from Central CityRail or #380 from Bondi Junction CityRail), shows classic, arthouse and cult films. Throughout January and February, the **Open Air Cinema** (Ⓦ www.stgeorgeopenair.com.au) is erected at Mrs Macquaries Points in the Royal Botanic Gardens (tickets from 6.30pm or bookings on Ⓣ 13 6100; $23), screening mainly mainstream recent releases and some classics. Other opportunities to watch films under the stars are detailed in the "Film festivals" box on pp.224–225.

Locals and independents

Chauvel Cinema Paddington Town Hall, corner of Oatley Rd and Oxford St, Paddington Ⓣ 02/9361 5398, Ⓦ www.chauvelcinema.net.au. **Bus #378 from Central CityRail, or #380 from Circular Quay or Bondi Junction CityRail.** A Sydney cinema institution, the arthouse Chauvel, with its varied programme of Australian and foreign films plus classics, has been operating in Paddington Town Hall (with a brief interruption) since 1977.

Hayden Orpheum Picture Palace 380 Military Rd, Cremorne Ⓣ 02/9908 4344, Ⓦ www.orpheum.com.au. **Bus #243 from Wynyard CityRail or #246 & #247 from Clarence St.** Charming heritage-listed six-screen cinema built in 1935 with a splendid Art Deco interior. The main cinema keeps up a tradition of Wurlitzer organ recitals preceding the Sat evening and Sun afternoon films, and a jazz quartet plays 1940s' swing on Sundays. Mainstream and foreign new releases. Discount Tues.

Govinda's Movie Room 112 Darlinghurst Rd, Darlinghurst Ⓣ 02/9380 5155, Ⓦ www.govindas.com.au. **Kings Cross CityRail.** Run by the Hare Krishnas (but definitely no indoctrination), Govinda's shows two films every night from a range of classics and recent releases in a pleasantly unorthodox cushion-room atmosphere (you're encouraged to take off your shoes if you lie on the cushions, so choose unsmelly footwear). The movie and dinner deal (all-you-can-eat vegetarian buffet) is popular – $19.80 for the meal and then an extra $8.80 to see the movie. Buy your film ticket after you've ordered your meal, or you may miss out on busy nights; you can just see the film for $12.80, but diners always get preference.

Randwick Ritz 45 St Paul St, Randwick Ⓣ 02/9399 5722, Ⓦ www.ritzcinema.com.au. **Bus #339 from Central CityRail or #372, #373, #374 or #377 from Circular Quay CityRail.** Characterful old cinema that's handy if you're staying in Coogee. Five screens show mainstream new releases, always at discount prices ($11, though all sessions on Tues are just $7). Now shows 3-D digital movies ($15), while "Bubs Clubs", child-friendly sessions for parents, take place every Mon (10.30am). The surrounding area, known to the locals as "the Spot", holds lots of cafés and culturally diverse restaurants to eat at, before or afterwards.

16

Gay Sydney

S ydney is indisputably one of the world's great gay cities – indeed, many people think it capable of snatching San Francisco's crown as the Queen of them all. There's something for everyone – whether you want to lie on a beach during the warmer months (Oct–April) or party hard all year round. Gays and lesbians are pretty much accepted, particularly in the inner-city and eastern areas.

If you can't be here for gay Sydney's two big events – **Mardi Gras** and the **Sleaze Ball** (see both below) – you'll still find the city has much to offer. **Oxford Street** (mostly around Taylor Square) is Sydney's official "pink strip" of gay-frequented restaurants, coffee shops, bookshops and bars, where you'll find countless pairs of tight-T-shirted guys strolling hand-in-hand, or checking out the passing talent from hip, streetside cafés. However, the gay-straight divide in Sydney has less relevance for a new generation, perhaps ironically a result of Mardi Gras' mainstream success. Several of the long-running gay venues on and around Oxford Street have closed down, while many of those that remain attract older customers, as younger gays and lesbians embrace inclusiveness and party with their straight friends and peers, or choose to meet new friends online (particularly at Ⓦgaydar .com) instead of in bars. **King Street**, Newtown, and nearby **Erskineville** are centres of gay culture, while lesbian communities have carved out territory of their own in **Leichhardt** (known affectionately as "Dykehart") and **Marrackville**.

The Mardi Gras and Sleaze

The year's highlight and international drawcard is the **Sydney Gay & Lesbian Mardi Gras** (Ⓣ02/9568 8600, Ⓦwww.mardigras.org.au), which starts the second week of **February**, kicking off with a free Fair Day in Victoria Park, Camperdown, and culminating with a massive parade and party, usually on the first weekend of March. The first parade was held in 1978 as a gay-rights protest and today it's the biggest celebration of gay and lesbian culture in the world. In 1992, an unprecedented crowd of 400,000, including a broad spectrum of straight society, turned up to watch the parade and two years later it began to be broadcast nationally on television. By 1999, the combined festival, parade and party was making the local economy a hundred million dollars richer annually, and the increasing commercialization of Mardi Gras was drawing criticism from the gay and lesbian community. Its bubble burst in 2002, after financial mismanagement saw the Mardi Gras organization in the red to the tune of $500,000. Instead of throwing in the towel, the fundraising organization was rebuilt as the "New Mardi Gras"; although less cash-rich, New Mardi Gras has drawn on the resources and creativity of its talented community, along with the desire to keep the festival going, and has continued building.

▲ Mardi Gras

The festival, parade and party

Three weeks of exhibitions, performances and other events – including the **Mardi Gras Film Festival** (Ⓦ www.queerscreen.com.au), in late February at the Palace Academy cinema (see p.225), showcasing the latest in queer cinema – represent the largest lesbian and gay arts festival in the world. This paves the way for the main event, an exuberant nighttime **parade** down Oxford Street, when up to half a million gays and straights jostle for the best viewing positions, before the Dykes on Bikes, traditional leaders of the parade since 1988, roar into view.

Participants devote months to the preparation of outlandish floats and outrageous costumes at Mardi Gras workshops, while even more time is devoted to the preparation of beautiful bodies in Sydney's packed gyms. The parade begins at 7.45pm (finishing around 10.30pm), but people line the barricades along Oxford Street from mid-morning (brandishing stolen milk crates to get a better view). If you can't get to Oxford Street until late afternoon, your best chance of finding a spot is along Flinders Street near Moore Park Road, where the parade ends.

Otherwise, AIDS charity the Bobby Goldsmith Foundation (Ⓦ www.bgf .org.au) sells around seven thousand grandstand ("Glamstand") seats on Flinders Street, at $120 each.

The post-parade, wild-and-sexy, all-night **dance party** is one of the hottest tickets in Sydney. More than twenty thousand people sashay and strut through several differently themed dance spaces, mostly based around the Hordern Pavilion at the Entertainment Quarter in Moore Park. Past performers have included Kylie Minogue, Boy George and Grace Jones, and Paul Oakenfold headlined in 2009. If that's still not enough, the *Homesexual* recovery party keeps the ball rolling at *Home* megaclub (see p.219) at Darling Harbour.

You may have to plan ahead if you want to get a dance party **ticket**: party tickets ($135 from Ticketek on Ⓣ13 2849, Ⓦ www.ticketek.com .au) sometimes sell out by the end of January. Your local gay-friendly travel agent can also organize tickets. The **Sydney Gay & Lesbian Mardi Gras Guide**, available from mid-December, can be picked up from bookshops, cafés and restaurants around Oxford Street or downloaded from the website.

The Sleaze Ball

Sydney just can't wait all year for Mardi Gras, so the **Sleaze Ball** (tickets $120 through Ticketek) is a very welcome stopgap in early October that also serves as a fundraiser for the Mardi Gras organizers. Similar to the Mardi Gras party, it's held at the Entertainment Quarter, and goes on through the night. For those who miss the parties themselves, the **recovery parties** the next day are nearly as good; virtually all the bars and clubs host all-day sessions after the parties, especially the lanes behind the *Flinders Bar*, which are packed with exhausted but deliriously happy party-people.

Information, accommodation and eating

A good starting point for **information** is The Bookshop, 207 Oxford St, Darlinghurst (℡02/9331 1103, Ⓦwww.thebookshop.com.au), which has a full stock of gay- and lesbian-related books, cards and magazines, including the free gay and lesbian weeklies, *Sydney Star Observer* (Ⓦwww.starobserver.com.au) and *SX* (Ⓦwww.eevolution.com.au). Both come out on Thursdays and include weekly event listings; monthly publications include the free lesbian-specific *LOTL* (*Lesbians on the Loose*; Ⓦwww.lotl.com), and the nationally distributed *DNA* ($9; Ⓦwww.dnamagazine.com.au). Check the websites of all these magazines before you leave home.

The inclusiveness of modern, cosmopolitan Sydney has led to a significant decline in exclusively **gay accommodation**. On the positive side, just about everywhere in the city centre or inner suburbs is gay-friendly and you shouldn't find it unpleasant booking in anywhere. This is doubly true around the gay heart of Oxford Street (particularly the suburbs of Darlinghurst, Paddington and Surry Hills, where you will still find a couple of predominantly gay places. We've listed several in our general accommodation listings – flick to *Governors on Fitzroy* (p.169) and *Brickfield Hill B&B Inn* (p.169) and the male nudist *Oasis on Flinders*. Other gay-friendly contenders in the area include *The Wattle* (p.165), *De Vere* (p.163), *Sullivans* (p.165), *Medusa* (p.164) and *Kirketon* (p.164).

The parts of town popular with the gay community are full of good **cafés** and **restaurants**. Again, none is exclusively gay, so we've included the best places in our general "Eating" listings (see Chapter 12). Good hunting grounds include the section of Oxford Street from Taylor Square to Hyde Park, particularly *Battuta*, *Grumpy Baker*, *Mahjong Room*, *Pink Peppercorn*, *Thai Nesia*, and *Una's*.

Gay and lesbian contacts

AIDS Council of NSW (ACON) 9 Commonwealth St, Surry Hills ℡1800 063 060, Ⓦwww.acon.org.au.

Albion Street Centre 150–154 Albion St, Surry Hills ℡02/9332 9600, Ⓦwww.sesiahs .health.nsw.gov.au/Albionstcentre. Counselling, testing clinic, information and library.

ALSO Foundation Ⓦwww.also.org.au. Based in Victoria, they have a good website with an excellent nationwide business and community directory.

Gay & Lesbian Counselling Service ℡02/8594 9596, Ⓦwww.glcsnsw.org.au. Daily 5.30–10.30pm.

Gay traveller Ⓦwww.gay-traveller.com.au. A good resource for gay-owned apartment rentals and B&Bs.

GALTA (Gay and Lesbian Tourism Australia) Ⓦwww.galta.com.au. A non-profit organization set up to promote the gay and lesbian tourism industry. Its website has links to accommodation, travel agents and tour operators.

Pinkboard Ⓦwww.pinkboard.com.au. Popular, long-running Australian website featuring personal ads and classifieds sections with everything from houseshares, party tickets, employment and a help and advice section. It's free to run your own personal or classified ads.

The Pink Directory Ⓦwww.thepinkdirectory.com.au. An online and print directory of gay and lesbian businesses and community information.

Qbeds Ⓦwww.qbeds.com.au. Handy general guide giving information on where to stay Australia-wide.

Pubs and bars

A few of the **bars** listed here have dance–floor–type areas, open at weekends; most have regular DJs, and could easily be included in the club listings (see below). Our bar and club listings have not been split into separate gay and lesbian listings, as the scene – thankfully – doesn't split so neatly into "them and us".

Bank Hotel 324 King St, Newtown 02/8568 1900. Newtown CityRail. This stylish bar is a dyke favourite; "Wednesday night in the Velvet Room" attracts large crowds with great DJ's, cocktails and a fun atmosphere. 24hr licence: Mon & Tues noon–12.30am, Wed & Thurs noon until 1.30am or 2am, Fri & Sat noon–4am, Sun noon–midnight.

Clarence Hotel 450 Parramatta Rd, Petersham, 02/9560 0400, www.clarencehotel.com.au. Bus #338 or #440 from Central CityRail. Currently the only exclusively gay and lesbian venue in the Inner west. Both its two bars, Manacle and Outbar, hold numerous saucy evening events from guy-on-guy jelly-wrestling to fetish dress-ups. Mon–Sat 10am–6am, Sun 10am–midnight.

The Colombian 117–123 Oxford St, corner of Crown St, Darlinghurst 02/9360 2151. Bus #378 from Central CityRail or #380 from Circular Quay CityRail. Mixed-clientele bar where people come to get revved-up in the evenings and renew their energy the day after. The fun and funky faux South American-style interior in the ground-floor public bar makes an airy and comfortable space to drink, bop and chat, with open windows onto the street. Upstairs, there's a more intimate cocktail bar – which includes a giant red tribal mask. Different DJs and musical styles (Wed–Sun), from R&B to funky house and drag-cum-variety nights Wed & Thurs. Thursday is glamour night in the cocktail lounge. Hip but not pretentious. Mon & Tues 10am–4pm, Wed–Sun 9am–5am.

Flinders Bar 63 Flinders St, Darlinghurst 02/9356 3622, www.flindershotel.com. Bus #378 from Central CityRail, or #380 from Circular Quay CityRail. With a welcoming and very mixed crowd, this hotel offers a funky, sleek modern environment to drink or dance with friends. Once very popular with younger gays and their admirers, this bar is now a much more varied after-work drinks place and late-night groove lounge. There's something on most nights – quiz and $10 curry on Tues, Bears night on Fri etc: see website for details. It also has an international restaurant upstairs that serves meals from $14. Tues–Sun 3pm until late.

Imperial Hotel 35 Erskineville Rd, Erskineville 02/9519 9899. Erskineville CityRail. This gay icon, brought to the world's attention in the hit film *The Adventures of Priscilla, Queen of the Desert*, which both started and ended here, was closed for renovations and undergoing the painful negotiation of development plans with the council when this book went to press. When operational, drag shows never fail to delight all manner of patrons while, downstairs, the basement jumps, jiggles and jives on full-throttle gay club nights.

Oxford Hotel 134 Oxford St, Darlinghurst www.theoxfordhotel.com.au. Bus #378 from Central CityRail, or #380 from Circular Quay CityRail. Right on Taylor Square, this four-floor establishment was once the macho pillar of the gay community but has gone a little straight of late. That's least true in the open-to-the-street ground floor bar, with its dim lights, hard and handbag house and regular clientele. The basement holds *Gilligans* (Thurs–Sun 11pm–3am; $5–10), a popular cocktail bar with a mixed clientele and a vibrating dancefloor, while the upper two floors hold the Supper Club (Wed–Sun 7pm until late), with light meals accompanied by anything from DJs to burlesque, and the Polo Lounge (Tues–Sun 6pm until late), a cocktail and champagne bar dominated by a huge black horse lamp.

Stonewall Hotel 175 Oxford St at Taylor Square, Darlinghurst 02/9360 1963, www .stonewallhotel.com. Bus #378 from Central CityRail, or bus #380 from Circular Quay CityRail. Extending over three action-packed levels, this pub is a big hit with young gays and lesbians and their straight friends. The airy downstairs bar (with a few outside tables) plays commercial dance music, the cocktail bar on the next level accelerates on uplifting house, while the top-floor, weekend-only VIP Bar gets off on campy, "handbag" sounds (Fri & Sat 11pm–6am; free). Expect theme nights like karaoke, celebrity drag, or Mailbox (a dating game), and DJs in the various bars Wed–Sat. Daily 11am–6am.

Clubs

As ever, the scene is rapidly changing, and bars and **clubs** seem to close down at an alarming rate: try to check recent listings magazines before going out of your way for a big night. Entry is free unless otherwise indicated.

Arq 16 Flinders St, corner of Taylor Square, Darlinghurst ⓦ www.arqsydney.com.au. **Bus #378 from Central CityRail, or #380 from Circular Quay CityRail.** Huge 900-person capacity, state-of-the-art mainstream club with everything from DJs and drag shows to pool competitions. Two levels, each with a very different scene: the Arena, on the top floor, is mostly gay, while the ground-floor Vortex is a quieter, less crowded mix of gay and straights, with pool tables. Chill-out booths, laser lighting, viewing decks and fish tanks add to the fun, friendly atmosphere. Sunday is the big night. Thurs–Sun from 9pm; Thurs free, Fri $10, Sat $15 before 11pm, $25 after, Sun $5. Check website for specific events.

Burdekin Hotel 2 Oxford St, Darlinghurst ⓦ www.burdekin.com.au. **Bus #378 from Central CityRail, or #380 from Circular Quay CityRail.** Around once a month, Friday is lesbian dance night here at the first-floor Mini Bar, where Girl Friday kicks off at 8pm (free entry until 9pm) and goes until the small hours. $10.

Exchange Hotel 34 Oxford St, Darlinghurst ⓣ 02/9331 1936. **Bus #378 from Central CityRail, or #380 from Circular Quay CityRail.** The downstairs Phoenix Bar, is one of the more firmly gay places on the Strip. After midnight it's at its peak and a more raunchy, bacchanalian crowd you won't find anywhere else on the strip. This is also the place to be from around 6am on Sat and Sun mornings when Phoenix Rising day club keeps the clubbing ball rolling. Entry free–$15.

Midnight Shift 85 Oxford St, Darlinghurst ⓣ 02/9360 4319, ⓦ www.themidnightshift.com. **Bus #378 from Central CityRail, or #380 from Circular Quay CityRail.** Commonly known as "The Shift", this veteran of the Oxford St scene has now been running for over 25 years. On the ground floor, the Video Bar is a large drinking and cruising space to a music-video backdrop, with pool tables out the back. Upstairs, the massive weekend-only club looks rather splendid, with everything from a waterfall to a cutting-edge laser light show. The club hosts drag shows (usually Fri nights), DJs and events; cover charge $5–20, depending on the event. Mainly men. Bar daily noon–6am, club Fri & Sat 11pm–7am.

Taxi Club 40 Flinders St, Darlinghurst ⓦ www.thetaxi.com.au. **Bus #378 from Central CityRail, or bus #380 from Circular Quay CityRail.** Last stop. It's a Sydney legend and famous (or notorious) for being the only place you can buy a drink on Good Friday or Christmas Day; but don't bother before 2am or 3am, and you'll need to be suitably intoxicated to appreciate it fully. There's a strange blend of drag queens, taxi drivers, lesbians and boys (straight and gay) to observe, and the cheapest drinks in gay Sydney. An upstairs dance club (free) operates Fri & Sat from 1am. Bring ID to show you're from out of town: draconian liquor licensing laws do allow clubs to serve alcohol to those "visiting from afar", so it could come in handy. Mon–Thurs 4pm–midnight, Fri & Sat 2pm–6am, Sun 2pm–4am.

Trademark Hotel 1 Bayswater Rd, Kings Cross ⓦ gazesunday.com. **Kings Cross CityRail.** Head here Sunday late afternoon and evening for GazeSundays, and hot house in cool surroundings with a handful of resident DJs. Sun from 5pm.

Gyms

The prices below are for a casual pass, which can last all day if you want it to, and includes any fitness classes on offer. Many **gyms** allow one free trial session, which is a cheeky way for travellers to do the rounds and get a buff bod for nothing.

City Gym 107–113 Crown St, East Sydney ⓣ 02/9360 6247, ⓦ www.citygym.com.au. **Museum CityRail.** Unbelievably popular (at all hours) among gay men, lesbians and straights. Plenty of weights, aerobics, body combat and yoga classes and male and female steam rooms – which can be cruisey. Mon–Fri 5am–midnight, Sat 6am–10pm, Sun 8am–10pm; $22.

Gold's Gym Level 1/58 Kippax St, Surry Hills ⓣ 02/9211 2799, ⓦ goldsgymsydney.com.au. **Central CityRail.** Low-key gym over three levels in the heart of Surry Hills with a large gay clientele. Neither cruisey nor full of muscleheads, it's a friendly place to work out either on weights, on their separate cardio level or at one of their classes – power yoga, aerobox, Pilates etc. Mon–Fri 5.30am–9pm, Sat 8am–8pm, Sun 8am–6pm; $19.

Newtown Gym Level 1, 294 King St, Newtown ⓣ 020/9519 6969, ⓦ www.newtowngym.com.au. **Newtown CityRail.** Large lesbian membership. Step, body pump and yoga classes, weight training, solarium and sauna. Free childcare facilities (Mon–Sat 9am–noon). Mon–Fri 6am–10pm, Sat & Sun 8am–8pm; $15.

Beaches and swimming pools

During Sydney's hot summer, a popular choice among the gay set is **Tamarama** (known locally as Glamarama, see p.134), a fifteen-minute walk from the southern end of Bondi Beach. But if showing off is not your thing, **Bondi** (p.133) or nearby **Bronte** (p.135) may suit you better. The calm harbour waters of **Redleaf** at Double Bay (p.119) also lure a big gay crowd, while if you want to get your gear off, try **Lady Jane Beach** at Watsons Bay (p.123).

Pools of choice are Redleaf harbour pool at Double Bay and the appropriately named Andrew "Boy" Charlton pool in the Domain (p.268). The Coogee Women's Baths, at the southern end of Coogee Beach, is popular with lesbians.

Kids' Sydney

W
ith its sunny climate, fabulous beaches and wide open spaces, Sydney is a great place to holiday with kids. There are lots of parks, playgrounds, sheltered bays and public pools for safe swimming, and a range of indoor options for rainy days. Museums are mostly child-friendly, in particular the **Powerhouse Museum** and the **Australian Museum**, both of which have exhibits and activities designed to entertain as well as educate, and most offer special school-holiday programmes. Three areas, **The Rocks**, **Darling Harbour** and the **Entertainment Quarter** have much to keep children amused, and all offer plentiful free activities during the school holidays. Check these websites for the latest goings on: Ⓦwww.therocks.com, www.darlingharbour.com.au and www.eqmoorepark.com.au.

Also see our "Sports and activities" chapter for details on the many options for children, from renting bikes to the free pony rides and jumping castle at Rosehill Gardens racetrack (p.264). And check out the "Festivals" chapter, where everything from Sydney's kite festival at Bondi to the balmy evening Christmas carols in the Domain will keep the kids happy. Out of town, rail-enthusiast kids will love the Zig Zag Railway (p.312) near Lithgow, the Toy and Railway Museum at Leura (p.303), and the Sydney Tramway Museum and tram rides at the Royal National Park (see p.316); fire-engine-mad children should experience the Museum of Fire at Penrith (p.298).

Costs and access

Children under 5 get **entry into museums** for free, while those aged from 5 to 15 have a half-price or reduced rate (teenagers 16 or older should bring a student card or get hold of an ISIC card – see p.39); most places also offer discounted **family tickets**, usually based on two adults and two children. We give the child and family entry prices in this chapter; where we don't list these rates in the rest of the Guide, assume they are available.

Children under 4 travel on **public transport** for free, while children from 4 to 15 travel at a fifty percent discount.

There are also "family fares" – when one fare-paying adult travels with their children, the first child travels at normal price and the rest are free. Family Funday Sundays enable all family members unlimited travel on trains, buses and ferries every Sunday until 4am the following day at a cost of only $2.50 each member – making it a great day to explore the harbour by ferry or take a day-trip to the Blue Mountains, Central Coast or Royal National Park (visit Ⓦwww.131500 .com.au/faresandpasses/funday). Special family discounts are also available on the Sydney Pass, Sydney Explorer and Bondi Explorer services, ferry cruises, and with the Wild Australia Pass (involving a ferry ride to Darling Harbour, Aquarium and Sydney Wildlife World visits). Our "Travellers with disabilities" section in Basics, which gives information about accessible transport and even bushwalks, is all relevant to those with prams and pushchairs.

Public toilets and parents' rooms

Sydney is well serviced with free **public toilets**, and those in shopping malls and department stores invariably have a separate unisex **parents' room** attached, where you can change nappies. There's often even a microwave to heat bottles or baby food, and curtained booths with vaguely comfy chairs for breastfeeding. However, it's your legal right to breastfeed in public and on the whole most people are pretty unfazed, given the amount of flesh routinely bared on Sydney's beaches.

Information and childminding

Sydney's Child, an excellent free monthly magazine, contains intelligent articles, detailed listings of **what's on**, and adverts for a range of services including **babysitting**; pick up a copy at libraries, major museums and many kid-oriented shops and services, or check out Ⓦwww.sydneyschild.com.au. Two popular books detailing activities for kids in Sydney are also available at bookshops, and are reviewed in "Contexts" (see p.350).

Some hotels, usually the most expensive, offer in-house babysitting; enquire when you're booking. Should your accommodation not provide this, consider Wright Nanny, a childcare service providing rigorously screened first-aid trained nannies and babysitters from across Sydney. Babysitters (evenings only), and day nannies cost $18–22 per hour – minimum four hours – plus a flat fee of $20; Ⓣ02/9660 6621; Ⓦwww.thewrightnanny.com.au). Casual **childminding**

▲ Skateboarding at the beach

Summer, six weeks, beginning roughly ten days before Christmas, to last week in January; **autumn**, two weeks coinciding with Easter (normally early to mid-April); **winter**, two weeks, beginning the second week of July; **spring**, two weeks, beginning the last week of September. Check the public schools section of the New South Wales Department of Education website for exact dates: ⓦwww.schools.nsw.edu.au/calendar.

services are available at many gyms and swimming pools (see Leichhardt Park Aquatic Centre, p.269, and Victoria Park Pool, p.269), usually with a limit of up to two hours.

Museums and galleries

The dynamic **Historic Houses Trust of New South Wales**, including the Justice and Police Museum (p.62), the Museum of Sydney (p.76), Hyde Park Barracks (p.72), Susannah Place Museum (p.57), Elizabeth Bay House (p.96), Vaucluse House (p.120), Government House (p.68), and Elizabeth Farm in Parramatta (p.155) and Rouse Hill estate, offer a huge range of school-holiday programmes for children aged 6 to 12 (ⓣ02/8239 2211, ⓦwww.hht.net.au), from theatrical performances exploring pioneering history at Elizabeth Farm and feeding the farm animals at Rouse Hill estate to drawing classes at Vaucluse House.

In addition to the listings below, the Powerhouse also runs the **Sydney Observatory** (see p.58), where the 3-D Space Theatre and the animated Aboriginal Dreamtime stories are a big hit with kids; The Observatory also has a big school holiday programme, from making and launching rockets and electronic workshops to star- and planet-related fun days, though these are mostly aimed at small groups.

Art Gallery of New South Wales The Domain ⓦwww.gallerykids.com.au. **Martin Place or St James CityRail.** The gallery's free Sunday Performances (2.30pm) for families – art appreciation, drama, storytelling, dance and mime – run most of the year, and also daily except Sat during school holidays. Also kids' practical art workshops during the vacation periods (1hr 30min–2hr; $25–30; 5–8-year-olds & 9–13-year-olds; booking essential on ⓣ02/9225 1740). Daily 10am–5pm and Wed until 9pm; free; see also p.69.

Australian Museum Corner of College and William sts ⓦwww.australianmuseum.net.au. **Museum or Town Hall CityRail.** The people here clearly know a thing or two about the special relationship kids have with dinosaurs – their dino exhibition is aimed squarely at 5–12-year-olds. The museum's Search & Discover room comes complete with microscopes, specimens (and books to help identify them). Kidspace, for under-5s, has a shipwreck and all sorts of crawling pits and cubby houses to explore,

plus a baby-change area. Thurs during term time is "Family Day", with organized activities for under-5s (10.30–11.30am; no bookings), while there are occasional weekend scientific workshops for 7–12-year-olds and school scientific and craft programmes (from $20; bookings on ⓣ02/9320 6225). Daily 9.30am–5pm; adult $12, child 5–15 $6, family $30; see also p.81.

Australian National Maritime Museum Darling Harbour ⓦwww.anmm.gov.au. **Harbourside Monorail.** Free entry makes this modern museum particularly inviting for families. Sunday is the big family day, when free films are shown in the theatrette in the early afternoon and the Kids Deck activity area is in full swing (11am–3pm; $7); activities include exhibition-related stories, games and craft activities. There's also an imaginative school-holiday programme in Kids Deck (10am–4pm; $7 per session), which could include a session pretending to be an eighteenth-century sailor or something involving stories, drawings, dress-ups and games. Information and bookings ⓣ02/9298 3655. Daily 9.30am–5pm, to 6pm in Jan; free; see also p.87.

Powerhouse Museum 500 Harris St, Ultimo Ⓦ**www.powerhousemuseum.com. Central CityRail or Paddy's Market monorail.** Each level of this science and technology museum has a noisy and colourful corner aimed at small children, with hands-on exhibits exploring machines and movement, domestic activities, music, film and television. The general exhibits, from the huge steam engine to the chiming Strasbourg clock, will interest older kids. On weekends kids can get creative musically at "Soundhouse openhouse" (noon–1pm, book ahead), a music and multi-media lab on level 2; organized kids' activities take place between 11am and noon, from craft activities and science experiments to historical dress-ups. These weekend activities are extended to daily sessions during the school holidays – information and bookings on ⓣ02/9217 0111. There are also kids' discovery areas for under-8s and the excellent outdoor Cogs Playground on Level 1. The Powerhouse Shop in the foyer is crammed with quirky and educational toys. Daily 10am–5pm; adult $10, child 4–14 $5, family $25; see also p.90.

Parks and wildlife

Sydney and the surrounding area provide plenty of opportunities to see – and in some cases touch – **native wildlife**. The kids can pat koalas at **Taronga Zoo** (see p.127), at **Featherdale Wildlife Park** (p.153) and the **Koala Park Sanctuary** (p.153). They can also feed kangaroos, wallabies and birds or picnic in interactive yards with baby roos and emus at **Hunter Valley Zoo** (p.288) They can meet Elvis the giant crocodile and watch snakes and spiders being milked at the **Australian Reptile Park** on the Central Coast (p.281). Children also love observing the sea creatures, seals and fairy penguins, and dipping their hands into the touch-and-feel rockpool at **Sydney Aquarium** (see p.86), and seeing the scary sharks at Manly's **Oceanworld** (see p.140). And if you're visiting during June or July, be sure to take the kids on a **whale-watching cruise** (see p.27).

Centennial Park Corner of Oxford St and Lang Rd, Paddington Ⓦ**www.cp.nsw.gov.au. Bus #378 from Central CityRail or #380 from Circular Quay CityRail.** Besides typical park pleasures such as feeding ducks and climbing trees, you'll also find bike paths (and a learners' cycleway) and bridleways. You can rent kids' bikes nearby (see p.270), and the Equestrian Centre offers horse and pony rides. Children over 7 can join escorted horse rides around the park, while ages 5 and 6 can take an escorted pony ride in the centre grounds, with Centennial Stables, in Pavilion B (ⓣ02/9360 5650; $55 for 30min). See also p.271 for more on horseriding. If you can't afford a ride, it's great fun and perfectly fine for kids to wander through the Equestrian Centre and see the different horses in their stables. Back in the park, during the school holidays ranger-led dusk "Spotlight Prowls" search for possums, flying foxes and other night creatures ($11 per adult or child; bookings essential on ⓣ02/9339 6699). Other ranger-led nature-based activities are aimed at varying age groups from 2 years up ($10–25), and there's a child-friendly café (with kids' playground). Daily 8am–6pm, to 8pm during Daylight Saving; free.

Cumberland State Forest 95 Castle Hill Rd, West Pennant Hills ⓣ**02/9871 3377,** Ⓦ**www.forest.nsw.gov.au/cumberland. Pennant Hills CityRail, then bus #631–635.** Australia's only metropolitan state forest is in Sydney's northwestern suburbs with over half a century of native forest growth. The Information Centre (Mon–Fri 9am–4.30pm, Sat & Sun 10am–4.30pm) has displays and videos and a café, and sells great wooden toys. There are bushwalking trails, a native plant nursery and family activities at weekends, from a lesson in animal tracking (1hr; $5.50, family $18), to nocturnal wildlife-spotting walks (2hr; 6 years and over $11 or $35 per family) and bird-watching bush break-fasts (over-10s only; 2hr; $11, $35 family). The school-holiday programme includes activities such as making an animal mask or bushpainting (most are for kids 6–12 and over but some "mini-ranger" activities are suitable for kids aged 3–6), which usually last an hour and cost $5.50 (bookings necessary). Free barbecue and picnic areas.

Sydney Harbour National Park Cadman's Cottage, 110 George St, The Rocks ☏ **02/9247 5033,** ⓦ **www.npws.nsw.gov.au** The NPWS offers special ranger-led walks for families in the school holidays (from $9.90 per child; $13.20 per adult), detailed on their website. They also lead a Kid's Ghost Tour of the Quarantine Station near Manly on Fri and Sat nights (2hr; $22 child or $34 adult).

Taronga Zoo Bradleys Head, Mosman Bay ⓦ **www.taronga.org.au. Ferry to Taronga Zoo Wharf.** Taronga Zoo occupies an enviable position high over the harbour, and the ferry ride there plus the cable car up the hill are half the fun. Favourites with the kids are the lumbering Kodiak bears, reptiles, playful gorillas, poised meerkats, the native animal walkabout enclosure, and aviaries where you wander among birds. There's also a nocturnal animal house, seal show (11am & 2pm), an impressive free-flight bird show (noon & 3pm), and a chance to be photographed with a koala (11am & 2.45pm), plus keeper talks and feedings throughout the day. Daily 9am–5pm; $39, ages 4–15 $19, family $98.50, under-4s free.

Shops

Suburban K-Mart, Target, Best and Less, and Pumpkin Patch stores sell affordable **kidswear**, while the department stores in the city centre stock a full range of quality clothes and toys. Huge Toys "R" Us stores are found at various suburban locations. More interesting shops are detailed below. A delightful selection of **kids' books** set in Sydney are reviewed in "Contexts" on p.347, and are available at the bookshops listed on p.242, as well as the specialist Gleebooks store, below.

ABC Shop Level 1, Queen Victoria Building, 421–481 George St ⓦ **www.shop.abc.net.au. Town Hall CityRail.** ABC (and BBC) television's merchandizing outlet – books, audio, video, toys, clothing and accessories – sells all the Australian favourites, from *Bananas in Pyjamas* to the *Wiggles*. Mon–Fri 9am–5.30pm (Thurs to 8pm), Sat 9am–5pm, Sun 11am–5pm.

Gleebooks Children's Books 191 Glebe Point Rd, Glebe ⓦ **www.gleebooks.com.au. Bus #431–434 from Central CityRail.** Children's bookshop, attached to the well-respected Gleebooks secondhand store (see p.243); 9am–9pm.

Hobbyco Levels 2 & 3, Queen Victoria Building, 421–481 George St ⓦ **www.hobbyco.com.au. Town Hall CityRail.** Established in 1935, this huge hobby shop has everything from dolls' houses to kites, Meccano sets, trains, and bubble-headed storm troopers. The working model railway is a major attraction. Mon–Sat 9am–6pm (Thurs to 9pm), Sun 11am–5pm.

The Kids Room 83 Paddington St at Elizabeth St, Paddington ⓦ **www.thekidsroom.com. au. Bus #378 from Central CityRail or #380 from Circular Quay or Bondi Junction CityRail.** Quality clothes and shoes, for babies through to early teens. Australian brands like Fred Bare and Gumboots. Mon–Fri 10.30am–5.30pm, Sat 10am–5.30pm, Sun 12.30–4.30pm.

The Puppets Shop At The Rocks 77 George St, The Rocks ⓦ **www.thepuppetshop.com.** A dungeon-like Shop where a great selection of puppets, marionettes and toys adorn sandstone walls and rustic timber shelving. From Pinocchio to Charlie Chaplin to Tin Tin to witches and goblins to bipedal humanoid animals in colonial attire, the crafted creatures here range from endearingly rudimentary to decidedly sophisticated works of art – an entertaining, though possibly frightening, experience for the kiddies (and it's all for sale).

Swimming and water sports

Beware Sydney's **strong surf** – young children are safer swimming at sheltered harbour beaches or ocean pools. Public swimming pools (typically outdoor and unheated) generally have a toddlers' **paddling pool**. For year-round swimming there are heated pools at North Sydney (p.269), right beside Luna Park, and the

Sun protection

The sun in Australia is punishing. The country's proximity to the ozone hole over Antarctica means ultraviolet (UV) radiation levels are much higher than in Europe. Australia also comes closer to the sun in summer than does the northern hemisphere, meaning an increase of seven percent solar UV intensity. Skin burns in early childhood have been shown to contribute to skin cancer in later life, which kills 1600 Australians every year, so be safe. A broad-spectrum, water-resistant **sunscreen** (minimum SPF 20) is a must, and colourful zinc cream on nose and cheeks is a good extra protectant when swimming. Most local kids wear UV-resistant lycra **swim tops** or wetsuit-style all-in-ones to the beach, and schoolchildren wear **hats** in the playground – the legionnaire-style ones are especially popular, as they shade the face and the back of the neck. All these items can be purchased at surfwear shops, department stores, or at the NSW Cancer Council Shop in the Westfield Centrepoint shopping centre, Castlereagh Street entrance (Town Hall, CityRail) or Westfield Bondi Junction, Oxford Street entrance (Bondi Junction, CityRail; Ⓦ www.nswcc.org.au).

indoor Sydney Olympic Park Aquatic Centre at Olympic Park (p.269), which has a rapid water ride and slides. The Cook and Phillip Park Aquatic and Fitness Centre (p.268) is another good place to take kids, while the Leichhardt Park Aquatic Centre, overlooking Iron Cove (p.269), and Victoria Park Pool (p.269) have crèche facilities.

If you're going to be in Sydney for a while and your children can't swim, or are weak swimmers (or you're envisaging a future Olympic career for them), the NSW Department of Sport and Recreation conducts excellent inexpensive small-group **Swimsafe courses** at local swimming pools, held over nine consecutive days (information and bookings Ⓣ 13 1302, Ⓦ www.dsr.nsw.gov.au; pre-schoolers from 18 months, 30min per day, $41.95; school-age, 40min per day, first child $55.95 and 41.95 for each additional child).

Bondi's Lets Go Surfing (Ⓣ 02/9365 1800, Ⓦ www.letsgosurfing.com.au) offers Saturday and Sunday group lessons in **board-riding** and **surf safety** for kids aged 7–11 and 12–16 (1.5hr; $40), including longer surf camps in school holidays (5 days; 1hr 30min per day; $180), plus individual and family lessons. On the northern beaches, Manly Surf School, opposite Jellyfish on North Steyne (Ⓣ 02/9977 6977, Ⓦ www.manlysurfschool.com), offers small-group surfing classes (5–17 years; 1hr; $55), and school-holiday surfing classes at Manly, Collaroy and Palm beaches (1hr 30min per day over 4 days; $120).

Balmoral Windsurfing, Sailing and Kayaking School at Balmoral Beach holds a **learn to sail** camp during summer and Easter holidays (ages 5–12; 1–5 days; 9.30am–3pm; $145–370; Ⓣ 02/9960 5344, Ⓦ www.sailingschool.com.au).

Northside Sailing School, Spit Bridge, Mosman (Ⓣ 02/9969 3972, Ⓦ www .northsidesailing.com.au), specializes in weekend dinghy sailing courses on Middle Harbour during the sailing season (Sept–April), and also offers lessons for kids (7–15 years; 2hr lesson for 1–2 children $100) and holiday camp programmes (3-, 4- or 5-day programmes; $240/320/400) during all school holidays except the winter break.

Beaches

Balmoral Beach On the north side of the harbour, around the corner from Taronga Zoo, this is the pick of the harbour's family beaches for its wide sandy bays, sheltered from the wind and waves, and sheer beauty (spacious parks, bush-clad promontories arcing from its sides, and an Edwardian crenellated esplanade). Much of the southern end is shaded by big trees, and there's a great children's playground next to the beach kiosk that sells ice creams and takeaway coffee (there's also great fish'n'chips across the road at *Bottom of The Harbour Seafoods*). See p.129.

Bronte Beach The most popular of the eastern beaches for families, fronted by an extensive and shady park with picnic shelters and barbecues (plus a stash of good alfresco cafés across the road), a mini-train ride (Sat & Sun 11am–4pm) and an imaginative children's playground. A natural rock enclosure provides a calm area for swimming. See p.133.

Coogee Coogee Bay is popular with families, with a grassy park with picnic shelters and barbecues. Past the southern end of the beach, Coogee Women's Pool (see p.138) is for women and children only (boys are welcome up to age 3). Grant Reserve, opposite the pool, holds a big adventure playground. See p.136.

Manly On the north side of the harbour, tucked in beside Manly Wharf, Manly Cove has a small harbour beach with a netted-off swimming area, while the sheltered beaches of Fower Bower (with a rock pool) and Shelly Beach (fronted by a big park) lie on Cabbage Tree Bay on the ocean side of Manly. The ferry ride over is lots of fun, and the area holds plenty of attractions for kids, including an aquarium and a water slide. You can rent bikes or rollerblades and get onto the Manly bike path, which is shared with pedestrians. See p.141.

North Bondi The northern end of Bondi Beach has a shallow enclosed seapool for children. It's backed by a grassy park rising up the hill with electric barbecues and a playground on the next level up the steps. Consequently this is the child-overrun "family" end of the beach; an ice-cream van takes advantage of the situation, and a couple of beachfront cafés stand across the street. See p.133.

Northern beaches Stretching from Manly, the northern beaches also have some good family choices – Dee Why Beach is backed by a sheltered lagoon, Long Reef's creature-filled rock pools provide wonderful exploration opportunities, while Narrabeen Beach fronts extensive, swimmable lakes. Beyond Narrabeen, sheltered Bongin Bongin Bay, with a headland reserve and rocks to clamber on, is ideal for children. See pp.143–145.

Shark Beach (Neilson Park) A harbour favourite for many Sydney families, on the southern shore of the harbour in Vaucluse. Don't let the name put you off, Shark Beach is net-protected and safe, with glorious views taking in much of Sydney Harbour National Park. Backed by an expansive park filled with gnarled and majestic Morton Bay figs, historic buildings, and a gorgeous Edwardian kiosk fronting the beach and esplanade (serving good coffee and snacks), this is a great option for a relaxed day of swimming, ballgames and lounging around with the family. You might consider reaching Neilson Park via the vista-packed Hermitage Foreshore Walk (see p.265), but you can also get the bus.

Theatre

Marian Street Theatre for Young People 2 Marian St, Killara bookings ☎02/9645 1611. **Killara CityRail.** Bookings are essential for the popular matinees for kids aged 3–10, often involving audience participation (Sat 1pm; school holidays: Mon–Fri 10.30am & 1pm; $15, child $12).

Sydney Opera House Bennelong Point, Circular Quay ☎02/9250 7770, ⊛www .sydneyoperahouse.com. **Circular Quay CityRail/ ferry.** The popular Kids At The House programme includes "Babies Proms" for

2–5 year olds (interactive concerts in which the kids learn about and participate in orchestral music, African percussion or the singing of exquisite Dreamtime lullabies from around the world; 35min; $18) – and numerous other highly inventive music, theatre and dance performances aimed at school-age children ($18–26). The Australian Ballet holds twice yearly "Introduction to the Ballet" sessions, for anyone aged 10 and upwards (May & Nov; 1hr 30min).

Theme parks, playgrounds and activities

Sydney's first theme park, harbourfront **Luna Park**, opened in the 1930s and remains an essential visit (see p.123). You can head south to **Jamberoo Recreation Park** (below), or, if you're in town around April, to Homebush Bay for the biggest annual funfair at the **Royal Easter Show** (see p.258).

Darling Harbour is never short of kids' amusements, and is big on family festivals, especially during school holidays. The area around **Tumbalong Park** is particularly child-focused – there's a watery playground with fountains to race among, colourful stationary bikes, and a children's play area with a charming nineteenth-century **carousel** right next door.

The **Entertainment Quarter** holds plenty on tap for everyone from little kid to teenager: a big choice of movies at its cinemas, an outdoor music screen, a food market with kids' petting zoo (Wed, Sat & Sun 10am–3.30pm), lots of shops to browse in, two outdoor adventure playgrounds and, beside them, a carousel ($2.50 per ride) and a (pricey) indoor playground, Lollipops (see below), that's perfect for rainy days.

Jamberoo Action Park Jamberoo Rd, Jamberoo, 7km from Kiama (see p.331)
Ⓦ **www.jamberoo.net.** Running daily Sept–April, this is a water-themed fun park with a mix of thrilling and gentle water-rides and -slides and an artificial lagoon to swim in. There are non-watery attractions, too: a chairlift, toboggan rides, a park train, racing cars and a mini-golf course. A picnic area holds coin-operated barbecues, and there are several fast-food outlets. A sit-down licensed eatery, *The Loft*, serves healthier food. Entry 4–12 year olds $29, over-13s & adults $37.

Lollipops Playground 122 Lang Rd, Entertainment Quarter, Moore Park Ⓦwww .lollipopsplayland.com.au. **Bus #339 from Central CityRail.** Indoor playground, aimed at children aged 1–9, that's guaranteed to exhaust them, with a jungle gym, giant mazes, tunnels, jumping castle and everything from a ball pool to a tea-cup merry-go-round ride, books, toys, dress-ups and games as well as organized activities. Socks are obligatory. There are also two free playgrounds, and a carousel

▲ Luna Park

outside. Daily 9.30am–6pm; under-1s free; 1–2 midweek $10, weekends $14; 2 and over $14; adults $5.

Sydney **festivals**

From the word go, Sydney's annual calendar is packed with lively, spectacular festivals and events. The year kicks off in grand style with a magnificent firework display at midnight on New Year's Eve, when the skyline over Sydney harbour explodes in pyrotechnic flowers, showers and cascades. Highlights throughout the rest of the year include the exuberant family-oriented celebrations for Australia Day, the gloriously over-the-top Mardi Gras carnival, and some great film and music festivals.

Sydney Festival ▲

Australia Day ▼

Sydney Festival

The lively, three-week-long **Sydney Festival** in **January** – Australia's most extensive cultural event – celebrates the arts, and summer in the city. Many events are free and held outdoors, including hugely popular night-time symphony and jazz concerts in The Domain. Besides the free stuff, international musicians, theatre companies and art exhibitions, most charging hefty ticket prices, appear in venues all over the city (Ⓦwww .sydneyfestival.org.au).

Australia Day

January 26, 1788, the day that the First Fleet arrived to settle Sydney Cove, is celebrated nationally as **Australia Day**, but nowhere more so than in Sydney. The whole extravaganza is free and action-packed, so be prepared to roam the city all day and into the night to make the most of it. The Rocks, Hyde Park and Darling Harbour burst with live entertainment, while there's half-price museum entry, yacht and boat races on the harbour, aerial displays, a vintage car show, and 9pm fireworks at Darling Harbour (Ⓦwww.australiaday.gov.au).

Tropfest ▼

Tropfest

From humble beginnings as a short film screening in the *Tropicana Cafe* in 1993, **Tropfest** has become the world's largest short film festival. The free outdoor event takes over The Domain on the **last Sunday in February**, with entertainment from mid-afternoon, and screening of the sixteen finalist films at 8pm. Films must be made specifically for Tropfest, incorporating an item announced several months in advance (Ⓦwww.tropfest.com).

Mardi Gras

The month-long **Sydney Gay & Lesbian Mardi Gras** runs through hot, sweaty February, before climaxing in **early March** in an outrageous street parade that pulsates down Oxford Street. What began as a gay rights protest in 1978 now celebrates all things "Queer". A high percentage of straight Sydney turns out to watch the antics and cheer on the floats, which are traditionally led by the Dykes on Bikes (Ⓦwww.mardigras.org.au).

▲ Mardi Gras

▼ Royal Easter Show

Royal Easter Show

Every **April**, cosmopolitan Sydney is invaded by visitors dressed in Akubra hats, moleskins, R.M. Williams boots and Drizabone coats: not tourists overdoing "Outback", but country folk here to exhibit prize cows and pumpkins, and compete in rodeos and wood-chopping competitions. Part agricultural festival, part fun-fair and attracting a million people over two weeks, the **Sydney Royal Easter Show** dates back to 1822 (Ⓦwww.eastershow .com.au).

Manly Jazz Festival

As spring sunshine starts to make the outdoors appealing again, five outdoor stages in beachside Manly host the three-day **Manly International Jazz Festival**, held over the Labour Day long weekend in **early October**. The massive community-based festival, mostly free, has attracted Sydneysiders for over 25 years: the water may still be chilly, but the combination of beach views from the oceanfront stage, warm sun, and live jazz is irresistible. Restaurants and bars put on a fringe program, and there's a beachfront market (Ⓦwww.manly.nsw.gov.au/manlyjazz).

▼ Manly International Jazz Festival

Sculpture by the Sea ▲

Sydney to Hobart Yacht Race ▼

Food and Wine Fair

On a Saturday in **late October**, Hyde Park's huge **Sydney Food and Wine Fair** launches the picnic season. Around 30,000 grazers flock to more than a hundred stalls, representing restaurants, coffee houses, breweries and wineries, all raising funds for AIDS research. Restaurants produce entree-sized portions of their signature dishes, which sell out fast after the noon start. Live music, dance and drag on two stages accompany the food frenzy (Ⓦgfm.smh.com.au).

Sculpture by the Sea

As the weather hots up in **early November**, the stunning coastal path between Bondi and Tamarama is transformed into an outdoor sculpture park for eighteen days. During **Sculpture by the Sea**, more than a hundred Australian and international sculptors reach an audience of over 400,000. The sandstone cliffs and crashing ocean create a sublime setting for often playful works, encouraged to "incorporate the sun, sea, wind and rain" (Ⓦwww.sculpturebythesea.com).

Sydney to Hobart Yacht Race

Up there with the less frequent America's Cup and the Whitbread Around the World Race in terms of excitement and media interest, the annual **Sydney to Hobart Yacht Race** on **December 26** has been contested for over sixty years. Huge post-Christmas crowds gather around Sydney Harbour to watch more than a hundred vibrantly coloured yachts set sail through the Heads for Tasmania, 630 nautical miles and several days southwest.

Shopping and galleries

Sydney's prime shopping area, the rectangle bounded by Elizabeth, King, York and Park streets, holds several beautifully restored **Victorian arcades** as well as the main **department stores**. The city also has plenty of sparkling shopping complexes where you can hunt for fashion and accessories without raising a sweat. The Rocks is packed with Australiana and **souvenir shops**, if you feel the urge to buy boomerangs, didgeridoos and stuffed toy koalas, and it's also the best place for duty- and GST-free shopping.

Paddington's Oxford Street is best for stylish one-stop shopping, with its enticing array of designer shops, funky fashion, some of the city's most appealing bookshops – and the best **weekend market** in town. The more avant-garde **Darlinghurst** and **Surry Hills** (notably the stretch of Crown Street between Devonshire and Oxford streets) have become a focus for retro-influenced interior design and clothes shops. In the inner west, **Balmain** has chic shops and gourmet delis to supplement its Saturday market, while cheerfully offbeat **Newtown** and neighbouring St Peters are great for secondhand fashions and quirky speciality stores. Down at the beach, **Bondi Pavilion** has an excellent souvenir shop, and the Campbell Parade strip offers lots of beachwear and surf shops.

The main **sales** take place immediately after Christmas and into January, and in June and into July; there are also stock clearances throughout the year, often around public holidays.

Finally, if you've run out of time to buy presents and souvenirs, note that **Sydney Airport** has one of Sydney's largest shopping malls, with outlets for everything from surfwear to R.M. Williams bush outfitters, at the same prices as downtown stores; see box below.

Duty-free shopping

If you have an air ticket out of Australia, you may be able to save around thirty percent on goods such as perfume, jewellery, imported clothing, cameras and electronic equipment. One of the main outlets is DFS Galleria, with a major store on four floors at 155 George St in The Rocks (Mon–Fri & Sun noon–7.30pm; Sat 11am–7.30pm; Ⓦwww.dfsgalleria.com).

Books

In addition to the small selection of places listed below, King Street in Newtown and Glebe Point Road in Glebe hold concentrations of **secondhand bookshops**, and Glebe, Balmain, Paddington and Bondi markets have good **secondhand stalls** (see p.253). Gertrude & Alice Cafe Bookstore at Bondi (see p.198), Delizia in Haymarket in the city (see p.183), and the well-organized Sappho Books and Café in Glebe (see p.193) also sell secondhand books. The Bookshop, a specialist **gay and lesbian** bookshop in Darlinghurst, is detailed on p.229.

The worldwide book **superstores** also have a presence in Sydney – there's Borders at the Skygarden shopping centre (see p.249), and a Books Kinokuniya at The Galeries Victoria (see p.248), but the Australia-owned Dymocks at Broadway Shopping Centre, Glebe, also offers high-comfort-level browsing – and this has prompted many bookshops to offer added value, in terms of in-store coffee shops, internet terminals, discounted bestsellers and author talks. For extended opening hours and knowledgeable staff, though, you'll still do better with the independents.

The bookshop at the State Library (see p.71) has one of the best collections of **Australian-related books** in Sydney, while if you're interested in Australian art, try the extensive bookshop at the Art Gallery of New South Wales (p.71). The shop at the Museum of Sydney (see p.76) has plenty on the city and there's a National Trust bookshop at the S.H. Ervin Gallery (p.59). If you're after Australian **first editions**, seek out Nicholas Pounder, who now only operates online (Ⓦ www.nicholaspounder.com); for **antiquarian books**, check out Berkelouw (below) and Hordern House (p.253).

Abbey's 131 York St at Market St ☎ 02/9264 3111, Ⓦ www.abbeys.com.au. Town Hall CityRail. This big academic and general bookstore, established in 1968 and still mostly family-run, is among Sydney's best-known independent booksellers – great at ordering in books – and in a prime spot opposite the QVB. The Language Book Centre on the first floor is the place to buy foreign-language books in Sydney. Mon–Wed & Fri 8.30am–7pm, Thurs 8.30am–9pm, Sat 8.30am–6pm, Sun 10am–5pm.

Ariel 42 Oxford St at West St, Paddington ☎ 02/9332 4581, Ⓦ www.arielbooks.com.au. Bus #378 from Central CityRail or #380 from Circular Quay CityRail. Not too large, lively and very hip, Ariel is especially good for design books and cutting-edge fiction. A great place to browse in the evening after a movie (the Palace cinemas Verona and Academy are just across the road; see p.225). It often has author readings and book launches. The branch at 103 George St (Circular Quay CityRail) also offers respite from the stuffed-koala overdose that frequently afflicts shoppers in The Rocks. Both daily 9am–midnight.

Berkelouw Books 19 Oxford St at Verona St, Paddington ☎ 02/9360 3200, Ⓦ www.berkelouw.com.au. Bus #378 from Central CityRail or #380 from Circular Quay CityRail. Catering to collectors as well as casual browsers, Berkelouw has been dealing in antiquarian books since 1812. New books are downstairs, and their upstairs coffee shop, with huge windows overlooking the busy Oxford Street strip, is a popular pre- and post-movie meeting place (the Palace Verona is next door). Sun–Thurs 9am–11pm, Fri & Sat 9am–midnight.

Berkelouw Books and Music 70 Norton St, Leichhardt ☎02/9560 3200, Ⓦ www.berkelouw .com.au. **Bus #438 or #440 from Central CityRail.** New and secondhand books and CDs (including a big range of world music), plus two in-store cafés, the streetfront Berkelouw Cafe and the second floor Booklounge Cafe, which hosts fortnightly Philo Cafe philosophy discussions (first & third Tues; 8pm; $5 includes coffee) and monthly poetry readings (last Thurs in the month; $5 includes glass of wine or a coffee) and even a performance space. Sun–Wed 9am–10pm, Thurs–Sat 9am–11pm.

Books Kinokuniya Level 2, The Galeries Victoria, 500 George St, corner of Park St ☎02/9262 7996, Ⓦ www.kinokuniya.com. **Town Hall CityRail.** Now Sydney's biggest book superstore, the Japanese-owned Kinokuniya has seventy percent of its estimated 300,000 titles in English. A range of books in Japanese and Chinese make up the rest. As you'd expect, there's a good range of comics, including Manga. The art and design section is also impressive and there's an antiquarian books section, an art gallery, a selection of world globes, a fossil collection and the now-obligatory bookstore café. Mon–Wed, Fri & Sat 10am–7pm, Thurs 10am–9pm, Sun 10am–6pm.

Dymocks Broadway Level 2, Broadway Shopping Centre, Broadway, near Glebe Ⓦ www.dymocks .com.au. **Bus #431–434 from Central CityRail.** Previously Collins Superstore – Sydney's first book superstore – this vast bookstore has curving bookshelves, soft lighting and comfy sofas and seats in the arched windows where you can easily lose yourself for an afternoon. When it's time to face the real world again, make for the in-store coffee shop to ease the transition. Mon–Wed & Fri 10am–7pm, Thurs 10am–9pm, Sat 9am–6pm, Sun 10am–6pm.

Dymocks Sydney 424 George St Ⓦ www .dymocks.com.au. **Town Hall CityRail.** Sprawled across several floors, this central store has a particularly impressive Australian selection, and an upstairs café where you can slurp generous smoothies; Mon–Wed & Fri 8.30am–6.30pm, Thurs 8.30am–9pm, Sat 9am–6pm, Sun 10am–5pm.

Galaxy 143 York St ☎02 9267 7222, Ⓦ www.galaxybooks.com.au. **Town Hall CityRail.** Sydney's science fiction, fantasy and horror bookshop, run by Abbey's. Mon–Wed &

Fri 8.30am–7pm, Thurs 8.30am–9pm, Sat 8.30am–6pm, Sun 10am–5pm.

🏃 **Gleebooks 49 Glebe Point Rd, Glebe** Ⓦ www.gleebooks.com.au. **Bus #431–434 from Central CityRail.** Legendary independent Sydney literary bookshop specializing in academic and alternative books, philosophy and cultural studies, contemporary Australian and international literature, plus author appearances and book-signings upstairs. Gleebooks Secondhand and Children's Books is further up the hill, at 191 Glebe Point Rd. Daily 9am–9pm.

▲ Gleebooks

Gould's Book Arcade 32–38 King St, Newtown ☎02/9519 8947. **Newtown CityRail.** Chaotic piles of books greet you in this near-legendary secondhand bookstore run by Bob Gould. The incredible range of non-fiction includes a whole host of leftie political tomes; you'd never find anything specific here unless you were incredibly lucky, but it's great for browsing. Daily 7am–midnight.

Lesley McKay's Bookshop 118 Queen St at Moncur St, Woollahra ☎02/9327 1354, Ⓦ www.lesleymckay.com.au. **Bus #378 from Central CityRail or #380 from Circular Quay CityRail.** Excellent range and knowledgeable staff, and a big children's section; Mon–Wed, Fri & Sat 9am–6pm, Thurs 9am–8pm, Sun 9am–5pm.

Macleay Bookshop 103 Macleay St, Potts Point ☎02/9358 2908, ⓦwww.macleaybookshop.com.au. Kings Cross CityRail. When you're sick of all the bigger stores, this tiny, independent and very literary bookstore is a peaceful place for browsing, with a well-chosen selection. It also stocks books by local Kings Cross writers. Mon & Tues 10am–7pm, Wed–Sat 9.30am–9pm, Sun 10am–5pm.

Sappho Books and Café 51 Glebe Point Rd ⓦwww.sapphobooks.com.au. Bus #431–434 from Central CityRail. Good-condition secondhand books, next door to Gleebooks in an easily navigable two-storey building (see the genre locating floor plan on the wall near the front desk), plus a highly recommended courtyard café in which to enjoy them (see p.193). Daily 8am–7pm.

Clothes and accessories

For interesting **fashion** to suit a range of budgets, Oxford Street in Paddington is the place, along with the glitzy Sydney Central Plaza on Pitt Street Mall in the city. With more time to explore, take a stroll down Crown Street, near the junction with Oxford Street, where great stores are stuffed with Hawaiian shirts, frocks from the fifties and cool clubbing gear. Or check out the **secondhand stores** on Newtown's King Street – though you'll probably find prices are higher than for similar stuff in the UK or US. If you want to peek at expensive Australian **designer fashion**, head for David Jones department store (see p.248), or the shops of the designers themselves, mostly on Oxford Street in Paddington or the Strand Arcade in the city centre – see p.249.

High street fashion

Country Road 142–144 Pitt St at King St ⓦwww.countryroad.com.au. Town Hall CityRail. Classic but stylish (if a little preppy) Australian-designed clothes for men and women, plus a high-quality range of shoes and accessories. Several other stores include one on the ground level of the QVB (see p.248) and another at 255 Oxford St, Paddington, near Taylor Square. Store hours Mon–Wed, Fri & Sat 9am–6pm, Thurs 9am–9pm, Sun 11am–5pm.

Dangerfield Lower Ground Floor, Galeries Victoria ⓦwww.dangerfield.com.au. Town Hall CityRail. Edgy street fashion, "from punk to funk", for both sexes. Also at 268 King St, Newtown, and Market City, Hay St, Haymarket. Mon–Fri 9am–6pm, Sat 10am–5pm, Sun 11am–5pm.

Mambo 80 The Corso, Manly ⓦwww.mambo.com.au. Ferry to Manly. Influenced by comic-strip and graffiti art, Reg Mombassa's designs are now emblazoned on T-shirts, surf gear, beach towels, watches and wallets around the world, promoting his tongue-in-cheek philosophy of "salvation through shopping". Also at David Jones. Daily 9.30am–6pm.

Marcs Ground Floor, QVB, corner of George St and Druitt St ⓦwww.marcs.com.au. Town Hall CityRail. The place to buy great shirts for men and women. Also hip European and US lines such as Diesel. Several other locations including 270 Oxford St, Paddington, Bondi Junction and Myer and David Jones department stores.

▲ Mambo

Mooks Clothing Co Shop 2, The Galeries Victoria, 500 George St at Park St ⓦ www.mooks.com. Town Hall CityRail. Internationally known brand of trendy streetwear which originated in Melbourne; clothing and footwear. Mon–Fri 9am–6pm, Sat 10am–5pm, Sun 11am–5pm.

Sarah Jane 133 King St, Newtown ⓦ www.sarah -jane.com.au. Newtown CityRail. Gorgeous, highly feminine frocks, from silky slip dresses to ethereal, floaty chiffon numbers, embroidered velvet coats and appliquéd tops, all with a vintage feel. Prices are mid-range, somewhere between chain store and designer levels, with substantial reductions during summer and winter clearances. Also at 338 Darling St, Balmain.

Surf Dive N Ski 462 George St ⓣ 02/9267 3408, ⓦ www.sds.com.au. Town Hall CityRail. Chain of surfwear shops stocking all the major labels. As well as casual clothes, swimming and surfing gear and shoes, there are great accessories – sunglasses, jewellery and watches, hats, beach towels, and bags to stash it all in.

Zomp Shoez 255 Oxford St, Paddington ⓣ 02/9360 1546. Bus #378 from Central CityRail or #380 from Circular Quay CityRail. A shoe fetishist's heaven, with styles (and prices) that run the gamut from sensible to extravagant; women's shoes only. Mon–Wed, Fri & Sat 10am–6pm, Thurs 10am–8pm, Sun noon–5pm.

Designer fashion

During **Australian Fashion Week** (ⓦ www.rafw.com.au), held annually in late April, around sixty designers from Australia and the Asia-Pacific region show their collections. Since Fashion Week's inception in the mid-1990s, there's been a stronger focus both at home and abroad on Australian designers, many of whom, such as **Collette Dinnigan**, have made a name for themselves internationally. We have listed designers with their own outlets below, all on (or just off) Oxford Street in Paddington and Woollahra and in the Strand Arcade. Some designers don't have their own shops, but **David Jones** department store stocks a big range of home-grown designers. The top-end boutiques are mostly opposite

Victoria Barracks around the junction of Oxford Street and Glenmore Road; for high-street fashion head further west to the strip opposite Paddington Markets (see p.98). Visit on Saturday and you can combine shopping with a market visit, though expect big crowds. All the stores below are open daily. To get to Oxford Street (Queen St is just off it), Paddington and Woollahra, take bus #378 from Central CityRail or #380 from Circular Quay or Bondi Junction CityRail; the nearest train station to the Strand Arcade in the city is Town Hall CityRail.

Akira Isogawa 12A Queen St, Woollahra ⓦ www.akira.com.au. Japanese-born designer Akira Isogawa has lived in Sydney since the mid-1980s. His ethereal, Japanese-influenced designs, which also include clothes for men, have found favour overseas, with stockists including Barney's in New York and Browns in London. Mon–Wed, Fri & Sat 10.30am–6pm, Thurs 10.30am–7pm, Sun 11am–4pm.

Alannah Hill 118–120 Oxford St at Glenmore St, Paddington ⓣ 02/9380 9147; Level 1, The Strand Arcade. Over-the-top, vintage-look, feminine clothing in rich fabrics; boudoir-like stores. Mon–Sat 10am–6pm.

Bettina Liano Shop 74–78, Level 1, The Strand Arcade ⓦ www.bettinaliano.com. Well-cut designer jeans for women. Mon–Wed, Fri & Sat 9.30am–5.30pm, Thurs 9.30am–8pm, Sun noon–4pm.

Wayne Cooper 16 Oxford St, Paddington ⓦ www .waynecooper.com.au. Hip but practical clothes for women in the latest high-tech fabrics; even the store feels futuristic. Mon–Wed, Fri & Sat 10am–6pm, Thurs 10am–8pm, Sun 11am–5pm. There's also a Wayne Cooper store at Level 1, The Strand Arcade.

Colette Dinnigan 33 William St at Underwood St, Paddington ⓦ www .collettedinnigan.com. Australia's most internationally recognized designer has her own shop in London and her designs stocked in Harrods in the UK and Barneys in the US. In Sydney, she's also in David Jones. Dinnigan is known for her very feminine, finely made clothes for women – lots of beading and embroidery.

Grandma Takes a Trip 263 Crown St, Darlinghurst ⓣ 02/9356 3322, ⓦ www .grandmatakesatrip.com.au. Vintage and retro clothes reinvented, including some fabulous

1950s and 1960s dresses. Mon–Wed, Fri & Sat 10am–6pm, Thurs 10am–8pm, Sun noon–5pm. Also stores at 79 Gould St, Bondi. Daily 10am–6pm (Thurs to 7pm).

Lisa Ho Shop 2A–6A Queen St, Woollahra; Level 1, The Strand Arcade ⓦ www.lisaho.com. Girly frocks; lots of evening wear. Mon–Wed, Fri & Sat 10am–6pm, Thurs 10am–8pm, Sun 11am–5pm.

Morrissey 372 Oxford St, Paddington ☎ 02/9380 7422. Peter Morrissey designs sexy clothes with an edge, for men and women; also accessories. Mon–Wed, Fri & Sat 9.30am–6pm, Thurs 9.30am–7pm, Sun 11am–5pm. Other locations include Sydney Central Plaza and Direct Factory Outlets, Homebush (see "Factory outlets" box below).

Pretty Dog 1 Brown St, Newtown, just off King St ☎ 02/9519 7839, ⓦ www.prettydo.com.au. **Newtown CityRail.** Boutique clothing store with a well-picked selection of great Aussie designers.

Saba Sydney Central Plaza, 450 George St at Market St ⓦ www.saba.com.au. **Town Hall CityRail.** Understated, urbane range of clothing for men and women by veteran designer Joe Saba. Other locations include 80 Queen St, Woollahra and the QVB. Mon–Wed & Fri 9.30am–6pm, Thurs 9.30am–7pm, Sat 9.30am–5pm, Sun 11am–4pm.

sass & bide 132 Oxford St, Paddington ⓦ www.sassandbide.com. The hot Australian designer duo, Heidi Middleton and Sarah-Jane Clarke, who burst onto the world fashion scene in early 2000 with their low-slung jeans, now have their own Oxford Street flagship store featuring entire collection of funky, glam clothes for skinny young things. Mon–Wed, Fri & Sat 10am–6pm, Thurs 10am–8pm, Sun noon–5pm. Also at Ivy, Shop 6, 320–348 George St.

Scanlan & Theodore 122 Oxford St at Glenmore Rd, Paddington ⓦ www.scanlanandtheodore .com.au. Original, stylish clothes for women; great cuts and fabrics. Mon–Wed, Fri & Sat 10am–6pm, Thurs 10am–8pm, Sun noon–5pm.

Wheels & Doll Baby 259 Crown St, Darlinghurst ⓦ www.wheelsanddollbaby .com. This quirky store with its own label has

---

Factory outlets

If you like **designer labels** and fashion but not the price tags, check out Sydney's **factory outlets**. The best, the vast **Direct Factory Outlets** (DFO), is out in the 'burbs on the corner of Homebush Bay Drive and Underwood Rd, Homebush (daily 10am–6pm; ⓦ www.dfo.com.au; Strathfield CityRail then bus #525 to Underwood St). Around 120 clearance outlets here sell men's, women's and children's wear and underwear, jewellery, shoes, handbags and luggage, with big fashion brands including Esprit, Jigsaw, Laura Ashley, Polo Ralph Lauren, Portmans, Colorado and Rivers; surfwear outlets Billabong Mambo and Ripcurl; Pumpkin Patch for kids; and Australian designer fashion at Country Road, Marcs, Charlie Brown, Morrissey and Lisa Ho (see above); there are also two food courts. A more pleasant spot for samples and seconds hunting, the competing **Birkenhead Point Outlet Centre** at Roseby Street, Drummoyne (ⓦ www.birkenheadsc.com.au), can be reached on a very pleasant ferry trip from Circular Quay to Birkenhead Ferry Wharf (ⓦ www.131500.info /realtim/timetableentry.asp; alternatively any #500–508, #510, #515, #518, #520 bus departing from George Street in the city and alighting at Victoria St). Fashion and accessory outlets include Oroton, French Connection, Country Road, Esprit, Marcs, Mambo, Sunglass Hut and David Jones bargain warehouse; there's Shoes'n'Sox Wharehouse for kid's shoes; outdoor/climbing/bushwalking gear at Kathmandu and Mountain Designs; sportwear at Insport; Australian designer outlets are Alannah Hill and Ojay; and you can enjoy water views from the alfresco cafés.

If you don't want to stray from the city, try **Market City shopping centre** in Chinatown (see p.248) which has dropped most of its designer seconds shops, but has good mainstream fashion factory outlets including mixed fashions at Dangerfield and Esprit, and women's fashion chains Bracewell, Seduce, Sisco and Supre. For more detail on the best places to head for discounts, shopaholics should get hold of the excellent *Bargain Shoppers Guide to Sydney*, sold at newsagents.

been here – just off Oxford Street – since 1987 but the fru-fru French bordello fashion by Australian designer Melanie Greensmith (with her own rock star husband of Divinyl fame) has taken off in the UK and Europe. Mon–Wed, Fri & Sat 10am–6pm, Thurs 10am–8pm, Sun noon–5pm.

Zimmermann 387 Oxford St, Paddington ⓦwww.zimmermannwear.com. Simone Zimmermann is known for her trendy women's swimwear. Also corner of 2 Glenmore Rd, Paddington and Level 1, The Strand Arcade. Mon–Wed, Fri & Sat 10am–6pm, Thurs 10am–8pm, Sun noon–5pm.

Secondhand

The best picking grounds for **second-hand clothes** are the Newtown area (from Broadway to St Peters), and a short section of Crown Street in northern Surry Hills between Goulburn Street and Campbell Street.

The Look 230 King St, Newtown ⓣ02/9550 2455. Newtown CityRail. A stylish variant on the charity shop, run by the Wesley Mission and worth a look for bargain buys. Mon–Thurs 10am–6pm, Fri–Sat 10am–10pm.

Blue Spinach 348 Liverpool St, Darlinghurst ⓣ02/9331 3904, ⓦwww.bluespinach.com.au. Kings Cross Cityrail. Secondhand, designer men's and women's clothing, shoes and accessories, mostly in tip-top condition. Expect Gucci, Paul Smith, Costume National and the like. Mon–Sat 10am–6pm.

Broadway Betty 259 Broadway, Glebe, ⓣ02/9571 9422. All westbound buses from Railway Square, Central/CityRail. Well-picked garb, in a selection of styles covering the best of the twentieth century, from the outlandish to the sublime. Also some great vintage footwear.

🏃 **The Vintage Clothing Shop** St James Arcade, 80 Castlereagh St, City ⓣ02/9238 0090, ⓦwww.thevintageclothingshop .com. St James CityRail. Sydney's (and probably Australia's) premier vintage clothing store, established in 1976. It has a fabulous range from the 1890s to the 1970s, including an incredible collection of beaded and sequinned tops and dresses from the 1960s, and couture to the 1990s. Mon–Wed & Fri 10am–5.30pm, Thurs 10am–7pm, Sat 10am–4pm. Sun closed.

Zoo Emporium 180b Campbell St, Surry Hills ⓣ02/9380 5990. Bus #378 from Central CityRail or #380 from Circular Quay CityRail. The very best in 1970s disco gear, from a world where day-glo never died. Mon–Wed, Fri & Sat 10.30am–6pm, Thurs 10.30am–8pm, Sun noon–5pm.

Outdoor and workwear

R.M. Williams 71 George St, The Rocks ⓦwww.rmwilliams.com.au. Circular Quay CityRail. This quality bush outfitters is great for moleskin pants and shirts, Drizabone coats and superb leather riding and dress boots. Also 389 George St at King St, and the airport.

Strand Hatters The Strand Arcade, 412 George St at King St ⓣ02/9231 6884, ⓦwww .strandhatters.com.au. Town Hall CityRail. For the widest range of Akubra hats and other Australian classics, this old-fashioned store is the place. Mon–Wed & Fri 8.30am–6pm, Thurs 8.30am–8pm, Sat 9.30am–4.30pm, Sun 11am–4pm.

Accessories and jewellery

In addition to the following shops, it's worth checking out the markets (see p.253) and museum shops (especially the MCA, see p.61, the Powerhouse Museum, see p.90, and the Art Gallery of New South Wales, see p.69) for unusual treasures and trinkets, as well as the smaller, private galleries (see p.251).

Dinosaur Designs Level 1, Strand Arcade, 412 George St (through to Pitt St) ⓦwww .dinosaurdesigns.com.au. Town Hall CityRail. Dinosaur's trademark chunky resin and silver jewellery, and beautifully tactile tableware in muted shades of amber and earth, are terribly hard to resist. Mon–Wed & Fri 9.30am–5.30pm, Thurs 9.30am–8pm, Sat 10am–4pm, Sun noon–4pm. Also at 339 Oxford St at William St, Paddington. Mon–Sat 10am–4pm, Sun noon–4pm.

Love and Hatred Level 1, The Strand Arcade, 412 George St (through to Pitt St) ⓣ02/9233 3441. Town Hall CityRail. Funky Australian jewellery incorporating Gothic and medieval imagery. They will also make commissioned pieces. Mon–Wed & Fri 9.30am–5.30pm, Thurs 9.30am–8pm, Sat 10am–4pm, Sun noon–4pm.

a has followed the American trend in shopping and you're bound to
urself in mall-land at some stage. Although lacking in neighbourhood
er, big city and suburban malls and department stores are handy for
familiarizing yourself with prices and variety, especially if time is short. Mall
air-conditioning, too, can be a big plus on hot, sticky days.

Department stores

David Jones **86–108 Castlereagh St** ⓦ www
.davidjones.com.au. **St James or Town Hall
CityRail.** Straddling Market St, David Jones'
flagship store offers an utterly civilized
shopping experience. Women's clothing
(including lots of Australian and International
designer labels) is mostly in the Elizabeth
St store where the ground floor is graced
with seasonal floral displays and a coiffured
pianist playing tasteful tunes. A tunnel
links the basement to the Market St store
where there's a fantastic gourmet food hall,
and men's clothing and homeware on the
floors above. A less salubrious version is
located at 500 Oxford St, Bondi Junction
(Bondi Junction CityRail), and there's a
warehouse outlet at Birkenhead Point (see
box, p.246). Mon–Wed 9.30am–6pm, Thurs
9.30am–9pm, Fri & Sat 9.30am–7pm, Sun
10am–6pm.

Myer **436 George St** ⓦ www.myer.com.au.
Town Hall CityRail. The more workaday of
Sydney's two main department stores,
the Myer store, at the heart of the Sydney
Central Plaza mall, nevertheless has several
gleaming floors of fashion and elegant
minimalist homeware. Mon–Wed 9am–6pm,
Thurs 9am–9pm, Fri & Sat 9am–7pm, Sun
10am–6pm.

Shopping malls

Broadway Shopping Centre **Corner of Broadway
and Bay sts, Broadway** ⓦ www.broadway
-centre.com.au. **Bus #431–434, #438 or #440
from Central CityRail.** On Broadway, between
Central Station and Glebe, this mall benefits
from its proximity to Sydney University
and the arty enclave of Glebe, with a less
run-of-the-mill mix of street fashion and
chain stores. A Hoyts multiplex cinema
shows art-house and mainstream movies
(see p.224); for books there's Dymocks,
plus there's a big Rebel Sport store, a vast
K-Mart, a great Harris Farm Markets for fresh
fruit and vegetables, and an extensive Asian

section in the Coles supermarket. The three-
hour free parking is handy, as Glebe Point
Road's street parking is all metered.

The Galeries Victoria **500 George St, corner of
Park St** ⓦ www.tgv.com.au. **Town Hall CityRail.**
Diagonally opposite the Town Hall, this
upmarket shopping mall is given a great
sense of space by its central glass-roofed
piazza and a series of arcades throughout.
The fashion stores are virtually all mixed
clothing or menswear – including funky
Mooks Clothing Co and Dangerfield. Its
main attraction, however, is the city's biggest
book superstore, Kinokuniya (see "Books"
section). There are lots of cafés, patisseries, sandwich bars, a sushi shop and an
ice-cream parlour on the lower ground floor.
You can enter the heritage *Arthouse Hotel*
(see p.205) from one end of the ground floor,
where there are also cheap eats by day.

Market City **9–13 Hay St, Haymarket**
ⓦ www.marketcity.com.au. **Central CityRail.**
Cavernous mall above Paddy's Market,
with a distinctly Eastern feel, thanks to
Asian supermarkets, two food courts strong
on Asian cuisines, plus factory outlets for
big-name stores like Esprit, and smaller
boutiques selling cute street and club wear
imported from Asia (think smaller sizes).
There's also the multiplex Reading Cinema
(see p.225) and a bar.

QVB (Queen Victoria Building) **455 George St,
City** ⓦ www.qvb.com.au. **Town Hall CityRail.** This
splendid Victorian arcade is a sight in its
own right, attracting more visitors than either
the Harbour Bridge or the Opera House.
The interior is magnificent, with beautiful
woodwork, elevated walkways and antique
lifts. Brave the weekend hordes for a wistful
look at the designer shopfronts upstairs
and a wander around the ubiquitous Esprit,
Jigsaw or the Country Road at ground
level. Or just come for a coffee fix at *QVB
Jet* (see p.182), at street level. From Town
Hall Station you can walk right through the
basement level (mainly bustling food stalls)
and continue via the Sydney Central Plaza to
Myer, emerging on the Pitt St Mall.

In recent years, Aussie skincare companies have wowed the world with their minimalist approach to packaging, lavish use of essential oils and vibrant lippy colours – not to mention some savvy marketing. All the following are available at David Jones and/or Myer, or their own stores detailed below.

Aesop ⓦ www.aesop.net.au. Divine skin balms and haircare products packed in pharmaceutical-grade brown glass, which rely on essential oils for their beneficial properties and fragrance, and eschew the usual exaggerated claims and hype. Store at 72A Oxford St, Paddington ☎02/9358 3382.

Bliss ⓦ www.blissaromatherapy.com. Aromatherapy range of pure essential oils, massage oils and incense.

Bloom ⓦ www.bloomcosmetics.com. Whimsically packaged cosmetics, candles and body range, including hugely popular fruity lip balms and lipsticks, from young entrepreneur Natalie Bloom. Available David Jones, Myer and elsewhere.

Jurlique ⓦ www.jurlique.com.au. Pure, hypoallergenic skin and haircare based on essential oils produced from herbs grown biodynamically in South Australia. Not tested on animals. Jurlique has its own stores, including the flagship Jurlique Day Spa, Shop 33, Ground Floor, 193 Pitt St Mall ☎02/9231 0626.

Napoleon Perdis ⓦ www.napoleoncosmetics.com. Individually colour-matched cosmetics to suit all types and shades of skin, as you might expect from a company that also runs a school for make-up artists. Napoleon has a chain of its own stores, including one on Level 2 of the Skygarden shopping centre (see below) and on the fashionista strip, Oxford St, at no. 74.

Skygarden 77 Castlereagh St and off Pitt St Mall ⓦ www.skygarden.com.au. Town Hall CityRail. Stylish shopping centre with lots of fashion for men and women, and the Borders book superstore. Level 2 is virtually devoted to homeware, plus Napoleon Perdis (see box above). Places to eat include the stylish Sky Phoenix Chinese restaurant, serving a big range of *yum cha*.

The Strand Arcade 412 George St (through to Pitt St) ⓦ www.strandarcade.com.au. Town Hall CityRail. Built in 1892, this elegant arcade with its wrought-iron balustrades houses tiny fashion boutiques including outlets of several of Australia's top designers on level 1, jewellers including Dinosaur Designs and Love and Hatred, an outlet of Jurlique (see box above), plus gourmet coffee shops and tearooms.

Sydney Central Plaza 450 George St, City ⓦ westfield.com.au/sydneycentralplaza. Town Hall CityRail. Sprawling from George St through to Pitt St Mall, this maze of shops and fast-food outlets takes in Myer and a whole host of mostly clothing and fashion stores, not to mention a stage where variable, but free, entertainers perform for the munching masses.

Westfield Centrepoint Corner of Pitt St Mall and Market St, City ⓦ westfield.com.au /centrepoint. Town Hall CityRail. At the base of the landmark Sydney Tower, Westfield Centrepoint holds more than 130 speciality stores, 60 of them focusing on fashion and accessories, though nothing terribly exciting. There's an excellent basement food court, and the Australian Geographic Shop (p.255) is good for quality souvenirs.

Camping and outdoors equipment

Kent Street in the city behind the Town Hall is nicknamed "adventure alley" for its plethora of outdoor equipment stores, mostly between Druitt St and Bathurst St. Here you'll find almost a dozen outdoor gear and clothing shops including Kathmandu, Macpac, Snowgum, Paddy Palin, Mountain Equipment, and Mountain Designs.

Cheaper options include suburban K–Mart stores (closest stores to the city are at Spring St, Bondi Junction and at the Broadway shopping centre, Bay St) or hostel notice boards. For **gear rental** try Alpsport.

Alpsport 1045 Victoria Rd, West Ryde, 13km northwest of central Sydney ☎ 02/9858 5844, Ⓦ www.alpsport.com.au. West Ryde CityRail. One of the few outdoor sports and ski shops that rents gear: 2-person tent ($50–80 a weekend, $80–170 a week); backpack ($50/80); sleeping bag ($40/60). Mon–Wed & Fri 9am–5.30pm, Thurs 9am–8pm, Sat 9am–4pm, Sun 10am–4pm.

Larry Adler 497 Kent St at Druitt St ☎ 1800 235 377, Ⓦ www.larryadler.com. Town Hall CityRail. Australia's largest ski store (including rentals) with winter stock all year plus hiking gear and clothing. Mon–Wed & Fri 9am–6pm, Thurs 9am–9pm, Sat 9am–5.30pm, Sun 9am–5.30pm.

Kathmandu Corner of Kent St & Bathurst St ☎ 02/9261 8901, Ⓦ www.kathmandu.com.au. Town Hall CityRail. Moderately priced, fair

quality outdoor clothing and footwear from this Australasian chain. Especially good value during their frequent sales. Mon–Wed & Fri 9am–5.30pm, Thurs 9am–8.30pm, Sat 9am–5pm, Sun 10am–4pm.

Mountain Equipment 491 Kent St at Druitt St ☎ 02/9264 5888, Ⓦ www.mountainequipment .com. Town Hall CityRail. Top brands but still at reasonable prices. Mon–Wed & Fri 9am–5.30pm, Thurs 9am–9pm, Sat 9am–5pm, Sun 10am–4pm.

Paddy Pallin 507 Kent St ☎ 02/9264 2685, Ⓦ www.paddypallin.com.au. Town Hall CityRail. The best known outdoor gear shop in the city, with high-quality clothing, camping and climbing gear. Mon–Wed & Fri 9am–5.30pm, Thurs 9am–9pm, Sat 9am–5pm, Sun 10am–5pm.

Food and drink

The handiest **supermarkets** for the city centre are Woolworths, opposite the Town Hall (Mon–Fri 6am–midnight, Sat & Sun 8am–midnight), and the three small Coles supermarkets in the Wynyard Station complex (Mon–Fri 6am–midnight, Sat & Sun 8am–midnight), and at 388 and 650 George St (both daily 6am–midnight). The larger Coles in Kings Cross, at 88 Darlinghurst Rd, is also handy for travellers (same hours), as is the one in the Broadway Centre near Glebe (see p.248). The Asian supermarkets on Sussex and Burlington streets in Chinatown and in the Market City complex offer more exotic alternatives, while for deli items and impromptu picnic supplies head for the splendid food hall at David Jones (see p.248), or one of the gourmet stores listed below. In the suburbs, the big supermarkets such as Coles now stay open until midnight, and there are plenty of (overpriced) 24-hour convenience stores in the inner city and suburbs, often attached to petrol stations.

There are also several **food markets**: Paddy's Market in Chinatown has been selling fruit and vegetables since the nineteenth century, and there's a bigger version at far-flung Flemington beside the city's wholesale markets (Fri 10am–4.30pm, Sat 6am–2pm & Sun 9am–4.30pm; Flemington CityRail). Rural growers and producers of gourmet goods also distribute direct to Sydney's regular **produce markets**: at Pyrmont Bay Park in front of the Star City Casino on the first Saturday of the month (7–11am); in The Rocks on Argyle Street every Friday (10am–3pm) and Saturday (9am–3pm); at the Showring at the Entertainment Quarter every Wednesday, Saturday and Sunday (10am–3.30pm); and at the Northside Produce Market at the Civic Centre, Miller Street, North Sydney, between Ridge and McClaren streets, on the third Saturday of the month (8am–noon). A hugely popular, quite festive **organic market** takes place every Saturday morning (9am–2pm) within the grounds of the Orange Grove Public School, at the corner of Perry Street and Balmain Road, in Leichhardt.

SHOPPING AND GALLERIES | Food and drink

(18)

Australian Wine Centre Shop 3, Goldfields House, 1 Alfred St, corner of George St, Circular Quay ☎02/9247 2755, ⓦwww.australianwinecentre .com. Circular Quay CityRail/ferry. Basement store stocking more than a thousand wines from more than 300 wineries around Australia. Regular tastings, or you can just buy a test-drive glass of wine at its in-house wine bar during the week. They also ship overseas. Mon–Wed & Sat 9.30am–7pm, Thurs & Fri 9.30am–8pm, Sun 10am–6pm.

Camperdown Cellars 233 Victoria St, Darlinghurst ☎02/9380 6133. Kings Cross CityRail. Handy for BYO supplies around Kings Cross and Darlinghurst, this place has an exceptional selection and well-informed, friendly staff. Mon–Thurs & Sun 11am–10pm, Fri & Sat 11am–midnight.

GNC LiveWell 53–55 Glebe Point Rd, Glebe ⓦwww.gnclivewell.com.au. Bus #431–433 from Central CityRail. International chain offering a vast range of wholefoods, organic fruit and vegetables, speciality foods and supplements.

Infinity Sourdough 225 Victoria St at William St, Darlinghurst ☎02/9360 1011. Kings Cross CityRail. A great place for breakfasts on the hoof, and for the sheer pleasure of wonderful bread baked on the premises – from sourdough and wholemeal to the more exotic spelt or soy and linseed loaves. Also tasty cakes and coffee to go. Daily 5.30am–8pm.

jones the grocer 68 Moncur St, Woollahra ⓦwww.jonesthegrocer.com. Bus #389 from Circular Quay CityRail. Stylishly packaged, outlandishly priced and utterly delicious groceries and gourmet treats to eat in or take away; includes a cheese room. Also at Shop 45, The Grove, 166 Military Rd, Neutral Bay. Mon–Sat 7.30am–5.30pm, Sun 9am–5pm.

Simon Johnson 181 Harris St at Miller St, Pyrmont ☎02/9552 2522, ⓦwww .simonjohnson.com.au. Pyrmont Light Rail. When only the best will do, try Simon Johnson's superb cheeses (kept in a dedicated conditioning room), teas and coffees, top-of-the-range pastas, oils and vinegars, as supplied to discriminating restaurateurs. Also at 55 Queen St, Woollahra and Quadrangle Shopping Village, 100 Edinburgh Rd, Castlecrag. Mon–Fri 10am–6.30pm, Sat 9am–5pm, Sun 10am–4pm.

Sydney Fish Markets Pyrmont Bay, Pyrmont ⓦwww.sydneyfishmarket.com.au. Fish Market Light Rail. Sydney's seafood comes straight off the fishing boats here, from where it's sold to retailers at the fish market auction and then goes on to the several fishmonger outlets. There's also excellent fruit and veg, flowers, a reliable deli, a bottle shop, plus takeaway (and eat-in) sushi and fish'n'chips' for the picnic tables by the water's edge (if you don't mind the seagull invasion). See also p.184. Daily 7am–4pm.

Galleries

Sydney's diverse arts scene is reflected in a myriad of **small art galleries**, which are concentrated in Paddington and Surry Hills, with a new gallery precinct developing on the southwestern fringes of Surry Hills at Banks Street, Waterloo (bus #343 from central CityRail). The useful *Artfind Guide* (ⓦwww.artfind.com.au) to selected Sydney art galleries and antique dealers includes maps, and the website links to the galleries selected. Alternatively, you can buy a copy of *Art & Australia* magazine (ⓦwww.artaustralia.com), Australia's authoritative quarterly national art journal, which has major exhibition reviews and listings. The Citysearch Sydney website, ⓦwww.sydney .citysearch.com.au, has comprehensive listings of art galleries and current exhibitions, while Friday's "Metro" section of the *Sydney Morning Herald* (ⓦwww.smh.com.au) offers reviews of recently opened shows. For shops attached to Sydney's major galleries and museums, see the individual reviews in the main Guide section.

If you're interested in buying **Aboriginal art and crafts**, try some of the galleries that direct profits back to Aboriginal communities, rather than settling for the standard tourist tat.

For background on Aboriginal art styles and communities, visit the Art Gallery of New South Wales (see p.69) or check out the excellent Aboriginal Art Online website, ⓦwww .aboriginalartonline.com.

Boomalli Aboriginal Artists Co-operative 55–59 Flood St, Leichhardt ⓦwww.boomalli.org.au. Bus #438 or #440 from Central CityRail. Boomalli, initiated by ten indigenous artists in the late 1980s, is still wholly Aboriginal-operated and now has a membership of seventy. Unlike many other Aboriginal galleries, it prioritizes the work of New South Wales urban and rural Aboriginal artists: expect controversial, cutting-edge contemporary art including photography and mixed media. Tues–Sat 10am–4pm.

Gavala Aboriginal Art Centre Level 1, Harbourside Shopping Centre, Darling Harbour ☎02/9212 7232, ⓦwww.gavala .com.au. Town Hall CityRail. Highly credible Aboriginal-owned and -run arts and crafts store – all profits go to the artists and their communities, and the centre aims to raise awareness of indigenous cultures through education programmes. Also music, books, clothes, jewellery and souvenirs. Daily 10am–9pm.

Gallery Gondwana 7 Danks St, Waterloo, ☎02/8399 2492, ⓦwww.gallerygondwana.com .au. Buses #301–304 from Circular Quay. Supporting the contemporary indigenous art of Australia and the Pacific with both established and emerging artists, Gallery Gondwana is a superb introduction to the increasingly exciting experimentation and development of contemporary art from traditional indigenous art forms. Wed–Sat 10am–5.30pm.

Hogarth Galleries Aboriginal Art Centre 7 Walker Lane (off Brown St), Paddington ☎02/9360 6839, ⓦwww.aboriginalartcentres .com. Bus #378 from Central CityRail or #380 from Circular Quay CityRail. This long-established gallery has a sound reputation for its support of contemporary Aboriginal artists, and its broader commitment to reconciliation. Extensive collection of work by contemporary Aboriginal artists, both tribal and urban, and special exhibitions. Tues–Sat 10am–5pm.

2 Danks Street Galleries 2 Danks St Waterloo. ⓦwww.2danksstreet.com.au. Buses #301–304 from Circular Quay. For lovers of contemporary art, 2 Danks St Galleries is an essential port of call. The nine galleries (separately owned but collectively run) are bright and expansive, showcasing everything from contemporary Aboriginal and Pacific island art to exquisite jewellery and object design to 3-D painting. Tues–Sat 11am–6pm.

Art House Gallery 66 McLachlan Ave, Rushcutters Bay ☎02/9332 1019. Kings Cross CityRail. This cavernous gallery showcases Australian artists and always has interesting exhibits, as well as pieces for sale. Tues–Fri 10am–6pm, Sat 10am–5pm.

Australian Galleries: Roylston Street 15 Roylston St, Paddington ☎02/9360 5177, ⓦwww.australiangalleries.com.au. Edgecliff CityRail. Serene gallery exhibiting and selling contemporary Australian art, including works by Gary Shead, Jeffrey Smart and John Coburn. Mon–Sat 10am–6pm.

Ray Hughes Gallery 270 Devonshire St, Surry Hills ☎02/9698 3200, ⓦwww.rayhughesgallery .com. Central CityRail. Influential dealer with a staple of high-profile contemporary Australian and New Zealand artists. Tues–Sat 10am–6pm.

Sherman Contemporary Art Foundation 16–20 Goodhope St, Paddington ☎02/9331 1112, ⓦwww.sherman-scaf.org.au. Bus #389 from Circular Quay or Bondi Junction CityRail. Influential Australian and international painters and artists feature at this cutting-edge gallery, whose huge interior is echoed in the 350-square-metre outdoor sculpture garden. Tues–Fri 10am–6pm, Sat 11am–6pm.

Artspace 43–51 Cowper Wharf Rd, Woolloomooloo ☎02/9356 0555, ⓦwww.artspace.org.au. Kings Cross CityRail. In a wonderful location, showing provocative young artists with a focus on performance, installations and new media. Daily except Mon 11am–5pm.

CarriageWorks 245 Wilson St at Corrington St, Eveleigh ☎02/8571 9099, ⓦwww.carriageworks .com.au. Redfern CityRail. Opened during 2007 in the former Eveleigh railway carriage and blacksmith workshops, this massive, industrial venue has quickly become a lynchpin in the Sydney performance scene. Playing host to a cross-disciplinary arts complex it is home to the Performance Space contemporary arts company, the Anna Schwartz Gallery (Tues–Fri 11am–7pm, Sat 1–7pm), and several other dynamic arts companies.

Ivan Dougherty Gallery Corner of Albion Ave and Selwyn St, Paddington ⓦ www.cofa.unsw.edu.au. Bus #378 from Central CityRail or #380 from Circular Quay CityRail. The exhibition space for the College of Fine Arts (COFA), University of New South Wales. The ten shows per year focus on international contemporary art with accompanying forums, lectures and performances. Mon–Sat 10am–5pm.

Roslyn Oxley9 Gallery 8 Soudan Lane, off Hampden St, Paddington ⓣ 02/9331 1919, ⓦ www.roslynoxley9.com.au. Edgecliff CityRail. Avant-garde videos and installations among the Australian and international offerings. Recently controversial for showing Bill Henson's pubescent nudes. Tues–Fri 10am–6pm, Sat 11am–6pm.

Photography, drawing and prints

Australian Centre for Photography 257 Oxford St, Paddington ⓣ 02/9332 1455, ⓦ www.acp .au.com. Bus #378 from Central CityRail or #380 from Circular Quay CityRail. This non-profit organization is part-funded by various government agencies. Exhibitions of photo-based art from established and new international and Australian artists in four galleries. It attracts many developing (and visiting) photographers, with basic and specialist courses and a digital studio available for use (daily noon–6pm). There's also free wi-fi in the courtyard. Tues–Fri noon–7pm, Sat & Sun 10am–6pm.

Australian Galleries: Glenmore Road 24 Glenmore Rd at Oxford St, Paddington ⓣ 02/9380 8744. Bus #378 from Central CityRail or #380 from Circular Quay CityRail. Works for sale here include drawings by William Robinson, Brett Whiteley and Arthur Boyd, as well as prints and sketches by young Australian artists. Mon–Sat 10am–6pm, Sun noon–5pm.

Hordern House 77 Victoria St, Potts Point ⓣ 02/9356 4411, ⓦ www.hordern.com. Kings Cross CityRail. Eminent antique dealer, trading in colonial art including antiquarian prints and maps, rare books and manuscripts. Tues–Fri 9am–5pm.

Josef Lebovic 34 Paddington St, Paddington ⓣ 02/9332 1840, ⓦ www.joseflebovicgallery.com .au. Bus #378 from Central CityRail, #380 from Circular Quay CityRail. Renowned print and graphic gallery specializing in Australian and international prints and posters from the nineteenth, twentieth and twenty-first centuries, as well as vintage photography. Wed–Fri 1–6pm, Sat 11am–5pm.

Stills Gallery 36 Gosbell St, Paddington ⓦ www .stillsgallery.com.au. Kings Cross CityRail. Among Sydney's highest-profile photography galleries, exhibiting contemporary Australian and international work. Tues–Sat 11am–6pm.

Markets

Weekend **markets** have become a feature of the leisurely lives of Sydney-siders, so be prepared for crowds. The best for general browsing are the trendy Paddington Markets, the more arty Balmain Markets and the relaxed market on Glebe Point Road. There are also several produce markets, detailed on p.250, including Sydney's oldest, Paddy's Market, where you can also buy cheap and cheerful clothes and souvenirs. We've picked the best of the events, but our list is far from exhaustive. If you're an addict, or just fancy smaller, more specialized markets, visit ⓦ www.you.com.au/market-sydney .html for guidance.

Balmain Markets St Andrews Church, corner of Darling St and Curtis Rd, Balmain. Bus #433 from Central CityRail or #442 from the QVB. Assorted books, handmade jewellery, clothing and ceramics, antiques, home-made chocolates, cakes and gourmet foods and organic produce. The highlight is an eclectic array of food stalls in the church hall where you can snack your way from the Himalayas to South India. Sat 8.30am–4pm.

Bondi Markets Bondi Primary School, corner of Campbell Parade and Warners Avenue. Bus #380 or #389 from Bondi Junction CityRail. In the grounds of a lucky beach-facing primary school, these relaxed Sunday markets place great emphasis on hip fashion – both

new and secondhand – and jewellery.
Sun 10am–5pm.

**Glebe Markets Glebe Primary School, 38 Glebe
Point Rd. Bus #431–434 from Central CityRail.**
The market is shady, relaxed and quietly
sociable, like Glebe itself. A mixture of funky
new and secondhand clothes and accessories, including beach dresses, handbags,
jewellery – plus plants, records and CDs,
and the inevitable New Age knick-knacks
and secondhand books. A jazz band usually
plays to a grassy stretch of earth where
friends gather to relax and soak up the
atmosphere. Chinese masseurs ply their
trade, but the small range of food stalls
is disappointing; there is, however, a strip
of great cafés opposite, including *Badde
Manors*, *Iku*, *Well Connected* and *Sappho*
(see p.193). Sat 10am–4pm.

**Kirribilli Markets Bradfield Park, corner of
Alfred and Burton sts, Kirribilli. Milsons Point
CityRail or ferry from Circular Quay to Milsons
Point wharf.** Fantastically sited market just
across the North Shore and practically
under the Harbour Bridge. Nearly 200 stalls
– lots of food stalls, secondhand clothes
and bric-a-brac plus plants, jewellery and
arts and crafts. There are typically lots
of small stalls, many where locals sell off
unwanted gear – however, given the North
Shore's wealth, the pickings are good.
The atmosphere is festive, with live music
throughout the day. Fourth Sat every month
7am–3pm.

**Paddington Markets 395 Oxford St, Paddington
Ⓦ www.paddingtonmarkets.com.au. Bus #378
from Central CityRail or #380 from Circular**
Quay or Bondi Junction CityRail. As well as
being a great location for people-watching
in the shady church grounds, these
markets offer contemporary Australian
crafts – particularly leather goods and
jewellery – plus original fashion, both old
and new. Even if you're just here to browse,
the atmosphere, music and buskers come
free, and it's all conveniently located in
the middle of an excellent shopping and
grazing strip. Sat 10am–4pm.

**The Rocks Market George St, The Rocks.
Circular Quay CityRail/ferry.** Completely taking
over The Rocks end of George St and
feeding into Playfair St, this collection of
more than a hundred stalls offers jewellery,
antiques and art and crafts, mostly with an
Australiana/souvenir slant. Sheltered from
the sun and rain by a long row of conjoined
geometric white canvas parasols. Sat & Sun
10am–5pm.

**Rozelle Markets Rozelle Public School, Darling
St, Rozelle. Bus #433 from Central CityRail
or #442 from the QVB.** Secondhand goods
with numerous garage sale stalls selling
everything from vintage LPs to clothes to
characterful furniture or books. The exotic
smells of numerous international food stalls
waft across the historic school grounds,
and musicians perform blues and jazz
between 11am and 2pm in two areas. Sat
& Sun 9am–4pm.

**Sydney Opera House Market Sydney Opera
House forecourt.** Quality handmade Australian
arts and crafts stalls in a spectacular
location, with most artists on hand to talk
about their work. Sun 9am–5pm.

Music

**Australian Music Centre Shop Level 4, The Arts
Exchange, 10 Hickson Rd, The Rocks Ⓦ www
.amcoz.com.au. Circular Quay CityRail/ferry.**
Specialist Australian music store of the
Australian Music Centre, set up in 1974 to
provide information, publications and scores
relating to Australian music. The retail outlet
covers genres from classical through jazz and
electroacoustic and experimental sounds.
With its relaxed, listen-before-you-buy policy
and knowledgeable staff, this is a great place
to get a taste for antipodean music; you are
also welcome to visit the centre's resource
library, which has listening facilities (Mon–
Thurs 10am–5pm). Mon–Fri 9am–5pm.

Birdland Records Ⓦ www.birdland.com.au.
Currently without premises (but still
operating online), this has long been one
of Sydney's premier jazz and blues stores
(with a dedicated Australian section which
aims to stock everything available), helped
along by some soul and a big world music
section. CDs and vinyl available. Check the
website for possible future store location.

**Central Station Records 46 Oxford St at Riley St,
Darlinghurst Ⓣ 02/9361 5222, Ⓦ www
.centralstationsydney.com.au. Museum CityRail.**
Sydney's dance specialist, stocking the latest
imported and local sounds on vinyl and CD.
At the heart of the gay scene in Darlinghurst,

If you forget that vital present for your pet-minder or plant-waterer, your conscience can be salved at the international terminal of the airport, which holds enough surfwear shops, branches of R.M. Williams (see p.247) and Australian wine and craft shops (including boomerangs, didgeridoos and the like), to cover most eventualities. And, if you've trawled Sydney for the height of kitsch without success, this is your chance to buy a furry toy kangaroo or a set of shot glasses adorned with paintings of koalas in incongruous primary colours – your mantelpiece will thank you. A full list and details of all the airport stores can be checked out at Ⓦwww.sydneyairport.com.au.

they also put together and sell the official Mardi Gras compilations. Mon–Wed & Fri 10am–7pm, Thurs 10am–9pm, Sat & Sun 10am–6pm.

Fish Records 261 King St, Newtown Ⓦwww.fishrecords.com.au. Newtown CityRail. Australia's largest independent music chain but catering to eclectic tastes – indie, top 40, dance, jazz, soundtracks and some classical. Also at 289 Darling St, Balmain and Norton Plaza Shopping Centre, Norton St, Leichhardt. Fish Fine Music at 350 George St specializes in classical and jazz (Town Hall or Martin Place CityRail). Also Fishtix, in-store (and online) ticket sales for the best gigs. Mon–Wed 9am–10pm, Thurs–Sat 9am–10pm, Sun 9.30am–9pm.

Folkways 282 Oxford St at Heeley St, Paddington ☎02/9361 3980. Bus #378 from Central CityRail or #380 from Circular Quay CityRail. Long catering to Sydney's folk-music devotees; with a comprehensive selection of folk recordings, plus some world music. Mon–Wed, Fri & Sat 9.30am–6pm, Thurs 9.30am–8pm, Sun 11am–5pm.

Red Eye Records 66 King St, City ☎02/9299 4233, Ⓦwww.redeye.com.au. Martin Place CityRail. Sydney's largest independent record store is the place to track down your favourite Australian bands on hard-to-find independent labels, plus rare, out-of-print and collectable items. The ground floor is all new, with everything from alternative to jazz; upstairs there's a huge range of secondhand vinyls, CDs and memorabilia. This is also where you can plug into the live music scene, with heaps of flyers available. They also ship overseas. Their shop at 370 Pitt St (Central CityRail) offers a larger secondhand range. Mon–Wed & Fri 9am–6pm,Thurs 9am–9pm, Sat 9am–5pm, Sun 11am–5pm.

Title 499 Crown St, Surry Hills ☎02/9699 5222, Ⓦtitlespace.com. Bus #301–303 from Circular Quay CityRail or Castlereagh St, City. A grown-up CD and DVD shop that concentrates on specialist genres – jazz, soul, funk, electronic – with a handpicked range and knowledgeable staff. Also at 90 Willoughby Rd, Crows Nest. Mon–Sat 10am–6.30pm, Sun 10am–5pm.

Souvenirs

Aussie Koala Shop Shop 8, The Rocks Centre, 10–26 Playfair St, The Rocks ☎02/9247 6388. Circular Quay CityRail. The place for those kitsch souvenirs: lots of furry koalas plus Opera House snowdomes and even mini-boomerangs. Daily 9am–6pm.

Australian Geographic Shop Lower Ground Floor, QVB, 455 George Street Ⓦwww .australiangeographicshop.com.au. A great place for quality souvenirs including portable indigenous art, coffee-table and travel books, and quirky novelty items. Perfect for last-minute shopping. There's another store in the Westfield Centrepoint. Mon–Wed,

Fri & Sat 9am–6pm, Thurs 9am–9pm, Sun 11am–4pm.

Done Art and Design 123 George St, The Rocks Ⓦwww.done.com.au. Circular Quay CityRail/ferry. Love the stuff or loathe it, there's no doubt that Ken Done's loud and colourful knitwear, T-shirts and other design oddments are as identifiably Sydney as the Harbour Bridge. The bridge, Opera House and harbour grace items from duvet covers to swimwear. Also at 1 Hickson Rd, The Rocks (daily 10am–6pm) and in the Harbourside shopping centre in Darling Harbour (daily 10am–9pm).

Festivals and events

The Sydney year is interspersed with festivals, both sporting and cultural, with summer being the peak time for big events. The **Sydney to Hobart Yacht Race**, starting on Boxing Day (Dec 26), is followed by the **New Year's Eve fireworks**, subsequently eclipsed in turn by the big extravaganza of the **Australia Day** celebrations (Jan 26). Highlights of the **Sydney Festival**, which runs throughout January, include the opening night's free multi-zoned extravaganza, and free outdoor concerts in The Domain. The summer winds up in a whirl of feathers and sequins at the **Sydney Gay & Lesbian Mardi Gras**, held in late February/early March. An entirely different side of Sydney life is on view at the impressive summer **surf carnivals**, staged regularly by surf life-saving clubs; for details contact Surf Life Saving NSW (☎02/9984 7188, ⓦwww.surflifesaving.com.au) or check newspapers. For other sporting events, see "Sports and activities". The "What's on" section of Sydney council's website (ⓦwww.cityofsydney.nsw.gov.au) lists events including a rundown of the Sydney Festival. See also our "Sydney festivals" colour section.

▲ Sydney Festival

January

New Year Sydney sees in the New Year with a spectacular multimillion-dollar fireworks display on Sydney Harbour. The more family-focused part of the proceedings begins at 9pm with a short fireworks display at various points, with plenty for the kids at Darling Harbour (for more information check ⓦwww.darlingharbour.com.au). The main event is at midnight, when longer themed fireworks are set off at a number of harbour and habour-side spots (including CBD skyscrapers); the most impressive displays pulse, rocket or cascade from the Harbour Bridge itself, all synchronized to music. People crowd out vantage points including The Rocks, Cremorne Point, Blues Point, Neutral Bay and Neilson Park – anywhere with the Bridge in sight is good – and many bag their spots from early morning; for information, see ⓦwww.cityofsydney.nsw .gov.au. Thousands of vessels also anchor on the water to take in the views; contact any of the ferry cruise companies listed on p.28, as well as Sydney Ferries (ⓦwww. sydneyferries.nsw.gov.au), or, if you can sail yourself, check the boat and yacht charters on p.267 of "Sports and activities" to organize getting out on the water.

Sydney Festival After the New Year celebrations, there's a week's hiatus before the Sydney Festival starts around January 10 (ⓣ02/8248 6500, ⓦwww.sydneyfestival .org.au). This exhaustive (and exhausting) arts event lasts until a few days after the Australia Day celebrations (Jan 26), and ranges from concerts, plays and outdoor art installations to circus performances. A lot of events are free, and based around urban public spaces, focusing on Circular Quay, The Domain, Darling Harbour and Sydney Olympic Park; the remainder – mostly a fantastic roster of international performances – can cost a packet. Highlights of the free outdoor programme include the opening night, in which multiple city precincts are blocked off from traffic, with multiple stages, roaming performers and a big international act (Grace Jones in 2009) at The Domain, and the Jazz in the Park and Symphony in the Park concerts, also in The Domain, in the weeks that follow. A dynamic bar is set up in the grounds of the Hyde Park Barracks. The general programme is usually printed in the *Sydney Morning Herald* in October or November, while a full eighty-plus-page (free) programme is available nearer the time from the Town Hall. A weekly listing of events appears in the *Sydney Morning Herald* during the festival.

Flickerfest International Short Film Festival Week-long film festival, held mostly outdoors in the amphitheatre of the Bondi Pavilion in early January; some films in the auditorium. More details on ⓦwww .flickerfest.com.au; see also box on p.224.

Sydney Fringe Festival ⓣ02/9130 3325, ⓦwww.sydneyfringe.org.au. Runs for two weeks from mid-January, and encompasses performance, music, visual art, workshops, kids' shows and some very unusual, irreverent sporting events, from the very camp Drag Race Meet to the Nude Night Surfing competition.

Australia Day January 26 is the anniversary of the arrival of the First Fleet in Sydney Harbour in 1788, and Australia Day activities are focused on the harbour (Australia Day Council of NSW; ⓦwww.australiaday .com). Sydney's passenger ferries race from Fort Denison to the Harbour Bridge, via Shark Island, the Tall Ships Race goes from Bradleys Head to the Harbour Bridge, and military planes put on an aerial display. The Australia Day Regatta takes place in the afternoon, with hundreds of yachts racing all over the harbour, from Botany Bay to the Parramatta River. There are also free events at The Rocks, Hyde Park, and at Darling Harbour, where the day culminates with the Australia Day Spectacular at around 9pm, a "multimedia symphony of light, sound and music" concluding with a massive fireworks display. In addition, many museums let visitors in free or half price. Besides all this, at least two outdoor festivals take place. Yabun (formerly "Survival"), which celebrates Aboriginal culture and acts as an antidote to the mainstream white Australia Day festivities, is held at Victoria Park, Broadway (free; contact Koori Radio on ⓣ02/9384 4000 or check ⓦwww.gadigal .org.au). And Rocksong at the Rocks, an all-day festival, featuring high-calibre singers and songwriters of assorted genres from all over Australia, takes place at The Rocks.

Big Day Out Held at the end of January in the Showground at Homebush Bay, this features around sixty local and international bands and DJs; more details on ⓦwww .bigdayout.com and box on p.218.

February

Chinese New Year Towards the end of January and into the first weeks of February, Chinese New Year is celebrated in and near Chinatown at Belmore Park (opposite Central Station) – where the festivities commence with firecrackers, dragon and lion dances, food stalls and music – and at Darling Harbour, where traditional dragon boat races occur (more details on Ⓦ www .cityofsydney.nsw.gov.au)

Tropfest Hugely popular competition festival for short films, at the end of February, with an outdoor screening in The Domain. More details on Ⓦ www.tropfest.com.au; see also box on p.224.

Sydney Gay & Lesbian Mardi Gras Running through February, the festival features films, theatre and exhibitions that range from cheeky to outrageous. It all culminates in one of the world's largest street parades, when up to a million people line the streets on the last Sat in February or first Sat in March. More details on Ⓦ www.mardigras .org.au; see also p.227.

March–April

Greek Festival of Sydney This month-long celebration kicks off with the two-day Greek Fest at Darling Harbour in late March, featuring food and wine stalls, plus live entertainment, including traditional dance (and dance workshops). More information on Ⓦ www.greekfestivalofsydney.com.au.

Surry Hills Festival Held in mid-April, this colourful community festival, in Prince Alfred Park, Surry Hills (near Central Station), features six stages of established and emerging (usually riotous) artists, up to 250 market stalls bursting with creative fashions, arts and crafts and wafting aromatherapeutic international cuisines, plus thousands upon thousands of Sydney's funkiest residents, dressed to impress. More details at Ⓦ www .shnc.org/festival.

Royal Easter Show Agricultural and garden show in the Sydney Showground at the Olympic site at Homebush Bay. For fourteen consecutive days in late March/early April (the Easter weekend is neatly sandwiched in between), the country comes to the city with parades of prized animals and various farm/agriculture related displays, plus a frantic array of amusement-park rides, and frenzied consumerism in the Showbag Pavilion. At night in the main arena, there's a celebration of Australian bush heritage, stunt shows, a rodeo and fireworks displays; by day, there are usually horse-related events, judging of show animals, and the traditional, and very popular, wood-chopping competitions. Open 9.30am–10pm, last admission 8.30pm. Tickets include public transport to the show from anywhere in the greater Sydney area; adults $32, ages 4–16 $21.50; rides extra; ☏02/9704 1111, Ⓦ www.eastershow.com.au.

May–July

Kings Cross Food & Wine Festival On a Sunday at the beginning of May, Fitzroy Gardens, Kings Cross, hosts a one-day food fair with local restaurateurs (around twenty stalls) and NSW wineries (around sixteen) showing their wares, plus entertainment and community stalls. Sponsored by the City of Sydney Council, more information on Ⓦ www.cityofsydney.nsw.gov.au and www .kingscrossonline.com.au.

Sydney Writers Festival Week-long, high-profile, mid-May event, with readings, workshops and discussions, mostly free; Australian and international writers. Events take place in and around town, but most of the action is in a very scenic location at the Wharf Theatre, Hickson Rd, Millers Point. Details on Ⓦ www.swf.org.au.

Sydney Italian Festival From the end of May into early June, this festival celebrates Sydney's strong Italian community and includes everything from Italian fashion parades, lectures on Italian culture, theatre performances and recitals in venues all over the city. Major events include Primo Italiano, a street festival along the Stanley St strip of cafés and restaurants in Darlinghurst (late May), with Italian food stalls, a produce market, motorcycle and scooter displays and three stages for entertainment; the Official Celebration Of Italian National Day at Pyrmont Point in early June with much of the same; and Viva Leichhardt, a weekend festival of Italian food and culture in Leichhardt (early June). Details on Ⓦ www.cityofsydney.nsw.gov.au or www .sydneyitalianfestival.com.au.

Biennale of Sydney Every alternate (even-numbered) year, this international contemporary art festival takes place over

Christmas Day on Bondi Beach

For years, backpackers and Bondi Beach on **Christmas Day** were synonymous. The beach was transformed into a drunken party scene, as those from colder climes lived out their fantasy of spending Christmas on the beach under a scorching sun. The behaviour and litter began getting out of control, and after riots in 1995, and a rubbish-strewn beach, the local council began strictly controlling the whole performance, trying to keep a spirit of goodwill towards the travellers while also tempting local families back to the beach on what is regarded as a family day. Nowadays, alcohol is banned from the beach and surrounding vicinity on Christmas Day, and police enforce the rule with on-the-spot confiscations. However, a **party** is organized in the Pavilion, with a bar, DJs, food and entertainment running from noon to 10pm. Up to 3000 revellers cram into the Pavilion, while thousands of others – including a greater proportion of the desired family groups – enjoy the alcohol-free beach outside. In 2008, **tickets** for the Pavilion bash were $65 in advance from backpacker hostels, ⓦMoshtix.com.au (☎1300 438 849) or from ⓦTicketek.com.au (☎13 2849).

six weeks from early June until mid-August, featuring artists from every continent. Provocative contemporary exhibitions and events at venues and outdoor spaces around town, including the Art Gallery of New South Wales, the Opera House, Customs House, Cockatoo Island and the Museum of Contemporary Art. Usually free. Details on ⓦwww.bos2008.com

Sydney Film Festival Takes over several of the city's screens for two weeks from early June. More details at ⓦwww.sydneyfilmfestival.org; see also box on p.224.

August

Sun Herald City-to-Surf Race A 14km fun run from Park St in the city to Bondi, held on the second Sun of August, that attracts up to 60,000 participants. Entry forms are in the *Sun Herald* from June 1 or available online. More details on ⓦcity2surf.sunherald.com.au or www.coolrunning.com.au/citytosurf.

September–October

Festival of the Winds In September, as the skies get bluer, Australia's largest kite festival takes over Bondi Beach. Details on ⓦwww.waverley.nsw.gov.au.

Manly International Jazz Festival As Sydney gets into the swim of summer, and the beaches officially open for the year, this jazz-fest by the sea is a wonderful way to enjoy the warming weather. Held over the Labour Day weekend in early October, it consists of mostly free outdoor, waterfront events; some indoor concerts charge entry for bigger Australian and international acts. Details on ⓦwww.manly.nsw.gov.au/manlyjazz or www.manlytourism.com.au; also see p.218.

WOW (World of Women's Cinema) Film Festival Held over five days in early October at the Chauvel Cinema, Paddington and surrounding venues. More details on ⓦwww.wift.org/wow/; see also box p.224.

Sydney Food and Wine Fair Part of the *Sydney Morning Herald*-sponsored Good Food Month. On a Saturday in late October or early November, Hyde Park is taken over for a day by a hundred stalls representing restaurants, wineries, cheese-makers and the like, plus live entertainment from the concert stage. The usually sunny event attracts around 30,000 visitors and is an important fundraiser for the AIDS Trust of Australia. Details on ⓦgfm.smh.com.au

November

Sculpture By the Sea The coastal walk between Bondi and Tamarama becomes crowded during this 18-day installation (from late Oct to mid-Nov) of around a hundred wonderfully playful and provocative sculptures by Australian and international artists, many designed to be site-specific. Details on ☎02/8399 0233, ⓦwww.sculpturebythesea.com.

Newtown Festival One of Sydney's largest community festivals, held on the second Sun in November, when nearby Camperdown

Memorial Park is overtaken by a bazaar with food, community and market stalls, and a mixed bag of upbeat live music on three stages. Details on ☎02/9516 4755, Ⓦwww.newtowncentre.org/festival.

Glebe Street Fair Second to last Sun in November. Thousands flock to one of Sydney's great eat-streets, Glebe Point Rd, for a vibrant street festival – notably fabulous food for sale, representing local restaurants and cafés, plus lots of arts and crafts, live music, and roaming performers. Details on Ⓦwww.glebestreetfair.com.

December

Homebake Australian (and New Zealand) music is celebrated in The Domain with a line-up of bands from around the country. More details on Ⓦwww.homebake.com.au; also see box, p.218.

Sydney to Hobart Yacht Race It seems like almost half of Sydney turns out at around 1pm on December 26 to cheer the start of this classic regatta, and watch the colourful spectacle of a hundred or so yachts setting sail on their 630-nautical-mile slog. The toughest bit is the crossing of Bass Strait, which is swept by the "Roaring Forties" (conditions were so rough in 1999 that six sailors died and many crews abandoned the race). Good vantage points include South Head, Lady Bay and Nielson Park on the eastern shores, or Georges Head, Middle Head, Chowder Bay, North Head and Bradleys Head on the North Shore. Details on Ⓦwww.rolexsydneyhobart.com.

Carols in The Domain A balmy mid-December night of Christmas carols under the stars. Details on Ⓦwww.cityofsydney.nsw.gov.au.

FESTIVALS AND EVENTS

Sports and activities

Sydneysiders are **sports** mad, especially for the ostensibly passive spectator sports of Rugby League, Aussie Rules football, cricket, tennis and horse racing. No matter what it is, from surf life-saving competitions to yacht races, it'll draw a crowd. They're keen participants, too, whether it's a game of tennis or horseriding in Centennial Park, but getting into (or onto) the water is their greatest joy. The *Sydney Morning Herald*'s Friday listings supplement, "Metro", has an Active section, with details of the best events around town. Most seats can be booked through Ticketek (☎13 2849, Ⓦwww.ticketek.com.au).

See the "Festivals and events" chapter for details of the annual City-to-Surf race, a fourteen-kilometre fun run.

Rugby League

Rugby League is *the* football code in Sydney, and was for many years a bastion of working-class culture. Run by the National Rugby League (NRL; Ⓦwww.nrl.com.au), there are sixteen clubs, the majority of them Sydney-based. The Sydney teams are the Canterbury Bulldogs, Manly Sea Eagles, Parramatta Eels, Penrith Panthers, Sydney Roosters, Cronulla Sharks and South Sydney Rabbitohs, St George Illawarra Dragons and West Tigers, all with associated "leagues clubs" where you can drink, eat, be entertained and above all gamble on the "pokies" (see Penrith Panthers, p.298). The western-suburbs clubs Canterbury Bulldogs, Parramatta Eels and Penrith Panthers have the most loyal and boisterous supporters – expect any of their matches to be well attended.

The season starts in early March, and the **Grand Final** is played in early October, when huge crowds pack out the ANZ Stadium at Sydney Olympic Park.

The hard-fought **State of Origin** series, contested between New South Wales and Queensland with players selected according to the state in which they played their first senior game, takes place over three matches from early June to mid-July. At least one game is held in Sydney, and coverage of these matches consistently produces the highest ratings on Australian television. In recent years Queensland have been dominant.

Tickets for the less popular games can start as low as $15, though $30 would get you a seat in the grandstand. Finals and State of Origin games command prices of at least $60.

Australian Rules

Victoria has traditionally been the home of **Australian Rules** ("Aussie Rules") football, and Victorian sides are still expected to win the AFL Flag – decided at the Grand Final in Melbourne in September – as a matter of course. However, the enormously popular **Sydney Swans** (ⓦ www.sydneyswans.com.au), New South Wales' contribution to the AFL, have ensured Aussie Rules a place in the city. The game itself is a no-holds-barred, 18-a-side brawl, closely related to Gaelic football, and dismissively known north of the Victorian border as "aerial ping pong". The ball can be propelled by any means necessary, and the fact that players aren't sent off for misconduct ensures a lively, skilful and, above all, gladiatorial confrontation. Aussie Rules stars have delightful sobriquets such as "Tugger" and "Crackers", and their macho garb consists of tiny butt-hugging shorts and bicep-revealing tank tops. The game is mostly played on cricket grounds, with a ball similar to that used in rugby or American football. The aim is to get the ball through the central uprights for a goal (six points). There are four 25-minute quarters, plus lots of time added on for injury. Crowds tend to be very well behaved; you'll be surrounded by boisterous fans, but perfectly safe, if you go to watch the Swans at their home base at the Sydney Cricket Ground (see opposite). See the website of the Australian Football League, ⓦ www.afl.com.au, for more details.

The **season** runs from late March to late September, and **tickets** cost $35–75 with finals series tickets starting around $70.

Rugby Union

Despite the huge success of the national team, the Wallabies, **Rugby Union** still lags behind Rugby League in popularity in New South Wales. That said, there's always an enthusiastic following for the nine-game **Tri-Nations** series held annually between the national sides of Australia, New Zealand and South Africa from mid-July to mid-September. One of the three home games is usually played at ANZ Stadium at Sydney Olympic Park, but tickets are hard to come by.

You've got a better chance of catching something during the **Super 14** competition (ⓦ www.super14.com), which runs from the end of February to the end of May, and involves regional teams from Australia, New Zealand and South Africa. The only NSW team is the Waratahs, who play about six times per season in Sydney. **Tickets** are around $20–60 when they play at the Sydney Football Stadium, but more like $16–40 for the less frequent games at the ANZ Stadium. For more details and the latest rugby info check out the Australian Rugby Union (ARU) website at ⓦ www.rugby.com.au.

Soccer

Soccer is still a minority sport in Australia, traditionally played by teams evolved from communities of postwar immigrants – mainly Italians, Greeks and Yugoslavs. In the mid-1990s, a ban on clubs with these nation's flags in their team logos won considerable support, but also came in for accusations of "ethnic cleansing". The main competition is the Australasian A-League (ⓦ www.a-league .com.au), played from October to April by ten teams – Adelaide, Brisbane, Melbourne, Perth, Sydney, Central Coast, Newcastle, Gold Coast, and Townsville, plus the sole New Zealand team, Wellington. Sydney FC (ⓦ www.sydneyfc.com) play their home games at the Sydney Football Stadium, and tickets cost $20–40.

▲ Soccer in the park

They usually place in the top four, which gives them entry to the end-of-season finals series, but they've never won it.

Australia's best **players** invariably head off to play in Europe: Harry Kewell is currently at Galatasaray in Turkey, while Tim Cahill and Mark Viduka both play in the English Premiership, for Everton and Newcastle United respectively. All are frequently called up to play for the national side, the **Socceroos**. Currently ranked 32nd in the world, they played at the 2006 World Cup (making it to the final 16 and losing to eventual winners, Italy), and as this book went to press were topping their Asia Group 1 table, with high hopes of reaching the 2010 World Cup in South Africa. Their home matches are played at the Sydney Football Stadium.

Cricket

Cricket is the most popular summer spectator sport in Australia. Sydney's cricket season runs from October to March, and offers some of the year's best sporting days out (locals go for the atmosphere, the sunshine and the beer as much as the game). The **Sydney Cricket Ground** (see p.100) is home to most four-day, interstate Sheffield Shield matches (not much interest for spectators, but a breeding ground for Australia's Test cricketers); five-day international **Test matches**; the colourful, crowd-pleasing **one-day internationals**; and the thrills-and-spills **Twenty20** matches. The Test to see here is, of course, the Sydney leg of the five- or six-test **Ashes** series against England, which takes place every four or five years, and lasts five days, starting on New Year's Day. Subject to availability, you can buy tickets for all matches at the gates on the day, or purchase them in advance from Ticketek (☏13 2849, ⓦwww.ticketek.com.au).

Tennis and squash

Sydney's major **tennis** event, the **Medibank International** (Ⓦwww
.medibankinternational.com.au), takes place during the second week of January as
a lead-up to the Australian Open in Melbourne, at the 10,500-seat centre court of
the **Olympic Park Tennis Centre** at Homebush (see p.181).Tickets ($25 rising
to $90) are available from September.You can play tennis on one of the fifteen
outdoor courts (Mon–Fri 8am–10pm, Sat & Sun 8am–5pm; $20–24 per hr;
bookings Ⓣ02/9764 1999, Ⓦwww.sydneytenniscentre.com.au). A more central
place to play is **Rushcutters Bay Tennis Centre**, in picturesque Rushcutters
Bay Park, by the marina at 7 Waratah St (daily 7am–11pm; Ⓣ02/9357 1675; $20
per hr, $26 after 4pm and Sat & Sun; racket rental $3; Kings Cross CityRail).

A handy place to play **squash** is Hiscoe's Fitness Centre, 525 Crown St, Surry
Hills (Mon–Thurs 6am–9pm, Fri 6am–9pm, Sat 8am–8pm, Sun 9am–1pm &
4–8pm; squash bookings essential on Ⓣ02/9699 9222, Ⓦwww.hiscoes.com.au;
$30–41 per 45–60min session; racket rental $4.65; gym casual visit $20).

Horse and greyhound racing

Australians lose approximately $1000 per head each year succumbing to the
temptation of a flutter. This eagerness to bet, coupled with relaxed **gambling**
laws, has tax-collectors rubbing their hands as the revenue rolls in. Sydney offers
plenty of opportunities for any punter heading for the fast lane to millionaire's
row – or the slippery slope to the poorhouse. Every Friday the *Sydney Morning
Herald* publishes its racing guide,"The Form". Bets are placed at TAB (Totalisator
Agency Board) shops, scattered throughout the city; most pubs also have TAB
access, as does Star City Casino (see p.88).

Horse-racing meetings take place on Wednesday, Saturday and most public
holidays.They're well attended, due mainly to the accessibility of courses, the high
quality of racing, the presence of bookmakers and cheap admission prices ($7–12,
$25–35 for carnivals).The venues are well maintained and peopled with colourful
characters and often massive crowds. Best times to hit the track are during the
spring and autumn carnivals (Aug–Sept & Feb–April respectively), when prize
money rockets, and the quality of racing rivals the best in the world.The principal
racecourses are: **Royal Randwick**, Alison Road, Randwick (Ⓣ02/9663 8400,
Ⓦwww.ajc.org.au), which featured in *Mission Impossible II*; **Rosehill Gardens**,
James Ruse Drive, Rosehill (Ⓣ02/9930 4000, Ⓦwww.stc.com.au; Rosehill
Gardens CityRail), which also has loads of free kids' entertainment including a
bouncy castle and pony rides (entry for children is also free); and **Canterbury
Park** King St, Canterbury (Ⓣ02/9930 4000, Ⓦwww.stc.com.au; Canterbury
CityRail), which has midweek racing, and floodlit night racing from November
to February.There are also plenty of picturesque country venues to choose from;
contact the Australian Jockey Club for more details on Ⓣ02/9663 8400 or at
Ⓦwww.ajc.org.au.

If the chariot scenes of *Ben Hur* are more to your taste, a trip to the trots might be
the ticket. **Harness racing** occurs at **Harold Park Paceway**, Ross Street, Glebe
(Fri 7–11pm; Ⓣ02/9660 3688, Ⓦwww.haroldpark.com.au; $10). The excitement
reaches its peak with the **Miracle Mile** on the last Friday of November. Some
find watching horses lope around the course too sedate, but just around the
corner, money is thrown away at greater speed as the **greyhounds** hurtle around
Wentworth Park (Mon & Sat, gates open at 5.30pm, races 7.30–10.30pm;
Ⓣ02/9552 1799, Ⓦwww.wentworthparksport.com.au; $5.50).

Walking and hiking

Walking is one of the best ways to experience Sydney, whether it be exploring the urban landscape and architecture around The Rocks, sampling the delights of the Inner West, or heading out for a few hours into the Blue Mountains. Below we've given a rundown of some of our favourites, several of them more fully explored in the rest of the Guide.

In the city

City Centre Walking Tour 5km loop; 2hr; easy.
Give your central city wanderings some structure, by following this tour of Sydney's urban highlights. See box, p.77.

Harbour Bridge Walk 2km; 2–3hr; easy. From Circular Quay, wander through the historic streets of The Rocks, then use Bridge Steps off Cumberland St to reach the walkway across the Harbour Bridge. Drop down to Milsons Point for an hour or so at Luna Park, then catch the ferry back to Circular Quay.

The suburbs, harbour and coast

Eastern Beaches Coastal Walkway 10km; 2hr 30min–4hr; easy. Walk the entire coastal stretch from Bondi south to Maroubra, or just pick a short section and spend the day lazing and swimming. Either way this is a gorgeous walk along the sea cliffs, dipping repeatedly into bays, all equipped with cafés and pubs. See p.134.

Hermitage Foreshore Walk 1.5km one-way; 1hr; easy. This is a cracker. After catching a ferry from Circular Quay to Rose Bay or Watsons Bay, grab a bus (#324 or #325) to Bayview Hill Rd. From here, the walk follows a thin strip of gorgeous bushland between Vaucluse mansions and the harbour. The views of the harbour and the city framed by lush plant life are as spectacular as the grand houses, while small secluded beaches, graveyards and historic buildings are dotted along the way. You end up at ravishing Neilson Park, which besides a great beach has a Federation-era kiosk fronting the water, with alfresco tables and good coffee.

Hunters Hill Village Walk 3km; 2–3hr, easy. Spend a few hours exploring the sylvan streets and historic mansions of one of Sydney's prettiest suburbs. See p.121.

Inner West Lifestyle Walk 5km; 3–8hr; easy. This walk is best done as a slow meander, broken into instalments over a whole Saturday, to coincide with the Inner west's many Saturday markets. From Circular Quay, catch a ferry to Balmain East, then wander up Darling St past pretty historic buildings before calling in at the Balmain or Rozelle Markets and stopping at a café for a wholesome late breakfast. Then catch a bus (#432, #433, or #434) to Glebe and walk up tranquil Glebe Point Rd, soaking up the atmosphere, maybe taking in a live performance at Glebe Markets, dipping into a book shop or two, and relaxing over lunch in a café courtyard. Next call in at at least one of the museums on the Sydney University campus (see p.106), before walking up King St, through Newtown to St Peters – an essential stop for its fascinating fashion, gift and speciality shops. Finally, double back to Newtown for dinner at an ethnic restaurant followed by a sunset beer or cocktail on a rooftop bar (see ZanziBar, p.212).

Manly Scenic Walkway 10km one-way; easy. Wonderful harbourside walk, following the shore inland from Manly Cove all the way west to Spit Bridge on Middle Harbour. For details, see p.141.

Taronga Zoo/Bradleys Head to Balmoral 12km; 3–4hr; moderate. This superb harbourside walk weaves through stunning bushland and past secluded, often deserted beaches with great views of the city and harbour, Middle Head offers history and drama, with its massive nineteenth-century gun emplacements overlooking North and South heads.

Blue mountains

Federal Pass 5.3km one-way; 3hr; moderate to hard. This popular route from Katoomba's Echo Point follows the Giant Stairway down 170 metres, then contours around the base of the cliff past Katoomba Cascades to the base of the Scenic World Railway. At this point you can either catch the railway back to Echo Point or hike up the steep Furber Steps (additional 45min), through rainforests with great views of the Three Sisters. See p.309.

National Pass 5.4km one-way; 4hr; moderate to hard. One of the finest walks easily accessible from Sydney, this track loops down from the cliff tops at Wentworth Falls to skirt a precipitous-looking (though in fact perfectly safe) track halfway up the sheer cliffs. Great views, waterfalls and a pretty finish along the Darwin Walk (strolled by the great botanist in 1836), back to Wentworth Falls Station.

Surfing and surf carnivals

In the peculiarly Australian institution known as a **surf carnival**, teams of volunteer life-savers demonstrate their athletic skills in mostly inflatable life-saving boats. They're usually held on summer weekends, which makes for a great day out at the beach. Community surf life-saving organizations began forming across Australia in 1905, and the Surf Life Saving Association was established in 1907. Women have been allowed to join since 1980, and now make up about forty percent of members (also see box, p.134). Contact Surf Life Saving NSW for details of the current season's carnivals (☎02/9984 7188, Ⓦwww.surflifesaving.com.au). **Surfing** competitions are good opportunities to catch some hot wave-riding action. Check the Surfing NSW website for details (Ⓦwww.surfingaustralia.com).

Surf schools can teach you the basic skills, and enlighten you on surfing etiquette and lingo. In the eastern beaches, the best is Lets Go Surfing, 128 Ramsgate Ave, North Bondi (daily 9am–6pm; ☎02/9365 1800, Ⓦwww.letsgosurfing.com.au), which sells surfing gear, rents boards ($25 for 2hr, $40 all day, plus $5–10 for a wetsuit) and offers lessons: a two–hour group lesson ($79–89) includes board and wetsuit, or go for a private lesson (1hr; $130 one person, $70 each extra person). Up on the northern beaches, visit Manly Surf School (☎02/9977 6977, Ⓦwww.manlysurfschool.com), who charge similar rental rates, run $55 group lessons and offer private lessons for $80 an hour per person. Nearby, Dripping Wet, 93 North Steyne, Manly (☎02/9977 3549, Ⓦwww.drippingwetsurf.com), rent Malibu boards ($35 for 4hr), bodyboards and wetsuits ($15 for 4hr).

Check daily **surf reports** at Ⓦwww.coastalwatch.com.au (which has surfcams) and Ⓦwww.swellnet.com.au. Also see the box "Beach and sun safety" on p.135.

▲ Manly Beach

Canoeing, kayaking, rafting, sailboarding and sailing

The **sailing season** and best time to sail in Sydney is from April to September; some sail schools only offer lessons and rental during these months. For other sailing courses and yacht rental, contact Yachting NSW (℡02/8116 9800, ⓦwww.nsw.yachting.org.au). You can also take a thrilling **white-water rafting** circuit at the Penrith Whitewater Stadium, a former Olympic venue at the foothills of the Blue Mountains (see p.299).

Balmoral Windsurfing, Sailing and Kayaking School Balmoral Boatshed, southern end of the Esplanade, Balmoral Beach ℡02/9960 5344, ⓦwww.sailingschool.com.au. Bus #247 from Wynyard CityRail. Sailboard rental ($50 first hour then $20 per hr) and Hobie Cat dinghies ($50 per hr) as well as lessons. Group windsurfing courses for beginners (two 2hr sessions; $270) plus Hobie Cat sailing courses (two 2hr sessions; $270). For classes for children, see p.238. Open all year.

Natural Wanders ℡02/9899 1001, ⓦwww.kayaksydney.com. Guided sea-kayaking in the harbour with trips around Balmain and a shorter, beginner-oriented jaunt around the sheltered waters of Blues Point. There's also the Bridge Paddle (4hr; experience needed at weekends; $90), which starts from Lavender Bay near Luna Park, goes under the Harbour Bridge and explores the bush-clad, yacht-filled North Shore, usually with a brief stop on a beach near Taronga Zoo. Trips meet at Lavender Bay Wharf, just west of Milsons Point. Year-round, weather permitting.

Northside Sailing School Middle Harbour Skiff Club Spit Bridge, Mosman ℡02/9969 3972, ⓦwww.northsidesailing.com.au. Bus #169, #175, #176, #178, #L90 or #180 from Wynyard CityRail. Weekend dinghy sailing courses on Middle Harbour (Sept–April); start with a lesson (1hr $70 solo, $95 for two; 2hr

$110/$165), and progress at your own pace (four lessons equal an Australian Yachting Federation beginners' course). Also lessons for kids (see p.238).

Rose Bay Aquatic Hire 1 Vickery Ave, Rose Bay ℡02/9371 7036. Rose Bay Wharf; bus #323, #324 & #325 from Edgecliff CityRail. Rents out catamarans ($50 first hour, $30 thereafter), kayaks ($25 per hour), and motorboats (weekends $80 for the first two hours, $15 for each subsequent hour, plus charge for petrol). No boat licence required, only a drivers' licence. Closed Mon & Tues.

Sydney by Sail Based at the National Maritime Museum, Darling Harbour ℡02/9280 1110, ⓦwww.sydneybysail.com.au. Harbourside Monorail. Bookings are essential for their popular hands-on sightseeing sail (daily 1–4pm; $150), which gives you a chance to help trim sails or helm a yacht (normally a 33- or 44-footer) out on the harbour with a professional skipper. They also run Learn To Sail programmes throughout the year for all levels, from a Level 1 Introductory Course (12hr over 2 days; $425), which includes the opportunity to join in two social races which take place on the third Saturday of the month, up to a Level 4 Inshore Skipper Course (3-day, 2-night live-aboard; $695, includes all meals). Experienced sailors can also charter the yachts, from $570 half-day to $995 for a weekend.

Diving and snorkelling

Visibility in the waters around Sydney is good – and **divers** can expect to see to a distance of 10–15m, with the best visibility typically in winter and spring. One of the best places to dive, at **Gordon's Bay** in Clovelly, gives easy access to Sydney's only underwater nature trail – a sort of beneath-the-sea bushwalking track, marked by a series of chains connected to concrete drums. The trail includes typical Sydney shoreline life: sponges, sea jellies, anemones, shrimps and crabs, molluscs, cuttlefish, octopus, sea stars and sea squirts. The 700-metre trail takes around 35–40 minutes to cover, with a maximum depth of 14m. Diving off North and South heads is also popular, and in spring (Aug–Oct) you can dive with timid Port Jackson sharks at La Perouse. When there's a swell running, you can always head for the harbour which has its own unique flora and fauna. All the operators below also offer diving courses.

Aquatic Explorers 40 Kingsway, under Cronulla Beach YHA, Cronulla ℡ 02/9523 1518, ⓦ www.aquaticexplorers.com.au. **Cronulla CityRail.** Local coordinated shore dives on the weekend (free; full gear rental $85; tank refills $9), including Ship Rock and the Botany Bay National Park on the Kurnell Peninsula. Also two-dive boat trips ($85; including all gear $150), night dives and weekends away up and down the New South Wales coast.

Dive Centre Bondi 198 Bondi Rd ℡ 02/9369 3855, ⓦ www.divebondi.com.au. **Bus #380 from Bondi Junction CityRail.** Shore dives at Camp Cove (Watsons Bay) and Ben Buckler at North Bondi (double dive $120), and boat dives (double $170) to South Head and Maroubra where there's a chance to see sharks.

Dive Centre Manly 10 Belgrave St, Manly ℡ 02/9977 4355, ⓦ www.divesydney.com.au. **Ferry to Manly Wharf.** Shore dives at Shelley Beach, Fairlight, and Little Manly plus Harbord if conditions are good, and boat dives off North and South Head and Long Reef (boat dives Fri–Sun 9am, 11am, 1pm & 3pm; single boat dive $145, double $185; shore dives daily 9am & noon; single shore dive $75, double $95; rates include full gear).

Prodive Coogee 27 Alfreda St, Coogee ℡ 02/9665 6333, ⓦ www.prodive.com.au. **Bus #373 & #374 from Circular Quay CityRail.** Equipped boat and shore dives anywhere between Camp Cove (Watsons Bay) and La Perouse (4hr double boat dive $189 weekend, $125 mid-week, double shore dive $135), plus dives all over Sydney.

Swimming

While Sydney is blessed with abundant ocean and harbour beaches, sometimes it's more convenient to head for a **swimming pool**. Most public, council-run pool complexes are outdoors and have a fifty-metre pool, a smaller children's pool and a wading pool, all usually unheated. The **swimming season** is generally the warmer months, from the long weekend in early October until Easter. Many pools are closed to the public for several days in February when school swimming carnivals traditionally take place. There are over seventy public pools, as well as 74 enclosed sea pools at beaches and on the harbour; several of the latter are detailed in the Guide, including the Dawn Fraser Swimming Pool in Balmain (p.113), Women's Pool (p.138), and Wylies Baths (p.138), both in Coogee; the pool at the Bondi Icebergs (p.133); and the Mahon Pool at Maroubra (p.138). What follows is a selection of favourites in popular areas; check "Swimming pools" in the *Yellow Pages* for a full list.

Andrew "Boy" Charlton The Domain ℡ 02/9358 6686. **Martin Place CityRail.** See map on p.67 and coverage on p.69. Chic outdoor pool with its own café-restaurant and yoga and Pilates classes, plus a regular Thursday night biathlon (running and swimming; Nov–March only) open to all competitors. Sept–April daily 6am–7pm or 8pm; $5.70.

Annette Kellerman Aquatic Centre Enmore Park off Enmore Rd, Enmore ℡ 02/9565 1906. **Bus #423, #426 & #428 from Central CityRail.** Not far from Newtown, and known to the locals simply as Enmore Pool, the heated 33m indoor pool stays open all year. Mon–Sat 5.30am–8.30pm, Sun 8am–6pm; $4.20.

Cook and Phillip Park Aquatic and Fitness Centre 4 College St at William St ℡ 02/9326 0444, ⓦ www.cookandphillip.org.au. **Museum CityRail.** State-of-the-art undercover complex with a 50m heated indoor pool for laps, a 25m leisure pool with a wave-making machine at weekends and during school holidays, a bubbling "river run" feature and toddlers area with its own beach, a hydrotherapy pool with disabled access and a gym. There's access to an outdoor courtyard and café, plus the vegetarian *Bodhi in the Park* (see p.182) is adjacent. Mon–Fri 6am–10pm, Sat & Sun 7am–8pm. Swim $6.20, swim & gym $16.50.

Cronulla Sports Complex 1 The Esplanade,
Cronulla ☎ 02/9523 5842. **Cronulla CityRail.**
Beachfront complex with heated indoor
pools and a gym. Mon–Fri 7am–3.45pm,
Sat 7am–5pm, Sun 8am–5pm. Swim $4.50,
swim & gym $18.

Ian Thorpe Aquatic Centre 456 Harris St,
Ultimo ☎ 02/9518 7220, Ⓦ www.itac.org.au.
Exhibition Centre Light Rail. All white tiles
and sensuous curves, this modern pool
was one of the last things designed by
renowned Sydney architect Harry Seidler
(see p.88). Centrally located, with a leisure
pool, sauna, steam room, gym and swim
school it also has a 50m indoor pool
suitable for the pool's swimming legend
namesake. Mon–Fri 6am–10pm, Sat & Sun
6am–8pm. Swim $6.20, swim & sauna
$12, swim & gym $16.50.

Leichhardt Park Aquatic Centre Mary St
Leichhardt ☎ 02/9555 8344, Ⓦ www.lmc
.nsw.gov.au. **Bus #440 from Central CityRail.**
A great spot for a swimming centre, on
an extensive park on Iron Cove, an inlet
of the Parramatta River. The pool grounds
themselves are green and spacious. The
heated outdoor 50m pool is a great place
to swim in winter and there's also a diving
pool. Alternatively, you can stay inside
in the smaller 18m heated pool (with an
indoor toddlers'pool and spa beside it).
Just outside there's a popular, landscaped,
gate-surrounded toddlers' pool. The
gym has aerobics, aqua aerobics and
yoga classes. There's a handy weekday
childminding service, too (Mon–Fri
9am–1.30pm; max 2hr; bookings essential
$3.70 per hr). Daily 5.30am–8pm. Swim
$6.20, swim & gym $16.80.

North Sydney Olympic Pool 4 Alfred St
South, Milsons Point ☎ 02/9955 2309,
Ⓦ www.northsydney.nsw.gov.au. **Milsons Point**
CityRail. The heated 50m outdoor pool here
is open all year; situated by the water in
the shadow of the harbour bridge, it's one
of Sydney's best. The site also includes an
indoor 25m pool, a gym, sauna, spa and
café, and a crèche (Mon, Wed & Fri 9am–
noon; $3.70 per hr). Mon–Fri 5.30am–9pm,
Sat & Sun 7am–7pm; $5.80.

Sydney Olympic Park Aquatic Centre Olympic
Blvd, Sydney Olympic Park, Homebush Bay
☎ 02/9752 3666, Ⓦ www.aquaticcentre.com.au.
Olympic Park CityRail. As well as being a
great place to swim laps in the competition pools, there are landscaped leisure
pools with amusements such as the rapid
river-ride, as well as water slides. Also
spas, steam rooms and saunas, a gym
and fitness classes. A crèche is available
(Mon–Fri 8.45am–1.45pm; max 2hr; book
in advance; $7.50). Nov–March Mon–Fri
5am–9pm, Sat & Sun 6am–8pm; April–Oct
Mon–Fri 5am–9pm, Sat & Sun 6am–7pm.
Swim & spa $6.60, child $5.20 ($13.50
includes steam rooms and sauna; also
including gym and fitness classes $20).

Victoria Park Pool Corner of City Rd and
Broadway, Camperdown ☎ 02/9298 3090 4181.
Bus #431, #433, #434, #438 or #440 from
Central CityRail. Heated outdoor pool next
to Sydney University and close to Glebe
Point Rd, in a landscaped park, and with
a shaded toddlers' wading pool. Great
café (daily 7.30am–3pm), plus a gym and
crèche (Tues, Thurs & Fri 9.15am–1.45pm;
book in advance; $3.30 per hr). Mon–Fri
6am–7.15pm, Sat & Sun 7am–5.45pm;
$4.80, swim & gym $13.20.

Cycling

The narrow maze of streets in Sydney's CBD, combined with traffic congestion,
means that **cycling** has never been too popular, though the current government
is trying to address the situation with plans that should build on recent spending
on new cycleways and bike routes. **Cycleway maps** (complete with off-road
paths, suggested bicycle routes and cycling difficulty ratings) can be downloaded
from Ⓦ www.rta.nsw.gov.au (search for "cycleway maps"). The *Sydney and
Parramatta* map covers the City, Inner east, Inner west, the Harbour and most
of the Ocean Beaches. For leisure cycling, head for **Centennial Park** or the
cycleway at Manly.

Bikes cannot be taken on buses, but taking them on other forms of **public
transport** is fairly easy. They travel free on ferries at all times, and are always

allowed on trains, though if part or all of your journey is during peak hours (Mon–Fri 6–9am & 3.30–7.30pm) you must pay a child fare for the bike, even a folding one. Wearing a **helmet** is a legal requirement – police issue fines for non-compliance.

The best source of information is the very helpful advocacy organization Bicycle NSW, based at Level 5, 822 George St (Mon–Fri 9am–4.30pm; T02/9218 5400, W www.bicyclensw.org.au). Two useful publications available here are *Bike It Sydney* ($20), which has backstreet inner-city bike routes, and *Cycling Around Sydney* ($20), detailing 25 of the best rides. They also hand out free council and RTA bike route maps.

Critical Mass is an activist group "reclaiming the streets for cycling" that began in San Francisco and now has groups all over the world. The Sydney movement organizes a cycling event on the last Friday of the month; meet at the Archibald Fountain in Hyde Park for an hour-long ride through the city leaving at 6pm (or you can skate, jog, rollerblade; even runners turn up, too).

Sadly, liability and insurance issues make finding bike rentals ever more difficult. We've listed a few candidates.

Bike sales, repairs and rentals

Centennial Park Cycles 50 Clovelly Rd at Avoca St, Randwick T02/9398 5027, W www.cyclehire.com.au. Ideal for a leisurely ride in Centennial Park with a base in Randwick and rental outlet in Centennial Park. They rent hybrid mountain bikes ($12 per hr, $35 per day), road bikes ($20/55), kids' bikes ($10/30), tandems ($20/55) and off-road mountain bikes ($75 for 24hr). They also deliver almost anywhere in Sydney. Daily 9am–5pm.

Cheeky Transport 3a Georgina St at King St, Newtown T02/9557 5424, W www .cheekytransport.com.au. Urban/transport cycling oriented shop with a focus on quality repairs, parts and cycling advocacy. Also touring and commuting bike sales. Mon–Wed & Fri 10am–6.30pm, Thurs 10am–8pm, Sat 10am–4pm.

Clarence Street Cyclery 104 Clarence St at King St, City T02/9299 4962, W www.cyclery.com.au. Large, city centre sales and repair shop for roadies and off-roadies. Also rents out pricey hybrids ($33 for 4hr, $65 for 24hr), perfect for cruising around town. Mon–Wed & Fri

8.30am–5.30pm, Thurs 8.30am–8pm, Sat & Sun 10am–4pm.

Inner City Cycles 151 Glebe Point Rd at Norton St, Glebe T02/9660 6605, W www .innercitycycles.com.au. Sales and repair shop that also rents hardtail mountain bikes ($33 a day, $55 a weekend, $88 for a week), good for exploring Darling Harbour or taking up to the Blue Mountains. Mon–Wed & Fri 9.30am–6pm, Thurs 9.30am–8pm, Sat 9am–4pm, Sun 11am–3pm.

Manly Cycles 36 Pittwater Rd, Manly, a block back from the beach T02/9977 1189, W www.manlycycles.com.au. Bike sales and repairs plus hybrid rentals ($15 per hr, $35 per day), ideal for Manly's bike paths. Also proper off-road MTBs ($75 per day including map), if you fancy heading off to the entertaining trails around Manly Dam. Open daily.

Woolys Wheels 82 Oxford St, Paddington T02/9331 2671, W www.woolyswheels.com. No rentals, but good repairs and lots of shiny bikes for sale from retro cruisers to carbon fibre rockets. Mon–Fri 9am–6pm, Sat & Sun 10am–4pm.

Rollerblading, skateboarding and ice-skating

Rollerblading is banned in the CBD. The most popular areas for bladers are along the bike track at Manly; along the Luna Park concourse and Lavender Bay walkway at Milsons Point (which you can reach by rollerblading across the Sydney Harbour Bridge along the cycle path on the western side); in Centennial Park; and along the Esplanade at Bondi Beach – teenagers also use the skateboarding ramp at Bondi. **Rental places** charge $15 for the first hour for either inline skates or skateboards, inclusive of protective gear, then up to around $25–30 for the day: try Skater HQ, 49 North Steyne (☎02/9976 3833, ⓦ www.skaterhq.com.au), close to Manly's bike track.

Ice-skating mostly takes place out in the distant suburbs, including the Macquarie Ice Rink, corner of Waterloo Rd and Herring Rd, North Ryde (☎02/9888 1100, ⓦ www.macquarieicerink.com.au; $20 for a 2hr session includes skate hire), 16km northwest of the city centre. Get there by train to Epping CityRail then bus #288, #611 or #630.

Horseriding

The vast expanse of **Centennial Park** holds extensive **horseriding** tracks, and people stable their horses at the Centennial Parklands Equestrian Centre at the southeast corner of the Fox Studios site, on the junction of Cook and Lang roads just through the Showground gate to Centennial Park. Several **stables** offer **rides**; you can just wander into the centre and enquire, or book in advance with one, such as Centennial Stables in Pavilion B (☎02/9360 5650, ⓦ www.centennialstables.com.au; 1hr escorted rides $95; 1hr lesson weekdays $95, weekends $125). There's more scenic horseriding in the Blue Mountains' Megalong Valley and in the Hunter Valley; for operators see p.301.

Abseiling, canyoning and climbing

For **thrill sports**, from abseiling to skydiving and aerobatic flights, contact Adrenalin (☎1300 791 793, ⓦ www.adrenalin.com.au). A popular spot for **hang-gliding** is Stanwell Park just south of the Royal National Park; the Sydney Hang Gliding Centre (☎02/4294 4294, ⓦ www.hanggliding.com.au) offers tandem flights with an instructor for $195 during the week, $220 at weekends or courses from $275 per day.

See the Blue Mountains chapter for operators offering **abseiling** and **canyoning** trips. Sydney's best **indoor climbing centre** is 6km southwest of the city centre, near Newton: Sydney Indoor Climbing Gym, Unit 4C, 1 Unwins Bridge Rd, St Peters (Mon–Wed & Fri 9.30am–10pm, Thurs 9.30am–11pm, Sat & Sun 9.30am–9pm; ☎02/9519 3325, ⓦ www.indoorclimbing .com.au; St Peters CityRail; casual entry $16, harness, shoes and chalk bag rental $10).

Gyms

Most **gyms** charge between $15 and $22 for a casual visit, which applies all day, and includes access to aerobics and even yoga classes. In their quest for new members, many gyms have a no-obligation free introductory offer (anything from a day to a week), which provides a cheeky way for travellers to do the rounds and get fit for free. Several gyms are reviewed in the "Gay Sydney" chapter, with the (nearly) 24-hour City Gym (see p.231) recommended. Many swimming pools also have gyms, and with a swim usually thrown in, the rates are much more reasonable (see p.268). Hiscoe's Fitness Centre (p.264), also has a gym.

Yoga

Yoga is popular in Sydney. Most gyms organize classes, costing around $16–20 (see above), and you can find both schools and teachers near where you're staying from the excellent ⓦ www.findyoga.com.au, which also includes retreats and events in all sorts of yoga styles. Their **Yoga Pass** (5 classes for $60 over 6 months or 10 classes for $100 over 12 months) is great value if you're in Australia for a while, and gives access to over 200 yoga schools around the country. The website also details community-based classes, where a $5–10 "donation" is the norm. The following three dedicated **yoga schools** allow casual visits.

Dharma Shala 108 Brighton Boulevard, Bondi ☎ 02/9365 5033, ⓦ www.dharmashala.com.au. Bus #333 or #380 from Bondi Junction CityRail. Predominantly flowing hatha yoga with classical postures, meditation and chanting, close to Bondi Beach. Also free group chanting on the last Sun of each month at 5.30pm, and frequent retreats about 3hr south of Sydney. Casual $17; 10 classes $150.

Samadhi Yoga The Gallery, 36 Lennox St, Newtown (Newtown CityRail) ☎ 02/9517 3280, ⓦ www.samadhiyoga.com.au. Popular school practicing a flowing style of hatha yoga and often hosting international guest teachers and workshops. Lots of well-patronized weekday classes for $6.

Yoga Synergy 115 Bronte Rd, Bondi Junction; Bondi Junction CityRail; and 196 Australia St, Newtown; Newtown CityRail; ☎ 02/9389 7399, ⓦ www.yogasynergy.com.au. The directors here are also physiotherapists: the yoga taught is a synthesis between hatha yoga and modern medical science. Classes 1hr 30min, beginners to advanced; $20.

Dance classes

The prestigious Sydney Dance Company, Pier 4, Hickson Rd, Millers Point (☎ 02/9221 4811, ⓦ www.sydneydancecompany.com; Circular Quay CityRail), holds day and evening open **dance** classes at their waterfront studios on an atmospheric converted wharf. Just turn up for an $18 casual class, ranging from funk, jazz and hip-hop, through contemporary to ballet.

Out of the City

The City

21

The Hawkesbury River and the Central Coast

N orth of Sydney, the Hawkesbury River widens and slows as it approaches the South Pacific, joining **Berowra Creek**, Cowan Creek, Pittwater and Brisbane Water in the system of flooded valleys that form the jagged jaws of the aptly named **Broken Bay**. The bay and its surrounding inlets are a haven for anglers, sailors and windsurfers, while the entire area is surrounded by bush, with the huge spaces of the **Ku-Ring-Gai Chase National Park** in the south and the **Brisbane Waters National Park** in the north. Beyond Broken Bay, the **Central Coast** between Gosford and Newcastle is an ideal spot for fishing, sailing and lazing around.

The **Pacific Highway** up here, partly supplanted by the **Sydney–Newcastle Freeway**, is fast and efficient, though not particularly attractive until you approach Ku-Ring-Gai Chase; if you want to detour into the park or towards Brooklyn on the Hawkesbury River, don't take the freeway. The **rail** lines follow the road almost as far as Broken Bay, before they take a scenic diversion through Brooklyn and Brisbane Waters to Woy Woy and Gosford.

Ku-Ring-Gai Chase National Park

Much the best known of New South Wales' national parks, **Ku-Ring-Gai Chase** (daily sunrise–sunset; $11 per vehicle per day) is also, with the Pacific Highway running all the way up one side, the easiest to get to. The bushland scenery is crisscrossed by walking tracks, which you can explore to seek out Aboriginal rock paintings, or just to get away from it all and see the forest and its wildlife. Only 24km north of the city centre, the huge park's unspoiled beauty is enhanced by the presence of water on three sides: the Hawkesbury, its inlet Cowan Creek, and the expanse of **Pittwater**, an inlet of Broken Bay. With access from several sides, but few roads linking within the park, it's easiest to pick one section to explore.

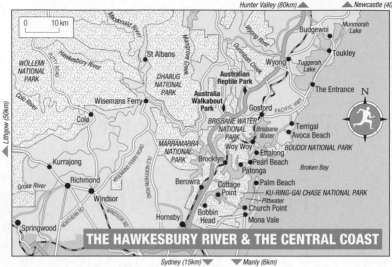

Hunter Valley (80km) ▲   ▲ Newcastle (40km)

Sydney (15km) ▼   ▼ Manly (6km)

THE HAWKESBURY RIVER & THE CENTRAL COAST

Pittwater and Scotland Island

The northeastern corner of Ku-Ring-Gai Chase National Park is accessed along West Head Road which leads to West Head, jutting out into Broken Bay and marking the entrance to **Pittwater**, a deep ten-kilometre-long sheltered waterway. Superb views from here look across to Barrenjoey Head and Barrenjoey Lighthouse at Palm Beach on the eastern shore of Pittwater. From West Head, the **Garigal Aboriginal Heritage Walk** (3.5km loop; 2–3hr) leads past a rock-engraving site, the most accessible Aboriginal art in the park.

Without your own transport, it's more rewarding to explore the Pittwater and eastern Ku-Ring-Gai by **ferry**, which provides access to a couple of great places to stay. The only place to **camp** is *The Basin* ($14 per person; bookings ☎02/9974 1011, ⓦwww.basincampground.com.au) on Pittwater, reached via the Palm Beach Ferry Service. Facilities at the site are minimal, so bring everything with you. If you want to stay in the park in rather more comfort, head for one of New South Wales' most scenically sited hostels, the very popular *Pittwater YHA* (☎02/9999 5748, ⓔpittwater@yhansw.org.au; dorms $28, rooms $72; bookings essential and well in advance for weekends). A rambling old house overlooking the water (kayaks available), it's surrounded by spectacular bush walks, and can be accessed by regular **ferries** from Church Point Wharf (15min; $12.50 return; last departure Mon–Fri 7pm. Sat & Sun 6.30pm; ☎02/9999 3492, ⓦwww.churchpointferryservice.com), or water taxi (free-phone at the wharf), alighting at Halls Wharf and walking 15 minutes up the hill. Bring supplies with you – the last food (and bottle) shop is at Church Point.

Two direct **buses** run to Church Point: #E86 from Central Station (Mon–Fri only) or #156 from Manly Wharf. The Church Point–Halls Wharf ferry also calls frequently at the bush-clad and residential **Scotland Island**, at the southern end of Pittwater. The island has no sealed roads or shops, just a school, a kindergarten and a bush-fire brigade, and makes for an interesting wander.

Bobbin Head

Ku-Ring-Gai Chase National Park's best-loved picnic spot, **Bobbin Head**, 6km east of the Sydney–Newcastle Freeway, is essentially just a colourful marina with a café, a picnic area and visitor centre beside Cowan Creek. Driving in from the freeway, you'll pass the volunteer-run **Kalkari Discovery Centre**, Ku-Ring-Gai Chase Road (daily 9am–5pm; ℡02/9472 9300, ⓦwww.environment.nsw.gov .au), where you can watch videos about the area's Aboriginal heritage and stroll around a short nature trail spotting kangaroos and brush turkeys.

Some 3km on, at Bobbin Head itself, the NPWS **Bobbin Head Information Centre** (daily 10am–4pm; ℡02/9472 8949) can give you details of local trails like the **Birrawanna Track**, immediately behind, which loops though the gum forest and back (2km loop), and the steep uphill hike to the Kalkari Discovery Centre (2.5km one-way; 180m ascent). From the picnic area near the Information Centre, the **Mangrove Boardwalk** (10min return) pleasantly traces the water's edge past thousands of bright red crabs. It continues as the **Gibberagong Track** (additional 20min return) through a small sandstone canyon to some Aboriginal rock art featuring figures and axe-grinding grooves.

You can also access Bobbin Head by **cruise** from Palm Beach with Palm Beach and Hawkesbury River Cruises (ⓦwww.sydneysceniccruises.com), though you only get an hour for lunch at Bobbin Head.

The Hawkesbury River

One of New South Wales' prettiest rivers, lined with sandstone cliffs and bush-covered banks for much of its course and with some interesting old settlements alongside, the **Hawkesbury River** (ⓦwww.hawkesburyaustralia .com.au) has its source in the Great Dividing Range and flows out to sea at Broken Bay. Indeed, it's navigable up to 100km inland, as far as the foothills of the Blue Mountains.

Exploring the Hawkesbury River system

If time is short, the best way to explore the Hawkesbury River is with the *Riverboat Postman* (see p.278) or a paddlewheeler from Windsor (see p.280), but there are a number of other useful cruises, and boat rentals. **Gosford's** Public Wharf is the starting point for the *MV Lady Kendall II* (℡02/4323 1655, ⓦwww.starshipcruises.com.au), which cruises both Brisbane Water and Broken Bay (daily except Thurs & Fri, daily during school hols, 10.15am & 1pm; 2hr 30min; $27; bookings essential; licensed kiosk on board).

Boat and houseboat rentals
Barrenjoey Boating Services at Governor Phillip Park, Palm Beach (℡02/9974 4229, ⓦwww.barrenjoeyboathire.com), hires out boats that comfortably seat six people (2hr for $60, 4hr $80, 8hr $130) and are perfect for fishing expeditions around the mouth of the Hawkesbury or Dangar Island. Barrenjoey Boating also has a fishing shop that sells bait supplies and hires out rods. Otherwise, if you're keen to fish and can get four people together, you can charter a boat, including all the gear and bait, plus a skipper who knows exactly where to go, from Fishabout Tours (℡02/9451 5420; $175 per person; 7hr), who have a great reputation on the Hawkesbury. **Houseboats** can be good value if you can assemble a group; prices start from $700 for a weekend and $1200 for a week for four people. Try Able Hawkesbury River Houseboats, on River Road in Wisemans Ferry (℡1800 024 979, ⓦwww.hawkesburyhouseboats.com.au), or Ripples Houseboats, 87 Brooklyn Rd, Brooklyn (℡02/9985 5534, ⓦwww.ripples .com.au).

▲ Picnic beside the Hawkesbury River

For information about the many national parks along the river, contact the NPWS (Sydney ☎02/9995 5000; Richmond ☎02/4588 5247; Ⓦwww .environment.nsw.gov.au). Short of chartering your own boat (see box, p.277), the best way to explore the river system is to take a cruise with the *Riverboat Postman*.

Brooklyn and the Riverboat Postman

For a brief taste of the bucolic pleasures of the Hawkesbury River, turn east off the Sydney–Newcastle Freeway to **Brooklyn**, 40km north of Sydney, a small riverside community made more important by the presence of the Hawkesbury River train station. Here the train line crosses the Hawkesbury on a causeway and bridge, an image immediately familiar if you've seen the movie *The Oyster Farmer*, which was set on the banks of the Hawkesbury.

The main reason to stop is to ride the Hawkesbury River Ferries' **Riverboat Postman** (Mon–Fri 9.30am excluding public hols; $50; booking essential on ☎02/9985 7566, Ⓦwww.hawkesburyriverferries.com.au), which still takes letters, as well as tourists, up and down the river on a four-hour cruise, including morning tea. Boats leave from Brooklyn Wharf on Dangar Road, about 50 metres from the train station. A connecting CountryLink train leaves Sydney's Central Station at 8.15am.

Brooklyn is also home base for houseboat rentals (see box, p.277), and has a few places to **eat**. For good, modestly priced seafood and water views go for *Leah's Alfresco*, on the wharf, who do half a dozen oysters for $12 and a plate of fish, chips and salad for $15.

Upstream: Wisemans Ferry and around

The first ferry across the Hawkesbury River was opened by ex-convict Solomon Wiseman in 1827, ten years after he was granted 200 acres of river frontage at the spot now known as **WISEMANS FERRY**. The crossing forged an inland connection between Sydney and the Hunter Valley via the convict-built Great

North Road. Unfortunately, travellers on this isolated route were easy prey for marauding bushrangers, and it was largely abandoned for the longer but safer coastal route. Today Wisemans Ferry is a large village with a post office, a handful of places to stay and eat, and a free 24-hour car **ferry** that runs every few minutes. Just a little over an hour from Sydney by car, it's a popular recreational spot for day-trippers, particularly water skiers and those keen to explore the **Dharug National Park** on the north side of the river. Dharug's rugged sandstone cliffs and gullies shelter Aboriginal rock engravings that can be visited only on ranger-led trips during school holidays; there's a **camping** area at *Mill Creek*, 8km east of Wiseman's Ferry ($10 per adult; book on ☎02/4320 4203 for summer weekends and hols).

One of the park's most interesting features, the **Old Great North Road**, (ⓦ www.environment.nsw.gov.au/nswcultureheritage/TheOldGreatNorthRoad .htm), was literally carved out of the rock by up to 700 convicts from 1826 to 1836. Planned as the 264km main route from Sydney to the Hunter Valley, it soon lost favour to coastal shipping and was abandoned almost before it was completed. The 43km section from Wiseman's Ferry north to Bucketty (and well away from any other roads) is the best preserved, with beautiful convict-built stonework and the oldest stone bridges on the Australian mainland. Open to walkers, cyclists and horse-riders but not vehicles, the route can be walked in one moderate and one long day, with camping en route at the Ten Mile Hollow, and at the end at Mogo Creek (both free; no guaranteed water).

Also on the north side of the ferry, a scenic 19km river drive leads north along Settlers Road, another convict-built route, to **St Albans**, where you can partake of a cooling brew (or stay a while) at a pub built in 1836, the sandstone-hewn *Settlers Arms Inn* (☎02/4568 2111, ⓦ www.settlersarms.com.au; en-suite rooms Sun–Fri $130, Sat $150). The pub is set on 2.5 acres, and many of the vegetables and herbs for its delicious home-cooked food are organically grown on site (lunch daily, dinner Fri–Sun).

Accommodation and eating

The settlement of Wisemans Ferry was based around Wiseman's home, Cobham Hall, built in 1826. Much of the original building still exists in the cream-painted *Wisemans Ferry Inn*, 1 Old Northern Rd (☎02/4566 4301, ⓦ www .wisemansinnhotel.com.au; pub $75, motel $75), with unglamorous but characterful, shared-bath **rooms** upstairs, and aging and poky en-suite motel-style rooms outside at the back. Acceptable bistro meals are served daily on a vast deck with distant river views, and there's live entertainment on Sunday afternoons. Just across the road, with extensive grounds fronting onto the river, the contrastingly modern *Retreat at Wisemans* (☎02/4566 4422, ⓦ www.wisemans.com.au; B&B $160 midweek, $240 weekend), is a 54-room resort with upmarket motel-style rooms. The location is superbly scenic and facilities include a restaurant, golf course, tennis courts, swimming pool and in-house masseuse. Other local accommodation includes the *Del Rio Riverside Resort* (☎02/4566 4330, ⓦ www .delrioresort.com.au; camping $25–35 per site, studio cabins $90–120, water-view villas $170–260), a **campsite** in Webbs Creek across the Webbs Creek car ferry, 3km south of Wisemans Ferry; facilities include a bistro, swimming pool, tennis court and golf course.

The Upper Hawkesbury: Windsor and beyond

About 50km inland from Sydney and just a few kilometres apart, Windsor and Richmond are two of five towns founded by Governor Macquarie early in the nineteenth century to capitalize on the fertile, well-watered soil of the Upper

Driving via the Hawkesbury River area from Sydney makes a very scenic way to get to the Blue Mountains via the Bells Line of Road or Hawkesbury Road, and to the Hunter Valley via Putty Road.

From Windsor, **Putty Road** (Route 69) heads north through beautiful forest country, along the eastern edge of the Wollemi National Park, to Singleton in the Hunter Valley.

From Richmond, the **Bells Line of Road** (Route 40) heads northwest through Kurrajong to Lithgow (see p.311). It follows a beautiful route through the Blue Mountains originally discovered in 1823 by a 19-year-old Richmond local, Archibald Bell Jr; fruit stalls all along the way are stacked with produce from the valley. There's a wonderful view of the Upper Hawkesbury Valley from the lookout point at **Kurrajong Heights**, on the edge of the mountains.

Another scenic drive from Richmond to the Blue Mountains, emerging near Springwood (see p.301), is south along the **Hawkesbury Road**, with the **Hawkesbury Heights Lookout** halfway along providing panoramic views. Not far from the lookout, the modern solar-powered *Hawkesbury Heights YHA* (☎02/4754 5621; dorm beds $24–27), offers more views from its secluded bush setting.

Hawkesbury River area. Both are reached easily by train from Central Station via Blacktown.

Windsor is probably the best preserved of all the historic Hawkesbury towns, with a lively centre of narrow streets, spacious old pubs and numerous historic colonial buildings. It's terrifically popular on Sundays, when a **market** takes over the shady, tree-lined mall end of the main drag, George Street, and the *Macquarie Arms Hotel*, which claims to be the oldest pub on the Australian mainland, puts on live music – raucous rock'n'roll to befit the crowd of bikers and assorted cliques crowding the front veranda – on Thompson Square, the grassy village green opposite. Around the corner from the pub, the **Hawkesbury Regional Museum and Tourist Information Centre** (Mon–Fri 10am–4pm, Sat–Sun 10am–3pm; free; ☎02/4560 4655, ⓦwww .visitnsw.com/town/Windsor) doles out local information. There are picnic tables along the river from where Hawkesbury Paddlewheeler (☎02/4575 1171, ⓦwww.paddlewheeler.com.au), runs a good-value Sunday afternoon Jazz Cruise: live jazz and a BBQ lunch for $35 (Sun 12.30–2.30pm; advance bookings essential).

Just seven kilometres northwest of Windsor, **Richmond**'s attractions include its unspoiled riverside setting, an old graveyard and settlers' dwellings. Cinema buffs could take in a bargain-priced film at the beautifully preserved Regent Twin Cinema, on the main road through town at 149 Windsor St (☎02/4578 1800, ⓦwww.richmondregent.com.au).

The Central Coast

The shoreline between Broken Bay and Newcastle, known as the **Central Coast**, is characterized by large **coastal lakes** – saltwater lagoons that are almost entirely enclosed, but connected to the ocean by small waterways. To travel anywhere on the Central Coast, you need to go through sprawling **GOSFORD**, near to which lie two excellent **national parks** – Brisbane Water and Bouddi – and a couple of wildlife attractions: the **Australia Walkabout Park** and the nearby **Australian Reptile Park**. Beyond the national parks, **Pearl Beach** and nearby **Patonga** are idyllic bay beach retreats, while on the ocean, **Avoca**, **Terrigal**, and **The Entrance** are all enjoyable holiday resorts.

For tourist information on the whole region, and accommodation bookings, contact **Central Coast Tourism** (☎1300 130 708, ⓦwww.cctourism.com.au).

Gosford and around

Perched on the north shore of Brisbane Water, **GOSFORD** is just about within commuting distance of Sydney. Hence its uncontrolled residential sprawl, which has put a great strain on the formerly unspoiled lakes nearby. While the area holds plenty of accommodation, there's little incentive to stay any longer in Gosford than it takes to visit **Central Coast Tourism**, near the train station at 200 Mann St (Mon–Fri 9.30am–4pm, Sat 9.30am–1.30pm; ☎1300 132 975, ⓦwww.cctourism.com.au), and the NPWS office, 207 Albany St, Gosford (☎02/4320 4203), which has details on local national parks.

Australia Walkabout Park

About 10km west of Gosford, **Australia Walkabout Park**, just off the F3 freeway at Peats Ridge Road, Calga (daily 9am–5pm; $22; ⓦwww.walkaboutpark.com .au), was set up by the former Federal Minister for the Environment, Barry Cohen, and his son in an attempt to save Australian wildlife from introduced species. Entry fees to the 170-acre site, with its huge range of native plants, birds and animals – including red-nicked pademelons, long-nosed bandicoots, sugar gliders, emus and much more – cover a knowledgeable guided tour along its 2km of walking trails, passing Aboriginal rock engravings.

Australian Reptile Park

Also just off the Pacific Highway, around 5km west of Gosford, the privately run **Australian Reptile Park** (daily 9am–5pm; $22.50; ⓦwww.reptilepark .com.au) has a long history of providing snake and funnel-web spider venom for the nation's stock of anti-venins. You can see some of the snakes and watch the funnel-web being milked (daily 9.45am). Ranged around a lake filled with American alligators and a picnic area populated by four species of kangaroos that you can pat and feed, the park has a good selection of native reptiles, many of

Transport on the coast

If you're **driving**, and want to enjoy the coastal scenery and lakes, follow the older Pacific Highway, which heads to Newcastle via Gosford and Wyong, rather than the speedier Sydney–Newcastle Freeway that runs some way inland. The frequent **train** service from Central Station (Country Trains) to Gosford or Woy Woy also follows a very picturesque route. Aussie Shuttles (see "Airport Buses" box, p.25) gets you to the area direct from Sydney airport.

The fit and intrepid can get here by **bike**: from Manly, head up the northern beaches and hop on a ferry from Palm Beach (see p.145) to **Ettalong** (departs Palm Beach 8–10 daily; $9.10 each way; ☎02/9974 2411, ⓦwww.palmbeachferry.com.au), then continue up through Woy Woy and Gosford to the coast.

You can also reach **Patonga** by **ferry** with Palm Beach and Hawkesbury River Ferries (☎041/446 6635, ⓦwww.sydneysceniccruises.com), departing from Palm Beach daily at 11am (also 9am & 3.45pm hols & weekends) and returning from Patonga at 4.15pm (also 9.30am & 3pm hols & weekends); Hawkesbury River Ferries (see p.278) also run a service between Brooklyn and Patonga Beach. Walkers can alight from the ferry and hike to Pearl Beach (see p.282), a walk of 3km.

Within the Central Coast area, a well-developed **bus service** is mostly run by Busways (☎02/4368 2277, ⓦwww.busways.com.au) and Red Bus Services (☎02/ 4332 8655, ⓦwww.redbus.com.au). For **taxis**, call Central Coast Taxis ☎13 1008.

which you would be lucky to spot in the wild. Elvis, the largest saltwater crocodile in NSW; Leonardo, a hefty turtle found in a Sydney sewer; and the Perentie lizard of central Australia are highlights. Regular reptile shows and talks take place throughout the day, including giant Galapagos tortoise feeding (daily 10.45am), alligator feeding (Sat & Sun noon), and a crocodile show (Sat & Sun 1.30pm) featuring Elvis. Come also for displays of other native mammals including koalas, wombats and Tasmanian devils that are bred here. Juveniles are visible all year, but they first emerge from their mothers' pouches just before Christmas.

Brisbane Waters and Bouddi national parks

Brisbane Waters National Park ($7 per vehicle), immediately south of Gosford, is the site of the **Bulgandry Aboriginal engravings**, in a style unique to the Sydney region, with figurative outlines scratched boldly into sandstone. The site, no longer frequented by the Guringgai people – whose territory ranged south as far as Sydney Harbour and north to Lake Macquarie – is 7km southwest of Gosford off the Woy Woy Road.

Tiny **Bouddi National Park** ($7 per vehicle) lies 20km southeast along the coast, at the mouth of Broken Bay, and is a great spot for bushwalking, with **camping** facilities at: the popular, drive-in *Putty Beach* ($14 per person), which has flush toilets and gas barbecues but no power; *Little Beach* ($14) which requires a 750m walk from the car park and has gas barbecues and composting toilets; and *Tallow Beach* ($10) which requires a 1.2km walk and has composting toilets and no water. All can be booked through the NPWS office in Gosford.

Pearl Beach and Patonga

Surrounded by Brisbane Waters National Park, friendly, undeveloped **PEARL BEACH**, just over 25km south of Gosford via Woy Woy and Umina, is a small community that expands at weekends. The very pretty, sheltered beach is popular with families, and has a relaxing (if somewhat dilapidated) open-access saltwater pool at the south end. Commerce is clustered nearby with the casual *Pearl Beach General Store and Café* and the classy *Pearls on the Beach*, 1 Tourmaline Ave (Thurs–Sun noon–3pm & 6–9pm; licensed and BYO; bookings ☏02/4342 4400, ⓦwww.pearlsonthebeach.com.au) which serves contemporary Australian cuisine at around $35 a main course. It's one of the best restaurants on the Central Coast, and eating at a veranda table overlooking the beach can be delightful. The only **accommodation** is in holiday houses, rented through the local real estate agent (☏02/4341 7555, ⓦwww.pearlbeachrealestate.com.au; from $900 per week in peak season).

The neighbouring beach settlement of **PATONGA** (with its ferry from Palm Beach) is 7km away by road, but a path through the bush (3km one-way; 45–60min), from the end of Crystal Avenue, makes a much more pleasant link with views over Broken Bay and over Pearl Beach's Crommelin Native Arboretum. Patonga itself is just a general store and fish'n'chip shop.

To get to Pearl Beach or Patonga, take the Busways Peninsula bus #50 or #52 (☏02/4392 6666) from Woy Woy station, or the ferry to Patonga from Palm Beach or Brooklyn (see p.278).

Avoca Beach

Fifteen kilometres east of Gosford, laid-back **AVOCA BEACH** is especially popular with surfers. A large, crescent-shaped and sandy beach between two headlands, it has its own surf life-saving club at the south end with a safe children's rock pool right outside. West of the beach are the still waters of **Avoca Lake**. Avoca's pleasant small-town atmosphere is enhanced by the Avoca Beach

Picture Theatre (⊛www.avocabeachpicturetheatre.com.au), a little-changed early-1950s cinema near the surf club on Avoca Drive. You can **learn to surf** with Central Coast Surf School, 14 Pozieres Ave, Umina (1hr lesson $25; ☎0417 673 277, ⊛www.centralcoastsurfschool.com.au), who offer $40 group lessons and rent boards for $30 per half-day. Aquafun, by the bridge in Heazlett Park (☎0413/808 394, ⊛www.aquafun.net.au) charge a single fee ($15 for 1hr plus $4 each extra 30min) for combined use of pedal boats, kayaks and surf skis, plus a little more if you want to use their double kayaks and waterbikes.

To get to Avoca, take Busways #65 or #69 from Gosford or #69 from Terrigal.

Accommodation and eating

Limited overnight **accommodation** in Avoca includes the self-contained cabins and villas of *The Palms*, Carolina Park, off the Round Drive (☎02/4382 1227, ⊛www.palmsavoca.com.au; villa sleeping four $185–205), an upmarket, family-oriented holiday resort with garden-set swimming pools, spa, and games room. There's a similar approach at *Treetops Resort Avoca Beach* (☎02/4382 2322, ⊛www.treetopsavocabeach.com.au; rooms $110, villas $165) set amid bush, with pool, tennis court and villas with full kitchen and laundry, plus some simpler rooms.

For **eating**, grab fish'n'chips, gourmet and veggie burgers, or Turkish-bread sandwiches from the groovy, colourful *Burger Girls*, at the end of the main set of shops at 168 Avoca Drive (Mon–Wed 9am–3pm, Thurs–Sun 9am–8pm). Alternatively, head to the south end of the beach for the classy *Blue Bar and Restaurant*, 85 Avoca Rd, near the surf club (☎02/4381 0707; daily noon–3pm & 6–9pm), with fabulous sea views and a contemporary menu strong on seafood (mains $25–40). The licensed *Point Café*, next to the surf club, serves simpler food at tables almost on the beach.

Terrigal

Eight kilometres by road north of Avoca Beach, beautiful **TERRIGAL** comes backed by bush-covered hills. One of the liveliest spots on the Central Coast, it's a thriving beach resort with a strong café culture. The big curve of beach has a picturesque sandstone headland, and the sheltered eastern end, the Haven, where the boats moor, is popular with families. With rocketing house prices all along the Central Coast, Terrigal's main street has been invaded by real estate agents and the town has taken a decidedly upmarket turn, helped along by the pink, hulking presence of the enormous five-star *Crowne Plaza Hotel* at the southern end of **The Esplanade**. With its grand marble lobby, pricey boutiques, three restaurants, two bars, nightclub, pool, gym and tennis courts, the hotel is the centre of this small town's social life.

Terrigal is a popular spot for **water-based activities**. Operators include Central Coast Charters (☎0488/123 474, ⊛www.centralcoastcharters.net; ocean and river cruises, deep-sea and game fishing); Central Coast Surf School (☎0417/673 277, ⊛www.centralcoastsurfschool.com.au); and the long-running, well-respected Terrigal Dive Centre (☎02/4384 1219, ⊛www.terrigaldive.com.au; five-day diving courses $385, two boat dives $90 plus gear rental).

To get to Terrigal, take Busways #67 or #68 from Gosford; #69 links Terrigal to Avoca Beach (see above).

Accommodation and eating

Accommodation is limited: try the swanky *Crowne Plaza Hotel Terrigal*, Pine Tree Lane (☎02/4384 9111, ⊛www.crowneplaza.com; $230), or *Tiarri Terrigal Beach*, a boutique motel at 16 Tiarri Crescent (☎02/4384 1423, ⊛tiarriterrigal.com.au; queen rooms from $125, spa suites from $150).

Plenty of places to **eat and drink** lie within a couple of blocks of the *Crowne Plaza*, which itself has a typically packed beer garden – the *Florida Beach Bar* – and the posh *Lord Ashley Lounge* upstairs. The best fish'n'chips are from *The Snapper Spot*, 108 The Esplanade, where you can sit on the few tables outside or take your haul across the road to the beach. A block back from the beach, the cheap and cheerful *N Thai Sing*, 18 Church St (☎02/4385 9800) is the best of several Thai places, while the *Hungry Wolf*, 88 The Esplanade, serves the best pizza in town. A few hundred metres south, beside Dive Terrigal, you'll find sister restaurants. Upstairs, *The Reef* (☎02/4385 3222; Tues–Sat noon–2pm & 6.30–9pm) offers some of the finest dining in town with an Asian-influenced modern Australia menu (mains $30–35) and great sea views. The vistas are just as good from the relaxed café, *Cove*, downstairs, where breakfasts are a particular speciality.

The Entrance

Further north, Tuggerah and Munmorah lakes meet the sea at **THE ENTRANCE**, a beautiful place where water extends as far as the eye can see. It's a favourite fishing spot with anglers – and with swarms of **pelicans**, which turn up for the afternoon fish-feeds (daily 3.30pm; free) at Memorial Park, near the visitor centre (see below).

The beaches and lakes along the coast from here to Newcastle are crowded with caravan parks, motels and outfits offering the opportunity to fish, windsurf, sail or waterski; although less attractive than places further north, they make a great day-trip or weekend escape from Sydney. Pro Dive Central Coast, 163 Wyong Rd, Killarney Vale (☎02/4389 3483, ⓦwww.prodivecentralcoast .com.au), arranges **scuba-diving** lessons and daily boat dives, and rents out snorkelling and dive gear.

The **Entrance Visitors Centre**, on Marine Parade (daily 9am–5pm; ☎1300 132 975, ⓦwww.cctourism.com.au), offers a free **accommodation** booking service. Several workaday places to eat are located around the park next to the visitor centre, including the cheery *Mojo's Café*.

Get to The Entrance **by bus**, use Red Bus Services #21, #22 or #23 from Gosford station; or #24, #25, or #26 from Tuggerah or Wyong train stations.

The Hunter Valley

N ew South Wales' best-known wine region is the **Hunter Valley**, an area long synonymous with fine **wine** – in particular its golden, citrusy **semillon** and soft and earthy **shiraz**. In recent years the region has become equally synonymous with culture. Visitors are treated to some of the best Australia has to offer in fine dinning restaurants, gourmet delis, arts and crafts, and outdoor events and festivals featuring delectable foods, high-profile jazz, opera and theatre performances and sell-out shows by international acts like Alicia Keys and Leonard Cohen.

While South Australian wines dominate the nation in terms of volume and popularity, the wineries of the Hunter Valley are mainly boutique operations, where many of the wines offered for tasting can only be bought at the cellar door or through wine clubs. The first vines were planted in 1828, and some of the area's current wine-making families, such as the Draytons, date back to the 1850s. In what seems a bizarre juxtaposition, this is also a very important **coal-mining region**: in the **Upper Hunter Valley**, especially, the two often go hand-in-hand, but there's a big cultural divide between "the mineries" and "the wineries", as the locals put it. By far the best-known wine area is the **Lower Hunter Valley**, nestled under the picturesque **Brokenback Range**, which fans north from the main town of **Cessnock** and centres beneath the wine-tasting area of **Pokolbin**.

Pokolbin, however, can seem a little like an exhausting winery theme park. To experience the real appeal of the Hunter Valley wine country – stone and timber cottages surrounded by vast vineyards somehow lost among forested ridges, red-soiled dirt tracks and paddocks with grazing cattle – explore the region's periphery. Take the scenic, winding, Wollombi Road to the charming historic Aussie town of **Wollombi**, 28km southwest of Cessnock; or follow the Lovedale/Wilderness Road area, to the northeast and the unspoiled **Upper Hunter**, west of Muswellbrook, with its marvellous ridges and rocky outcrops. A number of alternative activities can spice up your stay nicely – for information on gaining a bird's-eye perspective, bonding with beasts or working on your golf swing, see p.288.

The Lower Hunter

CESSNOCK, two hours' drive north of Sydney, makes a depressingly unattractive introduction to the salubrious wine culture surrounding it. Its big old country pubs are probably its best feature; for a real taste of Australian rural life, past and present, you might even consider staying in one. Most

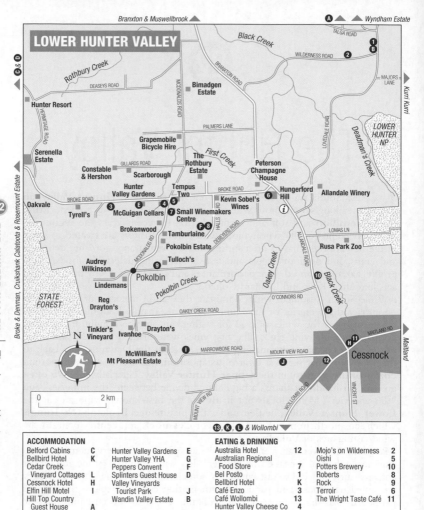

LOWER HUNTER VALLEY

Branxton & Muswellbrook
Wyndham Estate
Black Creek
Rothbury Creek
TALGA ROAD
WILDERNESS ROAD
DEASEYS ROAD
MAJORS LANE
Kurri Kurri
Hunter Resort
HERMITAGE ROAD
Bimadgen Estate
BRANXTON ROAD
McDONALDS ROAD
PALMERS LANE
LOWER HUNTER NP
Deadman's Creek
Serenella Estate
Grapemobile Bicycle Hire
First Creek
The Rothbury Estate
GILLARDS ROAD
Peterson Champagne House
LOVEDALE ROAD
Constable & Hershon
Scarborough
Hunter Valley Gardens
Tempus Two
BROKE ROAD
Hungerford Hill
Allandale Winery
Oakvale
BROKE ROAD
Kevin Sobel's Wines
Tyrell's
McGuigan Cellars
Small Winemakers Centre
HALLS ROAD
DEBEYNS ROAD
LOMAS LN
ALLANDALE ROAD
Brokenwood
McDONALDS RD
Tamburlaine
Rusa Park Zoo
Audrey Wilkinson
Pokolbin Estate
Tulloch's
Lindemans
Pokolbin
Pokolbin Creek
Oakey Creek
Black Creek
STATE FOREST
Reg Drayton's
O'CONNORS RD
OAKEY CREEK ROAD
MAITLAND RD
Tinkler's Vineyard
Ivanhoe
Drayton's
Cessnock
N
McWilliam's Mt Pleasant Estate
MARROWBONE ROAD
MOUNT VIEW ROAD
VINCENT ST
MOUNT VIEW RD
WOLLOMBI ROAD
Maitland
Broke & Denman, Cruikshank Calabota & Rosemount Estate

0   2 km

Branxton & Wollombi

ACCOMMODATION		
Belford Cabins	C	
Bellbird Hotel	K	
Cedar Creek Vineyard Cottages	L	
Cessnock Hotel	H	
Elfin Hill Motel	I	
Hill Top Country Guest House	A	
Hunter Valley Gardens	E	
Hunter Valley YHA	G	
Peppers Convent	F	
Splinters Guest House	D	
Valley Vineyards Tourist Park	J	
Wandin Valley Estate	B	

EATING & DRINKING		
Australia Hotel	12	
Australian Regional Food Store	7	
Bel Posto	1	
Bellbird Hotel	K	
Café Enzo	3	
Café Wollombi	13	
Hunter Valley Cheese Co	4	
Mojo's on Wilderness	2	
Oishi	5	
Potters Brewery	10	
Roberts	8	
Rock	9	
Terroir	6	
The Wright Taste Café	11	

of the **wine-tasting** is around the area called **Pokolbin**, spread over three kilometres at the heart of the vineyards, 12–15km northwest of Cessnock, which holds some luxurious accommodation and a fine-dining scene – all very much appreciated by Sydneysiders up for a weekend pamper. Some extraordinary modern architecture stimulates the optic nerves, but it's not all pretty, and with its overabundance of B&Bs, resorts packed with cafés, restaurants and shops, and a huge number of wineries offering tours, tastings and courses, the area can be less than relaxing. While its main focus, the resort, shopping and dining complex known as the **Hunter Valley Gardens Village**, bears an unfortunate resemblance to an expensive retirement village, it does hold a handy general store, highly recommended cafés and restaurants, plus specialist outlets for books, gifts, homewares, chocolates, art, fashion and antiques. Flanking the village, the impressive sixty-acre, **Hunter Valley**

Gardens makes for pleasant meandering, and children will love the many fairytale characters displayed in its kitsch, but pleasing, Storybook Garden. For entertainment, nocturnal crowds and beer and wine-fuelled community, *Harrigan's* Irish pub, a vast complex, 500 metres west of the village, is usually the best option.

Information and events

Pick up the excellent free visitors guide, with a handy pull-out map, from the **Hunter Valley Wine Country Visitor Information Centre** on Wine Country Drive, Pokolbin (Mon–Sat 9am–5pm, Sun 9am–4pm; guides available outside after hours; ☎02/4990 0900, ⓦwww.winecountry.com.au), scenically sited among vineyards and home to the pleasant, affordable *Wine Country Café*. Try to tour the wineries during the week; at weekends both the number of visitors and accommodation prices go up, and it can get booked out completely when there's a concert on in the valley.

In late October, Wyndham Estate (see p.291) hosts the night-time **Opera in the Vineyards** (☎1800 675 875, ⓦwww.4di.com.au), followed a week later by a day of fine food, wine and music at **Jazz in the Vines** (☎02/4930 9190, ⓦwww.jazzinthevines.com.au; tickets $55–70) based at Tyrell's vineyard (see p.291). On multiple dates between November and February, Bimbadgen Estate holds **A Day on the Green**, featuring local and international performers (tickets through Ticketek; $105–129; ⓦwww.adayonthegreen.com.au). For information on numerous other events – like the Raggamuffin Reggae Festival (late Jan), Strings in the Winery (mid-Nov) and international acts performing at Tempus Two and Hope Estate wineries – visit ⓦwww.winecountry.com.au/events. Between early October and mid-January the Wollombi region hosts **Sculpture in the Vineyards**, in which surreal and innovative site-specific sculptures dazzle among the vineyards, valleys, dirt roads and bushy ridges of picturesque Wollombi's wineries.

Getting there

By car, the Lower Hunter Valley lies two hours north of Sydney along National Highway 1 (F3 Freeway). For a more scenic route, and eminently more pleasurable start to your stay, turn off the F3 to join Peats Ridge Rd, later taking a slight left into George Downes Drive and continuing on Great North Rd. Stop off at the pretty village of **Wollombi** (on the Hunter Valley regions periphery), admiring its nineteenth-century sandstone architecture and great Aussie tavern, before starting off with some of its local picturesque wineries. A meandering route from the Blue Mountains via **Putty Road** is also popular with motorcyclists. Rover Coaches (☎02/4990 1699, ⓦwww.rovercoaches.com.au) leave daily from Sydney Central Station, The Rocks and Chatswood to Cessnock and on to Pokolbin resorts. Cashed-up lovers of the fine life might consider arriving in style on a scenic amphibious seaplane flight from Sydney Harbour with Sydney Seaplanes (see p.119).

Tours and activities

Lots of **vineyard tours** are available. The excellent, long-established Hunter Valley Day Tours (☎02/4951 4574, ⓦwww.huntervalleydaytours.com.au) offers a wine-and-cheese tasting tour ($95 for Hunter Valley pick-ups; restaurant lunch included), with very informative commentary, while the family-run Hunter

Vineyard Tours (☎02/4991 1659, ⓦwww.huntervineyardtours.com.au) visits five wineries (Hunter Valley pick-up $60, Newcastle, Maitland or Wollombi $65; restaurant lunch $30 extra).

Also recommended are **Trek About 4WD Tours** (☎02/4990 8277, ⓦwww .hunterweb.com.au/trekabout; half-day $45; full day $55), and **Aussie Wine Tours** (☎0412/735 809, ⓦwww.aussiewinetours.com.au; $50), both supportive of small local wineries and flexible. Should you wish to discover the secrets of a different kind of beverage, visit *Potters Hotel & Brewery* on Wine Country Drive, Nulkaba (tours daily noon, 2pm & 4pm).

Otherwise, you can **rent bikes** from Grapemobile, on the corner of McDonalds Road and Palmers Lane, Pokolbin (☎02/0418 404 039, ⓦwww.grapemobile .com.au; $25 per day; bookings required; free delivery), or hire a **taxi** (Cessnock RadioCabs ☎02/4990 1111). The more extravagant can get around in horse coaches (☎0408/161 133, ⓦwww.pokolbinhorsecoaches.com.au), limousines (☎02/4984 7766, ⓦwww.huntervalleylimosines.com.au), or convertible Cadillacs (☎02/4996 4959, ⓦwww.cadillactours.com.au).

Less sophisticated, but thoroughly enjoyable, activities include sunrise hot-air **balloon rides** (ⓦwww.balloonaloft.com), **horse rides** (ⓦwww.Huntervalley horseriding.com.au), **helicopter** flights (ⓦwww.hunterwinehelicopters.com .au), aerobatic warbird, sport and vintage **aircraft** flights (ⓦwww.airaction.com .au), and **golf** (ⓦwww.thevintage.com.au). If you'd like to get close and personal with Australian wildlife, visit the **Hunter Valley Zoo** ($8–14; ⓦwww.huntervalley zoo.com.au), where you can picnic with adorable baby roos and emus.

Accommodation

Since the Hunter Valley is a popular weekend trip for Sydneysiders, accommodation **prices** rise on Friday and Saturday nights, and most places only offer two-night deals; the price ranges below indicate the substantial midweek to weekend variable. Advance **booking** is essential for weekends, or during the October–November events.

▲ Callatoota Estate, Hunter Valley

Belford Cabins 659 Hermitage Rd, Pokolbin
☎02/6574 7100, ⊛www.belfordcabins.com.au.
Family-run, fully equipped self-catering
two- and four-bedroom (6–12 person)
wooden bungalows set in bushland. Comfy,
spacious and clean cabins – renovated
ones are quite stylish – each with its own
barbecue. Games room with pool table,
table tennis and TV, outdoor pool and
playground. Good value midweek $100;
$35 each extra adult. Minimum four adults
on weekends $225.

Bellbird Hotel 388 Wollombi Rd, Bellbird,
5km southwest of Cessnock ☎02/4990 1094,
⊕4991 5475. Classic country pub, circa
1908, with wide iron-lace veranda and a
bar full of rustic charm. Check available
rooms as some are more charming than
others. Eat inexpensive no-frills bistro
food in the pleasant beer garden, which
has an adjacent playground. All rooms
share bathrooms. Midweek, light breakfast
included, $69; weekend $85.

Cedar Creek Vineyard Cottages
Wollombi Rd, Cedar Creek, 10km
northwest of Wollombi ☎02/4998 1576,
⊛www.cedarcreekcottages.com.au. An idyllic
choice away from the busy Pokolbin area
on a 550-acre deer- and cattle-stocked
farm. Run by the delightful Stonehurst
Wines, whose tiny chapel-like tasting
room, stocked with wine from insecticide-
free, handpicked, estate-grown grapes,
well illustrates the owner's philosophy.
Delightful self-catering cottages, for
couples or big groups, are made from
recycled timber with views over vineyards
and bush-clad mountainsides. Expect
queen-sized beds, wood combustion
stoves, ceiling fans and a/c, CD-players,
stylish decor, breakfast hampers and a
BBQ; civilized noon check-out. $149–189
for two, $40 per extra person.

Cessnock Hotel 234 Wollombi Rd, Cessnock
☎02/4990 1002, ⊛www.huntervalleyhotels.com
.au. Renovated pub with a great restaurant,
the *Wright Taste Cafe*. Rooms all share
bathrooms but they're huge with high
ceilings, fans and really comfy beds. Big
veranda to hang out on and cooked breakfasts served in the café. B&B $90.

Elfin Hill Motel Marrowbone Rd, Pokolbin
☎02/4998 7543, ⓔelfinhill@hunterlink
.com.au. Friendly, family-run hilltop motel
with comfortable timber-cabin-style a/c
units and extensive views – particularly

good value midweek. Facilities include
a pool, BBQ area and spacious, well-
furnished, glass-walled common room
with table tennis table and guest kitchen.
Rates include hearty continental breakfast.
$130–200.

Hill Top Country Guest House 288 Talga Rd,
Rothbury ☎02/4930 7111, ⊛www
.hilltopguesthouse.com.au. Rural retreat
on three hundred acres with nice views.
Explore the property on foot, by horse
or 4WD night wildlife safari ($90–290).
The modern brick building's interior has
the feel of an old-fashioned guesthouse,
with a piano, billiard table and wood fires.
Mock-antique-style bedrooms have TV.
Also a large unit with a spa. Light breakfast
included (lunch and dinner available).
Rooms $110–160, spa unit $154–220.

Hunter Valley Gardens Broke Rd, Pokolbin
☎02/4998 7854, ⊛www.hvg.com.au. Set in
extensive lakeside gardens, this resort has
a handy upmarket shopping mall complete
with cafés – including the recommended
Bliss Coffee Roasters – and restaurants.
The modern combined motel and hotel
complex overlooks the vineyards, and holds
a popular Irish pub and bistro, *Harrigan's*, a
fine-dining restaurant, *The Cellar,* a heated
pool, spa, sauna, tennis courts and three
standards of accommodation: pricey
72-room *Grand Mercure* ($169–239 B&B
midweek; weekend $239–399); smart four-
star motel-style behind *Harrigan's* (midweek
$220–385, weekend $660–960 for two
nights' minimum stay); or in self-contained
one- and two-bedroom cabins at *Grapeview
Villas* ($82–105).

Hunter Valley YHA 100 Wine Country Drive,
Nulkaba, ☎02/4991 3278. The obvious choice
for the budget traveller. A long single-storey
timber building with wrap-around balcony,
offering everything one would expect from
a YHA – communal kitchen, refrigerator,
laundry, TV/lounge area, plus a sauna and
swimming pool. Rental bicycles, plus cheap
tours to local vineyards and, for nightlife,
Potters Hotel and Brewery is only 400m
away. Multi-share rooms $26–32, doubles
$70–78, en suite $82–92.

Peppers Convent Halls Rd, Pokolbin
☎02/4998 7764, ⊛www.peppers.com.au.
The swankiest place to stay in the Hunter
Valley, with a price to match. The guesthouse, converted from an old nunnery, is
decidedly regal, with fireplaces, low beams

Nearly 150 wineries cluster around the Lower Hunter Valley, and fewer than twenty in the Upper Hunter; almost all offer **free wine tastings**. Virtually all wineries are open daily, at least between 10am and 4pm, and many offer **guided tours**. These include: McWilliams Mt Pleasant Estate, Marrowbone Rd, Pokolbin (daily 11am; $3.30; no bookings required); Hermitage Road Cellars, Hunter Resort, Hermitage Rd, Pokolbin (daily 11am & 2pm; $10; bookings ℡02/4998 7777); and Drayton's, Tyrell's, Wandin Valley and Wyndham Estate, all detailed below.

The Hunter Resort also runs a recommended **wine course** (daily 9–11am; $50; bookings essential) including a tour followed by a tasting instruction tutorial. Antique enthusiasts should check out the "Old Shop" museum at Oakvale (Broke Rd, Pokolbin), consisting of a slab cottage replicating a nineteenth-century general store – the cellar door here also sells a great selection of **wine-related books**.

Impressive new **state-of-the-art wineries** include the space-station-like **Hungerford Hill** (Broke Rd, Pokolbin ℡02/4998 7666), with its fine-dining restaurant *Terroir* (mains $39–59; degustation menu $110) and chic wine bar (evenings Wed–Sat) serving a light day menu (10am–5pm; $12–20). Enjoy fine panoramic **views** at Audrey Wilkinson (Debeyers Rd, Pokolbin) and Tinklers Vineyard (see p.292), from where you can continue to the Pokolbin Mountains Lookout. The award-winning Pepper Tree Wines, Halls Rd, Pokolbin, with its French-rustic feel, has beautiful **gardens**. Below are a few more of our favourites, but by meandering you'll inevitably discover your own gems.

Allandale Lovedale Rd, Pokolbin. Picturesque, medium-sized winery established in 1978. Set on a hill, with great views overlooking the vineyard and the Brokenback Range. All their wines are highly recommended but make sure you try the prize-winning chardonnay. Mon–Sat 9am–5pm, Sun 10am–5pm.

Constable Estate Vineyards Gillards Rd, Pokolbin. Established in 1981 by two best friends, this small establishment feels like a personal dream come true (wine is made by contract winemaker Neil McGuigan; the owners visit on annual holiday from England). The vineyard under the Brokenback Ranges has five formal gardens – Sculpture, Camellia, Rose, Herb and Secret – and you're encouraged to wander around with a glass of semillon; or at 10.30am the gardener leads a tour. Unhurried sit-down tastings. Daily 10am–5pm.

Cruikshank Callatoota Estate Wybong Rd, Wybong, Upper Hunter Valley, 18km north of Denman. Owner John Cruikshank has been making red wine here since 1974. All grapes are estate-grown and everything is in-house, including the bottling. The slow pace and unpretentious cellar door suits the remote feel of the place whose vineyards nestle below bush-covered ridges. BBQ and picnic facilities, or light lunch available. Daily 9am–5pm.

Drayton's Family Wines Oakey Creek Rd, Pokolbin. Friendly, down-to-earth winery, established in 1853. Everything is still here and the excellent free tours (Mon–Fri

and luxurious rooms, and is part of the Pepper Tree Winery (see box above), with fine-dining at *Roberts* restaurant (see p.293) just a stroll away. Midweek $396, weekend $849 for two nights' minimum stay.
Splinters Guest House 617 Hermitage Rd, Pokolbin ℡02/6574 7118, @ www.splinters.com.au. The mezzanine-bedroomed cottages on this 10-acre property come with slate floors, wood-combustion stoves, leather armchairs and kitchens

with coffee machines (cook-your-own breakfast supplied). En-suite rooms have mini espresso machines (light breakfast included); port and chocolate in every room, and guests are served with cheese and wine on arrival. There's a covered BBQ area, a practise golf green, swimming pool and walking tracks. Cottages $180–425 for two couples; rooms $140–200.
Valley Vineyards Tourist Park Mount View Rd, 2km northwest of Cessnock

11am; 40min) show the whole process. A pretty picnic area with wood-fired BBQ overlooks a small dam and vineyards. Mon–Fri 8am–5pm, Sat & Sun 10am–5pm.

Peterson House Corner of Broke and Wine Country Drive, Pokolbin. The only Hunter Valley winery to specialize in sparkling wines; they also use their *méthode champenoise* expertise to produce for other wineries. The pretty duck-pond-set stone building makes a pleasant tasting and eating spot: the *Restaurant Cuvée*'s fantastic, well-priced cooked breakfast. For more indulgence, the Hunter Valley Chocolate Factory is right next door. Daily 9am–5pm.

Scarborough Gilliards Rd, Pokolbin. Small, friendly winery with a reputation for outstanding wines; specializes in chardonnay and pinot noir. Pleasantly relaxed sit-down tastings are held in a small cottage on Hungerford Hill with wonderful valley views. Daily 9am–5pm.

Tamburlaine McDonalds Rd, Pokolbin. The jasmine-scented garden outside offers a hint of the flowery, elegant wines within. Tastings are well orchestrated and delivered with heaps of experience. Daily 9.30am–5pm.

Tempus Two Broke Rd, Pokolbin. This huge, spectacular winery – all steel, glass and stone – looks worth every cent of the $7 million it cost. A high-tech urban-chic exterior – terrace, fountains and amphitheatre – meets a rural landscape of vineyards and dam; its contemporary interior continues down even to the sinuous bottles with their distinctive pewter labels. Owned by Lisa McGuigan, of the well-known winemaking family, whose unique-tasting wines are the result of using lesser-known varieties such as pinot gris, viognier and marsanne. The attached Japanese-Thai *Oishi* (11.30am–9pm; ℡02/4999 7051) restaurant charges surprisingly moderate prices and there's a lounge area where you can relax over an espresso. Daily 9am–5pm.

Tyrrell's Broke Rd, Pokolbin. The oldest independent family vineyards, producing consistently fine wines. The tiny ironbark slab hut, where Edward Tyrrell lived when he began the winery in 1858, still stands in the grounds, and the old winery with its cool earth floor remains much as it was. Beautiful setting against the Brokenback Range. One of the best. Mon–Sat 8.30am–5pm, with free tour 1.30pm.

Wandin Valley Estate Corner of Wilderness and Lovedale roads. Picturesquely sited on a hundred acres of vineyard with magnificent views across the Wategos and the Brokenback Ranges, especially from the balcony of the European-style *Bel Posto* café/restaurant (℡02/4930 9199; mains $30; cellar-door priced wine). Daily 10am–5pm.

Wyndham Estate, Dalwood Rd, Dalwood. A scenic drive through the Dalwood Hills leads to the Lower Hunter's northern extent, where Englishman George Wyndham first planted shiraz in 1828. Now owned by multinational Pernod Ricard, there's an excellent guided tour (daily 11am; free), which covers the vines and winemaking techniques and equipment, including the original basket press. The idyllic riverside setting – grassy lawns, free BBQs – makes a great spot for picnics and the annual opera concert. Restaurant open for lunch Thurs–Sun. Daily 9.30am–4.30pm.

℡02/4990 2573, ☒www.valleyvineyard.com.au. High-standard camping site with camp kitchen, BBQ area, pool and on-site Thai restaurant. Cabins (BYO linen) have external en suites, cottages (linen included) internal. Cabins $65–85; cottages $95–130.

Wandin Valley Estate Wilderness Rd, Lovedale ℡02/4930 7317, ☒www.wandinvalley.com.au. One to four-bedroom cathedral-ceilinged, two-level Tuscan-style villas situated on a wonderful winery estate (see box above). You can wander from your villa through vineyards, where grazing kangaroos are a common sight. Comfortable and stylish with everything from wood fires to wine books. Expect two bottles of wine and generous cook-your-own breakfast provisions. Portable BBQ, swimming pool and tennis court. Midweek $150–175, weekends $212–425.

Eating and drinking

Many of the Hunter's excellent (and pricey) restaurants are attached to wineries or are among vineyards rather than in the towns (see box, pp.290–291), while the large old pubs dish out less fancy but more affordable grub – see the "Accommodation" section above for bistro options. Every year over a mid-May weekend around eight wineries along and around the scenic Lovedale and Wilderness roads team up with local restaurants to host the **Lovedale Long Lunch** (℡02/4990 4526, ⊕www.lovedalelonglunch.com.au). The Hunter **olive-growing** industry has also taken off: check out the Hunter Olive Centre (Pokolbin Estate Vineyard, McDonalds Rd, Pokolbin; ℡02/4998 7524, ⊕www .hunterolivecentre.com.au), and ask about the weekend-long **Feast of the Olive Festival** (⊕www.hunterolives.asn.au/feast) in late September. Other places where you can taste local wares include the Hunter Valley Cheese Company at the McGuigans Complex, McDonalds Road (⊕www.huntervalleycheese .com.au); the newer Binnorie Dairy, just across the road from the Hunter Resort, which specializes in soft fresh cheeses; and fresh farm produce at Tinkler's Vineyard, Pokolbin Mountain Road. You can also try local-brewed beer at *Potters Hotel & Brewery* on Wine Country Drive or the *Blue Tongue Brewery*, Hunter Resort. Just about every winery and accommodation place in the valley has a BBQ or cooking facilities – for picnic or self-catering supplies (a budgeter's necessity in this area) there's the large Coles **supermarket** in Cessnock, at 1 North Ave (Mon–Sat 6am–midnight, Sun 8am–8pm), or the small supermarket in the Hunter Valley Gardens Village. Delectable deli supplies are available at the Australian Regional Food Store at the Small Winemakers Centre on McDonalds Road, and Stone Pantry @ Peppers Creek on Broke Road. For a real treat, head to *Mojo's on Wilderness Deli*, Lovedale Road (see resturant review below; Mon–Fri 10am–5pm, Sat–Sun 9am–4pm), where you can buy scrumptious gourmet pizzas ($9) tasty paninis ($8), wicked sweets ($2–12) and richly scented coffee, to eat on brightly coloured bean bags on a lush green lawn, or take away.

Australia Hotel 136 Wollombi Rd, Cessnock.
The excellent bistro here is popular with the locals, and the pub showcases the Hunter's coal-mining roots with mining paraphernalia and related art. Though steaks hit the $28 mark, mains average $15–25, and the menu encompasses stir-fries, gourmet salads and vegetarian dishes.

Café Enzo Peppers Creek, Broke Rd, Pokolbin.
Charming café of stone and timber with an old-world earthy interior and regal garden seating; feels like it's been lifted from the south of France; light Mediterranean menu ($19–32) and excellent Italian-style coffee, or start the day with a cooked breakfast ($16–22). Daily 9am–5pm.

The Upper Hunter

If you plan to tour the **Upper Hunter**, ask the tourist office at Pokolbin for the useful booklet and map, *Get Lost in the Upper Hunter Valley*. The little settlement of **SANDY HOLLOW** on the Golden Highway (Route 84), in the Goulburn River Valley, close to the Goulburn River and Wollemi national parks, makes a good base; try the excellent *Sandy Hollow Tourist Park*, set in twenty grassy acres backed by bush-covered outcrops, with a large swimming pool, camp kitchen and open fires (℡02/6547 4575, en-suite cottages and cabins with kitchen facilities and linen $75–140, plus camping $19). The country pub, *Tourist Hotel*, serves pretty good pizzas (daily 6–9pm), and there's excellent coffee at *David Mahoney Art Gallery and Coffee House* on the edge of town.

Café Wollombi Wollombi Rd, Wollombi
☎02/4998 3220. In a beautiful old timber
building on a hill, with delightful views of the
leafy and historic surrounds of Wollombi
from the seating on its wrap around
balcony. Cheap and delicious eats (with
good vegetarian options) include Turkish
toasties ($13), salads ($14–17), pizza ($16),
laksa ($17) and burgers, with gorgeous
home-made patties ($12–14).

🏃 **Mojo's on Wilderness** Wilderness Rd,
Lovedale ☎02/4930 7244. A British
Michelin-rated chef and his Australian
chef-wife create the divine modern British/
Australian food at this bush-set restaurant.
Warm, local-art decorated interior, flowery
courtyard with hillside views, cheerful staff
and a laid-back vibe. Set dinner menu
(2-courses $56, 3-courses $70) has
suggested wines for each course, many
from the immediate area and all available by
the glass. Dinner daily from 6.30pm.

🏃 **Roberts** Peppertree Winery, Halls Rd,
Pokolbin ☎02/4998 7330. Fine-dining
restaurant in a fairy-tale 1876 wooden
farmhouse – as romantic a dining experience as one could possibly wish for.
Oodles of dark polished timber contrast
beautifully with cream walls and gleaming
white tablecloths while Gothic antiques,
candles and flowers do the rest. The
European-influenced modern cuisine from
head chef, Daniel Hunt, and his team, is
blissful – so long as you can forget about
price. Mains $38–56; Degustation Menu
(highly recommended) $150.

🏃 **Rock** 576 DeBeyers Rd, Pokolbin,
☎02/4998 6968. Rated Sydney's
best regional restaurant by the *Sydney
Morning Herald* in 2009, *Rock*, with its
industrial warehouse chic, dashings of
desert landscape aesthetics and dining-
hall glass walls overlooking rolling hills of
vineyards, drains the wallet and pleases the
soul in equal measure. The contemporary
Australian cuisine with a French influence
(including a full vegetarian menu) is superb
and worth every penny. Mains $42–72.

The Blue Mountains region

The section of the Great Dividing Range nearest Sydney gets its name from the blue mist that rises from millions of eucalyptus trees and hangs in the mountain air, tinting the sky and the range alike. In the early days of the colony, the **Blue Mountains** were believed to be an insurmountable barrier to the west. The first expeditions followed the streams in the valleys until they were defeated by cliff faces rising vertically above them. Only in 1813, when explorers Wentworth, Blaxland and Lawson followed the ridges rather than the valleys, were the mountains finally conquered, allowing the western plains to be opened up for settlement. The range is surmounted by a plateau that's over a kilometre high, where, over millions of years, rivers have carved deep valleys into the sandstone. Winds and driving rain have helped to deepen the ravines, creating spectacular

▲ Touring Jenotan Caves

From Sydney

Several operators run day-tours from Sydney; we've listed recommended outfits below. Some operators also package accommodation and activity deals.

Oz Experience 761–763 George St, near Central Station (T02/9213 1766 or 1300 300 028, Wwww.ozexperience.com). Their active one-day tour ($95) includes a 2- to 3-hour Wentworth Falls walk, a descent into the Jamison Valley and a ride on the Scenic Railway. You can go back the same day, or stay overnight at Katoomba YHA for an extra charge.

Oz Trek (T02/9666 4662 or 1300 661 234, Wwww.oztrek.com.au. Active full-day tours to the Blue Mountains ($55), with a choice of bushwalks. Small groups (max 20). The trip can be extended to overnight packages with either abseiling ($255) or a Jenolan Caves visit ($210–230). City, Glebe, Kings Cross, Bondi and Coogee pick-ups.

Wildframe Ecotours (T02/9440 9915, Wwww.wildframe.com). Two full-day tours to the Blue Mountains (both $85) and overnight tours starting at $136. The Grand Canyon Eco-tour, for fit walkers, includes a small-group bushwalk (maximum 21) through the Grand Canyon (5km; 3hr); BYO lunch in Katoomba. The more relaxed Blue Mountains Bush Tour offers several short bushwalks and BYO lunch in Blackheath. Kangaroo spotting promised on both trips.

From the Blue Mountains

Blue Mountains Walkabout (T0408/443 822, Wwww.bluemountainswalkabout.com). Excellent half-day (3hr 30min; $75) and all-day (8hr; $95), off-the-beaten-track bush roam (around 10km) between Faulconbridge and Springwood led by an Aboriginal guide; expect to look at Aboriginal rock carvings, taste bushtucker and swim in waterholes in summer (BYO lunch; own train journey to Faulconbridge).

Fantastic Aussie Tours Main St, by Katoomba station (T02/4782 1866 or 1300 300 915, Wwww.explorerbus.com.au). Operate the **Blue Mountains Explorer Bus**, red double-decker former London buses that link Katoomba and Leura, taking in all attractions with more than thirty stops (departs Katoomba hourly 9.45am–4.15pm, last return 5.15pm), with a half-hourly shuttle service between Katoomba, Echo Point and Scenic World; $33 all-day pass valid for up to seven days; includes discounts to attractions. There's no commentary on the bus, but you get a 48-page guide with maps detailing bushwalk and sightseeing options en route. The same company also do large-group coach tours to the Jenolan Caves: a day-tour (daily; $70–78 with one cave entry), or adventure caving ($105). A small-group half-day 4WD tour takes in the Blue Mountains National Park ($110).

Tread Lightly Eco Tours (T02/4788 1229, Wwww.treadlightly.com.au). Small-group expert-guided off-the-beaten-track half-day and full-day bushwalk and 4WD tours, picking up from Katoomba accommodation; their two-hour morning Wilderness Walk takes in some of the Six Foot Track (see box, p.306).

Trolley Tours Main St, by Katoomba train station (T1800 801 577, Wwww.trolleytours .com.au). A minibus decked out like a tram, which does a scenic circuit with commentary from Katoomba to Leura around Cliff Drive to the Three Sisters and back, taking in 29 attractions along the way (departs Katoomba hourly Mon–Fri 9.15am–4.15pm, Sat & Sun 9.45am–3.45pm; $20 all-day pass includes local Blue Mountains Bus Co services (see p.299) and discounts to attractions; wheelchair accessible.

scenery of sheer precipices and walled canyons. Before white settlement, the Daruk Aborigines lived here, dressed in animal-skin cloaks to ward off the cold. An early coal-mining industry, based in Katoomba, was followed by tourism which snowballed after the railway arrived in 1868; by 1900 the first three mountain stations, **Wentworth Falls**, **Katoomba** and **Mount Victoria** were fashionable resorts, extolling the health-giving benefits of eucalyptus-tinged mountain air. In 2000 the Blue Mountains joining the Great Barrier Reef as a World Heritage Listed site; the listing came after abseiling was finally banned on the mountains' most famous scenic wonder, the **Three Sisters**, after forty years of clambering had caused significant erosion. The Blue Mountains stand out from other Australian forests, in particular for the recently discovered **Wollemi Pine** (see p.308), a "living fossil" that dates back to the time of the dinosaurs.

All the villages and towns of the romantically dubbed "**City of the Blue Mountains**" – the main ones being Glenbrook, Springwood, Wentworth Falls, Leura, Katoomba and Blackheath – lie on a ridge, connected by the Great Western Highway. Around them is the **Blue Mountains National Park**, the fourth-largest national park in the state and to many minds the best. The region makes a great weekend break from the city, its stunning views and clean air complemented by a wide range of accommodation, cafés and well-regarded restaurants, especially in Katoomba and Leura. But be warned: at weekends, and during the summer holidays, these two spots in particular are thronged, and prices escalate accordingly. Even at their most crowded, though, the Blue Mountains always offer somewhere where you can find peace and quiet, and even solitude – the deep gorges and high rocks make much of the terrain inaccessible except to bushwalkers and mountaineers. Climbing schools offer courses in rock-climbing, abseiling and canyoning for both beginners and experienced climbers, while Glenbrook is a popular mountain-biking spot.

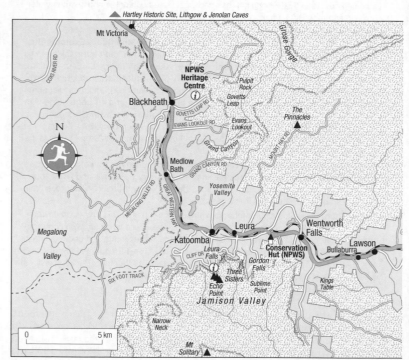

Practicalities

Although **public transport** to the mountains is quite good, bringing your own vehicle gives you much greater flexibility, allowing detours to old mansions, cottage gardens and the lookout points scattered along the ridge. **Trains** leave from Central Station for Mount Victoria and/or Lithgow and follow the highway, stopping at all the major towns en route (frequent departures until about midnight; 2hr; $12.30 one-way to Katoomba, $16.80 off-peak day return). If you're dependent on public transport, Katoomba makes the best base: facilities and services are concentrated here, and Blue Mountains Bus Co (℡02/4751 1077, ⓦwww.bmbc.com.au) has half-hourly **bus** services to Blackheath, Mount Victoria (no service weekends), Echo Point and the Scenic World complex, Leura, Wentworth Falls and North Katoomba. Buses leave from Katoomba Street outside the *Carrington Hotel*, and opposite the *Savoy*.

The two Katoomba-based, hop-on-hop-off tour buses detailed on p.295 have offices by the train station exit on Main Street; passes include discounts to some of the attractions en route.

Information

The **Blue Mountains Information Centre** (9am–4.30pm; ℡1300 653 408, ⓦwww.bluemts.com.au), on the Great Western Highway at Glenbrook, the gateway to the Blue Mountains, has a huge amount of information, including two free publications: the *Blue Mountains Wonderland Visitors Guide* (ⓦwww .bluemountainswonderland.com), which has several detailed colour maps and

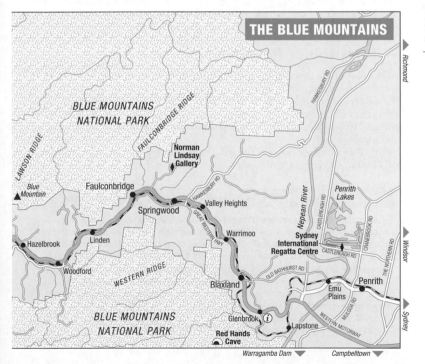

bushwalking notes, and an events guide. The other official tourist information centre is at **Echo Point**, near Katoomba (see p.309); both offices offer a **free accommodation booking** service.

At the main ranger station for the **Blue Mountains National Park**, at Blackheath (see p.310), you can get comprehensive walking and camping information. Car-accessible NPWS camping and picnic sites are located near Glenbrook, Woodford, Wentworth Falls, Blackheath and Oberon, and bush camping is allowed in most areas. The only point where you must pay vehicle entry into the park is at Glenbrook ($7).

Accommodation

Katoomba holds the mountains' greatest concentration of **accommodation**. Bear in mind that rates rise on Friday and Saturday nights – aim to visit on weekdays when it's quieter and cheaper. The tourist offices at Glenbrook and Echo Point can make bookings. **Katoomba** is the obvious choice if arriving by train, particularly if you're on a budget, since it has several **hostels**, but if you have your own transport you can indulge in some of the more unusual and characterful **guesthouses** in **Blackheath** and **Mount Victoria**.

Many charming **holiday homes** are also available. Contact Soper Bros, 173 The Mall, Leura (℡02/4784 1633, 🌐www.soperbros.com.au) and check out homes like the idyllic Brookside Cottage, overlooking the Charles Darwin Walk, in Wentworth falls (sleeps 4; 3-night weekend, $475), or the less exotic bargain of Geebung Cottage, Katoomba (sleeps 8; 3-night weekend $480).

There are two council-run **caravan parks**: *Katoomba Falls,* at Katoomba Falls Road (℡02/4782 1835; en-suite cabins $77 – bring your own bedding) and *Blackheath,* at Prince Edward Street (℡02/4787 8101; cabins $46 en suite $64). You can **camp** at both, as well as in the grounds of *Flying Fox Backpackers* (see p.306), and in the bush at several NPWS sites.

The foothills: Penrith

At the foot of the Blue Mountains in a curve of the Nepean River, **PENRITH** is the most westerly of Sydney's satellite towns. Penrith has an old-fashioned Aussie feel about it – a tight community that is immensely proud of the Panthers, its boisterous rugby league team. The huge *Panthers Leagues Club* on Mulgoa Road (℡02/4720 5555) is the town's eating, drinking, entertainment and gambling hub.

From Penrith Station, you can't miss the huge lettering announcing the **Museum of Fire**, on Castlereagh Road in a former power station (daily 9.30am–4.30pm;

Festivals

Katoomba's **Blue Mountains Music Festival** (🌐www.bmff.org.au) is a three-day mid-March bash featuring folk, roots and blues from Australian and international musicians on several indoor and outdoor stages; it includes food and craft stalls and kids' entertainment ($165 whole weekend, $95 full-day ticket, $65–70 night ticket).

Winter Magic (🌐www.wintermagic.com.au) is a day-long, pagan-inflected fancy-dress celebration of the Southern Hemisphere winter solstice, held on a Saturday in mid-June. Katoomba Street is closed to traffic and lined with market and food stalls; there's a morning street parade, music stages dotted around town, and a firework display from the roof of the *Carrington Hotel*. On Sunday, the gardens at Everglades (see p.302) are the scene for a marvellous kids' treasure hunt and live entertainment.

Bookshops Katoomba Street holds several interesting secondhand bookshops, as do Blackheath and Mount Victoria. The best place to buy new books, and great for browsing, is the very literary Megalong Books, 183 The Mall, Leura ℡02/4784 1302, Ⓦwww.megalongbooks.com.

Bus services Blue Mountains Bus Co ℡02/4751 1077, Ⓦwww.bmbc.com.au. See p.295 for details.

Camping equipment Paddy Pallin, 166 Katoomba St, Katoomba (℡02/4782 4466), sells camping gear and good topographic maps, bushwalking guides and supplies, as does nearby Mountain Designs, at no. 131 (℡02/4782 5999). For cheap gear, go to K-Mart (next door to Coles supermarket, Katoomba St). Otherwise, rent it in Sydney (see p.250).

Car rental Redicar, 121 The Mall, Leura (50 metres from Leura Station) ℡02/4784 3443, Ⓦwww.redicar.com.au.

Hospital Blue Mountains District Anzac Memorial, Great Western Highway, Katoomba ℡02/4784 6500.

Internet access Katoomba Book Exchange, 34 Katoomba St, Katoomba, ℡4782 9997 (17 cents per min, 15min free with a cup of coffee, daily 10am–6pm).

Laundry The Washing Well, K-Mart car park, Katoomba (℡02/4782 2377). Daily 7am–6pm.

Pharmacies Blooms Springwood Pharmacy, 161 Macquarie Rd, Springwood (Mon–Fri 8.30am–9pm, Sat & Sun 9am–7pm); Greenwell & Thomas, 145 Katoomba St, Katoomba (Mon–Fri 8.30am–7pm, Sat & Sun 9am–6pm).

Post office Katoomba Post Office, Pioneer Place, off Katoomba St, Katoomba, NSW 2780.

Supermarket Coles, Pioneer Place off Katoomba St, Katoomba (daily 6am–midnight).

Taxis Taxis wait outside the main Blue Mountains train stations to meet arrivals; otherwise, for the upper mountains call Katoomba Radio Cabs (℡02/4782 1311), or for the middle mountains call Blue Mountains Taxi Cab (℡02/4759 3000).

Trains Katoomba station general enquiries ℡02/4782 1902. Transport Infoline ℡13 1500.

$8.50; Ⓦwww.museumoffire.com.au), which focuses on one of Australia's greatest and most widespread perils, with a serious message about fire safety. The museum has around fifty fire-fighting vehicles (dating from the late eighteenth century) – which kids especially love – and other fire-fighting memorabilia.

Penrith is also home to the extensive International Regatta Centre on Penrith Lakes, between Castlereagh and Cranebrook roads north of the town centre. **Penrith Whitewater Stadium** here was the 2000 Olympics competition venue for the canoe/kayak-slalom events. You can take part in a thrilling, ninety-minute **white-water rafting** session, completing five to eight circuits of the 320-metre-long, grade-three course ($85; bookings ℡02/4730 4333, Ⓦwww.penrithwhitewater.com.au).

Visitors can also experience the splendour of the spectacular **Nepean Gorge** from the decks of the paddle steamer *Nepean Belle* (range from 1hr 30min morning tea cruises, $22, to longer lunch and dinner cruises $42–65; bookings ℡02/4733 1274, Ⓦwww.nepeanbelle.com.au), or head 24km south to the **Warragamba Dam**, the source of Sydney's water supply. The dam has created the huge reservoir of **Lake Burragorang**, a popular picnic spot with barbecues and a kiosk, and some easy walking trails through the bush.

Glenbrook to Faulconbridge

Off the busy highway and away from the information centre, **GLENBROOK**, 10km on from Penrith, is a pleasant village arranged around the train station. As well as a great cinema (see box below), it has some great cafés, like the charming *Blue Tongue Lizard Cafe* at 6 Ross Street, and *Mash Café*, across the road at no. 19. The local section of the **Blue Mountains National Park** is popular for **mountain biking** along the thirty-kilometre **Oaks Fire Trail** (it's best to start the trail higher up the mountain in **WOODFORD** and head downhill, ending up at Glenbrook; bike rental is only available at Katoomba). The park entrance (cars $7) is just over a kilometre from the train station, following Burfitt Parade then Bruce Road alongside the railway line. Several bushwalks start from the part-time NPWS office at the end of Bruce Rd (hours variable; ☎02/4739 2950), including the easy 2km return trip to the **Blue Pool** and **Jellybean Pool**, swimmable in summer. Another good hike

Mountain activities

There's heaps to do in the mountains, from bushwalking to canyoning, meditation and yoga. The free **local newspaper**, *Blue Mountains Gazette*, comes out every Wednesday and has good entertainment and activities listings (80¢ from newsagents but usually found floating around cafés).

Adventure activities

Loads of outdoor adventure companies line Main and Katoomba streets in Katoomba. The town's original abseiling outfit, the **Australian School of Mountaineering** at Paddy Pallin, 166 Katoomba St (☎02/4782 2014, ⓦwww.asmguides.com), offers daily day-long courses ($145), plus canyoning to Grand, Empress or Fortress canyons (Oct–May daily 9am; $165; also less frequent trips to other canyons), rock-climbing and bush-survival courses. Another long-established operator, **High'n'Wild Mountain Adventures**, 3–5 Katoomba St, Katoomba (☎02/4782 6224, ⓦwww.high-n-wild .com.au), has great beginners' courses in abseiling (half-day $90, full day $145), canyoning (from $179), rock-climbing (half-day $159, full day $179), plus guided bushwalking and bushcraft courses. If you're unsure, check out the website's videos. Both companies include lunch on the full-day courses. If the weather is bad, you can train at the **climbing wall** at Leading Edge Fitness in Leura, 166–188 The Mall (☎02/4784 3733).

Bike rental

The friendly Vélo Nova, 182 Katoomba St, Katoomba (☎02/4782 2800), offers mountain bikes from $40 half-day, $50 full day.

Cinemas

The Edge Maxvision Cinema 225–237 Great Western Highway, Katoomba (☎02/4782 8928, ⓦwww.edgecinema.com.au), shows *The Edge – The Movie* (see p.308), a Blue Mountains movie, as well as new-release feature films on a giant screen (cheap tickets all day Tues).

Mount Vic Flicks Harley Ave, off Station St, Mount Victoria (☎02/4787 1577, ⓦwww.bluemts.com.au/mountvic/), is a quaint local cinema in an old hall with an old-fashioned candy bar; it shows a fine programme of prestige new releases and independent films (Thurs–Sun, daily during school holidays; good-value $10 tickets).

Glenbrook Cinema Corner of Ross Street and Great Western Highway, Glenbrook (☎02/4739 4433, ⓦwww.glenbrookcinema.com.au), is a quality, family-run cinema, costing just $10 for all sessions.

leads to the Aboriginal hand stencils on the walls of **Red Hands Cave** (3hr return; medium difficulty). You can also drive or cycle to the cave, and on to the grassy creekside Eoroka picnic ground (camping available), where eastern grey kangaroos usually abound.

SPRINGWOOD, 11km northwest of Glenbrook and the Blue Mountains' second largest town, has the feel of a commuter suburb, with its express train links to Sydney, but has several cafés, and offers bushwalks in **Sassafras Gully** (8km circuit; easy). Turn off here onto Hawkesbury Road to take a scenic drive down to Richmond (see p.279). Many artists and writers were first drawn to the mountains 3km further west in **FAULCONBRIDGE**, following in the footsteps of controversial artist and poet **Norman Lindsay** (1879–1969). His nude studies scandalized Australia in the 1930s, and his story was told in the 1994 film *Sirens* (starring Sam Neill, with Elle McPherson as one of his life models). From 1912, Lindsay spent a great part of his life at the 42-acre bush property "Springwood", set among extensive gardens at 14 Norman Lindsay

Horseriding

Below Blackheath, the scenic Megalong Valley offers horse-riding opportunities.

Blue Mountains Horse Riding Adventures (☎02/4787 8188, ⊛www.megalong.cc) offers escorted trail rides in the valley and along the Cox's River, from a beginners' 1hr Wilderness Ride ($45) to an experienced riders' all-day adventure ride along the river (from $165).

Werriberri Trail Rides (☎02/4787 9171) offers horseriding for all abilities and pony rides for children (from $5.50 for 5min); their 2hr ride costs $90; full day $190.

Massage

Yindi Day Spa *Carrington Hotel*, Katoomba St (☎4782 1111, ⊛www.yindi.com .au). This award-winning spa offers everything from 30–90min massages ($50–150) to body exfoliation treatments and manicures. Special couples' treatments are well worth investigating.

Spa Sublime 9 Penault Ave, Katoomba (☎02/4782 3113, ⊛www.spasublime.com .au), offers a wide range of therapies, including numerous styles of massage, from Swedish to deep-tissue (30min $90; 60min $85; 90min $125) and other treatments, like body wraps (90min $125), and hot stone therapies (90min $155).

Meditation

Australian Buddhist Vihara 43 Cliff Drive, Katoomba (☎02/4782 2704), hosts free meditation sessions Sunday 8–11am and 1hr sessions daily 8am & 6pm.

Swimming

Katoomba Aquatic Centre Gates Ave, Katoomba (Mon–Fri 6am–8pm, Sat & Sun 8am–8pm, winter weekends closes 6pm; ☎02/4782 1748), Outdoor pools, with heated Olympic-sized and children's pools, plus an attached year-round complex with heated 25m indoor pool, toddlers' pool, sauna, spa, a gym and kids' play area. Entry is $5.10 (plus sauna and spa $9.10; plus gym, sauna and spa $12.50; gym only $9). For details of pools at Glenbrook, Springwood, Lawson and Blackheath, contact the Blue Mountains City Council (☎1300 653 408 or 02/4780 5500, ⊛www.bmcc.nsw .gov.au). You can swim at waterholes at Glenbrook (see above) and in the Megalong Valley (see p.310).

Yoga

The **Blue Mountains Yoga Studio** 4/118 Main St, Katoomba (☎02/4782 6718, ⊛www .bmyogastudio.com.au), is a highly regarded Iyengar Yoga school where you can join in casual yoga classes for beginners to advanced (around $15 per class).

Crescent, and now owned by the National Trust as the **Norman Lindsay Gallery** (daily 10am–4pm; $9; ☎02/4751 1067, ⓦwww.normanlindsay.com .au). The exhibition of paintings and drawings, many of them erotic, and some from his famous, enduring and very funny children's tale, *The Magic Pudding* (itself made into a movie in 2001), is well worth visiting.

Wentworth Falls

The small town of **WENTWORTH FALLS**, 23km further west, was named after William Wentworth, one of the famous trio who conquered the mountains in 1813. A signposted road leads from the Great Western Highway to the **Wentworth Falls Reserve**, with superb views of the waterfall tumbling down into the Jamison Valley. You can reach this picnic area from Wentworth train station by following the easy creekside 2.5-kilometre **Darwin's Walk**, which traces the route followed by the famous naturalist in 1836, when he described the view from the great precipice as "magnificent".

Most of the other local bushwalks start from the national park's **Conservation Hut** (Mon–Fri 9am–4pm, Sat & Sun 9am–5pm; ☎02/4757 3827), about 3km from the railway station at the end of Fletcher Street. Blue Mountains Bus Co services run from Wentworth Falls train station (Mon–Fri 2 daily, Sat & Sun 4 daily), with more frequent services from the highway, outside the *Grand View Hotel* (Mon–Fri 7 daily, Sat & Sun 4 daily), and from Katoomba (Mon–Fri 10 daily, Sat 8 daily, Sun 4 daily). The hut is in a fantastic location overlooking the Jamison Valley, and from its *Conservation Hut Cafe* you can take full advantage of the views through the big windows or from the deck outside; in winter an open fire crackles in the grate. Bushwalks, detailed on boards outside, range from the two-hour **Valley of the Waters track** to the rewarding 5.4-kilometre, four-hour circuit walk, along the strenuous **National Pass**.

A great place to **eat** in Wentworth Falls is the relaxed BYO café *Il Postino*, at 13 Station St, opposite the train station. Housed in the original post office, this relaxed café is light and airy, with outside tables on a street-facing courtyard. The menu is Mediterranean- and Thai-slanted, with plenty for vegetarians and nothing over $16. Also opposite the station is the wonderful *Patisserie Schwartz* – divine German-style pastries to eat in or take away make the perfect reward after a long bushwalk.

Leura

Just 2km west of Wentworth Falls, and 2km east of Katoomba, wealthy **LEURA**, packed with cafés, classy antique and craft stores, elegant boutiques and a hugely popular old-fashioned sweet shop, retains its own distinct identity and a quaint village atmosphere and is well worth exploring. It's a very scenic spot: arriving by train, you get stunning views across the Jamison Valley to the imposing plateau that is **Mount Solitary**. The main shopping strip, **Leura Mall**, with its central road island lined with cherry trees makes a popular picnicking spot. Leura is renowned for its beautiful **gardens**, eight of which can be visited during the **Leura Gardens Festival** (early to mid-Oct; $18 all gardens, or $5 per garden; ⓦwww.leuragardensfestival.com.au). On busy days, a hop-on, hop-off shuttle service links the gardens ($4.50 all-day ticket). The gorgeous National Trust-listed **Everglades Gardens**, 2km southeast of the Mall at 37 Everglades Ave (daily 9am–sunset; $7), remain open all year, with a colourful display of azaleas and rhododendrons, an arboretum, a gallery and a simple tearoom, and offering superb Jamison Valley views from formal terraces.

Just over a kilometre south of the Mall, the **NSW Toy and Railway Museum**, 36 Olympian Parade (daily 10am–5pm; $12, $8 garden only; ☎02/4787 1169, ⓦwww.toyandrailwaymuseum.com.au) is located within a brilliant-white Art Deco mansion set in twelve acres of gardens. Inside you'll find a huge collection of dolls, cartoon figurines and fantasy paraphernalia – almost every significant twentieth-century childhood fancy is represented. As well as massive toy dioramas and push-button model trains, a miniature railway in the grounds tracks its way around a six-metre replica of the Matterhorn ($2 extra). A separate $2 entry fee gets you into **Olympian Park** opposite, where a natural ampitheatre gives more breathtaking Jamison valley views.

From the nearby **Gordon Falls** picnic area on Lone Pine Ave, Leura's mansions and gardens give way to the bush of the **Blue Mountains National Park**. An easy ten-minute return walk gets you to and from the lookout over the falls, or a somewhat harder two-hour canyon loop walk, via Lyre Bird Dell and the Pool of Siloam, which takes in some of the Blue Mountains' distinctive hanging swamps, an Aboriginal rock shelter, and cooling rainforest. From Gordon Falls, a 45-minute bushwalk, partly along the Prince Henry Cliff Walk (see p.310), heads to the **Leura Cascades** picnic area off **Cliff Drive** (the scenic route around the cliffs which extends from Leura to beyond Katoomba), where among several bushwalks a two- to three-hour circuit hike leads to the base of the much-photographed **Bridal Veil Falls**. To the east of Gordon Falls, Sublime Point Road leads to the aptly named **Sublime Point** lookout, with panoramic views of the Jamison Valley.

Accommodation

Staying in Leura, so close to the attractions of Katoomba, is well worth considering. Only expensive luxury options are available, however. Along with those listed, several attractive B&Bs – such as *Llandrindod Bed & Breakfast* (☎02/4784 3234, ⓦwww.llandrindod.co.au), and *Megalong Manor* (☎02/47841461, ⓦwww .megalongmanor.com) – lie close to the Mall's shopping precinct, national park walks and Jamison Valley views.

Broomelea Bed & Breakfast 273 The Mall ☎02/4784 2940, ⓦwww.broomelea.com.au. A gorgeous Edwardian home (built 1909), with pleasant gardens and luxurious rooms in the original style. Average $400 per couple for minimum two-night weekends.

York Fairmont Resort 1 Sublime Point Rd ☎02/4784 4144, ⓦwww.fairmontresort.com.au. This huge 4.5-star luxury resort, a significant distance from the town, has more than 200 rooms, fantastic recreational facilities, and peaceful grounds with Jamison Valley views. From $180.

Eating

Leura has several delightful cafés where you can relax after a hard few hours of bushwalking or knick-knack browsing. Coffee is high-calibre, and hot chocolate is a winter speciality, while all the restaurants except *Hana* aim for the expensive, fine-dining end of the market.

Café Bon Ton 192 The Mall ☎02/4782 4377. Casual yet sophisticated café; bistro by day, fine-dining European-influenced modern Australian restaurant by night, all set in an expansive courtyard arbor and stately two-storey building, distinctly reminiscent of an English manor house. For lunch try a simple focaccia ($14.50) or the popular house-made beef shank pie with parmesan mash and red wine reduction ($21.50). Among numerous dinner options, the slow-braised pork cheeks with star anise cassia bark and shitake mushrooms are a hit ($34.50). Daily 8.30am–4pm & 6–9pm.

Hana 121 The Mall. Cheap Japanese restaurant serving delicious sushi rolls, teriyaki hot plates and udon noodle soups. Mains average $13.50. Closed Sun & Mon.

Lily's Pad Café **19 Grose St**. A delightful water-lily themed courtyard café, tucked away behind the Mall (access from the car park behind the Aspects of Leura Arcade). Coffee and food is consistently good – breakfasts in particular – and staff are friendly and patient. Daily except Mon 8am–5pm.

Silk's Brasserie **128 The Mall** ☎ **02/4784 2534**. Parisian-style bar with excellent service and great food. For dinner, the classy European dishes, from confit of duck to Tasmanian salmon, range from \$29–34. Lunch offers relaxed, cheap dishes (\$17–28), plus the option to order from the dinner menu. Licensed, with many wines available by the glass.

Stockmarket Cafe **179 The Mall**. Rustic hole-in-the-wall serving consistently good coffee, delicious breakfasts, gourmet pies, great salads and paninis, and mood-altering desserts. Mon–Fri 7.30am–3.30pm, Sat & Sun 8am–3.30pm.

Katoomba and around

KATOOMBA, 103km west of Sydney, is the largest town in the Blue Mountains. Besides being the area's commercial heart, it's also the best base for the major sights of Echo Point and the Three Sisters. Its main drag, **Katoomba Street**, which runs downhill from the train station, hosts a lively café culture, and is full of vintage and

KATOOMBA & LEURA

EATING & DRINKING
Arjuna	5
Avalon	7
Bamboo Box	10
Café Bon Ton	6
Café Zuppa	8
Elephant Bean	11
Fresh	12
Hana	1
Lily's Pad Café	4
Papadino's	9
Silk's Brasserie	3
Solitary	13
Stockmarket Cafe	2

ACCOMMODATION
Blue Mountains YHA	I
Broomelea Bed & Breakfast	G
Carrington Hotel	C
Cecil Guesthouse	E
The Clarendon	H
Echoes Boutique Hotel	L
Flying Fox Backpackers	A
Jamison House	J
Katoomba Mountain Lodge	F
Kurrara Guesthouse	K
No 14 Budget Accommodation	B
York Fairmont Resort	D

Of the many guides to the area, the best is the sturdy paperback *Exploring the Blue Mountains* (Leonard Cronin et al), in the immaculately researched Key Guides series. It's aimed at bushwalkers, cyclists and adventure sports enthusiasts as well as visitors on a driving tour. The Pocket Pals series comprises small bushwalking guides to specific mountain walks, including *Federal Pass*, *The Giant Stairway* and *Prince Henry Cliff Walk*. The NPWS also publishes a series of walking track guides for the Blue Mountains National Park and the Wollemi National Park, including *Glenbrook and the Eastern Blue Mountains*, *Bushwalking in the Wentworth Falls Area*, and the most popular, *Bushwalking in the Katoomba and Leura Area*. All are available at Megalong Books, Leura.

retro clothes shops, secondhand bookstores, antique dealers and gift shops. When the town was first discovered by fashionable city dwellers in the late nineteenth century, the grandiose **Carrington Hotel**, prominent at the top of Katoomba Street, was the height of elegance, with its lead lighting and wood panelling. It's recently been returned to its former glory, with elegant sloping lawns running down to the new **town square**; for historical tours of the hotel, call ☏02/4754 5726. Katoomba also boomed during the **Art Deco** era, and many of its cafés and restaurants feature the style, notably the **Paragon Cafe** at 65 Katoomba St (closed Mon), also known for its handmade chocolates and sweets.

Accommodation

Katoomba offers a broad range of quality accommodation to suit all budgets. Guesthouses, hostels and hotels, on the whole, occupy charmingly furnished Federation or nineteenth-century buildings, their timber tones and old-world mystique providing the perfect aesthetic accompaniment to the beauty of the natural environment.

Hotels and guesthouses

Carrington Hotel 15–47 Katoomba St ☏02/4782 1111, ⊛www.thecarrington.com.au. When it opened in 1882, the *Carrington* was the region's finest hotel. Now fully restored, its original features include stained-glass windows, open fireplaces, a splendid dining room and ballroom, cocktail bar, snooker and games room, library and guest lounges. The spacious, well-aired en-suite rooms are beautifully decorated in rich heritage colours. Cheaper rooms share bathrooms. Rooms $125–145, en suite $195–240, deluxe $230–310.

The Clarendon Corner of Lurline and Waratah sts ☏02/4782 1322, ⊛www.clarendonguesthouse .com.au. Classic 1920s guesthouse on three levels, with its own cocktail bar and restaurant, and a music and cabaret programme (see p.308). Also pool, sauna, gym, open fires, games room and garden. The guesthouse rooms aren't flashy, but they're atmospheric in an old-fashioned

way. Mostly en suite ($130–176), but budget rooms without bathroom (but with TV) are also available ($90–130) and exude a faded charm. They also offer modern motel rooms along the front at $130–176.

🏃 **Echoes Boutique Hotel 3 Lilianfels Ave** ☏02/4782 1966, ⊛www.echoeshotel.com .au. The views are incomparable, the luxury suites faultlessly stylish and the ravishing restaurant's Australian cuisine a culinary elevation. For the ultimate, money-is-not-an-issue Blue Mountains holiday experience, try *Echoes*. Rooms $495–650.

Jamison House 48 Merriwa St, corner of Cliff Drive ☏02/4782 1206, ⊛www.jamisonhouse .com. Built as a guesthouse in 1903, this seriously charming place has amazing, unimpeded views across the Jamison Valley. The feel of a small European hotel is enhanced by the French restaurant downstairs, *The Rooster*, with its gorgeous dining room full of original fixtures. Upstairs, a breakfast room gives splendid views, and there's a sitting room with a fireplace. All rooms en suite, $150–170.

 **Kurrara Guesthouse 17 Coomonderry St** ℡ 02/4782 6058, ⓦ www.kurrara.com. The ultimate in cosy old-fashioned mountains' atmosphere – the eight characterful guestrooms, each different, are filled with antique or four-poster beds, huge armchairs, books and bric-a-brac, all with an eclectic charm. Rooms are en suite, and some even have spa baths. The two-storey 1903 building has original features including working fireplaces (plus central heating). Evening drinks are offered in the parlour, and a buffet breakfast in the dining room ($10, or $15 cooked). A loyal Sydney-escapee following means you should book in advance. Prices change week to week; check website. Rooms $80–110 midweek, $150–180 weekend, suites $110–160.

Hostels

No 14 Budget Accommodation 14 Lovel St ℡ 02/4782 7104, ⓦ www.numberfourteen.com. This relaxed hostel in a charming restored former guesthouse – polished floors, cosy fire, and original features – is like a home from home, run by an informative, friendly young couple who put in a lot of effort. Mostly twin and double rooms, some en suite, plus four-share dorms with comfy beds instead of bunks; all centrally heated. Peaceful veranda surrounded by pretty plants and valley views. Dorms $25, rooms $69; en suite $79.

Blue Mountains YHA 207 Katoomba St ℡ 02/4782 1416, ℮ bluemountains@yhansw.org.au. Huge 200-bed YHA hostel in the town centre. The former 1930s guesthouse has been modernized but retains its charming lead-lighted windows, Art Deco decor, huge ballroom and an old-fashioned mountain-retreat ambience, with an open fire in the reading room, separate games room (with pool table), internet access, pleasant courtyard, plus typical YHA attributes. Most rooms and some of the four-bed dorms are en suite (also 8-bed dorms). Friendly reception staff are very helpful. Dorms $27–30, rooms $75–84, en suite 84–94.

Cecil Guesthouse 108 Katoomba St ℡ 02/4782 1411, ⓦ www.ourguest.com.au. Very central choice, set back from the main street with great views over the town and Jamison Valley from the common areas and some bedrooms (these ones go first). A little dilapidated, but charming with original 1904 wallpaper, dark polished timber, log fires, games room, alfresco white metal lace tables and chairs, and an abandoned overgrown tennis court all providing an old-fashioned atmosphere with a pleasing sense of regal decay. Dorms $25; rooms $85.

Flying Fox Backpackers 190 Bathurst Rd ℡ 02/4782 4226 or 1800 624 226, ⓦ www.theflyingfox.com.au. Colourfully painted, homely and comfortable bungalow near the station, with spacious seven-bed dorms and artistically furnished doubles (no en suites). Cosy inside lounge area with instruments; outside, there's a courtyard and a popular "chill-out" hut

The Six Foot Track

Along the Great Western Highway, about 2.5km west of Katoomba train station, stands the **Explorers Tree**, initialized by Blaxland, Lawson and Wentworth during their famous 1813 expedition. Nellies Glen Road here marks the start of the 42-kilometre **Six Foot Track** to the Jenolan Caves (2–3 days; carry plenty of water), and shorter walks to Pulpit Rock and Bonnie Doon Falls. Four basic campsites lie along the way, plus well-equipped cabins at Binda Flats. Blackheath NPWS can provide more bushwalking and camping information. Blue Mountains Guides (℡ 02/4782 6109, ⓦ www.bluemountainsguides.com.au) offers a guided walk along the track (3-day $750; camping), while Fantastic Aussie Tours (see p.295) provides a return service from Jenolan Caves for those who have completed the walk (1.5hr; $35). A more unusual way to complete the track is to enter Australia's largest annual off-road marathon, the **Six Foot Track Marathon** held in March (more details at ⓦ www.coolrunning.com.au).

with a fire, and a bush-outlook camping site ($18 per person; $26 with tent, mattress, sleeping bag and pillow). Free wi-fi, free tea and coffee, a kitchen and fridge space. Camping gear is rented out at reasonable rates and the knowledge-able managers offer info on bushwalks and camping, and free transport to walks. Rates include continental breakfast. Dorms $29, rooms $71.

Katoomba Mountain Lodge 31 Lurline St ℡ 02/4782 3933, ⊛ www.katoombamountainlodge .com.au. Everything a mountain lodge should be, with lots of timber panelled walls and quaint rooms – eighteen in all – on three floors. The best lead on to verandas with magic mountain vistas. There's also a communal kitchen and dining area. Free wi-fi. Good value and central. Dorms $21–24, rooms $68–80, en suite $78–90.

Eating

A huge number of cafés line thriving **Katoomba Street**, along with some great bakeries: top of the list is *Hominy* at 185 Katoomba Street, with public picnic tables just outside.

Cafés and light meals

Café Zuppa 36 Katoomba St ℡ 4782 9247. Wall-to-wall waist-high mirrors, crystal ball light shades and an undulating glass and timber street facade are just some of the attributes that make this charming Art Deco café endearing. Tasty coffees bring it a little closer, while the food – from burgers to salads to pastas to pizzas (like the sublime roasted veg and fetta "Zuppa Pizza"; $12.95) – could feasibly inspire a sonnet. Daily 7.30am–late.
Elephant Bean 159 Katoomba St. Great coffee is the focus at this spunky little café with its local gig-posters, timber floors and sound-track of jazz and world music. The simple menu of organic sourdough sandwiches ($9.50) is a hit, however, and house-made cakes are plain tasty. Mon–Sat 7am–4pm, Sun 7am–3pm.

Fresh 181 Katoomba St. This spacious goldfish-bowl at the bottom end of the main street, by the busy pedestrian lane heading to the health-food co-op, post office and supermarket, is the most popular café with locals, from cops to arty types. Has an open kitchen, wooden interior, good music, sunny tables outside and a big magazine stash. Serves great breakfasts – from build-your-own egg'n'bacon bonanzas to ricotta hotcakes with house-made butter-scotch sauce ($12.90), to organic toasted muesli with rhubarb compote and creamy greek yoghurt ($10.90). Raved about lamb burgers, risotto and wraps ($12.50–15.50) tweak lunchtime taste buds, while from open to close the coffee is the best in town. Daily 8am–5pm.

Restaurants

If money is not an issue, for exceptional fine dining and amazing views of the Jamison Valley, head to *Darley's* (at *Lilianfels Resort*, Lilianfels Ave) or *Echoes* (3 Lilianfels Ave) – both near Echo Point. *Darleys* wins out with the quality of its cuisine, but *Echoes* isn't far behind and pulls up trumps with its "yes, there is a God" vista.

Arjuna 16 Valley Rd, just off the Great Western Highway ℡ 02/4782 4662. Excellent, authentic Indian restaurant (dinner-only). A bit out of the way but positioned for spectacular sunset views, so get there early. Good veggie choices, too. BYO. Evenings from 6pm; closed Tues & Wed.
Avalon 18 Katoomba St ℡ 02/4782 5532. Stylish place with the ambience of a quirky café, in the dress circle of the old Savoy Theatre, with many Art Deco features intact. Moderately expensive menu, but generous

servings and to-die-for desserts – or come here just for a drink. BYO & licensed. Lunch & dinner Wed–Sun.
Bamboo Box 50 Katoomba St ℡ 02/4782 6998. Very friendly clean white simple place, with ergonomic seating and appealing tropical-plant-life-inspired box-canvas art along the wall. A favourite with locals for its many cheap'n'tasty Asian eats (the *laksas* are particularly delicious $11.80–14.80) Eat in or takeaway (sushi packs are a good option for bushwalk picnics); be sure to check

out the cheap lunch specials. Tues–Sat 10am–9pm.

Carrington Hotel 15–47 Katoomba St ☎02/4782 1111. The splendid "Grand Dining Room", all columns and decorative inlaid ceilings, offers a high-tea buffet on Sundays (2.30–5.30pm; $27.50), or a full dinner, with mains around $34; there's also an earth-toned and stately award-winning brasserie above the Carrington's *Old City Bank Bar*, at the bottom of the drive, with great wood-fired pizzas, pastas and gourmet burgers.

Papadino's 48 Katoomba St ☎02/4782 1696. Affordable charming little place filled with intoxicating aromas. Churns out tasty authentic Italian pizzas from its busy little wood-fired oven – pastas and salads aren't bad either. Daily 6–11pm.

Solitary 90 Cliff Drive, Leura Falls ☎02/4782 1164. The views of the Jamison Valley and Mount Solitary from this former kiosk, now modern Australian restaurant, perched on a hairpin bend on the mountains' scenic cliff-hugging road, are sublime. Expect beautifully laid tables, eager service, a well-chosen and reason-ably priced wine list, and a jazz soundtrack to accompany a superb meal. There's a fireplace in the back room and rattan tables and chairs beneath parasols on the lawn outside overlooking the valley. You can enjoy it all cheaply for tasty affordable breakfast or lunch when it morphs into the laid-back *Solitary Kiosk* (little above $16.50). Kiosk daily 10am–4pm, restaurant lunch Sat & Sun, dinner Wed–Sun.

Drinking and nightlife

Katoomba has several **nightlife** options. The salubrious cocktail bar and cabaret room at the *Clarendon* hosts eclectic folk, blues, jazz, and world music (Fri–Sun; $12–35; dinner plus show extra $35). On the other side of the tracks, opposite the station, the huge and now rather hip *Gearin Hotel* (☎02/4782 4395) is a hive of activity, with several bars where you can play pool, see touring bands (Fri & Sat nights) or boogie at the club nights. There's more mainstream action at the *Carrington*, on Katoomba Street (☎02/4782 1111), which has a host of bars in and around its grand old building. Inside, *Champagne Charlie's Cocktail Bar*, has a decorative glass ceiling dome and chandeliers. You can order tasty polysyllabic cocktails and down them in one of the classic Kentia-palm-filled lounges or out on the front veranda overlooking the lawns. Cheaper drinks and a livelier atmosphere are found at the bottom of the *Carrington's* curved driveway at stately *Old City Bank Bar* (live music most Fri & Sat evenings) and the down-to-earth *Carrington public bar*, with a separate entrance around the corner, on Bathurst Street opposite the train station. Fittingly, upstairs here is the up-to-heaven fantasy of *Baroque Bar & Nightclub*, a dimly illuminated Art Deco escape hosting a mix of DJ's and live music (Fri & Sat 10pm until late).

The Edge Maxvision Cinema

Across the railway line (use the foot-tunnel under the station and follow the signs), a stunning introduction to the ecology of the Blue Mountains can be had at the **Edge Maxvision Cinema**, at 225 Great Western Highway (☎02/4782 8900, Ⓦwww.edgecinema.com.au), a huge six-storey cinema screen created as a venue to show *The Edge Movie* (daily 10.20am, 11.05am, 12.10pm, 1.30pm, 2.15pm & 5.30pm; $15.00). The highlight of the forty-minute film is the segment about the "dinosaur trees", a stand of thirty-metre-high **Wollemi Pine**, previously known only from fossil material over sixty million years old. The trees miraculously survive deep within a sheltered rainforest gully in the **Wollemi National Park** north of Katoomba, and made headlines when they were first discovered in 1994 by a group of canyoners. To film the pines, whose exact location is kept secret, it was necessary to work closely with the NPWS. After the discovery, the first cultivated Wollemi Pine was planted in 1998 at Sydney's Royal Botanical Gardens. There are now also Wollemi Pines at Taronga Zoo, and you can see them in the Blue Mountains at the Mount Tomah Botanic Garden (see p.311).

Echo Point

A 25-minute walk south from the train station, or a tour or regular bus from the top of Katoomba Street, will bring you to **Echo Point**. From the projecting lookout platform between the **information centre** (daily 9am–5pm; ☎1300 653 408, Ⓦ www.bluemts.com.au) and souvenir shops and eateries at the Three Sisters Heritage Plaza, breathtaking vistas take in the Kedumba and Jamison valleys, Mount Solitary, the Ruined Castle, Kings Tableland and the Blue Mountains' most famous landmark, the **Three Sisters** (910m). These three gnarled rocky points take their name from an Aboriginal Dreamtime story which relates how the Kedumba people were losing a battle against the rival Nepean people: the Kedumba leader, fearing that his three beautiful daughters would be carried off by the enemy, turned them to stone, but tragically was killed before he could reverse his spell. An easy half-hour return stroll from the information centre will get you closer to the Sisters at Spooners Lookout.

The Three Sisters stand atop the **Giant Stairway** (1hr 45min one-way), a very steep 800-step staircase leading into the three-hundred-metre-deep **Jamison Valley** below, passing Katoomba Falls en route. A popular walking route, taking about two hours and graded medium, leads down the stairway and part way along the **Federal Pass** to the **Landslide**, and then on to the Scenic Railway or Skyway (see below), either of which you can take back up to the ridge.

Scenic World and beyond

If you want to spare yourself the trek down into the Jamison Valley – or the walk back up – head for the very touristy **Scenic World complex** at the end of Violet Street off Cliff Drive (daily 9am–5pm; $28 combined ticket for Scenic Railway, Cableway and Skyway; $19 for Railway down, Cableway up or vice versa; $10 one-way railway or Skyway; Skyway return $16; Ⓦ www.scenicworld.com.au). Here you can choose between two modes of transport, the original Scenic Railway and the modern Scenic Cableway, or, for a purely "Scenic" experience, take a thrilling return ride on the Skyway, a glass-floored gondola across an arc in the ridge, carved by the pretty Katoomba Falls.

The **Scenic Railway** (every 10min; last train up leaves at 4.50pm), originally built in the 1880s to carry coal, is a funicular that glides down an impossibly steep gorge to the valley floor. Even more vertiginous, but not as nail-bitingly thrilling, is **Cableway** (same times), an AUS$8-million, high-tech cable car (wheelchair accessible), with floor-to-ceiling windows – the views of the Three Sisters as the car drops 545m are really spectacular. At the base, a 330-metre elevated boardwalk (also wheelchair accessible) heads through the forest – en route you can drink clean rainwater from a spring – to the base of the Scenic Railway via the entrance to the old coal mine, active when the railway still hauled coal; an audiovisual display tells the story. A further 1.5km of boardwalk on various levels, with interpretative boards detailing natural features, is worth exploring, and there's access to longer bushwalks in the national park, including a 12km return walk (medium difficulty) to the Ruined Castle (see p.310).

Back up on the ridge, you can get your legs trembling again with the state-of-the-art **Skyway** (daily 9am–5pm), the 2005 replacement for the rickety-looking cable-car contraption that had been plying its way 350m across to the other side of the gorge and straight back again since 1958. As if the bird's-eye view of **Orphan Rock**, the Three Sisters and Katoomba Falls weren't exhilarating enough, the new gondola has a glass floor which starts out opaque then becomes crystal clear, revealing the 270-metre drop to the ravines and waterfalls below. Though the price for a few minutes is high, the thrill is worth it.

To satisfy visitors who have missed the fabulous views on wet and misty days, the **Scenic Cinema** (entry included with ticket purchase) shows a 17-minute film of the mountain sights. Both the complex's **revolving** *Skyway Restaurant*, and the terrace at *Cableway Cafe-Bar* – where you need only grab a take-away ice cream or coffee – offer more views.

A short walk from the Scenic World complex along Cliff Drive, at the **Katoomba Falls picnic area**, there's a kiosk and several bushwalking options. The **Prince Henry Cliff Walk** (9km one-way; 1hr 30min; easy) is a long but pleasant stroll along the plateau clifftop via Echo Point all the way to **Gordon Falls** (see p.303), with glorious lookouts along the way; a great refreshment/lunch stop en route is *Solitary* (see p.308) across Cliff Drive from the Kiah Lookout. A scenic drive following Cliff Drive southwest of Katoomba Falls leads to several spectacular lookouts: Eaglehawk, the Landslide, and Narrow Neck. The last-named is a great sunset spot, with views into both the Jamison and Megalong valleys. To get to Narrow Neck peninsula itself, popular with mountain bikers, take the unsealed, winding Glen Raphael Road. From here, the top of the **Golden Stairs** provide access down to a difficult 14km-return, eight- to ten-hour walking route to **Mount Solitary**, where you can bush camp overnight (but take NPWS advice first). The track to Mount Solitary goes past the turn-off to the **Ruined Castle**, which is a six-hour medium to hard return walk from the Golden Stairs (or it can be reached via the base of Scenic World).

Medlow Bath and Blackheath

One train stop beyond Katoomba, and 6km further northwest along the Great Western Highway, the quiet village of **MEDLOW BATH** is based around the distinctively domed **Hydro Majestic Hotel**, built as an exclusive health resort in 1904 on an escarpment overlooking the **Megalong Valley**. The hotel was given a meticulous make-over by the Mercure chain in 2000 and was experiencing another as this book went to press (check ⓦ www.hydromajestic.com.au for updates). Even if you're not tempted to stay, it's worth a stopoff to gaze at the interiors and the stunning bush views from the balcony.

Five kilometres north of Medlow Bath along the Great Western Highway, there are more lookout points at **BLACKHEATH** – just as impressive as Echo Point and much less busy. One of the best is **Govetts Leap**, at the end of Govetts Leap Road (just over 2km east of the highway through the village centre), near the **Blue Mountains National Park** headquarters, the **Blackheath Heritage Centre** (daily 9am–4.30pm; ⓣ02/4787 8877). The two-kilometre **Fairfax Heritage Track** from the NPWS Centre is wheelchair- and pram-accessible and takes in the Govetts Leap Lookout with its marvellous panorama of the **Grose Valley** and Bridal Veil Falls. Many walks start from the centre, but one of the most popular, the **Grand Canyon** (5km; 3hr 30min; medium difficulty), begins from **Evans Lookout Road** at the south end of town, west of the Great Western Highway.

Govetts Leap Road and its shady cross-street, Wentworth Street, hold lots of antique and craft shops, an antiquarian bookshop, and great cafés and restaurants (see opposite). Ten kilometres southwest of Blackheath, across the railway line, the beautiful unspoilt **Megalong Valley** is reached via winding Megalong Road; it's popular for **horseriding** (see box, p.301), and there are creeks with swimmable waterholes.

Accommodation

Great **accommodation** in Blackheath includes *Glenella* on Govett's Leap Rd (ⓣ02/4787 8352, ⓦ www.glenellabluemountainshotel.com.au), a guesthouse in a charming 1905 homestead with its own licensed restaurant (dinner Fri & Sat) and antique-furnished rooms, mostly en suite, and a few cheaper share-bathroom options ($100–120, en suite $110–130).

If you have your own transport, you can easily indulge in some of the more unusual and characterful guesthouses in Blackheath. Pricier bush-set cabins and retreats line Evans Lookout Road, backing onto the national park. One highly recommended option is 🎋*Jemby-Rinjah Lodge*, 336 Evans Lookout Rd (☎02/4787 7622, 🌐www.jembyrinjahlodge.com.au), where accommodation is in distinctive one- and two-bedroom timber cabins with wood fires, sleeping two to six people ($170–219; $30 per extra adult), and luxurious eco-lodges sleeping up to 16 ($225 per person). The focal point of the licensed common area is a huge circular "fire pit"; a restaurant operates here on demand so be sure to make a booking.

Eating

Govett's Leap Road and Wentworth Street have the pick of places to **eat**. *Bakehouse on Wentworth*, 105 Wentworth St, is the original outlet of a cottage-like bakery selling European-style and organic bread and delicious pies and pastries, along with excellent coffee. Phenomenally popular with locals, and offering seating in a shady front courtyard, the *Bakehouse* has recently expanded with branches in Leura (by the fire station) and Springwood (opposite the train station). The *Victory Café*, 17 Govetts Leap Rd (☎02/4787 6777), is a very pleasant space at the front of an old Art Deco theatre now converted into an antiques centre. The gourmet sandwiches are good, and there's an all-day breakfast, plus plenty of choice for vegetarians. Bookings are also essential at the raved-about and highly recommended **restaurant** 🎋 *Vulcan's*, at 33 Govetts Leap Rd (☎02/4787 6899; lunch & dinner Fri–Sun). Housed in a century-old bakery, the wood-fired oven is used to produce sensational, seasonal food and there are fantastic desserts, such as the trademark chequerboard pineapple and star anise ice cream. It's expensive, with mains around the $30 mark, though BYO makes it more affordable.

Mount Victoria and around

At the top of the Blue Mountains, secluded and leafy **MOUNT VICTORIA**, 6km northwest of Blackheath along the Great Western Highway and the last mountain settlement proper, is the only one with an authentic village feel. The beautifully restored nineteenth-century resort, the *Imperial Hotel*, (rooms: budget $60–89, standard $79–109, en suite $100–145; ☎4784 1978, 🌐www.hotelimperial.com.au) has lovely accommodation and is good for a drink or **meal**, as is *Bay Tree Tea Shop* opposite, with raved-about meals like beef Wellington with truffle mash and tasty teas to have with old-fashioned scones in the charming atmosphere of an 1870s cottage. Mount Victoria is also fondly regarded for its tiny **cinema**, Mount Vic Flicks, in the public hall (see box, p.300). Several antique and secondhand bookshops are also worth a browse. Short **walks** start from the Fairy Bower Picnic area, a ten-minute walk from the Great Western Highway via Mount Piddington Road.

Beyond Mount Victoria, drivers can circle back towards Sydney via the scenic **Bells Line of Road**, which heads east through the fruit- and vegetable-growing areas of Bilpin and Kurrajong to Richmond, with growers selling their produce at roadside stalls. **Mount Tomah Botanic Garden** is on the way (daily: April–Sept 10am–4pm; Oct–March 10am–5pm; $5.50; 🌐www.rbgsyd.nsw.gov.au; no public transport), where the collection of southern-hemisphere cool-climate species includes Wollemi Pine. The popular *Restaurant Tomah* (lunch daily; licensed; mains $22–28.50; ☎02/4567 2060, 🌐www.restauranttomah.com.au) serves a contemporary Australian menu, and has fantastic north-facing views over the gardens, Wollemi National Park and Bilbin orchards. Cheaper light lunches are also available and there's a kiosk, plus free electric barbecues and picnic tables in the grounds. By car, you can continue west along the Bells Line of Road to the Zig Zag Railway at Clarence, just over 35km away (see below).

The **Hartley Historic Site** (Ⓦ www.npws.nsw.gov.au; no public transport), a well-preserved but deserted nineteenth-century village, lies at the foot of the scenic Victoria Pass, 11km from Mount Victoria on the Great Western Highway. As settlers headed west and forged roads through the mountains, the need for a police centre led to the construction of a courthouse here in 1837, but Hartley was eventually bypassed by the Great Western Highway in 1887. Looking at the site costs nothing, and the NPWS information centre and shop provides a map (daily 10am–1pm & 2–4.30pm; ☎ 02/6355 2117). To enter the buildings, however – only the courthouse is currently visitable – you have to take a guided tour (contact the information centre).

The Zig Zag Railway

En route to Bathurst and the Central West on the Great Western Highway, **Lithgow**, 21km northwest of Mount Victoria, is a coal-mining town nestled under bush-clad hills, with wide leafy streets, quaint mining cottages and some imposing old buildings. About 13km east of the town on the Bells Line of

▲ Zig Zag Railway

Road, by the small settlement of **Clarence**, is the **Zig Zag Railway**. In the 1860s, engineers were faced with the problem of how to get the main western railway line from the top of the Blue Mountains down the steep drop to the Lithgow Valley, so they came up with a series of zigzag ramps. These fell into disuse in the early twentieth century, but tracks were relaid by rail enthusiasts in the 1970s. Served by old steam trains, the picturesque line passes through two tunnels and over three viaducts. You can stop at points along the way and rejoin a later train.

The Zig Zag Railway can be reached by ordinary State Rail train on the regular service between Sydney and Lithgow, by requesting the guard in advance to stop at the Zig Zag platform; you then walk across the line to Bottom Point platform at the base of the Lithgow Valley. To catch the Zig Zag Railway from Clarence, at the top of the valley, you'll need to have your own transport. Zig Zag trains depart from Clarence daily (11am, 1pm & 3pm; from the Zig Zag platform 11.50am, 1.50pm & 3.50pm; single $19, return $25; ☎02/635 2955, ⓦwww.zigzagrailway.com.au).

The **Lithgow Visitor Information Centre**, 1 Cooerwull Rd (daily 9am–5pm; ☎1300 760 276, 02/6350 3230, ⓦwww.tourism.lithgow.com), can advise on the **motels** that abound in and around Lithgow, especially on the Great Western Highway.

The Jenolan Caves and Kanangra Boyd National Park

Kanangra Boyd National Park shares a boundary with the Blue Mountains National Park. Further south than the latter, much of it is inaccessible, but you can explore the rugged beauty of **Kanangra Walls**, where the Boyd Plateau falls away to reveal a wilderness area of creeks, deep gorges and rivers below. Reached via Jenolan Caves, three **walks** leave from the car park at Kanangra Walls: a short lookout walk, a waterfall stroll and a longer plateau walk. Contact the NPWS in **Oberon** for details (38 Ross St; ☎02/6336 1972). Vehicle entry to the park costs $7. *Boyd River* and *Dingo Dell* camping grounds, both off Kanangra Walls Road, have **free bush camping** (pit toilets; limited drinking water at Dingo Dell). You can get to **Oberon**, a timber-milling town and the closest settlement to Kanangra, by Countrylink bus from Mount Victoria (3 weekly).

The Jenolan Caves

The **Jenolan Caves** lie 30km southwest across the mountains from Katoomba on the far edge of the Kanangra Boyd National Park – over 80km by road – and contain New South Wales' most spectacular limestone formations. Guided tours explore the ten "show" caves throughout the day (daily 9.30am–5.30pm; 2hr adult-oriented ghost tours depart 8pm Sat only). If you're just coming for a day, plan to see one or two caves: the best general cave is the Lucas Cave ($25; 1hr 30min), and a more spectacular one is the Temple of Baal ($33; 1hr 30min), while the extensive River Cave, with its tranquil Pool of Reflection, is the longest and priciest ($38; 2hr). The system of caves is surrounded by the **Jenolan Karst Conservation Reserve**, a fauna and flora sanctuary with picnic facilities and walking trails to small waterfalls and lookout points. All is administered by the Jenolan Caves Trust (☎02/6359 3911, 1300 763 311, ⓦwww .jenolancaves.org.au), which also offers **adventure caving** in various other caves (2hr Plughole tour $60, 7hr Central River Adventure Cave tour $187.50).

There's no public **transport** to Jenolan Caves, but you can get here with Fantastic Aussie Tours (see p.295; 1hr 30min; $35; departs Katoomba 11.15am; departs Jenolan Caves 3.45pm), designed as an overnight rather than a day-return service; otherwise the same company offers day-tours from Katoomba, as do several other operators, or for tours from Sydney see p.295. You can actually **walk** from Katoomba to the Jenolan Caves along the 42-kilometre-long **Six Foot Track** (see box, p.306).

Accommodation

Apart from the caves themselves, the focus for the area is a rather romantic old **hotel**, which found fame as a honeymoon destination in the 1920s and is now part of the *Jenolan Caves Resort* (contact details as for Jenolan Caves Trust, above). In the old hotel, which also has a good restaurant, you'll find *Chisholm's Grand Dining Room* (3-course dinner $45), plus a bar and a more casual bistro; there are en-suite rooms ($185; $215; $265), and cheaper shared-bathroom versions ($115), all with a minimum two-nights' stay on weekends.

The newer annexe, the *Mountain Lodge*, holds motel-style rooms ($160) and two bedroom units ($270; $35 per extra adult); family rooms sleep four to six in the *Gatehouse* ($60; $25 for each extra child; BYO linen), which has shared communal areas, including a kitchen. For big groups and families, Jenolan Karst Conservation Park is also dotted with well-equipped cottages (sleep 6–8; $135; $198 – *Binoomea Cottage*, which accommodates 12, costs $345 for 6 and $25 each extra person – BYO linen). Another place to stay, 4km west of Jenolan Caves on Porcupine Hill, is *Jenolan Cabins*, 42 Edith Rd (☏02/6335 6239, ⓦwww .jenolanccabins.com.au; $98–125). These very reasonably priced, well-equipped, modern, two-bedroom timber cabins with wood fires accommodate six (BYO linen; $15 for each extra adult) and offer magnificent bush views; 4WD tours of the area are also offered (from $80 half-day, including lunch).

The Royal National Park and beyond

The Princes Highway and the Illawarra railway – the two main transport arteries out of Sydney's bustling southern reaches to the unspoiled NSW south coast – hug the edge of the **Royal National Park**, a huge nature reserve right on the city's doorstep, for more than 20km. Though the park is only 32km out, just over an hour's drive on a good day, it marks Sydney's southern extent, separating it from the gradual suburban sprawl of **Wollongong**, a working-class industrial centre 85km south. A stunning **coastal route** heads through the Royal National Park to **Thirroul**, outside Wollongong, where D.H. Lawrence wrote most of his novel *Kangaroo*. Eight kilometres south of **Wollongong**, Australia's largest **Buddhist temple**, **Nan Tien**, has an irresistibly peaceful atmosphere.

The Royal National Park

In 1879, the **Royal National Park** was established as only the second national park in the world, after Yellowstone in the US. On the eastern side, from Jibbon Head to Garie Beach, the park falls away abruptly to the ocean, creating a spectacular coastline of steep cliffs that's broken here and there by creeks cascading into the sea and little coves with fine sandy beaches. The remains of **Aboriginal rock carvings** are the only traces of the original Dharawal people.

Apart from the beaches and tracks, the main goals are the NPWS visitor centre at the tiny hamlet of **Audley**, and the small town of **Bundeena**, on Port Hacking, which holds cafés, and a few places to stay. Advance information is available from the NPWS Office, Level 14, 59–61 Goulburn St, Sydney (Mon–Fri 9am–5pm; ☎0300/361 967).

Approaching the park

The railway between Sydney and Wollongong marks the Royal National Park's western border. From the train, the scenery is fantastic – streams, waterfalls, rock formations and rainforest flora fly past the window. If you want to explore further, get off at one of the **stations** along the way: Loftus, Engadine, Heathcote, Waterfall or Otford. All are starting points for walking trails into the park, but since there is no public transport inside the park you're a bit limited without your own vehicle.

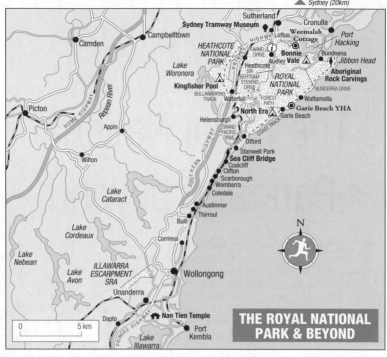

A more interesting way to reach the park is the 25-min **ferry** ride across Port Hacking from the southern beachside suburb of Cronulla (see p.150) to little **Bundeena** (see p.318) at the park's northeast tip. Cronulla & National Park Ferry Cruises operate from Cronulla's Tonkin Street wharf, just below the train station (Mon–Fri hourly 5.30am–6.30pm except 12.30pm, continuous during school hols; Sat & Sun Sept–March 8.30am–6.30pm hourly, April–Oct 8.30am–5.30pm; returns from Bundeena hourly: Mon–Fri 6am–7pm except 1pm; Sat & Sun Sept–March 9am–7pm, April–Oct 9am–6pm; $5.40; ☎02/9523 2990, ⓦwww.cronullaferries .com.au). They also run three-hour **narrated cruises** around Port Hacking (Sept–May daily 10.30am; June–Sept Mon, Wed, Fri & Sun 10.30am; $20).

Finally, you can **drive** into the park. If you plan to use any of the day-use areas or park anywhere you'll incur the park **entry fee** ($11 per vehicle per day), payable at booths at each road entrance. With entrances off the Princes Highway in the north (at Loftus) and south (at Otford on Lady Wakehurst Drive), drivers can loop off the main road en route between Sydney and Wollongong. Roads through the park are always open and if you're just driving through there is no charge: just tell the officer in the pay-booth. It's also possible to visit the fringes of the park by tram from the Sydney Tramway Museum.

Sydney Tramway Museum

Pull off the Princes Highway just north of the park, or get off the train at Loftus, to visit the **Sydney Tramway Museum** (Wed 10am–3pm, Sun & public hols 10am–5pm; last entry 1hr before closing; $15 including unlimited tram rides; ⓦwww.sydneytramwaymuseum.com.au), right next to Loftus train station.

Trams operated in Sydney for a century until 1961, and examples of the old fleet, including a Bondi tram, as well as trams from around the world, are on display here. You can ride a tram either 1.5km north through bushland towards the suburb of Sutherland, or take the two-kilometre Parklink route (trams hourly when open) to the start of the Bungoona Lookout walk (see below). From there, a one-kilometre walk leads downhill to the NPWS Visitor Centre (see below) and Audley, where there's a kiosk and picnic facilities.

Accommodation

There's little roofed accommodation in the park. The emphasis is on **camping**, primarily on the shores of the Hacking River just west of Bundeena at the NPWS *Bonnie Vale Camping Ground* (no powered sites; $14 per person), or at the *North Era* walk-in **bushcamp** ($5 per person) along the Coast Track. Both campgrounds should be booked in advance, either through the NPWS office in Sydney (see p.47), or by phone (Mon–Fri 10.30am–1.30pm; ☎02/9542 0683): the permit can be posted out to you, and may take up to seven days. The *North Eva* site is often booked out weeks in advance for weekends.

A small, very basic but secluded **YHA hostel**, with no electricity (except for solar lighting) or showers, stands inside the park, one kilometre from Garie Beach (book in advance at any YHA hostel; key must be collected in advance; dorms $14). If you want to stay in more comfort, opt for the B&Bs and holiday rentals in Bundeena (see Ⓦwww.bundeena.com), or the NPWS-run *Weemalah Cottage* ($190–220 a night), a three-bedroom place on the shores of Port Hacking with a two-night minimum. Reserve through the camping booking line, above.

The park

Approaching the park from the north, stop 3km south of Loftus at the easy, concrete, wheelchair-accessible Bungoona Lookout **nature trail** (1km return; 20min; flat), which has information panels on local history, flora and fauna, and ends with panoramic views north and east across the park.

Roughly one kilometre south, you cross the Hacking River on a low causeway at **Audley**, which is just a picturesque picnic ground (with kiosk) and a shed for renting rowboats, canoes and kayaks (all $28 for 2hr) and mountain bikes ($22 for 2hr, $34 all day).

The park's **NPWS Visitor Centre** here (daily 8.30am–4.30pm; ☎02/9542 0648, Ⓦwww.environment.nsw.gov.au), stocks the excellent fold-out *Royal National Park* **brochure** ($1), detailed enough to use for bushwalks and camping. They also sell the more comprehensive *Royal National Park Tourist Map* ($6.50) and *Discovering Royal National Park on Foot* by Alan Fairley ($12.95), which includes maps and commentaries on the best walks in the park.

The ultimate trek in the park, the spectacular 26-kilometre **Coast Track**, takes in the park's entire coastal length. Hiking it can be tough, as you need to carry your own water, but is thoroughly rewarding. Give yourself two days to complete it, starting at either Bundeena (see p.318) or Otford, and camping overnight either at the YHA, the *North Era* campsite (see above), or one of several other officially designated bushcamps (check with the NPWS office or visitor centre). En route you'll pass the vehicle-accessible Wattamolla and Garie **beaches**, both with kiosks (generally open weekends only), and good surfing. An easier but still satisfying option is to hike just part of the route, such as the popular trail from Otford down to beachfront **Burning Palms** (2hr one-way; no camping).

▲ Little Marley Beach

Also in the south of the park, consider **Forest Path** (4.5km loop, 1hr 30min; easy) which winds through some of the finest rainforest in the Sydney area. Take your time and walk quietly to appreciate an area rich in wildlife, with many butterflies, lizards, water dragons, snakes and birds.

Bundeena

Park roads meet ferries from Cronulla at **Bundeena**, a small town on the shores of Port Hacking with a golden beach. It marks the northern end of the Coast Track, reached by following the Avenue and Lambeth Walk for 1km to the national park gate. Other less strenuous options include the pleasant walk south to pretty sheltered **Little Marley Beach** (9km return, 4hr; moderate) for a swim and a picnic, while heading down a signposted pathway east to **Jibbons Beach** (3km return, 1hr; easy) will take you past some Dharawal rock engravings, where faint outlines of a kangaroo, stingrays, whales and a six-fingered man can be seen. Get directions from *The Fringe*, the best of the local cafés, 300m south of the ferry dock at 44 Brighton St, which acts as a visitor information point.

Heathcote National Park

The Princes Highway separates Royal National Park from the much smaller and quieter **Heathcote National Park** (entry free) to the west. Heathcote is a serious bushwalkers' park, with no roads and a ban on trail bikes; you can walk its entire length in a morning and see no one along the way. From the best **train** station for the park, Waterfall, you can follow the fairly hilly **Bullawarring Track** north (12km one-way, 5hr; moderate), and join a later train from Heathcote. The track weaves through assorted vegetation, including scribbly gums with their intriguing bark patterns, and spectacular gymea lilies with bright red flowers atop tall flowering spears in the spring. En route, Heathcote Creek feeds several swimmable pools – the carved sandstone of the **Kingfisher Pool** is the largest and most picturesque. The *Royal National Park Tourist Map* ($6.50 from NPWS) is needed for route finding.

There's a small, very basic 18-person **campground** at Kingfisher Pool, and another at Mirang Pool (12 people; $5 each). Water is not guaranteed, and you'll need to book through the NPWS camping booking line (Mon–Fri 10.30am–1.30pm; ☎02/9542 0683).

By car, you can reach the picnic area at Woronora Dam on the western edge of the park: turn east off the Princes Highway onto Woronora Road (free entry); parking available.

South of the parks

A stunning **coastal drive** leads from the Royal National Park to **Thirroul**, just north of Wollongong. The route runs between rugged sandstone coastal cliffs on one side and bush-covered Illawarra Escarpment on the other, with some beautiful beaches and great pubs and cafés along the way.

Follow the Princes Highway south out of Sydney, exiting into the Royal National Park after Loftus onto Farnell Drive; the entry fee at the gate is waived if you are just driving through without stopping. The road through the park emerges above the cliffs at **Otford**, beyond which runs Lawrence Hargreave Drive (Route 68), part of the **Grand Pacific Drive** to Wollongong and beyond.

A couple of kilometres south of Otford is the impressive clifftop lookout on **Bald Hill**, a great viewpoint looking down the coast past the 665 metre-long **Sea Cliff Bridge**, which curls around the seacliffs circumventing a massive landslip which temporarily closed the coast road in the mid-2000s. At Bald Hill you're also likely to see **hang-gliders** taking off and soaring down. You can join in with the Sydney Hang Gliding Centre (☎02/4294 4294, ⓦwww.hanggliding.com.au), which offers tandem flights for around $195 during the week, $220 at weekends (available daily depending on the weather); the centre also runs courses from $275 per day. Head south along the Sea Cliff Bridge and past impressive cliff scenery, and you soon pass through **Scarborough**, just over 7km south, best appreciated from the historic *Scarborough Hotel*.

Austinmer

By the time you get to **AUSTINMER**, 5km south of Scarborough, you've come to a break in the stunning cliffs and into some heavy surf territory. This down-to-earth former coal-mining town is typical of small coastal settlements in the area, with the Pacific to the east and the soaring Illawarra Escarpment looming over the town, it's easy to see why it has attracted an influx of "downsizers", who lend the place its relaxed atmosphere. A popular, very clean, patrolled **surf beach** gets packed out on summer weekends. Across the road, the excellent *Austi Beach Café*, 104 Lawrence Hargrave Drive, serves great food and coffee in a casual setting, daily, and stays open for dinner (Thurs–Sat) in summer. Alternatively, seek out the arty *Fireworks Café*, a locals' secret at 40 Moore St, just back from the beach on the way to the train station.

Thirroul

Just 2km south of Austinmer, **THIRROUL** is the spot where English novelist **D.H. Lawrence** wrote *Kangaroo* during his short Australian interlude in 1922.

Lawrence renamed the then-sleepy village "Mullumbimby" in the novel, but the bungalow he stayed in at 3 Craig St, the town and the surrounding area are described in some depth. Today, Thirroul is gradually being swallowed up by the suburban sprawl of Wollongong, but makes a lively spot to stop for a coffee at the *Tin Shed*, 364 Lawrence Hargrave Drive, or a sophisticated but moderately priced dinner at *Samuels*, 382 Lawrence Hargrave Drive (☎02/4268 2244; closed Mon), which opens for lunch at weekends.

At the southern end of Thirroul's beach, **Sandford Point** (labelled Bulli Point on maps) is a famous surfing break. A sixty-kilometre cycle track runs from Thirroul south along the coast, through Wollongong to Lake Illawarra.

The Illawarra Escarpment

A kilometre south of Thirroul, Lawrence Hargrave Drive joins the Princes Highway, which heads south to Wollongong (Route 60) or northwest, up to a section of the forested Illawarra Escarpment and the **Bulli Pass**. You can enjoy fantastic views from the Bulli Lookout, which has its own café, and from the appropriately named **Sublime Point Lookout**, a couple of kilometres further north heading back towards Sydney. Explore the escarpment using the various **walking tracks** that start from the lookouts, or visit the extensive portion of the **Illawarra Escarpment State Recreation Area** that lies about 10km west of Wollongong's city centre on Mount Kembla and Mount Keira.

Wollongong and around

With a quarter of a million residents, **Wollongong**, 80km south of Sydney, is the state's third largest city, but is often ignored by visitors in favour of quainter beach towns either side. Certainly the large steelworks just south of town doesn't help, but "The Gong" is a nice enough place, with a good beach and a lively atmosphere thanks to the local university students.

One of the most pleasant activities is simply to wander along the coastal **City Walk**, which starts at the eastern end of Crown Street and runs 2km north to **North Wollongong Beach**. The walk passes Flagstaff Point, a grassy headland overlooking the lovely **Wollongong Harbour**, with its fishing fleet, a fish market, a few seafood restaurants, and a picturesque nineteenth-century lighthouse on the breakwater. Around the middle of October, the **Viva la Gong** festival (ⓦwww.vivalagongfestival.org) spices up the city with a sculpture exhibition along the seafront and nightly events including circus, dance, music and the like.

Excellent café-style **lunches** can be had beside North Beach at *Diggies*, 1 Clift St (daytime daily, plus Fri & Sat dinner in summer). If you stick around for dinner, go for the modestly priced Vietnamese at *Mylan*, 193 Keira St (☎02/4228 1588; BYO; closed Sun), or the French *Caveau*, 122 Keira St (☎02/4226 4855; closed Sun & Mon), a match for many of Sydney's best, with three courses for $72.

Nan Tien Temple

Eight kilometres south of Wollongong, the vast **Nan Tien Temple**, Berkeley Road (Tues–Sun, and all public hols, 9am–4pm; free; ⓦwww.nantien.org.au), is the largest Buddhist temple in Australia. Entry is through a traditional Chinese-style roofed triple gate to a truly impressive complex of shrines, a museum, meditation hall and seven-tier pagoda, erected to house the cremated remains of up to seven thousand devotees. The main shrine contains five large Buddhas, while a thousand smaller ones line the walls. Well signposted off the Princes Highway, it's a twenty-minute walk from the Unanderra CityRail train station, reached direct from either Sydney's Central Station or Wollongong. Premier Illawarra (℡02/4271 1322) route #34 from Crown Gateway in the centre of town passes close to Nan Tien every half-hour or so.

The Fo Guang Shan Buddhists welcome visitors to the temple and offer all-you-can-eat **vegetarian lunches** (Tues–Fri 11.30am–2pm, Sat & Sun 11.30am–2.30pm; $9).

There are also Buddhist retreats with **accommodation** in the peaceful and surprisingly upmarket *Pilgrim Lodge* (℡02/4272 0500; $80–160 per room, sleeping up to 4; all activities included in accommodation price). Their weekend-long annual cultural festival in December, which includes food stalls, dance performances, traditional craft demonstrations and workshops, provides a good antidote to the commercial frenzy of Christmas; check the website for details.

25

The Southern Highlands and around

T hanks to their beautiful countryside – rolling hills, pasture and forest – and pretty, historic towns, crammed with cafés, restaurants, antique shops and secondhand book stalls, the **Southern Highlands** have been a popular weekend retreat for Sydneysiders since the 1920s. Located about an hour and a half's drive down the South Western Freeway from the city, the area is also home to a young, yet increasingly important **wine industry**, and provides a good alternative to the Hunter Valley.

The Southern Highlands and surrounding area are well served by public transport. Frequent **trains** from Sydney's Central Station stop at Mittagong, Bowral, Moss Vale, Exeter and Bundanoon, while the South Coast line can take you to Kiama, Gerringong, Berry and Bomaderry ($13.60–15.80 one-way, better deals on off-peak return tickets). Priors Scenic Express operate a **coach** service from Campbelltown train station, on Sydney's western fringes (daily except Sat 3.30pm; ☎1800 816 234), to Mittagong, Bowral, Kangaroo Valley and on to Bateman's Bay. Premier Motor Service runs from Pitt Street outside Central Station to Kiama, Bomaderry and Nowra (daily 9.15am & 3.20pm; ☎13 3410, Ⓦwww.premierms.com.au). Plenty of **local buses** can get you around once you are there, including Berrima Buslines (☎02/4871 3211).

Accommodation is generally more expensive at weekends and public holidays, but you can get good deals on rooms if you visit during the week. There are also plenty of self-catering character cottages, and a few campsites.

If you **drive** to the Southern Highlands, a good scenic route back to Sydney passes through **Kangaroo Valley**, and on to **Berry** and **Kiama**, both lovely spots south of Wollongong.

Mittagong

Just over 100km south of Sydney, the small agricultural and tourist town of **MITTAGONG** doesn't quite have the twee weekender appeal of Bowral or Berrima, but increasingly attracts visitors for its epicurean delights and as a staging post for the limestone **Wombeyan Caves**. Mittagong's **visitor information centre** (Mon–Fri 9am–5pm Sat & Sun 9am–4pm; ☎1300 657 559, Ⓦwww.southern-highlands.com.au) provides a free accommodation booking service, and has masses of information on bushwalks. The characterful ten-room *Fitzroy Inn*, 1km north of town at 1 Ferguson Crescent (☎02/4872 3457,

ⓦwww.fitzroyinn.com.au; $190 midweek, $240 weekend), is a great **place to stay**. Once used to house prisoners, it has been restored with a surprising touch of European chic and still retains its old stone cells. Its excellent **restaurant** offers modern Australian dishes with provincial Italian leanings (Wed–Sat noon–3pm & 6–10pm, Sun noon–3pm; mains $25–34; licensed and BYO). Mittagong also holds a handful of motels, while the *Mittagong Caravan Park* is 300m north of the information centre at 1 Old Hume Hwy (ⓣ02/4871 1574, ⓦwww.mittagongcaravanpark.com.au; $20 per site, cabins from $60).

For good lunch or just a coffee and cake, visit *Just Bite Me*, 24 Bowral Rd (Mon–Sat 7am–5pm, Sun 8am–4pm) which produces its own gluten-free cakes and breads.

Wombeyan Caves

From Mittagong, a tortuous, mostly unsealed road winds 65km up into the hills to the west, to **Wombeyan Caves** (daily 9am–5.30pm; ⓣ02/4843 5976, ⓦwww .nationalparks.nsw.gov.au), amid some of the state's finest karst landscape. The effort is rewarded with a selection of caves to visit, some easy and well-packaged, others more adventurous. Take as long as you like in the self-guided Figtree Cave ($13), where the wild formations are inventively lit. Other caves are visited on tours ($16 each; 60–90min each), whether individually or with the Explorer Pass ($28), which covers two tours and the Figtree Cave.

Above ground there are bush walks, picnic areas with barbecues, and a **campsite** with cabin and cottage accommodation and pitches along the pretty Wombeyan Creek; good amenities include hot showers, a communal kitchen and campfire facilities (sites $10 per person; en-suite cabins $72–78, cottage $95–110, both with two-night minimum weekends & hols). You'll need your own linen, towels and food, though the kiosk sells limited groceries.

Bowral

Six kilometres southwest of Mittagong, the busy, well-to-do town of **BOWRAL** hums with activity at weekends, when the upper echelon of Sydney society pitch up to cruise the streets in flash cars, sip cappuccinos and catch up on gossip before retiring to their country hideaways. The main strip, Bong Bong Street, is full of upmarket clothes and homeware shops; pick up a leaflet at Bong Bong Books, at no. 42, which highlights literary stops on the region's **BookTrail** (ⓦwww .booktown.com.au).

Bowral was the birthplace of **cricket** legend **Don Bradman**. Cricket fans will want to head straight for the **Bradman Museum of Cricket** on St Jude St (daily 10am–5pm; $12; ⓦwww.bradman.org.au), set in an idyllic spot between a leafy park and the well-used cricket oval and club. Inside, a history of the game and its development in Australia leads to a cinema showing great 1930s' and 1940s' footage of "The Don" in his pomp, along with patronizing film of women's cricket. Elsewhere you can learn about the operation of stump cameras, marvel at a collection of tour blazers and "baggy green" caps, and admire the shabby bat that Bradman was given when playing for the local senior team, aged 12. You can even try your hand at Bradman's childhood game using a golf ball, a stump as a bat and playing knock back against the brick base of a water tank. He attributed this game as the foundation of his skills.

The Shepherd Street house where he grew up is now a station on the **Bradman Walk** (45min) around town: pick up a leaflet from the museum. The cricket fan who owns it is turning it into a B&B, and is apparently recreating the long-gone tank stand.

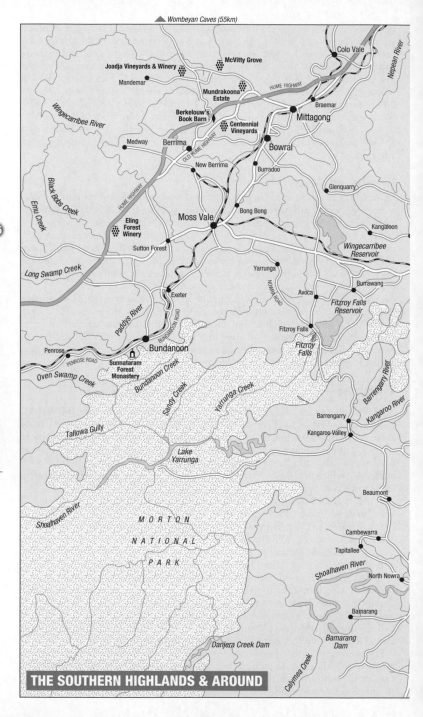

▲ Wombeyan Caves (55km)

Colo Vale

McVitty Grove

Joadja Vineyards & Winery

Mandemar

Mundrakoona Estate

HUME HIGHWAY

Braemar

Berkelouw's Book Barn

Mittagong

Centennial Vineyards

Medway   Berrima

OLD HUME HIGHWAY

Bowral

New Berrima

Burradoo

HUME HIGHWAY

Glenquarry

Eling Forest Winery

Bong Bong

Moss Vale

Kangaloon

Sutton Forest

Wingecarribee Reservoir

Yarrunga

Long Swamp Creek

Burrawang

Exeter

Avoca

Fitzroy Falls Reservoir

NOWRA ROAD

Paddys River

BUNDANOON ROAD

Fitzroy Falls

Fitzroy Falls

Penrose

Bundanoon

PENROSE ROAD

Sunnataram Forest Monastery

Oven Swamp Creek

Bundanoon Creek

Sandy Creek

Yarrunga Creek

Barrengarry

Kangaroo River

Barrengarry River

Kangaroo Valley

Tallowa Gully

Lake Yarrunga

Beaumont

Shoalhaven River

M O R T O N

Cambewarra

N A T I O N A L

Tapitallee

Shoalhaven River

North Nowra

P A R K

Bamarang

Danjera Creek Dam

Bamarang Dam

Calymea Creek

Wingecarribee River

Black Bobs Creek

Emu Creek

Nepean River

THE SOUTHERN HIGHLANDS & AROUND

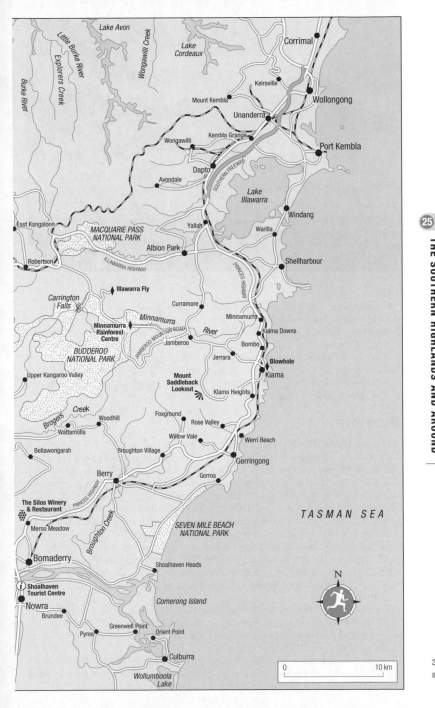

Lake Avon

Little Burke River

Explorers Creek

Burke River

Wongawilli Creek

Lake Cordeaux

Corrimal

Keiraville

Mount Kembla

Wollongong

Unanderra

Kembla Grange

Port Kembla

Wongawilli

East Kangaloon

MACQUARIE PASS NATIONAL PARK

Avondale

Dapto

SOUTHERN FREEWAY

Lake Illawarra

Windang

Yallah

Warilla

Albion Park

ILLAWARRA HIGHWAY

Robertson

Shellharbour

Carrington Falls

Illawarra Fly

Curramore

PRINCES HIGHWAY

Minnamurra

Minnamurra Rainforest Centre

Minnamurra

River

Kiama Downs

BUDDEROO NATIONAL PARK

JAMBEROO MOUNTAIN ROAD

Jamberoo

Bombo

Jerrara

Blowhole

Kiama

Upper Kangaroo Valley

Mount Saddleback Lookout

Kiama Heights

Brogers

Creek

Woodhill

Foxground

Rose Valley

Wattamolla

Willow Vale

Werri Beach

Bellawongarah

Broughton Village

Gerringong

Berry

Gerroa

The Silos Winery & Restaurant

PRINCES HIGHWAY

Meroo Meadow

Broughton Creek

SEVEN MILE BEACH NATIONAL PARK

TASMAN SEA

Bomaderry

Shoalhaven Heads

Shoalhaven Tourist Centre

Nowra

Comerong Island

Brundee

Greenwell Point

Pyree

Orient Point

Culburra

Wollumboola Lake

N

0   10 km

▲ Bradman Oval, Bowral

The Bradman museum holds the pleasant *Stumps Tea Room* (daily 10am–4pm), with a garden terrace, while plenty more good **eating** options lie on or near Bong Bong Street. *Coffee Culture*, hidden at the end of a lane behind Empire Cinema Complex on Bong Bong Street, is a slick city-style café with the best coffee in town and outstanding food including all-day breakfast. The best Italian restaurant is *Onesta Cucina*, Wingecarribbee St (℡02/4861 6620; lunch Thurs–Sun, dinner Tues–Sun), where you might sample a porcini risotto or salmon pasta: mains $25–30.

Berrima

Picturesque little **BERRIMA**, 7km west of Bowral on the Old Hume Highway, is set around an English-style village green and is considered one of the country's best preserved and restored 1830s towns. Of particular note is the *Surveyor General Inn*, which has been serving beer since 1835, making it the oldest continually licensed hotel in Australia. The **visitor centre** (daily 10am–4pm; ℡02/4877 1505) can be found inside the 1838 sandstone **Courthouse Museum** (same hours; $7; ⓦwww.berrimacourthouse.org.au), on the corner of Argyle and Wiltshire streets, while across the road the still operational **Berrima Gaol** once held the infamous bushranger Thunderbolt, and acted as an internment camp for POWs and immigrants in wartime; it also has the dubious distinction of being the first place in Australia to execute a woman, in 1841. Continue up Wiltshire Street to reach the **River Walk**, a 200-metre path that ends at a nature reserve with **picnic tables**.

If you'd like to **stay**, try the *White Horse Inn*, The Marketplace (℡02/4877 1204, ⓦwww.whitehorseinn.com.au; midweek $80, Fri $100, Sat $150), a large old 1832 sandstone hotel with accommodation in modern motel units in the garden.

Berrima itself holds a handful of good cafés, while *Berkelouw's Book Barn & Café*, 3km north along the Old Hume Highway, is a vast converted barn that sells secondhand and rare books alongside good **food** and coffee.

Bundanoon and the Morton National Park

Five kilometres southwest of Berrima on the Old Hume Highway is the turn-off south to **BUNDANOON**, famous for its annual celebration of its Scottish heritage. Exploiting the autumnal atmosphere of mist and turning leaves, Bundanoon becomes Brigadoon for one Saturday in April, overtaken by **Highland Games** – Aussie-style. It's only a small place, but its charm and easy atmosphere make it a good place to break a journey or relax for a few days' bushwalking or cycling.

The town is in an attractive spot set in hilly countryside scarred by deep gullies. It enjoys splendid views over the gorges and mountains of the huge **MORTON NATIONAL PARK** (car parking fee $7; bring coins), which extends from Bundanoon to near Kangaroo Valley. Start your explorations by setting off at sunset armed with a torch on an evening stroll to **Glow Worm Glen**; after dark the small sandstone grotto is transformed by the naturally flickering lights of these insects, and you may be lucky enough to see wombats along the way. It's a 25-minute walk from Bundanoon via the end of William Street, or an easy forty-minute signposted trek from Riverview Road in the national park.

Five kilometres southwest of town, a community of Thai Buddhist monks provide residential meditation retreats and teaching programmes at the **Sunna-taram Forest Monastery** (visitors welcome; ☏02/4884 4262, ⓦwww.sunnataram.org for details and directions).

Southern Highlands wineries

With most producers only producing vintages since the mid-1990s, the wine industry in the Southern Highlands is still emerging, but the financial investment in some of the larger labels is significant, and awards are rolling in. The climate here is cooler than most other Australian wine regions and the harvest later, resulting in more varietal flavours, an enhanced fruity character and increased complexity.

Centennial Vineyards Centennial Road, Bowral ☏02/4861 8700, ⓦwww.centennial.net.au. Large set-up, with an extensive range of wines for tasting, plus its own restaurant, which gets busy at weekends. Cellar door with free tasting, daily 10am–5pm.

Eling Forest Winery Hume Highway, Sutton Forest (between Berrima & Bundanoon) ☏02/4878 9499, ⓦwww.elingforest.com.au. Boutique winery established in 1990 in the area's original schoolhouse, set on 200-acre grounds that visitors are free to roam. It's a very friendly place, producing some excellent wines, has a prize-winning restaurant (Thurs–Sat noon–3pm & 6–9pm, Sun noon–3pm; mains $25–31), which couples modern Italian food with wines produced on site. Cellar door daily 10am–5pm.

Joadja Vineyards and Winery Joadja Road, Berrima ☏02/4878 5236, ⓦwww.joadja.com. The area's first boutique winery offers the chance to walk through the working winery. Look out for "Brambelini", a fruit liqueur made from grape spirit, grape juice and seasonal berries. Cellar door daily 10am–5pm.

McVitty Grove Wombeyan Caves Rd, Mittagong ☏02/4878 5044, ⓦwww.mcvittygrove.com.au. Beautifully situated winery, with stunning views over the valley from the cellar door. The restaurant serves dishes (lunches $15–24, dinner mains $20–25) made from home-produced olives and trout; book in advance. Cellar door daily 10am–5pm.

Mundrakoona Estate Sir Charles Moses Lane, off Old Hume Highway, 5km west of Mittagong ☏02/4872 1311, ⓦwww.mundrakoona.com.au. Small family-run winery with its own working blacksmith shop, where you can buy ironwork bookstands, rocking chairs or even full sets of gates. Cellar door Mon–Fri 10am–5pm, Sat & Sun 10am–6pm.

The national park, and Bundanoon, are popular with **cyclists**. The long-established Olde Bicycle Shoppe, 9 Church St, near Bundanoon railway station, rents out bikes (Mon–Fri 9am–4.30pm, Sat & Sun 9am–5pm; $18.50 per hr, $28 half-day, $45 full day; ☏02/4883 6043). Opposite the station, the cosy *Bundanoon Hotel* (ⓦwww.bundanoonhotel.com.au), is a good place to recover with a pint of stout and a filling meal after a cycling adventure, serving plain, affordable **food** in its *Thistle* carvery (lunch Wed–Sun, dinner Wed–Sat); book ahead at weekends.

Accommodation options in Bundanoon include the good-value *Bundanoon Country Inn Motel*, Anzac Parade (☏02/4883 6068, ⓦwww.bundanoonmotel .com.au; midweek $85, weekend $110), a central motel with great facilities including a pool, tennis court and barbecue. About a kilometre northeast is the ⚐ *Bundanoon YHA* on Railway Ave (☏02/4883 6010; camping $15.50, dorms $25, rooms $60; book ahead), a spacious Edwardian-era guesthouse complete with open fireplaces, set in extensive grounds where you can also camp; and a few metres away, the stylish *Tree Tops Country Guesthouse*, 101 Railway Ave (☏02/4883 6372, ⓦwww.treetopsguesthouse.com.au; midweek $160, weekend $200), occupies the other end of the scale in an elegant guesthouse dating from 1910, furnished top to bottom with antiques. Prices include a sumptuous breakfast and you can stay for dinner ($45) preceded by canapés and sherry.

There's also drive-in **camping** inside the national park at *Gambells Rest*, 1km south of Bundanoon station ($10 per person; bookings essential on ☏02/4887 7270), which has flush toilets, hot showers and drinking water.

Macquarie Pass and Budderoo national parks

Three main routes run from the Southern Highlands to the coast, via Moss Vale: one (see below) heads southwest past Fitzroy Falls to Kangaroo Valley and Berry, while the other two initially follow the Illawarra Highway due east. The fastest route heads to Shellharbour through **MACQUARIE PASS NATIONAL PARK**, 30km east of Moss Vale, one of the southernmost stands of Australia's subtropical rainforest. The car park on the highway is the trailhead for the **Cascades Walk**, a two-kilometre loop through the forest to the twenty-metre Cascades Waterfall.

The small town of Robertson, 5km west, marks the start of the second route, this time southeast through **BUDDEROO NATIONAL PARK** to the coast at Kiama. The impressive, fifty-metre **Carrington Falls**, 8km southeast of Robertson off Jamberoo Mountain Road, can be accessed by a short bush walk that leads to lookout points over the waterfalls.

Some 6km further southwest, **Illawarra Fly**, 182 Knights Hill Rd (daily 9am–5pm; $19; ⓦwww.illawarrafly.com.au), gives you the chance to walk out on a massive 500m-long treetop walkway cantilevered out over the edge of the Illawarra Escarpment. On a fine day the views can seem never ending, north and south along the coast, and down into the gumtrees below.

Continuing southwest, Jamberoo Mountain Road heads down the escarpment, twisting and turning until, when you feel you've reached the foothills, a turn-off leads to the **Minnamurra Rainforest Centre** (daily 9am–5pm; $11 per vehicle; ☏02/4236 0469), which hugs the base of the escarpment. From the centre you can wander along a wheelchair-accessible elevated boardwalk (1.6km loop, 30min–1hr; last entry 4pm), which winds through cabbage tree palms, staghorn ferns and impressive Illawarra fig trees, with the distinctive call of whip birds and the undergrowth rustle of lyre birds for company. Midway along the boardwalk, a path (2.6km return; last entry 3pm), spurs off steeply uphill (quickly gaining 100m) to a platform with views of the delicate 25-metre **Upper Minnamurra Fall**. A second platform allows you to peer down the fifty-metre lower fall as it cascades into a dark slot canyon.

Coastal Kiama lies a further 17km west from Minnamurra.

Fitzroy Falls and Kangaroo Valley

Nowra Road heads directly southeast from Moss Vale, to reach **Fitzroy Falls** after 15km (daily: Oct–April 9am–5.30pm, May–Sept 9am–5pm; parking $3), on the fringes of Morton National Park. A short boardwalk from the car park takes you to the falls, which plunge eighty metres into the valley below, with glorious views of the Yarrunga Valley beyond. The **NPWS visitor centre** at the falls holds a buffet-style café with a very pleasant outside deck, and can provide detailed information about the many walking tracks and scenic drives in the park.

From Fitzroy Falls, Kangaroo Valley Road winds steeply down 20km to **KANGAROO VALLEY**. Hidden between the lush dairy country of Nowra and the highlands, the town is a popular base for walkers and canoeists, and is brimming with cafés, craft and gift shops, plus an imposing old pub, *The Friendly Inn*.

Just over a kilometre west of the township, the road from Fitzroy Falls crosses the Kangaroo River on the picturesque 1898 **Hampden Suspension Bridge**, with its castellated turrets made from local sandstone. Lying to one side of the bridge, the **Pioneer Museum Park** (Fri–Mon: Nov–April 10am–4pm; May–Oct 11am–3pm; $4; ⊛ www.kangaroovalleymuseum.com) provides an insight into the origins of the area, in and around an 1850 homestead. The shop next door is the base for Kangaroo Valley Safaris (☎02/4465 1502, ⊛ www.kangaroovalleycanoes .com.au), who offer leisurely **self-guided kayak trips** along the placid Kangaroo River, and between the escarpments of the Shoalhaven Gorge. Rates include basic instruction, maps, waterproof containers and a return bus trip, so you only need to paddle downstream. Opt for a day-trip ($35–65 per person depending on kayak type), or an overnight trip ($85–130), camping beside the river. They also offer tent ($40 one-off) and cooking stove ($30) rentals.

Some of the same waters are also accessible on kayaks and canoes rented from the very pleasant Kangaroo Valley Tourist Park **campsite**, on Moss Vale Road (☎1300 559 977, ⊛ www.kvtouristpark.com.au), which has camping ($11–13 per person), a bunkhouse ($20–25 per person), and en-suite timber cabins equipped with DVD and air-conditioned, sleeping from two to seven people (midweek $70–150, weekend $120–180). A kilometre east of Kangaroo Village, *Tall Trees B&B*, 8 Nugents Creek Rd (☎02/4465 1208, ⊛ www.talltreesbandb.com.au; midweek $135, weekend $185), is a home from home, with great views across the valley and hearty breakfasts. Self-contained accommodation in a studio or treehouse is also available (studio midweek $180, weekend $435 for two nights).

Of the many **cafés** in Kangaroo Valley, *Café Bella*, 151 Main Rd (☎02/4465 1660; BYO; closed Mon–Wed) stands out from the crowd with its relaxed, friendly feel, good-value breakfast and delicious lunches. It's also open on Friday and Saturday evenings with a small but well-chosen menu (mains $20–30). Alternatively, you can sit beneath a shady veranda and enjoy a cup of tea at *Jing Jo Café Restaurant* by the Hampden Suspension Bridge, which serves a modern Australian daytime menu and Thai in the evening (Thurs–Mon). A service station near the bridge sells **groceries**.

Bus access to Kangaroo Valley is with Priors (☎1800 816 2340; not Sat), on their run from Campbelltown train station on the outskirts of Sydney through Bowral to Narooma on the coast. They stop at 5.25pm southbound and 10.45am northbound.

South of Wollongong

The twin town of **NOWRA-BOMADERRY**, 22km southeast of Kangaroo Valley, straddles the wide **Shoalhaven River**. Bomaderry lies north of the river, with Nowra to the south. The river itself is great for sailing, windsurfing and boating, while the nearby coast is dotted with popular holiday settlements and numerous beaches. **SHOALHAVEN HEADS**, a sleepy resort on Seven Mile Beach, a stunning sweep of sandy beach with its own small oceanfront national park, is north of the river mouth, while **GREENWELL POINT** fishing village is south; both are within 15km of Nowra.

The region's most interesting towns are inland **Berry**, with its restaurants and wineries, pretty **Gerringong**, and **Kiama**, an attractive stop with an occasionally spectacular blowhole. The rail line running south from Sydney terminates at Bomaderry, but there's no local public transport, so you need your own vehicle to explore.

Berry

On the Princes Highway some 25km south of Kiama and 65km south of Wollongong, **BERRY** is an appealing historic town with many listed buildings, surrounded by dairy country and green hills. The main reason to stop is to eat well, do a little craft and homeware shopping, then eat some more. The main drag, **Queen Street**, is packed with upmarket shops, little art galleries, cafés and restaurants, and is home to two country pubs. As a favourite weekend getaway for Sydneysiders, Berry gets unbearably crowded on fine weekends. The town's popularity is further enhanced by the proximity of **Kangaroo Valley** (16km west) and the beach at **Gerringong** (18km east), and a monthly market (first Sun of the month).

Wineries are another draw, two of the best being: the Coolangatta Estate (daily 10am–5pm; ☎02/4448 7131, ⓦwww.coolangattaestate.com.au), just 5km southeast on Bolong Road, and the Silos Estate, 8km southwest at Jasper's Brush (Wed–Sun 10am–5pm; ☎02/4448 6082, ⓦwww.thesilos.com).

Arrival and information

Berry is easily reached by **train** on CityRail's South Coast Line from Sydney. The Shoalhaven **visitor centre** (daily 9am–5pm; ☎1300 662 808, ⓦwww.shoalhavenholidays.com.au) can help you out with any queries and accommodation bookings – it's on the Princes Highway, 18km south of Berry just after the road bridge between Nowra and Bomaderry.

Accommodation

In addition to our recommendations below, dozens of rural **B&Bs** are scattered in the hills around town (check ⓦwww.shoalhavenholidays.com.au for listings).

The Berry Hotel 120 Queen St ☎02/4464 1011, ⓦwww.berryhotel.com.au. A really lovely old coach-house offering pretty, old-fashioned rooms, including a huge family flat sleeping eight. A full country breakfast is included in the (higher) price at weekends. Weekdays $70, weekends $110.

Berry Orchard 17A George St right in town ☎02/4464 2583, ⓦwww.berryorchard.com.au. Lovely, central B&B with a delightful self-contained cottage for two, a smaller studio; both are provided with fresh flowers, cheese, bubbly and orange juice on arrival. Two-night minimum. $160.

The Bunyip Inn 122 Queen St ☎02/4464 2064. Good-value 13-room B&B, mostly in an imposing National Trust-classified former bank, with a lovely leafy garden and swimming pool. Every room is different (nearly all en suite), and the modern stables accommodation includes a wheelchair-accessible unit and another with a kitchen. $80.

Great Southern Hotel 95 Queen St, Berry
☎02/4464 1009. These wackily decorated
and hand-painted rooms attached to the
hotel are fun and cheap, and you don't have
to stumble back far after a night at the pub.
Weekday $70, weekend $100.

Silo Estates Jaspers Bush, 8km south
☎02/4448 6082, @www.thesilos.com. Boutique
accommodation on a vineyard with four
delightfully appointed suites, some with spa.
Two-night minimum at weekends. Suite
$175–195, spa suite $195–235.

Eating and drinking

Berry has easily the best dining selection for some distance, most of it right
in town.

The Berry Hotel 120 Queen St. This much-
loved place boasts the best value food in
town, served in either the pub itself, the large
courtyard at the back, or a cosy-cottage
dining room with open fire. Food consists of
posh pub tucker at lunch (around $15) and
affordable Mod Oz offerings in the evening,
including the likes of cumin-spiced lamb
rump with puy lentils, aubergine and yoghurt
($26). Entertainment Sat evenings. Daily
11am–11pm or later.

🏃 **Berry Woodfired Sourdough Bakery**
23 Prince Alfred St. Virtually everything
is made on the premises at this wonderful
bakery/café just off the main street. A coffee
and one of their delectable tarts is a treat,
but aim to come for breakfast or lunch,
which might be toasted brioche with lemon
curd ($8) or corn fritters with caramelized
prosciutto and tomato relish ($14). Some
outdoor seating. Wed–Sun 8am–3pm.
Cuttlefish 98 Queen St. Stylish pizza-bar
located over the top of the *Hedgehog Café*,
overlooking a beautiful nursery. Also serves

modern Italian mains and desserts. Lunch
Sat & Sun, dinner Thurs–Sun.
Emporium Food Co. 127 Queen St. This
gourmet deli serves posh sandwiches,
savoury pies, beautiful little cakes and
excellent coffee – try to grab one of the little
tables at the front of the shop. Mon–Sat
9am–5pm, Sun 10am–4.30pm.
The Posthouse 137 Queen St ☎02/4464 2444.
Quality contemporary Oz dining at moderate
prices is the motif at this lively restaurant
with seating either in the former post office
or in the leafy patio. Lunch mains $15–18;
dinner mains $19–28. Closed Wed.
Silos Winery Princes Highway, Jaspers Bush,
8km southwest ☎02/4448 6160, @www
.thesilos.com.au. The area's finest dining,
with an eclectic, Asian-inspired Mod Oz
menu, beautifully crafted desserts and
idyllic views over the vineyard. Expect five-
spice duck with scallops ($36) and their
own variation on moussaka ($27). Lunch &
dinner Wed–Sat, lunch Sun.

Gerringong

Gerringong, 10km northeast of Kiama, is wonderfully scenic, set against green
hills with glorious sweeping views. There's little specific to do but you can eat
well at *Gerringong Deli & Café* on Fern Street, the best café in town, with divine
fish'n'chips and gourmet burgers, or try *Perfect Break Vegetarian Café*, just along
the street, for outstanding veggie food such as nachos and lentil burgers, washed
down with a freshly squeezed fruit juice.

    Seven Mile Beach, 4km south of Gerringong, is beautiful: you can camp
beside the beach at *Seven Mile Beach Holiday Park* (☎02/4234 1340, @www
.kiamacoast.com.au; suites $29–35, cabins $95, safari tents $105, en-suite cabins
$140), located beside Crooked River almost 4km south of Gerringong but with
cafés and a restaurant close by.

Kiama and around

Of the coastal resorts south of Sydney, **KIAMA**, 35km south of Wollongong, is
probably the most attractive. Kiama is famous for its star attraction, the **Blowhole**,
which you can drive right up to, or walk to in five minutes from the train station.
Lying beneath the lighthouse at Blowhole Point, and stemming from a natural
fault in the cliffs, the blowhole explodes into a water spout and booms loudly

when a wave hits with sufficient force. It's impressive when the sea is right, but also potentially dangerous as freak waves can be thrown over sixty metres into the air, and have swept several over-curious bystanders to their deaths – stand well back. The **visitor centre** nearby on Blowhole Point Road (daily 9am–5pm; ☏02/4232 3322, ⓦwww.kiama.com.au), books accommodation and has plenty of information on other local attractions, including **Cathedral Rocks**, a few kilometres north, where dramatic rocky outcrops drop abruptly to the ocean.

There's abundant **accommodation** (mostly motels) along the Princes Highway, and a few places downtown. Budget alternatives include the rather basic *Kiama Backpackers*, 31 Bong Bong St (☏02/4233 1881, ⓔkiamabackpackers @hotmail.com; dorms $20, rooms $49), in the stark 1970s building next to the train station. Management is perhaps a little too laid-back, but the good location near the beach makes up for it. The hostel sometimes closes in winter – ring ahead. Next door, the *Grand Hotel*, corner of Manning and Bong Bong streets (☏02/4232 1037; singles $40, doubles $70), is one of Kiama's oldest hotels, with shared-bath rooms – the pub restaurant serves decent filling meals for lunch and dinner daily. There's convenient **camping** right in town at *Surf Beach Holiday Park*, Bourrool St (☏02/4232 1791, ⓦwww.wiama.net/holiday; sites $26, on-site vans $90, cabins $135), and swankier accommodation at *Kiama Harbour Cabins*, Blowhole Point Rd (☏1800 823 824, ⓦwww.kiama.net/holiday /blowhole; en-suite cabins $195), which has great views of the harbour and coast, but a two-night minimum at weekends.

Kiama holds plenty of **places to eat** – Thai, Chinese, Italian restaurants and lots of cafés – largely concentrated on Manning and Terralong streets. The best is *55 on Collins*, 55 Collins St (☏02/4232 2811; daytime daily plus dinner Thurs–Sat), which is casual enough for coffee and cake in the daytime, and serves very good contemporary cuisine in the evening (mains around $30).

Contexts

Contexts

History

Aboriginal tribes have inhabited the region of what is now Sydney for more than forty thousand years. Around fifteen thousand years ago, when the polar ice caps melted and the salty Pacific rose to fill the deep valley carved by the ancient Parramatta River, the people of the **Eora** were living in rich and complicated tribal cultures, hunting, fishing and gathering along the shores of Sydney Harbour.

The history of the city itself began when Sydney was founded in 1788, amid brutality, deprivation and despair, as a British **penal colony**. Its development was facilitated by a system in which convicts worked as bonded domestics and labourers, serving the bureaucracy, military and, from 1793 onwards, **free settlers** arriving in the colony.

While initially cordial, relations between settlers and the native tribes were soon strained by violent encounters, and sullied by huge numbers of Aboriginal deaths from European diseases. As the settlement expanded, destroying sacred sites and traditional food sources, an Aboriginal guerrilla resistance began, continuing for more than ten years and causing serious losses to both sides.

After a trio of **explorers** successfully traversed the Blue Mountains, the opening up of the western plains saw more white settlers arrive, and the long era of transportation to the colony of New South Wales ended in the 1840s. Soon the **goldrushes** of the 1850s attracted many more free settlers from all corners of the world; some were **Chinese**, whose descendants still operate businesses in Haymarket today. However, the notorious **White Australia policy** was developed after a goldrush-induced xenophobia, and it wasn't until the period after World War II, when Australia desperately needed workers and a larger population, that waves of culturally varied migrants began to arrive, transforming Sydney into the cosmopolitan city it is today.

Prehistory and Aboriginal occupation

The area around Sydney was home to about three thousand Aboriginal inhabitants at the time of colonization, divided into two tribes organized and related according to complex kinship systems, and speaking two different languages and several dialects: the **Eora**, whom settlers called the "coast tribe", and the **Dharug**, who lived further inland. Common to the two tribes was the belief that land, wildlife and people were an interdependent whole, which engendered a sympathy for natural processes, and for maintaining a balance between population and natural resources. Legends about the mythical **Dreamtime**, when creative forces roamed the land, provided **verbal maps** of tribal territory, and linked natural features to the actions of these Dreamtime ancestors.

The early records of the colony mainly describe the lifestyle and habits of the **Eora people**, who, because their staple diet was fish and seafood, made temporary camps close to the shore, usually sleeping in the open by fires. Shaping canoes from a single piece of bark, they would fish on the harbour using hooks made from shells attached to lines of bark fibre, or spear fish from rocks with multi-pronged wooden spears spiked with kangaroo teeth. The fish diet was supplemented by the hunting of kangaroo and other game, and gathering plants such as yams. Besides storytelling and ceremonial dancing, other cultural expression was through **rock engraving**, usually of outlines of creatures such as kangaroo and fish.

The first Europeans

Although the Dutch, Spanish and French had previously attempted to locate and map the "Great Southern Land", only with the *Endeavour* expedition, headed by Captain **James Cook**, was a concerted effort finally made. Cook had headed to Tahiti (where scientists observed the movements of the planet Venus), then mapped New Zealand's coastline before he sailed west in 1770.

The British arrived at **Botany Bay** in April 1770; Cook commented on the Aborigines' initial indifference to seeing the *Endeavour*, but when a party of forty sailors attempted to land, two Aborigines attacked them with spears and were driven off by musket fire. The party set up camp for eight days, while botanist **Sir Joseph Banks** studied, collected and recorded specimens of the unique plant and animal life. They continued up the Queensland coast, entered the treacherous passages of the Great Barrier Reef, ran aground and stopped for six weeks to repair the *Endeavour*. When they set off again, Cook successfully managed to navigate the rest of the reef, and claimed Australia's eastern seaboard – which he named **New South Wales** – on August 21, 1770.

Founding of the colony of New South Wales

The outcome of the American War of Independence in 1783 saw Britain deprived of anywhere to transport convicted criminals; they were temporarily housed in prison ships or "hulks", moored on the Thames in London, while the government tried to solve the problem. Sir Joseph Banks advocated Botany Bay as an ideal location for a **penal colony** that could soon become self-sufficient. The government agreed and on May 13, 1787, the **First Fleet**, carrying over a thousand people, 736 of them convicts, set sail. The eleven ships – two of them navy vessels, the *Sirius* and the *Supply* – were commanded by Captain **Arthur Phillip**. Reaching Botany Bay on January 18, 1788, they expected the "fine meadows" that Captain Cook had described. What greeted them was mostly swamp, scrub and sand dunes, which Phillip deemed unsuitable for his purposes, so he moved the fleet north, to well-wooded **Port Jackson**, on **January 26**, a date marked nationwide as Australia Day (see p.257).

Camp was set up on what was named **Sydney Cove** (after Viscount Sydney, then secretary of state in Great Britain), beside the all-important freshwater source, the **Tank Stream**, which now runs under the city streets. Government officials camped on the eastern side of the stream, while the marines and convicts were relegated to the west – a geographic demarcation of social standing that endures to this day. Ranging from a boy of nine to a woman of 82, the **convicts** were a multicultural bunch, including English, Scots, black and white Americans, Germans and Norwegians; 188 were female.

Once Phillip had read the Act of Parliament founding the new colony of New South Wales and was commissioned as **governor**, he gave a speech enjoining the assembled convicts to be industrious, decent and righteous.

Directed by the marines, they were used as labour to build the city or became bonded servants, but unless they were found guilty of further crimes, they were not imprisoned or shackled, and were free to marry (fourteen convict marriages occurred in the first weeks of settlement alone). Aged mostly between 15 and 25, the convicts had youth on their side. Phillip's method of "the gallows and the lash" and chain-gang justice deterred most from committing more crime, and there was also nowhere to escape to. The lure of a "ticket of leave", which rewarded good behaviour with self-employment and the opportunity to own land, proved a strong incentive to reforming, though not necessarily refining, this former underclass.

In the first three years of settlement, the colonists and convicts suffered from erratic weather and **starvation**, soil which appeared to be agriculturally worthless, and Aboriginal hostility. When much-anticipated ships from Britain arrived, they carried hundreds more malnourished convicts to additionally burden the colony. Not until 1790, when land was successfully farmed further west at **Parramatta**, did the hunger begin to abate.

Quarantined in Australia, Sydney's Aboriginal population succumbed tragically and dramatically to European diseases, especially smallpox. Within the first three years, up to ninety percent of Aborigines in the Sydney region are thought to have been wiped out. Driven to establish cordial relations and desperate for a means to engage in open communication, Phillip ordered the kidnapping of two Eora men in November 1789. One of them, Bennelong, learned rapidly, soon revealing a playful wit and above-average intelligence, and forged a strong friendship with Phillip. In August 1790, at Manly Cove, Phillip was non-fatally speared by an Aboriginal wise man in what modern anthropologists characterize as a "payback" ritual, most probably for the kidnapping and his settlement's regular contravention of Eoran law. Knowing it to be a formalized occasion, Phillip accepted without retaliation. Retiring and returning to Britain in 1792, Phillip took Bennelong with him, where his intelligence, humour and charm greatly impressed the English parliament and gentry.

The first **free settlers** reached Sydney in 1793, while war with France reduced the numbers of convicts being transported to the colony.

The rum corps

After Phillip's departure, the military, known as the **New South Wales Corps** (or more familiarly as the "rum corps"), soon became the supreme political force in the colony. Headed by **John Macarthur**, the 500-strong corps soon manipulated the temporary governor, Major Francis Grose, into serving their interests. Grose gave out land grants and allowed the officers liberal use of convict labour to develop their holdings. The corrupt corps' members became rich farm-owners, and virtually established a currency based on their monopoly of rum.

Aboriginal Resistance

From 1790 onwards, as the land grab and clearing proceeded, increasingly depriving the Eora of their traditional food sources, a guerrilla war against the settlers began under the leadership of Pemulwuy, a skilled warrior. Raids were executed against outposts and homesteads: crops were burned, buildings destroyed, the legs of livestock broken. In 1794, thirty-six British and fourteen Eora were killed in an attack on the border of the Sydney settlement at Brickfield Lane (near the end of today's George St). Other major attacks occurred at Prospect, Parramatta, Toongabbie and the Hawkesbury River. The numbers and firepower of the settlers proved overwhelming, however. Pemulwuy was captured and killed in 1802, and his severed head sent back to England. Aboriginal resistance continued for a number of years, but soon ended.

The conditions of Sydney's Aboriginal population rapidly deteriorated. In 1819 the visiting Frenchman Jacques Arago was appalled to find wealthy merchants, for their amusement, entreating luckless Eora men to fight one another, often to the death, by plying them with liquor (to which Aboriginal minds and bodies were by no means accustomed).

The Rum Rebellion and Governor Macquarie

Successors to Governor Grose struggled to regain the powers he had abandoned. Events culminated in the **Rum Rebellion** of 1808, when the military, supported by merchant and pastoral factions, ousted mutiny-plagued Governor **William Bligh**, formerly of the *Bounty*, who had attempted to restore order. Britain finally took notice of the colony's anarchic state, and resolved matters by appointing the firm-handed Scotsman Colonel **Lachlan Macquarie**, backed by the 73rd Regiment, as Bligh's replacement in 1810. Macquarie settled the various disputes – Macarthur had already fled to Britain – and brought the colony eleven years of disciplined progress.

Macquarie has been labelled the "Father of Australia" for his vision of a country that could rise above its convict origins; he implemented enlightened policies towards former convicts or **emancipists**, enrolling them in public offices. The most famous of these was **Francis Greenway**, the convicted forger whom he appointed civil architect, and with whom Macquarie set about an ambitious programme of public buildings and parks. However, he offended those who regarded the colony's prime purpose as a place of punishment.

In 1813, the **explorers** Wentworth, Blaxland and Lawson became the first white men to cross the Blue Mountains, opening up the western plains to agricultural and pastoral development. Here again, one of Australia's largest Aboriginal tribes, the **Wiradjuri**, resisted – this time under the leadership of the charismatic Windradyne (also known as "Saturday"). Martial law was declared in response, and large numbers of Aboriginal men, women and children were rounded up and massacred. Faced with no other option, Windradyne made peace to save his tribe.

With the opening up of the west, more settlers arrived, and in 1821 Macquarie's successor Sir Thomas Brisbane was instructed to segregate, not integrate, convicts. To this end, New South Wales officially graduated from being a penal settlement to become a new **British colony** in 1823, and convicts were used to colonize newly explored regions – Western Australia, Tasmania and Queensland – as far from Sydney's free settlers as possible.

The Victorian era

Australia's first **goldrush** occurred in 1851 near Bathurst, west of Sydney. Between 1850 and 1890, Sydney's population jumped from 60,000 to 400,000; terraced houses were jammed together, and with their decorative cast-iron railings and balconies, they remain one of Sydney's most distinctive heritage features. The first railway line, to Granville near Parramatta, was built in 1855.

However, until the tramway system was constructed in the 1880s, most people preferred to live in the city centre, within walking distance of work.

During the Victorian era, Sydney's population became even more starkly divided into the haves and the have-nots: self-consciously replicating life in the mother country, the genteel classes took tea on their verandas and erected grandiloquent monuments such as the Town Hall, the Strand Arcade and the Queen Victoria Building. Meanwhile, the poor lived in slums where disease, crime, prostitution and alcoholism were rife.

An outbreak of the plague in The Rocks in 1900 made wholesale **slum clearances** unavoidable, and with the demolitions came a change in attitudes. Strict new vice laws meant the end of the bad old days of drunken taverns and rowdy brothels.

Federation, World War I and World War II

With **federation** in 1901, the separate colonies came under one central government and a nation was created. Unhappily for Sydney, Melbourne was the capital of the **Commonwealth of Australia** until Canberra was built in 1927, roughly halfway between the two cities. The **Immigration Act** was the first piece of legislation to be passed by the new parliament, reflecting the nationalist drive behind federation. The act heralded the **White Australia policy**, which greatly restricted non-European immigration until 1958.

With the outbreak of **World War I** in 1914, Australia promised to support Britain to "the last man and the last shilling", and there was a patriotic rush to enlist in the army. This enthusiasm tapered when the slaughter at **Gallipolli** in 1915 – 11,000 **Anzacs** (Australian and New Zealand Army Corps) died in the eight-month battle in Turkey – prompted the first serious questioning of Anglo-Australian relationships. The aftermath of Gallipolli is considered to be the true birth of Australian national identity.

As the **Great Depression** set in, in 1929, Australia faced collapsing economic and political systems; pressed for a loan, the Bank of England forced a restructuring of the Australian economy. This scenario, of Australia still financially dependent on Britain but clearly regarded as an upstart nation, came to a head as a result of the 1932 controversy over England's "**Bodyline**" bowling technique during that year's series of England–Australia cricket matches. The loan was virtually made conditional on Australian cricket authorities dropping their allegations that British bowlers were deliberately trying to injure Australian batsmen during the tour. In the midst of this troubled scenario, it was a miracle that construction continued on the **Sydney Harbour Bridge**, which opened in 1932.

During **World War II**, Labor Prime Minister **John Curtin**, concerned about Australia's vulnerability after the Japanese attack on Pearl Harbor, Hawaii (on Dec 7, 1941), made the radical decision to shift the country's commitment in the war from defending Britain and Europe to fighting off an invasion of Australia from Asia. In February 1942 the Japanese unexpectedly bombed Darwin, launched **submarine raids** against Sydney and Newcastle, and invaded New Guinea. Feeling abandoned by Britain, Curtin appealed to the USA, who quickly adopted Australia as a base for coordinating Pacific operations under **General Douglas MacArthur**, who made his headquarters in Sydney at the Grace Building, on York Street (now the *Grace Hotel*).

The postwar generation

Australia came out of World War II realizing that the country was closer to Asia than Europe, and began to look to the USA and the Pacific, as well as Britain, for direction. **Immigration** was speeded up, fuelled by Australia's recent vulnerability. Under the slogan "Populate or Perish", the government reintroduced assisted passages from Britain – the "ten-pound-poms" – and also accepted substantial numbers of European refugees. The new European migrant populations ("New Australians", a substantial number of Italians, Greeks and Eastern Europeans among them), colonized the inner city, giving it a more cosmopolitan face.

Anglo-Australians took on board postwar prosperity during the conservative **Menzies era** – Robert Menzies remained prime minister from 1949 until 1966 – and headed for the suburbs and the now affordable dream of their own home on a plot of land. Over the next few decades, Sydney settled into comfortable suburban living as redbrick, fibro and weatherboard bungalows sprawled west and southwards into the new suburbs, while the comfy parochialism of the Menzies years saw Australian writers, artists and intellectuals leave the country in droves.

Modern Sydney

Immigration continued in waves, with a large influx of people from postwar Vietnam and Southeast Asia aided by Gough Whitlam's tolerant Labor government (before it was famously sacked by the Governor General in 1975). Concentrated ethnic enclaves include a vibrant Vietnamese community at Cabramatta, a Filipino focus in Blacktown, and an emerging Chinese community in Ashfield, resulting from the thousands of Chinese students whom the prime minister **Bob Hawke** allowed to remain in Australia on humanitarian grounds after the Tian'anmen Square massacre in 1989.

Other developments were more concrete. When the restrictions limiting the height of buildings was lifted in 1957, the development of Sydney's high-rise skyline really took off. Notably tall office blocks include the 183-metre Australia Square Tower (1961–67) and the 244-metre MLC Centre (1975–78), designed by Sydney's most prominent architect, **Harry Seidler** (see p.88). Though the 259m Sydney Tower (1981) is the tallest and most recognizable structure on the skyline, the **Sydney Opera House** was the most striking and controversial of Sydney's postwar buildings. Originally designed by Danish architect Jørn Utzon in 1957, it finally opened in 1973.

This building boom saw many heritage buildings unthinkingly demolished. The New South Wales premier, Robin Askin (1965–74), was keen for many residential areas of the inner city to make way for new office blocks and hotels. Locals began to protest against developments, and a radical union, the Builders' Labourers Federation (BLF), put its might behind the dissent. BLF secretary Jack Mundey coined the term **Green Ban**, meaning the withdrawal of union labour for projects opposed by the community and potentially damaging to the environment. In 1971 a Green Ban was placed on demolition of The Rocks: two-thirds of the city's most historic area would have been redeveloped if the Sydney Cove Redevelopment Authority had had its way. In 1973, non-union workers poised to start demolition were stopped by eighty members of the Rocks Resident Action Group. A compromise in 1975 saw some development, but the residential areas were extended and historic buildings restored.

When Sydney beat Beijing in 1993 for the 2000 Olympics, the city rejoiced. But in January 1994 the world watched stunned as the future Olympic city went up in flames: front-page images of the two icons of Australia, the Opera House and the Harbour Bridge, were silhouetted against an orange, smoke-filled sky during the Black Friday **bushfires**, which destroyed 250 homes and cost four lives. Bushfires continue to endanger Sydney's bushland – recurrent and long lasting **droughts** have provided perfect conditions. While Sydney's main water source, Warragamba Dam, is no longer at an all-time low, the beloved suburban garden hose continues to be subject to restrictions.

In 1995, a New South Wales Labor government was elected under the leadership of the outspoken ex-journalist **Premier Bob Carr**. When Labor was re-elected for a third term in the 2003 state elections, Carr seemed intent on staying in office indefinitely, but he shocked everyone by suddenly retiring in July 2005. He was replaced by media-shy **Morris Iemma**, who despite leading Labor to victory in 2007, faced a series of service delivery problems and local government scandals, which lost him support. After caucus disputes over a proposed cabinet reshuffle, he was forced to resign in turn in September 2008, and was replaced by current Premier, **Nathan Rees**.

Carr's decade at the helm saw him increase the size and number of national parks, improve educational standards and, in preparation for the Olympics, undertake the task of coordinating the city's biggest infrastructure project since the construction of the Sydney Harbour Bridge. More than $2.5 billion of public money was spent on major road and rail projects, including a $630 million rail link from the airport to the city, and a $93 million rail link to Olympic venues at the $470 million Homebush Bay site.

The great success of the 2000 Sydney Olympics sent the city's self-confidence skyrocketing. However, in the heightened climate of fear since the 2001 New York terrorist attack and Bali bombings of October 2002, in which 88 Australians were killed, simmering racial tension in Sydney's relatively tolerant multicultural society has been on the increase. On December 11, 2005, a spontaneous anti-Muslim protest gathered at North Cronulla beach following reported confrontations between Middle Eastern youths from Sydney's west and Anglo locals. The demonstration turned violent when one man of Middle Eastern appearance was chased and sought refuge in a hotel. Several more assaults took place as the crowd turned against police who tried to lead victims away. Car-loads of Middle Eastern youths from Sydney's western suburbs retaliated that evening, smashing cars and assaulting pedestrians in the Cronulla area. The violence continued on 12 October, soon ending, however, when pressure from community leaders and "lockdown" powers given to police took effect. State and federal government responded to the crises by increasing funding to educational and community-based programs that promote cultural awareness and racial harmony, and there has been very little racial violence since.

While the long-term effects of the 2008 global economic crisis remain to be seen, real estate prices are at record highs, with a generation now effectively priced out of the market. Apartment living in the Central Business District has been on the increase, with an injection of residential life and everyday facilities such as supermarkets into an area that used to be quiet at weekends once the workers had cleared out. The gap between rich and poor in Sydney continues to increase, and as the upwardly mobile move closer to the centre while remaining in the eastern suburbs and by the North Shore, less affluent renters are forced towards the increasingly troubled, poorly serviced western suburbs.

Books

M any of the best books by Australian writers or about Australia are not available overseas, so you may be surprised at the range of local titles available in Australian **bookshops**; we have reviewed several favourite Sydney stores on p.242, with websites where available for online sales. A good website to check is ⓦwww.gleebooks.com.au, one of Australia's best literary booksellers, with a whole host of recent reviews; you can order books online, to be posted overseas. Titles marked 🏃 are especially recommended.

History and politics

🏃 **John Birmingham** *Leviathan: the Unauthorised Biography of Sydney*. Birmingham's 1999 tome casts a contemporary eye on the dark side of Sydney's history, from nauseating accounts of The Rocks' slum life and the 1900 plague outbreak, through the 1970s' traumas of Vietnamese boat people, to scandals of police corruption.

Manning Clark *A Short History of Australia*. A condensed version of this leading historian's multi-volume tome, focusing on dreary successions of political administrations over two centuries, and cynically concluding with the "Age of Ruins".

Ann Coombs *Sex and Anarchy: The Life and Death of the Sydney Push*. The legendary Sydney Push, a network of anarchists and bohemians who met at pubs through the conservative 1950s and 1960s, experienced the sexual revolution a generation before mainstream society, and influenced everyone from Germaine Greer to Robert Hughes.

David Day *Claiming A Continent: A New History of Australia*. Award-winning, general and easily readable history, concluding in 2000. The possession, dispossession and ownership of the land – and thus issues of race – are central to Day's narrative. Excellent recommended reading of recent texts at the end of each chapter will take you further.

Colin Dyer *The French Explorers and the Aboriginal Australians*. From the expeditions of Bruny d'Entrecasteaux (1793) to Nicolas Baudin (1802), the French explorers and on-board scientists kept detailed journals providing a wealth of information on Aboriginal Australians. Dyer provides engaging access to much recently translated material.

Jack Egan *Buried Alive, Sydney 1788–92: Eyewitness Accounts of the Making of a Nation*. A fascinatingly detailed, almost day-by-day view of the first five years of the city's settlement, culled from diaries and letters, and connected by Egan's narrative.

Bruce Elder *Blood on the Wattle: Massacres and Maltreatment of Aboriginal Australians Since 1788*. A heart-rending account of the horrors inflicted on the continent's indigenous peoples, covering infamous nineteenth-century massacres as well as more recent mid-twentieth century scandals of the "Stolen-Generation" children.

🏃 **Tim Flannery** (ed) *Watkin Trench 1788*. A reissue of two accounts – "A Narrative of the Expedition to Botany Bay" and "A Complete Account of the Settlement of Port Jackson" – written by Trench, a captain of the marines who came ashore with the First Fleet. Trench, a natural storyteller and fine writer, was a young man

Australian writing came into its own in the **1890s**, when a strong nationalistic movement, leading up to eventual federation in 1901, produced writers such as Henry Lawson and the balladeer A.B. "Banjo" Paterson, who romanticized the bush and glorified the mateship ethos. Outstanding women writers, such as Miles Franklin and Barbara Baynton, gave a feminine slant to the bush tale and set the trend for strong female authorship.

During the **twentieth** and **twenty-first centuries**, Australian novelists came to be recognized in the international arena: Patrick White was awarded a Nobel Prize in 1973, Peter Carey won the Booker Prize in 1988 and again in 2001, and Kate Grenville scored the 2001 Orange Prize for Fiction. Other writers who have made a name for themselves include David Malouf, Julia Leigh, Tim Winton, Thomas Keneally, Richard Flanagan, Chloe Hooper and Robyn Davidson. Literary journals such as *Meanjin*, *Southerly*, *Westerly* and *Heat* provide a forum and exposure for short fiction, essays, reviews and new and established writers. The big prizes in Australian fiction include the **Vogel Prize**, for the best unpublished novel written by an author under the age of 35, and the country's most coveted literary prize, the **Miles Franklin Award**.

Many British and multinational **publishers** have set-ups in Australia, publishing an Australian list which is never seen overseas, and the same goes for Australian publishers. As booksellers usually have separate Australian fiction and non-fiction sections, you can easily zero in on the local stuff. Gleebooks (p.243), Ariel (p.242) and Dymocks (p.243) hold readings and literary events, but the best chance to see a host of Australian (and international) writers read and talk about their work is at the Sydney Writers Festival in May (see p.258). Also check out the Writers' Walk at Circular Quay (p.60).

C

in his twenties, and the accounts brim with youthful curiosity. *The Birth of Sydney*, an anthology of writings from the 1770s to the 1850s, includes accounts by Captain Cook, Charles Darwin, Anthony Trollope and Mark Twain, as well as Flannery's essay, "The Sandstone City", which draws connections between ecology, Aboriginal history and present-day Sydney.

Alan Frost *Botany Bay Mirages: Illusions of Australia's Convict Beginnings*. Historian Frost's well-argued attempt to overturn many long-cherished notions about European settlement.

Robert Hughes *The Fatal Shore*. A minutely detailed epic of the origins of transportation and the brutal beginnings of white Australia.

Grace Karskens *The Rocks: Life in Early Sydney*. Karskens' social history draws a vivid picture of Australia's earliest neighbourhood from 1788 until the 1830s.

Mark McKenna *Looking For Blackfellas Point: An Australian History of Place*. McKenna uncovers the uneasy history of Aboriginals and European settlers on the south coast of NSW, and widens his scope to the enduring meaning of land to both Aboriginal and white Australians.

Geoffrey Moorhouse *Sydney*. All the latest developments – from Mardi Gras to police corruption and inner-city Aboriginal poverty – are analysed by internationally renowned British historian and travel writer Moorhouse, with their roots traced back to the city's beginnings.

Maria Nugent *Botany Bay: Where Histories Meet*. Botany Bay was where Captain Cook famously first landed in 1770, and in 1788 was the British choice for an Antipodean convict colony. A substantial and enduring Aboriginal settlement at La Perouse is the focus of Nugent's cultural history.

Portia Robinson *The Women of Botany Bay*. Based on painstaking research into the records of every woman transported from Britain between 1787 and 1828, and the wives of convicts who settled in Australia.

Gavin Souter *Times & Tides: A Middle Harbour Memoir*. Esteemed historian Souter weaves his intimate knowledge of Middle Harbour's bush-covered suburban shores – so close to the city yet so idyllic – into the cultural and natural history of the area, from Aboriginal to European occupation.

Peter Spearitt *Sydney's Century: A History*. A very readable academic history, following Sydney's social and physical development in the twentieth century. Archival photographs, maps, cartoons, advertisements and snippets from novels and magazines help flesh out a fascinating portrait.

Martin Thomas *The Artificial Horizon: Imagining the Blue Mountains*. Taking a thought-provoking cultural studies approach to the Blue Mountains, Thomas focuses his lens on explorers, Aboriginal people, the tourism industry and even the long tradition of suicidal cliff-leapers, supported by maps and photographs.

Larry Writer *Razor*. A satisfyingly lurid account of the mean streets of inner-city Sydney of the 1930s, with its vicious gang wars and rule by two blood-enemy vice queens, Tilly Devine and Kate Leigh. Engrossing photos and crims' mugshots accompany the text.

Ecology and environment

Meredith and Verity Burgmann *Green Bans, Red Union*. The full political ins and outs of the Green Bans of the 1970s – when the radical New South Wales Builders' Labourers union, led by Jack Mundey, resisted developers' plans for The Rocks and other areas of Sydney.

Tim Flannery *The Future Eaters*. Palaeontologist Flannery explains how, as the first human beings migrated down to Australasia, Aborigines, Maoris and other Polynesian peoples changed the region's flora and fauna in startling ways, consuming the resources needed for their own future; Europeans made an even greater impact on the environment, of course, continuing the "future eating" of natural resources.

Tim Low *Bush Tucker: Australia's Wild Food Harvest* and *Wild Food Plants of Australia*. Guides to the bountiful supply of bushtucker that was once the mainstay of the Aboriginal diet; the latter is pocket-sized and contains clear photographs of more than 180 plants, describing their uses.

Mary White *The Greening of Gondwana*. Classic work on the evolution of Australia's flora and geography.

James Woodford *The Wollemi Pine: The Incredible Discovery of a Living Fossil from the Age of the Dinosaurs*. The *Sydney Morning Herald's* award-winning environment writer tells the story of the 1994 discovery in Wollemi wilderness near Sydney (see p.308).

Biography and autobiography

John Dale *Huckstepp: A Dangerous Life*. The still-unsolved 1986 murder of Sallie-Anne Huckstepp, herself steeped in Sydney's criminal underworld of drugs and prostitution, continues to capture the public imagination. When her drug-dealing boyfriend, Lanfranchi, was shot dead in 1981 by detective Roger Rogerson (later proved to be one of New South Wales' most corrupt officers), the young, beautiful and articulate Huckstepp went to the national media to accuse the police force of cold-blooded murder.

Robin Dalton *Aunts Up the Cross*. Dalton, a prominent London literary agent, spent her childhood in the 1920s and 1930s in Kings Cross, in a huge mansion peopled by the eccentric aunts (and uncles) of the title.

Robert Holden *Crackpots, Ratbags & Rebels: A Swag of Aussie Eccentrics*. From *Eternity* graffiti-guy Arthur Stace to Shakespeare-spouting bag-lady Bea Miles and the "Witch of the Cross" Rosaleen Norton, the majority of the famous eccentrics here hail from Sydney.

Clive James *Unreliable Memoirs*. The expat satirist humorously recalls his postwar childhood and adolescence in Sydney's southern suburbs.

Jill Ker Conway *The Road from Coorain*. Conway's childhood, on a drought-stricken Outback station during the 1940s, is movingly told, as is her battle to establish herself as a young historian in sexist, provincial 1950s' Sydney.

Hazel Rowley *Christina Stead: A Biography*. Stead (1902–83) has been acclaimed as Australia's greatest novelist. After spending years in Paris, London and New York with her American husband, she returned to her native Sydney in her old age.

Bernard Smith *The Boy Adeodatus: The Portrait of a Lucky Young Bastard*. Art historian Smith is author of several books including *Australian Painting*, but his best writing is in this prize-winning memoir. Writing honestly about growing up as a state ward in Sydney, Smith beautifully captures the atmosphere of the city from the first World War to the 1930s.

Shane Weaver *Blacktown*. This working-class survival autobiography provides a harsh but compelling account of life in Sydney's socio-economically deprived outer west. From a difficult childhood in the 1950s and 1960s, involving a violently abusive stepfather, and immersion in a culture of drugs and alcohol as a young adult, the late Weaver went on to become a champion boxer, a psychiatric nurse and finally creative director of a multinational advertising agency.

Travel writing

Bill Bryson *Down Under* (published in the US as *In a Sunburnt Country*). The famously funny travel writer devotes a chapter of his Australia book to "the frappaccino heaven that is modern Sydney".

Peter Carey *30 Days in Sydney*. Based in New York, renowned Australian writer Carey set himself a thirty-day time frame and subtitled his book "A wildly distorted account", to defuse ideas that it might be a comprehensive guide. As he hangs out with old friends, it is their lives, the tales they tell and the often nostalgic trips around Sydney that form the basis of this vivid city portrait.

Michael Duffy, David Foster et al *Crossing the Blue Mountains: Journeys Through Two Centuries.* Eleven personal Blue Mountains' journeys, including Gregory Blaxland's famous expedition with Wentworth and Lawson in 1813 when they found a route across; Charles Darwin's visit in 1836 as part of his world trip on the *Beagle*; and contemporary novelist David Foster's reflections on wilderness and solitude as he walks from Mittagong to Katoomba.

Richard Hall (ed) *The Oxford Book of Sydney.* This wide-ranging collection of writing – including journalism, letters, poems and novel excerpts – spans 1788 to 1997.

Jan Morris *Sydney.* An insightful and informative account of Australia's favourite city by one of the world's most respected travel writers, written in the early 1990s.

Ruth Park *Ruth Park's Sydney.* Parks is one of Australia's most loved storytellers (see p.101). Her historically detailed, impressionistic and personal look takes the form of a walking guide full of anecdotes and literary quotations – a wonderful companion for solo exploration. Written in 1973, and long out of print, it was revised and expanded in 1999.

Sydney and around in fiction

Murray Bail *Eucalyptus.* A beautifully written novel with a fairy-tale-like plot. A NSW farmer has planted nearly every type of eucalyptus tree on his land. When his extraordinarily beautiful daughter is old enough to marry, he sets up a challenge for her legion of potential suitors to name each tree.

Peter Corris *The Coast Road.* Australia's answer to Raymond Chandler, former academic Corris brings a glittering but seedy Sydney alive in all his detective novels. Private eye Cliff Hardy, chucked out of his Paddington terrace office, operates from his Glebe home. His clients include a Sydney University linguistics professor, and his investigations take him down the coast south of Sydney. Corpses, bikie gangs and undercover cops all feature.

Eleanor Dark *The Timeless Land.* Classic historical novel, written in the 1940s, which recounts the settlement of Sydney in 1788.

Tom Gilling *Miles McGinty.* Nineteenth-century Sydney comes alive in this colourful historical fable. The riotous, entertaining love story of Miles, who becomes a levitator's assistant and begins to float on air, and Isabel, who wants to fly.

Kate Grenville *The Secret River.* Inspired by research into the author's convict ancestry, and her troubled imaginings of her forebears' interaction with indigenous people, Grenville's novel vividly evokes the landscape of the Hawkesbury River, where emancipated convict William Thornhill takes up a land grant, but also the London where he worked as a Thames waterman, using transcripts of his Old Bailey trial to great effect.

Linda Jaivin *Eat Me.* Billed as an "erotic feast", the story opens with a memorable fruit-squeezing scene. Three trendy women (fashion editor, academic and writer) hang out in Darlinghurst cafés and swap stories of sexual exploits.

Malcolm Knox *Summerland*. Narrator Richard has been coming to Palm Beach, Sydney's summer playground for the wealthy, every year to stay with friend and golden boy Hugh Bowman, and now, in adulthood, with their partners. Richard's telling of the disintegration of a friendship and the downfall of Hugh gives a critical insight into an exclusive, less-than-perfect social milieu.

Gabrielle Lord *Baby Did a Bad, Bad Thing*. One of Australia's best crime-fiction writers bases her immaculately researched novels in hometown Sydney. Former police officer and private investigator Gemma Lincoln's policeman boyfriend has gone undercover to investigate the city's biggest crime boss. Meanwhile Gemma deals with her own investigation into the rape and murder of local prostitutes and an insurance case involving the death of a millionaire.

Roger McDonald *Mr Darwin's Shooter*. The shooter of the title is Syms Covington, Charles Darwin's servant on the famous *Beagle* expedition. He eventually settled in Sydney's Watsons Bay, and is captured here in the 1850s as, now middle-aged and troubled by the theory of evolution he helped to evolve, he awaits with trepidation the publication of *The Origin of the Species*. Finely written and immaculately researched.

Ruth Park *The Harp in the South*. First published in 1948, this first book of a trilogy is a well-loved tale of inner-Sydney slum life in 1940s Surry Hills. The spirited Darcy family's battle against poverty provides memorable characters, not least the Darcy grandmother with her fierce Irish humour.

Christina Stead *For Love Alone*. Set largely around Sydney Harbour in the 1920s, where the late author grew up, this novel follows the obsessive Teresa Hawkins, a poor but artistic girl from an unconventional family, who scrounges and saves to head for London and love.

Kylie Tennant *Ride on Stranger*. First published in 1943, this is a humorous portrait of Sydney between the two world wars, seen through the eyes of a newcomer.

Sydney in children's fiction

Gabrielle Carey and Kathy Lette *Puberty Blues*. This hard-hitting novel for teenagers explores the sexist underworld of Sydney's surf culture. Set at Cronulla Beach in the late 1970s, the reality of peer pressure and the temptations of sex and drugs are examined with frankness and gritty honesty. A 1981 film brought this story to the big screen.

Jean Chapman *Opera House Mouse* and **Lindy Batchelor** *ZOOming in on Taronga*. These delightful picture books give the very young a glimpse behind the scenes at two of Sydney's best loved attractions, Sydney Opera House and Taronga Zoo, and are suitable as either a pre-visit introduction or a post-visit souvenir.

Jean Chapman *A Day with May Gibbs at Nutcote*. This picture book introduces the world of May Gibbs, Australia's much-loved children's book author and illustrator, during the 1930s, when she lived at Nutcote, in the harbour-side suburb of Neutral Bay. May Gibbs is best remembered as the creator of the gumnut babies and the big bad banksia men, found most famously in the classic of Australian Children's literature, *Snugglepot and Cuddlepie*.

Deirdre Hill *Bridge of Dreams.* This novel is a detailed retelling of the story of the Sydney Harbour Bridge. The construction, associated accidents and controversial opening, together paint a complex picture of not only the bridge but Sydney itself in the first third of the twentieth century.

Victor Kelleher *Taronga* and **John Heffernan** *CBD.* These novels for older readers are set in a future, post-apocalyptic Sydney, and present bleak but compelling visions of the city's possible destiny.

Melina Marchetta *Looking for Alibrandi.* A passionate and gently humorous novel that tells the story of Josie, a teenager in her last year at a strict Sydney Catholic high school in the late 1990s, whose world is thrown into turmoil by the revelation of family secrets and the suicide of a friend. Made into a highly successful film in 2000, it presents the complex, multicultural face of contemporary Sydney.

Lilith Norman *A Dream of Seas.* In this novel for young readers, a boy and his mother move to Bondi Beach in Sydney's east after the drowning death of the boy's father. A misfit at his new school, the boy finds peace and solace through the affinity he feels with the sea and its resident seals.

Ruth Park *Playing Beatie Bow.* Set in the historic Rocks district, this novel takes older readers on an exciting adventure as they follow troubled teen Abigail Kirk back through time to Sydney's colonial era. Park vividly re-creates the sights, sounds and smells of the area's slums in 1873, as Abigail uses her experiences in a Sydney of old to put her twentieth-century problems into perspective. In 1985 the story became a film, beautifully shot on location in The Rocks.

John Pye *Ferryboat Fred: The Big Race.* Sydney's answer to *Thomas the Tank Engine* is a little ferryboat called Fred. This picture book takes the pre-school set along on Fred's adventures, as he plies the waters of Sydney Harbour accompanied by his trusty friends.

Ethel Turner *Seven Little Australians.* The lives of the seven Woolcot children take readers around late nineteenth-century Sydney, from the rambling family home, Misrule, by the Parramatta River, to their father's job as Captain at Victoria Barracks. The misadventures of the bright and precocious Judy and her brothers and sisters charm young readers as much today as they did when the book was first published more than a hundred years ago. The story was made into a successful television series in 1974, which has recently been released on DVD.

Nadia Wheatley *My Place.* This fascinating picture book depicts the multi-layered evolution of a Sydney street through time, up until the present day. A lovely way to introduce the very young to Sydney's history.

Food and wine

Ben Canaider and Greg Duncan Powell *Drink Drank Drunk.* Fun, no-nonsense guide to Australian wine by an irreverent duo.

Bill Granger *Sydney Food.* Self-taught chef Granger – his cooking style is based on using the freshest ingredients in simple combinations – runs three very popular *bills* restaurants (see p.185) in his adopted city. A great souvenir, with gorgeous photographs of city settings.

James Halliday *Australian Wine Companion*. Released every year, the venerable Halliday's authoritative guide not only covers the best wines but also more than 1800 of the wineries themselves. A great accompaniment to a Hunter Valley visit.

Huon Hooke and Ralph Kyte-Powell *The Penguin Good Australian Wine Guide*. Released every year, this is a handy book for a wine buff to buy on the ground, with the best wines and prices detailed to help you navigate around the bottle shop.

Kylie Kwong *Kylie Kwong: Recipes and Stories*. Sydney chef Kylie Kwong cooks contemporary Chinese at her stylish restaurant *Billy Kwong* (see p.191). Her cookbook not only provides some great recipes but also gives an insight into Chinese-Australian culture, from shopping in Chinatown to memorable family meals.

R. Ian Lloyd *Australian Wine Regions: Hunter Valley*. With informative text by Lloyd and beautiful photographs by Steve Elias, this glossy coffee-table tome, published in 2001, is one of a series introducing Australia's premier wine-producing areas.

Joanna Savill *The SBS Eating Guide to Sydney*. This annual guide to the best of ethnic food in Sydney will help you hunt down authentic cuisines. Researchers work at Australia's multicultural TV station, SBS.

Art and architecture

Wally Caruana *Aboriginal Art*. An excellent illustrated paperback introduction to all styles of Aboriginal art.

Philip Drewe and Jørn Utzon *Sydney Opera House*. A study of one of the world's most striking pieces of contemporary architecture, designed by Jørn Utzon, with detailed photographs and notes.

Robert Hughes *The Art of Australia*. The internationally acclaimed art historian, author of *The Shock of the New*, cut his teeth on this seminal dissection of Australian art up to the 1960s.

Sylvia Kleinert & Margo Neale (eds) *The Oxford Companion to Aboriginal Art and Culture*. Weighty 644-page tome, illustrated in colour, emphasizing visual art – photography to rock art and body painting – while also covering Aboriginal music, writing and even theatre.

Alice Spigelman *Almost Full Circle: Harry Seidler*. Biography of Australia's most notable architect, the Viennese-born Seidler, who migrated to Australia in 1948 after wartime internment in Canada. He went on to build Sydney's first skyscraper, the fifty-storey Australia Square on George Street, in 1963, and has continued to revolutionize Sydney's skyline.

Specialist guides

Bruce Ashley *Sydney: The Complete Guide to Sydney's Best Rides*. Published in 2005 by cycling advocacy group Bicycle NSW: 25 cycling routes take in the city, the suburbs, the beach and the bush.

Peter and Gibson Dunbar-Hall *Deadly Sounds Deadly Places*. Comprehensive guide to contemporary Aboriginal music in Australia, from Archie Roach to Yothu Yindi; includes a handy discography.

Alan Fairley *Sydney's Best Bushland Walks.* The "Top 30" walks detailed – which include nature notes and maps – are all accessible by public transport.

Wendy Preston *The Choice Guide to Sydney For Kids.* The updated 2007 edition features more than 400 fun activities, plus practical detail from transport to baby-changing facilities. Categories include cycling, swimming, animals and "freebies and cheapies". Preston also manages a useful website ⓦwww.sydneyforkids .com.au.

Greg Pritchard *Climbing Australia: The Essential Guide.* A comprehensive guide for rock-climbers, with a section on the Blue Mountains.

Seana Smith *Sydney For Under Fives: The Best of Sydney For Babies, toddlers and Preschoolers.* A bible for locals with small children, with more than 450 pages. Smith ensures that parents enjoy themselves, too, including information on kid-friendly cafés and restaurants, baby-friendly cinemas, and child-care contacts.

Tyrone Thomas *120 Walks in NSW.* A comprehensive guide to some great walks in NSW, with something to appeal to everybody. Readers are given a choice of long, medium or short walks with insight into levels of difficulty, maps, information on safety and navigation.

Mark Thornley and Veda Dante *Surfing Australia: A Guide to the Best Surfing Down Under.* One of the *Periplus Guides* series, with loads of full-colour photos and maps, and more than thirty pages on the Sydney area, including the Central and South coasts.

Jeff Toghill *Walking Sydney: Over 20 Original Walks In and Around Sydney.* This wide-ranging walking guide covers city, harbour, suburban and coastal walks. Includes maps.

Small print and
Index

A Rough Guide to Rough Guides

Published in 1982, the first Rough Guide – to Greece – was a student scheme that became a publishing phenomenon. Mark Ellingham, a recent graduate in English from Bristol University, had been travelling in Greece the previous summer and couldn't find the right guidebook. With a small group of friends he wrote his own guide, combining a highly contemporary, journalistic style with a thoroughly practical approach to travellers' needs.

The immediate success of the book spawned a series that rapidly covered dozens of destinations. And, in addition to impecunious backpackers, Rough Guides soon acquired a much broader and older readership that relished the guides' wit and inquisitiveness as much as their enthusiastic, critical approach and value-for-money ethos.

These days, Rough Guides include recommendations from shoestring to luxury and cover more than 200 destinations around the globe, including almost every country in the Americas and Europe, more than half of Africa and most of Asia and Australasia. Our ever-growing team of authors and photographers is spread all over the world, particularly in Europe, the US and Australia.

In the early 1990s, Rough Guides branched out of travel, with the publication of Rough Guides to World Music, Classical Music and the Internet. All three have become benchmark titles in their fields, spearheading the publication of a wide range of books under the Rough Guide name.

Including the travel series, Rough Guides now number more than 350 titles, covering: phrasebooks, waterproof maps, music guides from Opera to Heavy Metal, reference works as diverse as Conspiracy Theories and Shakespeare, and popular culture books from iPods to Poker. Rough Guides also produce a series of more than 120 World Music CDs in partnership with World Music Network.

Visit www.roughguides.com to see our latest publications.

Rough Guide travel images are available for commercial licensing at www.roughguidespictures.com

SMALL PRINT

Rough Guide credits

Text editor: Greg Ward
Layout: Nikhil Agarwal
Cartography: Maxine Repath
Picture editor: Sarah Cummins
Production: Rebecca Short
Proofreader: Susanne Hillen
Cover design: Chloë Roberts
Photographer: Helena Smith, Graham Sutch
and Guy Bailey
Editorial: Ruth Blackmore, Andy Turner, Keith
Drew, Edward Aves, Alice Park, Lucy White,
Jo Kirby, James Smart, Natasha Foges, Róisín
Cameron, Emma Traynor, Emma Gibbs, Kathryn
Lane, Christina Valhouli, Monica Woods, Mani
Ramaswamy, Harry Wilson, Lucy Cowie, Helen
Ochyra, Amanda Howard, Lara Kavanagh, Alison
Roberts, Joe Staines, Peter Buckley, Matthew
Milton, Tracy Hopkins, Ruth Tidball; **Delhi**
Madhavi Singh, Karen D'Souza, Lubna Shaheen
Design & Pictures: **London** Scott Stickland,
Dan May, Diana Jarvis, Mark Thomas, Nicole
Newman, Emily Taylor; **Delhi** Umesh Aggarwal,
Ajay Verma, Jessica Subramanian, Ankur Guha,
Pradeep Thapliyal, Sachin Tanwar, Anita Singh,
Sachin Gupta

Production: Vicky Baldwin
Cartography: **London** Ed Wright, Katie Lloyd-
Jones; **Delhi** Rajesh Chhibber, Ashutosh Bharti,
Rajesh Mishra, Animesh Pathak, Jasbir Sandhu,
Karobi Gogoi, Alakananda Bhattacharya, Swati
Handoo, Deshpal Dabas
Online: **London** George Atwell, Faye Hellon,
Jeanette Angell, Fergus Day, Justine Bright, Clare
Bryson, Aine Fearon, Adrian Low, Ezgi Celebi,
Amber Bloomfield; **Delhi** Amit Verma, Rahul Kumar,
Narender Kumar, Ravi Yadav, Debojit Borah,
Rakesh Kumar, Ganesh Sharma, Shisir Basumatari
Marketing & Publicity: **London** Liz Statham,
Niki Hanmer, Louise Maher, Jess Carter, Vanessa
Godden, Vivienne Watton, Anna Paynton, Rachel
Sprackett, Libby Jellie, Laura Vipond, Vanessa
McDonald; **New York** Katy Ball, Judi Powers,
Nancy Lambert; **Delhi** Ragini Govind
Manager India: Punita Singh
Reference Director: Andrew Lockett
Operations Manager: Helen Phillips
PA to Publishing Director: Nicola Henderson
Publishing Director: Martin Dunford
Commercial Manager: Gino Magnotta
Managing Director: John Duhigg

Publishing information

This fifth edition published October 2009 by
Rough Guides Ltd,
80 Strand, London WC2R 0RL
14 Local Shopping Centre, Panchsheel Park,
New Delhi 110017, India
Distributed by the Penguin Group
Penguin Books Ltd,
80 Strand, London WC2R 0RL
Penguin Group (USA)
375 Hudson Street, NY 10014, USA
Penguin Group (Australia)
250 Camberwell Road, Camberwell,
Victoria 3124, Australia
Penguin Group (Canada)
195 Harry Walker Parkway N, Newmarket, ON,
L3Y 7B3 Canada
Penguin Group (NZ)
67 Apollo Drive, Mairangi Bay, Auckland 1310,
New Zealand
Cover concept by Peter Dyer.

Typeset in Bembo and Helvetica to an original
design by Henry Iles.

Printed in Singapore

© Margo Daly 2009

No part of this book may be reproduced in any
form without permission from the publisher except
for the quotation of brief passages in reviews.

360pp includes index

A catalogue record for this book is available from
the British Library

ISBN: 978-1-84836-083-9

The publishers and authors have done their best
to ensure the accuracy and currency of all the
information in **The Rough Guide to Sydney**,
however, they can accept no responsibility for
any loss, injury, or inconvenience sustained by
any traveller as a result of information or advice
contained in the guide.

1   3   5   7   9   8   6   4   2

Help us update

We've gone to a lot of effort to ensure that the
fifth edition of **The Rough Guide to Sydney** is
accurate and up-to-date. However, things change
– places get "discovered", opening hours are
notoriously fickle, restaurants and rooms raise
prices or lower standards. If you feel we've got it
wrong or left something out, we'd like to know,
and if you can remember the address, the price,
the hours, the phone number, so much the better.

Please send your comments with the subject
line "**Rough Guide Sydney Update**" to ©mail
@roughguides.com. We'll credit all contributions
and send a copy of the next edition (or any
other Rough Guide if you prefer) for the very
best emails.

Have your questions answered and tell others
about your trip at
@ community.roughguides.com

Acknowledgements

Paul Whitfield: for the kind use of their wonderful house in Paddington I owe a huge debt to Miriam, Martine and Louis. Thanks too, to Clive and Terry for dragging me around Sydney's gay bars, Debbie Elkind for considered restaurant advice, and all the others who suggested favoured activities and haunts from their favourite city – Chris and Sarah in particular. Gratitude is also due to my co-author, Ben, for sticking with it through difficult times and most of all to Marion, for great times in Sydney and hanging in there through long absences.

Ben Connor: special thanks to Amy Nancarrow, for all your suggestions, support and care; Joy, John, Tim, Rachel and Paddy Connor; Ben, Judie and Colin Nancarrow; Jake Waddell, Dave Kalmar, Rachel Hills, Thushara Dibley, Eloise O'Hare, Louise Coad and the many Sydney locals who kindly shared their thoughts and ideas.

Readers' letters

Thanks to all those readers of the fourth edition who took the trouble to write in with their amendments and additions: Nicole Burchill, Josiah Fisk, Katrina Stevenson, Rebecca Giglia, Chris Seward, Jorie Woods.

SMALL PRINT

Photo credits

All photos © Rough Guides except the following:

Title page
Fort Denison © TNSW

Full page
Bondi Beach © R.Ian Lloyd/Masterfile

Introduction
Surfer in Sydney © Clifford White/Corbis

Things not to miss
02 Giraffe © Courtesy of Taronga Zoo
08 South Head, Sydney Harbour © Hamilton Lund/TNSW
09 Strand Shopping Arcades © Frank Chmura/Alamy
10 Ocean baths at Coogee © 3 stroke photography/TNSW
11 Tourists with bikes looking over Hunter Valley © Paul Blackmore/TNSW
12 Old Courts Art Gallery © Jenni Carter/Courtesy of NSW Art Gallery
13 View over Hawkesbury River and Valley © Paul Blackmore/TNSW
15 People eating at Bill Granger © David Hancock/Alamy
16 Wentworth Falls, Blue Mountains © Hamilton Lund/TNSW

Black and whites
p.70 Exterior of New South Wales Art Gallery © Jenni Carter/Courtesy of NSW Art Gallery

p.228 Mardi Gras © Hamilton Lund/TNSW
p.256 Sydney Festival, Opera House © Jann Tuxford/TNSW
p.288 Boy and dog, Callatoota Estate © Philip Quirk/TNSW
p.294 Walkabout Tours, Blue Mountains © Paul Blackmore/TNSW
p.312 Zig Zag Railway © TNSW
p.318 Little Marley Beach, Royal National Park © Nick Green/Photolibrary.com
p.326 Bradman Oval, Bowral © Claver Carroll/Photolibrary.com

Sydney festivals colour section
New Year's fireworks, 2009 © Hamilton Lund/TNSW
Sydney Festival © Hamilton Lund/TNSW
Tall ship *New Endeavour* at wharf, Sydney Cove, Australia Day © Jann Tuxford/TNSW
Tropfest 2009 © Belinda Rolland/Courtesy of Tropfest
Mardi Gras 2009 © Daniel Munoz/Reuters/Corbis
Royal Easter Show © Corbis
Manly Jazz Festival © Courtesy of Manly Jazz Festival
Annual Sculpture by the Sea exhibition © Jeremy Sutton-Hibbert/Alamy
Sydney to Hobart Yacht Race © Hamilton Lund/TNSW

Selected images from our guidebooks are available for licensing from:

ROUGHGUIDESPICTURES.COM

Index

Map entries are in colour.

Map symbols

maps are listed in the full index using coloured text

	Expressway		Lighthouse
	Main road		Statue
	Minor road		Fountain
	Pedestrianized street		Golf course
	Steps		Swimming pool
	Path		Post office
	Waterway		Information office
	Railway		Hospital
	Metro Monorail		Monastery
	Metro Light Rail		Temple
	CityRail		Buddhist temple
	Ferry route		Campsite
	Sydney ferries		Accommodation
	Airport		Parking
	Mountains		Gate
	Peak		Building
	Rocks		Market
	Waterfall		Church
	Cave		Stadium
	Lookout		Park/forest
	Place of interest		Christian cemetery
	Wine/vineyard		Beach
	Museum		

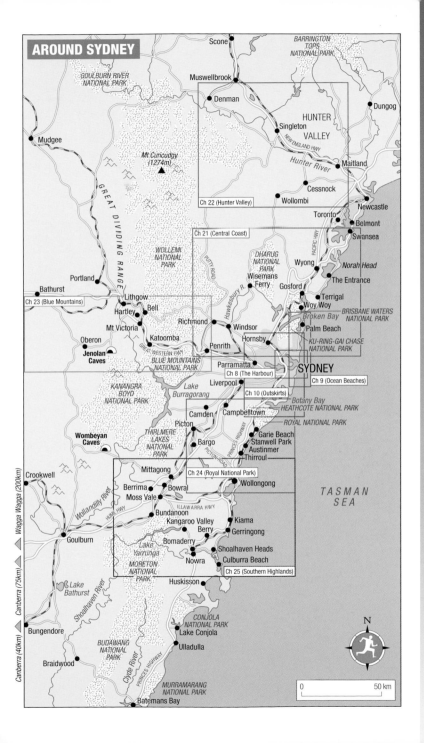

AROUND SYDNEY

Scone

BARRINGTON TOPS NATIONAL PARK

Muswellbrook

GOULBURN RIVER NATIONAL PARK

Denman

Dungog

HUNTER

Mudgee

Mt Curicudgy (1274m)

Singleton

VALLEY

NEW ENGLAND HWY

Hunter River

Maitland

Cessnock

Wollombi

Newcastle

Ch 22 (Hunter Valley)

Toronto

Belmont

PACIFIC HWY

Swansea

Ch 21 (Central Coast)

WOLLEMI NATIONAL PARK

PUTTY ROAD

DHARUG NATIONAL PARK

Wyong

Norah Head

Portland

Wisemans Ferry

The Entrance

Gosford

Bathurst

Hawkesbury R.

Terrigal

BRISBANE WATERS NATIONAL PARK

Ch 23 (Blue Mountains)

Lithgow

Bell

Woy Woy

Hartley

Richmond

Windsor

Broken Bay

Mt Victoria

Palm Beach

Oberon

Katoomba

Hornsby

KU-RING-GAI CHASE NATIONAL PARK

Jenolan Caves

Penrith

GREAT WESTERN HWY

BLUE MOUNTAINS NATIONAL PARK

Parramatta

Ch 8 (The Harbour)

SYDNEY

KANANGRA BOYD NATIONAL PARK

Lake Burragorang

Liverpool

Ch 9 (Ocean Beaches)

Ch 10 (Outskirts)

Botany Bay

Camden

Campbelltown

HEATHCOTE NATIONAL PARK

Wombeyan Caves

THIRLMERE LAKES NATIONAL PARK

Picton

ROYAL NATIONAL PARK

Garie Beach

Crookwell

Bargo

Stanwell Park

Austinmer

PICTON ROAD

PRINCES HIGHWAY

Thirroul

Mittagong

Ch 24 (Royal National Park)

Wollondilly River

Berrima

Bowral

Wollongong

TASMAN SEA

Moss Vale

HUME HWY

ILLAWARRA HWY

Bundanoon

Kangaroo Valley

Kiama

Goulburn

Berry

Gerringong

Bomaderry

Shoalhaven Heads

Lake Yarrunga

Nowra

Culburra Beach

MORTON NATIONAL PARK

Ch 25 (Southern Highlands)

Lake Bathurst

Huskisson

Bungendore

CONJOLA NATIONAL PARK

Lake Conjola

BUDAWANG NATIONAL PARK

Ulladulla

Braidwood

Clyde River

PRINCES HIGHWAY

MURRAMARANG NATIONAL PARK

Batemans Bay

◁ Canberra (40km) ◁ Canberra (75km) ◁ Wagga Wagga (200km)

GREAT DIVIDING RANGE

Shoalhaven River

N

0   50 km

SYDNEY SUBURBS

0   2 km

Ettalong (10km)
Barrenjoey Head

MOOGAMURRA
NATURE
RESERVE

Juno Pt   West
           Head

PALM
BEACH

Whale
Beach

The Basin

Cowan Creek

Pittwater YHA   Pittwater

Berowa Creek

BEROWA
WATERS

BEROWA
HEIGHTS

Scotland
Island

ARCADIA

Church
Point

Newport
Beach

BEROWRA VALLEY
REGIONAL PARK

KU-RING-GAI CHASE
NATIONAL PARK

MONA
VALE

GALSTON

SYDNEY-NEWCASTLE HIGHWAY

INGLESIDE

BEROWRA
VALLEY
REGIONAL
PARK

DUFFYS
FOREST

TERREY
HILLS

Narrabeen
Head

GARIGAL
NATIONAL PARK

NARRABEEN

ASQUITH

HORNSBY

COLLAROY

LONG
REEF

St IVES

GARIGAL
NATIONAL
PARK

FRENCHS
FOREST

DEE WHY

M2

CUMBERLAND HIGHWAY

CURL CURL

CHELTENHAM

PACIFIC HIGHWAY

KILLARA

QUEENSCLIFF

M2

MANLY

Middle
Harbour

BALGOWLAH

WILLOUGHBY
M2

North
Head

LANE COVE ROAD

VICTORIA ROAD

LANE COVE

SYDNEY HARBOUR
NATIONAL PARK

South Head

RYDE

CROWS NEST

MOSMAN

WATSONS
BAY

Lane Cove River

Taronga Zoo

Watsons
Bay

PARRAMATTA

HUNTERS
HILL

NEUTRAL
BAY

VAUCLUSE

Parramatta River

Port Jackson

HOMEBUSH
BAY

BALMAIN

WESTERN FREEWAY

CONCORD

ROZELLE

CITY

KINGS
CROSS

ROSE
BAY

BONDI

STRATHFIELD

HABERFIELD

GLEBE

PADDINGTON

Bondi Beach

LEICHHARDT

BURWOOD

PARRAMATTA ROAD

SURRY HILLS

CENTENNIAL
PARK

RANDWICK

BRONTE

NEWTOWN

MARRICKVILLE

HUME HIGHWAY

CANTERBURY

MASCOT

COOGEE

BANKSTOWN

CANTERBURY ROAD

KING GEORGE'S ROAD

ROCKDALE

PRINCES HIGHWAY

Kingsford
Smith
Airport

BOTANY

MAROUBRA

MALABAR

SOUTH WESTERN MOTORWAY

BRIGHTON-
LE-SANDS

LA
PEROUSE

EAST HILLS

Botany
Bay

Georges River

KURNELL

Cabramatta (6km)

Cronulla (8km)

N

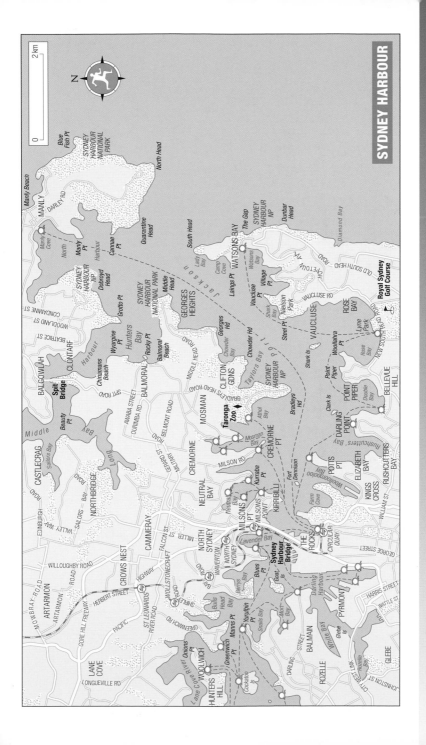

SYDNEY HARBOUR

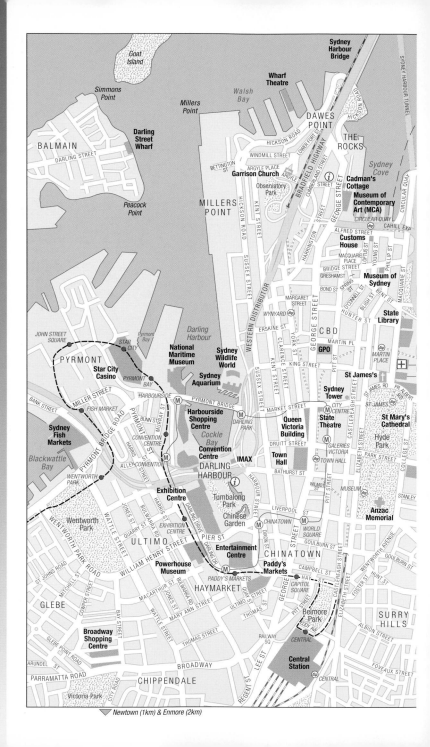

Newtown (1km) & Enmore (2km)

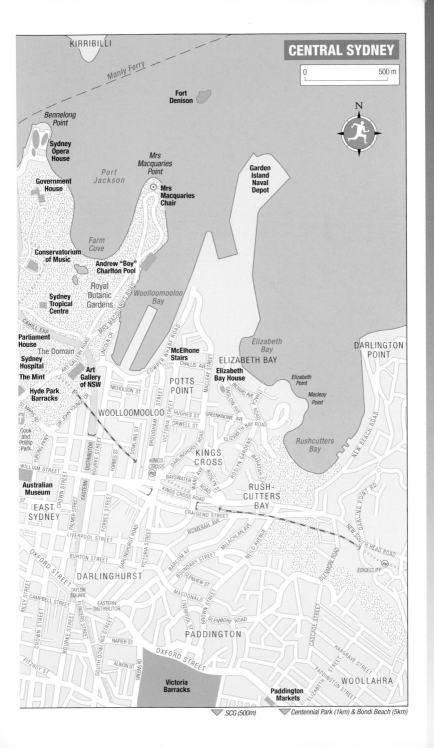

CENTRAL SYDNEY

0   500 m

N

KIRRIBILLI

Manly Ferry

Fort Denison

Bennelong Point

Sydney Opera House

Government House

Port Jackson

Mrs Macquaries Point

Mrs Macquaries Chair

Garden Island Naval Depot

Farm Cove

Conservatorium of Music

Andrew "Boy" Charlton Pool

Royal Botanic Gardens

Woolloomooloo Bay

Elizabeth Bay

DARLINGTON POINT

Sydney Tropical Centre

CAHILL EXP

Parliament House

The Domain

Sydney Hospital

The Mint

Hyde Park Barracks

MRS MACQUARIES ROAD

ART GALLERY ROAD

LINCOLN CR

McElhone Stairs

COWPER WHARF ROAD

CHALLIS AVE

ELIZABETH BAY

Elizabeth Bay House

Elizabeth Point

Macleay Point

Art Gallery of NSW

NICHOLSON ST

POTTS POINT

MACLEAY STREET

BILLYARD AVE

ITHACA ROAD

ONSLOW AVE

GREENKNOWE AVE

Rushcutters Bay

ST MARYS RD

ST JAMES RD

SIR JOHN YOUNG CR

WOOLLOOMOOLOO

BROUGHAM STREET

VICTORIA STREET

HUGHES ST

ORWELL ST

DARLINGHURST ROAD

ELIZABETH BAY ROAD

ROSLYN GARDENS

WARATAH ST

NEW BEACH ROAD

Cook and Philip Park

TUFPONG PKWY

DISTRIBUTOR

BOURKE STREET

FORBES ST

DOWLING ST

KINGS CROSS

KINGS CROSS

WARD AVE

ROSLYN ST

RUSH- CUTTERS BAY

WILLIAM STREET

BAYSWATER ROAD

KINGS CROSS ROAD

Australian Museum

EASTERN

CROWN STREET

PALMER STREET

FORBES STREET

DARLINGHURST ROAD

VICTORIA STREET

CRAIGEND STREET

WOMERAH AVE

McLACHLAN AVE

NEILD AVENUE

GLENMORE ROAD

NEW SOUTH HEAD ROAD

DARLING PVANT RD

EAST SYDNEY

OXFORD STREET

LIVERPOOL STREET

BURTON STREET

BARCOM AV

BOUNDARY STREET

GLENVIEW ST

EDGECLIFF

DARLINGHURST

RILEY STREET

CAMPBELL STREET

CROWN STREET

BOURKE STREET

FLINDERS STREET

TAYLOR SQUARE

EASTERN DISTRIBUTOR

NAPIER ST

SOUTH DOWLING STREET

ALBION ST

GREENS RD

MACDONALD

LIVERPOOL ST

BROWN STREET

GLENMORE ROAD

PADDINGTON

OXFORD STREET

FITZROY ST

Victoria Barracks

Paddington Markets

CASCADE STREET

HARGRAVE STREET

PADDINGTON STREET

ELIZABETH STREET

WOOLLAHRA

▽ SCG (500m)   ▽ Centennial Park (1km) & Bondi Beach (5km)

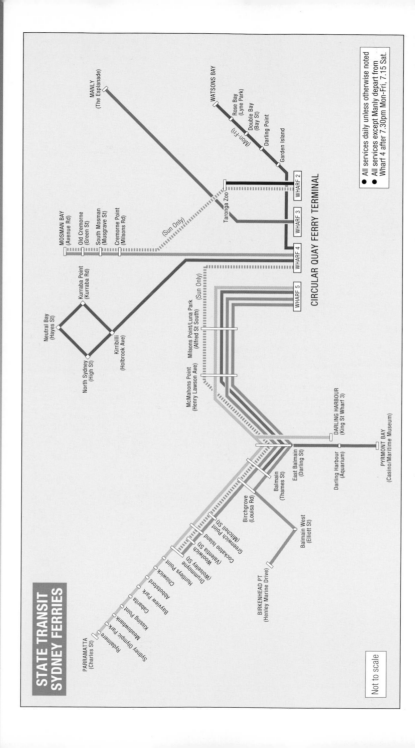

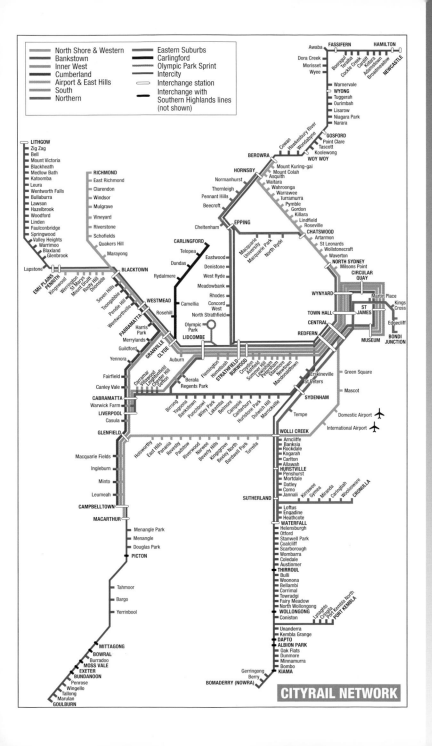

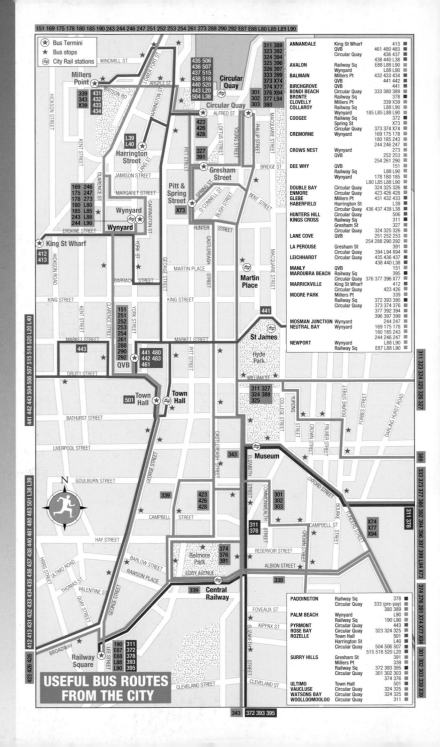